UNVEILING THE MYSTERY OF DANTE

The Empyrean, *engraving by Gustave Doré to illustrate Dante's* The Divine Comedy

UNVEILING THE MYSTERY OF DANTE

An Esoteric Understanding of Dante and his Divine Comedy

ERIC L. BISBOCCI

LINDISFARNE BOOKS | 2017

LINDISFARNE BOOKS
An imprint of SteinerBooks / Anthroposophic Press, Inc.
610 Main St., Great Barrington, MA 01230
www.steinerbooks.org

Copyright © 2017 by Eric L Bisbocci. All rights reserved.
No part of this publication may be reproduced, stored in
a retrieval system, or transmitted, in any form or by any
means, electronic, mechanical, photocopying,
recording, or otherwise, without the prior
written permission of the publisher.

Cover image: *The Queen of Heaven in Glory*. William Blake, c. 1825
(National Gallery of Victoria, Melbourne)
Design: Jens Jensen

The author gratefully acknowledges permission to use the following texts:

From the DIVINE COMEDY by Dante Alighieri, translated by John Ciardi.
Copyright © 1954, 1957, 1959, 1960, 1961, 1965, 1967, 1970
by the Ciardi Family Publishing Trust.
Used by permission of W. W. Norton & Company, Inc.

Brief quotations from: Mark Musa.
Dante's "Vita Nuova": A Translation and Essay.
Indiana University, 1973

LIBRARY OF CONGRESS CONTROL NUMBER: 2016960786
ISBN: 978-1-58420-971-3 (paperback)
ISBN: 978-1-58420-972-0 (ebook)

Contents

Acknowledgments vii

Preface ix

Introduction xii

PART ONE: The Esoteric Background of the Divine Comedy . 1

    The Tower of Babel and the Problem of Dialecticism 3

    Metamorphoses of the Soul 16

    Behind the Scenes 32

    The Secret Message 43

    Deciphering the Meaning of Love 59

    Goddess of the Sun 83

    Resurrecting the Temple 127

    "The Cross and the Eagle" 138

    The Heresy of Romantic Love:
        The Manichean Stream of Thinking 145

    Sufis and their Influence 175

    Unearthing the Forces of Darkness 184

PART TWO: RE-IMAGINING THE *DIVINE COMEDY*
IN THE LIGHT OF THINKING, FEELING, AND WILLING . . 191

The Tripartition of the Divine Comedy 193

The Inferno: Confronting the Dragon 209

The Purgatorio: Ascending the Slopes of Redemption . . . 301

The Paradiso: Into the "I" of God 409

Notes 573

Bibliography 581

Index of Illustrations 591

Acknowledgments

In our journey of life, little of what we express is attributable only to ourselves. From others we constantly gather ideas and impressions that are instrumental in helping us form our conception of reality. And so it is with this work. Many have contributed to its writing, some without even knowing it. Friends, acquaintances, and those with whom I may have had the slightest brush of contact, have through the years provided me with valuable insights into life and the nature of human consciousness. To all of them, I owe my gratitude.

From the time I encountered the writings of Rudolf Steiner and Massimo Scaligero in Rome in 1979, I have sought to apply their teachings to my life. They have been a guiding light, without which my life would not be the same. I am forever indebted to them, as well as to those interpreters of Dante's work who braved criticism and derision for proposing ideas outside the accepted norm. I owe thanks to John Ciardi, whose translation of Dante's *Divine Comedy* I used exclusively throughout the book and whose footnotes I leaned upon heavily for historical and mythological references. I am especially grateful to Christopher Bamford, Gene Gollogly and the staff at SteinerBooks for their encouragement and support. Without them, none of this would be possible.

In ending, I wish to acknowledge my parents who had always felt that they provided me with so little while I was growing up, not realizing that they had given me the keys to my never-ending search for truth and understanding.

To my daughter
Erika

May your path lead you to the light

Preface

This work arose from the crossfire between my love for Anthroposophy and my disenchantment with the rigidities of academic thinking. It attempts to reconcile the gap between those two worlds by explicitly drawing attention to the role of thinking itself, which lies at the heart of their divergence.

Gripped by the harrowing and the luminous depictions of Dante's *Divine Comedy*, I was unable to grasp the meaning of this work in my early years. The problem, as I see it now, arose from my failure to consider the *function* of literature, particularly as it relates to the evolution of human consciousness. For I believe that our relationship to thinking lies at the heart of each and every attempt that we make to decipher the world around us. With the gradual passing of time, I came to realize how the fundamental aim of literature has, indeed, always been to unveil the mystery of our existence to give direction and purpose to our lives. I came to accept the notion that the great writers of antiquity were not inspired to produce transformational works of art—or what might even be called metaphors of life—merely to appease the playful curiosities of those who approach them solely through the contrived use of literary devises, many of which, of course, did not even exist then. Instead, I began to perceive writers such as Homer and Dante as beacons of light whose primary aim was to open up vistas by which we could understand our place in the evolution of this most enigmatic weaving of events that we call "life." I began to see how the question of human consciousness had often been ignored by literary analysts, save applied "psychological" approaches—Freudian, Jungian, etc. —that sought to explain behavioral patterns relative to a given character at a given point in time. Hardly anywhere, however, did much attention seem devoted to *how* a piece of literature reflects the human struggle for meaning in the context of an ever-evolving consciousness. As far as I have been able to see, modern-day theoretical approaches to literature in academia have largely failed in this regard. Morris Berman in his book, *The Twilight of American Culture*, alludes to this when he says,

> Finally, we come to the phenomenon of postmodernism and deconstruction, a philosophical viewpoint that seems to have taken over much of the academy, and that has become part of the air we breathe: the notion that nothing is absolute, that one value is as good as another, that there is no difference between knowledge and opinion, and that any text or set of ideas is merely a mask for someone's political agenda. This lends itself well to the new world of microchip technology, inasmuch as it promotes a valueless universe.... A philosophy of despair masquerading as radical intellectual chic, postmodernism is, in fact, the ideological counterpart of the civilizational collapse that is going on around us...[1]

More than at any time in history, we need to resurrect the failing social and religious structures around us. The existential nihilism that increasingly surfaces amidst an ever-pervasive technological apparatus that oppresses the human spirit can only be answered by questioning the functionality of our own thinking and its role in the evolution of human development. Unfortunately, so often, though certainly not always, institutions of "higher" learning fail to even acknowledge how they contribute to this crisis. All too often, guided by economic forces, they reduce art or literature to mechanical or abstractly contrived representations of reality that have little to do with our essential nature as human beings. As a consequence, the role that art or literature *could* play in helping to shape human destiny fades evermore into oblivion.

Preface

My reason for writing this work is not to defend one particular interpretation of the *Divine Comedy* over another but, rather, to show how it can be *imagined* to help elucidate our search for an ever-greater understanding of our spiritual nature. In so doing, I try and examine some of the various esoteric streams of thought relevant to Dante's great poem and somehow place them into the context of Rudolf Steiner's cosmology as it relates to human consciousness. I hope that, in one way or another, this work will serve as a blueprint by which students of classical literature can find ways of their own to configure a work of art imaginatively and, thereby, better understand its relation to their own lives.

Introduction

This work began many years ago when I was too young to know who Dante Alighieri was, let alone realize his profound influence on Western Civilization. As a child, I often listened to my mother who, having only completed the fifth grade, would recite selected verses from the *Divine Comedy* by heart, twenty years after having heard them from her brother outside a small mountain village in central Italy. Not only could she recite them word for word, she would often take me on brief excursions through the various realms of Dante's vision, absolutely convinced that his description of the afterworld bore the stamp of truth.

With time, I began to realize the extent to which Western society had become permeated by Dante's conceptual representation of the spiritual world, and how much the Catholic Church, whose corruption he bitterly opposed and sought to reform, would utilize his harrowing descriptions of Hell to manipulate human thought and, thereby, subjugate human beings through fear and coercion.

During my university years, I slowly found myself gravitating toward the *Divine Comedy* once again, but this time with the aim of taking those initial steps on the path described to me as a child, to see for myself what it was about this poem that so gripped my soul and that of humanity throughout the centuries. The more I read, the more I became convinced that what lay hidden behind the works of Dante—and his contemporaries—was not so clearly visible in the light of traditional scholarly views.

Introduction

Only later, having already encountered the works of Rudolf Steiner, did I come across a small group of Italian writers who had gradually, over the course of a century, each uncovered "keys" to what appeared to be a "secret understanding" that Dante and his circle of friends shared among themselves. I began to connect their findings to the cosmological insights of Anthroposophy. What seemed important to me was how the love poetry of Dante and his circle of poets—though *apparently* innocent and devoid of profound philosophical and religious significance—was hermetically imbued with a *sacred knowledge* that permeated the evolution of philosophical thought from the Greeks to the Neo-Platonists to the writings of St. Thomas of Aquinas. Some of these Italian writers sought to demonstrate how Dante and his circle were connected to various esoteric orders or movements, such as the Knights Templar. Because of the enormous scope of the historical and philosophical traditions of which the *Divine Comedy* was a part, I have chosen to focus (among other things) primarily on the inner workings of the order to which Dante belonged—the *Fedeli d'amore*. In so doing, it is partly my aim to show how the *sacred knowledge* that they sought, embodied in the "Lady Philosophy," reemerges today in Anthroposophy—namely, a knowledge conducive to an initiation into the spiritual world and the founding of a spiritual community on Earth for all humankind.

Portrait of Dante (c. 1495), by Sandro Botticelli

The first chapter of this work, "The Tower of Babel and the Problem of Dialecticism," is intended not only for anthroposophists, but also for members of academia who are inclined to acknowledge the presence of a spiritual foundation in the world. It represents a modest attempt to isolate *thinking* as that aspect of human consciousness whose "unredeemed" nature accounts for the seemingly irreconcilable division between Anthroposophy and postmodern philosophical theories. The predominance of such literary theoretical constructs, I believe, has inadvertently been responsible for the failure to interpret much of the poetry of Dante's time as it relates to the esoteric nature of human thought. In effect, this chapter is largely a response to the profusion of literary paradigms—born of rationalistic thinking—that attempt to explain the essence of ancient texts while too often provoking the opposite effect. Besides underscoring the importance of thinking as a basis for comprehending our relation to the spiritual world, I have felt the need to give a brief account of its esoteric historical development in the chapter entitled, "The Metamorphosis of the Soul," with the hope that the reader may better comprehend how the *Divine Comedy* can be envisioned as a poetic expression of an initiatory experience. This, in turn, is followed by a brief historical overview of Dante's time in "Behind the Scenes," where I discuss the impulses that worked in society and provoked the need to create what some have called a "secret society," known as the *Fedeli d'amore* (The Faithful of Love). Through the construction of a subtle means of communication, this secret society became the vehicle that could give freedom of expression to individuals who sought *sacred knowledge* in the face of persecution by the Catholic Church. In the chapter "The Secret Message," this "secret language" is examined to reveal how an understanding of the universal aspect of *Divine Wisdom (Sophia)*—to which the *Fedeli d'amore* aspired—was shared and individually transmitted by each of its members. Thus, the tenuous communicative network itself, as it became the means by which each member could identify the other without drawing the attention of the Church, is taken into account. Having examined various aspects related to the *Fedeli d'amore*, I then seek to explore Dante's relationship to Beatrice in his quest for the being Sophia (*Divine Wisdom*), which forms the basis of his journey throughout the *Divine Comedy*.

The initial part of this book also includes two separate outlines of the process of initiation somewhat relevant to that time. The first led to a type of initiatory experience known as *excessus mentis*, which Luigi Valli—a prominent exponent of Dante's esoteric nature—believes was sought by the *Fedeli d'amore*; the second, given by Rudolf Steiner, regards Rosicrucianism, which was to come a bit later. I also explore Dante's connection to other so-called esoteric groups such as the Knights Templar in "Resurrecting the Temple," as well as his relation to the Troubadours and the Cathars in "The Heresy of Romantic Love." In so doing, I try to give a wider more inclusive picture of how certain spiritual forces were at work in humanity during the time of the *Divine Comedy*. Especially important in this context was the School of Chartres, where the Platonic and Aristotelian streams find expression in helping to prepare humanity for what Rudolf Steiner describes as the coming Age of Michael. Also having to do with this Manichean stream is the *Fedeli d'amore's* relationship to the Sufi poets of their time, which I examine in "The Sufi's and Their Influence." Finally, I end this first part by examining Dante's characterization of evil and how it is reflected in the *Divine Comedy*.

These preliminary chapters represent part one of this book and set the stage in part two for an esoteric interpretation of the *Divine Comedy* in its entirety. This interpretation, in the form of a narrative, is not founded on the constructs that abound today in the realm of literary theory. Instead, it is an attempt to fathom the inner dynamics of this literary piece—if at all possible—by trying to comprehend the nature of consciousness reflected in the poem, itself. In so doing, I lay aside modern-day theoretical models of interpretation. What, instead, becomes the basis for my interpretation is the threefold constitution of human consciousness—i.e., thinking, feeling, and willing. I believe that by examining the *Divine Comedy* on the basis of the threefold nature of our being, we can begin to comprehend within it a spiritual knowledge that *relates* to our own time.

The universality of Dante's epic poem lends itself to a multitude of interpretations, each reflective of the nature of consciousness that attempts to embrace it. There are a myriad of ways to interpret the *Divine Comedy*, each of which is valid with respect to one's individual interest. Therefore, my aim is not to try and give the reader a so-called definitive interpretation of the *Divine Comedy*. Nor do I wish to dismiss the valiant attempts of countless scholars who have done much to further an appreciation of it. Instead, my objective is twofold. First, I simply wish to provide an outline by which we can approach this great literary work to better comprehend what underlies Dante's *imaginative* experience as it relates to our time and, thereby, acknowledge the possibility of beholding the *light* by which we can come to the realization of our own "I." Secondly, it is to reveal the ethical imperatives by which, according to Dante, we must live our lives, to experience the *grace* that allows for the possibility of such an imaginative experience.

It is this path, traversed by Dante, that awaits us all—one to which I, again, was led as a child by she who, to this day, seventy years after hearing them herself, still recalls the indelible words of Dante as the shadows begin to lengthen on his journey toward immortality.

PART ONE

THE ESOTERIC BACKGROUND
OF THE DIVINE COMEDY

There may be times when what is most needed is, not so much a new discovery or a new idea as a different "slant"; I mean a comparatively slight readjustment in our *way* of looking at the things and ideas on which attention is already fixed.

Draw a rectangular glass box in perspective—not too precise perspective (for the receding lines must be kept parallel, instead of converging)—and look at it. It has a front and a back, a top and a bottom. But slide your hand across it in the required direction and look again: you may find that what you thought was inside of the top has become its outside, while the outside of the front wall has changed to the inside of the back wall, and vice versa. The visual readjustment was slight, but the effect on the drawing has been far from slight, for the box has not only turned inside out but is also lying at quite a different angle.

—Owen Barfield,
Saving the Appearances[2]

The Tower of Babel
and the Problem of Dialecticism

When analyzing literature of the distant past, we may occasionally feel beset by a curious problem. Do we interpret it by means of a *consciousness* that mirrors that of the artist who produced it? If not, how is it different? Or, better yet, how has human consciousness transformed through time? It seems to me that the modern-day literary theorist often takes such questions for granted, choosing instead to focus on the socioreligious or political realities of a particular period as they have been customarily interpreted and accepted as truth. One need only read a book on modern literary theory to realize how the kind of "critical" thinking employed by literary analysts to define or interpret an ancient text can prevent them, inadvertently, from entering into the "field of imaginative forces" responsible for its creation. In other words, is the dialectical process of thinking from which literary explanations arise often *by nature* antagonistic to the work's intrinsic living reality? By focusing attention on *outer* "factual" representations, such theorists presume the authority to proclaim the veracity of their particular interpretations, even though the conceptual models that they use are themselves constantly being supplanted through time. Where is the basis for an objective analysis to be found? Can it truly be uncovered in the externalized, interpreted *fact* that has been inherited, or is it buried somewhere deep within the current of an ever-changing consciousness?

At the root of such ambiguity is the pervasive notion that, save an increase in "scientifically verifiable knowledge" and the apparent complexity of dialectical thought, our thinking is fundamentally similar in nature to that of earlier times. That is to say, we believe that our consciousness has, for the most part, remained unchanged and that we *behold* the world in much the same way we did two thousand years ago. Furthermore, we commonly assume that our increasingly complex system of thought and the countless tidbits of information accumulating in libraries and on computer screens provide a "sufficient" key to deciphering the enigmas contained in ancient writings. What often seems lacking, however, is the realization that the *qualitative* nature of thinking may have changed. The same holds true for the literary devises often used to express a given reality. Take the metaphor or allegory as an example. Whereas humanity could once look at a given phenomenon, perceive the very forces that shaped it, and convey its inner reality through picture, today this picture has often been reduced to a mere physical representation used to depict a given reality through outer association. Herein lies the basis upon which psychoanalysis, for example, has been conceived and applied to the study of literature. Because literary theorists interpret an epic or myth separate from the *nature* of thought that brought it into being, they have, in a sense, charted a course similar to modern religions, which seek the existence of God outside the boundaries of human consciousness.

Such thinking has also, one might add, given rise to hesitation on the part of many scholars to classify folktales as "literature." The reasons for this are often nebulous. One explanation has been that neither folktales nor myths, for the most part, can be attributed to a particular author. In other words, what differentiates *The Odyssey* from the *Myth of Gilgamesh* is that, in the former instance, one solitary individual (Homer) can tenuously be singled out for having brought it into manifestation. Whereas myths, on the other hand, are representations of a collective consciousness, which, as Terry Eagleton says in his book *Literary Theory: An Introduction,* "unfold their 'concrete logic' with supreme disregard for the vagaries of individual thought, and reduce any particular consciousness to a mere function of themselves."[3] Yet, is a so-called individualized literary expression, itself, not but a *reflection* of the universal consciousness from which it arises? In other words, are not both aforementioned works (each in their own way) but quintessential *reflections of consciousness during different points in humanity's evolutionary development?* Excluded from consideration, of course, is *how* both works reflect human consciousness. Though the example set forth may seem inconsequential, it is indicative of the arbitrary values by which we often evaluate what is passed down through time. This is done regardless of the fact that even the most eminent literary theorists may, in effect, take into consideration how our view of Homer may be very different from, let us say, that of someone living in the fourteenth century. Terry Eagleton goes on to say,

> The fact that we always interpret literary works to some extent in the light of our own concerns—indeed that in one sense of "our own concerns" we are incapable of doing anything else—might be one reason why certain works of literature seem to retain their value across the centuries. It may be, of course, that we still share many preoccupations with the work itself; but it may also be that people have not actually been valuing the "same" work at all, even though they may think they have. "Our" Homer is not identical with the Homer of the Middle Ages, nor "our" Shakespeare with that of his contemporaries; it is rather that different historical periods have constructed a "different" Homer and Shakespeare for their own purposes, and found in these texts elements to value or devalue, though not necessarily the same ones.[4]

Implied here, of course, is how through time we interpret a literary work differently in relation to our sociohistorical context. What most literary theorists do not seem to insist upon, however, is how such interpretations in no way enable us to uncover the *nature* of thinking out of which an ancient text was born. Such interpretations are, instead, continually born of a thinking that associates with external reality. Though the value placed on a piece of literature may change in its relation to our interpretation of a particular sociohistorical context, such interpretations do not change the fact that the original work, in itself, is the product of a consciousness *particular* to a given point in time. The universality of literature is not to be sought *merely* in its applicability to one's social environment but, more important, in the stage of consciousness of which it is an expression, since each developing social configuration is, itself, a manifestation of an *evolving* human consciousness. Thus, the universality of a literary work can only be understood within the context of this ever-changing consciousness.

Present-day dialectical consciousness can in no way enable us to capture the essential thinking out of which a given work was written. By means of it, we can only *speculate* as to its past nature. Though this speculative process has become increasingly refined, all present-day exhibitions in conceptual dexterity seem to lack the essential quality of ancient thinking. Dialectical, sense-based thinking is *devoid* of life and, by nature, unable to *conjure* the pictorial quality of the consciousness that operated in the past. Astute observations, such as Eagleton's, merely have the inadvertent effect of acknowledging the reader's lack of orientation when confronted by a classic work of antiquity, while justifying yet another refabricated interpretation of it. They provide no bridge toward a true comprehension of the evolutionary stages in between by which one can understand how the thinking behind a given literary work has developed to its present stage.

During the last hundred years, the rise of conceptual models stemming from literary analysis has been impressive, so that one who chooses to understand past literature is faced with deciphering a monstrous edifice of signs and symbols. This edifice, for the most part, is merely the invention of a thinking process, which, itself, has become reduced to a mere concatenation of symbols. From the emergence of formalism (which declared literature to be a "'special' kind of language, in contrast to the 'ordinary' language we commonly use"[5]), to semiotics (which considers literature by means of a "systematic study of signs"[6]), to deconstructionism (which "is the name given to the critical operation by which oppositions can be partly undermined, or by which they can be shown to partly undermine each other in the process of textual meaning"⁷) namely, abolishing the binary oppositions into which structuralism sought to reduce a piece of literature, we witness the gradual *mechanization* of human thinking. This process of mechanization is, itself, superimposed onto a work of art so that the latter may be torn asunder. Consider, for example, the so-called fundamental kinds of signs common to the study of semiotics. Says Eagleton:

> There was the "iconic," where the sign somehow resembled what it stood for (a photograph of a person, for example); the "indexical," in which the sign is somehow associated with what it is a sign of (smoke with fire, spots with measles), and the "symbolic," where as with Saussure the sign is only arbitrarily or conventionally linked with its referent. Semiotics takes up this and many other classifications: it distinguishes between "denotation" (what the sign stands for) and "connotation" (other signs associated with it); between codes (the rule-governed structures which produce meanings) and the messages transmitted by them; between the "paradigmatic" (a whole class of signs which may stand in for one another) and the "syntagmatic" (where signs are coupled together with each other in a chain). It speaks of "meta-languages" where one sign system denotes another sign system (the relation between literary criticism and literature, for instance), "polysemic" signs that have more than one meaning, and a great many other technical concepts. ⁸

Here, we seem to witness how each conceived "system of signs" is a mere reflection of other so-called systems all to be related to one another in whichever way seems most applicable. Yet, if one probes the many applications invented to justify the mere existence of such a system, whose main function is thought to be the uncovering of meaning in a text, one realizes that, in so doing, such a meaning can never be found, for meaning so often largely arises from within one's *ineffable* experience of the text itself and not in the systematic relationships or paradigms artificially devised outside the parameters of such an experience. In the end, individual dialectical thoughts are but themselves the very signs by which a systematic ordering is construed, all with the aim of uncovering meaning. Unfortunately, the highly complex systematic ordering that is derived from such dialecticism is not intrinsic to the *quintessential experience* itself, but, instead, taken to the extreme, begins to be figuratively aligned to the inner configuration of a microchip, which would, in effect, be tantamount to seeking answers regarding the essential nature of a piece of literature within the inner workings of a computer. Rudolf Steiner, in a series of lectures entitled *The Karma of Untruthfulness* (vol. 1), states:

> Ancient knowledge is lost, and for the most part we speak in the way we do just because the ancient knowledge is lost and we are surrounded by maya, which gives us nothing but mere words. Now we must once again seek the spiritual life that gives the words their content. We live, in a way, in a mechanism of words, just as externally we shall gradually completely lose our individuality in a mechanism of technology until we are at the mercy of external mechanisms.[9]

In light of this, who can argue with the fact that many modern-day literary theorists have merely become literary "technicians," whose very preoccupation with literature, often poses its greatest threat. In *The Arts and their Mission,* Steiner says:

> Abstract thoughts deaden artistic phantasy. Becoming more and more logical, one takes to writing commentaries on works of art. This is a terrible product of the materialistic age: scholars write commentaries of art. But these academic explanations, *Faust* commentaries, *Hamlet* commentaries, learned descriptions of the art of Leonardo, Raphael, Michelangelo, are coffins in which genuine artistic feeling, living art, lie buried. If one picks up a *Faust* or *Hamlet* commentary, it is like touching a corpse. Abstract thoughts have murdered the work of art.[10]

We now come to Dante. More than seven hundred years have passed since he wrote his immortal depiction of the human condition—the *Divine Comedy.* Yet, the literary world has seemingly failed to divine the significance of this "eternal poem" as it relates to the evolution of human consciousness. Many explanations have been conceived to elucidate the theological and philosophical questions that comprise Dante's cosmological view of life, only to resignedly attribute the greatness of his poem to its multidimensionality, or even to its obscurity. In addition, modern scholars have often repudiated metaphysical insights that have failed to accord themselves with the formalistic rigidities of modern-day philosophical, scholarly thought. Our inability to comprehend the function of poetry as it relates to the consciousness of a particular historical era has greatly obscured our ability to decipher the enigmas concealed within it. How can centuries of intellectual scrutiny by many traditional literary scholars overlook the *nature* of consciousness in their analysis of ancient texts and, at the same time, ostracize those few individuals who, in the face of academic prejudice, had inadvertently striven to rectify this shortcoming by *unveiling* what lay behind the nebulous jargon employed by Dante and his contemporaries?

To understand the answer to these questions, we will have to describe the impulses that gradually arose during the waning decades of the Middle Ages and that firmly took hold of humanity during the beginning of the fifteenth century. We know from the various lectures given by Rudolf Steiner that what occurred during that time was a subtle transformation of consciousness, in which humanity acquired a more conceptual and abstract relationship to nature. No longer was it readily possible for human beings to behold the living forces that weave the material world into being. Instead, those forces had slowly receded from view so that what was, for the most part, left for humanity to behold was a "crystallized" representation of the world, which became evermore devoid of life and differed substantially from the more pictorial consciousness of earlier times. Yet, in spite of this, there still existed *a "residual" of the atavistic clairvoyance* that Steiner says was a lingering characteristic of the "Intellectual Soul Age"—a term used by him to denote a particular stage of largely "un-individualized" human consciousness connected to hereditary forces, lasting roughly 2,160 years from 747 BC up until the early fifteenth century (AD 1413).

The abstract thought forms that humanity had begun to experience, on the other hand, were lifeless. They could be arranged in the most varied ways and, thereby, generate a multiplicity of conceptual models by which human beings could seek to fathom the past. The tragedy in this was that had human beings been able to perceive the *force*, itself, which binds these materialized thoughts, they would have been able to recapture the *living force* of thinking in such a way as to eventually awaken what Rudolf Steiner calls "Cosmic Memory," thus enabling them to perceive the unfolding of human consciousness. This, however, was not at all possible, for human beings had yet to attain a spiritual constitution that would have permitted them to tread the path of initiation proper to the Consciousness Soul Age—a period that marked the beginning of a purely "individualized" consciousness, initially reflected to a large degree in the discoveries of such individualities as Copernicus, Kepler, and Galileo. Instead, human beings were left, as we have stated, to construct representational models of spiritual reality so that, as their dialectical dexterity increased, so, too, did their inner conviction in the validity of abstractions to uncover truth. Each new concept was analyzed and expanded so that a systematic process gradually unfolded. Now, as this so-called Tower of Babel increasingly took hold of human hearts, it fervently denied that there be any other way toward a more comprehensive representation of reality, and therefore, repudiated the employment of elements that did not conform to its mechanized network. This "nominalistic" perspective was to be the foundation of nineteenth century Positivism, and only of late have cracks begun to form along the surface of this great dialectical edifice.

While this mechanized apparatus, known to us as intellectualism, conformed all disciplinary endeavors to its sense-based grasp of reality, so, too, did religion follow suit and seek to rectify its inability to substantiate the spiritual foundation underlying earthly phenomena by pointing to the limitations inherent in sense-based thinking. This realization, however, did not come about through the capacity to "behold" the very essence of thought—i.e., the *light* of thinking. Rather, it was *itself* a mere product of the kind of thinking that it had put into question in the first place. In the end, religious adherents sought to rectify their own penetrative incapacities by fostering the notion that the only bridge between these two realms was "faith," a word that inferred the absence of dialectics. Thus, in a most peculiar way, the dialectical mode of thinking that characterized science had also become an intrinsic characteristic of religion, even though it tried to dismiss dialectics as a vehicle toward comprehending such mysteries as the Resurrection.

Owing to the lack of insight, by philosophy and religion, to apprehend the spiritual impulses during the period preceding the Consciousness Soul Age, modern humanity has been stripped of the ability to resolve the inherent shortcomings to which it has fallen prey. This can clearly be evidenced in the assertion (even to this day) that the *mere* physical presence of Beatrice Portinari at the age of nine eventually led Dante, one of the great minds in human history, to the realization of his spiritual being. Such myopia arises out of a thinking whose limitations we fail to perceive, for it was not *only* the physical presence of Beatrice but, just as important, *the spiritual aspect of her being* that was the inspirational force that led him toward the realization of his "I." As Steiner says in his lecture on Dante (February, 11, 1906), humanity experienced both the physical aspect and the spiritual aspect of reality *equally* during the Middle Ages.[11] In fact, many have argued that "Beatrice" was the name given by Dante to denote the realization of *Divine Wisdom* (Sophia). Therefore, like many of the feminine names used by Dante's contemporaries (i.e., Laura/Petrarch and Fiammetta/Boccaccio), the name "Beatrice" denoted the attainment of a particular transcendent state of consciousness.

Thus, the unwillingness of modern theorists to consider the limitations of the method they employ to explicate ancient literary works of art reveals, at the very least, their dismissal of the very basis of understanding—the nature of thinking itself. They merely employ, unconsciously, a *systematic* thought process to decipher the incomprehensible enigmas they encounter. By ignoring the *nature* of thinking, how can we ever ascertain the validity of our suppositions? In the end, all modern literary movements such as structuralism, deconstructionism, semiotics, etc. are but highly polished variations of an intellectual dialecticism whose validation (or comprehension) is rarely, if ever, objectified. Reassurance as to the plausibility of its postulations seems to rest in the preponderate ability to make ever complex and incomprehensible its theoretical models to the general populace, which is to essentially create a systematic paradigm that is taboo to the average layman. In so doing, it proclaims itself to be irrefutable. Opposing voices can find but few means to challenge it without finding themselves entangled in the very dialectical jargon that they contest. No wonder little opposition has, in fact, succeeded in slowing the perpetuation of such a proliferation of dialectical thinking, which, in turn, has inevitably resulted in a lack of orientation within literary circles where one literary theory often invalidates another. The supplanting of one theoretical model of reality by another is, in turn, symptomatic of an underlying premise pervading all hypothetical models of reality, especially Marxist ideology—namely, that material dialecticism is the unquestionable authority, by which we decode the enigmas that surround us. This notion is unknowingly predicated on the belief that just as matter generates life, so, too, is the physical brain the creator of thoughts. In other words, materiality becomes the basis for understanding life. Georg Lukács states, "Marxism searches for the material roots for each phenomenon, regards them in their historical connections and movement, and ascertains the laws of such movement..."[12] The ascertainment of such laws, however, does not stem from a perceptive process which bridges itself to the heart of creative activity in the suprasensory realm. Thus, there is, so to speak, no place at all for a spiritual world. In light of the historical emergence of dialecticism, this is most natural, for how can a thinking that adheres only to materiality acknowledge the presence of a reality it cannot behold experientially?

Nevertheless, in his book regarding the immaterial nature of thinking, *Il Pensiero come Anti-Materia*, the Italian anthroposophical thinker, Massimo Scaligero, states *"il sistema materialistico muove da una metafisica...*"¹³ (the materialistic system proceeds from suprasensory reality...). If the adherents to modern-day literary ideologies sincerely take this into account and begin to probe experientially the thinking that they employ, they may themselves come to perceive the limitations of dialectical thinking. They may see that thinking, steeped in materialism, cannot, in and of itself, lead us to the essence of its own nature. In other words, sense-based dialectical thinking alone does not enable us to *perceive* the process of its own becoming. It does not allow us to witness the activity of thinking, but only the end product of that activity—i.e., static thought forms, the very foundation of present-day thought. Again, all too often, modern-day theorists do not take any of this into account, for the spiritual world is, of course, to most of them nothing but an intellectual construct and not a perceptible reality. So, too, Dante's *Divine Comedy* has been construed, for the most part, as nothing more than a fanciful intellectual creation, reflective of his speculations on the spiritual world.

So, whether we speak of deconstructionism, structuralism, Foucault, Barthes, Benjamin, and so on, we are, in effect, speaking of the same thing. There exists no worldview, no underlying conception based on the *perception* of forces that manifest outer reality or, even thought itself, for that matter. Such literary constructs are, again, mere intellectual speculations on reality that continually supplant one another while reaching exasperate levels of complexity. Thus, it is easy to see how in analyzing literary works of the past, little is taken into account of the impulses that generate an historical reality—impulses that can be perceived without the implementation of theory. Likewise, there is no coherent picture of the spiritual development of humanity that would suffice as a context within which to place a particular work of art, unless of course, one seeks to *understand* the essential factors that comprise such a context. For this to occur, much attention, again, would by necessity have to be given to the nature of thought and perception as the foundation by which an understanding of the world and its spiritual evolution can be ascertained.

A worldview that does take all of this into account, however, though little known in academic circles, is Anthroposophy. It places the *activity of thinking* at the very heart of its attempt to probe outer reality. It is founded on the ability to *behold* the very forces that manifest the material world. The cognitive mode of perception is, itself, transformed so that no longer is reality understood based on the associative capacity of thoughts but, rather, on the transformation of thinking itself, whereby the *force* of thinking is initially beheld as an objective nonmaterialized entity. The ability to perceive the force that brings dialectical thought into manifestation, as a visible reality, marks the beginning of modern initiation. It is this ability that can gradually allow us to consciously enter into what Steiner calls the "etheric" realm, the world's formative interplay of forces, wherein it is possible to behold a tableau of all that has transpired since the creation of the world.

Rudolf Steiner was able to penetrate into this sphere where the Christ, Himself, can be experienced. In so doing, he could describe the philosophical and religious impulses that arose during the creation of the present-day world from many points of view. He was not guided by the mere ability to cleverly arrange concepts into a systematic whole that he then could apply as a hypothesis to be proved or disproved. Instead, he could *perceive the very forces themselves*, at the heart of consciousness, responsible for the manifestation of an artistic form of expression. Herein lies the importance of Steiner's contribution to the world of art and literature. By formulating a worldview based on suprasensory perception, Steiner could perceive the relation between historical transformation and the nature of thinking and was, thus, able to show *how* the human deeds that shaped outer historical development were born of a consciousness particular to a given period of time. It is, of course, a comprehensive worldview such as his that is lacking in present-day literary circles. In the absence of such a view, the intellectual world has failed to provide society with a coherent understanding of human development. The fragmentation of thought has precluded the emergence of a coherent worldview by which one can place a work such as the *Divine Comedy* into context and hope to understand it as an *imaginative expression* conducive to the realization of the "I."

A principle aim of this work is to show how what is urgently needed today can be gleaned from Dante's *Divine Comedy*, namely a path that enables us to transform our being by immersing ourselves into the creative *act* of life.

Metamorphoses of the Soul

To unveil a number of hidden esoteric aspects embodied within the *Divine Comedy* as they relate to the threefold aspect of our being, it would be helpful to focus attention on the evolution of human consciousness and its intimate relation to the being of Christ. For central to this is the quest for *Divine Wisdom*. How can we even begin to study the theological implications of Dante's poem without taking into consideration the manner in which the Christ impulse gradually manifested in human consciousness up to Dante's time? In this way, we not only gain a clearer idea of *how* the aims of Dante and his circle of poets, the *Fedeli d'amore*, fall into this evolutionary process, but, more specifically, how Dante, himself, embodies the emergence of what Rudolf Steiner calls "personality," which, in effect, characterizes the stage of human development arrived at during the Middle Ages. This "personality," which arose through the gradual strengthening of the egoic forces, harbored the possibility of connecting humanity, by way of thinking, to the creative impulses issuing from the Godhead. Thus, it is important to trace the development of thinking as a suprasensory activity experienced by human beings in our relation to the outer world. It is difficult to arrive at a coherent picture of human evolution by merely stringing together outer pictorial representations of events, which we have come to call history. Instead, we must take into account how the visible configurations that we deem historical are but reflections of impulses working imperceptibly in the realm of human nature. Only then can history, as it is commonly understood, be placed into context.

As Rudolf Steiner repeatedly shows, if we delve back in time to the farthest reaches of antiquity, we find that sense-based thinking, as we presently experience it, did not exist. Because of this, the impulses leading to human freedom were also inexistent, for free will is inextricably linked to thinking. Humanity, at one time, beheld, in a somewhat unconscious manner, the interplay of cosmic forces that resulted in the manifestation of physical world. In other words, we human beings could actually perceive the "gods" or spiritual hierarchies at work, but we were, in effect, mere *spectators* of this cosmic interplay. What we perceived was, in fact, pure (divine) willing. This stage of human development was symbolically depicted as the "Garden of Eden" in the *Old Testament*. There, we find Adam and Eve representing the embryonic separation of the sexes, but, just as important, the initial separation of the feminine and masculine polarities of human consciousness—i.e., thinking and willing.

This biblical parable is of profound significance, for it portrays the first so-called conscious act of humankind, namely, the "eating of the apple" forbidden to humanity by God. This "premeditated" act, induced by the luciferic forces that were symbolized by the Serpent, was more than an allegory depicting the emergence of "good" and "bad." Instead, it depicted a significant transformation undergone by human consciousness, one from which sense-based thinking was to gradually emerge in humanity—a thinking that slowly severed our connection to the spiritual worlds. As a result, our ability to perceive the cosmic interplay of forces, to which we have just alluded, gradually diminished. The emergence of this thinking also signaled the gradual separation of human willing from Divine Willing. At the same time, it harbored the *potentiality* of our eventual reintegration into the sphere of cosmic activity as active participants, as co-creators of life. It is important to remember that in spite of the gradual unfolding of this process, the atavistic clairvoyance, to which we have just alluded, remained a part of human consciousness for quite some time.

To gain a more systematic understanding of this transformational process, we must note that a strict interrelationship exists between the materialization of thinking forces and the gradual solidification of the Earth's substantiality. As we know from the numerous indications given by Rudolf Steiner, the Earth of past planetary epochs differed greatly from that upon which we walk today. During the period of earthly evolution known as Old Moon, for example, Steiner describes the Earth's state of materiality as being "vegetative" in nature, resembling what he called "cooked spinach." Only with time did the Earth undergo a further process of densification that, among other things, led to the gradual formation of rocks and other hardened materials. This reflected the degree to which death or despiritualization had taken place. Just as the materiality present on the Earth indicated a recession of creative etheric (life) forces, so, too, was the eventual emergence of dialectical thinking a sign of the dying process taking hold of human consciousness. We must not imagine this hardening process, which occurred simultaneously within the human being, as happening overnight. It was imperceptibly slow, encompassing large stretches of time. Human beings gradually realized that direct perception of the spiritual worlds was becoming lost, for within the communities there existed, to an ever-lesser degree, particular individuals who still possessed the ability to perceive spiritual reality. These people were recognized, by the ever-growing majority, as humanity's only remaining link to the spiritual world receding from view. They were known as priests, kings, shamans, and chieftains. (A remnant of this, incidentally, was reflected in the headgear of the American Indian chief, in that its size and coloration represented the degree of spiritual vision that he or she possessed.) For most of humanity, however, the ability to behold suprasensory forces gradually disappeared.

Rudolf Steiner describes how after the fall of Atlantis the metamorphoses of thinking became, in essence, the *principle* that differentiated the successive cultural epochs. These epochs known as the Indian, Persian, Egyptian–Babylonian–Chaldean, Greek–Roman, and that of which we are a part, the fifth post-Atlantean epoch, each reflect how *nature* gradually inserted itself into human consciousness.

During the Indian epoch, the first to succeed the disappearance of Atlantis, humanity's relationship to time and space differed significantly from our own. Human beings perceived time in "simultaneous moments" and space as being "immeasurable." This reflected the extent to which the materialization of thinking had yet to take hold of human consciousness. There existed virtually no perceptible distinction between the spiritual and physical worlds for humanity at that time. In other words, the distinction between the forces of willing and thinking had yet to manifest, although such a separation was in its germinal phase. It is important to note that this embryonic separation echoed the dichotomous relationship between inner and outer warmth during the first stage of such an evolution, which Steiner called Old Saturn. The zodiacal configuration under which the Indian epoch unfolded is the sign of Cancer, ♋. Here, the representation of inverted vortexes depicts the gradual separation of thinking from willing—i.e., the external manifested form-to-be (thought) from the creative forces that are responsible for bringing it into manifestation. In other words, we witness the gradual emergence of thought, still contained within the forces from which it was individualized in embryonic form. We must, however, bear in mind that, in no way, was this thinking completely independent from the forces of willing, for it still existed *within the womb* of creative activity.

It is no wonder that the constellation of Cancer symbolizes the maternal aspect of human development. While the seeds of materiality had imperceptibly taken root in the consciousness of humanity, the Indian of this first post-Atlantean epoch was able, through the inspiration of the Seven Holy Rishis, to reach up into the hierarchy of the Spirits of Movement, and acknowledge (though unconsciously) the lofty being, Vishvakarman (Christ), descending from the sphere of the Sun. The arrival of this being was to gradually *counter* the forces of materialization that, if left unchecked, would have eventually fettered humankind to the Earth. However, humanity was able to have only the knowledge (Sophia) of this being. It would be a long time before this being would actually permeate the Earth.

During the Persian epoch, humankind interpreted the world in "shades of light and darkness." Moral order was understood in such a way that beings of good nature were perceived as "light," whereas those who were selfish, often manifesting their lower nature, were perceived as "dark." Though the dichotomy between good and evil, during the Persian epoch, revealed how human consciousness had fallen from a loftier state of spirituality during the Indian epoch, natural necessity and human freedom were still nonexistent, for thinking had yet to sufficiently materialize so as to permit their entrance into the stream of human evolution. Human beings still saw everything as a unity of physical and spiritual forces.

The Persian epoch, governed by the constellation of Gemini (duality), symbolized as ♊, marks the point in which the embryonic separation, witnessed during the Indian culture, became more differentiated. Thus, two individualized streams emerged in the consciousness of humanity, in spite of the fact that they were intrinsically interdependent. Thinking and willing, in a sense, can be designated as "dark" and "light." For just as willing, representative of the purest forces issuing from the creative hierarchies, was experienced as "light," its submergence into the materiality of the earthly forces, manifesting as thinking, was experienced as "darkness." Thus, the question of "good" and "bad," in the so-called moral sense, should be understood in this connection. To experience "darkness" was to behold, more and more, the fall of willing into thinking. This cultural epoch, however, was one in which a transformation occurred in the light ether of human consciousness. Incidentally, it brings to mind, as a faint echo, what Steiner called the Sun Stage of the earthly development, for there, too, we witness a similar duality manifested—i.e., a separation of the light ether from the denser air element which, at that point of the Earth's evolution, comprised the substantiality of the Earth.

The Persian epoch had, as its great initiate, Zarathustra, who was able to perceive more than mere differentiations between light and darkness. Rather, he perceived the *beings* behind such contrasts of light and darkness. While the Spirits of Form were somewhat visible, Zarathustra perceived the solar being, known to the Indians as Vishvakarman, descending from the Sun. He named it Ahura Mazda. Zarathustra also perceived, behind the shades of darkness, the presence of a "retarded" archangelic being whom he called Ahriman. Therefore, Zarathustra beheld the very forces that we human beings would begin to experience, more and more, *within* our consciousness.

The Egyptian–Babylonian–Chaldean period marked the point in which something of the human being's conception of the world began to somewhat resemble that of the present day. Steiner maintains that a certain "necessity of nature" began to find its way into human thinking. Providence and nature were seen as one, in as much as natural events themselves were assumed to be *manifestations* of Divine Willing. When we moved a part of our body, it was divinity moving within us. While, in the Persian epoch, thinking and willing each reached a greater degree of individualization, during the Egyptian epoch, thinking begins to manifest itself as *form*. Guided by the influence of Taurus, ♉, thought is represented in its tangible separation from the creative forces directed from above. The closed circle, of course, is indicative of self-containment, or *form*. However, this form is connected to impulses streaming down from the sphere of cosmic activity, as is illustrated by the half circle facing up toward the Heavens. What the Egyptian–Babylonian–Chaldean perceived in the movement of the Heavens was the reflection of movements of the Spiritual Hierarchies. In other words, the will of the "gods" was embodied in celestial movements and their configurations. Human beings could experience the Music of the Spheres. Whereas "light" was the principle element by which the ancient Persian differentiated his or her environment, "tone" became the means by which the Egyptian–Babylonian–Chaldean could experience the spiritual forces of the cosmos. The emergence of tone in human consciousness is reminiscent of the Old Moon, where it first arose in its separation from the watery element of the Earth. The being that Zarathustra called Ahura Mazda was the very same being that the Egyptians named Osiris. Human beings could now perceive only into the sphere of the Spirits of Personality (Archai). Up to that point in time, the being who was given the names Vishvakarman, Ahura Mazda, and Osiris was perceived as being separate from earthly development. Instead, *it was the knowledge (Sophia) of Him as He descended from the Sun that humankind possessed. This knowledge was represented in Egyptian mythology as Isis.*

During the time of the Greeks, humanity began to feel itself separate from nature—i.e., nature was gradually perceived to exist outside human consciousness. The spiritual nature of human beings began to recede and was perceived to be less intrinsically related to the physical self. Dialectical thinking became evermore manifest, while humanity's capacity to behold beings of a higher order was lessening. This cultural epoch was under the stellar configuration of Aries, ♈. Here depicted is the crystallization of the thinking forces in the human head, as they flow down from the spiritual hierarchies. This period marked the dawn of intellectuality, though the spiritual world was still visible within nature. When a person from Greece spoke of the highest of all Greek gods, Zeus, his or her perception was directed to the realm of the archangelic and/or angelic hierarchies. No longer was he or she able to witness the activity of the most sublime beings.

By the time of the Romans, humanity had virtually (but not completely) severed its contact with the suprasensory world. Though many of the Roman myths paralleled those of Greece, it was the *physical* human being, as emperor, who was now considered a "god." The Romans represented the point in which earthly forces imprinted themselves, so to speak, onto human consciousness in a more pronounced way. It thus corresponded to the Earth phase of earthly evolution—i.e., the point in which the hardening forces of the Earth began to materialize to an ever-higher degree. It was a civilization where individualized consciousness manifested more than ever before. Largely through the interbreeding of cultures (mixing of the blood), group consciousness began to diminish. Human beings gradually started to interrelate or communicate more and more through the forces of the "I," and less and less through the forces of heredity.

Up to and including the time of the Romans, the possibility for humanity to experience the spiritual world had, as we have stated, gradually receded. Only in mystery centers such as Delphi and Ephesus did there exist, for those prepared, the possibility of being more fully initiated into the spiritual worlds. This initiation, however, could only take place when the aspirant was put into a "sleeping" state. Under the guidance of a hierophant, one's etheric and astral bodies rose up into the spiritual worlds, leaving behind the "I" and the physical body. In this way, one was able, though unconsciously, to reconnect oneself to the cosmic forces, especially the descending Sun being who was known to humankind throughout the ages. Nonetheless, the possibility of such an initiation was also to gradually disappear as thinking took ever-greater precedence.

In conjunction with this evolutionary process so far described, Steiner points out, in a lecture given on July 18, 1915,[14] two extremely important developments that occurred with respect to the relationship between language and thinking. The tendency of the luciferic forces was to tear away the conceptual content, once inherent in language, from the language itself. Words were "peeled away from the mental images." Language and thinking worked, from here on, independently of one another. This was particularly important, for not only did this reflect the separation of a thought form from the force (of thinking) intrinsic to it but, as a result, it marked the inception of dogma. This was because these same luciferic beings induced a state whereby uniformity could be established for all human beings to the degree in which thought was emancipated from the influence of language differences. While this was occurring, the ahrimanic forces "allowed the character of language to sink a stage lower," so that languages were separated from one another. Whereas the luciferic beings sought a principle of *uniformity* based on dogma, the ahrimanic beings sought a *division* of humanity predicated upon the separation of the languages, which was to eventually lend itself to the rise of nationalism.

During Roman times, human development was in crisis. For having fallen more and more into a state devoid of spirituality, humanity faced the influential dangers of these ahrimanic and luciferic beings. Had no regenerative impulse made its way to the Earth, human beings would have, in effect, been reduced to an "animalistic state." It was at this most crucial time that the cosmic spirit, known through the ages as Vishvakarman, Ahura Mazda, and Osiris, descended to the Earth and provided the impulse toward a revitalization of humanity's fallen nature. These names were in reference, of course, to the Christ whose experience of death on Golgotha and subsequent resurrection represents, as Rudolf Steiner suggests in *The Foundation Stone*, the "turning point in time"—i.e., the moment after the Fall in which humanity could begin its re-ascension into the cosmic heights. Whereas before, humanity had knowledge (*Sophia*) of Christ but lacked His substantiality, now that substantiality had descended into the human being and would one day give us the opportunity to eventually reconnect to the spiritual world by way of *living* thinking. Says the Christ, "Follow me. I am the Way. I am the Light. I am the Life." The presence of Christ can be found in *living thinking.* It is the *light* that shines in the darkness of dialecticism. ("In Him is the Life, and *this Life is the Light of humankind."* Moreover, *"The Light shone in the darkness, but the darkness comprehended it not!"*) As Christ resurrected himself from death, so, too, must we follow his example and resurrect our thinking from materiality, so as to reconnect ourselves to spiritual world. *Freedom lives in living thinking*; we can only manifest free will to the degree in which thinking is not influenced by the physicality of our being. Given all this, a most astonishing fact arose. Though human beings now had the being of Christ living within the world (and within them), they had lost the *knowledge (Sophia)* of this fact. As Steiner points out in his book, *The Search for the New Isis, Divine Sophia*, from the time of the birth of Christ into the physical world, "it is not the Christ we lack...but the knowledge and wisdom of the Christ, the Sophia of the Christ, the Isis of the Christ.[15] Therefore, humanity was compelled to seek the knowledge of Christ's being—i.e., *Sophia*."

Meanwhile, because the spiritual constitution of human beings was such that only very few could actually grasp the esoteric significance of Christ's presence upon the Earth, most were obliged to rely on an emerging dialecticism to fathom the profundity of the mystery before them. *Religion,* as the etymological root of the word connotes, is the *process* by which human beings "reconnect" (Latin: *religare*) to the spiritual world or, more precisely, to the Christ (through *living* thinking). Yet, humanity, by institutionalizing religion, created a structure that to a large extent inevitably prevented this process from unfolding within the human being. Instead, humanity became subjected to a dogma that had first begun to manifest by way of the luciferic influences during the Indian cultural epoch. The time had yet to come in which the impulses leading to *nationalism* would take hold of human thought and, thereby, subject humanity more strongly to the ahrimanic influences that had first instilled themselves in language.

This brings us to Dante and his circle of poets, known as the *Fedeli d'amore,* for they lived during a period in which the dogma of the Church, having reached its highest pitch, coincided with the impulses of nationalism *about* to surface. Though humanity found itself more and more besieged by the influences of these ahrimanic and luciferic forces, there emerged from the depths of human consciousness the impetus that led many toward an esoteric comprehension of the nature of the Christ, which is to say, they sought *knowledge (Sophia) of the Christ*—embodied in the figure of the Virgin Mary. We can see this manifested in both the profusion of replicas depicting the archetypal Goddess of Nature known as the Black Virgin, which René Querido says, harbored "the promise of the birth of the child fulfilled,"[16] and the formation of the many so-called secret societies, some of which, having arisen throughout all of Europe during that time, were in large part connected to the Gnosticism of early Christianity. Though the existence of such esoteric orders goes back to antiquity, rarely had their presence been so pervasive. Their emergence seemed to be a response to the unconscious intuitions of a new age that harbored the impetus toward humanity's re-ascension into the spiritual world.

This new era that Steiner called the "Consciousness Soul Age," begun in the early fifteenth century, was largely the result of a thinking that would, during the course of the next few centuries, extinguish itself of unconscious atavistic forces and, thereby, adhere solely to the impressions gained of the materialized Earth. It would thus mark the time in which *thought* as a detached and so-called objective phenomenon reflected the degree to which nature, as a materialized reality, had inserted itself into human consciousness. Just as the natural surrounding world was a "crystallized" expression of the suprasensory forces imperceptible to human beings, so too were their thoughts. Nonetheless, through this process, we were given the inherent possibility of one day *consciously* creating our own destiny, by willing our own thinking. This could eventually result in our ability to perceive the will forces (*light*) intrinsic to thinking. These forces are the very ones, which epochs ago, human beings perceived outside in nature. The new age in which this has become ever more possible and in which we presently find ourselves, Steiner called the fifth post-Atlantean epoch.

Thus, just before the dawning of the Consciousness Soul Age when the adversarial forces of humanity sought to take absolute hold of human thinking and willing, there arose a profusion of esoteric or even "heretical" movements that strove to carry humanity onto a new phase of development. The most important order to arise relative to that time was Rosicrucianism. It sought to direct human beings, by way of a sevenfold path, toward perceiving the interplay of microcosmic and macrocosmic forces. This sevenfold path was, in effect, a re-adaptation of the path to initiation of the early Christians, insofar as it corresponded directly to the steps of initiation outlined by the Christ in the seven miracles performed by Him—miracles that culminated with the transformation of Lazarus to John. Many other "religious" groups such as the Knights Templar, the Albigenses, and the Cathars had previously appeared, all of which also sought a deeper relationship to the *being* of Christ. The widespread proliferation of these groups resulted in a brutal campaign of extermination by the Church, which perceived them as undermining its authority. (Of course, we must realize that the Church, by means of the mere slaughter of thousands of people known as the Inquisition, could never have eradicated the *impulses* streaming from the spiritual world.)

Finally, in addition to the many spiritual groups in existence, there was the School of Chartres, whose teachers included Bernardus Sylvestris, Bernard of Chartres, and Alanus ab Insulis, all of whom taught that the Goddess Natura could only be experienced by direct perception. This Goddess Natura, in reference to the living force behind nature, was, of course, what had become hidden from human beings within the depths of their own consciousness—i.e., the presence of *Sophia* leading to the being of Christ. It was, in fact, at this school that Dante's teacher, Brunetto Latini, was said to have participated. We shall deal with Brunetto Latini's importance in a subsequent chapter. Indeed, one sees his profound sensitivity to the divine aspect of Nature (the Goddess Natura) reflected in his homage to the Earth entitled *Il Tesoretto*. In his cycle of lectures on karmic relationships, Steiner makes mention of how the School of Chartres embodied the influences derived from Platonism and Aristotelianism. For, in the spiritual world at the time, a great number of souls shared in bringing down to Earth those impulses that were to eventually prepare humanity for the dawning of the Michaelic Age at the end of the nineteenth century. In essence, all of these movements, if we may call them so, can be thought of as manifestations of Christ consciousness, *countering those adversarial forces that attempted to render humanity unprepared for the future guidance of Michael* during the period following the end of Kali Yuga in 1899, our present time.

As we have stated in the previous chapter, the transformations of what we might call the evolution of human thinking are often mirrored by various literary manifestations through time. Rudolf Steiner, in his *Transforming the Soul,* vol. 2, shows how, by taking into consideration Homer, Dante, Shakespeare, and Goethe, we can witness this transformation as it proceeded from a "fallen" clairvoyant nature (Homer), to one in which "personality" becomes the vehicle toward exploring the spiritual worlds (Dante), to the stage where personality is dispersed among the whole of humanity (Shakespeare), to finally arriving at the point in which personality is transcended (Goethe). Thus, we can witness how the preparation for the Michaelic Age was not only reflected in the formation of religious or "heretical" streams seeking to counter the adversarial forces manifesting themselves through the Church, but also in the literary expressions as witnessed, for example, in the transition from Dante to Goethe. For unlike Dante, whose journey through the *Divine Comedy* is undertaken by himself, we do not find in *Faust* a representation of Goethe's own personal relationship with the spiritual world. Instead, Faust is representative of *all* humankind. Goethe, by not identifying himself with Faust, points to the transcendence of the egoic forces that impede human beings from acknowledging how one's salvation depends upon the salvation of all humanity.

To better comprehend the stage of consciousness attained by humanity during the time of Dante, we must, as Rudolf Steiner shows, compare Dante himself to a representative of a preceding stage—i.e., Homer. Homer lived during the Intellectual Soul Age in which humankind possessed, to a greater degree, the ability to behold the suprasensory world. The principle characteristic of Homer's works was "poetic imagination," which, as Steiner says, attempted to recapture what it could of the forces manifesting life. Even though the "I"-consciousness of human beings slowly began to assert itself more and more with the passing of time, they still drew their inspiration from the gods that they invoked. This is evident in *The Odyssey*, which begins with Ulysses uttering, "Sing, O Muse, of the man, the much travelled one...."

We see, here, that Ulysses appeals to the higher spiritual powers for guidance, for though direct observation of them was receding, there still existed the awareness that spiritual beings directed the movements of human beings. By Dante's time, we find that the spiritual forces once addressed by Homer had now descended into humanity. In fact, this is intimated in the *Divine Comedy*, where Dante's appeal is no longer directed to the Muses, as was Homer's, but, rather, to the forces inherent within human consciousness. Says Dante,

> O Muses, O high Genius! Be my aid!
> O *Memory*...
> > (*Inferno II*, 7–8; italics mine)

The development of this individualized consciousness fostered the emergence of the "personality" to which Steiner refers. This "personality" may be seen to have a correlation to the human embodiment of the gods during Roman times. Whereas, then, the Roman emperor declared himself the visible manifestation of the Godhead, in Dante and those living during his time, the Logos, which had already begun to live within thinking, was reflected outwardly as personality. Nonetheless, during Dante's time, the emergence of pure dialectical thinking was still in its developmental phase and could not yet lead to a conscious perception of the spiritual world, as is appropriate to the Michaelic Age. In other words, the resurrection of thinking was not yet possible for most of humanity, for a remnant of clairvoyant perception still lingered within human consciousness. Human thinking could not yet totally divorce itself from lingering atavistic forces. Thinking had yet to become hardened or materialized to the point in which the living forces intrinsic to it could be lifted out and beheld as an objective reality. Nonetheless, this did not preclude Dante and others from partaking in the developmental process itself and, thereby, from participating, at least to some degree, in the stage of initiation attainable by humanity at that time—though conditioned by the Catholic world of which he was a part. In his previously mentioned lecture on Dante given on February 11, 1906, Steiner says,

> Dante's poem is a vision. It is a vision that an Initiate can experience, a reality of the Spiritual World that Dante can truly perceive. He perceives with spiritual organs what is found in the world of the Spirit and represents it as a Christian–Catholic Initiate can represent it. In this vision, he brings that of the Catholic world, which has penetrated into his being, but he is nevertheless capable of penetrating spiritually.... At each point in time, we catch sight of the Spiritual through the lenses of our own experience.

The relationship between the physical world and the life of an unborn child in the maternal womb corresponds to the relation between the Spiritual World and the fabric of our experiences that we fulfill on Earth. Here, in the course of our earthly existence, we mature, so to speak, as if in our mother's womb, in order to one day be born spiritually. The senses that we have fashioned for our spiritual vision depend on our existence on Earth.... Dante therefore had his spiritual organs fashioned thanks to the influence that the Christian–Catholic world had exerted on him. (tr. mine from Italian)[17]

As in the case of Ulysses in *The Odyssey*, we find Dante, in Canto II of the *Inferno*, imploring the Muses to help him retell his experience of the journey undertaken by him. These forces, however, are now within *him*. Says Dante,

> O Muses! O high Genius! Be my aid!
> O *Memory*, recorder of the vision,
> here shall your true nobility be displayed!
>   (*Inferno II*, 8–9; italics mine)

Interestingly, this word *memory,* used to express *"mente"* (mind) in Italian, is something that we do not find in Homer when he addresses the Muses. If anything, it shows how the cosmic activity experienced outwardly by Ulysses had become "personalized" in Dante through *his* "individualized" experience of his spiritual journey. In other words, the Intelligences (Muses) that Homer had experienced outside of him now exist within Dante. Retrieving such an experience depends on the ability to grasp, free of the senses, the impressions originating from the suprasensory realm. This is precisely the case with Dante. If we are to understand that he, in his *Divine Comedy*, attempts to depict the spiritual vision that his teacher, Brunetto Latini, had *conveyed* to him, we must accept the fact that in the very act of transference, the living reality of such a vision is at least felt, if not directly experienced, by Dante. This living aspect, again, reflects the presence of a consciousness that is free of the influences of the material world. Says Steiner,

...the same living reality is reflected in the descriptions of such men as Brunetto Latini, the celebrated teacher of Dante. The vigorous, creative spirit of the time can be readily imagined, for the characters and splendid pictorial descriptions of Dante's *Commedia* are inspired by the graphic descriptions of his teacher Brunetto Latini....[18]

Thus, what is it that the *Divine Comedy* symbolizes? How is it to be understood? The answer to these questions will form the basis of this work. For now, we can say that Dante's poem was, itself, a direct manifestation of a consciousness particular to a given point in time that invariably sought to show how humanity could reconnect itself to the suprasensory world. It contains characterizations that delineate the moral underpinnings of Dante's journey as they relate to human thinking. Though the nature of human consciousness at the time of Dante was yet not ripe for modern initiation, we will later see how the *Divine Comedy* can nonetheless be *imagined* in such a way as to embody the path of human initiation relevant to our times.

Behind the Scenes

As we begin to consider the social climate surrounding Dante and his contemporaries, it would be helpful to ponder a statement made by Rudolf Steiner in a lecture given on October 18, 1918 in Dornach, Switzerland. He said, "External events, what are usually called historical facts, are in reality only symptoms."[19] In other words, the so-called historical facts by which we attempt to understand human development are merely markers that invariably point to a *suprasensory process* underlying their formation. Consequently, Steiner's remarks suggest the need of cultivating the perceptive capacity to decipher the inexplicable events that comprise much of what we call history. We would thus need to behold the *forces* responsible for manifesting such events, which would, in turn, enable us to contextualize what we deem "historical" with respect to the evolution of human consciousness. Implicit in Steiner's words is the notion that events inevitably spring from the inner depths of being, that is, from the spiritual foundation of human consciousness—thinking, feeling, and willing. This gives rise to an interesting correlation between historical representations and thinking itself, in that, what we construe as an historical event buried in time is often little more than the materialized embodiment of thought. Thus, just as an "historical fact" can, by nature, be likened to the materialized thought from which it takes its form, so, too, can the suprasensory impulses that manifest an isolated event in time be likened to the *force* of thinking from which such a thought form arises, once this force has been taken hold of by the physical body.

Thus, we can infer from Steiner's statement that the meaning we attribute to the mere appearance of such an outer representation (or "historical fact") should not be given too much weight, for without understanding the underlying forces responsible for its manifestation, one can easily misinterpret its inherent relevance to the spiritual development of our being. In effect, we are normally confronted by what seems to be a succession of historical events, which thinking has systematically linked, just as objects strewn about us in a room are connected by thought the moment we perceive them. Nevertheless, the manner in which events are interconnected can, in no way, *fathom* the impulses responsible for their manifestation. Without adequate spiritual preparation, we can (at best) try to interpret such events by placing them within a context that traces the unfolding of human consciousness—a context such as that provided by Rudolf Steiner, who was able to *penetrate the sphere of pure spiritual activity*. In so doing, we can begin to visualize Dante as a human personality who enters the stream of human evolution at a time in which the nature of human consciousness is about to undergo a drastic transformation.

Born in 1265, Dante signals the *initial* stirring of the Consciousness Soul Age that would take root roughly 150 years later, when the human *personality* begins its struggle for emancipation within the social framework. It is a period that witnesses the birth of pure abstract thinking, which in many ways, is the basis for today's social interrelations. This is in marked contrast to the Intellectual Soul Age preceding it, in which we find human communities established largely through blood-ties. In such an instance, blood was the vehicle through which group consciousness expressed itself. Folk Souls, governing the various races, were able to bring the thinking of human beings—not fully individualized—into a sort of collective expression. Only with the emergence of the Consciousness Soul Age does the differentiation arise that permits human beings to gradually step out of their so-called group soul and allow each person to begin establishing their individualism. In this case, the blood played an essential role in the human being's growing predilection toward self-expression. It did so in such a way that, now, with the dawning of the Consciousness Soul Age, the "I" begins to assert its autonomy. Blood now becomes *the vehicle of the "I"* that leads to the emergent individual freedom. Though blood-ties gradually became less a determining factor in forming interrelations between people in the West—due largely to the mixing of cultures during Roman times[20]—the atavistic clairvoyant consciousness, connected to blood ties, somewhat persisted *residually* on into the Middle Ages. With the exception of Church dogma, society, up to that time, did not function according to conceptual models, but largely according to impulses born of blood-ties characteristic of Intellectual Soul Age. That is to say, there existed no philosophical framework among the common people that could unify them, at least conceptually, in their quest toward freedom. Only with the birth of personality could this *gradually* become manifest. In *From Symptom to Reality in Modern History*, Steiner says,

> When this new epoch dawns, the budding Consciousness Soul is operative in it and manifests itself in historical symptoms. On the one hand, we see the national impulses at work, on the other hand we see, striking at the very roots of religious faith, the revolt of the personality that strives for autonomy because the Consciousness Soul seeks to burst its bonds.[21]

Though Dante was clearly a man of the Middle Ages, he heralds the birth of a dawning new age. In *Transforming the Soul*, vol. 2, Steiner shows that Dante can be differentiated from Homer or Aeschylus (both of the Intellectual Soul Age) insofar as he is "alone with his personality." He "relies on the inner development that was possible in the Middle Ages, with the strength of human *personality* as its only aid" (italics mine).[22]

In spite of the fact that Dante was, to some degree, representative of this emerging element in humanity, he still had to struggle against the countering forces of the Intellectual Soul Age. We can see this conflict working itself out in his individuality. On the one hand, there stands a man who strives to establish both a new sociopolitical order (*De Monarchia*) and a religious impulse based upon the spiritual aspect of the human being. On the other, both of these initiatives take effect within the framework that had already manifested during the Intellectual Soul Age, namely the Roman Empire and the Catholic Church. Although Dante, as we shall witness, seeks to establish a deeper, more esoteric connection to the Christ, this was done, in large part, with the hope of transforming or *spiritualizing* the Church in Rome. Likewise, he sought to establish a new political impulse, separate from the Church, which would be based on restoring (and reforming) the Roman Empire. This "bipartition" of the social sphere is reflective of the changes that human beings inwardly were soon to experience with the dawning of the Consciousness Soul Age, and illustrates how the transition from one age to the other was gradually reflected in the human soul. Interestingly, the spiritualization that Dante hoped to see in the Church was fostered most notably through his use of language, for, unlike his predecessors who exclusively used Latin, Dante was the first Italian poet to write a major work in the vernacular. Largely, for this reason, he has been called "The Father of the Italian language." In a lecture held on June 28, 1923, Rudolf Steiner points to the importance that Latin held throughout the centuries in relation to the development of human consciousness. He states that nearly everything that one has learned by way of formal education (at least up to his time) came under the influence of the Latin language. The peculiar thing about Latin, according to Steiner, is that it had developed in such a way during ancient Rome, that it could actually "think on its own in the human being." Says Steiner,

> It is interesting how Latin is taught in high schools. One learns Latin; and then one learns thinking, correct thinking according to Latin syntax. So one's whole way of thinking does not depend on anything one does, but on what the Latin language does. You understand, don't you, that this is something quite significant. Anybody who has learned something does not think for himself: the Latin language thinks in him, even if he has not learned Latin.[23]

Now this chief characteristic of the Latin language is such that it stifles independent thinking and makes the human being into somewhat of an automaton, thus providing the ahrimanic forces with a most suitable vehicle through which to operate. Since Latin, as developed and employed by the Romans, is the language that, as Steiner says, reflects more than any other, humanity's fall into materiality, it can readily be understood how it fetters thinking to the physical brain, thereby precluding human beings from perceiving the spiritual world. In light of all this, one can never underestimate the profound significance that Dante's conversion to the vernacular in the *Vita Nuova* and the *Divine Comedy* had for the future development of humanity. Not only can he be thought of as having planted the seeds for the gradual disintegration of Latin's influence upon human thinking but, in so doing, he helped prepare the groundwork for the usurpation of the Church's influence over society, an influence which, as Steiner shows in *Three Streams in Human Evolution*, arose from the efforts of the Roman Emperor Augustus to return to the initiatory practices of remote antiquity—i.e., to direct humanity to the rituals and initiatory practices of the Egyptian epoch. Says he,

> ...the Catholic Church is a continuation, the true continuation of the Augustan age.... The most active element that runs through the Catholic Church is at best its ritual. And into this ritual there are woven only some threads derived from the Mystery of Golgotha; in its forms and ceremonies, it has come over from the age of the Sentient Soul.[24]

Nevertheless, the relevance of Dante's desire to spiritualize the Church is implicitly reinforced by Steiner's affirmation that the Mass, while pointing to the highest Mystery of human evolution, was itself in need of *new life,* for no longer could the Sentient Soul serve humankind with that which only the Consciousness Soul could provide it. We see this manifested to the degree in which the rituals employed by Catholicism, inadvertently led to mere dogma by inducing humanity's strict adherence to symbolic forms unfathomable to a dialectical intellect that was about to take an ever-greater hold on human consciousness. This was to have the inevitable effect of circumventing the process of thinking, which alone could eventually harbor the possibility of reenlivening one's inner world. In other words, the strict adherence to the symbolism of ritual, devoid of understanding, precluded humanity from entering a new age in accordance with the development of being. Thus, the inception of dogma, which, as we have seen, occurred during the Indian epoch when mental images were stripped of their content, reached its height through the Church, insofar as humanity witnessed this separation of content from meaning in the form of ritual. For this reason, the connection that Augustus sought to the spiritual world was one inspired by luciferic forces. One must not think, however, that the luciferic forces alone were responsible for establishing the Church's authority. For the effect of dogma upon human consciousness was to undermine the inclination toward independent thinking and induce conformity, and it was Latin (which, again, "thinks on its own in the human being") that provided the basis for dogma to take hold in human beings in such a way that the makings of a surrogate "nationalistic" impulse that functions from *within* the institution of the Church itself could take root. The uniformity that the Church sought to impose by way of dogma was predicated on the basis of what once united its people, namely the non-individualized consciousness (Intellectual Soul) connected to the forces at work in the blood. And so, the imposition of this kind of uniformity could only arise through (and result in) the suppression of individualized thinking. In the end, the Church sought to undermine the emergence of individuality by subjugating humanity to the decrees of established law, enforced by willful manipulation through fear. Here, incidentally, is where the ahrimanic forces make their presence felt, for they make religion a sociopolitical force whose influence, predicated on fear—often for the salvation of one's own soul—is virtually insurmountable. With the dawning of the Consciousness Soul Age, however, the Church began to lose its power. We see this loss of power manifested in the widespread proliferation of new religious movements, which presaged the emergence of individualized thinking.

Thus, this Consciousness Soul Age, marking a change in the spiritual constitution of humanity, took place around the year 1413, at a time when the influence of Catholicism had weakened. This weakening was poignantly reflected in the fact that, in 1309, the Papacy transferred residency to Avignon, which Steiner says would have been "inconceivable in earlier times."[25] It was during this period, and even later, that we witness the Papacy exerting tremendous force in suppressing those elements that were precursors to the rise of nationalism. Steiner says, "just as this Roman Catholic impulse had relegated the guilds and other corporate bodies to a subordinate role, so, too, national identity suffered the same fate," adding "at the time when Roman Catholicism exercised its greatest dynamic power, national identity was not regarded as the most important factor in the structure of the human soul."[26] In fact, the Church's suppression of individuality had the effect of inhibiting the emergence of a "national identity" in the regions where it held temporal power. This "national identity," in effect, represented, on a collective level, what on an individual level Steiner describes as "personality"—i.e., the degree to which self-consciousness began to assert itself in the individual.

To achieve its aims, the Catholic Church implemented a most menacing institution to regulate social activity—the Inquisition. Though it would exist for centuries, the Inquisition was never more brutal than during the waning years of the Middle Ages and early Renaissance, when thousands of people were persecuted and tortured for being suspected of trying to usurp the Church's influence. Charles William Heckethorn states, in his *Secret Societies of All Countries and Ages*, that in his eighteen-year reign as the Grand Inquisitor of Spain, Father Thomas de Torquemada, for example, condemned an average of ten thousand people annually to death by fire, torture, and starvation. In the first six months of his sanguinary rule 298 *marranos* (Moors and Jews) were burnt at the stake in Seville alone. Two thousand were condemned to death in other places, while 17,000 people accused of heresy underwent various forms of punishment.[27] This does not even take into consideration the near total extermination of the Cathars, Albigenses, and especially the holiest of orders dedicated to renewing and spreading the Christ impulse through its relation to the Sophia—the Knights Templar.

It is against such a backdrop that we must understand the motivations of individualities such as Dante and his contemporaries in both their political and spiritual endeavors. As we shall see, what is necessary in comprehending the enigmatic nature of the *Divine Comedy* and countless love sonnets during the period in which Dante lived is precisely this force of oppression that the Roman Catholic Church then embodied in society. Though the Middle Ages can be said to be the period in human evolution when the Church manifested its greatest power, it should not be assumed, however, that its subversive tendencies—in which fear was used as an instrument to manipulate the freedom of thought—arose spontaneously as a mere aberration of its teachings. In fact, the Inquisition, as Heckethorn states, existed "from the earliest days of Christianity... in the *spirit*, if not in the *form*."[28]

It seems that Constantine's success in greatly empowering the Church did more than anything to instigate a condemnation of heretics. This became civil law when Pope Urban II determined that the execution of an excommunicated was not a crime. In 1228, at the request of Pope Honorius III, an inquisition was organized into the death of Peter of Castelnau, who had been allegedly killed by the Albigenses for leading an expedition against them. According to Charles William Heckethorn, the *idea* of such an inquisition was initially due to the founder of the Dominican order, Dominique de Guzman. This led to the banishment of the heretics from their state and the confiscation of their property. In due time, Guzman also organized what was known as the "Militia of Christ," a band of religious enforcers, "an invisible troop of spies and denouncers... who formed a *secret* portion of the Inquisition."[29] From 1233 on into the

1300s, the Inquisition spread through Spain, France, Italy, and Germany and was soon responsible for the persecution of the Knights Templar. Thus, we see that what became the Inquisition was, in effect, a reemergence of Romanism in new form. It was a way to subjugate those who aspired toward the true teachings of Christ, just as the Romans brutalized the early Christians during the first centuries after the Mystery of Golgotha. In this way, the Catholic Church, which harbored the impulses of the Sentient Soul (brought on during the Intellectual Soul Age by Augustus), opposed the birth of the Consciousness Soul Age. This impulse was to penetrate into the deepest levels of society for centuries to come, that is, until humankind, under the influence of the Consciousness Soul Age, was able to develop scientific thinking to the point where the Church could not escape its influence and, thereby, had to accept the inevitable—the rise of the human being's will toward freedom.

In the meantime, due to the suppressive social conditions just described, elements of this new soul age could only emerge in strict secrecy, since it was not uncommon for men such as Dante and his teacher, Brunetto Latini, to be exiled from their native cities with the threat of persecution always at their heels. Though Dante's conflict with the Church is often reflected in the *Divine Comedy* and other writings, he had, at first, joined forces with the Guelfs, comprised of a middle-class merchant society, whose influence was orchestrated by the Church in an effort to overthrow the emperor Frederick II, King of Germany and Emperor of Rome who was, in turn, supported by the Ghibellines and overthrown in 1266. But this was not done in support of the Papacy, per se. Instead, its primary aim was to bestow upon the city-states of Italy the autonomy from foreign rule needed to establish a national identity connected to its Roman past. In demonstrating his opposition to the Church, Dante afterward declared that he would form a party "by himself" with the hope of establishing an empire that sought to enkindle Italy's future by proclaiming himself a "White Guelf," which was more philosophically allied to the Ghibellines. Though we can assume that Dante's need to form a party sought to abolish the secular power assumed by the Papacy, it can easily be overlooked as containing the seeds to one of the most constitutional elements characteristic of the Consciousness Soul Age, the rise of nationalism. Rarely, in the history of human evolution had members of the general populace, united by their ideological convictions, utilized what may be called rudimentary political parties as a vehicle toward social change.

The ideological foundation behind Dante's vision of the sociopolitical spheres of society was to appear in a work entitled *De Monarchia* (burnt by the Church), in which he conceived being governed by what we today would call the separation of Church and State. Though we will focus primarily on the nature of Dante's spiritual conception of the human being and the Cosmos, we must be mindful of the fact that the religious freedom he sought could only be attained through the segregated autonomy of the political and religious spheres. The insurgence of religious freedom, at that time, squelched as it was, could find no outer vehicles by which to manifest itself in the whole of society. Because the Church ruled with an iron fist, anyone who was, in the slightest degree, suspected of professing a differing conceptual relationship to God, would be deemed heretical, tortured, and often burnt alive. Modern scholars, seemingly oblivious of the many restrictions imposed upon members of society at that time, have often consequently forgotten to ask by which means did those of similar political or religious persuasions communicate with one another so as to avoid the ever-present watchful eye of the Church. Furthermore, was it possible for someone like Dante to nurture the profound spiritual knowledge that he possessed without any connection to those around him of like mind?

It is precisely this point, rarely taken into account by modern scholars, that I believe has often led them astray in uncovering the ingenious paradoxes contrived in medieval Italian literature. For, as we shall see, the effort to make unintelligible many of the enigmatic references in the poetry of Dante and the *Fedeli d'amore* was intentional. Only by obfuscating the explicit communications by means of a jargon, secretive and well constructed, could Dante and his closest friends (Guido Cavalcanti, Guido Guinizelli, and others) avoid persecution. Herein lies the key to unveiling many of the most puzzling mysteries contained in the Italian literature of that era and, thereby, understanding how the esoteric knowledge of that time connects with the stream of Anthroposophy.

The Secret Message

"O voi c'avete intelletti sani, mirate la dottrina che s'asconde sotto il velame de li versi strani."

(O, you of sound intellect and probity, weigh with good understanding what lies hidden behind the veil of my strange allegory.)
(*Inferno* IX: 58–60, tr. John Ciardi)

As we probe the challenges faced by Dante and his circle of poets, the *Fedeli d'amore*, it becomes apparent that much more than is traditionally imagined lay behind the sweet poetic images of courtly love. Through the exquisitely refined adulations of womanhood, there emerged the constitutional elements of a philosophy that, at the time, extended far beyond the common understanding of humanity. Because the pursuit for such knowledge threatened to shake the roots of ecclesiastical authority, the sharing of information amongst the group required careful planning and deliberation. The dilemma in establishing a secure and reliable network of communication seems to have been twofold. First, how could the transmission of secret information forbidden by the Church be executed so as to avoid detection, thereby leaving unscathed the "sacred knowledge" toward which these poets yearned? Secondly, what were the precautions needed to conceal the appearance of a conspiracy that the Church might have interpreted as a threat to its security? As we will gradually discover, the answer to the second question hinges on the first. To maintain a cohesive inner structure, the circle to which Dante belonged could display no outer administrative configuration. Instead, such unity could solely arise out of an *understanding* made implicit within the jargon of their literary works. The inclusion of new members, communicated messages, accounts of journeys, and knowledge of related sects in other cities had to be *coded* so as to transmit the desired information and, at the same time, misdirect the wary eyes of the Church without stirring the slightest suspicion of the circle's true motives. And what were those true motives? What was the knowledge that the *Fedeli d'amore* really sought to disseminate amongst its members? These are some of the questions that (as many have come to believe) unveil one of the great "schemes" in the history of literature.

Arising out of the School of Frederick II in Sicily, around the early 1200s, was what many scholars have construed as an attempt by Frederick II to initiate a national lyric poetry. However, as this poetic movement spread to the central regions of Italy, it was to undergo numerous refinements and transformations under the name *"Il Dolce Stil Novo"* (The Sweet New Style). The apparent objective of this poetry was the "beatification of woman," a theme that seems to have had its origins in Islam and whose tradition survived on into the Middle Ages in Europe via the love sonnets of the Provencal Troubadours.

Now, if we bear in mind the many allusions made by Steiner to the impulse of Arabism during the Middle Ages and its influence on the philosophical nature of European thought, and couple this with the fact that Dante himself was versed in the *Koran*, it is not hard to imagine how such an impulse—having spread up through Spain into Western Europe and through Turkey into Eastern Europe, thereby permeating a great part of Western Civilization—might have affected the thinking of these poets. But this is not quite the case! In spite of the fact that Dante may have been acquainted with the writings of Averroes, which were at odds with Aristotelianism, it was certainly not the materialistic impulse—begun at the court of Haroun al Raschid—by which Averroes was guided, that was reflected in the poetry and the spiritual striving of Dante and his circle. For such themes as the "beatification of women" were earlier used in the poetry of the mystical Sufi orders in Persia, which were certainly *not* representative of this materialistic impulse—an impulse later embodied in the teachings and writings of Lord Bacon of Veralum and Amos Comenius. This materialistic impulse sought to implant Arabism in the thinking of humanity and, thereby, counter the influences of Scholasticism, a form of "Christianized Aristotelianism."

Instead, it must also be remembered that in the West the theme "beatification of woman" became directly connected to the cult of Mary, initiated largely through the efforts of St. Bernard of Clairvaux, Dante's final guide in the *Paradiso*. The figure of Mary, symbolic of the Archetypal being, *Sophia*, represented the feminine stream of human consciousness. Through the contemplation of an individualized representation of this Archetypal force, the *Fedeli d'amore* strove to realize the being of Christ. In his book, *Rites, Symbols and Initiation*, Mircea Eliade says,

> "Woman" symbolizes the transcendent intellect, Wisdom. Love of a woman awakens the adept from the lethargy into which the Christian world had fallen because of the spiritual unworthiness of the pope. In the writings of the *Fedeli d'Amore* we find allusions to a "widow who is no widow"; this is the *Madonna Intelligenza,* who was left a widow because her husband, the pope, died to spiritual life by devoting himself entirely to things temporal.
>
> Strictly speaking, this is not a heretical movement, but simply a secret group that no longer accorded the pope the status of spiritual leader of Christianity. We know nothing of their initiation rites; but they must have had such rites, for the *Fedeli d'Amore* constituted a militia and held secret meetings. But they are chiefly important because they illustrate a phenomenon that will become more marked later—the communication of a secret spiritual message through literature. Dante is the most famous example of this tendency—which already anticipates the modern world—to consider art, especially literature, the paradigmatic method of communicating a theology, a metaphysics, and even a soteriology.[30]

"Il Dolce Stil Novo" maintained that only by the *love* of woman (divine) could humankind come to the realization of its own divine nature. Yet, this "idealization of woman" was fraught with ambiguity, for what did it mean to idealize or beatify? Such a nebulous

characterization thus had the effect of inscribing, in the minds of the *"gente grossa"*—i.e., the ignorant masses—a term used by Luigi Valli (a leading exponent of Dantean esotericism) to describe those unable to recognize and penetrate the secret jargon of the *Fedeli d'amore*—the notion that beatifying woman was, in and of itself, a divine act, and that only by showing love toward one's "lady" could one hope to find "salvation."

This is where the shrewdness of such a characterization asserts itself, for it inevitably gave rise to the inference that earthly love was synonymous or interchangeable with Divine Love. Whereas, this was not quite the case, for again the word *beatification* had more to do with the *feminine principle* of human consciousness, namely, human thinking. In other words, thinking itself was to be "idealized," that is, it was to lead to the contemplation of the Archetypal Idea (Sophia). This, in turn, prompted the transformation or purification of the impulses arising from the lower aspect of human nature. *The ultimate aim of this "purging of desire" was, again, to enable human beings to experience the being of Christ.* Only in this way could a true spiritualization of the Church arise, as Dante himself had envisioned.

Such deliberate ambiguity regarding the term *beatification* had the desired effect of perpetrating the obscurity intended—i.e., inhibiting the Church Fathers from inferring that woman (divine) was, in essence, the Virgin Sophia or *Divine Wisdom*—namely, what Goethe later referred to as the Eternal Feminine. This *Divine Wisdom*, incidentally, as we have shown, referred to the true *knowledge* leading to the Christ—a knowledge from which humanity had been forsaken from the time of His entry into the world. We must remember that the Church had declared *itself* to be the so-called Bride of Christ, thereby replacing, in the form of institutionalized dogma, the "wisdom" inherent within thinking, inasmuch as this represented the feminine principle at work within human consciousness. Thus, we see that the *Fedeli d'amore* could not declare that they were the sole proprietors of this Sophia without incurring the wrath of the Church. This would have essentially been the greatest threat that the Church could have possibly faced, namely, the widespread realization that it did not embody the wisdom/Sophia that could lead to the Christ. Realizing the dangers associated with all of this, the *Fedeli d'amore* could not risk exposing such knowledge without fearing prosecution. Hence, great care was taken to shift attention away from the representation of the archetypal being (*Sophia*) that the Church falsely claimed for herself, by indirectly addressing this being through the concept of the "beatification of woman." In this way, only those who would not let themselves be deceived by the outer representations of the Church could take part in the *genuine* pursuit of this sacred being. Such confusion was largely made possible because each member of the circle (or sect, as Valli called them) acknowledged this *feminine principle* by a different name that, in turn, resulted from the apparent individualization of this Archetypal Wisdom. Of importance was the fact that, as Henry Corbin states in *Avicenna and the Visionary Recital*,

> The angelic mediation that is the very form, necessary and each time unique, of the revelation of the hidden and inaccessible deity completes a process of individualization that brings the self to the threshold of the trans-consciousness in which it receives the announcement of the true Subject who thinks it by individuating it and individuates it by thinking it—that is, by revealing *it* and revealing this revelation to *it* (consciousness of its consciousness!). And that is why the *Fedeli d'amore* could profess the same cult for the same Intelligence–Sophia, yet at the same time could perceive its archetypal Figure under the features of a Figure that was each time another, unique for each unique.[31]

We can thus view this individualization of the *Intelligence–Sophia*, in its most occult sense, as each person's attempt to *actualize* the *Active Intelligence* within consciousness, that is, to cognize thinking to the degree that it was possible, with respect to the human being's spiritual constitution. One need only think of Dante's poem in the *Vita Nuova*, "*Donne ch'avete l'intelletto d'amore*" ("Women, you who have the intellect of love"). Here, the *intellect of love* is the faculty of cognition whose very contemplation leads to the Christ.

Thus, *donne* (women) can be thought to symbolize the group's individual representations of the Archetypal being, Sophia, whereby each member of the *Fedeli d'amore* could then be seen as having shared in its contemplation, while giving the illusion of being afflicted by sensual love. As a result, the Church was left thinking that members of this poetic circle, the *Fedeli d'amore,* uttered sentimental rhymes of love, which the Church ultimately found innocent, puerile and, of course, acceptable.

Incidentally, as we shall later see, *donne* could also have been in reference to the individual members of the poetic circle who sought to actualize the "intellect of love"—i.e., the *Divine Wisdom (Active Intelligence)* conducive to realizing the Christ.

The success of the *Fedeli d'amore* in deceiving the Inquisition and the *"gente grossa"* lay in their ability to construct, through allegory, a jargon that would often connote a meaning opposite to that suggested. In uncovering the implementation of such a jargon, we are greatly indebted to a relatively obscure group of individuals who, one after another, began to explore the inner connections between the writings of the various members of the sect. As Willy Schwarz succinctly shows in his *Studi su Dante e spunti di storia del cristianesimo*, this unfolding awareness began with the Italian poet, Ugo Foscolo, when he noticed that there existed correlations between the *De Monarchia* and fundamental ideas in the *Divine Comedy*. Then, in 1840, Gabriele Rossetti in his *Il Mistero dell'Amor Platonico del Medioevo* traced Dante's separation from the Church and showed how he had connections with the Knights Templar. It was Rossetti who also intuited a "secret language" after having perceived inconsistencies in the lyric poetry of that time. In 1852, Michelangelo Caetani of Sermoneta and, later, the renowned Italian poet Giovanni Pascoli recognized the symbolism in the dichotomy of Church and State. It was Luigi Valli, however, one of Pascoli's disciples, who went on to make a systematic study of this symbolism and, thus, uncover the function that this "secret language" had for Dante's circle of friends—the *Fedeli d'amore*. These efforts have been substantiated by a number of scholars during the last century such as Robert John, who in his book entitled, *Dante,* provides convincing evidence to verify Rossetti's intuitions regarding Dante's affiliation with the Templar order.

Each scholar, such as Valli or Rossetti, while revealing a particular esoteric aspect, passed on the torch by which future Dantean scholars could unveil yet even more enigmas obscured by rationalistic thinking. If we are to assume that greater clarity can only arise from a vision of reality that is in consonance with the unfolding of human consciousness over time, how can it be otherwise? It is, therefore, no coincidence that the esoteric nature of Dante's writings gradually became revealed centuries after he had written them, just at the time the Michaelic forces began raying down, once again, onto the Earth.

Nonetheless, as Henry Corbin points out in *Avicenna and the Visionary Recital,* the findings of people such as Rossetti came very close to being *lost* during the course of the late nineteenth century. Says he,

> All the ground gained by phenomenology in this domain from the time of Dante Gabriele Rossetti was in the danger of being lost without even being missed. The fact is that a false dilemma was set up by the supposed obligation to decide whether it was a question of real feminine figures *or* of the Intelligence–Sophia, just as elsewhere it is shutting oneself in a false dilemma to begin by limiting the spheres of being to the intelligible sphere *or* the sensible sphere.[32]

Having stated this, it would be useful to remember a statement made by Rudolf Steiner in *Karmic Relations,* vol. 6. There, he shows how, just preceding the advent of Michael, forces at work from within the Earth had begun to take possession of human thinking in an effort to *counter* the archangelic impulse of Michael, an impulse, incidentally, that had manifested itself just as the secret knowledge hidden within the writings of Dante and the *Fedeli d'amore* had gradually begun to be uncovered. In a great many instances, these ahrimanic forces worked in opposition to Michael through the printed word. Steiner states,

Ahriman's influence in the printing art of the modern age, however, has assumed a deep significance. Authorship has, so to speak, been popularized. And something has become possible, something that is as great in a wonderful, brilliant, dazzling way as, on the other hand, the necessity is great to receive it in absolute equableness of soul and to estimate it according to its true significance. First attempts have been made, attempts that from Michael's realm may be characterized by saying: Ahriman has appeared as an author.[33]

We must understand that here we are dealing with a spiritual force that seeks to weaken human thinking so that it becomes lifeless, devoid of will. Thus, we find individualities, such as Nietzsche, whose thinking embodies the materialistic impulses that arise, as a consequence. Steiner adds, "works written by men will appear, but some individuals must be aware that a being is training himself to become one of the most brilliant authors in the immediate future."[34] In the attempts of modern criticism (whose foundation rests firmly on nineteenth century positivism) to strip Beatrice, for example, of all her spiritual attributes as they relate to the *knowledge* of Christ, can we not possibly perceive the workings of these anti-Michaelic forces? As a result, regardless of whether Dante may have known and been inspired by the figure of Beatrice Portinari as a child, most of the characterizations regarding the divine aspects of Beatrice have been, at best, nebulous fabrications of the so-called official criticism, whereby the words *divine* or *spiritual* are themselves mere empty shells—indiscriminate nominal projections of a thinking divorced from its source of spiritual activity.

These attempts to obscure the esoteric relevancy of Dante's writings, as well as those of the *Fedeli d'amore*, have primarily arisen from positivistic thinking. Rarely, if ever, do we find that the objections to the "esoteric" interpretations of Dante result from a true understanding of the "esoteric mind." More important, rarely, if ever, do such critics reveal to the reader their *own* understanding of the world's esoteric foundation by means of which they can level their criticism.

The Secret Message

Theirs is a criticism whose perspective is largely derived from *outside* the circle of understanding.

Although the implicit connections between thinkers such as Rossetti, Pascoli, and Valli have not always been systematically delineated, those connections exist by virtue of the fact that they each intuitively partook in what Dante called the anagogic meaning of his works, namely, a meaning not easily fathomed by purely sense-based consciousness and elucidated by dialectical explications. Positivistic thinking is, *by nature,* precluded from fathoming the deeper levels of esoteric thought underlying Dante's *Comedy*, because of its incapacity to *perceive* the inner dynamics of consciousness, as we have shown. Furthermore, positivistic thinking only gives credence to what can be systematically categorized—a categorization often not conducive to esoteric thought. Just as Dante himself states that there exists a level of cognitive experience responsible for the manifestation of the ineffable vision of the *Divine Comedy,* so, too, is it only by means of such cognition that the meaning of his work can be fully grasped.

When all is said and done, what seems to me most implicitly advocated by many opponents of Dante's esotericism, besides an unabashed adherence to the traditional positivistic means of interpretation, is an appreciation for the aesthetic and structural attributes of Dante's work, and the leeway by which one is free to boundlessly speculate on them. Certainly, these aesthetic and structural attributes are plentiful and often extraordinary. However, such perspectives do not shed light on the intrinsic meaning of Dante's work as it relates to the nature of human consciousness. Such adherence to the aesthetic properties of the *Divine Comedy*, for example, is exemplified by the work of Italian literary philosophers such as Benedetto Croce, who justified the validity of positivistic thinking when he said "to say, as has often been said, that Dante would burn with indignation against his major modern-day admirers and critics...taken *only* by the sensitive and poetic beauty of [his] work is not an argument against, but in favor of, such [positivistic] criticism, which from Dante's time until today has come a long way" (tr.

mine).³⁵ In testimony to the fact that writers and critics can often be seen to live in divergent universes from the writers whose works they examine, Croce essentially goes on to say that just as Dante's aesthetics and criticisms were his affair, the aesthetics and criticisms of his critics must be seen as their affair.

Not to diminish the validity of the aesthetics attributable to Croce and others like him, but is it possible that Dante wrote what he did primarily for aesthetic reasons alone, namely, for "beauty's sake"? If so, why is there rarely, if ever, an explication on the *function* of beauty as it *specifically* relates to the spiritual nature of our being, *or* on exactly *how* beauty itself can be the vehicle of transformation by which spiritual reality reveals itself? Besides, what *concrete* understanding can aesthetics or positivistic thinking give us with regard to our *spiritual* (nondialectical) nature, in the first place?

Rudolf Steiner, on the other hand, often spoke on the function of beauty with regard to the spiritual aspect of the human being. Among his many allusions to beauty, we are, for example, told of its relationship to the etheric body and to the human being's pre-earthly state in a lecture entitled, *Truth, Beauty and Goodness,* in which he says

> *When we develop the right feeling for beauty, this means that we are properly fitted to our etheric body, the body of formative forces....*
>
> Through a true and genuine feeling for beauty we can, as it were, *reestablish a link with pre-earthly life during life on Earth.* In all aspects of education, in all our outward manifestations of culture and civilization, therefore, we should never underestimate the significance of beauty. A cultural environment full of nothing but ugly machinery, smoke, and unsightly chimneys, where beauty is entirely lacking, is a world that does not want human beings to create a link to their pre-earthly existence, so to speak.

And later:

> Saying that we should be warmly enthusiastic about beauty means that in our soul life we should create at least an image of a new link to the spiritual world of pre-earthly existence.³⁶

If we as uninitiated seekers of truth are to find the inner wisdom at work in the poetry of Dante and his circle, we must begin by taking into consideration the fact that Dante himself drew "on the ancient method of the fourfold interpretation of scripture." As William Anderson outlines in his book, *Dante the Maker*, these four levels of meaning are:

> ...the literal or the true story as it is told; the allegorical, which revealed the relation of that story to the requirement of faith, to the history of humanity as a whole and to the coming of Christ; the moral, which revealed the inner psychological truth to be discovered in the story and the right direction of the will by charity, that an understanding of this truth would encourage; and the anagogic meaning which is *understanding beyond the senses*, which concerns celestial things and which reveals the relationship of the soul to God in the expectation of hope.[37] (italics mine)

He adds, "Dante then goes on to stress the importance of starting with the literal as the sense within the expression of which all the others are included. We cannot reach the meanings without first reaching the outside." By *literal*, however, Dante did not mean that the outer events recounted throughout the *Comedy* were necessarily as he experienced them, himself. Rather, they are often embodiments of historical realities rendered imaginatively so as to capture an intended underlying meaning. An example of this would be the episode of Paolo and Francesca, whose passion for one another is depicted by the winds (of passion) that buffet them. Within this image, there is the literal truth, namely, the passionate union of Paolo and Francesca, as well as the allegorical representation of passion—the winds.

Thus, it is from material and allegorical depictions that we must move toward moral and spiritual meanings. We must consequently understand that such allegorical or metaphorical connotations contained within the literal descriptions given by Dante did not arbitrarily refer to some hypothetical reality, as modern scholasticism so often devises while it seeks to rectify the seemingly irreconcilable ambiguities it encounters. Instead, such connotations specifically harbored an ulterior function, namely, the establishment of a relationship to the Christ by means of a *Wisdom (Sophia)*, whose roots had become buried and forgotten through time. On the basis of this, we can begin to get a feel for how words used both literally and allegorically conveyed a different meaning altogether to those individuals "with eyes to see and ears to hear." This is evidenced most clearly in the earthly figure of Beatrice and other "beatified" women of the *Fedeli d'amore*. Once again, it would be useful in this regard to quote Henry Corbin, who states,

> ...so the Figures contemplated by the *Fedeli d'amore* could perfectly well be concrete and terrestrial Figures and yet be visible only to them. For what was visible to them was not the sensible Figure, indifferently and identically perceptible by any visual organ; it was a Figure whose beauty made itself visible only in these Figures, and also only for the mode of perception proper precisely to a *Fedele d'amore*—that is, for a soul that transmutes the epiphany and simultaneously makes it possible by welcoming the metamorphosis. This is why what the *Fedeli d'amore saw* was at once the Angel Intelligence–Wisdom and some particular earthly figure, but this simultaneity was actual and visible to each one of them. The organ for such a perception is not the sensible faculties but the active Imagination; the sensible is not thereby abolished, but transmuted into symbol; correlatively, the intelligible can reveal itself to the mental vision of a human soul only through an Image–symbol, yet without this making it necessary to say that it is *merely* a symbol; rather, it has *all* the eminent value of a symbol.[38]

One of the basic characteristics of the metaphors employed by the *Fedeli d'amore* was that words were often used to mean the exact *opposite* of what was normally intended. In this way, the language could be constructed so as to contain both an exoteric and an esoteric meaning. As Rossetti states in his book, *Disquisition on the Antipapal Spirit that Produced the Reformation*,

> The mystic language of this society was taught by means of a vocabulary, called the Grammar of the *Gay Science*; founded chiefly on

The Secret Message

the ideas and words put in opposition to each other. The antithesis of *gay science* was *sad ignorance*...[39]

In addition to concealing meaning on the basis of "words put in opposition to each other," Luigi Valli, in his *Linguaggio Segreto di Dante e "dei Fedeli d'amore,"* presents a series of words that he says contains "the true key to the jargon" employed by the *Fedeli d'amore*. We shall only choose a number of examples, some of which we will later apply to a few poems to demonstrate the veracity of the claims made by Valli, who left it up to us to ascertain the validity of his findings. According to him, *"love"* (*amore*), aside from its obvious meaning, often denoted *Divine Wisdom* (*Sapienza Santa*), that is, "that Divine Wisdom personified in the Madonna." One can experience this love, says Valli, in such a way that when the intellect is joined to *Divine Wisdom*, it has those two effects. The first is to awaken the slumbering intellect to new life, for *without Divine Wisdom* (*Sapienza Santa*) *the intellect is, in essence, dead*. At the same time, this revivification of the intellect incites a transformation of the human emotions—i.e., the heart, whereupon the emotions (heart) are said to have been killed (tr. mine).[40] Valli says, "when the mind lives in the human being in amorous contemplation and human emotions are dead, animality—i.e., the soul, the lower human, or what has something in common with the animal—*is sacrificed*" (tr. mine).[41]

The word *love* was used also in reference to the sect (or poetic circle) of the *Fedeli d'amore*, its doctrine, and pact of initiation. *Madonna*, like the word *love*, meant "sacred wisdom"; it, too, could refer to the sect. The word *death* had a multiplicity of meanings. For example, it meant *"mystical death,"* in regard to the death of one's lower self. It also meant *"death in sin,"* often implying the corruption of the Church, especially in persecuting those who sought "sacred wisdom." Thus, *life* was in reference to the spirituality sought within the sect, and those who were *alive* were, of course, the *Fedeli d'amore*. The *"aspect of death"* or the *"color of death"* referred to members of the sect who, for reasons of fear, made as if they were believers in the Church. The word *donna* (woman), that so many critics through the years have interpreted literally, was actually in reference to the adepts within the sect. The word *flower* had the same connotation as the word *love* or *Madonna*. *River* or *fountain* meant the stream of spirituality from which the members of the sect nourished themselves. To *cry* meant pretending to follow the Church. The word *greeting* (*saluto*) was in reference to the ritual that welcomed new members of the sect. *Boredom* (*noia*) meant all that was cultivated outside the sect. Words like *jealousy, cold, ice, rock, stone* were used to imply the hostile nature of the Church. A "savage" (*selvaggio*) was a follower of such an evil Church. *Gentile* or *cortese* (gentile one, polite one) was, of course, the opposite of *selvaggio*. *Shame*, or "to be ashamed," was in reference to those who, through fear, stayed their distance from the *Fedeli d'amore* while still remaining faithful to it. These are just some of the many word meanings uncovered by Valli, which, when applied to the poems exchanged between Dante and his contemporaries, reveal a secret pathway of communication, whereby they could cultivate and spread their spiritual teachings and avoid persecution. Truth could only be arrived at through the freedom of expression.

Thus, one can see how the works of Rossetti, Valli, and others represent a divergence from the approach of orthodox scholarly views. They do not speculate indiscriminately on the metaphorical meanings of Dante's *Comedy*, divorced from an historical context that takes into consideration the impositions of the Church upon the freedom of human thought. Instead, their work attempts to seek out the intentions underlying the work of the *Fedeli d'amore* in the context of the social restrictions imposed by the Catholic Church. In so doing, we understand that history, as it has come to us in its traditional form, does not always readily provide the insights necessary by which a work of literature can become *living* and, thereby, engender a search for truth and meaning. What we, again, see taking shape in the work of individuals such Rossetti, Valli, etc. is an expression of the impending

Michaelic Age, in which true knowledge of the Christ being, as it has manifested itself in the works of enlightened thinkers throughout history, unfolds.

Dantis Amor, *Dante Gabriele Rossetti*,
(1860. Tate Britain)

Deciphering the Meaning of Love

As mentioned in the previous chapter, according to Valli, the word *love* for the *Fedeli d'amore* had two distinct meanings, aside from what we normally associate with it. The first signified *Divine Wisdom* as "personified in the Madonna," so that even the words *love* and *Madonna* were, themselves, often interchangeable. Falling in *love* referred to the awakening of *Active Intelligence*, which was said to have a transforming effect on the "region of the heart." This necessitated the "killing" of strong emotional impulses (connected to the Sentient Soul) arising from the depths of the subconscious, thus resulting in the "sacrifice" of one's lower nature. Secondly, *love* also referred to the circle of poets, the *Fedeli d'amore*, its doctrine, pact of initiation, etc. Though the word *love* formed the basis of the underlying philosophy of *"Il Dolce Stil Novo"* (The Sweet New Style), its successful implementation depended upon the adoption of many other words whose meanings were likewise "modified." In this way, a whole new way of *seeing* could take root within the context of the existing linguistic apparatus and, thus, remain undetected by the Church. Since a comprehensive study of such poetry would take us far beyond the scope of this work, our primary consideration, here, will be to examine a handful of poems of this period, which, in many ways, is illustrative of both the "philosophy" of the *Fedeli d'amore* and their system of communication. In so doing, I will reiterate a few of the interpretations provided by Luigi Valli, himself. For, after all, it was he who disclosed, in great detail, the nature of operations between Dante and his poetic circle.

The first poem that we will take into consideration, "Love to a gentle heart runs evermore," has been described by Valli as the "Magna Carta" of the poetry arising from *"Il Dolce Stil Novo."* It was written by the person to whom some attribute the founding of this so-called Sweet New Style, and whom Dante called "the wise one" or "the illustrious doctor"—his "literary father," Guido Guinizelli. As one of Guinizelli's most famous poems, it demonstrates that even without many key words that comprise a so-called secret code or language, an underlying theme or motif that permeates much of the poetry of this era is present, namely, *Love (Divine Wisdom) rises to the soul that is made "pure."* In other words, a tainted soul cannot, by its very nature, partake in *Divine Love.* According to Valli, this concept existed among the Persian mystics and was in consonance with a basic tenet of Augustinian philosophy, which claimed that the human mind is unable to participate in *Divine Intelligence* if it does not succeed in purging itself of influences derived from the senses. "Love to a gentle heart runs evermore" begins,

> Love to a *gentle* heart runs evermore
> for safety, as a bird to the green shade:
> for neither Love by Nature was before
> a *gentle* heart, nor this before *Love*, made.
> The very hour the Sun
> shone forth, was born the splendor of the day,
> not this before the sun.
> And *Love* finds soon in *gentleness* its home
> precisely in that way
> warmth has its place in clarity of flame.
>   (tr. J. Tusiani; italics mine)[42]

In this first stanza, as in most of the poem, the key word is *gentle*. We find it repeated here three times. In conjunction with it are the words *heart, Love, Sun, splendor, warmth,* and *flame*. It is evident from the start that "Love" (*Divine Wisdom*) finds its home in a "gentle" heart. Indeed, it is intrinsic to a "gentle (pure) heart" as "warmth" is to a "flame," or "splendor" to the "Sun." These words, if we observe them attentively, have one thing in common, namely, they have all, at one time or other, been attributed to the Christ, the *heart* of creative activity. "Through Him (the Word) all things were made" (John 1:3). We see this creative principle expressed by Guinizelli when he says, "the splendor of the day was born" the moment the "Sun (Word) shone forth." This light of day is "the light of man" (John 1:4), as it, too, lies hidden in day consciousness. Similarly, *Love*, itself, is the spiritual foundation that gives life to a "gentle heart." Just as the light that issues from the "Sun" is but a manifestation of a spiritual activity that our physical eyes cannot behold so, too, is the "heart" (the *solar* region within us) made ever so "pure," that it becomes an expression of the unseen (etheric) forces responsible for forming a "gentle (etheric) heart"—one capable of being permeated by the force of *Love*. Says Guinizelli, "for neither Love by Nature was before a gentle heart, nor this before Love made." Here, let us remember that "in the Beginning was the Word" (Life), the "Light of man"—namely, that "through which all things were created." The created could, of course, also refer to the darkness—the darkness that could not grasp the source of its own creation. Nonetheless, this darkness contained the Light, by means of which it, too, became a manifestation of *Love*. Thus, just as a "heart" made "pure" is a manifestation of *Love*, so, too, is "Love by Nature." "*Love*," as Steiner says, "*is the creative force of the world.*"[43]

The second stanza builds upon the first, for just as "warmth" is an intrinsic property of a "flame" so, too, is this "fire" an essential characteristic of *Love*, but a love whose lower nature (the reflected aspect of its higher principle) must be redeemed like "virtue in a precious stone." "Fire," of course, is the element of purification, the "Holy Spirit" burning within a "gentle heart."

> Fire of love hides within a *gentle* heart
> as height of virtue in a precious stone;
> but from the star no value can depart
> till the Sun makes it *gentle* and its own:
> as soon as he draws out,

through his sole virtue, what was there impure,
the star's worth shines about.
Thus, *lady*, all men's hearts by Nature are
made *gentle*, *fair*, and *pure*,
and each grows soon enamored like a star.
      (tr. J. Tusiani; italics mine)

However, not until the Sun (Christ) becomes manifest can the *light* of the star begin to shine forth from within the human being. Thus, it is the work of a higher spiritual force, "Sun," that consummates the purification by "fire" (Holy Spirit), thus making the "heart" a true vessel for the Word. "Fire" (Christ) had come to replace water (John the Baptist) as the means by which one can enter the spiritual world. And so, we find that "He who baptizes with the Holy Spirit" had descended amongst humankind, so that the *light* might become manifest ("the star's worth shines about"). Note here incidentally that Guinizelli addresses the reader as "lady," a possible reference to the *Fedeli d'amore*.

In the third stanza, we are told that *Love* (or *Divine Wisdom*) finds its abode in a "pure heart" as naturally as "fire" upon a "taper's top":

Love in a *gentle* heart dwells for the reason
whereby fire lodges on a taper's top:
for its own joy it, bright and thin, does glisten—
so proud indeed, it otherwise would stop.
A man depraved and bold
does against *Love* what water does to heat
with its outpouring *cold*.
Love in a *gentle* heart has shore and shrine
as its congenial seat,
just like a diamond in an iron mine.
      (tr. J. Tusiani; italics mine)

Here, the "fire" that "lodges upon a taper's top" rekindles the image of the Holy Spirit as a "tongue of fire." A person "depraved and bold" (i.e., who fails to acknowledge such a Light) is antagonistic toward *Love,* just as water, "with its outpouring cold" is to heat. Here, the word *cold* is used to denote the forces opposed to *Love*. Such opposing forces may be envisioned as the flow of thoughts arising from the cold intellect, precluding our access to the realm from which they arise. The word *outpouring* pictorially represents the force of this opposition. This "outpouring" may also connote a clash of the two elements of baptism, "water" and "fire," whereby adherence to ancient rituals of initiation ("water") as symbolized by the baptism in the river Jordan (perpetuated in deadened form by the Church) "extinguishes the modern form of initiation in the form of the Holy Spirit ("fire"), brought into being through Christ's entry into the world. The "bold and depraved" are the *"gente grossa"* to whom Valli refers, namely, those who are unable to cultivate the "gentleness" needed for the resurrection of being. They are the ignorant masses guided by the Church, into whose hands *Sacred* or *Divine Wisdom* would prove disastrous. "Love" in a "gentle" heart has sacredness "as its congenial seat." It shines outward through our physical nature as "a diamond in an iron mine."

In the fourth stanza, Guinizelli depicts the *effect* of *Love* or *Divine Wisdom* upon the human being:

> The sun strikes on the mud the bright day long:
> the mud is mud, the Sun still warm and *fair.*
> The proud man says, "By birth I do belong
> to gentleness": to mud I do compare
> such men, and to the Sun a gentle worth.
> For no one must believe
> that with no merits of one's own one may
> through fame of father *gentleness* achieve
> unless one's heart be made by virtue bright:
> the sea reflects the ray,
> and the skies hold the star and all its light.
>   (tr. J. Tusiani; italics mine)

Just as the physical Sun, beating upon the ground ("mud"), does not ennoble it (for "mud is mud"), so, too, is a person unprepared (without "pure heart") for *Divine Wisdom* altered by it in any way. In other words, those who have not become "pure" cannot, by their very nature, be transformed by *Divine Wisdom*. Furthermore, those who deem themselves "pure" because of their ancestry are mistaken, for they have as little to do with purity as does "mud" touched by the rays of the Sun; "purity" is not an inherited characteristic. Nor does purity arise from wealth—an obvious reference to the Church. Only by *virtuous deed* can the heart become "bright." Guinizelli concludes this stanza by reasserting the idea that just as water is unaffected by the rays that shine down from the stars, so, too, is an "impure heart" not made "warm" by *Divine Wisdom*. Heaven and Earth can unite only when we witness the Holy Spirit in the depths of our being, namely, when we perceive the *"light,"* which darkness cannot grasp, as *"life"* itself. By the word *warm*, he intends the life engendering impulses of feeling, from which issues Love.

In stanza five, Guinizelli, in making reference to "the Intelligence of Heaven," implies that the spiritual hierarchies receive their immediate light from God (the Creator), for He shines in them more brightly than the Sun's light shines in our eyes.

> Up in the Intelligence of Heaven shines
> God the creator, more than to our glances
> the Sun: He knows all its deep-hidden signs;
> and as that sky, obeying Him, advances,
> from God Himself it showers
> upon the first, complete and proper bliss.
> A *lovely lady* with her sunlit glance
> must so reveal the powers
> of inborn *gentleness*
> to one who never scorns obedience.
> (tr. J. Tusiani; italics mine)

Because the spiritual beings—i.e., Higher Intelligences, are without physical bodies, they can receive God's *light* directly, without suffering any diminution of its splendor. This is not true of humanity's relationship to the "Sun," namely, the spiritual aspect of the Christ, hidden within the "darkness." Given this, we can see how Guinizelli intimates that it is God who sets Heaven in motion, imbuing it with the Wisdom reflected in the activity of the spiritual hierarchies. God comprehends the very depths of spiritual activity, in all its infinite nature, far transcending our inability to perceive beyond the limits of the Heavens as they reveal themselves to us. Just as the Heavens are aligned with *Divine Wisdom* and, thus, dutifully follow the Will of God, Guinizelli shows that humankind should experience one's lovely "lady" (*Divine Wisdom/Intelligence*) so that Divine Will may be revealed and realized.

Guinizelli's reference to "a lovely lady" can, as has been suggested by Valli, also be a reference to the members of the *Fedeli d'amore*, encouraging them to disclose their knowledge or wisdom ("gentleness") to those inwardly inclined toward "obedience"—i.e., the capacity to maintain secrecy by following the dictates of the order.

In the last stanza, Guinizelli reveals that to which he himself has directed his love—i.e., *Divine Wisdom*. If asked by God whether he had mistaken "futile love" (love of the senses) for Him, or if he had sought the "Queen" (*Divine Wisdom*) with vain (impure) love, Guinizelli would respond that he had directed his heart (love) toward that which had the "features of an angel"—*Divine Wisdom*. In fact, apart from death, only by way of *Divine Wisdom* could Guinizelli "cross the skies" to find himself before the face of God. Only with a "gentle" heart could this have even been possible. Thus, he would not have sinned (erred) in his love. For being of a pure ("gentle") heart, it is impossible for him to manifest a propensity toward the lower forces of nature.

> And God will ask, "Why have you been so base?"
> the day my soul will in his presence be:
> "Crossing the skies, you've come before my face,
> who did mistake a futile love for me:
> to me is fit each laud,
> and to the *Queen* of this my blest domain,
> wherein ends every fraud."

> But I will answer: "*She* had features of
> an angel of your reign:
> I did not sin in giving her my love."
> (tr. J Tusiani; italics mine)

We see conveyed in this poem the factors necessary for the creation of a vessel by which the Christ can enter into humankind. Only with a "gentle heart" is it possible to gather within oneself the capacity to receive the force of the Christ, as He rays down into humanity through the Holy Spirit. This, of course, is but another way of suggesting the need to cultivate *Divine Wisdom*—i.e., the Sophia, wherein resides the "life" or "light" "ungraspable" by the "darkness." Here, again, we refer to thinking which, upon finding its place within the "gentle heart," is reintegrated with willing, its masculine counterpart, so that the Will of God is made manifest.

As we mentioned before, this theme of "purity" or "gentleness," which runs through the whole of the poem, can, in large part, be attributed to Augustine, a philosopher who had a profound influence upon Dante and the *Fedeli d'amore*. Though Augustine lived during the fourth century, Rudolf Steiner, in his book, *Redemption of Thinking*, tells us that his inner development corresponded more to that of human beings living during the Middle Ages, for he possessed "a strong sense of individuality." This was particularly reflected by his unwillingness to accept the dualism of Manichaeism. For he rejected the notion that God could be imagined in material form. In fact, here lay the basis for Augustine's struggle with Manichaeism. Steiner says, "He needed a point of view to which he could look up as having its foundation in the essential being of Man, something which did not, like Manichaeism, regard the whole sense-world as being in itself directly spiritual–material."[44] Born within him was the impulse that sought to free thinking from the senses, for as Steiner further relates, Augustine is said to have even asked the Earth itself such burning questions as "what is the Divine," to which the Earth replied, "I am not it." Manichaeism would, says Steiner, have replied, "'I am it as Earth, in so far as the Divine expresses itself through earthly creation.'"[45] Moreover,

Augustine could not accept the premise that "all is spirit" as did Plotinus who, according to Steiner, still had a constitution of soul that permitted him to perceive, as did the Greeks in ancient times, the inseparability of the material and spiritual worlds. Instead, Augustine discovered Plotinus' concept of the "One"—synonymous with Plato's "World of Ideas"—embodied in the "figure of Christ." Augustine, in his effort to bring the "One" into Christianity, related it as "being." This represented the Father principle of the Trinity. He referred to The Son—i.e., the Idea-World, as "Knowing," while he knew the Holy Spirit as *Love* or *Life*—that to which the *Fedeli d'amore* refer in their many poems. This, along with his early experience of Manichaeism, led Augustine to acknowledge the fact that humankind cannot experience the spiritual world solely by means of the material. In fact, Steiner tells us that Augustine "strove to reach a soul experience of the spiritual which is entirely free from sense experience, and so to escape from a material view of life."[46] The material could not, as it did for Plotinus, represent "the lowest method for revealing the spiritual," that is to say, one could not experience the spiritual world by conceptualizing the material as a mere expression of it. This, again, was due to the fact that he could not perceive matter as Spirit, as did Plotinus. Instead, he was gradually to develop a view that would become a model for those who believed that, to reach the spiritual, one had first to transform those inner forces connected to Nature.

Thus, in deepening our understanding of what was meant by "pure heart" and its relation to Love or *Divine Wisdom*, we must begin by briefly taking into consideration the very process at which Augustine was unable to arrive due to the unpreparedness of his spiritual constitution. Only as of the last century is humankind finally able to *fully* realize what Augustine unconsciously strove to achieve with the full force of his being. As Massimo Scaligero states in his book, *Graal: Saggio sul Mistero del Sacro Amore*,

> In feeling, as we have seen, Lucifer can still operate to the degree in which the human being requires reflective thinking, or cerebral thinking. The era of self-consciousness is that which harbors the

possibility of passing from reflective thinking to living thinking. This cannot mean that reflective thinking must be abolished: it must become the *instrument* of true thinking, ceasing to submit to illusory appearances or to the expression of instincts. Thought, in rising to pure ideation, contains the key that can reconnect feeling to the heart—the feeling that reconnects itself to the heart contains the key to sacred love, which is the feeling that discovers within itself the power of life capable of reestablishing the purity of the soul's relationship to the forces operating in reproduction. (tr. and italics mine)[47]

Here, as we can see, the concept of "purity" is intrinsically related to the spiritual constitution of humanity in the Consciousness Soul Age, for only within the last hundred years or so could reflective thinking be "an *instrument* of living thinking." In fact, this is precisely what may be described as the most important characteristic of this present age. Yet, what about Dante and the circle of friends to which he belonged? They lived during a time when thinking had not yet developed to the point in which it could transform feeling in the manner just outlined. Instead, the whole of Italian society was guided largely by what Rudolf Steiner calls the Sentient Soul. To understand the kind of initiation that Dante may have experienced, we can refer to Steiner, who revealed how Dante received his inspiration for the *Divine Comedy* from his teacher, Brunetto Latini. Given his inner constitution of soul, Latini was able to undergo a profound, spiritual experience equivalent to a real initiation, upon having suffered a heat stoke. Now, having taken part in the School of Chartres where the active forces in Nature were acknowledged to be receding from humanity's ability to perceive them, Latini was able to transfer, in a pictorial way, the *effect* of his experience to Dante. Steiner tells us that the effect of that experience upon Dante was so profound that it could actually inspire the creation of the *Divine Comedy*. In *True and False Paths in Spiritual Investigation*, Steiner describes this event and how it was reflected in the soul mood of that time. He says,

The mood in which the students of the School of Chartres—the majority were of the Cistercian Order—came out of their lectures was vastly different from the mood of students leaving their lecture rooms today! Their response was vitally alive and a deeper expression of their inner being. And the same living reality is reflected in the descriptions of such men as Brunetto Latini, the celebrated teacher of Dante. The vigorous, creative spirit of the time can be readily imagined, for the characters and splendid pictorial descriptions of Dante's *Commedia* are *inspired* by the graphic descriptions of his teacher Brunetto Latini who owed his initiation to a karmic incident. (italics mine)[48]

In other words, Brunetto Latini was able to transfer the graphic *spiritual impressions* he received so as to enable Dante to represent them in poetic form. It was this ability to transfer a vivid spiritual experience that must be considered when attempting to understand the poetry of that time. For the constitution of the human being was such that, by describing their spiritual experience of *Love* (or *Divine Wisdom*) poetically, the *Fedeli d'amore* were often able to partake in one another's experience largely through *the feeling life*. Thus, two factors converge during Dante's time that may account for the nature of pictorial transference. First, as was stated earlier, Dante, born at the end of the Intellectual Soul Age, lived during a time when there still existed a "residual of clairvoyance" (or pictorial consciousness) amongst humanity. In fact, the ability of those at the School of Chartres to perceive the Goddess Natura (*Divine Wisdom*) is testimony to this fact. Secondly, the Sentient Soul which, according to Steiner, characterizes the spiritual constitution of the Italian people, made it conducive at that time for those people to live into archetypal images through the feeling life or mood. This also helps to explain why many individuals then were able to delve into what Steiner described as "mysticism." Such individuals in the Middle Ages, however, who sought a spiritual foundation of the world through "mysticism," often experienced what Steiner described as a distorted representation of their physiologies. The emotional forces working within individuals often obfuscated objectivity in perception. Nevertheless, this characterization should not obscure the importance that these spiritual experiences had for people at that time. Steiner relates how mystics "strove to transmute the urge of self-love into love of wisdom and to let love ray out in beauty. By sinking in contemplation into the depths of their own soul life, they strove to become aware of the Divine Spark within them."[49]

To gain an understanding of the interrelationships between Dante and his contemporaries with regard to the question of *Love*, I have chosen, in part, a poem that reveals the inner squabbles that at times seemingly arose when characterizing *Divine Wisdom* as the object of one's love. It sheds light on the fact that the various names attributed to the "ladies" of the *Fedeli d'amore* such as Fiore, Laura, and Beatrice, were, according to Valli, in reference to the same thing—Sapienza Santa (*Divine Wisdom*). In other words, the *Divine Wisdom* (Beatrice) that Dante sought, was also sought by other members of his circle in as much as their individualized representations of *Angelic Intelligence* (referred to by different names) were synonymous with Beatrice. The poem is by Cino da Pistoia, who condemns Dante for not lauding his Selvaggia in the *Divine Comedy*, instead of Beatrice.

> *In fra gli altri difetti del libello…*
> *che passo' poi nel bel coro divino*
> *la' dove vide la sua Beatrice.*
> *E quando ad Abraam guardo' nel sino*
> *non riconobbe l'unica fenice*
> *che con Sion congiunse l"Appennino*

> Among the faults we in that book descry…
> that when he says he came
> To see, at summit of sacred stair,
> *His Beatrice among the heavenly signs,—*
> *He, looking in the bosom of Abraham,*
> *Saw not that highest of all women there*
> *Who joined Mount Sion to the Apennines.*
>   (tr. D. G. Rossetti; italics mine)[50]

First of all, the penultimate line here translated into English by Dante Gabriele Rossetti is a bit misleading, for "l'unica fenice" could be translated more accurately as "the only phoenix" (or "the unique phoenix"), and not necessarily as "that highest of all women." Cino, a "disgruntled" member of the circle, *seemingly* directs his anger at Dante, who, by exulting Beatrice in the *Divine Comedy*, is accused of exulting his own personal conception of *Divine Wisdom*, without recognizing, as Valli claims, that this *Divine Wisdom* (Beatrice), was "the singular woman [the only doctrine] of every *Fedele d'amore*, namely, the unique phoenix that reunited Italy [Appennino] to true Christianity [Sion]" (tr. mine).[51] In such an inflammatory denunciation, Cino seems to accuse Dante of pride, the very sin to which Dante himself later confesses in the *Purgatorio*. Cino "wanted to reprimand Dante for having exulted *his own* Beatrice, namely *Divine Wisdom* as he himself conceived it, according to *his own* "doctrine," without recognizing that this *Divine Wisdom* was that unique Wisdom that all the adepts...shared."

The "unique phoenix" was, as Valli elucidates, none other than the *"holy truth, eternally being resurrected from the ashes of the persecutions and the burnings at the stake, the unique phoenix who joined the Apennines to Mount Sion, namely, that which connected Italy (Appennino) to Jerusalem (Sion), to Christ's true cult of faith in spite of the corruptions of the carnal Church"* (tr. mine).[52] Valli insists that this poem is fundamental for comprehending the "true spirit" of this whole movement known to us as the *Fedeli d'amore*, in which erupts "the revelation of that whole subterranean world of agreements, disputes, anger, religious and sectarian passions which is aggravated beneath the deceptive covering of many cold and insipid *mutterings of love!*" (tr. mine).[53] In condemning Dante, Cino da Pistoia suggests that *Divine Wisdom* is differentiated between members of the sect by the various names given "first by this poet then by that, each time *dying*, rather often, under a different name only to be resurrected again and again" (tr. mine).[54] It is this continual rebirth, as symbolized by the "phoenix," that discloses how, within the circle (or sect), the intellect, through "pain and trial" is able to "connect with the Christ." Furthermore, Valli states that the "phoenix" mentioned by Cino, is in reference to the "eternal truth," which is indestructible. This eternal truth—symbolized by the names of Beatrice, Selvaggia, Fiore, etc. —which seeks to connect humankind to the Christ, is, according to Valli, what all the members of the sect can share. One need only read *La Vita Nuova, XXI*, in which Dante himself states that his lady, Beatrice, could awaken love where it has been asleep, namely, in the *hearts of others*. Says he,

> The power of Love borne in my lady's eyes
> imparts its grace to all she looks upon.
> All turn to gaze at her when she walks by,
> and when she greets a man his heart beats fast,
> the color leaves his face, he bows his head
> and sighs to think of all his imperfections.
> Anger and pride are forced to flee from her.
> Help me to honor her, most gracious ladies.
> (tr. M. Musa)[54]

Thus, the *Vita Nuova*, having preceded the *Divine Comedy*, bears testimony to the fact that Dante did, indeed, acknowledge that others could share in the *Divine Wisdom* exemplified by Beatrice. Such a verse as this is a testament to Valli's assertion "that Beatrice was loved not only by him [Dante] but by all those who knew her" (tr. mine).[55] We shall see in the *Divine Comedy* that Dante's personal journey toward spiritual salvation (realization), guided in large part by Beatrice and interpreted by Cino as self-serving, was meant as an example for all humankind. It was a journey toward the Christ who lives within each human being whose *"cuor gentile"* (pure heart) becomes the vessel of *Love*. In the end, one is even left to wonder whether Cino's condemnation of Dante was nothing other than a clever ploy to trick the Church into believing that the *Fedeli d'amore* often bickered over earthly women.

When considering how members of the *Fedeli d'amore* secretly communicated with each other to share important information, few poems are as intriguing as two which were written by another famous member of the sect, one whom Valli considers as having, for a long time, been its leader—Guido Cavalcanti. In the first poem, Cavalcanti relates to his circle the existence of another seemingly related sect in the city of Toulouse (the center of Catharism!) where he had one day found himself. Though it was a sect that resembled his own in Florence, insofar as there was a "donna somigliante" (i.e., a similar woman), Cavalcanti chose, as a precautionary measure, not to reveal to this new sect the identity of his own.

> A young lady of Toulouse,
> Beautiful and *noble*, of chaste elegance,
> Is a creature so precisely similar
> In her sweet eyes to my *lady*
>
> That she made [my] soul within [my] heart
> Desirous, such that it strays from there
> And goes off to her: but it is so fearful
> That it does not tell her to which *lady* it belongs.
>
> It looks into her sweet glance
> In which Love makes it joyful
> Because there within is its precise *lady;*
>
> Then it returns full of sighs to the heart,
> Having been wounded mortally by a keen arrow
> That this *lady* in parting shoots at it.
>   (tr. L. Nelson, Jr. ; italics mine)[56]

Cavalcanti identifies "the young lady of Toulouse," whom he calls "beautiful and noble," as the member of a sect that greatly resembles that to which he himself belongs. For "in her sweet eyes" he questions whether there is reflected the *Divine Wisdom* sought by members of his own sect. Cavalcanti wishes to involve himself in the affairs of the sect that he encounters ("That she made [my] soul within [my] heart desirous, such that it strays from there and goes off to her") but he is afraid, and thus will not reveal the existence of his own sect ("but it [soul] is so fearful that it does not tell to which lady it belongs"). Nonetheless, he can perceive that the sect he encounters possesses the wisdom conducive to *Love* ("It [his heart] looks into her sweet glance in which Love makes it joyful..."). So, he returns without attaining what he yearned, his soul greatly afflicted by the force of the *Love* ("a keen arrow") that revealed itself to him through the "eyes" of the "lady" (sect or member).

In a related poem, as conveyed to us again by Valli, Cavalcanti tells how upon returning from Toulouse, where he encountered the sect just mentioned (similar to his own), he comes upon "a lady who sang," namely, a *Fedele d'amore* who is overcome by the force of *Love* (sect). Accompanying him is a "fake" *Fedele d'amore* (a woman or sect *"fatta di gioco in figura di amore"*) that tries to elicit the name of the sect in Toulouse that he (Cavalcanti) approached by asking him a question. To this question that appears "hard and fearsome" (but which if taken literally would seem insignificant and ingenuous), the poet replies that in Toulouse he met a "woman" that Love calls "Mandetta." The first of the two "women" (a true *Fedele d'amore*) praises Cavalcanti and is pleased, inasmuch as "she" thereby acknowledges the existence of the sect or source of *Divine Wisdom* (Love) for which he has been searching.

Cavalcanti does not say anything more about the second "woman" (a false *Fedele d'amore*), who fails to understand Cavalcanti's coded message. Cavalcanti is thus able, by way of the adept he encountered, to send a message to the sect, so that it may know that he (though tempted) did not reveal the secret of its existence. Note how in this poem it is not Cavalcanti who calls the lady appearing to him, "Mandetta," but, rather, *Love* (Sect) itself. In other words, it is within the *context of the sect* that the adept, "Mandetta," (whose eyes shone with *Divine Wisdom*) could be recognized. This poem is particularly important in understanding how intended communications were transmitted, for we see that in the poem, as a whole, there are specific directives coded in such a way as to convey an intended meaning to a trusted sect member while obscuring it for those who pose a potential threat to the sect.

Deciphering the Meaning of Love

I was deep in thought about *love* when I met
Two young little country *girls*.
One of them was singing: "It is raining
Joy of love in us."

The sight of them was so pleasant
And so calm, courteous, and benevolent
That I told them: "You have the key
Of every high and noble virtue."
Ah, little country girls, don't think me base
For the wound that I bear;
This heart of mine was killed
From the time I was in Toulouse."

They turned with their eyes just enough
To see how my heart was wounded
And how a little spirit born of tears
Had come out through the wound.
When they saw me so dismayed
One of them laughed and said:
"Look how the violence of Love
Has laid him low!"

The other one, pitying, full of mercy
Transformed by joy (gioco=game) into a figure of love
Said: "Your wound, that can be seen over your heart,
Was drawn by eyes of overwhelming strength
Which left within a radiance
Such that I cannot look at it.
Tell me if you can
Remember those eyes."

To the hard and fearsome question
That the little country girl put to me
I replied: "I am reminded that in Toulouse
A lady appeared to me, tightly laced,
Whom Love called L'Amandeta;
She arrived so briskly and forcefully
That her eyes struck me,
Deep within, to death."

The one who had *first laughed at me*
Answered me with great courtesy.
She said: "The lady who, with love's violence,
Set all her sights on your heart,
Looked inside you through the eyes so intently
That she made Love appear.
If suffering is burdensome for you
Address yourself to him."

Go off to Toulouse, my little ballad,
And quietly enter La Daurade,
And there request that you be brought,
By courtesy of some lovely lady,
Before her for whose sake I have bidden you,
And if she receives you,
Tell her in a soft voice:
"For mercy I come to you."
       (tr. L. Nelson, Jr. ; italics mine)[57]

It is therefore quite evident that, taken literally, the meaning of this poem does not easily reveal itself. Through the centuries, critics have reconciled the poem's ambiguity by accepting the premise that this, like so many other "love ballads," follow in the tradition of courtly love where it was believed that the Troubadours, while wandering through the countryside, entertained nobility merely as a means of survival. Little recognized is the fact that these poems (as well as those sung by the Troubadours) veiled the pursuit for a higher spiritual knowledge that the Church sought to suppress. Even if we closely observe the translation of the poem above, we can see how misleading the language was, for unless the translator is privy to the intentions of the poet, he or she can easily be led astray in his or her interpretation. We witness this tendency toward misinterpretation in the line, *"fatta di gioco in figura d'amore,"* which rightly translated reads "transformed by *game* into a figure of love." The translator has instead interpreted *gioco* as "joy." However, *gioco* (game) does not translate as a direct cognate of *gioia* (joy). The closest association between *gioco* and *joy* is found in the word *giocoso*, interpreted as "playful." "Transformed by game" denotes an act of deception on behalf of the second "woman," who seeks unsuccessfully to know from Cavalcanti the name of the sect to which he alludes. In fact, by misinterpreting *gioco* to mean "joy" instead of "game," the translater unknowingly loses the key by which to unveil the "secret jargon" shared by the *Fedeli d'amore*—which was their intended aim.

As we alluded earlier, the Church, in its determination to maintain secular power, provided the greatest barrier to the free exchange of religious ideas. Because of the many dangers present at that time, a subterranean network for the transmission of ideas was established to keep the movements of the Church at bay. In my attempt to reveal the attitude of the *Fedeli d'amore* toward the Church, I have chosen another poem by Cino da Pistoia, who in his correspondence with Onesto Bolognese, a critic and despiser of the sect, is urged to consider leaving the *Fedeli d'amore*. Cino agrees, at first, to do so and is accused by another member, Gherarduccio, of having two loves (Church and the sect). Meanwhile, in a sonnet addressed to Dante, Cino describes how, after failing to uncover a deeper connection to *Divine Wisdom*, he seeks consolation in Death (the Church).

> Dante, whenever this thing happeneth.—
> That *Love's* desire is quite bereft of Hope,
> (Seeking in vain at *ladies'* eyes some scope
> Of joy, through what the heart for ever saith),—
> I ask thee, can amends be made by *Death*?
> Is such sad pass the last extremity?—
> Or may the soul that never feared to die
> Then in another body draw new breath?
> Lo! *Thus it is through her who governs all*
> *Below*,—that I, who entered at her door,
> Now at her dreadful window must fare forth
> Yea, and I think through her it doth befall
> That even ere yet the road is travelled o'er
> My bones are weary and life is nothing worth.
>   (tr. D. G. Rossetti; italics mine)[58]

In his address to Dante, Cino makes known that he has lost hope in attaining *Divine Wisdom* through grace, for "Love's desire is...bereft of Hope." His search for a clear understanding as to the nature (and purpose) of the spiritual experience (joy) cultivated by the sect has not revealed itself to him through the vision of its members (ladies' eyes). Cino then asks if the Church (Death) can fulfill his aims. Does reducing oneself to accepting the precepts of the Church represent a final hope for humankind? ("Is such sad pass the last extremity?") Can the soul eternal (Christ in the human being)—unaffected by the earthly forces in nature ("that never feared to die")—be resurrected ("draw new breath") "in another body" (Church)? Cino laments entering the door of "her who governs all, Below" (the carnal Church), in which operate the forces that fetter human beings to their lower nature by imprisoning them within the sense world ("I...Now at her dreadful window must fare forth"). This passage that depicts Cino entering the world of the dead is reminiscent of Dante, who, upon entering the gates of Hell, encounters the infamous words "abandon all hope, ye who enter!" Unlike Dante, however, Cino seems to lack the will to go on ("my bones are weary"), that is, the will to resurrect life (Sapienza Santa) from within the realm of Death (Church), so that he, himself, might abandon the path "travelled o'er" by the "crude masses."

In still another related sonnet, Cino again makes known how he seeks refuge in Death (Church), when reprimanded by a member of the sect from whose eyes rayed forth *Divine Wisdom*. Here, however, Cino "cries abroad on Death," that is, he only pretends to follow its precepts. Yet, upon acknowledging the "hardness" of the Church, he quickly reverts to "God" (the spirit of Christ within humankind) for the peace he yearns.

> This fairest *lady*, who, as well I wot,
> Found entrance by her beauty to my soul,
> Pierced through mine eyes my heart, which erst was whole,
> Sorely, yet makes as though she knew it not;
> Nay, turns upon me now, to anger wrought,
> Dealing me harshness for my pain's best dole,

Deciphering the Meaning of Love

> And is so changed by her own wrath's control,
> That I go thence, in my distracted thought
> Content to *die*; and *mourning*, cry abroad
> On Death, as upon one afar from me;
> But *Death* makes answer from within my heart.
> Then, hearing her so hard at hand to be,
> I do commend my spirit unto God;
> Saying to her, too, "Ease and peace thou art."
>   (tr. D. G. Rossetti; italics mine)[59]

This "fairest lady" (sect member) who by her "beauty" (wisdom) entered and deeply stirred Cino's soul, doubts having made such a profound impression on him. Moreover, Cino becomes the object of his anger (probably because this "fairest lady" doubts the sincerity of Cino's claim and sees him as a potential threat to the sect). Thus, Cino goes away in "distracted thought" (indicating the absence of contemplation) "content to die" (abandon hope for *Divine Wisdom*). But his move toward Death (Church) is one that he simulates ("and, mourning, cry abroad on Death"). Nonetheless, Cino feels Death's "hard" (cruel) nature resound from within his being ("Death makes answer from within my heart"), and thus he "commends" his "spirit unto God."

These few poems, whose "secret" messages were largely deciphered by Valli, serve to show that there existed a system of communication that sought to unite the *Fedeli d'amore*, to preserve the sacred knowledge (known to them as *Love*) forbidden by the Church. The mere profusion of "such love poetry" should, at the very least, raise suspicions in the minds of literary theorists as to the ulterior motives concealed therein. When, during the history of Western literature apart from the Troubadours, have the stirring of such seemingly adolescent love been communicated in such a uniformly calibrated and systematic manner? In other words, can it be that this was little more than a frivolous period of human development whose connection to the higher principles of knowledge were embodied *solely* in the *physical* representation of womanhood? If not, how can we enter more deeply into the nature of *sacred knowledge* itself? Is there a particular stream to which the *Wisdom* sought by Dante and the *Fedeli d'amore* is connected? And lastly, how could we better characterize the initiatory experience associated with the attainment of *Divine Wisdom*? These questions must be taken into consideration before we embark upon an esoteric interpretation of the *Divine Comedy* as a whole. By following the insights of Rudolf Steiner, we shall be able to gain a better understanding of where such "knowledge" fits in with the evolution of human consciousness. First, however, it will be necessary to explore Dante's relationship to this most enigmatic figure who, in all her transcendent radiance, possessed the very core of Dante's soul, namely, the heavenly Beatrice herself.

Encounter of Dante and Beatrice
Biblioteca Nazionale Marciana, Venice
14th-century miniature painting

Goddess of the Sun

Perhaps no figure in the history of literature remains so enigmatic as Beatrice—the personification of "blessedness" that had "revealed itself" to Dante at the age of nine. While beholding the "glorious lady of his *mind*," Dante hears the "spirit of life" tremble within him, as it reechoes the infamous words of Homer, "Here is a god stronger than I who comes to rule over me."[60] So powerful is this "god," that she prompts the "animal spirit, the one abiding in the high chamber to which all senses bring their perceptions," to address the "spirits of seeing" and acknowledge her. From now on, "the nature spirit which inhabits that part where our nourishing takes place" will no longer drive Dante's actions, for this "nature spirit" will be met with "hindrance." Such is the force of this new revelation! These utterances not only serve as an introduction to Dante's *Vita Nuova*—the "prelude" to his *Divine Comedy*—but when examined a bit more closely, they may refer to the threefold nature of human consciousness hidden within the *Comedy* itself. For just as the "spirits of seeing" refer to the activity of the "I" in its relation to *thought and perception*, "the nature spirit" refers to the untransformed *feelings* (sexual drive) arising from the lower self in its connection to the *will*. These three spheres of activity in Dante—thinking, feeling, and willing—undergo a transformation through his encounter with Beatrice ("blessedness"), the *Divine Sophia*, who bears the archetypal force of *Love* (Christ). In this chapter, we shall examine this "god" (Beatrice/Sophia) from various points of view. In so doing, we will understand how, through the characterizations of her enigmatic nature, Dante tried to hide her role as the transformative force of human consciousness (as seen by him and the *Fedeli d'amore*) from the "malicious curiosities" of the Church.

In attempting to gain a clearer understanding of Beatrice and Dante's relationship to her, it would be useful to refer once again to Rudolf Steiner. In his book, *True and False Paths in Spiritual Investigation*, he speaks of the seven archangelic beings, which, in their role as Time Spirits, govern the evolution of humanity in successive stages. Each Time Spirit, as a regent of a particular planetary sphere, normally directs the course of human evolution for a period of roughly three hundred years before relinquishing it to another. Now, just as Michael is the *current* regent of all humankind, Steiner intimates that Raphael's influence guided the consciousness of Dante and his contemporaries. He states, "When we enter into the Raphael epoch, from the ninth to the fifteenth centuries, then the figures of a Dante, a Giotto and especially those whose names are unknown to posterity, as well as the others I have mentioned, appear to stand out in bold relief."[61] (We must note that, in other places, Steiner points out that the reign of Raphael ended in 1190. Nonetheless, we know from his writings that an archangel's influence can extend into that of the succeeding epoch.)

Now these Time Spirits, each in their own way, oversee the consciousness of human beings at different stages in their *individual* lives as well. Just as Michael guides human development between the ages of twenty-one and forty-two, Raphael is present between the ages of seven and fourteen. Thus, we can see that, according to Steiner, this lofty being was not only responsible for guiding the consciousness of humanity during Dante's time, but also during that period of human life in which Dante declared himself "reborn"—the ninth year—the year in which Steiner often said that a transition in life occurs primarily in the soul and spirit nature of the child. This age marks the point at which the child, for the first time, begins to feel a separation from others. As a result, such a child begins to experience his or her own individuality and is thereby more able to consciously acknowledge the *impressions* that arise from this transitory stage. Given this, the impact of Dante's "blessed" experience at the age of nine on his later life is *conceivable*. Yet, can it really be that the "god" to whom he alludes in the *Vita Nuova* and toward which he aspires for the remainder of his life referred *exclusively* to the mere *physical* presence of Beatrice Portinari, a nine-year-old child?

Rudolf Steiner, in his lecture on Dante on February 11, 1906, speaks of how the consciousness of humanity during the Middle Ages was one that is unimaginable to someone living today. He says that we "no longer imagine that people of that time could still see something spiritual in all material things," adding "nothing was only physical or only spiritual, for the mentality of that time; during those times, everyone naturally experienced the fact that the spiritual and physical interpenetrate." He adds,

> If we succeed in immersing ourselves in this point of view, we would live according to the feelings from which the *Divine Comedy* was able to arise. It makes no sense to discuss whether Beatrice was only symbol or even the woman loved by Dante; there is no contradiction between the two things. Beatrice was a real personality, *but also the expression of the spiritual*. Beatrice is truly the intact personification of *Theology*, with regard to the unaltered inner meaning. (tr. and italics mine)[62]

In *Isis Sophia Mary: Her Mission and Ours*, Steiner speaks more specifically of the concreteness of Dante's relationship with Lady Philosophy, a concreteness that sheds greater light on the physical–spiritual nature of Beatrice. He states:

> People who do not know how the times—into which our soul is ever growing with new life—change, lack any idea that Dante was just one among many of those with the capacity for a concrete experience of a passionate and personal relationship, immediate and of the soul, with Lady Philosophy, such as we today can feel only toward a man or women of flesh and blood. In this sense, Dante's time is past. The modern soul no longer approaches Lady Philosophy, the woman Philosophy, as a being of the same fleshy nature as itself, as Dante did. Or perhaps it is somewhat closer to

the honest truth to say that Philosophy was something, or someone, who went around as a being of flesh and blood—someone with whom one could have a relationship, the expression of which could not really be distinguished from the intense words of love one would use in relation to a being of flesh and blood. Whoever enters into the whole relationship Dante had with Philosophy will know that this relationship was concrete, the kind that modern human beings can only imagine between a man and a woman.[63]

Whether the mere physical presence of a nine-year-old girl named Beatrice Portinari actually incited the inner transformative experience mentioned above will always be a point of controversy in some academic circles. Nonetheless, we can at least agree with Steiner that the spiritual aspect of her being played an important role in arousing *inspirational forces* to take hold of Dante's soul and lead him to the realization of his Higher Self.

In our attempt to further characterize the figure of Beatrice, we can refer to Henry Corbin, who in his book, *Avicenna and the Visionary Recital*, tells of how Beatrice represented *Active Intelligence*. Says he,

> The mystical Iranian '*Ushshqq* and the *Fedeli d'amore*, companions of Dante, profess a secret religion that, though free from any confessionary denomination, is none the less common to them all. We must here confine ourselves to mentioning the delicate and accomplished studies that have shown how the Beatrice of the *Vita nuova* typifies the Active Intelligence or Wisdom–Sophia, and how the arguments that hold for Beatrice hold no less for all the "ladies" of the "Faithful in Love," who resemble her in every point—she, for example, who in Guido Cavalcanti takes the name of Giovanna, or, still more explicitly, she who in Dino Campagni appears as *"l'amorosa Madonna Intelligenza, Che fa nell'alma la sua residenza, Che co la sua bieltà' m'ha 'nnamorato."*
>
> Nothing could be clearer than the identity of this "amorosa Madonna Intelligenza, who has her residence in the soul, and with whose celestial beauty the poet has fallen in love. Here is perhaps one of the most beautiful chapters in the very long "history" of the Active Intelligence, which still remains to be written and which is

certainly not a "history" in the accepted sense of the word, because it takes place entirely in the souls of poets and philosophers.[64]

≈

In addition to these characterizations by Rudolf Steiner and Henri Corbin portraying the nature of Beatrice, is the one arrived at by deciphering the secret jargon that Dante and the *Fedeli d'amore* utilized in depicting *Divine Wisdom* in the face of the harrowing presence of the Church. Gabriele Rossetti and Luigi Valli point to chapter 5 of the *Vita Nuova*, where we discover that there existed an *intermediary* between Dante and his direct experience of *Divine Wisdom*. Says he:

> It happened one day that this most gracious of ladies was sitting in a place where words about the Queen of Glory were being spoken, and I was where I could behold my bliss. Halfway between her and me, in a direct line of vision, sat a gentlewoman of very pleasing appearance, who glanced at me frequently as if bewildered by my gaze, which seemed to be directed at her.... *At once I thought of making this lovely lady a screen to hide the truth, and so well did I play my part that in short time the many people who talked about me were sure they knew my secret. Thanks to this lady I concealed the truth about myself for several years and months, and to encourage people's false belief.* I wrote certain trifles for her in rhyme which I do not intend to include unless they could serve as a pretext to treat of that most gracious Beatrice... (tr. M. Musa; italics mine)[65]

Here, Dante seems to suggest that there literally stood between himself and the "Queen of Glory" (*Divine Wisdom*) someone that others were able to clearly perceive for themselves—i.e., a human figure that induced a "false belief." Thus, whenever Beatrice's name was mentioned, Dante was assured that the "lady" referred to was the one whose place rested halfway along the direct line extending from the Queen of Glory (*Divine Wisdom*) to him. In other words, Dante finds comfort in the fact that those who in a previous chapter (4) were "full of malicious curiosity" (Church) have mistaken *Divine Wisdom* for a physical woman, its earthly representational form.

Moreover, to add to the complication, this "lady" of whom he speaks could *also* (according to Rossetti and Valli) represent a member of the *Fedeli d'amore,* who not only harbors an understanding of *Divine Wisdom* but ensures that Dante's realization of such *Wisdom* would not be uncovered by the Church. Says he, "Then I was greatly relieved, feeling sure that my glances had not revealed my secret to others that day." He continues in chapter 6 by stating:

> Let me say that during the time that this lady acted as a *screen* for so great a love on my part, I was seized by a desire to record the name of my most gracious lady and to accompany it with the names of many others, and especially with the name of this gentlewoman. I chose the names of sixty of the most beautiful ladies of the city...it happened that the name of my lady appeared as the *ninth* among the names of those ladies, as if refusing to appear under any other number. (tr. M. Musa; italics mine)[66]

A number of important considerations arise here. First, are we to surmise, as Valli suggests, that the name Dante gives to his "most gracious lady" was derived from his "screen lady" (Beatrice Portinari) and then made to accompany the names of many other "ladies" chosen by the *Fedeli d'amore?* Secondly, as we see, Dante chooses "the names of sixty of the most beautiful ladies of the city," implicitly drawing a parallel to the fact that "the *Wisdom* of Solomon was the elect of over sixty queens" (tr. and italics mine)[67] and that the name of his lady (Beatrice) "appeared as the ninth...as if refusing to appear under any other number." Valli asks incredulously if we can seriously believe that "Dante, having sixty names to put into a sirventese, was unable to put the name of Beatrice in any of the other fifty-nine places (tr. mine).[68] In other words, what is so significant about the number nine that it is the *only* number with which Beatrice wishes to be identified? Furthermore, to which "city" does Dante refer, since in the whole of his *Vita Nuova,* there is really never any mention of a particular geographical location that might elucidate the historical ambiguities that arise from one's attempt to literally interpret this work? Though it is commonly assumed that Dante most often associates himself with

Florence, never is there any concrete description that could fix the events of the *Vita Nuova* to any specific time and place. Surely, this, in itself, is of great importance for it increases the possibility that the *Vita Nuova*, like Dante's *Comedy*, depicts a spiritual experience, primarily unassociated with space and time.

In order for us to rightly interpret a number of the events in the *Vita Nuova*, it would again be helpful to use the invaluable key provided by Luigi Valli, in particular, the interpretation of specific words that give Dante's work its intended meaning. Of special importance are the words *Love* and *Death*, as well as *lady* (or *ladies*)—when not in direct reference to Beatrice/*Divine Wisdom*. These words secretly allude to the protagonist(s) and antagonist of the *Vita Nuova*. As we have seen, the word *ladies* could refer to the members of the *Fedeli d'amore*, who collectively were often referred to as "Love." On the other hand, the word *Death* denotes the Church that opposed the efforts of the *Fedeli d'amore* to communicate their experience of *Divine Wisdom*, which harbored the forces of Love reaching down into humankind from the angelic hierarchies. We get a hint of this opposition in chapter 4 where we read how Dante, guided by the "reason of Love" (prudent advice of the sect), is able to conceal information regarding *Divine Wisdom* (Beatrice) from those whose questioning was "malicious" (informers of the Church). Says Dante,

> ...my natural spirit was interfered with in its functioning, because my soul had become wholly absorbed in thinking about this most gracious lady; and in a short time I became so weak and frail that many of my friends were worried about the way I looked; others full of malicious curiosity were doing their best to discover things about me, which, above all, I wished to keep secret from everyone. I was aware of the maliciousness of their questioning and, guided by Love who commanded me according to the counsel of reason, I would answer that it was Love who had conquered me. I said that it was Love because there were so many of his signs clearly marked on my face that they were impossible to conceal. And when people would ask: "Who is the

person for whom you are so destroyed by Love?" I would look at them and smile and say nothing. (tr. M. Musa)[69]

Here, Love (the prudent council of the sect) advises Dante to declare that *Love* itself (as traditionally understood) had conquered him. This "traditionally understood love" was thus falsely projected as the cause for Dante's frailty as evidenced by the "signs clearly marked on [his] face." This carnal love was to supplant, in the minds of the *"gente grossa,"* the *Love* denoting *Divine Wisdom*. As Valli intimates, however, such "signs" refer to the "facial expressions" by which the *Fedeli d'amore* were able to identify one another and glean intended information. Thus, those with "malicious" intent, interpreting them as manifestations of a broken heart, are completely led astray from intuiting Dante's true intentions and are thus prompt to ask a most natural question under the circumstances, namely, "for whom are you so destroyed by Love?" At this, Dante is able "to look at them and smile and say nothing," well aware of the efficacy of his secret jargon.

In chapter 7, we find but another instance of the efficacy of this jargon, for there Dante reveals his tenuous predicament when he no longer has his "screen lady" (physical representation) to hide behind, for

> *The lady I had used for so long to conceal my true feelings* found it necessary to leave the aforementioned city and to journey to a distant town.... *And realizing that if I should not lament somewhat her departure, people would soon become aware of my secret.* (tr. M. Musa; italics mine)[70]

In other words, only by lamenting her loss could Dante misdirect the Church from realizing that the true object of his "Love" was something other than his "screen lady." This Church is depicted in the following chapter (8) and verse. There, Dante speaks of a "lady" (adept) whose body lay "without a soul... in the midst of many ladies (adepts) who were weeping most pitifully." Having seen this person in the company of "his lady" (i.e., in close proximity to the *Wisdom* held by the sect), Dante writes a poem that indirectly alludes to his death. There, we discover the underhandedness of the Church.

> If Love himself weep, shall not lovers weep,
> learning for what sad cause he pours his tears?
> Love hears his ladies crying their distress,
> showing forth bitter sorrow through their eyes
> because villainous Death has worked its cruel
> destructive art upon the gentile heart
> and laid waste all that earth can find to praise
> in a gracious lady, save her chastity.

The second part continues as follows:

> Villainous Death, at war with tenderness,
> timeless mother of woe,
> judgment severe and incontestable,
> source of sick grief within my heart—a grief
> I must constantly bear—
> my tongue wears itself out in cursing you!
> I need only reveal
> your felonies, your guilt of every guilt;
> not that you are unknown for what you are,
> but rather to enrage
> whoever hopes for sustenance in love...
>   (tr. M. Musa)[71]

It is not difficult to see how these verses apply to the Church, as "Love" (the sect as a whole) hears its "ladies" (members) lament the loss of one of their own at the hands of the "villainous Death" (Church) that "worked its destructive art upon the *gentle* heart." The idea that Death is suggestive of the Church can be gleaned from the fact that its "judgment is suffered and incontestable" in as much as the Church declared itself to uphold the law of God on Earth (by way of the Inquisition). For what judgment is there to pass in the ordinary act of death? Moreover, who other than the Church could commit felonies that contain "the guilt of every guilt," namely, bearing false witness unto God? In his apparent attempt to exploit this realization, Dante reveals the connection between the words *Death* and *Church,* for if the nature of death is truly unknown until consummated, how could it be the object of Dante's invective, "not that you are unknown for what you are"? Surely, Dante alludes, here, to the knowledge that many had of the felonious nature of the Church during the Middle Ages.

So as to elucidate the reasons for the ambiguous settings in the *Vita Nuova,* we can point to one example in particular. We learn in chapter 9 that Dante ventures to the city where his screen lady was thought to have gone. There, Love, "scantily and poorly dressed," appeared to him in a sort of vision. Love (the sect) appears to Dante as if it were dissimulating its true nature, so that Dante can go undetected. For this reason, we are told that Love "stared at the ground." And what are the eyes of this Love looking at but "a beautiful river, swift and very clear, flowing by the side of the road..."[72]

Never is there any precise geographical location attributed to this river, nor to the city in which the screen lady has gone. Nonetheless, Valli reveals that the word *river* has a specific meaning, in that, it refers to the secret "tradition of initiation," or the "fountain of secret teachings," which had been taught to other *Fedeli d'amore* to dissimulate. In addition, we need only remember that in Canto IV of the *Paradiso,* Beatrice is referred to as "that stream so blest / it flows down from the Fountain of All Truth." Hence, the word *stream* represents the *light of wisdom* that flows from the fount of creative activity intrinsic to the Word. It is that which the Church—*having assumed for itself the role of Divine Wisdom*—had falsified. Two things are important here. First, such indirect reference to *a secret tradition* hints at the connection the *Fedeli d'amore* had to other esoteric streams at work in humanity. Secondly, had Dante mentioned the name of a river (which, of course, is an assumption based on a literal translation of the passage), he would have unintentionally run the risk of diverting those with *"verace intendimento,"* (i.e., those for whom his *Vita Nuova* was written) from inferring the implicit meaning of his text.

Thus, with the transposition of certain key words it becomes clear that an inner meaning arises. Valli demonstrates that even comments made by Boccaccio, Dante's biographer, regarding the existence of a Beatrice "in the flesh" must be approached with some degree of caution. According to him, Boccaccio was fully cognizant of the activities and "secret symbolism" of the *Fedeli d'amore,* given that he himself was a member. It must not be forgotten that through Boccaccio's efforts, the *Comedy,* unlike *De Monarchia,* survived being burnt. Boccaccio alludes to the veiled nature of Dante's work in his treatise on poetry, *The Genealogy of the Gods,* XIV. Boccaccio states,

> *"Or can anyone believe he (Aeneas) wrote such lines without some meaning or intention hidden beneath the superficial veil of myth?* Again let any man consider our own poet Dante as he often unties with amazingly skillful demonstration the hard knots of holy theology; will such a one be so insensible as not to perceive that Dante was a great theologian as well as philosopher? And, if this is clear, what intention does he seem to have had in presenting the picture of a griffon with wings and legs, drawing the chariot on top of the austere mountain, together with seven candlesticks, and the seven nymphs, and the rest of the triumphal procession? *Was it merely to show his dexterity in composing metrical narrative?"* (ed. C. G. Osgood; italics mine)[73]

Having written what was the first full account of this "historical" Beatrice nearly fifty years after the death of Dante, Boccaccio states that, until the age of nine, Dante frequented the house of Beatrice Portinari. Yet, Dante clearly states in his *Vita Nuova* that Beatrice "never directed a word at him." In light of Boccaccio's claim, how could Dante virtually not know the Beatrice whom he describes having met at the age of nine? Moreover, Dante himself states in chapter 2 of the *Vita Nuova* that "the glorious lady" of his mind" (*Divine Wisdom*) was called Beatrice "even by those who did not know what her name was." How strange a comment if Beatrice is understood to be a real person! Would it not seem much more comprehensible if the name "Beatrice" arose from Dante's experience of *Divine Wisdom*, given that the name "Beatrice" itself means "blessedness"? Needless to say, much confusion has been generated in the minds of *"la gente grossa"* throughout the centuries by Dante's obscure references. Valli says that, as a result of Boccaccio's allusion to the Portinari family, many of the *"gente grossa"*

> went searching to find out who this very famous woman of the Poet (Dante) was and nothing was easier than to stop at the house of a certain Beatrice *Portinari* who lived fifty meters from Dante's house, and who was part of a family that was friends with the Alighieri family, and who had died during Dante's youth. Naturally, the Portinari quickly held fast to this *"glory of the family."* And *for what reason* should Boccaccio have renounced this magnificent manner of not saying that the Beatrice of the *Vita Nuova* was the sacred Wisdom of his secret sect? It had directly to do at that time with making the *Vita Nuova* and the *Divine Comedy* understood as little as possible by the Church, which had just burnt the *Monarchia* (tr. mine).[74]

≈

One of the most important clues to understanding that Beatrice did, in fact, refer to *Divine Wisdom* is Dante's use of the number nine. Not only did Dante "meet" her when they were both nine years of age, but they were born nine months apart. After their initial "meeting" Dante and Beatrice did not see each other again for another nine years, which, incidentally, occurred during "the ninth hour" of that fateful day. What a strange coincidence! As we have said, Beatrice appeared to Dante in a dream as the ninth among sixty women. In fact, nine times is the number nine mentioned in reference to Dante's relationship with Beatrice in the *Vita Nuova!* Each of Dante's three visions of Beatrice's death is associated with the number *nine*. What can all of this possibly mean?

In her book, *The Sacred Science of Numbers*, Corinne Heline states that the number nine is that by which man comes into contact with his inner self, unfolds his latent divinity, and attains to that state of interior illumination which is known by the name of Initiation.[75]

She also states that the number *nine* can be represented by three triangles symbolizing the threefold aspects of each of the three principles of man, namely the body, soul and spirit." More important, it symbolizes the "potential" unification of the male and female polarities at work within the individual—i.e., willing and thinking. Thus, if we are to understand the *Divine Comedy* as a representation of humanity's quest toward the reunification of these polarities separated by the Fall, we cannot but acknowledge the important role that Beatrice—symbolized by the number nine—has toward such an end. Heline points out the fact that the book of *The Bible* from which the *Fedeli d'amore* modeled their theme of "beatification," *The Song of Solomon*, is "attuned to the number nine," in that, it is "a chant of the mystical marriage" and "voices the ecstasy of a soul that has glimpsed the heights of cosmic freedom and returned to sing of the glory of that liberation which none who still remain in bondage to the things of the earth can ever know."[76] Does this not, in effect, correspond to Dante's experience in the *Divine Comedy*?

It is interesting to note that not only is Beatrice symbolized by the number nine but so, too, is Virgil who leads Dante through Hell and part of Purgatory. We need only remember that *The Aeneid* (a work that, as Boccaccio alludes, depicts the inner stages of transformation), means "the Nine." In addition, we must bear in mind that in the *Paradiso* Dante journeys through the seven planetary spheres, the Fixed Stars, and the Primum Mobile, each governed by one of the nine Celestial Hierarchies. In fact, the number nine is therefore connected to the concept of angels. It is not for nothing that in the *Vita Nuova* Dante refers to Beatrice as "one of the most beautiful angels of Heaven" (ch. 26: 2). Related to this schematic delineation of *Paradiso*, Paolo Vinassa de Regny mentions in his book, *Dante e Pitagora*, that the *Inferno* and the *Purgatory* are each subdivided into nine circles or terraces. And just as the number nine is referenced nine times with respect to Dante's relationship with Beatrice in the *Vita Nuova*, so, too, does Dante within the three realms of the *Divine Comedy* dream nine times. Lastly, the word *nuova* in *Vita Nuova*, often written as "nova," bears close resemblance to *nove*—i.e., *nine*.

In the *Vita Nuova* (ch. 29), Dante himself *explicitly* points out the significance of the number nine. Says he,

> ...if three is the sole factor of nine, and the sole factor of miracles is three, that is, Father, Son, and Holy Spirit, who are Three in One, then this lady was accompanied by the number nine so that it might be understood that she was a nine, or a miracle, whose root, namely that of a miracle, is the miraculous Trinity itself. Perhaps someone subtler than I could find a still more subtle explanation, but this is the one that I see and which pleases me the most. (tr. M. Musa)[77]

These are the words Dante uses to speak of Beatrice upon her "death," which occurred during the ninth day of the ninth month, if one "counts the way they do in Syria." Valli, in *Il Linguaggio Segreto di Dante e dei Fedeli d'Amore*, states that the death of Beatrice signified "a certain transcendence, a transcendence of his spirit in a form of ecstasy, or near ecstasy, a certain form of real and true rapture, in which Dante, following the example of all his mystical teachers, had, in a certain way, crowned his love for the holy mystical Wisdom, or believed that he would be crowned for having reached the 'supreme hierarchy' of the sect" (tr. mine).[78] He adds that though this "mystical death" for the "profane" was represented as the death of a woman, it was a kind of "*acceptance into the heavens of man's mind and intellect.*"

Lastly, Beatrice was said to have died the year, during "that century in which she had been placed in this world," in which the perfect number (ten) "had been completed *nine* times" (9 x 10 = 90)—namely, 1,290. The numerological significance of her death is balanced with that of her birth, which occurred when this number *nine* reflected the harmony of the celestial spheres, for "at her birth all nine of the moving heavens were in perfect relationship to one another." These nine heavenly spheres "affect the earth below according to the relations they have to one another," so that the evolutionary development attained before one's reunion with God is "revealed by the numerical truth that all numbers—sequentially in increasing and decreasing combination—from 1 to 9, reduce to 9 (1 + 8, 2 + 7, 3 + 6, 4 + 5)."

In the end, Dante states in the *Vita Nuova* that **Beatrice is herself the number nine.** Says he, "If anyone thinks more subtly and according to infallible truth, it will be clear that this number was she herself—that is, by analogy."[79]

It is interesting to note that Dante uses the words *Syria* and *Arabia* with regard to the death of Beatrice. Again, he states that Beatrice's death occurs on the ninth day of the ninth month, if one "counts the way they do in Syria." As we shall later see, this reference to Syria intimates that the mystery surrounding Beatrice (*Sophia*) could be traced to the Sufi poets of the Middle East who often used the symbol of the "rose" to describe their beloved, a symbol that Dante, of course, adopts in his *Divine Comedy*. If we consider the fact that Beatrice appears in red both the first time she meets Dante as well as the last, and that this color "red" (as Heline intimates) is "the color of nine," then it is easy to see how such a description might very well be a veiled reference to *Divine Wisdom*. For "red" regards the "rose," which was also amongst the most prevalent of names then given to one's beloved. This tradition is knowm to have passed from the Sufis in Persia to the Troubadours to the *Fedeli d'amore*. (Incidently, in light of this series of relationships, it is also easy to imagine how a certain Durante, thought to have written *Il Fiore*—an Italian version of the Troubadour epic poem, *The Romance of the Rose*—was none other than Dante himself.)

Probably the most obvious clue regarding the number nine's relationship to the rites of initiation is conveyed by Gabriele Rossetti, who refers to the *Recueil precieux de la Massonerie adonhiramite* by Louis Guillemain de Saint-Victor, which states that when the adept was conventionally thought to be nine years of age, it meant that he had reached a certain level of (spiritual) perfection. Dante alludes to this attainment of spiritual perfection in the *Vita Nuova*, particularly in chapter 12, where, having fallen into a dream, he is spoken to by a young man who tells him that he has erred in his efforts, saying, "my son, it is time to do away with our false ideas." As a result, we witness Dante's attempt at contemplation in the next chapter, when he says:

> I do not know from which to take my theme.
> I want to speak, but what is there to say?
> Thus do I wander in a maze of Love!
> (tr. M. Musa)[80]

And what do we then discover is Dante's theme, but that which makes "the center of a circle, equidistant from all points on the circumference," namely, the point in the human heart from which flow the creative forces of life. This "center" was what the young man in Dante's dream described that he, himself, resembled. It represents the balance attained through contemplation of that which is symbolized by the number nine. Valli himself tells us that it is typical of modern thinkers to assume that Dante was unfamiliar with the "mystical ages" known to secret societies—i.e., to recognize seven as being the age of Master, nine as the age associated with a "Scozese" (Scot), and eighty-one as referring to a secret Master. Nonetheless, regarding the importance of the number 81 ($9 \times 9 = 81$, $8 + 1 = 9$), Valli quotes Dante in his *Convivio* (book IV, ch. 24) in which he says,

> Hence it is said of Plato, who may be said to have possessed a supremely excellent nature both for the perfection of its being and for the physiognomic image which Socrates observed in him when he first saw him, that he lived to the age of eighty-one.... I believe that if Christ had not been crucified and had lived out the term which his life could have encompassed according to its nature, *he would have undergone the change from mortal body to immortal in his eighty-first year.* (tr. R. H. Lansing (1990); italics mine)[81]

If Beatrice is truly representative of *Divine Wisdom* how can we better understand her relationship to the Christ impulse? More specifically, where in Dante's works is the relationship between the being of Sophia and Christ consciousness revealed?

To understand the answers to such questions better, we must bear in mind that when Dante alludes to the *activity* of the being Sophia, he reveals it as a triune aspect. In the *Divine Comedy*, for example, *Beatrice* sends *Lucia* to summon Virgil to Dante's aid the moment Dante is lost in the "Dark Wood," after which this same Beatrice, at the bequest of the *Virgin Mary*, appears to Dante in the "Garden of Earthly Paradise" to help him ascend the heavenly spheres. This threefold aspect of the *feminine* presents itself again in the "Garden of Earthly Paradise." There, Dante dreams about *Leah* and *Rachel*, representative of *active and contemplative life*, respectively. However, it is *Matilda* who leads him to the river Lethe and absolves him of his memory of sin. Lastly, there are the three divine graces, *faith, love,* and *hope,* which Dante initially sees as emerging stars once he has begun to ascend the slopes of Purgatory before witnessing them around the chariot upon which is seated Beatrice in the "Garden of Earthly Paradise."

These three groups of feminine individualities each form a sort of trinity and, as such, collectively comprise the number nine. In his book, *The Triple Goddess,* Adam McLean states, "The Goddess is triple, manifesting in a threefold form, because she unites within herself the complements and opposites of the psyche." Later on, he adds, "Once we have come to an inner relationship with the Feminine, we can begin uniting the masculine and feminine facets of our souls."[82] As previously stated, it is the unification of these opposite polarities that forms the basis of Dante's ascension toward the spiritual worlds, thus symbolizing the reintegration of human consciousness with that of the "Mystic Lamb of God." Thus, as McLean says,

> The triplicity of the Goddess is very important. This is not merely a multiplying by three, but rather a threefold manifestation; the Goddess reveals herself on three levels, in the three realms of the world and of humankind. Thus the human being is threefold, having body, soul and spirit, and the Goddesses' three facets are often

seen as corresponding to these three realms within the microcosm of the human being.[83]

This threefold aspect relating to body, soul, and spirit is particularly evident in the case of Lucia, Beatrice, and the Virgin Mary, in that the *light of reason* (Lucia) that awakens Virgil to Dante's predicament in the *Inferno*, can be thought to represent the earthly manifestation of the cosmic light (Christ) irradiating down from Beatrice and Mary. In the *Purgatorio*, Beatrice becomes manifest to Dante, for having arrived at the point in which the intellectual and heart forces are truly integrated (Virgil and Beatrice momentarily in close proximity), Dante is soon to witness the Archetypal Intelligence of the hierarchies revealed through ever-luminous eyes of Beatrice. Finally, not until Dante has arrived at the furthest reaches of Paradise in the *Paradiso* does the *suprasensory light* of this Cosmic Sophia or Virgin *fully* reveal itself to him, thus heralding his imminent encounter with the Godhead. Only when Dante is able to wholly *perceive* this light, is he truly capable of beholding the sacred Trinity. In Canto XXIII, the Sophia bears the "Radiant Substance of the vision of Christ" as it flashes before Dante. In other words, She bears the *light* leading humanity to the perception of the Christ. As She follows her Son "to the highest sphere," we are led to realize that only through our contemplation of *Divine Wisdom* can the Christ be actualized. Says Dante:

> Lady, thou art so near God's reckonings
> that who seeks grace and does not first seek thee
> would have his wish fly upward without wings.
> (*Paradiso*, Canto XXXIII, 13–15)

≈

In addition to all of this, Rudolf Steiner mentions the fact that Faith, Love, and Hope (to which we have just referred) are symbolic of the attainment of Manas, Buddhi, and Atma respectively, whereas the four cardinal virtues mentioned by Dante—justice, temperance, fortitudeand wisdom—are each representative of the lower aspects of the human being, namely the physical, etheric, astral, and "I." In other words, only through the entrance of Christ into the world can humanity *realize* the so-called theological virtues of the Middle Ages—Faith, Love, and Hope (*Manas, Buddhi,* and *Atma*)—and the remaining cycles of the Earth evolution become complete.

To further relate Beatrice to the threefold nature of the human being as outlined in Anthroposophy, it would be useful to consider what Pierre Mandonnet describes in, *Dante the Theologian,* as the three ladies at work in Dante's *Vita Nuova*—Beatrice, Poetry, and Philosophy, which, in essence, may be thought to characterize the threefold aspect in the development of human consciousness. We have seen how Beatrice, symbolized by the number nine, is herself representative of the Archetypal Sophia as it manifests in the individualized consciousness of human beings. It denotes the stage whereby concept and percept are transcended, that is, they are themselves cognized so that no longer do they appear as polarities. Instead, they become united as one. Their enlivening results in the perceptive capacity to penetrate the physical world, wherein lies the creative forces of life originating from the Mystic Lamb. Philosophy and Poetry correspond, on the other hand, to the faculties of concept and percept respectively, which, once integrated, provide for the emergence of Beatrice (*Divine Wisdom*).

Finally, it would be useful to think of Philosophy and Poetry as representative of thinking and feeling, so that their integration accounts for the emergence of Beatrice—i.e., the active imagination resulting from the emancipation of the human will. We could conclude by saying that Philosophy (concept) is indicative of the *Inferno* where depicted are the static representations that arise from our observation of the world around us. Poetry (percept) denotes the so-called imaginative world still tenuously bound to the static representations of a thought world on the verge of being liberated from the senses. And so, the *Purgatorio* reflects the feeling realm, namely, that in which the concept is torn from its sense-based foundation, so that no longer do we have relationships adhering to the fixed representations of the physical world.

There, the presence of Beatrice symbolizes the imaginative world free of physical influences, so that no longer does the dichotomy of concept and percept form the basis of experience. Instead, the will becomes the conscious motivating force that leads Dante to the realization of his "I." Therein function the moral impulses embodied in the *Paradiso*.

≈

Robert Powell, in his book, *The Sign of the Son of Man in the Heavens*, states that the reason Rudolf Steiner chose the word *anthroposophy* was revealed in 1913 at the founding of the Anthroposophical Society, where he pointed to its "development from philosophy," which originally meant "the love of divine wisdom" (*philo* = love, *sophy* = wisdom). Powell states that Steiner

> referred to the poet Dante almost as if Dante was in love with the being of Sophia, the personification of divine wisdom. There was still a feeling for the being of Sophia right up to the Middle Ages, at least up to the time of Dante (1265–1321). *Then followed the development of modern science, which arose from the time of the Renaissance onward. And a deeper feeling for Sophia, who had been central to the whole of philosophy, faded more and more into the background.* (italics mine)[84]

He continues:

> What was previously the divine wisdom weaving into philosophy became more and more a purely human affair. Sophia, having poured herself out, "died" into the human being—sacrificing herself so that human beings could begin to think for themselves, to experience their thoughts as their own thoughts. Now, however, at the start of the New Age that we have entered into since the end of the last century, we have the task of bringing Sophia alive within us, and this signifies the birth of anthroposophia, the wisdom of man, where the being of Sophia becomes resurrected within the human being.[85]

In fact, in *Isis Mary Sophia: Her Mission and Ours* (February 3, 1913), Steiner speaks of Dante by saying,

For a person such as Dante, as we may gather from his descriptions in the *Divine Comedy*, it was still possible to experience in a natural way, so to speak, *the last remnant* of an immediate connection with the spiritual worlds. (italics mine)[86]

This relationship for Dante came in the form of *Lady Philosophy*. Steiner states,

> Dante himself told us—and I don't think any modern critic will deny that Dante knew what he wanted to say—that the beloved lady, with whom he had so direct and personal relationship, was none other than *Philosophy*.[87]

He adds,

> Dante explicitly says that when his personal beloved, Beatrice, was torn from him, and he was required to continue without a personal relationship, it was the lady Philosophy who drew near to his soul, full of compassion and more human than any human thing.[88]

We must understand Philosophy to still contain the living aspect known to the Greeks as Sophia. Steiner tells us that this being must be sought today in Anthroposophy. He states,

> What, therefore, must be developed? It must unfold that, once again, as a matter of course, a "Sophia" becomes present. But we must learn to relate this Sophia to the consciousness soul, bring her down directly to human beings. This is happening during the age of the consciousness soul. And thereby Sophia becomes the being who directly enlightens human beings. After Sophia has entered human beings, she must take their being with her and present it to them outwardly, objectively. Thus, Sophia will be drawn into the human soul and arrive at the point of being so inwardly connected with it that a love poem as beautiful as Dante wrote may be written about her.
>
> Sophia will become objective again, but she will take with her what humanity is, and objectively present herself in this form. Thus, she will present herself not only as Sophia, but as *Anthroposophia*—as the Sophia who, after passing through the human soul, through the very being of the human being, henceforth bears that being within her. And in this form she will confront enlightened

human beings as the objective being Sophia who once stood before the Greeks.[89]

Though there are various ways to characterize Beatrice, we would not be wrong to envision her as the personification of *Active Intelligence*, namely, that which today is referred to as *living thinking* at the heart of Anthroposophy.

Excessus Mentis / Morte Mistica

As we have seen, it is impossible to visualize the relationship that Dante's *Divine Comedy* had to the love poetry of the *Fedeli d'amore* without taking into account their implementation of a literary jargon that allowed for the free exchange of ideas without fear of persecution by the Church. What was it about the knowledge they coveted that made them so wary of the Church? Though we have discussed the significance of various names that they employed to relate their experience of *Divine Wisdom*, never do they, themselves, clearly delineate the role of *Divine Wisdom* in relation to the Christ. Instead, meaning is always clothed in allegory. The philosophical foundation that lies at the core of this allegory can only be *inferred* by analyzing the stage of development at which thinking had arrived during that time. Strange as it may seem, one cannot truly uncover inner meaning by merely acknowledging the influence that Scholasticism—the principle philosophy of the age—may have had for these poets, nor by entering abstractly into questions posed by Dante in his *Comedy*, such as the role of Fortune or predestination. For these have inevitably fallen into the realm of dialectical speculation often accepted as Church doctrine, as is the case with Augustine and Aquinas. Instead, the Church must have recognized the existence of something that not only transcended the insoluble aspects of dialectics, but also put into clearer light the limitations incurred by submitting to the notion of "faith," as defined by Augustine and adopted and promoted by the Church fathers. This "something" could be none other than an actual *experience* of the spiritual world.

Our fundamental problem in attempting to fathom these enigmas lies in the very nature of our modern-day consciousness, for initiatory experiences change through time with respect to the evolution of human thinking. We have seen how the *Fedeli d'amore*, by invoking the name of a woman (Beatrice, Selvaggia, Fiore, etc.), were able to communicate their experience of *Divine Wisdom* (Sophia) without falling suspect to the Church. By doing so, they sought to maintain certain conditions necessary to the realization of this higher wisdom—e.g., a "pure heart." There, however, exist few clues in their works that elucidate the *internal dynamics* of their initiatory experience. What is necessary is a bridge by which we can better comprehend how a person of Dante's time perceived the spiritual—a bridge based on the evolution of consciousness as outlined by Anthroposophy.

While considering the historical foundations of the *Fedeli d'amore*, Luigi Valli shows that the convergence of five distinct traditions contributed to its emergence. These traditions, each of which had varying effects on different members of the poetic circle, reflect how intricate and obscure is the derivation of "sacred knowledge" for those critics who, by adhering to the percepts of positivistic philosophy, fail to enter into the esoteric or metaphysical aspects of medieval thought. The five streams, defined by Valli as having had a profound impact on Dante and his circle, are:

1. The "philosophic" tradition that personified *Active Intelligence* in the figure of a woman by differentiating it from the passive intelligence commonly acknowledged by all individuals. The aim of *Active Intelligence* was to lead the human being to the acquisition of supreme eternal ideas ungraspable by way of the senses.
2. The second tradition had enormous impact on the sect; it metaphorically represented the "wisdom that sees God" as a "*woman who is loved*" (*donna amata*).
3. The third tradition was more orthodox in so far as it related to Catholicism. It centered primarily on the figure of Rachel, who was thought to represent the "virtue of contemplative life."

4. The fourth tradition declared the Church to be corrupt and sought the process by which it could undergo a transformation of its "carnal" nature.
5. The fifth and final tradition was that of using language with double meaning so as to conceal certain "forbidden" aspects of esoteric knowledge from those who could not rightly understand them (*"gente grossa"*).

In a previous chapter, we discussed the efforts of the *Fedeli d'amore* to conceal their aims from the Church by "beatifying" women. However, the elements of this tradition existed long before Dante and his contemporaries came upon the scene. The "philosophic" tradition that personified *Active Intelligence* in the figure of a woman had its roots in Aristotelianism. Its main premise was that if the intellect reflects ideas in such a way as the eye sees things, or as a mirror reflects images, then an *active principle* must exist that is possibly connected to the intellect, just as light is to the eye or mirror. Since the union of intelligence and the will symbolically represented the act of (sacred) Love, the tendency of the intellect to connect with *Active Intelligence* manifested itself as the "will in action." And so, Aristotle, who, in a sense, signaled the dawning of the intellectual self evermore removed from the atavistic clairvoyance of earlier times, did not appear to have completely severed his connection to Platonism. Instead, this *Active Intelligence* to which Aristotle refers is that aspect in human thinking that Steiner describes as "living"—namely the active spirit working in the human being. Aristotle was able to see how the imperceptible forces of nature that weave the materially perceptible world into being, are the very forces responsible for the manifestation of thought itself. *Active Intelligence* can, thus, be said to be that element which is the *creative principle* that works in human consciousness. However, the human being's ability to perceive it cannot take place until the activity of the intellect has been intensified to the point in which the forces of willing are beheld. This possibility was precluded from ancient humanity, for willing was still perceived as a creative force outside the realm of thought. Aristotle, for example, was still able to perceive this *Active Intelligence* somewhat atavistically, without having to cultivate it as the fruit of his own inner experience. For Dante and the *Fedeli d'amore,* the time had yet to come in which such willing could be consciously elicited from within the depths of thinking. For this to take place, thinking *itself* had to undergo a further process of transformation. This occurred when materialistic impulses began to shape human consciousness to an ever-greater degree, thus gradually eclipsing one's perception of the spiritual forces behind nature. Such a process, which we may define as the "hardening of thinking," had yet to completely take hold of the general consciousness of humanity during Dante's time. This would, for one, explain how Dante could be greatly affected by the initiatory experience of his teacher, Brunetto Latini, for had Dante's thinking become excessively permeated by materialistic impulses (common in our day), he would not have likely been able to atavistically capture the imaginative forces that were part of Brunetto's vision, as he had done. Thus, modern initiation, which necessitates the complete autonomy (or materialization) of thinking, was something that Dante and many of his contemporaries, for the most part, could not quite yet attain.

The second tradition which, metaphorically depicted "wisdom that sees God" as a woman *loved,* had, as its underlying premise, the fact that we are connected to God by *divine thinking.* It was by way of this "divine thinking" that God created the whole of life, and that through a single "ray" one could bridge oneself to God. As Valli explains, this "divine thinking" was known as "Logos" in Neo-Platonism, and also as the second person of the Trinity (after the *Gospel of John* identifies it with the Christ). However, in Gnosticism it was known as *Sophia.* It recalled the *Active Intelligence* of Aristotelianism, insofar as it was considered to be the "mediator between the higher and lower aspect of the soul." Thus, it is not difficult to envision how the concept of *Sophia* or *Divine Wisdom* was synonymous with that of *Active Intelligence,* and how it was possible to acknowledge that the forces that manifest life are the very ones by which humankind is able to connect itself to God. The distinguishing feature between these two traditions was the degree to which the latter allegorically represented *Active Intelligence,* or "divine thinking" in the figure of an individualized woman.

The third tradition also uses the figure of "woman loved" to represent "wisdom beholding God," but it differentiates itself by pointing to the *Bible* as its source of reference, more specifically to the Sapienza (Wisdom) in the *Canticle of Canticles* (or *Song of Songs*) by Solomon. Valli believes that Dante, in characterizing Beatrice, adopts the idea of woman as a symbol of "Sapienza Santa" (*Divine Wisdom*) from the *Canticle of Canticles.* One need only to be reminded of how "ideal" human love was portrayed in "Love's Inquiry" (1:9–10):

> I liken you, my darling, to a mare
> harnessed to one of the chariots
> of Pharaoh.
> Your cheeks are beautiful with
> earrings,
> your neck with strings of jewels.
> We will make you earrings of gold,
> studded with silver.[90]

Interestingly, the Church, too, seems to have adopted the portrayal of woman found in the *Canticle of Canticles.* In fact, according to Valli, the Church not only proclaimed itself to be "Sapienza Santa" (*Divine Wisdom*), but it declared that only it *itself* could be the mediator between God and humankind, since it alone had the capacity to represent Him. Thus, we see how the wisdom of the Gnostics first became adopted, then distorted by the Church. While in the Orient, the mysterious "Sapienza Santa" reappeared in various gnostic forms culminating in the figure of the "Rose"—the object to which the Persians and also the *Fedeli d'amore* later felt drawn (again, one need only think of the Mystic Rose that Dante perceives at the end of his journey in the *Paradiso*)—the Church, on the other hand, presented "Sapienza Santa" as the "Chiesa Rivelatrice" (Church Revealer). Though words such as "Rose" or "Flower," at first, were used by the *Fedeli d'amore* to symbolize *Divine Wisdom,* there later sprang a multiplicity of names, as numerous as the men who aspired toward her, so that each *Fedele d'amore* addressed her by a different name. Thus, they "reconcile their faith in the sacred catholic Revelation with the certainty that the corrupted *carnal* Church now no longer speaks on behalf of that sacred Revelation, of that Divine Wisdom and...beneath the veil of that strange symbolism of love, they appeal to the incorruptible Wisdom of the Church against the Church itself, which became corrupt" (tr. mine).[91]

Later, in Augustine, the "wisdom that sees God," is "personified in Rachel"—yet another transformation of the "woman loved." Valli tells us that Augustine conceived this wisdom in Platonic terms, saying that we can affirm there exists a Supreme Divine Wisdom in which only by participating (in it) can one become a true Knower (tr. mine).[92] Augustine states, "though human minds are individualized and in great number, Intelligence is one, toward which everyone aspires and in which everyone participates. It is like the light of the Sun, which by remaining whole, is multiplied by as many eyes that perceive it."[93] (Note the influence of Plotinus in his life!) Herein lies the reason for which this *Intelligence*, in as much as it multiplies by the number of people who behold it, has the name Beatrice for Dante, Vanna for Guido Cavalcanti, Selvaggia for Cino da Pistoia, etc.

According to Valli, Pascoli showed that both Leah and Rachel are two lives reflected in the Christ. He also makes note of the fact that one need only look to St. Augustine's *Contra Faustum* (XX, 52–58), where mention is made of the connection between Rachel (sister of Leah and daughter of Laban) and *"Sapienza Santa" (Divine Wisdom)*. While Leah is the temporal aspect that resides in work, Rachel is the eternal aspect that rests in contemplation. In fact, the name, Rachel, which personifies *active contemplation*, is interpreted as *Visum principium*. Valli reiterates the fact that Rachel (*Visum principium*) represents *Active Intelligence* that "*sees* the principles, the eternal ideas in things." In Dante, she is synonymous with Beatrice. In fact, in the *Vita Nuova*, Beatrice appears saying, "I am to see the principle of Peace" (tr. mine).[94] Only after Dante has perceived Leah at work and

Matilda the seer is he finally led to "pure vision and contemplation," namely, to the "pure wisdom" in Beatrice.

Having thus characterized the "Sapienza Santa" (*Divine Wisdom*), what significance lay in Rachel's (or Beatrice's) death? Is it not so that only *from the afterworld* is Beatrice (in the *Divine Comedy*) able to incite Dante's spiritual awakening by sending Virgil to his aid in the "Dark Wood"? Here, we arrive at a most unusual prerequisite for Dante's attainment of the *Divine Wisdom—death*. For Richard of St. Victor (a contemporary of Saint Bernard), Rachel's death signified "an act of pure contemplation," or "an ascension into contemplative perfection" (tr. mine).[95] Such an act of transcendence was known as *excessus mentis*. It represented the highest degree of perfection for the *Fedeli d'amore*. As long as Rachel (Beatrice, Vanna, etc.) was alive, she was merely the "embodiment" of "Sapienza Santa" (*Divine Wisdom*). Her death, on the other hand, symbolized self-purification—i.e., the highest level of mystical intuition attainable by the "initiate." In other words, the death of Beatrice, to which Dante makes reference in the *Vita Nuova*, signaled the direct intuition of Divine Truth.

Valli lists four stages (or ways) by which love leads to *excessus mentis*. The first stage is by completely abandoning the use of the senses. The second is by totally withdrawing from the external world and by introducing "imaginative vision." Then comes "intellectual vision," whereby one perceives things deemed intellectual not by way of the physical manifestation of the thing itself, but by way of revelation. Finally, when the mind is no longer connected to the lower aspect of human nature—thereby allowing direct access to God—it intuits, by way of "intellectual vision," the divine essence. Again, these four paths culminate in the experience of *excessus mentis*, "the highest level of love" and, in fact, the highest level of wisdom (initiation) "attainable by the *Fedeli d'amore*."[96]

Though nowhere does Dante actually describe the internal dynamics of his initiatory experience, in chapter 27 of the *Vita Nuova* he tells us of his desire to relate the *effect* that *Divine Wisdom* had on him. Says he, "...I decided to write a poem telling how I seemed to be disposed to her influence, and how her miraculous power worked in me."⁹⁷

To understand the effect of Beatrice's death upon Dante, Valli points to Richard of St. Victor, who claimed that the state of earthly transcendence known as *excessus mentis*, is directly related to the death of Rachel. Ray C. Petry quotes Richard of St. Victor in his book, *Late Medieval Mysticism*, as saying, "the soul not only breaks its normal bounds and attains realities which are above and beyond its reason, but it is so absorbed by its object that its faculties fail and it loses consciousness of the external world and of itself"⁹⁸ (from *Benjamin Major V*). In elaborating on the death of Rachel as described in Genesis 35:16–20, Valli quotes Richard's *Benjamin Minor*,

> But the mind, still crude, *cannot elevate itself to the contemplation of celestial things*, since only the forms of sensory things are revealed to it. It tries to see what is invisible and cannot. Therefore, what does it do? What it does best. Since it cannot see with pure intelligence, it accommodates itself to see with imagination.... Rachel unites her servant "Bilhah with Jacob and so she has her first children."
> ...Finally, the grace of contemplation is granted: Benjamin; but as soon as this last child is born, *Rachel dies; nor are there those who believe they can elevate themselves to contemplation if Rachel does not die*. (tr. and italics mine)⁹⁹

Richard of St. Victor elaborates further by saying that *Benjamin* represents

> *the act of pure intelligence, the intuition of things that do not fall under the influences of the senses*.... Benjamin is born and *Rachel dies: in as much as the mind is abducted above itself, the limits of every human argument are transcended, and as soon as it sees, in ecstasy, the divine light, human reason succumbs. This is the death of Rachel giving life to Benjamin.* (tr. and italics mine)¹⁰⁰

Pascoli, in his book *La Mirabile Visione*, points to the implicit relationship between Rachel and Beatrice. Says he,

Therefore the death of Rachel is declared as *mentis excessus*. And while such *mentis excessus* can be declared to be the death of oneself, insofar as the soul exits the body by way of the virtue of ecstasy, it seems as if it were recognized in the form of Rachel's death, of a woman, beautiful and loved. And also, therefore, with this example, we account for how Dante—who had already seen in his woman "the hope of the contemplation of God," or even his Rachel, by following the song *Donne che avete* with the song *Donna pietosa*—dreams that he dies and Beatrice dies. He exits from his mind, that is, he dies; his mind exits and leaves, that is, his woman dies. (tr. mine)[101]

William Anderson in *Dante the Maker,* says that Richard of St. Victor, a "supreme master of anagogic interpretation had described how Rachel must die for Benjamin, the youth symbolizing the ecstasy of contemplation, to be born."[102]

Thus, Beatrice is interchangeable with Rachel, so that the death of Beatrice to which Dante alludes even at the outset of the *Vita Nuova* is but an allusion to his suprasensory experience. We see this represented in the poem that Dante writes to end chapter 27.

> So long a time has love kept me a slave
> and in his lordship fully seasoned me,
> that even though at first I felt him harsh,
> now tender is his power in my heart.
> But when he takes my strength away from me
> so that my spirits seem to wander off,
> my fainting soul is overcome with sweetness,
> and the color of my face begins to fade.
>
> Then Love starts working in me with such power
> he turns my spirits into ranting beggars,
> and, rushing out, they call
> upon my lady, pleading in vain for kindness.
> This happens every time she looks at me,
> yet she herself is beyond belief.
>   (tr. by Mark Musa) [103]

Though not easily recognizable, what we have here is Dante's encounter with the death of Beatrice. He begins by describing his experience under the "lordship" of Love as "harsh." Yet, having endured such a state, Dante becomes "seasoned" so that he feels the power of Love become "tender" in his heart. It is not difficult to imagine, here, how Dante is, in essence, describing the hardships encountered on way toward an initiatory experience as overseen and administered by the *Fedeli d'amore*. In the beginning, he was a "slave" to Love— i.e., he had to discipline his will by conforming it to what we may assume to be the rituals of the sect. With time, what was most difficult and strenuous becomes "tender." (This, incidentally, brings to mind Steiner's description of the concentration exercises, which, at first, are exceedingly difficult but with time are welcomed by the meditant.)

Once Love has prompted this state, the "spirits" in Dante wander off, leaving behind a "fainting soul...overcome with sweetness." In other words, Dante is "outside himself" ("color of my face begins to fade")—i.e., *he experiences excessus mentis*. Love works in him so strongly that his "spirits" are as "ranting beggars" rushing out to call upon his lady (Beatrice). Here, Valli states that connected with this thought is "the interrupted song and one will understand how and why *it is interrupted by the death of Beatrice*," a song that Valli likens to "a stair of mystical exaltation which *rises toward mystical death* and for a profound symbolic drama *is interrupted by mystical death*" (tr. mine).[104] *In other words, Dante experiences the death of Beatrice, that is, a mystical death known to him as excessus mentis.* This is illustrated by his ascent toward his Lady who has risen. This "ascent" again culminates in the *Paradiso*, when Dante perceives the Virgin Mary within the Mystic Rose.

In chapter 28 of the *Vita Nuova*, Dante explains that there are three reasons for not revealing the death of his "beloved" Beatrice. Says Dante,

> The first is that such a discussion does not fit into the plan of this little book, if we consider the preface which precedes it; the second is that, even if this had been my intention, the language at

my command would not yet suffice to deal with the theme as it deserves; the third is that even supposing that the first two reasons did not exist, it still would not be proper for me to treat the theme since this would entail praising myself—which is the most reprehensible thing one can do. (tr. M. Musa)[105]

Valli holds all three of these reasons in suspect. Nonetheless, it is the third that is most interesting in light of what has thus far been described. Again, Dante says, "...it would not be proper for me to treat the theme, since this would entail praising myself—which is the most reprehensible thing one can do..." And so, he "leaves this subject to some other commentator."[106] How can speaking of the death of his beloved (Beatrice) constitute "the most reprehensible thing" unless, of course, such a death be not in reference to a human being but, rather, to *his* "mystical union with God." Only, then, could an *open* discussion of such a death constitute, in the minds of many, especially those of his circle who like him sought anonymity, an act of selfishness. Immediately in connection with this, Dante intimates that because "the number nine has appeared many times" in his *Vita Nuova*, this "clearly could not happen without a reason." Again, how strange, unless, of course, we remember that the number *nine* represents *Divine Wisdom* personified by Beatrice! As Valli says, "Dante does not therefore talk of the death of Beatrice because he *does not want to speak of it*...he wants to say of it that which suffices for those with the capacity for true discernment (*"verace intendimento"*) to understand it has to do with *mystical death*."[107]

≈

Even though Dante prefigures the birth of the Consciousness Soul Age, we must remember that the spiritual constitution of the human being during his time was not yet conducive to the threefold path of initiation outlined by Steiner—namely that of *Imagination, Inspiration,* and *Intuition*. Nevertheless, it would be interesting to imagine how the initiatory practices of the *Fedeli d'amore* might relate to the stream of Anthroposophy, for I believe that the *Divine Comedy* can (if we choose) be envisioned to embody many aspects of this modern path of initiation. First, we must analyze what appear to be the inherent similarities between the *Fedeli d'amore* and the Rosicrucians with regard to their spiritual practices, as both esoteric circles strove to preserve the sanctity of spiritual knowledge.

While it was possible for many highly developed individualities (of the *Fedeli d'amore*) to enter the fourth stage of initiation, *morte mistica (excessus mentis)* was attainable by only the highest of initiates—all this without the slightest intimation of reincarnation. For thinking, as Steiner says, had yet to develop sufficiently enough to afford human beings the possibility of fathoming some of the most enigmatic aspects of their spiritual being. In fact, philosophical thinking in the West did not come to embrace the notion of reincarnation until later, when "individuality" supplanted "personality" as the chief characteristic defining human nature. In his lecture on Dante on February 11, 1906, Steiner said:

> ...Upon presenting himself to Dante, Virgil tells him, "I cannot free you from the three beasts (leopard, lion and wolf), especially the wolf." This because Dante was raised on Italian soil, in an element that bears the imprint of ancient Roman qualities. Virgil, who in the *Aeneid* offered a picture of Initiation, had to be Dante's guide. It is precisely from Virgil that human beings of that time, learned what the conditions of the afterlife were, once the threshold of death was crossed. It appeared as divided into three parts: Inferno, Purgatory and Paradise. From a certain point of view, one can say only two coherent conceptions of the world exist: one is that of Augustine and the other is that of reincarnation and karma. Augustine says: "on this earth one part of humanity is predestined toward good, the other toward bad." The other conception is that, according to which, we evolve by way of repeated incarnations. Only these two conceptions are possible. Dante follows Augustine, for which humankind prepares itself for an eternal destiny in a single life.... This single earthly life is seen as determinate. It regards only the *personality* of the human being.

> If the personality becomes transcended, the boundaries of birth and death would die away. What lies beyond personality is what enters before birth and exits again with death. (tr. mine)[108]

Nonetheless, we can see some relationship between the fourfold initiatory path of the *Fedeli d'amore* outlined by Valli, and the sevenfold path of Rosicrucian initiation.

In his book, *Theosophy of Rosicrucianism*, Rudolf Steiner tells how the initiation arrived at during the thirteenth century by Christian Rosenkreutz, was an elaboration of the early Christian initiations during the first centuries after Golgotha. Though, according to Steiner, this early Rosicrucian initiation involved a sevenfold process, humankind could not, for the most part, arrive at the completion of all seven stages. For one, the mere conception of reincarnation and karma, as he states in *From Jesus to Christ*, had not even penetrated into the first stage of Rosicrucianism, known as "study."

The seven stages in Rosicrucian initiation were 1) study, 2) imaginative knowledge, 3) inspirational knowledge or reading of the occult script, 4) preparation of the philosopher's stone, 5) correspondence between microcosm and macrocosm, 6) entering the living macrocosm and finally, 7) divine beatitude.

The first of the seven stages of Rosicrucian initiation, known then as "study," differed greatly from what is usually implied by this term today. Then, the disciple deepened his or her understanding of reality—based not on the dialectical nature of thought, but on a content of the higher worlds, namely, the life in pure thought—in such a way as to be unaffected by the world of sentiment. By the word *sentiment* one associates all that which is connected to the sensorial impressions that fetter thinking to the influences arising from the lower self. This would seem to coincide with the first stage of the process leading to the *excessus mentis* (delineated by Valli)—i.e., abandoning the use of the senses. The kind of discipline sought by the Rosicrucians was ultimately one that necessitated the striving for total objectivity—i.e., a detachment from the influence of emotionality tied to the senses—an objectivity that Steiner often insisted could be cultivated, for example, through the study of mathematics. Here, of course, Steiner did not refer to the quantitative aspect of mathematics but, rather, to the thinking activity, which, divorced from the senses, is employed in the process of abstract mathematical computations. Only by way of this "willed" activity can it be revealed how thinking is rooted in the suprasensory sphere. Thus, it was with the impartiality of a mathematician that those initiated into the higher worlds were to perceive human nature.

Upon completion of the first stage, the aspirant of Rosicrucianism passed onto the "imaginative" stage of consciousness. Steiner relates how, here, the human being was led to perceive the physical world as an expression of spiritual forces, so that one could even perceive the spirituality of a rock or plant. This stage of initiation presupposes the attainment of a particular level of purification symbolized by the green stem of a plant through which flows the chlorophyll sustaining its existence. This was to be contemplated in such as way that, by superimposing an image of the red blood flowing in the human being, one could slowly begin to transform the "passions" (connected with blood) and, thus, gradually become more receptive of higher spiritual forces working within oneself, as well as the whole of nature. Again, it is not difficult to draw a relationship to the second stage of initiation sought by the *Fedeli d'amore*, for as Valli states, this stage required the initiate to withdraw from influences of the physical world to acquire "imaginative vision." In other words, one should not look to *physical* nature as the primal cause (or center) of creative activity, for there, one merely encounters the *effects* of things, whose cause is derived from the suprasensory realm. The need to develop "imaginative vision" could only arise by directing one's attention (as much as was possible) to that aspect which, in effect, manifests all outer reality—i.e., the suprasensory element within thinking.

During the third stage, the ability to read the occult script was acquired. One permitted a multitude of images to work on one's consciousness so as "to order in figures and color formations the lines of force that permeate the world" as creative activity. One also began to enter into the interrelationships that exist between such images, namely where the emanations of the musical spheres resound. Gradually, what one comprehended, during the second stage (spiritual forces manifesting nature) becomes more and more differentiated, so that, as Steiner says, the occult script of the etheric world finally became legible. In other words, the aspirant no longer merely acknowledged the creative activity of the world, but entered into it. In Rosicrucianism, this stage was called "inspiration consciousness." The *Fedeli d'amore* called this third stage "intellectual vision" for as Valli says, one perceived "things deemed intellectual" not by means of the objects themselves, that is, their sensorial attributes, but by "revelation." The key, here, lies in the word *intellectual*, in that the term *intellect*, for the Scholastics, referred to "something which brings into unity in man the 'vegetative principle, the animal principle, the lower human principle and finally the higher human principle.'"[109] Again, a relationship can be drawn between the description given by Steiner and that by Valli, for implicit in the latter is the capacity to enter into the heart of the creative spiritual activity of the world—wherein one can perceive *how* the physical world comes into manifestation.

Steiner refers to the fourth Rosicrucian stage as that of "preparing the philosopher's stone." Here, one learned to develop an organ, which in the future would replace the function that the plant world presently has for humanity—i.e., the conversion of carbon dioxide into oxygen. This stage, of course, could only be attained when one had purified oneself to the fullest extent.

In the fifth stage, one understood the relationship that one's bodily organs had to the cosmos. By going into oneself, one could see which part of the macrocosm was, for example, related to one's nose or eyes. Each part of the human body was in direct correspondence with a specific part of the universe, for Steiner says that everything that exists in the human being was once part of the cosmos. Herein, incidentally, is also connected the sixth stage. By entering into a particular organ, one could perceive the macrocosmic forces that corresponded to it and, thus, was led into the macrocosm itself. Finally, when a human being was able to enter fully into all of God's manifestations, then and only then, says Steiner was one able to know oneself, totally. Thus, by following the "impulses of universal will," one was initiated into the last stage—i.e., "divine beatitude." Again, the last stages of Rosicrucian initiation were virtually impossible for humanity at that time to attain, for thinking, connected with the "I" of human beings, had not yet fully developed.

In observing what lay in these final four stages of initiation, it is not easy to connect them to Valli's description of the fourth stage leading to *excessus mentis*. His description, however, becomes somewhat elucidated when we view the nature of initiation from a modern day anthroposophical perspective. As Valli states, "when the mind is removed from each act of lower human beings, and when nothing intervenes between it and God, it (mind) intuits, by way of *intellectual vision, the divine essence*" (tr. mine).[110] In other words, once one has overcome the influences of his astral body (lower self) and has become "purified" so as to possess sense-free thinking ("intellectual vision"), one then possesses the very instrument by which one can ascend to the higher stages of intuitive cognition, and, thereby, consciously experience spiritual, creative beings. For the "I," the eternal core of the human being, can unite itself in a most inward way with these beings and know them in their true form.

One was able to attain *morte mistica* only to the degree in which thinking manifested itself in its abstract form. In this way, it could provide a foundation from which the willing forces within thinking could be freed from thinking's adherence to the physical organism. Only, then, could "intellectual vision" become an organ for the perception of still higher worlds and one's immersion into the macrocosm take place. Only, then, could one truly realize one's spiritual nature.

≈

What can be said about the nature of *morte mistica* (mystical death)? We can begin to answer this question by devoting our attention to the words spoken by Paul when he said, "Not I, but the Christ in me," for contained in this statement is the resolution to one of the greatest of all mysteries—namely, life's relationship to death. In this statement there also lies the key by which we can later comprehend how the *Divine Comedy* is an allegorical representation of the human being's initiation into the spiritual world. Though, again, Dante lived at a time when initiation, in the modern sense, was unattainable owing to the "nonemancipated" nature of thinking, there existed the notion of a *mystical death*, in which one could be reborn by "dying in Christ." Luigi Valli mentions this in his book, *La Struttura Morale dell'Universo Dantesco*. There he says that *mystical death* is attributable to "the virtue of the Cross." Only by *dying* in Christ, does one overcome the death. Those that do not die mystically in Christ belong to "the true dead," even if they are alive physically. He says

> The fundamental oxymoron of the *Divine Comedy* and of all Christian mysticism is that only the *dead* (in Christ) are *alive* (with true life) and the living with respect to ordinary life are really the *dead, dead souls...* (tr. mine)[111]

"To die in Christ" means that the aspect of our individuality with which we identify in the physical world—i.e., the ego (personality, or reflected "I"), must give way to the *living* force (Christ) intrinsic to thinking. Our experience of thinking must be one that leads to the perception of the Christ, so that one beholds not what has hardened into form (materiality) but, rather, the *force of life* from which such form is able to manifest. The reemergence of life from death should not be viewed as a mere philosophical riddle, for the intellect by its very nature has never been able to experientially grasp the baffling mystery intrinsic to the idea of a *mystical death*, namely, the Resurrection. Logic is precluded from fathoming an experience that transcends the limits of the physical world, as we know it. In no other instance during the course of human evolution has life seemingly been known to have emerged from death, unless, of course, we consider the *fable convenue* of modern science, which insinuates (without openly saying so) that life results from the interaction of molecular or atomic substances—in other words, from death. Though modern thought cannot experientially fathom the Resurrection (and thereby discredits it), it conceives a view of reality based upon the principle it denounces, namely, that life springs from death, from the interaction of molecular structures. However, rarely does the scientific community as a whole ever seem to ask how the interaction of molecular structures comes about in the first place and what that would signify. As Owen Barfield intimates as the central question in his dialogical essay on the ontological aspects of human and earthly evolution in *Worlds Apart*, "is a mindless universe" responsible for what exists in the world today?

At the heart of such a philosophical dilemma is our inability to comprehend the interrelationship between the thinking as an activity—which we utilize to form such theories—and the theories themselves. Were we to actually *perceive* thinking as an activity, we would then understand how one's thoughts are lifeless manifestations of that process, just as a dead corpse is the shell, so to speak, of the spiritual forces that once imbued it with life. In a lecture entitled, "The Need for Understanding the Christ" on April 29, 1923, Steiner states, "With the same certainty with which one says that the corpse is the dead residue of a living person he can say also that abstract thinking such as we have at the present time is the dead residue of what we possessed during the pre-earthly existence in living thought."[112] Thus, we can see that what we possess during our life between death and new birth is lost to us once we have incarnated on Earth. Only when we are able to liberate thinking from the clutches of materialism will we actually see it as a force that weaves form into being. In other words, our thinking will itself determine the point of transformation between life and death.

This living pre-earthly thinking is what the Indians, Persians, and Egyptians of antiquity possessed, atavistically. With the emergence of the Greek–Roman epoch, it gradually faded from view in such a way as to be encapsulated in the form of an idea. Steiner intimates that the recollections of pre-birth were lost, but what remained was the thinking force itself that they had used before birth to give an intelligent meaning to the images. In other words, ideas replaced the imaginations themselves, but within these so-called ideas, unlike those of today, could still be seen the force of thinking. This, in essence, is what formed the basis of Gnosticism, so little understood throughout the centuries. Steiner states in, *How Can Mankind Find the Christ Again?*:

> The essential fact is that humanity became more and more incapable of taking in what streamed to it from the spiritual world, what had existed among the ancients as imaginative wisdom and then was active in Gnosis, what had evoked the power of acute thinking that still existed among the Greeks.[113]

If we were to visualize the diminishing power of pre-earthly human thinking and follow it through the centuries, we would find that it coincides with the development of what Steiner called the "personality," of which, again, Dante was a representative. Because this so-called personality emerges at a time in which the Intellectual Soul Age is about to give way to that of the Consciousness Soul, it can thus be understood to represent the point of germination from which the new forces of thinking are gradually to unfold. Thus, coinciding with the development of "personality," we witness a crossing point where the waning forces related to the imaginations of pre-earthly life, come to a close before providing the basis ("personality") for the rekindling of a thinking power that humankind must cultivate from within the inner depths of being.

What the early Gnostics perceived of the imaginative world, the Neo-Platonists, such as Plotinus, referred to as the "One." This "One" represented the *Universal Being* through which all of life was manifested. It was the so-called atom of antiquity that meant "indivisible whole." What existed in Plotinus as the ability to perceive the imaginative forces within the world of thought, albeit, atavistically, in Goethe was embodied by the "Idea," which came about through the conscious employment of will forces. Nevertheless, the nature of Goethe's spiritual constitution was itself still underdeveloped so as to enable him to enter fully into the imaginative forces. He could, instead, acknowledge the archetypal being present behind plant nature, which he mentioned in his study of plants and their metamorphosis. Just as the seasons mark the points of transformation of a plant from the state of "apparent" death to the burgeoning of new life, just as withering leaves of autumn point toward greening in the spring, so, too, does each plant species that seems confined to a particular shape and size represent but a given point of transformation in the development of the plant world toward its archetypal form. Therefore, just as each plant is not merely a self-contained entity, but exists in connection with other plants in further relation to its archetype, so, too, was the Idea for Goethe something that transcended individual concepts. It was, for Goethe, their archetype.

Thus, scientists and philosophers must strive to resurrect their thinking so as to perceive what Goethe called the "Idea." Only then is it possible to comprehend the Resurrection experientially. Again, what was known as "mystical death" has meaning only when we begin to penetrate the mystery of "dying in Christ," for Christ is *Life*. To "die in Christ" means to resurrect that abstract thinking, devoid of life and based upon a multiplicity of conceptual forms, into a living force whereby we are not subjected to the perception of materialized concepts but, rather, behold the center of creative activity—the Idea. We, then, begin to see the Christ working in and around us and, as a consequence, experience the birth of our spiritual being. In other words, by such a transformation we witness the disintegration of our personality, wherein is contained the living force of the Christ, which is liberated, just as a seed, which (not easily differentiated as living) sprouts visibly into life under the proper conditions, reveals the liberation of forces that are reflected in the continuous transformation of its form.

The possibility of experiencing *morte mistica* during Dante's time was exceedingly difficult for, as has been previously mentioned, the development of "personality" had just come into its own. And yet, it represented a flickering of light that heralded the dawning of a new age, one in which human consciousness could be made ripe for the Christ's appearance in the etheric realm. Even Scholasticism at that time sought, as its primary focus, to grasp the reality of the spiritual worlds by means of thought. As Steiner often points out in his essays on Thomism, the Scholastics were concerned with understanding "how Christ enters human thinking and leads it to a conscious experience of the higher spheres." Says he in a cycle of lectures entitled, *How Can Mankind Find the Christ Again?*, the Scholastics

> went back to Hellenism, to Aristotle, to find concepts with which to penetrate the religious revelations; and they elaborated these with the Greek intellect because the culture of their own time had no intellect of its own.... Only thereafter did there arise again, as from the hoary depths of spirit, an independent mode of thinking—the thinking of Copernicus and Galileo.[114]

Though the Scholastics were, in large part, unsuccessful, they helped to usher in the Consciousness Soul Age, for we see reflected in their very words how human beings gradually became conscious of themselves as individualities. As Georg Kühlewind states, "Thinking about thinking began with Scholasticism, which was a prelude to the Consciousness Soul." He adds, "Before the age of the consciousness soul, the possibility of observing finished thinking or of thinking about what has been thought did not exist."[115]

Thus, before the Middle Ages, when humans spoke of the Intelligences, they referred to the spiritual hierarchies that were responsible for the creation of the world. These Intelligences had now descended into humanity itself, so that "intelligence" now became a word that applied to the human being individualistically.

Could it be that the Church intuited the emergence of a new era, in which humanity would assume the responsibility of bridging itself to the Christ through a newly found connection to the Virgin Sophia? Could it also be that in the process, humanity would gradually begin to see that the Church misrepresented this *Divine Wisdom*, with which it yearned to be united, when the Church declared *itself* to be the "bride," namely, Sophia, and that, as a result, it had disingenuously lured many a bridegroom under its spell? Was not the "White Rose" that Dante employs to depict the eternal abode of the blessed (Cantos XXX and XXXI in the *Paradiso*), also utilized by the Church as the symbol for Mary, the Mother of Christ? There is no doubt that the Church, having accepted Aquinas' acknowledgment that reason alone could not bridge itself to Christ, found refuge in his account of "faith." The Church had, thus, found the means by which to lull human beings into somnambulism, and thereby, dispel its own premonitions and fears regarding the awakening of humanity. Faith—not that of which knowledge is the foundation (as Steiner intimated)—but, rather, faith in its contrived and degenerate form used as a vehicle of manipulation, was, in fact, the mighty sword by which the Church inadvertently sought to fend off the inevitable awakening of thought and its place in the world.

*Two Knights on Horseback
A Seal of the Knights Templar*

Resurrecting the Temple

René Guénon, in *The Esotericism of Dante*, speaks of two bronze medallions found in the Vienna Museum. One was of Dante and the other of the painter Pisanello. The reverse side of each medallion bears the letters F. S. K. I. P. F. T, signifying *Fidei Sanctae Kadosch Imperialis Principatus Frater Templaris*. Guenon argues that *Fidei Sanctae* refers to the *"Fede Santa,"* a tertiary order of the Templar association whose dignitaries bore the title of *Kadosch*, meaning consecrated. Guenon establishes this as proof that Dante belonged to the order of the Knights Templar. Luigi Valli, on the other hand, claims that these initials refer to the seven virtues—*Fides, Spes, Karitas, Justitia, Prudentia, Fortitudo* and *Temperantia*. Nonetheless, these medallions constitute the scant *physical* evidence linking Dante to the Knights Templar. To better understand his relation to the Order, we must venture toward a more symptomatic approach.

In his book, *The Temple Legend*, Rudolf Steiner states, "When you follow the teachings of the Templars, there at the heart of it is a kind of reverence for something of a feminine nature. This femininity was known as the Divine Sophia, the Heavenly Wisdom."[116] He continues by saying, "This wisdom is exactly what Dante sought to personify in his Beatrice." Furthermore, he points out that we are unable to truly understand the *Divine Comedy* unless we take into account Dante's Templar background. But where and how does his connection to the Knights Templar originate? What was it about the Templars that is so instrumental in helping us understand Dante's social and cosmological view of life?

We can begin by remembering that Dante sought, above all, the reformation of the Church. For him, the Church had overstepped its rightful place by taking upon itself the fundamental role of the State. He deemed it imperative that the Church be free of all corruption and that there be a separation of Church and State. In the book, *Thinkers, Saints, Heretics,* Manfred Schmidt-Brabant intimates that the purpose of the Knights Templar was "to bring about a new European sociopolitical order in a form through which the individual could be free and independent of both the emperor and the pope." He adds,

> The emperor or the pope would not be done away with, but the structure of the empire and the structure of the Church would be changed in such a way that each person would be able to develop his autonomy within these structures.... The Templar Order, which of course could not speak openly about such goals, had allies within society, people who stood in life, pursued their profession, but who were initiated into the esoteric purposes and often even the rituals and the esotericism of the Order. These were the so-called Affiliates.[117]

Schmidt-Brabant goes on to say that one of these Affiliates was Brunetto Latini, Dante's great teacher often mentioned by Steiner. Having been sent to Castile in 1260 as a diplomatic envoy to Alfonso X, Brunetto begins his return to Florence by way of the Pyrenees when he discovers that the Ghibellines (his rivals) had won their war against the Guelfs (to which he was aligned) and that his name appeared on a list of individuals banished from the city. The shock of this news causes him to fall unconscious. This, coupled with sunstroke, forces him to *excarnate* and "experience," according to Steiner, a spontaneous initiation into the being "Natura." Steiner says that it was as if he had been taken hold of by the still active aura of the School of Chartres. He then lives in exile in Paris. There he reads the works of the great masters of Chartres. In Paris, he does two things. Firstly, he writes in French the first encyclopedia ever produced entitled, *Li Livres dou Trésor*; secondly, he becomes an Affiliate of the Knights Templar and is initiated into their esotericism.

In 1266, the Ghibellines are defeated and he is able to return to Florence, where he soon meets Dante and guides him in his studies. Schmidt-Brabant states,

> Gradually he conveys to the young Dante the entire content of his own initiation knowledge and...stimulates in Dante the suprasensory capacities he already possessed; Dante had such a rich suprasensory experience, but it had to be set into motion.[118]

In fact, Latini publishes a second book in Italian called, *Il Tesoretto* (*The Small Treasure*), in which he describes his experience of initiation by way of the Goddess Natura. It is believed that this book was most likely intended for Dante, as some scholars maintain that it formed the basis of the *Divine Comedy*. In essence, Latini taught Dante how "the human being unfolds his eternal life," which Dante admits upon meeting Latini in the lower rings of the *Inferno*.

Latini initiates Dante into the Order of the Templars as an Affiliate. Such Affiliates, says Schmidt-Brabant, "could never meet openly with one another as such, so they camouflaged themselves in various secret associations," one of which was the *Fedeli d'amore*. Their dedication and extolment of love in all its various forms provided them with the "cover" by which to communicate important information about their esoteric practices.

Years later, after yet another battle between the Guelfs and the Ghibellines, Dante, a leading figure of Florence at the time, refuses to bow under the newfound rule of the Guelfs. As a result, he is forced to flee the city to save his life. He goes on to various places where he encounters benefactors who help sustain him. In France, he witnesses the burning of Jacques de Molay in 1314. It was during this period of exile that Dante works on the *Divine Comedy*. Says Schmidt-Brabant, "All of his knowledge about philosophy, theological problems, mythology, flow together. He was a quite highly educated man and everything he knew about the esotericism and the Mystery knowledge of the Templars flows into it as well." Schmidt-Brabant adds, "It was not just a matter of his worldly knowledge about these things but, according to Rudolf Steiner, *Dante had also seen clairvoyantly what he describes*" (italics mine).[119] This knowledge was put to use in helping to elucidate Dante's view on the problems of his time. Schmidt-Brabant again says,

> The *Divine Comedy* was permeated by Dante's view of how the problems of the time, the opposition of the pope and the emperor, could be solved. This was, of course, the Templar view.[120]

We will explore this in what follows.

Having established the importance that "women" had for the *Fedeli d'amore*, a curious question arises. If Beatrice is for Dante the object to which he devotes his love and the one who guides him up through the spiritual world, why is St. Bernard de Clairvaux chosen to lead Dante on that final stage of his journey where he can perceive God? In other words, if Beatrice represents the *Divine Wisdom* that leads to the Christ, why has a Cistercian monk been chosen as the intermediary between Dante and his Creator? Could it merely be because of Bernard's significant role as the founder of the Cistercian Order that he headed? If so, why did Dante not choose St. Francis, founder of the Franciscans, or even St. Dominic of the Dominicans? If one looks into the life of St. Bernard, one finds that among his many writings, one is of particular interest, for it reveals his connection to an esoteric order that Rudolf Steiner said had sought to make the West familiar with the Mystery of Golgotha. This writing, referred to by Thomas Merton as the "directory" of the Knights Templar, is entitled *In Praise of New Knighthood*. In it Bernard de Clairvaux states, "…to fight in a Holy War is to become an instrument of divine justice, reestablishing the order violated by sin."[121] The idea of Divine Justice plays a central role in Dante's vision for the birth of a New Jerusalem, and it is none other than the Order of the Knights Templar—which initially safeguarded pilgrims on their way to Jerusalem itself—that had, as its hidden aim, the task of imbuing Western humanity with the Christ impulse. Just as Beatrice symbolizes *Divine Wisdom*, leading Dante toward an ever-greater understanding of the Christ, St. Bernard—because of his influential role with the Knights Templar and his efforts to awaken an understanding of the Virgin Mary (the *archetype* of *Divine Wisdom*)—is chosen in the *Divine Comedy* to lead worthy *human beings* to the Mystic Rose to behold the "Glory of God."

In the attempt to explore the relation of the Knights Templar to the *Divine Comedy*, much credit must be given to Luigi Valli's successor, Robert John, who meticulously unveiled Dante's connection to the Knights Templar. We shall only concern ourselves here with the essential aspects of John's major work, simply called *Dante* in German. Though many of his conclusions are based upon the insights of Valli (who, in turn, developed them from his mentor, Giovanni Pascoli), John was able to reconstruct, from the bits of evidence uncovered by Valli, a coherent picture of the historical and philosophical realities underlying the *Divine Comedy*. For example, in his *Il Segreto della Croce e dell'Aquila nella Divina Commedia*, Valli points to thirty-one examples in the *Divine Comedy* where the symbols of "the Cross and the Eagle" form a polarity. For him, this polarity symbolized the interrelationship between the Church and State, which, once spiritualized through the Christ impulse, were thought by Dante to govern the eternal and temporal lives of human beings, respectively. Robert John, on the other hand, was able to intuit how Dante's representation of "the Cross and the Eagle" was symbolic of the Knights Templar. He shows how the "Cross" was representative of contemplative life, while the "Eagle" was symbolic of active life—both of which were considered necessary to realize the Christ. Given this, it would be possible to assume that the *Fedeli d'amore*, to which Dante belonged, were the vehicle by which Dante and many of his "philosophically allied" friends attempted to further the ideals of the Knights Templar and, thus, deflect the attention of the Church and King Philip the Fair. The fact that many *Fedeli d'amore* maintained possible relations with other esoteric orders (or even heretical sects) can be evidenced by Cavalcanti's poem that we have already discussed regarding the "woman" named Mandetta, whom he had met in Toulouse, the center of the Albigenses. There, in fact, exist similarities regarding both the

Knights Templar and the *Fedeli d'amore* in their relations to Islam. It is even suggested by Robert John that the Troubadours received much of their knowledge of Arab–Persian thought from the Knights Templar, and as we know from Dante's salutation of the Troubadour, Daniel Arnault in the *Paradiso*, there is, in turn, much that the *Fedeli d'amore* owe directly to this group of poets who entertained in the courts of kings. Though each sect or esoteric group existing during the Middle Ages functioned independently of the other, there is ample evidence to suggest that between them much was known.

What must be made clear is that the Templar Order connects itself to the ancient mysteries in such a way that its outer form merely reflects the metamorphosis of humanity's relation to the Godhead as it manifested itself during the Middle Ages. In fact, what materialized in 1118 as the Poor Fellow Soldiers of Jesus Christ (Templars) under Hugh de Payens, was part of a stream of consciousness that, through time, included other spiritual movements such as the Cathars, the Rosicrucians, the Freemasons. It was a stream opposed by the Church of Rome. Given that both of these streams have their roots in the Biblical story of Cain and Abel, the eventual opposition of the Church to the Knights Templar is related by the killing of Abel by Cain. As Rudolf Steiner shows, Cain and Abel represented the male and female principles, respectively.[122] Cain (masculine polarity), as tiller of the Earth, worked his way into the material world and, thus, separated himself from God, whereas Abel (feminine polarity), as keeper of sheep, merely received that which streamed down to him from the spiritual world. Steiner says that what humanity strove for in the Middle Ages was the nullification of the Rakshasas, a race born of the interrelation of the Cain and Abel impulses, which had destroyed Atlantis. These two principles find expression in the Greek myth of Prometheus and his brother Epimetheus, whose very names denote their essential natures. Prometheus (reflective of the feminine polarity) refers to thoughts that are yet to be (i.e., pre-dialectical), while Epimetheus (masculine polarity) refers to those thoughts that occur as "after the fact" (dialectical), which tend toward intellectualism, or material consciousness. Steiner tells of how humanity of the fifth cultural epoch is represented by Epimetheus who must be overtaken by Prometheus, the representative of spiritual thinking.

Now, as we have said, this dualistic aspect of human thinking first manifested during the second cultural epoch—i.e., the Persian epoch, when humanity largely perceived the opposition of light and dark, good and evil, as evidenced in the polarity of Ahura Mazda and Ahriman. This dualism finds its echo in what came to be known as Manichaeism, which, in turn, had its roots in Gnosticism. Manichaeism was founded by Manes, a Persian mystic who lived between AD 216 and 276, known as the "widow's son," a term that denoted the fact that his soul was widowed by the spirit. In other words, the feminine and masculine polarities had separated. Thus, Manes could be thought of as the initiator of a spiritual movement that sought to reintegrate them by drawing greater attention to the feminine aspect—thus the name, "widow's son."

As Manichaeism spread westward into Eastern Europe, it emerged during the tenth century in what came to be known as Bogomilism—named after its founder Bogomil—in and around what is presently the Balkans. From there, its impulse is said to have later spread primarily to Southern France and parts of Italy, where it became known as Catharism.

Belonging to this same spiritual stream is the Order of the Templars (and Freemasonry), which, as Steiner says, exemplifies a reverence to the feminine principle, or the *Divine Sophia*. This feminine principle is to play a major role in the development of Manas—the fifth principle or body in the human being—that will arise out of the transformation of our astral body. Like Manichaeism, the Templar Order had the mission of preparing humanity for its future development during the Sixth Cultural Epoch. It was from within this same feminine stream that Rosicrucianism arose. In fact, Rudolf Steiner, himself, says, "the Rosicrucians are none other than the successors to the Order of the Templars, wanting nothing else than the Templars did..."[123]

Thus, this stream, stretching from antiquity to the Middle Ages and beyond, out of which arose the Cathars, the Albigenses, the Templars, the Rosicrucians, and the Freemasons—a stream of which Dante was a part— sought to lead the spirit into the material world, so that Christianity could one day be understood in relation to the development of humanity's spiritual nature. In *The Temple Legend*, Steiner states that the "Temple of mankind's earthly culture, the great Temple of Soloman, has already been built, but what is to crown it must still remain a secret.... It [the secret] remains in the possession of a few initiated Christians. It is sealed up in the casting of the Molten Sea and in the Golden Triangle." He adds,

> The Molten Sea is what is created when the appropriate amounts of water and molten metal are cast. The three apprentices do it wrongly, and the casting is destroyed, but when the mysteries of fire are revealed to Hiram by Tubal-Cain, he is thereby enabled to unite water and fire in the proper way. This brings the Molten Sea into being. This is what the secret of the Rosicrucians is. It is brought about when the water of calm wisdom is united with the fire of the astral world, with the passion of fire and desire. A union must be brought about which is "of bronze," that is to say, is lasting and durable. It must endure into the next epoch, when the secret of the sacred Golden Triangle is added to it: the secret of Atma, Buddhi, and Manas. This Triangle, with all which it entails, will form the content of the renewed Christianity of the sixth cultural epoch. That is being prepared by the Rosicrucians and then what is symbolized by the Molten Sea will be united with a knowledge of reincarnation and karma. That is the new occult teaching, which will be united again with Christianity. The higher self of man, composed of Atma, Buddhi and Manas, will become an open secret when the man of the sixth epoch has become ripe enough to receive it.[124]

Steiner tells us that the Christianity of today is purely connected to the materialism of the fourth and fifth epochs and that "the true Christianity of the future, which contains the mystery of the Molten Sea and the Golden Triangle, only exists secretly." He adds that this future Christianity (of the Sixth Cultural Epoch), which is to replace its masculine polarity represented by the "crucified Son of God," will be one day represented by "the Cross encircled by roses." Whereas Hiram represents the initiates connected to the stream of Cain, the Queen of Sheba is the "soul of humanity," who during the fourth and fifth cultural epochs unites with Hiram, since he is "engaged in building the Temple." This Christianity of the Sixth Cultural Epoch, which will recognize the importance of the Molten Sea and the Golden Triangle, will thus arise out of the "Mystery of the Brotherhood of the Rose Cross."

Countering all of what has thus been described—namely, the necessary emergence of the feminine stream—was, of course, the stream issuing from Cain—the male principle—that has always sought to maintain its dominance by impeding the stream of Abel from asserting itself. As we have noted, this male principle is that which had separated itself from God through its adherence to the Earth. It is that aspect of human consciousness represented by Epimetheus—the thinking that arises as "after the fact," namely, dialectical thinking that has severed its relationship to the spiritual. Such thinking ultimately finds its source in Ahriman, who Zarathustra was able to perceive during the Persian epoch. The slaying of Abel by Cain is symbolic of the predominance of the male principle, which has resisted the feminine stream. We see this resistance manifested ardently in the person of Augustine, who accepted Christianity, but *only* if founded, as Steiner says, on the "authority of the Church."[125] This attitude differed greatly from those individuals (or movements) connected to the feminine stream, who believed that the teachings of Christianity should arise in freedom. Nonetheless, as Steiner continually pointed out, the life intrinsic to Christianity becomes lost in Catholicism, as it is permeated by the impulses arising from the Roman Empire, so that what was alive "becomes frozen into form." For this reason, the bishops of the Church represent a continuation of the official Roman state. The military religious order, known as the Jesuits, who later came into power as "brothers" of the Church, were *themselves* representative of this Roman impulse. The Jesuits, successors to Augustine who developed the *form* of the Church in his *City of God,* directly opposed the work done by the Freemasons. It is, therefore, not inconsequential that the predominance of the masculine principle helped obscure the knowledge of reincarnation beginning around the year AD 300 on through the Middle Ages and into the present time. Only due to the Michaelic impulse streaming into humanity, has it gradually begun to reassert itself in humanity. The gradual eradication of such knowledge was important in order for humanity to eventually realize the fundamental role of thinking in the life between birth and death. In this way, human beings could begin to utilize each lifetime as an opportunity to develop the fifth principle of Manas.

Because of the need for the feminine principle to assert itself in human consciousness for such a development to transpire, we see the "Cult of Mary" arising during the Middle Ages. In fact, it was none other than St. Bernard, himself, who was largely responsible for spreading the knowledge (Sophia) of Christ. He, more than any other, through his Order of the Cistercians and the founding of the Knights Templar, helped to incorporate this feminine principle into humanity so that it could find expression in the human heart. As Steiner points out in *Il Ponte fra la Spiritualita' Cosmica e l'Elemento Fisico Umano,* during Egyptian times what was embodied in the being Isis—the *knowledge* (Sophia) of Christ—had to be rediscovered on Earth. For it had been lost when the being of Christ (known to the Egyptians as Osiris) had entered the Earth. Only by understanding the importance of this female principle and the wisdom that it symbolized during the Middle Ages can we begin to understand the significance of the *Divine Comedy.*

It is no coincidence that, even in Islam, the Sufi poets used the image of woman to embody the wisdom sought by humanity, for there, too, it impressed itself upon human consciousness in opposition to the impulses of Arabism and Mohammedanism that arose. In fact, as we shall see, there exists a direct connection between the poetry of the *Fedeli d'amore* and that of Sufism. Thus, this feminine principle, manifesting in Beatrice and the other women of the *Fedeli d'amore*, or in the adulation of the Virgin Mary, arises as an impulse that helps to lift the consciousness of human beings toward the spiritualization of their own thinking. Whereas Beatrice represents for Dante this female principle on a personal level by leading him into the starry world, what we find celebrated in St. Bernard is that same feminine principle directing *all of humankind* toward a similar aim. By emphasizing the importance of the Virgin Mary and employing the Knights Templar to disseminate his message throughout Christendom, Bernard is chosen to lead Dante into the Mystic Rose from where he can behold the countenance of God. What is so interesting about Dante and what has made him difficult to categorize is the fact that he seems to adhere, in some ways, to both the masculine and feminine polarities. Even though, on the one hand, the Church was extremely corrupt in Dante's opinion and in great need of reform, he accepts the Catholic view of the afterlife initiated by Augustine, which claims that there is only one life by which we can find our way to God, thus reflecting, again, the emergence in the Middle Ages of what Steiner calls "personality"—which points to the limitations of human consciousness at that time.

The masculine polarity—reflective of a more earthly "militaristic" impulse—could not, by its very nature, have possibly embraced the idea of reincarnation and karma, as we have noted. On the other hand, the *Divine Comedy* and other works of Dante reveal, as we have seen, a philosophical adherence and sympathy to the various orders of the feminine stream, be they the Knights Templar, the Cathars, the Troubadours, or the *Fedeli d'amore*. Dante's recognition of Beatrice (*Divine Wisdom*) indicates that only by tapping into the feminine polarity—namely, that of Abel—could the Church undergo a reformation that would be reflective of its rightful purpose, that of preparing humankind for its future evolution. Of course, modern-day literary critics, whose thinking, by nature, is reflective of the more dominant masculine polarity, have done everything in their power—consciously or unconsciously—to discredit any attempt at more esoteric interpretation of Dante.

"The Cross and the Eagle"

Because of the Inquisition, Dante could not freely espouse the esoteric ideals of the Knights Templar (or, of course, the *Fedeli d'amore*) without fear of persecution. In fact, neither the word *Templar,* nor any of the prominent members of this Order (with the exception of St. Bernard and Brunetto Latini) are ever mentioned by name throughout the whole of the *Divine Comedy.* Moreover, Dante coded his work in such a way that there hardly existed the slightest intimation of the Templar's ultimate aim—that of heralding the being Sophia. The importance of the Knights Templar and their ideals was, however, reflected in his symbolic use of "the Cross and the Eagle." They were not only part of the insignia of the Templar Order but, as Robert John suggests, they were symbolic of the Church and State, both of which were idealized by Dante to have their seat in Rome.

When we speak of Church and State, we must not just envision them as variations of their present-day institutionalized forms. Instead, they must be associated with the *principles of contemplative and active life,* which, in turn, result in what was known during the Middle Ages as eternal and temporal beatitudes. These beatitudes lend themselves to the spiritual and temporal powers that here on Earth ultimately take the form of Church and State, respectively. They are, in effect, two ends willed by God for all humanity. These beatitudes are central to our reascension from the Fall, through which we can regain what was lost to us (in "Earthly Paradise") during the early stages of our spiritual development.

"The Cross and the Eagle"

In the *Divine Comedy*, Dante gradually purges himself of the materialistic impulses that impede his entrance into heavenly Paradise. He must attain temporal beatitude as a prerequisite for eternal beatitude, for it is through the development of reason that faith is acquired for the unveiling of revelation, which must manifest itself if heavenly Paradise is to become a reality for humanity. In Dante's *De Monarchia*, we find this twofold process elucidated. Says he,

> Unerring Providence has therefore set man to attain two goals: the first is happiness in this life, which consists in the exercise of his own powers and is typified by the earthly paradise; the second is the happiness of eternal life, which consists in the enjoyment of the divine countenance (which man cannot attain to of his own power but only by the aid of divine illumination) and is typified by heavenly paradise. These two sorts of happiness are attained by diverse means, just as one reaches different conclusions by different means. We attain to the first by means of philosophical teaching, being faithful to it by exerting our moral and intellectual virtues. We arrive at the second by spiritual teaching (which transcends human reason), in so far as we exercise the theological virtues of faith, hope, and charity. (tr. D. Nicholl)[126]

This idea, as we have said, was embodied in the symbol of the "Cross and the Eagle" as it had developed by the end of the thirteenth century. For, then, the insignia of the Knights Templar showed an eagle with outspread wings braced on a rock, surmounted by a cross and two stars. The rock, according to Robert John represents Rome, namely, the Church of Rome founded by Peter. It is easy to see how Dante was able to transpose this Templar symbol to represent the ideals by which he sought the transformation of the Catholic Church, which, as an institution, had contaminated the sanctity of the Christ impulse that Peter established on Earth (rock). This contamination occurred, of course, when the Church reigned as the temporal power regulating the social life of human beings.

Robert John believes that for Dante the spiritualization of the Church and the renovation of the Imperium "favored the hope of an almost miraculous rebirth of the Templar Order." Dante realized that the human thinking and willing needed to be resurrected for such an ideal to be realized, particularly for the fact that the materialistic forces, manifesting through the Church, were exceedingly rooted in the general consciousness of humanity.

Though the Council of Vienna had failed to halt the inner workings of the Knights Templar, it was ultimately the corruption of both the Church and State—headed by Clement V and Philip the Fair, respectively—that resulted in a reenactment of the slaying of Abel by Cain. Here, Rudolf Steiner in his *Inner Impulses of Evolution* gives us important insight into the impulses that worked through Philip the Fair in his brutal suppression of the Templar Order whose members spilled their blood so that one day the Christ impulse could stream through all humanity. The Knights Templar opposed the adversarial forces seeking to wrestle the Earth free of the spiritual impulses of the Christ. Though they accumulated great wealth, their riches belonged to no particular individual but, rather, to the Order itself, as it sought to spread the *knowledge* of the Christ impulse. For this reason, the ahrimanic adherence to earthly possessions that normally manifests in the human being did not take root in them. Nonetheless, the same ahrimanic forces from which they sought to free themselves, totally permeated the consciousness of the individual that would undo them—King Philip the Fair.

Steiner says that King Philip was so inspired by the properties of gold that he acquired what was known as "ahrimanic wisdom."[127] As a result, he sought to confiscate all the gold in France. Though he initially felt no threat from the Knights Templar, he recognized the influence of their wealth. What followed was of great consequence. Having witnessed the moral power that the Templar Order (regardless of their wealth) had over the people, he was overcome by the fear of not being able to manifest such power himself by way of the gold that he was able to obtain. This fear prompted him to take dominion over the Church and its riches, which was largely accomplished by having the papal seat transferred to Avignon, where he could exercise greater control over Clement V. During this period begun in 1309, known as the Babylonian captivity, King Philip began his final assault on the Knights Templar by trying to completely exterminate the order (which had been dissolved by Pope Clement V in 1307) while confiscating their riches. Rudolf Steiner describes the persecutions as having had such a strange effect on the King Philip that he experienced an "ahrimanic initiation."

On the other hand, many of the Knights Templar achieved an initiation based on their devotion to the Christ impulse. This initiation permitted them to look into the spiritual world. Nonetheless, they became susceptible to the influences brought upon them by torture, which dulled their consciousness. The enormous wealth achieved by the Knights Templar proved to be their undoing for it prompted Philip the Fair to surrender to the adversarial ahrimanic forces and become possessed by his desire for gold. Thus, we see the forces of the Cain impulse rising up against those of Abel. More important, as Steiner points out, the Knights Templar were, themselves, able to see the luciferic and ahrimanic impulses working through Philip, just as they were able to look within the depths of their own subconscious and perceive similar impulses that obscured their devotional attitude toward the Cross. Able to see instinctively what the Knights Templar experienced inwardly, King Philip stepped up his brutal persecution of them, so as to dull their consciousness and, thereby, coerce them into admitting things about themselves that were unfounded. The Knights Templar, under the duress of torture, actually confessed to the most heinous accusations (such as spitting on the Cross) made against them by the Inquisition, which formulated questions in such a way as to confound them. In this way, Steiner says that the luciferic forces, working within the subconscious realm, drew the Knights Templar toward their self-destruction. Meanwhile the ahrimanic forces, working through King Philip sealed their fate. Nonetheless, the spiritual impulses that had previously worked through the Order could not be eradicated and continued to work on into the spiritual world. Here, we can imagine them operating in conjunction with the Platonic and Aristotelian streams, which we shall address later, for as Sylvia Franck mentions in her work, *The Tree of Life and the Holy Grail*, the Knights Templar, "were very much in evidence in Chartres."[128] Nonetheless, the impulses that the Knights Templar sought to bring into the world did not have an immediate effect on humanity at that time, for human beings had yet to develop the thinking that could kindle a transformation of their spiritual faculties. Had the Knights Templar been able to directly impress their impulse onto the minds of human beings, it would have manifested in a luciferic way.

We see the protagonists of this abominable episode in human history regarding the Knights Templar represented by Dante in the figure of the harlot chained to a Giant atop the transfigured cart in the "Garden of Earthly Paradise" in the *Purgatorio*. There, the harlot represents the Church (Clement V) as it is seen glancing lustfully at Dante, while fettered to the Giant—Philip the Fair—to whom it is subjugated. The cart that delivers them is transformed into a seven-headed monster, a reference to the luciferic impulses described in the Book of Revelation. Thus, we have in the "Garden of Earthly Paradise"—the "land of humanity's innocent birth"—images arising from the depths of Dante's consciousness that point to the impulses impeding the development of the Christ forces in humanity. All the while, as the harlot beckons Dante with her glances, we witness the seduction of humankind by the luciferic impulses, which ultimately resulted in the demise of the Church and State that Dante hoped to see spiritualized. In this scene of the "Garden of Earthly Paradise" in the *Purgatorio*, we see Dante's denunciation of the Church—the masculine polarity symbolized by Cain—and the State.

Though, again, references to Dante's association with the Knights Templar are exceedingly well hidden in the *Divine Comedy*, we will briefly witness, in our examination of the *Inferno* and the *Paradiso*, Dante's unspoken allegiance to the principles of the Knights Templar, reflected in his use of "the Cross and the Eagle."

Troubadours 14th century, Archiv fur Kunst und Geschichte, Berlin, und Geschichte, Berlin; artist unknown artist unknown

Franciscan Friars witness a Cathar Consolamentum (Bible illumination, Bibliothèque Nationale de France)

The Heresy of Romantic Love
The Manichean Stream of Thinking

Throughout his life, Rudolf Steiner continually stressed how in our search for historical truth, the most obvious connections between events and people are often not realized because of prejudices arising from our inability to perceive the inner nature of things. Probing the cosmological wellspring of Dante's imaginative vision has proven to be no exception. Insight into the esoteric foundation of Dantean thought has largely been obscured by the lack of consideration that traditional literary scholars and historians have given to the influence of one of the most pervasive currents of thought to have affected the course of Western civilization, namely Manichaeism. By this, one should not immediately think that Dante openly propagated the tenets of the Manichean faith. Never, in fact, do we find in his any of works, especially the *Divine Comedy,* any overt reference to it. Instead, we must look at the degree to which Dante's work subtly reflects the permeation of this dualistic cosmology, rooted in religious and literary traditions spread throughout Europe for hundreds of years preceding him. In other words, could not Dante's *renunciation* of the Church and its false relationship to *Divine Wisdom* be symptomatic of an underlying spiritual impulse that, by nature, fostered the emergence of various heretical views at the time—some of which were offshoots of Manichaeism? Is it possible that his attempt to resurrect the Church from its "fallen state" reflects, in and of itself, a conscious realization of a fundamental cosmological principle underlying Manichaeism, namely, *the transformation of evil into good?* Put simply, was it the *spirit* of Manichaeism, rather than its doctrinal content, that formed the basis of his dissent with ecclesiastical authority?

We cannot speak of the effect that Manichaeism may have had on Dante unless, of course, we examine Catharism—the offshoot most likely familiar to him. In his book, *Love in the Western World*, Denis de Rougemont seeks to document evidence suggesting a likely relationship between the Troubadours (after whom Dante and the *Fedeli d'amore* modeled their poetry) and the Cathars. In showing the connection that Dante and other Italian poets had to the Troubadours, he quotes M. Charles Albert Cingria who stated,

> Between the eleventh and twelfth centuries, poetry—whether Hungarian, or Spanish, Portuguese, German, Sicilian, Tuscan, Genoese, Pisan, Picard, Champagne, Flemish, English, etc.—was at first Languedoc; which is to say, that the poet, who had to be a troubadour, was compelled to speak the troubadour language which is never other than Provencal.
>
> The whole of Occitanian, Petrarchian, and Dantesque lyric has but a single theme—love; and not happy, crowned and satisfied love (the sight of which yields nothing), but on the contrary love perpetually unsatisfied—and but two characters: a poet reiterating his plaint eight hundred, nine hundred, a thousand times; and a fair lady who ever says "No."[129]

As we have seen, the aim of such supplications on the part of poets like Dante was in no way arbitrary. Instead, they were directed toward the realization of knowledge that transcended their earthly experience, knowledge that could only be attained by means of a stream of consciousness that opposed the patriarchal authority in Rome. This particular form of gnosis, sought by both Dante and the Troubadours, was most prevalent in Manichaeism. Only by way of this seemingly untenable channel can the basis be formed by which to examine the influence that heretical thinking may have had in shaping Dante's cosmological understanding. Yet, if there truly was a connection between the Troubadours and the heretical Cathars, two regionally coexisting movements, a superficial glance at his *Comedy* unleashes

The Heresy of Romantic Love: The Manichean Stream of Thinking

an immediate, yet seemingly inescapable paradox. Why would Dante, in the sixth circle of Hell, place "Heretics" in eternal fiery tombs, and then, later, in Canto XXVI of the *Purgatorio*—shortly before stepping into the "Garden of Earthly Paradise"—exult the minstrels of courtly love songs, if, indeed, these Troubadours *had* (as Denis de Rougemont claims) intimate ties to the most widespread heretical movement of the Middle Ages—the Cathars? In other words, why would Dante place the Troubadours at the entrance to the "Garden of Earthly Paradise," heralding his entry into the higher regions of the spiritual world, if, in fact, they had assimilated heretical views of humanity's relationship to God, which he had previously condemned in the *Inferno?* Could it be that, for Dante, the word *heretic* referred to something *other* than what we might commonly ascribe to the term? Furthermore, was Eugene Aroux, the French literary and political thinker, correct in calling Dante a "heretic"?

In *Coming to Our Senses*, Morris Berman shows how the original source of De Rougemont's claim that romantic love was actually the vehicle of religious dissent initially surfaced in 1832, when Gabriele Rossetti published his previously mentioned book, *Disquisitions on the Antipapal Spirit Which Produced the Reformation.* This theme, says Berman, was continued in Rossetti's later book, *Il misterio dell'amor platonico del medioevo derivato da' misteri antichi,* which argued that Dante, Petrarch, and Boccaccio were part of a "love sect" that "exploited the language of erotic love for the propagation of Catharist beliefs, and that, in fact, the troubadours were ministers of the Albigensian heresy."[130] To glimpse this heretical tendency, however, we must trace, in part, the historical development of Catharism. Only then can we begin to understand the need for the use of opposite word meanings by the *Fedeli d'amore* to convey their esoteric striving.

Catharism is thought to have had its origins in the teachings of Mani, who in the third century essentially founded Manichaeism, which according to Walter Nigg, was possibly the "last offshoot of Gnosticism."[131] Some believe that Manichaeism sprung from a foundation of Mithraism. Charles William Heckethorn states that Mani divided the cosmos into two irreconcilable dominions, "that of light and that of darkness, in which one is superior to the other..." He goes on to say,

> The God of light has innumerable legions of combatants (aeons), at whose head are twelve superior angels, corresponding with the twelve signs of the zodiac. Satanic matter is surrounded by a similar host, which, having been captivated by the charms of the light, endeavors to conquer it; wherefore the head of the celestial kingdom, in order to obviate this danger, infuses life into a new power, and appoints it to watch the frontiers of heaven. That power is called the "Mother of Life," and is the soul of the world, the "Divine," the primitive thought of the Supreme Ens, the heavenly "Sophia" of the Gnostics. As a direct emanation of the Eternal it is too pure to unite with matter, but a son is born unto it, the first man, who initiates the great struggle with the demons. When the strength of the man fails him, the "Living Spirit" comes to his assistance, and having led him back to the kingdom of light, raises above the world that part of the celestial soul not contaminated by contact with the demons—a perfectly pure soul, the Redeemer, the Christ, who attracts Himself and frees from matter the light and soul of the first man. In these abstruse doctrines lies concealed the Mithraic worship of the sun.[132]

According to Franz Cumont, Manichaeism spread through the Roman Empire during the fourth century at a time when Mithraism was "expiring."[133] This would coincide with Steiner's assertion that Gnosis (or, the "living knowledge" of the Christ) had died out about the fourth century AD. Moreover, Mithraism could no longer effectively function in its truest form, for Christ, having been perceived in the Earth's etheric realm by Paul on the road to Damascus, had already penetrated the depths of the Earth and human consciousness. Ever since then, the gradual task of humankind has been to follow His example and thereby, one day, resurrect the *light* from the depths of thinking (the darkness). What we see transpiring in the extermination of Gnosis relates, of course, to definite cosmic happenings to which Rudolf Steiner makes mention. Steiner says that on Earth "Western ecclesiastical development took care that all external remains of the Gnosis were properly eradicated, root and branch."[134] He adds "that the Gnosis is only known from the writings of opponents, while anything that might have given some idea of it from an external, historical point of view has been thoroughly rooted out." This extermination of Gnosis on the part of a dogmatic and institutionalized religion reflects, above all else, the widening separation of the patriarchal and matriarchal streams of consciousness resulting from a growing materialistic impulse in human thinking. However, the very dogma of which Catholicism was the greatest exponent had its roots in Gnosis. Says Steiner,

> An intellectual study of the development of Western theology would make more people critical on this point as well—but such study is rare. It would show them, for instance, that Christian dogma must surely have its foundation in something quite different from caprice or the like. Actually, it is all rooted in the Gnosis. But its living force has been stripped away and abstract thoughts, concepts, the mere hulls are left, so that one no longer recognizes in the doctrines their living origin.[135]

In *The Driving Force of Spiritual Powers in World History*, Steiner shows how the mighty Imaginations of Gnosis were stripped of their living force and became abstract concepts as a result of the transference of power that occurred from the Exusiai to the Archai. He states:

> Turning to the suprasensory world, we find by means of suprasensory investigation that until the fourth century AD the thoughts through which human beings make the world comprehensible to themselves were borne, or perhaps one should say, poured forth (earthly expressions are little suited for the description of such lofty events and beings) by the beings of the hierarchy called the Exusiai, or Beings of Form.[136]

He later adds,

> And then came the fourth century AD in the evolution of humankind. For the suprasensory world it brought an event of the utmost

importance: the Exusiai, the Forces or Spirits of Form, transferred their thought forces to the Archai, the Primal Forces or Principalities.[137]

It was, at this very time, that Manichaeism made its way into the world. More than anything, it sought to further the knowledge of our spiritual being in an age in which earthly forces had taken hold of human consciousness, thus precluding us from a genuine insight into our divine nature. For this reason, the battle between the forces of light and darkness was thought to have been central to the plight of humanity. Thus, Manichaeism can be seen as a continuation of the Gnostic wisdom known as Mithraism. There, the "Mother of Life" or Sophia—i.e., "the soul of the world" that gives birth to a "human being," who, upon receiving the "Living Spirit" is led "back to the kingdom of light"—makes it possible for the Christ ("that uncontaminated part of the celestial soul") to "free from matter the light and soul of the first man." This "Mother of Life" is, of course, that to whom Dante, the *Fedeli d'amore,* and the Troubadours later sing their songs of praise—namely, *Divine Wisdom*, which had been lost to the patriarchal stream of consciousness embodied by the Church of Rome.

As a result of this transference of power (connected to the life of thought) from the Exusiai to the Archai, we see the battles raging in the physical world in the souls of such men as St. Augustine, who embraced Manichaeism for nine years before initiating an ecclesiastical movement that would eradicate all visible traces of Gnosis, until, of course, it reemerged in altered form nearly a thousand years later during the Middle Ages. Says Steiner,

> Then a personality appears who stands with his soul in the conflict between the newly empowered Spirits of Personality and the Spirits of Form who were no longer in authority. The personality, whose soul is entangled in the conflict, is *Augustine*, the Catholic Church Father. I have described the struggles of his soul to you from many different sides. When, however, we regard these struggles as the earthly reflection of a cosmic, suprasensory happening, we see in this individual, who in his youth inclined to Manichaeism, who

then became in the strictest sense an orthodox Roman Catholic believer—we see in this spectacle of a soul torn hither and thither, the earthly image, the earthly reflection of a cosmic happening behind the evolution of humanity. Augustine turned to the Manicheans while his soul was still influenced by the impulses of the Spirits of Form. These impulses brought to his soul treasures from earlier ages but these treasures were no longer suitable for the souls belonging to his time. Through the good and splendid fruits of culture which had come to him from the backward Spirits of Form, however, he was prevented from receiving with the full potentiality of his own personality the new form of thoughts that could be imparted by the Archai, the Spirits of Personality, the beings who had now assumed the rulership of the thoughts. And he could accept this new state of things only by surrendering unconditionally to the dogma of the Church.[138]

This behavior by Augustine is not of little importance, for it points to the fact (as was the case of the Knights Templar) that the spiritual impulses which had guided the unfolding of human consciousness were aligned with one of two streams: that of Epimetheus, leading to an outer exoteric realization of religious truth, or that of Prometheus, leading to an inner esoteric realization. Because the Archai, who had "assumed the rulership of thought," descended closer to humanity, the patriarchal stream could fully manifest itself and, in turn, paradoxically provide, by harboring the impulse of intellectuality, the possibility for a future reemergence (or reconstitution) of the lost Gnosis connected to the Christ.

Thus, as Steiner himself states in *The Temple Legend,* Augustine would not accept the teachings of Christ unless it was founded on the authority of the Church. This position taken by him, of course, lies in direct opposition to the teachings of Mani, who had warned his disciples to reject what comes by way of *outer* revelation—i.e., by means of the senses. These two polar and conflicting views were themselves again a reflection of the great battle raging within the spiritual world at that time. It should be noted that Augustine, in a way, provided the rudimentary beginnings for the establishment of what later came to be known as the Inquisition. Nevertheless, the presence of the Christ impulse, which, from that time on, worked unconsciously within humanity, as freedom of thought, continued to permeate Europe. As Steven Runciman has shown in his pivotal work, *The Medieval Manichee*, Manichaeism spread from Persia up into Europe through regions of Bulgaria, where in the tenth century it flourished as Bogomilism, a religious movement that harbored beliefs that gave rise to its most recognized offshoot, Catharism. Its ideas were spread by merchants traveling on trade routes through the northern regions of Italy and southern France.

These ideas were dispersed among the common folk by word of mouth, which impeded the Papacy from controlling their proliferation. In fact, by the end of the twelfth century, Catharism was located primarily in Languedoc, Provence, and Lombardy, but its teachings were so widespread that it posed an enormous political threat to the Church. Part of the problem for the Church in controlling Catharism could be attributed to the lack of an externally distinguishable organization. For one, there was no overriding figurehead to hold accountable. Neither was there much documented evidence that would elucidate the nature of the Cathars' beliefs or ritualistic practices. Few written works have been found that detail their philosophical or spiritual ideas in history. This merely fueled the Church's paranoia to the point in which it *institutionalized* the world's first police state, the Inquisition, nearly a thousand years after Augustine provided its initial impulse.

What was it about this heretical movement that by the beginning of the thirteenth century had become more widespread in Milan than Catholicism? As previously mentioned, the roots of Catharism are thought to have reached back to the time of the Mani. However, if we stop to consider the region of the world from which Manichaeism originated (Persia), we cannot help but be reminded of the *separation of light from darkness* that manifested in human consciousness there during the second cultural epoch. As with Manichaeism, light and darkness (or good and evil) are the polarities that form the basis of

Catharism. Though much debate was centered on whether evil was independent of God, the Cathars believed that the god of evil (darkness), namely, that of the Old Testament, had created the world. In other words, they perceived the physical world to have manifested out of the forces of darkness. Here, we can glimpse into the depths of heretical wisdom, for it was, in fact, Jehovah—connected to the Moon sphere while *reflecting* the light of the Christ—who was the God of the Old Testament. For this reason, the Cathars rejected the Old Testament, except when it prophetically foretold the coming of Christ. We can see how, unlike so many of the followers of the Church, the Cathars had begun the transition from Moon consciousness, which still marked the presence of the Intellectual Soul Age, to Sun consciousness. Thus, their rejection of the "suggestionism" *imposed* by the Church, indicates that they, in effect, were precursors of the Consciousness Soul Age. Another sign that reflects their affinity to the Sun sphere was their rejection of baptism by water. They were cognizant of the implications of John the Baptist's (the last of the "water-baptizers") infamous words during the baptism of Jesus at the River Jordan when he uttered, "I must decrease so that He (Christ) may increase." The Cathars perceived the insistence of the Church to baptize by water as evidence that the Church was an *instrument* of the "evil" god. The word *evil* suggested an impediment to the evolution of human consciousness with respect to the Christ being. For them, the rite of initiation known as the *Consolamentum*, was, as Morris Berman intimates, "the ritual...modeled on the practice of ancient soul travel or heavenly ascent..."[139] Moreover, the cross was rejected as an *image* of adornment for it was thought to be the instrument upon which the body of the Christ was made to suffer. Their rejection of the cross as an icon or image is consistent with their rejection of Jehovah, *the reflected light of the Christ.*

It remains to be seen to what degree, if any, the Cathars embraced the mystery of Christ in its relation to the resurrection of human consciousness. One thing we do know, however, is that they harbored the desire to escape the cycle of reincarnation (or *samsara*), leading some to believe that they adopted possible influences of Eastern spirituality. The highest members of the Cathar religion seemed to understand the connection that human deeds have to the unfolding of karma. For this reason, they sought to lead a most devout and pure life; thus the term *cathar* (*sis*) = purity. The degree of purification attained by the Cathars determined their rank within the order. For like the Church, they had their own hierarchy, though not outwardly so visible, or institutionalized. As Jeffrey Burton Russell states in *Dissent and Reform in the Early Middle Ages*,

> ...the Catharists had bishops of their own, but no pope. Local catharists were organized into groups in which a division was sharply drawn between the *perfecti* on the one hand and the *credentes* on the other. Admission to the sect was obtained through the rite known as the *convenientia*. This made one a *credens* and put one under the order of the *perfecti*.... After long instruction and practice in mortifying the flesh, including a year of exceptionally rigorous abstinence, the *consolamentum* was administered, and the *credens* became *perfectus*. The rigors of the period were so great that it sometimes ended in death, which, if it occurred after the administration of the *consolamentum*, the great sacrament of the Catharists, was not to be regretted, since it meant the final liberation of soul from body. Later, and in certain areas, the *endura*, or fasting unto death, was occasionally administered, especially to children or to the sick, with the express purpose of effecting such a liberation. In these instances the *consolamentum* was administered at the end of the ordeal; then, if one survived he became a *perfectus*. He was then a full initiate of the sect, wore special black clothing, and was expected to lead a life of utter purity.... They had three long fasts annually. They preformed public penance for public sin, private penance for private sin...[140]

Certainly, it was in light of such strict practices that the founder of the Knights Templar, Bernard de Clairvaux, who sought to contain the proliferation of Catharism, uttered what might be considered one of the most paradoxical claims imaginable at the time with regard to a heretical movement, namely, that their sermons were the most Christian and their morals most pure. At this point it would be appropriate to ask what connections could possibly have existed between such a strict religious order and what outwardly seems to be its polar opposite—i.e., the Troubadours who "turned love, the spring, dawn, the flowery gardens, and the Lady all into song"?

At first sight, there hardly seems to exist any tangible evidence that links the Cathars and Troubadours. Instead, one must search for possible connections in the literature of that time and in the relationship that these movements may have had to the matriarchal (or feminine) stream of consciousness, governed by the *Divine Sophia*. Only then will the German historian Fredriech Heer's allusion to Midi as "the feminine culture of the South"[141] not be seen as a curious notion.

There existed, again, two streams of consciousness throughout history, from a time long before the Intellectual Soul Age. The patriarchal stream, as previously stated, has been the bearer of the outer exoteric knowledge of the world, namely, that which easily reveals what can be identified on the physical plane, and the feminine stream, which, as Rudolf Steiner states, sought the knowledge of the Christ that had been lost—namely, the gnosis that contained the last breath of humanity's visible connection to the spiritual world at the time of Christ's descent into the Earth. The reemergence in the Middle Ages of this ancient Gnosis in the form of Catharism, represented the awakening of what Berman calls "interiority"—i.e., the *light* of knowledge that seeks to liberate humanity from the patriarchal stronghold of consciousness, of which the Church was its predominate manifested form of expression. Incidentally, the Cathars perceived this spiritual battle between Light and Darkness as raging within the human being. However, it was not the mere theoretical knowledge of this battle that induced them to suffer the hardships and trials that they bore, but a genuine conscious experience of its living reality. Had their knowledge been strictly theoretical, they would have inadvertently been part of the patriarchal stream, the stream of Darkness, which sought their eradication.

It is also not without reason that the Cathars, like the Manicheans before them, condemned the flesh. For one's adherence to the flesh guaranteed the permanent separation of the soul from the spirit. As de Rougemont says, the Cathars believed that there were two worlds: the world of good (created by God) and the world of evil (created by the devil, or lower forces). At one point, Lucifer tempted the "Angels or Souls" by saying in effect that "it is better to be down below, where you will be able to do both good and evil, than up above, where God allows you only to do good."[142] Moreover, the Cathars believed Lucifer further seduced the Angels/Souls by showing them a dazzling woman who "inflamed them with desire. Then he left Heaven with her, to descend into matter and into sensible manifestation."[143] Those Angel/Souls who followed Lucifer and the dazzling woman were, then, imprisoned in material bodies. The soul was thus seen as having parted from the spirit. If one looks closely into this parable, it becomes apparent that two hundred years or so after the Church had banned the existence of the spirit at the Ecumenical Council in Constantinople in 869—and unknowingly propagated a dualist philosophy of its own, which, incidentally, precluded the notion of Mystical Marriage, the union of Spirit and Soul—the Cathars still upheld the view of the threefold nature of human beings. In fact, it was precisely the marriage of soul to spirit that formed the basis for the poetry of courtly love and the *Divine Comedy,* itself.

In exploring the relationship between Catharism and the Troubadours, we are led to an article by Henry Corbin published in 1937, entitled "Pour l'hymnologie manicheenne," which contends that the structural essence of Manichaeism was lyrical in nature.[144] De Rougemont states,

> the nature of this faith made it unamenable to rational, impersonal, and "objective" exposition. Actually, it could only come to be held in being experienced, and the experience of it was one of combined dread and enthusiasm—that is to say, of invasion by the divine—which is essentially poetic.[145]

"Combined dread and enthusiasm" represent, of course, the dualistic poles of consciousness that are so inherent in the poetry of the twelfth and thirteen centuries, culminating in the "fiery-ice" sentiments central to the sonnets of Petrarch. De Rougemont immediately goes on to say "the cosmogony and theogony of this faith become "true" for a believer only when certitude was induced by his recital of a *psalm*. So Tristan, it will be recalled, cannot state his secret, only sing it." In light of this, we find that the lyrical poetry so prevalent in southern France at the turn of the twelfth century had its roots buried within the dualistic consciousness of Manichean heresy and its later offspring Catharism. Not only this, but there is something else of tremendous importance that cannot be overlooked, namely, the importance that death held for the Cathars. In spite of the fact that thousands of them died at the stake, Berman brings to light Heer's revelation of a Cathar text that says there is no happier death than death by fire. The Perfecti were even known to have stepped into the fire singing. How could this possibly be, one might ask? As de Rougemont tells us "death holds to be the *ultimate* good, whereby the sin of birth is redeemed and the human souls return into the One of luminous nondistinction."[146] At this point, it would be useful to remember that the death of Beatrice (Rachel), in effect, signified "the transcendence of wisdom in the act of pure contemplation" (Richard of San Victor). Only with the death of Beatrice—associated with her physical representation and, therefore, the lower egoic principle—could Dante ascend to the Father. Says de Rougemont,

> We may already attain to Light while here below through a gradual ascent which is achieved in the progressive death of a deliberate *askesis*. But the goal and the end of the spirit is also the end of limited life, of physical life obscured by immediate multiplicity. Eros, object of our supreme Desire, intensifies all our desires only in order to offer them up in sacrifice. The fulfillment of Love is the denial of any particular terrestrial love, and its Bliss of any particular terrestrial bliss. *From the standpoint of life*, it is this Love which is the absolute woe.[147]

What is he implicitly alluding to here if not the transformation of the astral nature of human beings? For the "fulfillment of Love" is only possible by redeeming the luciferic impulses that have directly taken hold of our lower nature. The redemption occurs when Eros "intensifies all desires only in order to offer them up in sacrifice." This "sacrifice" constitutes "denial"—i.e., the transformation of what would have permanently manifested itself as "terrestrial love." It is what Sergei O. Prokofieff points to as being most central to the Manichean concept of evil. In *The Occult Significance of Forgiveness*, he says "...the Christ within him [the human being] will be able to turn Lucifer and Ahriman toward the good; in this lies the essence of all true Manichean Mysteries."[148] In other words, *it is the transformation of the evil impulses at work within humanity that lies at the very heart of Manichaeism*. As Rudolf Steiner points out in *From Symptom to Reality in Modern History*, the question of evil is of great importance in our time. Just as Christ encountered and overcame the impulse of evil in the physical world during His incarnation—an evil that was repeated in the etheric realm during the latter half of the nineteenth century—we, at the present time, must overcome the impulse of the "forces of evil," as well. As Prokofieff states,

> The principle task of our epoch is that the forces of evil must enter into the inner world of men. But they must enter into it not in order to compel or entice human beings to engage in evil deeds but in order that man might be able to develop within himself a true spiritual life...[149]

He then goes on to quote Steiner who states, "Man must assimilate these forces of evil which exert their authority in the universe. By doing so, he implants in his being the seeds which enable him to experience the life of the spirit through the consciousness soul."[150] From our inner experience of evil, we will one day attain the capacity to spiritually behold the world. It is for this very reason that "evil"—through luciferic and ahrimanic impulses—came into the world in the first place! Is it any wonder why, during Dante's spiritual journey in the *Divine Comedy*, he must penetrate into the heart of darkness (evil) and actually confront the three-headed manifestation of evil (Satan), before scaling its tail to reach the starry-lit world of Purgatory?

With regard to the Cathars, some might wonder how their fear of being "ensnared in material bodies" may, or may not, have precluded them of the opportunity to *transform* darkness into light—i.e., to transmute and purify the earthly egoic passions necessary for experiencing the Passion of Christ. The Courtly Love Songs of the Troubadours, on the other hand, may very well have reflected the possibility of such a transformation since, in their case, *Eros sacrificially offers up the desire that has been intensified within the soul*. Therefore, "the fulfillment of Love" that ensues, arises not by circumventing passion, as was the case with the Cathars, but through a deliberate transformation of the heightened desire felt within the soul—a transformation of darkness into light.

For this very reason, the Troubadours were known as the "Messengers of Love," as Isabel Cooper-Oakley points out in *Masonry and Medieval Mysticism*. According to her, they "formed an integral portion of the mystic thread, and thus served in the weaving of the glorious traditions of eastern arcane lore into the young web of the Western child life."[151] According to Manly P. Hall in *Orders of the Quest: The Holy Grail*, the Troubadours were responsible for "those glorious myths and legends of the Age of Chivalry, the moral fables that right always conquers, and nobility of spirit is the only true nobility to which man can attain."[152] Cooper-Oakley reaffirms the nature of this chivalry when she goes on to quote Eugene Aroux in his *Le Mysteres de la Chevalerie*, who said, "not the feudal, fighting, iniquitous chivalry, as corrupt as it was ignorant." Instead, it was the chivalry whose "tone of thought which is well termed mystic, and which sees in all life only a manifestation of the Divine power; they fought for the purity of their ideal against the ever-increasing corruption of the Church."[153] Incidentally, it must be said that also Aroux claimed chivalry lay at the heart of the Troubadour quest.

Here, by the way, lies the basis for the relationship between the Troubadours and the Cathars. As later was the case for the *Fedeli d'amore,* they sought to preserve a living wisdom of our connection to the spiritual world in the face of a ruthless and brutal institution. If nothing else, their common disdain for the Church should have prompted literary analysts to openly examine Rossetti's claim that, among the Troubadours, there existed a "double" or "triple" language that permitted the existence of "secret schools," behind which they could propagate their knowledge. Says Rossetti,

> The existence of such a style of language is an historical fact affirmed by many, and denied by none; it is not a less notorious fact that the persecuted sect conformed in public to the language and ceremonies of the persecuting religion; while they gave in secret to every sentence of that language, and to every act of those ceremonies, an arbitrary and conventional meaning, corresponding with their own designs. There is scarcely a contemporary or succeeding historian who does not tell us that the Patarini, or Cathari, or Albigenses, were Manicheans; and we know that Silvanus, one of the successors of the murdered Manes, so artfully used that doctrine "that it seemed all drawn from the Scriptures, as they are received by Catholics. He affected to make use of Scriptural phrases and he spoke like the most orthodox among us, when he mentioned the baptism, death, burial or resurrection of our Lord Jesus Christ."[154]

This ability to conceal one's true ideas and sentiments regarding "religious subjects" in such a way as to "speak *in public like other men,* and only *in secret to express the thoughts*" (that one really harbors within), not only reveals itself as an Albigensian trait, but one that existed among many disenfranchised movements, such as the Canculars, a society of Anabaptists. Rossetti continues,

> Persecuted incessantly by the remorseless Inquisition, one of their chiefs had recourse to a cunning devise. He knew that he and his friends were accused of refusing to worship the saints, and of denying the supremacy of the Romish Church, and that they would be forced to make a profession of faith and to swear by the *Holy Mary* to have no other religion than that of the *Holy Church.* He was

resolved not to betray his inward sentiments, but he desired if possible, to escape *death*. "O, muses! O, high genius! Now vouchsafe your aid!" He shut himself up in a cave with two aged females of his own sect, and gave the name of *Holy Church* to the one and *Holy Mary* to the other, "in order, that, when the sectarians were interrogated by the Father Inquisitors, they might be able to swear by the *Holy Mary* that they held no other faith than that of the *Holy Church*." Hence, when we desire to estimate properly the devout and holy things written in those times, we must first consider who composed them; and thus we shall be able to reconcile the frequent contradictions which are apparent between the verses and the actions of the Troubadours and the Trouveurs."[155]

Before examining the poetry of courtly love, we must examine the social environment of both the Cathars and the Troubadours. For this, we can be grateful to the insights of de Rougemont. It was to his astonishment that, for centuries, no mention was made of the fact that both the Cathars and Troubadours may have had a connection between them in spite of living within the same geographical boundaries. He attributes this lack of connection to "Romanist scholars" and asks them, "Show us, then, how Cathars and Troubadours were able to rub elbows day after day, without making one another's acquaintance, and how they could live in two completely watershed worlds amid the same psychical revolution of the twelfth century!"[156] He adds that "to refuse to understand Heresy and courtly love each by means of the other and with but one movement of the mind looks very much like refusing to understand each of them one by one."

De Rougemont begins his examination by dispelling the once assumed notion that the Troubadours had first sprung from the region of Poitou and Limousin. Instead, he contends that their center was more likely to have been in the county of Toulouse—*the very region where the Albigenses had their stronghold!* For one, the very language that the courtly love poets used in their travels throughout Europe was that commonly spoken in the county of Toulouse. (Remember, incidentally, the poem of Cavalcanti where he mentions a "woman which *Love* called *Mandetta*" while in Toulouse!) De Rougemont dismisses the common assumption that the nobility comprising the courts harbored orthodox beliefs, by bringing to light a particular song by Pierre Vidal in which he states,

> My heart rejoices
> at the soft new season
> and at the Castle of Fanjeaux,
> which is like a paradise;
> for love and joy are enclosed here
> and all that honour and the true service of love
> encompass..."[157]

Little do most readers realize, says de Rougemont, that this so-called Castle of Fanjeaux was a *"mother-house" of the Cathars* and that Guilabert of Castres, the most famous heretical bishop directed it three years after Vidal composed the poem! It was also the castle where Esclarmonde of Foix, "the highest of heretical ladies," received the Consolamentum! Moreover, de Rougemont remarks that, within the poem, other houses are listed in which Vidal had stayed—Castles of Laurac, Gaillac, and Montreal—all of which harbored heresy! Zoe Oldenbourg, in her book, *Massacre at Montsegur,* defines the Troubadours at the courts of nobility as men "passionately devoted to poetry," who "tried to carry out in practice the literary ideals of their age." Oldenbourg claims that "honor" for the twelfth-century person of Midi "consisted in a certain disdain for the good things of this world, coupled with an unbounded exaltation of one's own personality."[158] In light of this, she asks whether the Troubadours' adoration of the "Lady" "was but the urge to proclaim a triumph of self-will." One must ask, however, "the triumph of self-will" in regard to what? Could this "triumph" that deals "not with love itself, so much as with a method of attaining moral and spiritual perfection through love's agency" as Oldenbourg declares, be subtly directed at anything other than that which they abhorred with vehemence, namely, the Church, which, as we have said, declared *itself* to be the embodiment of *Divine Wisdom*. If so, is it not likely that their silent crusade against the Church was one that they shared with the Cathars? How could they be unknowing of this? Moreover, is Oldenbourg's claim surprising that the very nobility which hosted these courtly love poets was "not only indulgent toward heresy but became its most steadfast (and, indeed, notorious) supporters"?[159] In short, can one truly imagine the Troubadours, themselves, to have really survived the extermination of both the nobility (which housed them) and the Cathars, whose subversive acts against the Church provided the cultural and spiritual soil for the blossoming of their poetry? It is easy to understand why many believe that the "Lady" to whom the Troubadours sang their "songs of love" was none other than the *Cathar Church*.

If all this is true, then there is a need to look at the poetry of the Troubadours with completely different eyes. It becomes evermore apparent that the similar themes that both they and the Cathars shared, such as the "virtue of chastity," are no mere coincidence. Not only did they share common themes, but also common ritualistic traditions. Both denoted initiation in the form of a single kiss received from their ladies. Both rejected marriage, and both "reviled the clergy" and its allies, namely, members of feudal castes. The Troubadours "distinguished two stages in the *domnei*," which was in likeness to the distinction made by the Cathars between Believers and the Perfect. Finally, de Rougemont mentions that the Troubadours and the Cathars each led a wandering life by setting *"off along the road in pairs"*—which, incidentally, brings to mind the symbol of two Knights Templar mounted together on horseback! Aroux reveals an interesting perspective regarding the interrelationship between the Albigenses and the Troubadours (or more explicitly the jesters). Cooper-Oakley (in *Masonry and Medieval Mysticism*) quotes from his *Le Mysteres de la Chevalerie*:

> As to the jesters, properly so-named jesters of song, of sayings, of romance, as they were called—they must be distinguished from *mimic* jesters, that is to say, from the mountebanks and buffoons. The clerical jesters were, as has already been said, evangelical ministers, still subject to the preliminary discipline of the priesthood.

Holding the rank of deacons in the sectarian church, they were with regard to the pastors to whom they were attached, in a position analogous to that of squires and knights, and it is under this title that they figure in the romances.

If distinguished troubadours are spoken of, and, among others, Giraud de Borneil, as accompanied by two jesters, it is unquestionably that these troubadours were *Albigensian bishops*, whose dignity and functions required the assistance of two deacons. This is why it is said of them that, "*They never went on a tour* (episcopal) without having both of them in their retinue."[160]

Hence, it becomes clear that the so-called Messengers of Love concealed their wisdom in the form of song, so as to avoid being conspicuous. For this reason, they had *per force* to be highly trained in the art of the *gay science* as Rossetti calls it, namely, that of being initiated into the mystery wisdom of *Love*. Thus, as Aroux proclaims,

> It would be a great mistake to think that the first comer could be admitted to the functions of a jester... it was necessary to have "an extraordinary memory, a fine voice, to be able to sing well, to play well on the accompanying instrument, and also to have a knowledge of history, of traditions of genealogies. Several jesters indeed are cited for their historical knowledge."[161]

He adds,

> Like the other aspirants to the sectarian priesthood, they went into seminaries or lodges to receive instruction; then, having become deacons or squires, having undergone tests, and even required pledges, they were admitted into the rank of the Perfect Knights, or Perfect Troubadours. Having thus graduated, they started in the character of missionaries or of *pilgrims of love* ("pellegrini d'amore") as Dante says, sometimes undertaking long and dangerous journeys.... Then it was that, in the symbolical language of the faithful in love, they were called by the name of Knights-errant.
>
> Preaching the doctrine of love, the true law of the Redeemer, their mission was to redress the wrongs of Rome, to take up the defense of the weak and oppressed; they were represented and celebrated as the true soldiers of the Christ... as comforters of the

widow Rachel, that Gnostic church so cruelly tried by the pontifical Herod; as devoted supporters of the *sons of the widow*...[162]

Now the "sons of the widow" was a term to denote the followers of Mani, which included the Albigenses. Rudolf Steiner makes reference to the "widow" as the feminine element abandoned by the masculine element, which had begun to recede through the centuries. Says Steiner,

> The soul was always known as the "mother" in all esoteric (mystical) teachings; the instructor was the "father." Father and mother, Osiris and Isis, those are the two forces present in the soul: the instructor representing the divine which flows directly into humankind; Osiris, he that is the father; the soul itself, Isis, the one who conceives, receives the divine, the spiritual into itself, she is the mother. During the Fifth Root Race, the father withdraws. The soul is widowed. Humanity is thrown back onto itself. It must find the light of truth within its own soul in order to act as its own guide. Everything of the soul nature has always been expressed in terms of the feminine. Therefore the feminine element—which exists only in a germinal state today and will later be fully developed—this self-directing feminine principle that is no longer confronted by the divine fructifier, is called by Mani the "Widow." And therefore he calls himself "Son of the Widow."[163]

In his book *Secret Societies of All Ages and Countries*, Charles William Heckethorn, states that the Albigenses and Troubadours "drew together in persecution; their friendship increased in the school of sorrow."[164] He mentions that the language of the Troubadours was called the "language of heresy" by the Popes, and adds, "It appears more easy and natural to think that those free champions of a heresy who were not permitted clearly to express their ideas, preferred the obscure turns of poetry and light forms that concealed their thoughts, as the sumptuous and festive courts of love perhaps concealed the 'Lodges' of the Albigenses from the eye of the Papal Inquisition."[165] This however does not mean that all the Troubadours concealed their rage and condemnation of the Church. One need only consider the poem of Peire Cardenal:

Clerics pretend to be shepherds,
but they are the *killers;*
the likeness of sanctity is on them
when you see them in their habit,
and it puts me in mind
that master Ysengrim, one day,
wanted to get into a sheepfold,
and because he feared the dogs
he put on the skin of a sheep
with which he tricked them all.
*Then he gobbled and glutted
as much as he liked.*

Kings, emperors,
dukes, counts, viscounts,
and knights, together,
used to rule the world.
*Now I see the power
in the hands of clerics
with stealing, betrayal,
hypocrisy,
violence, and sermons.*
And they are highly offended
if you don't hand it all over to them,
and so it shall be, though it may take a while.
The greater they are
the less they are worth
and the greater their folly,
the less their truth telling
and the greater their lying,
the less their friendship
and the greater their dereliction,
and the less they keep faith with their calling.
Of false clerics I say this:
*I have never heard of any man
so great an enemy to God
since the ancient of days.*
          (tr. F. Goldin; italics mine)[166]

Master Ysengrim here refers to the "wolf of the beast epic." It was, as Rossetti observes, part of the myth-making scheme to assign the symbol of the "wolf" to the clergy of the Papacy! To think that the poetry of the Troubadours merely propagated romantic ideals for the sheer proliferation of erotic love without heeding the menacing forces of the Inquisition is to overlook the fact that, by doing so, they themselves were heretical. In fact, in his book, *The Heresy of Courtly Love*, Alexander J. Denomy, a Catholic scholar and cleric, suggests this very thing. He says that since, in the eyes of the Troubadours, "love is ennobling, since it is the source of all virtue and good, since man is worthless unless he acts under the compulsion of love, there follows the absolute necessity, incumbent on everyone, of practicing love," later adding, "Courtly love not only condones fornication, adultery, sacrilege, but represents them as necessary sources of what it calls virtue."[167]

This evaluation of courtly poetry by Denomy precludes the assumption made by those such as Rossetti, that the nature of the poetry was to be interpreted on two or three levels. In fact, the concerted effort by the Troubadours to mask the inner meaning of their poetry reflected the emergence, at least on a collective level, of the "personality" (characteristic of the Middle Ages) as a force that sought to liberate human beings from the bondage of the Inquisition. For this very reason, the poetry of that time was devoid of personal attributes that would reveal the slightest insight into the nature of the philosophy that the poets tried to espouse. To merely denounce courtly poetry as heretical on the basis of its "erotic nature," without perceiving the connection that it may have had to the heretical thinking of the times, assumes, at the very least, that the noble courts, which protected the preservation of heresy, led two distinct and separate *philosophical* lives. In light of the dangers posed by the Inquisition, such an assumption is virtually unfathomable. Let us look, however, more deeply into the impulses that Denomy claims fostered the emergence of Courtly Love poetry.

According to him, "the origin of the courtly conception of love as ennobling is to be found not in Arabian literature but, rather, in

Arabian philosophy and specifically in the mystical philosophy of Avicenna."[168] He goes on to say,

> In his *Treatise on Love*, Avicenna treats of the love of external beauty. He assigns to human love, the love of the sexes, a positive and contributory role in the ascent of the soul to divine love and union with the divine. Hitherto, Arabian philosophy and mysticism had distinguished sharply between the animal and rational souls in man and had separated distinctly the orbits of their activity into natural and spiritual love. Man's destiny was to seek the highest beauty and this was solely the work of the rational soul. External beauty, though deriving from the beauty of the soul, belonged to nature and was the object of natural love. Love of external beauty, the love of man for woman, had a good in itself, that is, unification with the object loved, but that love remained an activity of the animal soul. Attraction to external beauty, therefore, was regarded as an impediment and obstacle to the soul's ascent to the divine in so far as it turned the rational soul away from its real good, spiritual beauty. It was to be suppressed and totally mortified. Avicenna, on the contrary, assigned to the lower soul a role of partnership with the rational soul whereby love of external beauty, sexual love, served as an aid in approaching the divine. Joined to the rational soul, the animal soul gained in excellence and nobility through its alliance with the higher faculty. In this state and condition it pursued sense pleasure with a fine, less gross intention so that its very actions were similar to those of the rational soul. Desire for union with external beauty, the beloved, therefore, is more than a yearning for voluptuous pleasure; it becomes a means of furthering the rational soul along its journey to the Supreme Good...[169]

Thus, the transformation of the "lower soul" by the "rational soul" into one of "excellence and nobility" is responsible for the creation of "pure love." Now opposed to this was what Denomy defines as "false love," what is "evil and impure, founded on sensuality for its own sake..." what "is but a counterfeit of true love, the source of evil...."[170] With these words, Denomy uncannily points to the fact that the love of which the Troubadours sang was Manichean in nature, for it sought to transform those animalistic impulses—which

The Heresy of Romantic Love: The Manichean Stream of Thinking

would normally lend themselves to the formation of "evil" within the human being—into an *unfulfilled* yearning for the beloved. In other words, it was a love he says that "consisted in the union of the hearts and minds of the lovers." But, once again, because Denomy does not conceive words to have multiple meanings, as does Rossetti, he fails to take note of a most apparent incongruity (especially for a believer of the Catholic faith, like himself), namely, that a love devoid of sexuality which seeks to unify the "hearts and minds" can be thought of as non-Christian. Can it be that he seriously fails to conceive of courtly poetry as metaphorical in nature? How else can such a discrepancy be explained? He fails to understand that the *desire* by which the poet arrives at courtly love, if ennobled, has itself been transmuted into Passion. This polarity of lower passion (related to the senses) and higher Passion (as it is ascribed to the Christ) echoes the duality between the principle of Evil (Darkness) and of Good (Light) intrinsic to Manichaeism. Denomy is able to isolate courtly poetry as that which makes the distinction between the two loves. When Denomy points out the fact that, though a number of Troubadours were Christians, there was no trace of Christianity in their lyrics, *he is always speaking from the point of view of the Church, or the so-called accepted orthodoxy, against which both the Cathars and the Troubadours struggled.*

One can thus understand the significance of the spiritual battle that raged during the Middle Ages between the "heretics" who sought to awaken humanity to the light within the soul, and the Church, which harbored the materialistic impulses of Roman times, later conducive to scientific positivistic thought. It is little wonder why the secret teachings of the Troubadours and the *Fedeli d'amore* had for centuries been lost, for, in fact, the (Church) forces that became metamorphosed into nineteenth-century thought were the same ones that considered courtly love poetry little more than a highly rhetorical passing fancy. The notion arises that the courtly jesters were perhaps themselves *"sons of the widow,"* if one considers the names given to the two main classes by which they were distinguished. Says Aroux,

> Besides the jesters attached to the person of the bishop or of the mere pastor, were those who, having already completed their probation, went forth, furnished with the recommendation of the one or the other, to give instruction or carry consolation into the courts and castles. It was these who were called *elder sons* [of age? "*fils majeurs*"], deacons of the first class. The others, designated *younger sons* [under age? "*fils mineurs*"], performed the same functions in towns and villages...[171]

If the Troubadours had, in fact, an inner connection to the Manichean principles of the Cathars, then there can be little doubt that their spiritual inclinations may have coincided with Dante's aversion to the papacy in Rome. Why would he have exulted the Troubadours if they *merely* provided him with the poetic model for his own work while harboring philosophical or theological proclivities adverse to his own?

What was it about this poetic model of the Troubadours that constituted the fundamental blueprint for poets of nearby countries during the succeeding years? Surely, it is a great mystery that there exists no evidence to prove that it had originated with any single individuality! Says de Rougemont, "the Troubadours, it should be borne in mind, displayed an admirable unanimity in composing their *coblas* and their *sirventes*. They all obeyed the same rhetorical canon."[172] Thus, there is no sign of "individualism" within this form of poetry that would, in turn, enable us to trace its specific roots. Outwardly, one may suppose that such poetry sprang as a manifestation of the collective unconscious forces at work within the region shared with the Cathars. De Rougemont remarks how strange it is to have a form of poetic expression emerge without the slightest clue of the philosophical beliefs that foster it, unless, of course, such poetry was formulated *intentionally* by the Troubadours so as to "not betray their faith, no matter what kind of death was in store for them," just as the Cathars themselves closely guarded the secrets to their *initiations*. Says he,

> For all the troubadours had to undergo the semblance of a "marriage" with the Church of Rome—they were clerks—while serving

in their "thoughts" another Lady—the Church of Love.... Bernard Gui, in his *Manuel de l'Inquisiteur*, shows that although the Cathars venerated the Blessed Virgin, she was not, in their belief, a woman of flesh and blood, the Mother of Jesus, *but their Church*.[173]

Evidence to elucidate their repudiation of the Church in Rome, which the Troubadours felt was in contrast to their total devotion to the "Lady," can be witnessed in the intimations set forth by a courtly poet mentioned by Dante in the *Purgatorio*, namely Arnaut Daniel.

> I do not want the empire of Rome,
> do not make me pope of it
> so that I could not turn back to *her*
> for whom the heart in me burns and
> breaks apart. (tr. F. Goldin; italics mine)[174]

In *Dante*, Robert John states that the casual dissociation, made by the likes of men such as Karl Bartsch, between the Troubadours and the Cathars means nothing, since there existed many Catholics amongst the ranks of the Albigenses. John claims that Neo-Manichaeism was cultivated in the castles of Southern France. He states that, "even if only one Troubadour is *proven* to have belonged to the Albigenses, the number of declared enemies of Rome, amongst the Troubadours, was too great for there not to have been many other secret followers of that diffused heresy, capable enough of dawning a Catholic mask" (translation and italics mine).[175] Interesting, too, is John's claim that the Troubadour's fight against the Church was directed against all its factions with the exception of the Knights Templar! According to John, never had a Troubadour ever directed a sirvente against the Templar Order. This, he says, can either be explained by that fact that the Knights Templar were responsible for spreading knowledge of Persian thought and, consequently, Sufi love poetry into Europe, or because the imprint of Gnosticism was inherent within the thinking of both the Albigenses and the Knights Templar. Moreover, John points to the fact that, in light of this, it was, indeed, "a strange way to "correct" certain punished heretics, during the war against the Albigenses, that of gathering them in the monasteries of the Knights Templar!"

Thus, based on his adherence to the feminine stream of consciousness, which he shared with the Troubadours, the Knights Templar and the Cathars, Dante could, by association, be, indeed, considered a heretic, as Eugene Aroux suggests. At the very least, his attempt to spiritualize or transform the "evil doings" (a Manichean trait!) of the Catholic Church made him an opponent of what was propagated in Rome. The Church certainly would have considered Dante a heretic had it understood his true spiritual orientation—one that enabled him to perceive the deviant or heretical nature of the Church's teachings with respect to *Divine Wisdom*. It is interesting to note that Dante never elaborates on the kinds of heresy perpetrated by those "heretics" entrapped within the fiery tombs in the sixth circle of Hell. Instead, we are merely led to surmise (by his inclusion of Farinata) that such tombs are largely comprised of Epicureans, who propagated a philosophy that valued "pleasure" as the only intrinsic "good." And so, for Dante, the unfettered desire of sense-based pleasure constituted the quintessential heresy. These Epicureans, unlike Dante, did not perceive such pleasure to be connected to a lower self in need of transmutation. Therefore, in the sixth circle of Hell we find them burning within their fiery tombs of passion, precluded from the possibility of transforming the love connected to the sense world into the *Love* born of the Christ.

*Muhammad-Sharif Musawwir's miniature
from a copy of* The Seated Princess
(*ca. 1600*), *perhaps from Bokhara
(The Smithsonian Institute)*

Sufis and their Influence

The connection between the Knights Templar and the Albigenses made by Robert John, unveils one of the ways in which the influences of Persia and of Manichaeism entered the regions of Southern France, thereby affecting both the Troubadours and, consequently, Dante. De Rougemont explains that within the religious poetry of Arabia, there occurred, in the ninth century, the "'unlikely' fusion of Iranian Manichaeism, Neo-Platonism, and Mohammedanism,"[176] which, he claims, contained the erotic metaphors used in the courtly poetry of the Troubadours. According to him, al Hallaj, al Ghazali, and Suhrawardi were "troubadours of supreme Love, of the Veiled Idea, which they treated as a beloved object but also as a symbol of a longing for the divine."[177] De Rougemont points specifically to Suhrawardi as having been greatly influenced by Plato—through the Neo-Platonism of his time—whom he, in turn, considered to be the successor to Zoroaster. In so doing, he borrowed a cosmic theme that "had 'inspired' Manes and had become the root of the Catharist faith,"[178] namely, the polar relationship between the Forces of Good (Light) and the Forces of Evil (Darkness).

This brings us to an interesting point that has not sufficiently been recognized, namely, that Dante and the *Fedeli d'amore*, in their idealization of woman—and, thereby, their idealization of love—were bringing to light Platonic ideals embodied in Divine Love. Though Dante largely adopts the tenets of Augustine in his tenuous adherence to the Church, he, nevertheless, without explicitly stating so, incorporates a Neo-platonic view of spiritual reality, particularly with respect to the *Paradiso*. George Santayana, in his *Interpretation of Poetry and Religion,* states "Nothing, for example, could be a better object lesson in Platonism than the well-known sentimental history of Dante."[179] He goes on to say that the "Platonism of Dante is, in any case, quite on its own," and that the *"lifelong devotion of Dante to Beatrice is something purely mental and poetical."* According to Santayana, Dante "never ventured *to woo...* " (italics mine).

In *Cosmosophia: Cosmology, Mysticism and the Birth of a New Myth,* Theodore Richards elaborates on Dante's relation to Plato and Aristotle by stating:

> From Plato, Dante inherited the notion of an ensouled cosmos in which the interiority of the soul was connected to the transcendent divine of the Empyrean. From Aristotle, Dante adopted the idea of a hierarchical order in which a divine intelligence permeates the universe, from the divine, through the planets and throughout creation. The Christian, Islamic, and Jewish traditions of angelology were adapted to this hierarchy, with the nine orders of angels corresponding to what was now nine cosmic spheres. He parted with Augustine, who advocated a more direct link between the soul and the divine, and agreed with Avicenna and Ibn 'Arabi in positing that we connect to the divine through an angelic cosmos, not by surpassing the Universe. Dante's was a living cosmos, and one in which every aspect, even hell, was part of the divine hierarchy.[180]

He adds,

> At the end of the *Commedia*, when Dante reaches the Empyrean, the hierarchy is inverted. The material periphery of the Universe is the spiritual center: the vastness of the stars is condensed into a single point of light, the divine consciousness.[181]

This single point of light, to which Richards refers, brings to mind the "One" of Plotinus, the indivisible light of which all things are a part and from which all things manifest. Thus, in his *Comedy,* Dante reflects both the Platonic and Aristotelian streams of consciousness working their way through humanity during the Middle Ages, as was also evident in the School of Chartres, where the spiritual vision of

Dante's teacher, Brunetto Latini, arose from his experience of the Goddess Natura—a vision which, again, according to Steiner, constituted the basis by which Dante could conceive the *Divine Comedy*.

Bearing in mind the connection of Manichaeism to the Neo-Platonic ideals as they concern Divine Love, De Rougemont argues that the cosmological principles of "Good" and "Evil" were transmuted into chivalrous love rhetoric. Furthermore, the problems faced by such mystical love poetry of the Middle East were similar to those of the West, for just as the Troubadours of Southern France were opposed by the orthodoxy of the Roman Church, so, too, were the mystical poets of Persia forced to overcome the influences of Mohammedanism. Again, we can witness here in both instances, the reciprocal opposition of the patriarchal and matriarchal streams of consciousness. One of the great problems that lay at the heart of the theological discord was the notion of what later came to be known as "mystical marriage"—i.e., the mystical union of one's soul to the divine (spirit). De Rougemont claims that with regard to many of the Sufi mystic poets, the fusion of the Creator (active creative principle) and the created was evidence of their attempt to harbor Manichaeism. That is to say, both institutionalized religions—Catholicism and Mohammedanism—*negated* the notion that there existed a principle (*Active Intelligence*) inherent within human consciousness *by which human beings could be connected to God*—a principle that formed the basis of the mystical poetry of the Sufis, as well as the poetry of the Troubadours and that of the *Fedeli d'amore*. This principle was veiled in the poet's *idealization of woman*. In essence, they referred to the mystical union of anima and animus, the soul and spirit, the matriarchal and patriarchal streams of consciousness whose union, of course, denoted the reintegration of one's whole being. It was, as mentioned previously, the separation of these two streams (resulting in the Fall) that these poets sought to reconnect, so as to realize the *light* of Christ within human consciousness.

In attempting to show how the mystical Persian poetry formed the basis for that of the Troubadours and the *Fedeli d'amore*, Valli quotes from the book of the orientalist Italo Pizzi entitled, *Storia della Poesia Persiana,* in which he writes,

> ...in his love for a woman, the Eastern ascetic saw the love of God. He created, out of a woman, the symbol and image of God Himself.
>
> *The mystics thus accepted this metaphor of "love for a woman"; the entire language of the love poets was largely taken and used in all their vast and complex literature.* This language...had already been discovered a long time before, even before this mystical doctrine was born, and used with all its richness of phrases, of images, and of artifices, in the Arab and Persian songs of earliest times. *And since they had found it as such, and found it suitable to their ideas, the mystics appropriated all of this for themselves and it [was done] in such a way as to not easily allow someone to understand whether this or that other poet...spoke of one's true love or of divine love.* For, like the impassioned love poet, the mystic who is inebriated with the love of God, enraptured in ecstasy and in the ardor of his beatific vision, *speaks to God as a lover speaks to his sweet friend. His love gives him complete trust. Doubt does not arise within his heart regarding his true friend, which is God...*
>
> ...therefore, when the mystical poet speaks of his friend's beautiful head of hair it must be understood that these hairs are the divine mysteries known to no one outside of God...
>
> *There is no doubt whatsoever...that this language* previously existed, in its true and literal sense as the language of true love poets; *but the mystics took it for themselves, not only because they found it readymade and suitable for being used as metaphor, but even more so, because with it, they could veil their dangerous doctrines so as to have it become more openly widespread—an object of loathing for all the orthodox.* And later we find that some mystics were persecuted "to death for their overly free and new doctrines." (tr. mine)[182]

What was the feature most common to all three currents of poetic thought that we have just mentioned, namely, that of the Sufi mystic poets, the Troubadours, and the *Fedeli d'amore?* It was none other than *Active Intelligence*, that which was referred to as "The Lady of Thoughts," or characterized by Dante as *"Donne ch'avete l'intelletto d'amore"*—namely, *Sophia*. It was that which Corbin and de Rougemont both intimate as the "spiritual and angelic part of man." The realization of *Active Intelligence* is, in our day, conducive to the attainment of the Spirit Self—born of the transformation of the astral body by the "I." Though the time, then, was not yet ripe for the attainment of the Spirit Self, the *knowledge* of its eventual realization by humanity was symbolized through the centuries by what was known as the "mystical marriage"—the union of masculine and feminine principles working within the human being. Herein lies the fundamental principle that forms the basis of Manichaeism, which was, in effect, originally brought forth during the second cultural epoch, and whose consummation will only be realized during the sixth cultural epoch—that which is to follow our own. Proof of the ritualistic practices binding all three poetic sects can be found in that to which Valli and others frequently referred as the *salutation*. We meet with it particularly in the poem by Cavalcanti, "The Lady in Toulouse." As we have said, Valli shows how Mandetta was the Lady (or code name) to whom Cavalcanti refers (salutes) when wishing to safely become recognized by those of like mind, given that Toulouse was a center of activity for both the Cathars and the Troubadours! Says de Rougemont in his chapter entitled "Arab Mystical Poetry,"

> Both the *salutation* and the *salute* that the initiated wish to give on approaching the Sage, but that the latter considerately gives first, are a constant poetic theme of the troubadours, and later of Dante, and eventually of Petrarch. All these poets attach extreme importance to the "salute" given by the Lady, and their doing so is easily understood if we bear in mind the two senses of *salutare*—namely "to greet" and "to save."[183]

However, this nuance in meaning conveyed by the word *salute* is somewhat clarified by Valli, who shows in *Il Linguaggio Segreto di Dante e dei Fedeli d'Amore* that there may have been a slight distinction in the use of *salute* as opposed to *saluto*. He states when Dante received the *saluto* (nine plus nine years, precisely!), he had a vision in which he perceived Beatrice (the "donna of salute") in the arms of Love. According to him, the word *saluto* (which we may here take to mean a "transformational experience," or even initiation) lends itself to the attainment of *salute* (salvation). Nevertheless, we can see the *impact* that this salutation by Beatrice had on Dante's soul in chapter XXI of the *Vita Nuova*. There, it says:

> and when she greets a man his heart beats fast,
> the color leaves his face, he bows his head
> *and sighs to think of all his imperfections.*
>   (tr. M. Musa; italics mine)[184]

Compare the effect of the *"saluto"* in this poem with various ones of the Troubadours. Let us consider a few lines by Cercamon, when he says,

> If she does not want me, I would have liked to die
> that day, when she took me as her servant;
> oh lord, how gently she slew me
> when she showed me the look of her love,
> and locked me in such an enclosure
> I never want to see another. (tr. F. Goldin)[185]

Notice that in both the poem of Dante and that of Cercamon there exists the feeling of captivity with regard to the love experienced by each of the poets—a love that they *desire*. Moreover, each finds himself at the mercy of his limited, mortal existence before the presence of his beloved. Remember, it is by looking into the eyes of Beatrice that Dante is able to rise through the celestial spheres of Paradise to encounter the Christ. Thus, for the *Fedeli d'amore*, the Troubadours and Dante himself, the "eyes of their women" form the gateway into a realm of consciousness that transcends the boundaries of the physical world. There is a poem by Marcabru, one of the earliest Troubadours, in which he seems to refer to the greetings of his beloved as a "food of everlasting life"—i.e., one not subject to the laws of corruption.

> I've got you a precious love:
> to a thousand admirers
> she has renders
> a thousand greetings,
> and sated them
> with dinners,
> never granting
> them the rotten fruit they crave. (tr. F. Goldin)[186]

This love of which these poets speak (as we have tried to show with that of the *Fedeli d'amore*) is not of the flesh. Says the Troubadour, Jaufre Rudel:

> My heart does not come to the end of desire
> for the one I love most;
> *and I think my will misleads me*
> *if lust takes her away from me;*
> far more piercing than a thorn
> is the pain only joy can cure;
> therefore let no man pity me.
>   (tr. F. Goldin; italics mine)[187]

What do we witness here but the striving for "purity," as exemplified by the Cathars—the "Pure Ones"! Thus, the "promiscuity" associated with the Troubadours throughout the centuries, because of the "romantic quality" of their verse, must be reconsidered on the basis of the inherent paradoxes in their idealizations. The "desire" of which Rudel speaks is not of the lower self, for "lust" will lead only to a separation from his beloved. *Is this not the same desire that enables Dante and others, to acknowledge all of their imperfections at the sight of their "Lady"?* This serves to show how we can perceive the influences of Manichean thought (having arisen in the form of mystical poetry roughly six hundred years after Mani) as an inherent trait in the concept of purification shared by the Troubadours and the *Fedeli d'amore*. Evidence elucidating the similar inner struggles of many Sufi poets can be seen in a short poem called "Fragment" by Ayn al-Qozat Hamadabi, who was executed on the charge of heresy in Baghdad at the age of thirty-three. There, he writes

> O would that the eye
> had never seen
> her face
> that the heart
> had never shared
> the sin
> of the eye!
> (tr. P. L. Wilson and N. Pourjavady)[188]

Thus, the mystical poetry of the Sufis that greatly influenced that of the Troubadours can be shown to have had some relationship to Manichaeism. In fact, de Rougemont states,

> There occurred during the twelfth century in Languedoc and in the Limousin one of the most extraordinary spiritual confluences of history. On the one hand, a strong Manichean religious current, which had taken its rise in Persia, flowed through Asis Minor and the Balkans as far as Italy and France, bearing the esoteric doctrines of Maria Sophia and the love for the Form of Light. On the other hand, a highly refined rhetoric, with its set forms, themes, and characters, its ambiguities invariably recurring in the same places, and indeed its symbolism, pushes out from Irak and the Sufis, who were inclined alike to Platonism and Manichaeism, and reaches Arabic Spain, then, leaping over the Pyrenees, it comes in the south of France upon a society that seems to have but awaited its arrival in order to *state* what it had not dared and had not been able to avow either in the clerical tongue or in the common vernacular. Courtly lyrical poetry was the offspring of that encounter.[189]

In effect, de Rougemont is pointing to the evolution of the two streams (Cathars and Troubadours) in southern France that existed side by side as spiritual impulses—each of which had originated and coexisted in Persia. In other words, what existed in the Arab world, as seemingly unrelated sects, manifests again in southern France in slightly altered forms, but with the same impulses, for both the Cathars and the Troubadours are rooted in common soil! In fact, de Rougemont states that Sufi poets such as Suhrawardi were "inspired by Persian Manichaeism." He states,

> Suhrawardi speaks of lovers as being *Brethren of the Truth*. This was a name given to all mystic lovers who were at one with their beloved in mutual idealization and who came to form a community analogous to the Catharist Church of Love. Mystics of the illuminative school of Suhrawardi were inspired by Persian Manichaeism....[190]

Finally, Morton M. Hunt, in his book *The Natural History of Love*, tells us that there is little wonder why courtly love poetry was so prevalent in the region of southern France, where, because of Catharism, chastity was such a strongly rooted concept. Says he, "Courtly love *did* catch on first by no mere coincidence in a heretic-dominated area of France with a tradition of chaste love..."[191] thus fueling the argument that "with its idealization of chaste love and its disinterest in procreation," courtly love was "only a poetic disguise for Manichean heresy."[192]

In light of this, it is important to reiterate how the "love" that the Sufi poets, the Troubadours, and the *Fedeli d'amore* had for their Lady, embodied both the principles of Eros and Agape, carnal and spiritual love—a dichotomy representative of the Manichean principle of creation, whereby Satan ruled the world of flesh and God the world of spirit. Says Eithne Wilkins in *The Rose-Garden Game*, "through all the erotic mysticism or mystical eroticism surrounding her, this Lady is venerated as a spiritual guide."[193] One may even wonder how the sudden rise in Mariolatry during the eleventh century, notably the creation of a new and sacred ideal or image toward which humanity could aspire, concealed that which (as we have said) lay at the heart of the Manichean faith—namely, a transformation of the principle of "evil" particularly embodied in the "promiscuity" of Eve.

Unearthing the Forces of Darkness

We have discussed how Dante and the *Fedeli d'amore*, in their search for *Divine Wisdom*, represented the initial stirring of the Consciousness Soul Age. Their striving posed a threat to the Church's authority, which inevitably forced them to communicate amongst each other through the implementation of a secretly coded language. The aim of this language was, in part, to identify and keep at bay, the forces of opposition that confronted them. Just like the Church sensed (and feared) the emergence of a consciousness that would eventually undermine its power, these poets feared the dangers posed by the Church in their quest for spiritual enlightenment. The increasingly ominous threat of the Church, outwardly visible to society, was a manifestation of seemingly impervious forces that arose in conjunction with the transformation of consciousness that humanity had begun to experience. Such forces impacted society with more consistency, entering evermore deeply into human *thinking*. At the same time, other forces worked strongly upon human souls, forces that were somewhat less attuned to the ever-growing dialectical nature of human thinking. Instead, they worked more on the *feeling* life of human beings, rendering them more vulnerable to the manipulative measures exercised by the Church in its struggle to exert and maintain power.

Though these two forces, ahrimanic and luciferic, respectively, worked independently of each other at that time, the Church efficaciously utilized them, inasmuch as it, *itself*, was a manifestation of their interrelationship. Their influence on the Church, the very institution that Dante had hoped could one day be reformed, were seemingly intuited by him, for we find aspects of both allegorically represented, albeit without clear distinction, in his *Divine Comedy*.

The impact of the luciferic forces upon the medieval Christianity is beautifully embodied in Dante's portrayal of Ulysses. There, Ulysses appears with Diomede as a shooting flame among the Evil Councilors in Canto XXVI of the *Inferno*. According to Dante's rendition, in his fervor to reach Purgatory—the point of contact between the earthly and spiritual worlds, represented as that promontory mount that rose up from the bottom of the world as a result of Lucifer's expulsion from Paradise into the center of the Earth—Ulysses set forth upon the seas and navigated his way to its shores with the intention of circumventing the depths of Hell. Passing through the "Pillars of Hercules," he and his crew sailed for five months until they were finally guided by the constellation above the South Pole. As they neared their goal, a hurricane struck their ship and caused it to sink to the depths of the ocean. The crew, including Ulysses, drowned.

Much has been made of this description given by Dante. Scholars, eager to attest to Dante's universal knowledge, have bestowed upon him the title of "myth-maker" for this refashioning of Homer's great epic. Others perceiving the *Divine Comedy*, itself, as a fabrication based upon the impulses of fantasy have called the Ulysses episode "a myth within a myth." Treatises have been written on the myth-making qualities displayed by Dante, often without, again, taking at all into consideration what *significance* such a "myth" might have in relation to the evolution of human consciousness. Nonetheless, there are those such as Theodore Richards who have judiciously contextualized the functionality of Dante's mythmaking. He states in his *Cosmosophia: Cosmology, Mysticism and the Birth of a New Myth*,

> More than a poet, Dante was a mythmaker. He was, in many ways, the last mythmaker in the West who understood that the task of the poet is to give a culture a sense of how it relates to the world. While he reinforced the established cosmologies in many ways,

Dante also showed that, as a mystic and poet, he could create a world of meaning that would transform politics and theology. [194]

If we penetrate the veil ingeniously placed by Dante in this episode, we will see raying forth the key by which to understand Dante's *need* to fathom the depths of Hell and experience it in all its horror. The fact that Dante strays into the "Dark Wood" and finds himself surrounded by the beasts of sensuality, pride, and greed (leopard, lion, and she-wolf) is not happenstance, for these beasts symbolize the obstacles on the path of life that all human beings must overcome to attain spiritual "salvation." What we see in Dante's characterization of Ulysses is the idea fostered by the Church during the Middle Ages that one should renounce earthly pleasures to find God—something that the Church with all its riches obviously did not do. Ulysses, in fact, exemplifies those who, in their fervor for spiritual self-realization, purposely shun penetrating into the core of materialism, and, thereby, close their eyes to the example set forth by Christ, Himself, who upon experiencing death, entered the depths of the Earth before resurrecting Himself.

Dante's Ulysses seems to recall the ancient knowledge that flowed from the East, most evident in the tradition of Buddhism, which taught that because the world contained so much suffering, the principle objective of humanity on Earth was to free itself as quickly as possible from its influences by entering permanently into a state known as "nirvana."

Now, the Ulysses of Homer lived at a time when humanity was still somewhat able to perceive the spiritual world, for materialistic impulses had yet to fully permeate human thinking. Because Ulysses belonged to another epoch in the evolution of human consciousness, his plight in the *Divine Comedy* is representative of what would befall human beings during Dante's time if they were to have followed his example. For it was inappropriate for people of the Middle Ages to pursue a path of initiation not in accordance with their own spiritual constitution. Thus, Ulysses brings to mind the ancient path of initiation, which was not based on the *light of thinking* possible because of Christ's entry into the world. Any other way for him to reach the spiritual world was, by nature, incomprehensible. Anyone living during Dante's time, attempting to enter the spiritual world without *knowledge* of the Christ, fell into err, as did Ulysses. Humanity's path to redemption lies not in dismissing the importance of the material world as the Church often proclaims but, rather, in penetrating its very depths to *redeem* it. We must do this, of course, by enlivening the fallen nature of our thinking. In fact, the *Inferno* as a whole can be seen to symbolize the thinking by which humankind is able to resurrect itself through the power of Christ. This being the case, Dante casts Ulysses into the circles of the Evil Councilors, for his example serves to show how luciferic impulses lead us astray from the true path of salvation.

On the other hand, the ahrimanic forces present in the Church were somewhat less recognizable, partly because they had yet to imprint themselves deeply onto human thinking. However, the characterization of their impending influence can be inferred from many of the descriptions connected with the *Inferno*. Take for example, Satan residing at the center of Hell. Not only does he have three heads, but also two sets of wings that flutter *mechanically*. His trine aspect is not merely a negative counterimage of the sacred Trinity, but it can be figuratively thought to represent the threefold nature of evil (Lucifer, Ahriman, and the Asuras). Though the influence of the Asuras lay far beyond the Dante's time, who could argue with the mechanical portrayal given to the Lord of Death, one that implies the absence of feeling and willing? In fact, this mechanization of Satan seeks to depict the lifeless nature of dialectical thinking. We see this beast acting as a magnetic force attracting all those who have fallen into error (sin) through thinking devoid of moral impulses. The center of Hell, itself, represented as a frozen lake and not a region of fire, denotes the crystallization of the etheric impulses (water). Frozen water symbolizing the materialization of etheric forces is to be understood as the effect of Ahriman on human consciousness as it deprives humanity of the movement of life. As Goethe's representation of Mephistopheles embodies both the luciferic and ahrimanic impulses, so, too, does Dante's characterization of Hell, governed by Satan.

In Canto XIX of the *Inferno,* Dante shows how the ahrimanic forces work through the hierarchy of the Church in an attempt to deviate humankind from its true course. We have shown that the Church *itself* assumed the role of *Divine Wisdom* while impregnating human souls with materialistic concepts of Christ and the spiritual world. As the Church fathers had largely lost all connection to the esoteric nature of Christ's teachings, they could only conceive of the Godhead anthropomorphically, thus giving greater power to idolatry. The "graven image of God," as an instrument to maintain unity among human beings by perpetuating the social order as it was conceived through Roman law, was something that arose spontaneously, at that time, from a thinking rooted in the physical world. Here, the materialistic impulses worked in effective collaboration with the luciferic influences as idolatry struck fear into human hearts—i.e., into humanity's feeling life, thus enabling the Church to exercise its power by psychologically manipulating the masses. The "graven image" that the Church fostered, found great success largely due to the inability of humanity, at that time, to comprehend the Resurrection by *experiencing* the light of thinking. In addition, the suggestive power of this "graven image" justified the embellishment of its own material means of expression. This was reflected by the Church's quest for material power that provided the impetus toward an ever-deepening temporal reign. Not only did the Church, in large part, "possess" the hearts of human beings, it effectively sought to "inherit the Earth" itself.

We encounter the punishment appropriated to such representatives of the Church in the third chasm of the eighth circle of the *Inferno.* There we find the souls of the Simonists, who, for the love of money, sold out the true values of the Church. They are depicted upside-down, with their heads placed in round holes, their legs and feet protruding out. There are, in fact, many such holes filled with the souls of popes who used their intellects for reasons of personal greed. Here, Dante dramatizes the characterization of those individuals whose thinking is rooted in earthly affairs. Instead of being positioned upright, whereby the head is directed, figuratively, toward the Heavens, we find the head set into the Earth projected in the direction of Satan. Dante seems to be affirming that those who utilize their intellects for material gain will experience an ever-greater degree of materialization of the thinking forces, which, of course, perpetuates the despiritualization of the Earth. Interesting to note is how, with each new "simonist" descending into the pit, the one preceding is thrust ever further into the depths of the Earth. What better way could Dante have depicted the karmic retribution allotted to those who have set into motion the ahrimanization of the Church? Those who find themselves pushed down into the furthest reaches of the pit are precisely those "simonists" whose actions have permitted similar exploitations by their successors. Thus, they must support the weight of all the future corruption connected to their actions.

If we bear in mind that the Consciousness Soul Age, which soon gave rise to empiricism, was yet to fully manifest, it becomes apparent that the Church, itself, became the vehicle by which the ahrimanic forces could lead humanity away from the Christ. Not only was it instrumental in impeding the search for a spiritual connection to Christ through the activity of thinking, by willfully manipulating humankind's adherence to the "graven image" of Christ, it had prepared the groundwork by which those adversary forces could take deeper root. In other words, the Church, through dogma, played a major role in accelerating the process by which reflective thinking could be brought to fulfillment. It helped to push thinking further down into the earthly sphere so that an anthropomorphic representation of the spiritual reality could supplant what little remained of a clairvoyance that allowed for the direct perception of spiritual realities. Strange as it may seem, the Church was, in large part, inadvertently responsible for ushering in a consciousness that could, in due time, unveil many of the truths that it sought to conceal. Those individuals who aspired toward a spiritual understanding of life by not conforming to the materialistic concepts espoused by the Church fathers were, of course, declared heretics. No wonder many considered Rome to be the dwelling place of the Antichrist, that is, the "Babylon" (corruption of *Divine Wisdom*) that would, one day, be overthrown and replaced by the New Jerusalem, namely, Christ-consciousness. In his *History of Magic*, Eliphas Levi tells of how Dante, finding himself positioned upside-down in relation to circles of Hell from which he had just descended, exits Hell by scaling the tail of Satan. This, according to him, represents the reversal of Church dogma that, for Dante, was essential in attaining the *perception* of higher states of creative activity.

Thus, we find humanity caught between two opposing forces, each vying to claim the soul. On the one hand, there exist those forces, represented by Ulysses, which tend to draw us away from the earthly realm. Such forces lead us toward a dream-like state, whereby we are unable to understand the function that both the Earth and human thought have in relation to the evolution of our being. On the other hand, humankind is beset by those forces manifesting themselves through the dogma of the Papacy, which have as their primary aim, the task of fettering thinking to the Earth. Just as Ulysses, in Homer's *Odyssey*, had to guide his ship through the strait between Scylla and Charybdis (ahrimanic forces and luciferic forces, respectively) to save himself, so, too, must humanity steer itself free of their influences by seeking the "straight path" leading to the Christ. Dante's journey is an illustration of this, as he must descend into the very center of Hell (ahrimanic and luciferic activity), into which there trickles the river Lethe, which, reminiscent of the "thread of Ariadne," guides him toward the gradual realization of the Christ.

PART TWO

RE-IMAGINING THE *DIVINE COMEDY*
IN THE LIGHT OF
THINKING, FEELING, AND WILLING

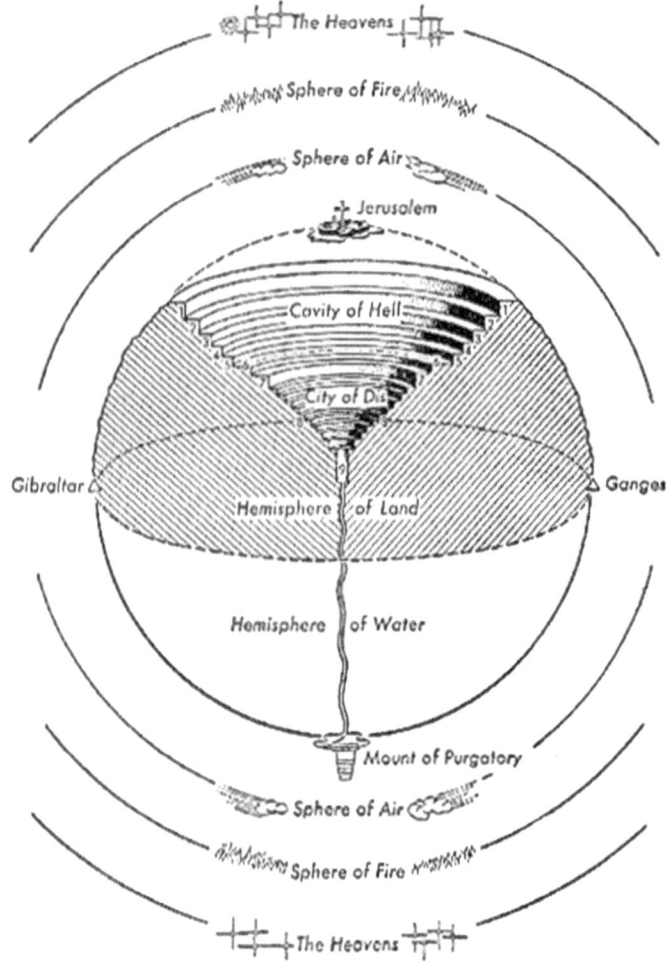

Diagram of the Earth at the Center of the Universe

The Tripartition of the *Divine Comedy*

Much has been written on the allegorical nature of Dante's *Divine Comedy*. His journey through the afterworld has, of course, always been thought to represent the path to "eternal salvation." As a result, many critics have sought to comprehend the *Inferno*, *Purgatorio*, and *Paradiso* in the light of theological interpretations that have done little to dispel the ambiguities that arise when relating Dante's cosmological scheme to the "inner" human being. The emphasis given predominantly to the outer significance of Dante's journey has thus inhibited the emergence of new ways by which the *Divine Comedy* may be "envisioned." It would be possible, for example, to imagine how the three realms comprising Dante's journey correspond to the threefold nature of the human being—i.e., thinking, feeling, and willing. If the principle objective of Dante's excursion is indeed that of self-transformation, how could they not portray those "spheres of spiritual activity" through which such a change must be incited? In other words, how can the purification and illumination he seeks not be reflected in aspects of his being that he *himself* transmutes? For centuries the esoteric nature of the *Divine Comedy* largely went unnoticed. This was partly due to the impact that the vivid characterizations, constituting the outer configuration of Dante's journey, had on the reader. Yet, in a number of instances Dante himself alludes to meaning hidden within the poem. At the Gates of Dis, for example, we hear:

> Men of sound intellect and probity, weigh with good understanding what lies hidden *behind the veil of my strange allegory.*
> (*Inferno* IX, 58–60; italics mine)

Another subtle hint of the esoteric nature of the *Divine Comedy* lies in the fact that the spirits of the dead, throughout the *Inferno*, proclaim Dante to be *alive*. One need only remember his crossing of the Styx where even the "Fallen Angels" rained the angry words:

> Who is it that invades Death's Kingdom in his *life*?
> (*Inferno* VIII, 81–82; italics mine)

These utterances intimate that Dante's path, extending into the depths of the netherworld and up through the planetary spheres, is not a mere allegorical representation of an after-death experience but, rather, an attempt by him to delineate the *path of initiation* into the suprasensory world. In fact, the human spirits who comprise Dante's "cast of characters" (sinners, penitent, and blessed) each reflect a level of consciousness determined by the degree to which thought has been transformed by willing. As Spiritual Science teaches that modern initiation begins by enlivening reflected thinking, it stands to reason that the *Inferno* corresponds precisely to the world of thought divorced from its fount of creative activity. Only when we enter the darkness of dialecticism, as Dante himself stepped into the "Dark Wood," can we direct ourselves to the *light* that has been lost. However, such light is not part of the world of dialectical thinking but, rather, *apart* from it, for mirrored thinking can only manifest through a separation from the act of creation (willing).

Thus, to extricate himself from the enveloping darkness, Dante must penetrate into the depths of Hell, into the darkest regions of thought. This eventually enables him to behold the stars, symbolizing Divine Will, wherein exists the *light* with which human thought forms a polarity. Here, incidentally, lies the key to understanding the nature of Dante's quest, for the polarities of thought/light and will/gravity (darkness) are portrayed in the *Divine Comedy* as having been separated and interchanged, so that the light that Dante seeks in thought (the *Inferno*) he later discovers in the will (the *Paradiso*). Meanwhile, within thought (the *Inferno*) resides the darkness from which his will (containing the light) is able to emerge.

Thus, Dante's poem reflects the polarity of thought/darkness and will/light. Self-transformation is only possible, however, when light (will) and thought (darkness) no longer exist as separate polarities but become one in the form of Divine Will. For now we can only say that Dante's entry to the darkness of thought lends itself to the gradual transformation of the emotional sphere where born is the "knowledge" of *Love*. It thus follows that the *Purgatorio* relates specifically to the feeling realm where we absolve ourselves of the "effects of sin." Only then may we rise (as Dante depicts) toward the "Garden of Earthly Paradise," symbolic of the reintegration of the feminine and masculine polarities of human consciousness—i.e., thinking and willing.

This "androgyny" reflects the attainment of love untainted by the influences arising from our lower nature—a love whose metaphysical foundations are described midway up the precipitous slopes of Purgatory, at the very *heart* of Dante's poem. There, Dante asks if love springs from outside the will of the soul, "what merit is there in loving good, or blame in loving ill?" Virgil explains that "all love springs from necessity," what Beatrice will later call the "Free Will." Nevertheless, he states that the age of reason appears imperceptibly like the unseen light of the human being's "first cognizance." Though he describes the birth of higher reason, it must be noticed that an interesting correlation is also made to the emergence of thought itself. Implicit in Virgil's statement is how each human act springs from a thought whose pre-dialectical force is but the light unseen. This is the "specific power" within the "substantial form" (essence of a thing) of which Virgil speaks when he says:

> Every substantial form distinct from matter
> and yet united with it in some way,
> has a *specific* power in it. This latter
>
> is not perceivable save as it gives
> evidence of its workings and effects
> as the green foliage tells us a plant lives.

> Therefore, *no man can know whence*
> *springs the light*
> *of his first cognizance...*
> (*Purgatorio* XVIII, 49–56; italics mine)

Virgil suggests that this very force that draws the mind toward manifested form is *Love* itself—the Christ inherent within thinking—i.e., the unperceived *Light* that descended from the Father to be *amongst humankind on Earth*:

> From that which really is, your apprehension
> extracts a form which it unfolds within you;
> that form thereby attracts the mind's attention,
>
> then if the mind, so drawn, is drawn to it,
> that summoning force is Love...
> (*Purgatorio* XVIII, 22–26)

Here we see how spontaneously Love gives itself over to thought, its creation. Yet, this Love is "crucified" by our lower self to the degree in which such thought is directed to the fulfillment of worldly pleasure. Only by uniting our "I" to the *force* of that Love, present in the *activity* of thinking, can we truly overcome the temptations of the lower self. In this way, Purgatory is the process by which the light of the Christ first becomes manifest. Interestingly, a tangible confirmation of Dante's intimate knowledge of the causal relationship between the physical and spiritual worlds can be evidenced if we consider Steiner's description of Purgatory as an after-death experience where the purging of "sin" occurs in the afterworld in the reverse order from its unfolding on Earth—i.e., from death to birth. In this way, we come to realize how this "mirroring" of earthly deeds in Purgatory is correctly depicted by Dante, for he in fact reveals the inner configuration of Purgatory as an inverted *reflection* of the upper region of Hell, where the transgressions furthest removed from the influences of the adversarial powers (Satan) are essentially the same as on Purgatory (see table).

	GARDEN OF EARTHLY PARADISE
Purgatory	lustful
	gluttonous
	avaricious
	slothful
	wrathful
Anti-Purgatory	proud
Upper Inferno	wrathful
	avaricious
	gluttonous
	lustful
Dark Wood	

It must be mentioned, however, that the difference between the lustful in the upper regions of Hell, for example, as opposed to those in Purgatory lies in the degree to which passions (astral) control thinking. In effect, all the "sins" of the *Inferno* are but the result of thought's inability to be *willed* free from the influences of the lower self.

Having reached the summit of Purgatory—i.e., the stage at which feeling (astral) has been "purified"—Dante becomes "transhumanized" as he enters Paradise, where his will conforms to the Will of God. Only in this way can he act in freedom—i.e., *out of the Love (Light) streaming through him*. This same *Light* is, in fact, the "thread of Ariadne" that initially led him out of the darkness of thought—i.e., the ray of starlight that faintly falls onto the Earth where Hell gives way to Purgatory. Only *now*, Dante truly lives within that *Light*. His will, having become an individualized expression of Divine Will, enables him to function out of the consciousness born in Christ, so that he can freely partake in the cosmic activity that all humankind had once beheld. This creative activity is symbolized by the "pollination" of the Mystic Rose on behalf of the angelic forces that descend into its petals bearing the *Love (light)* of God.

> (...like a swarm of bees who in one motion dive
> into the flowers, and in the next return
> the sweetness of their labors to the hive)
>
> flew ceaselessly to the many-petaled rose
> and ceaselessly returned into that light
> in which their ceaseless love has its repose.
> (*Paradiso* XXXI, 7–12)

By awakening to the consciousness of these co-creative forces, Dante thus acknowledges his future place among the beatitudes of God's creation seated upon the petals of the Heavenly Rose.

≈

Incidentally, we can see how the three realms traversed by Dante outwardly reflect the transformation of his soul. Whereas Hell (thought) is totally comprised of virtual darkness and Paradise (will) ever-ascending degrees of light, in Purgatory (the promontory mount jutting out from the bottom of the world), we witness the rhythmic alternation of light and darkness, for thinking and willing find their connection in the human *heart*, where "living" thinking is born. We see this same relationship of darkness to light also reflected in medieval alchemy where the process of self-purification was represented by the transition from raven to magpie to dove.

The Guiding Forces of Dante's Transformation

As we more deeply probe the spiritual nature of Dante's journey, it becomes apparent that an inextricable relationship exists between him and the forces that guide him along his path. In fact, by expanding upon what has just been presented, we shall find that, in each of the three realms, Dante is presented a different guide who, in turn, represents a particular stage of inner development that he must attain for himself. The first of course is Virgil who guides Dante through Hell and halfway up the slopes of Purgatory before being replaced by Beatrice. She then leads him through Paradise until finally relinquishing her role to St. Bernard. Virgil, symbolic of higher reason, is called upon by Beatrice to aid Dante in overcoming the impulses of the lower self that give rise to "sin," namely, pleasure, ambition, and avarice. These inner "drives" are represented by three beasts—leopard, lion, and she-wolf respectively—that accost Dante and prevent his return to the path that led him into the "Dark Wood." In other words, having acknowledged the primary causes of sin (that induced the Fall), Dante *can no longer follow the path of the past* (ancient initiation) to recover the *light* that has forsaken him. He must, instead, confront those impulses, which misguide the intellect, by penetrating into the very center of Hell, that is, he must enter into the materiality of thought, for there within the darkness "the will unfolds."[1]

Only in this way can he eventually rise to the Earth's highest regions to perceive the (astral) light radiating down from the starry world. Virgil, chosen to guide Dante through the regions governed by the three beasts below, prohibits him from establishing a fixed relationship with the sinners he meets, for this would in effect symbolize the adherence of his intellect to the influences arising from the lower self and would thereby preclude him from cultivating the will within which exists the light of thought. Throughout the *Inferno*, we witness a slow but significant transformation in Dante. At first, he seems to lack the fortitude (inner will) by which to endure the atrocities of the lower world. However, the more horrifying his experience, the greater his resolve, until he fearlessly reproaches those guilty of the most heinous of transgressions.

Thus, by confronting the manifestations of sin, Dante gradually empowers himself to overcome the ultimate cause of evil—i.e., thinking rooted in the earthly realm and, therefore, governed by "Satan," the mechanical beast anchored to the center of the Earth. Of particular importance is the fact that Virgil *has been sent by Beatrice* who, having descended into Limbo, arrives at the solitary castle occupied by the great thinkers of antiquity. Amongst them we find the likes of Aristotle, Plato, Seneca, Ovid, Averroes, etc., all of whom either preceded Christ's entry into the world or propagated a philosophy of life devoid of His influence. They are the "unbaptized," those who, according to the teachings of medieval theology, had no hope of ever bridging themselves to the Christ. This "noble" castle glows faintly in the darkness, thus illustrating the feebleness of intellectual forces bereft of Christ's *light*. Just as Virgil represents higher reason, within which reside the *imaginative* forces latent in the human being, Beatrice is emblematic of *Divine Wisdom* (Sapienza Santa), or shall we say, that which ultimately leads Dante to the awakening of *intuition*. Thus, Beatrice's summoning of Virgil depicts how dialectical thinking (Virgil) is itself guided by even higher forces of consciousness or wisdom. Says Virgil,

> ...I do not come this way
> of my own will or powers. A Heavenly Lady
> sent me to this man's aid in his dark day...
> *(Purgatorio* I, 52–54)

Having penetrated the very core of Hell, Dante begins his ascent of Purgatory. Still, Virgil remains by his side, for having fathomed the material depths of thought. Dante has yet to transform it into a vehicle for his ascension into the highest regions of spiritual world. Instead, he must free his will from the bondages of dialecticism that would, in turn, result in the acquisition of a new kind of thinking no longer linked to the forces of the terrestrial sphere. As he ascends the slopes of Purgatory, leading to the "Garden of Earthly Paradise" (purification of astral), his journey in fact becomes increasingly less arduous, for the stages leading to purification are, in effect, facilitated by thinking which gradually divorces itself from materiality. This "self-purification" is portrayed as weightlessness, so that we see how *thinking contains the mass /gravity (darkness) lost in willing*. Moreover, Dante can ascend Purgatory only by the light of day, so that the higher he climbs, the less obstruction there is of the light shining down upon him. In other words, the weightlessness he experiences on the higher terraces reflects the degree to which the *light* (Christ) intrinsic to willing is able to manifest within his thinking. As he purges himself from the effects of his earthly deeds, Dante is thus slowly able to actualize *Love*—the living force within thinking. This is, of course, all possible through the guidance of Beatrice.

Thus, we witness the gradual transformation from intellectuality into *Imagination* that arises through his encounter with Beatrice (*Divine Wisdom*). This process is incited by Virgil's (higher reason) entrance into Purgatory (feeling realm) where the movement and communication occurring between the penitents contrast remarkably to the isolated gestures of Hell. This characterizes the relationship between "etheric thinking" and the static representations we call thoughts. We see such movement or "visible speech" reflected, for example, in the bas-reliefs that Dante perceives carved into the wall in Canto X, each of which instructs the "Proud" on the virtues of humility. Gazing at them, Dante sees how the Archangel Gabriel

> stood carved before us with such force and love
> with such a living grace in his whole pose,
> *the image seemed to speak and move.*
> (*Purgatorio* X, 34–36; italics mine)

When he finally encounters Beatrice, Dante is overwhelmed by the sight of her and quickly turns to his beloved Virgil, no longer present. From now on, Dante cannot rely on Virgil (sense-bound thinking) for guidance. In fact, immediately preceding Virgil's departure, we witness his increasing inability to comprehend the more subtle questions of spirituality, such as the relationship of Love to Free Will. Says Virgil,

> ...As far as reason sees, I can reply.
> The rest you must ask Beatrice.
> The answer lies within faith's mysteries...
> (*Purgatorio* XVIII, 46–48)

Dante has entered the realm of *Imaginative* consciousness. What is most interesting is how he literally depicts the emergence of this consciousness from sense-based thinking through his incapacity to behold both forms of consciousness (Virgil and Beatrice) simultaneously. For in living thinking our immediate relationship to mirrored thinking is severed. Beatrice may be understood as the individualization of *Divine Wisdom* conducive to the attainment of *Imagination*. She has been summoned to be at Dante's side by the Virgin Mary (archetype of *Divine Wisdom*) via St. Lucia (who bestows *light*). Incidentally, this threefold relationship could be thought to represent a sort of feminine counterimage to the Holy Trinity or, as Adam McLean points out, the Triple Goddess whereby the Knowledge (Sophia) of the Father, permeated by the Love (Beatrice) of Christ, descends upon humankind through the Light (Lucia =Lux) of the Holy Spirit within the activity of thinking. Upon his entrance into the "Garden of Earthly Paradise," Dante is submerged into the river Lethe by Matilda, which outwardly reenacts the Baptism of Jesus Christ at the river Jordan. He is absolved of the "memory of sin" and, thus, no longer adheres to those impulses that had once resulted in humanity's separation from God. This may also be thought to represent the stage of *Inspiration* where the formative forces experienced during the stage of *Imagination* are completely erased. In his book, *Macrocosm and Microcosm*, Rudolf Steiner refers to this "Stream of Forgetfulness" as the point in which the human being "passes into the Great World."[2] In fact, Dante's submersion into the river Lethe is preceded by a long and intricate procession formally marking the beginning of Dante's *initiation* into the spiritual world.

Finally, he is led to drink from the river Eunoe, which rekindles his memory of the world free of error. It symbolizes the gradual awakening of *Intuition* in which the spiritual hierarchies slowly reveal themselves to him. Since the "Garden of Earthly Paradise" is the stage of reintegration whereby the human being is absolved of the impulses streaming in from the earthly realm, it is, thus, diametrically opposed to the "Dark Wood," which marked the stage of humanity's separation from God through the fall into materialization ("Fall of Humanity"). Able to enter into the heavenly realms, Dante is led by the *light in the eyes of Beatrice* up through the planetary spheres, the Fixed Stars and into the Empyrean where he beholds "countenance of God." Whereas in Hell and most of Purgatory, he exerts tremendous personal will to carry out his journey, in Paradise he is *drawn* toward the Holy Trinity by Divine Will. This can only happen through the unification of willing (containing light) and thinking (containing darkness), so that what arises as pure thinking, manifesting the force of creative activity, is synonymous with pure willing. (Note how once this reintegration is consummated, gravity reestablishes its natural polarity to willing!) The higher Dante ascends into the spiritual realms through Divine Will, the more capable is he of beholding ever-higher levels of luminosity. In short, his own thinking becomes increasingly imbued with the light of God, so that we, indeed, see how the *will contains the light lost in thought*. As Dante approaches the "eye" of God, he finds Beatrice replaced by St. Bernard, symbolic of *revelation*.

> Bernard, seeing my eyes so fixed and burning
> with passion on his passion, turned his own
> up to that height with so much love and yearning
>
> that the example of his ardor sent
> *new fire through me, making my gaze more ardent.*
> (*Paradiso* XXXI, 139–143; italics mine)

In fact, only by having attained the state of *Intuition* can the most sublime aspect of Divinity be revealed to him. Dante tells us,

> Bernard then, smiling sweetly, gestured to me
> *to look up, but I had already become*
> *within myself all he would have me be.*
>
> Little by little as my vision grew
> *it penetrated further through the aura*
> *of the high lamp which in Itself is true.*
> (*Paradiso* XXXIII, 49–54; italics mine)

≈

Though Virgil and Beatrice first appear to Dante in the *Inferno* and the *Purgatorio*, respectively, we have seen how the presence and influence of each extend far up into the neighboring realm. In other words, Virgil does not abandon Dante the moment he exits Hell, but assists him up the Mount until his powers begin to fail him. Similarly, Beatrice guides Dante beyond the planetary spheres and Fixed Stars of Paradise after having first appeared to him atop the treacherous slopes of redemption. In this way, Dante seems to illustrate the extent to which the higher intellectual forces must penetrate into the feeling realm before *Divine Wisdom*, resulting from a transformation of thinking (Imagination) can be realized. Likewise, *Divine Wisdom* cannot give way to the "Intuition" of higher spiritual realities until it has enabled this new thinking to totally absolve itself of its relationship to nature before merging with the forces of Divine Will. Thus, we have:

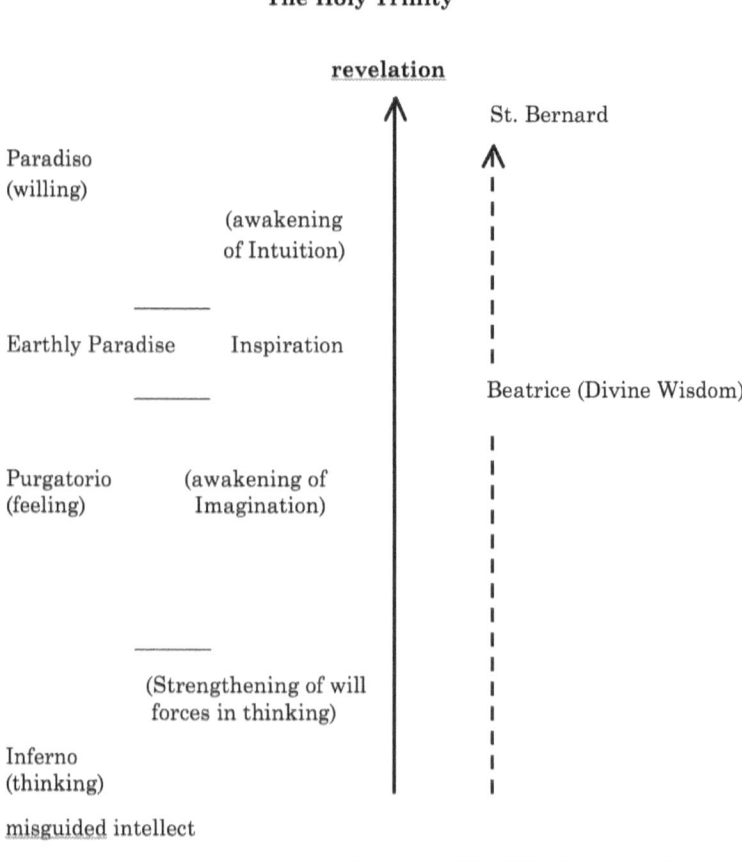

≈

In light of all this, what can be said regarding the importance of Dante's journey? To begin with, we witness the consummation of the "mystical marriage" as thinking (feminine polarity) is reunited with willing (masculine polarity); Heaven (light) and Earth (darkness) become one. Humanity thus reconnects itself to the being Sophia from which it had been separated at the time of Christ's entrance into the world, for, as Steiner points out in, *In Search of the New Isis*, "what we have lost is the *wisdom* and *knowledge* of Christ Jesus"[3] since He first appeared to humankind—an inevitable consequence of the separation of thinking from willing, begun when the lunar forces had separated themselves from the Earth. Having commenced his odyssey on Good Friday AD 1300, Dante reenacts the Mystery of Golgotha. Just as Christ resurrected himself from earthly forces, Dante resurrects himself from a despiritualized thought world, thereby showing how the resurrection of the Christ in human beings is initially attainable only through thinking.

It was not enough for Dante to merely posit theological solutions for overcoming the influences of adversarial forces at work in the spiritual world as did the Catholic Church, for such directives given by the Church were nothing more than refinements or extensions of Mosaic Law in the Old Testament, whereby humankind, lacking the sustenance of the Christ being, could not depend upon the moral impulses intrinsic to thinking. Though Dante precedes the Consciousness Soul Age by roughly a hundred years or so, in him can be seen the first signs of its emergence. Steiner states, "in Dante we see a poet who goes down into his own soul and remains entirely within his personality and its inner secrets. By pursuing this path of personal development he enters the spiritual world, and is thus able to present it in the powerful pictures we find in the *Divine Comedy*. Here the soul of Dante is quite alone with his personality."[4] Without the attainment of "personality," emblematic of medieval humanity, the development of the Consciousness Soul would have been impossible. Dante concludes his journey by contemplating the "Mystic Rose," whereupon he is bestowed the grace by which he can behold the Trinity "in a flash of light." Unable to encompass the radiance of God's *light* within the bounds of individual consciousness, he compares himself to a dreamer, who having lost the substance of the dream is only able to recall the feelings associated with it. Says he,

> What then I saw is more than tongue could say.
> Our human speech is dark before the vision.
> The ravished memory swoons and falls away.
>
> As one who sees in dreams and wakes to find
> the emotional impression of his vision
> still powerful while its parts fade from his mind—
> (*Paradiso* XXXIII, 55–60)

Nonetheless, he is able to transfer to humanity an image of his path of initiation in the form of the *Divine Comedy*. The lasting remains of Dante's vision is not so much to be found in its outer details but in the *force* of that revelation as it manifests itself in his feeling life. Dante thus provides the reader with the most essential clue to arriving at the Mystery before him. Only by not adhering to the static representations of our thought life, but by transforming them through the force of willing, can we awaken Love within our hearts. Only in this way can such representations be resurrected. Only then can we be seated upon the petals of the Mystic Rose among the *living*.

(This chapter originally appeared in *The Journal for Anthroposophy*, no. 56, spring 1993.)

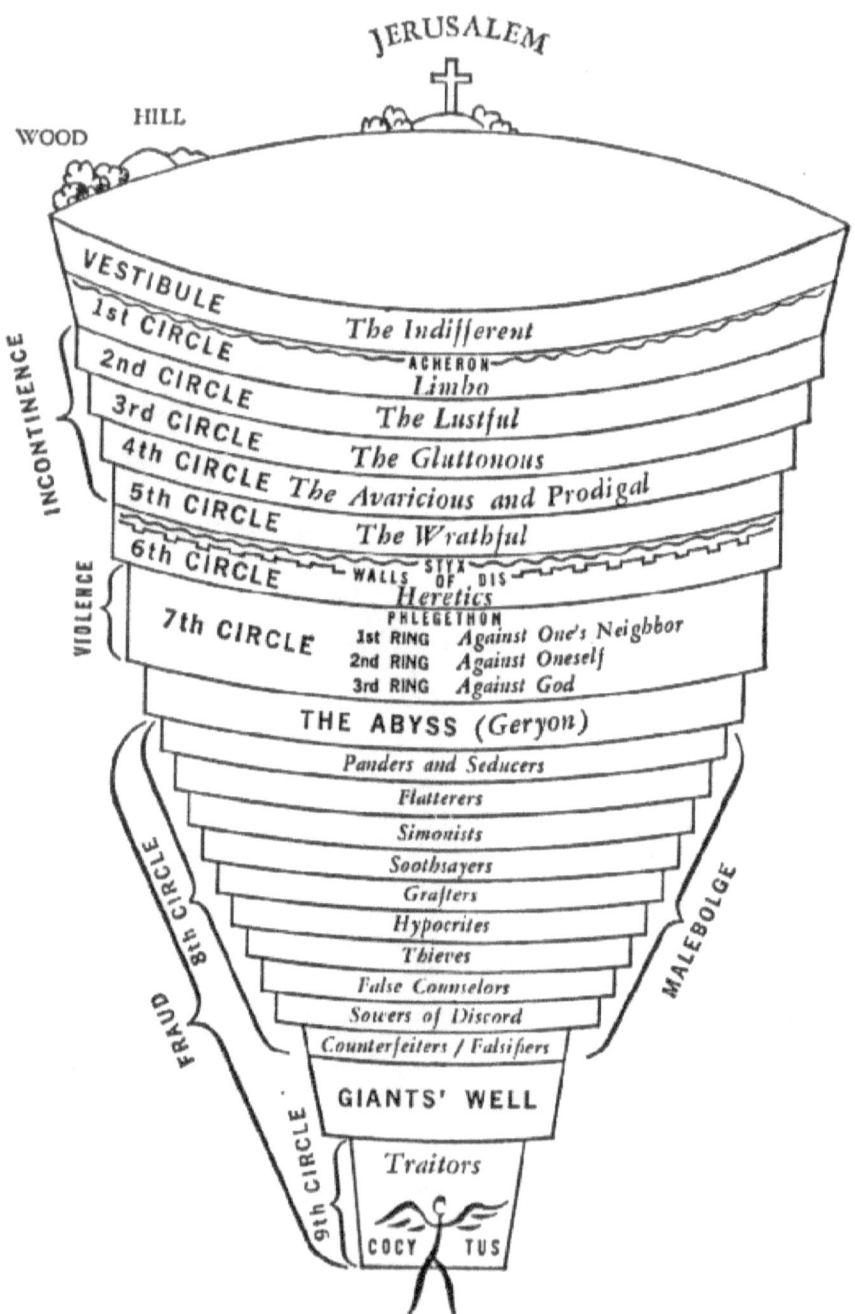

Map of Hell: Figurazione Generale dell'Inferno

THE *INFERNO*: CONFRONTING THE DRAGON

In the previous chapter, we saw how the threefold aspect of the *Divine Comedy* outwardly reflects the inner realms of human activity that must be transformed, if we are to fully realize our spiritual nature. We saw how the thinking sphere is represented by the *Inferno*; the feeling sphere by the *Purgatorio*; and the sphere of willing by the *Paradiso*. In addition, we analyzed the relationships that these three "realms" of activity have to the forms of sensory and suprasensory cognition necessary for their metamorphosis—forms personified by the figures of Virgil, Beatrice, and St. Bernard, respectively. Given this, we tried to show that the *Divine Comedy* can essentially be envisioned as a path of initiation into the spiritual worlds—a path whose transformation of these human activities was marked by the eventual attainment of three distinct stages of initiation, namely, *Imagination, Inspiration,* and *Intuition*. Nevertheless, many elements intrinsic to the whole of the poem demand a more detailed analysis of the intricate configuration of each realm through which Dante journeys. Only, then, can we better comprehend, among other things, the extent to which Dante in the *Inferno,* for example, tried to account for every conceivable transgression (or sin) as a measure by which to assess the degrees to which dialectical thinking can deviate us from the *act* of self-realization.

Upon reading the first canto of the *Inferno*, we are immediately made aware (even from its initial verses) that Dante is about to embark upon a journey into a world unknown. It is a world shrouded in darkness, for it *lacks* the *light* that streams from the Sun (Christ), which would illuminate the inner depths of his being, as well as the things around him. Dante does not just happen to wander into the "Dark Wood" at the age of thirty-five. Rather, at thirty-five, he *awakens* to the fact that somehow he *has strayed* from the right path. He is unable to explain *how,* and at what point, he became *lost*. These opening verses reveal that he has, for quite some time, led a life in error. The darkness that envelops Dante forces him to realize that he is without the *light* of God—the *light* that leads us to behold our divine nature, for the "Dark Wood" has obscured the rays of the Sun. Here, the "Dark Wood" represents the earthly forces that keep us bound to the sense world; it reflects the degree to which materialism takes hold of human consciousness. Dante's fall into darkness, though personal, represents the human condition. The nature of the realm in which he now finds himself—namely, materialized thinking—is so bitter that "scarcely more is death." Interestingly, Dante uses onomatopoeia to describe it:

> *Ahi quanto a dir qual era e' co*<u>*sa dura*</u>
> *questa selva selvaggia ed aspra e forte,*
>
> (What wood that was! I never saw so drear,
> So rank, so arduous a wilderness!)
> (Canto I, 4–5)

Note how the combination of the letters *s* and *g* (in Italian) draw the reader's attention to the snake-like *hissing* sounds that Dante evokes. This, of course, recalls the temptation of Adam and Eve in the "Garden of Eden," where they were confronted with a choice, namely, whether or not to eat the "forbidden" apple and thereby partake of the Tree of Knowledge. Their ability to *choose* symbolizes the birth of dialectical thought and, consequently, the beginning of humanity's separation from God. Likewise, it is this sense-based thinking (as evoked here by the serpent) through which we most directly relate to the outer world that has led Dante astray. Such thinking is devoid of *light,* devoid of the Christ force. It is lifeless, automatic, and mechanical; it lacks will. And in so being, it precludes us from comprehending just *how* it comes into existence, in the same way that Dante is unaware of how he finds himself in the "Dark Wood." Thus says Dante of the "Dark Wood"—i.e., the *state* in which he finds himself,

> How I came to it I cannot rightly say,
> so drugged and loose with sleep had I become
> when I first wandered there from the True Way.
> (Canto I, 10–12)

The darkness of the "Dark Wood," harboring the hidden light lost in thinking, naturally arouses *fear* in Dante. However, atop a little hill he witnesses the faint rays of the Sun that convey the possibility of hope.

> But at the far end of that valley of evil
> whose maze had sapped my very heart with fear!
> I found myself before a little hill
>
> and lifted my eyes. Its shoulders glowed
> already with the sweet rays of that planet
> whose virtue leads men straight on every road.
> (Canto I, 13–18)

Dante acknowledges his need of the Sun (Christ), for only its *light* can set him on the straight path. With this, his fear becomes "somewhat calmed." As Dante ponders his journey, he turns back to glimpse the "pass that none had ever left alive"—the pass leading into the depths of Hell. Here, the word *alive* refers specifically to a state of consciousness (or being), arising from the transcendence of death. It regards an initiatory experience, in which only by *dying* into Christ can we become *alive*. In order for this to happen, we must plummet the darkness and fathom the depths of Hell (material consciousness) during our earthly existence. All those individualities that Dante is about to encounter beyond this pass, failed to do so, and though they appear to be highly animated, they are effectively dead.

Dante Running from the Three Beasts, *William Blake*

As Dante struggles to reach the hill upon which he can better view the faint rays of the Sun, a leopard, a lion, and a she-wolf, accost him and prevent him from going back. These three beasts, symbolizing (among other things) worldly pleasure, ambition, and avarice respectively, represent, for Dante, the archetypal forms of egoism, which give birth to all sin. Each of these beasts represents a particular stage of transgression in the *Inferno* (thought) that must be overcome if he is to consciously tread the path leading to God. Dante has neither the courage nor strength (will) to confront these beasts and behold the faint *light* of the Sun upon the hill. And so, he is driven further away, "to where the Sun is silent." It is at this point that Virgil appears as his guide. He represents the glow of intellectuality and reason that can *initially* help Dante on his journey. However, as Virgil himself reveals, there shall appear, in due time, someone more capable of helping Dante further along his journey, for Virgil can lead him only so far.

Virgil speaks of the coming of the Greyhound, which many scholars (including Luigi Valli) believe symbolizes the imminent reign of the State, free from the corruption of the Church. With respect to Valli's elaboration of the Cross and Eagle, the greyhound ushers the

The Inferno: Confronting the Dragon

arrival of the Eagle, which as an instrument of Divine Justice, can overcome the injustices raging throughout the world. Valli reminds us that Virgil not only represents the intellect, but the Eagle as well, for he lived during the time of Augustus, when forces of benevolence had ruled Rome. And so, we have the Cross (Dante) as well as the Eagle (Virgil) penetrating the darkness of the underworld. Though this dual representation of Church and State pervades the whole of the *Divine Comedy*, it will be our intent and purpose to devote the bulk of our attention to the *process* of Dante's spiritual development, namely, Dante's initiation into the suprasensory world, which, symbolically portrayed, contains the key to the resolution of this duality.

Canto II signals the beginning of Hell. Lacking the *will* to face the challenges before him, Dante appeals to the Muses, which, as we have already seen, refer to the forces of memory at work within the human being—forces reflecting the activity of the Higher Self. Dante's lack of will, at this point, clearly shows how reflective thinking, by its will-less nature, can often inadvertently *un-will* what one has seemingly proposed for oneself.

> As one who un-wills what he willed, will stay
> strong purposes with feeble second thoughts
> until he spills all his first zeal away—
>
> so I hung back and bulked on that dim coast
> till thinking had worn out my enterprise
> so stout at starting and so early lost.
> (Canto II, 37–42)

Here, the word *un-will* does not denote a conscious act, but one that is a reflex born of fear. In fact, Virgil declares that Dante's soul is "sunken in...cowardice." Nevertheless, Virgil (reason) reassures Dante that he, Virgil himself, has been sent by Beatrice (*Divine Wisdom*) to help him find his way to her. Once, while in Limbo, Virgil had received a visit from Beatrice, to whom he asked,

> ...tell me how you dare to venture thus

> so far from the wide heaven of your joy
> to which your thoughts yearn back
> from the abyss. (Canto II, 82–84)

Here, Virgil seeks to know how she could *fearlessly* descend into the realm of the dead. She replies,

> ...Know then, O waiting and compassionate soul,
> that is to fear which has the power to harm,
> and nothing else is fearful even in Hell
>
> I am so made by God's all-seeing mercy
> your anguish does not touch me, and the flame
> of this great burning has no power upon me...
>   (Canto II, 88–93)

Beatrice reveals that earthly forces cannot affect the suprasensory nature of her being. In other words, it is not the material that works upon the spiritual, but *the spiritual that acts upon the material.* This is something that has not occurred to Virgil (reason). Having lived before Christ's entry into the world, his thinking, still imprisoned by the forces of darkness, is bereft of the *Light*. It will continue to be so until, of course, he, too, can one day be redeemed by the *reappearance* of the Christ. Interestingly, Dante did not perceive this encounter between Virgil and Beatrice. It is merely relayed to him, afterward. Had Dante perceived Beatrice and Virgil simultaneously, his excursion through the depths of Hell would have been unnecessary, for he would have beheld a thinking divorced from the influences of the material realm—namely, one that bears within it the *light* of the Christ. Instead, Dante merely draws our attention to the all-important fact that there exists a relationship between reflective thinking (Virgil) and sense-free thinking (Beatrice). This realization, in turn, enlivens him. It encourages him to face the obstacles before him and, thereby, proceed beyond the "vulgar crowd"—those who lack the key to spiritual redemption. Virgil tells Dante that Beatrice, herself, had been sent by St. Lucia at the request of the Virgin Mary. We are thus alerted to the fact that a principle aim of Dante's journey is to behold God

The Inferno: Confronting the Dragon

by way of the Virgin Sophia. To reach the heavenly spheres (Divine Will) would mark the reintegration of thinking and willing within Dante, namely, the feminine and masculine polarities of his being. The fact that scholars throughout the centuries have primarily been only concerned with the mere physical attributes of Beatrice reflects the degree to which modern consciousness has lost sight of the archetypal feminine (or the conscious feminine principle) intrinsic to the physical form. Says Massimo Scaligero in *Graal: Saggio sul Mistero del Sacro Amore*,

> Earthly woman continues to maintain an ancient relationship with the Moon: she is the holder of the connection, in as much as the transcendent principle, which in the Moon penetrates and governs lower matter, is present in her as a constitutional element of the soul, operating as far as the physical structure. *Such a structure, seen in its sense-based appearance, is illusory, but it is equally the symbol of that which the human soul had lost or forgotten; for this reason, when a man looks at a women he has the presentiment of having before him the being which can restore for him the lost spiritual world; by way of her figure, he feels blossoming the hope of resurrection of a level of beatitude and purity, of which his present existence is a deprivation.* (tr. and italics mine)[5]

And so, the words of Beatrice awaken greater *hope* in Dante. They enliven the forces of his will, which, in turn, will gradually become one with Virgil's. The second canto ends with Dante having set the forces of willing and thinking into motion. He says,

> ...Thy words have moved my heart to its first purpose.
> My Guide! My Lord! My Master! Now lead on:
> one *will* shall serve the two of us in this."
>
> He turned when I had spoken, and at his back
> I entered on that hard and perilous track.
> (Canto II, 133–137; italics mine)

Together, Virgil (Eagle) and Dante (Cross) begin their descent into the cone-shaped pit, where the manifestations of sin have been explicitly exaggerated or even, at times, caricatured. This descent proceeds to the left, or *sinistra* in Italian. It thus symbolizes the *sinister* path taken by humanity. Each character that Dante encounters embodies a particular aberration resulting from his or her fall into error. Thus, in this godforsaken realm of existence called Hell, which became manifest through our loss of the atavistic consciousness that once connected us to the divine world, each event or character is but an outer expression of an inner reality to which humanity has fallen prey. It is a world that threatens those who lack Christ consciousness, namely, the ability to penetrate into that sphere where the creative forces can be perceived. Thus, the *Inferno* depicts the realm of cause and effect; the action to which each character is subjected represents the *effect* that previously committed acts, born of ignorance, have had upon the soul. Unable to have perceived how the outer world is but a reflection of the creative forces imperceptible to them, the shades in Hell are consequently unable to counter the reaction that derives from their unconscious actions. In essence, *Dante's journey through the Inferno illustrates the realm of karma, where the light of the Sun—namely, the illuminating consciousness of Christ—has, thus far, failed to penetrate.*

Canto III opens with Dante and Virgil at the Gate of Hell, where the infamous words depicting the nature of what lies below are inscribed.

> I am the way into the city of woe.
> I am the way to a forsaken people.
> I am the way into eternal sorrow.
> (Canto III, 1–3)

This verse brings to mind the words uttered by Christ when he declared, "I am the Way. I am the Light. I am the Life. Through me is the way to the Kingdom of Heaven." The words inscribed before Dante are, of course, the antithesis of Christ's words, for those who do not seek Christ will be banished to a world of pain and anguish. However, it can also indicate the experience of confronting the outer configuration of one's karma, namely the Guardian of the Threshold, as later personified in the figure of Lucifer/Satan. Just as God created

The Inferno: Confronting the Dragon

Inscription over Hell-Gate, *William Blake*

Lucifer and Ahriman—who became "retarded beings"—the Guardian of the Threshold is but a manifestation of the creative forces working *unconsciously* within us. Thus, the inscription reads:

> Sacred justice moved my architect.
> I was raised here by Divine Omnipotence,

> Primordial love and ultimate intellect
> (Canto III, 4–6)

And so, the realm through which Dante ventures, was conceived by the eternal forces of creation and is, itself, eternal in nature:

> Only those elements time cannot wear
> Were made before me, and beyond time I stand.
> (Canto III, 7–8)

The realm of the *Inferno* must not be thought of as a "place" but, rather, as an aspect (or state) of consciousness, manifesting the materiality that we must penetrate and transform to eventually partake in the creative activity of our Maker. Those who fail to acknowledge this are told:

> Abandon all hope ye who enter here. (Canto III, 9)

Although Dante finds the inscription somewhat enigmatic, Virgil tells him that all distrust and cowardice must be overcome, for all the shades that Dante is about to perceive are essentially the expressions of a misguided intellect.

> ...Here you shall pass among the fallen people,
> *souls who have lost the good of intellect.*
> (Canto III, 17–18; italics mine)

The first group of shades Dante encounters is comprised of the uncommitted—those who refused to take a stand in life. Pursued by a swarm of hornets and stung into the act of movement, they endlessly and futilely chase an unmarked banner (rag), which reflects their lack of allegiance toward a noble cause. Since they refused to commit their sweat and blood to a noble ideal, the sweat and blood that now issue forth from the stings inflicted upon them, fall to the worms. Here, Dante makes obvious the fact that our lives must have purpose. *We must activate our **will** by dedicating ourselves to some noble ideal in life.* Those who fail to do so, not only abstain from contributing to the betterment of society, but they feed the blindness of those who are entrenched within earthly realm (worms). Though their lack of will results in painful stings meant to incite them to act, such actions do not arise from within and can, thus, never result in the realization of their true being. Since these uncommitted have utilized their thinking to abstain from actively participating in society, they occupy the vestibule *outside* of Hell proper—namely, the realm where all activity is intentional. Theirs is a realm neither here nor there, so to speak.

Soon after, Dante and Virgil find themselves by the banks of the Acheron where the boatman, Charon, takes the *dead* across to the other side. Charon tells Dante,

> ...And you who are *living yet, I say begone from these who are dead.*
> (Canto III, 85–86; italics mine)

Though he seems to notice that Dante is alive physically, he fails to acknowledge that Dante is also *alive* to the sacred knowledge that will get him through the very depths of Hell. Lacking the heaviness characteristic of death, Dante hears Charon utter,

> By other windings and other steerage
> shall you cross to that other shore. Not here! Not here!
> A lighter craft than mine must give you passage.
> (Canto III, 88–90)

Nonetheless, Virgil (reason) induces Charon to carry him across by telling him

> ...Charon, bite back your spleen:
> this has been *willed* where what is *willed* must be,
> and is not yours to ask what it may mean.
> (Canto III, 91–93; italics mine)

Here, again, we witness how the force of reason (Virgil) incites the will into action when Dante's path is impeded. And so, Charon agrees to guide them to the bank across the river, where assembled are those who do not fear God but, rather, hurl blasphemies at Him.

Divine Justice has cast them to the other side, within whose depths dwells Satan. There, they must learn to experience fear, which arises from the absence of God's grace. Only then can they begin to cultivate the desire to seek their Maker. The canto closes with Dante swooning after being startled by a terrifying earthquake. This episode calls to mind the death of Christ, when the Earth erupted as the body of Jesus was buried within it. Just as that eruption signaled the beginning of the Christ's resurrection, this quake signals the point in which Dante is about to begin the process of resurrecting his thinking from materiality.

In Canto IV, Dante awakens, at the edge of an abyss, to the deafening thunder of the sinners wailing below. The awful noise he hears represents the fragmentation of the "harmony of the spheres," which he will later encounter in all its glory upon initiating his journey into Paradise.

Now, gazing into the depths below, he sees, for the first and only time, the layout of Hell in its entirety. However, what he sees is "depthless deep and nebulous and dim." The light and music of the Heavens is transfigured into chaotic darkness, which seems to depict the state of an undisciplined mind that, divorced from the will, reechoes the confusion of voices surfacing haphazardly from its inner depths. This "blind world" lacks the light of the "I," or Higher Self.

As Dante and Virgil proceed, they come upon a dim light, glowing softly against the darkness. Therein sits a castle surrounded by seven walls, each containing a gate. This castle is populated by the great souls of antiquity, and so its seven walls have been thought to symbolize either the seven ancient virtues—i.e., prudence, justice, fortitude, temperance, the intellect, science and wisdom, or as Valli believes, the seven liberal arts. As they draw closer, Dante notices Virgil has changed expression and mistakes his pity for fear. Virgil reassures him by pointing out that they have come upon a place called Limbo, where the "unbaptized"—which include Virgil—reside. Here, no cries can be heard, only sighs. Though there are many good and noble souls amongst them, they had once sought understanding by the dim light of the intellect. Most had lived on Earth before the Christ and, therefore, were precluded from the possibility of a "Christian" baptism. And so many of them represent the old stream—namely, baptism by water, which ended with Christ's entry into the world. Since the coming of Christ, only those baptized by *fire* (Holy Spirit) could enter the Kingdom of Heaven. Thus, Dante beholds the many lost souls whose birth, Virgil says, fell

> ...before the age of the Christian mysteries
> and so they did not worship God's Trinity
> in the fullest duty. I am one of these.
>
> For such defects we are lost, though spared the fire
> and suffering Hell in one affliction only:
> that without hope we live on in desire.
> (Canto IV, 37–42)

Although there are many great luminaries among them, these souls, lacking the possibility of Christ consciousness, are depicted as yearning eternally for God. Among them, Dante spots Plato, Socrates, Cicero, Seneca, and "the one who knew" (Aristotle). These men are distinguished *merely* by the fact that they are set apart physically from the rest. This trivial mark of distinction reflects the feeble "glory" that thinking devoid of Christ's *light* is able to attain. Dante asks Virgil if anyone had ever left this realm to live among the blessed and is told that when Christ had descended into the Earth, He took with Him some of the ancient Patriarchs who believed in His coming. Thus, this episode may serve as an admonishment to those who seek an initiation into the spiritual worlds by returning to pre-Christian ways, for without the Christ, one can never hope for salvation.

The four circles immediately succeeding Limbo comprise transgressions of incontinence—namely, lust, gluttony, avarice and wrath. This upper realm of Hell embodies those actions that are not willfully executed, but that arise spontaneously (or unconsciously) out of one's lower self. Here, *thought lacks the will* by which the "I" can transform desire. Since these transgressions are not premeditated, the transgressors are physically further removed from the center of Hell where Satan dwells. And so, they find greater hope of redemption upon Christ's return. In fact, Dante seems to elucidate the dual nature of evil by the way in which Hell is divided. Those individuals, whose actions are influenced by luciferic impulses, find themselves further removed from the "mechanical beast" that rules from the depths below. Their actions are more redeemable than those whose actions were based on a *thinking that was willfully erroneous*—namely, the *cold* misguided intellect that can be described as ahrimanic. Those latter souls exhibiting such actions are more deeply entangled within the web of karma and are thus in closer proximity to the so-called Lord of Death at the pit of Hell—the material world.

As Dante and Virgil descend into the circle of the Lustful, they encounter Minos who—depicted as having a snake-like tail—symbolizes our inability to free ourselves from our unbridled animal nature. The son of Europa and of Zeus, Minos became the "mythological King of Crete and was so recognized for his wisdom and sense of justice that after his death he was made to judge the fate of the dead. Therefore, just as an Angel on Purgatory holds the keys of Peter while overseeing the entrance to its Gate, Minos is the "Guardian of Hell," who, upon hearing the sinners' confessions, ascribes a place for them below. As with Charon, Dante is initially refused entrance into the lower realms by Minos, until Virgil (reason) once again comes to his aid, declaring:

> …it is his fate to enter every door.
> This has been willed where what is willed must be,
> and is not yours to question. Say no more.
> (Canto V, 22–24)

Thus, the will once again rightfully asserts itself as the intellect seeks to penetrate the depths of Hell (materiality). In this circle, Dante says,

> I came to a place stripped bare of every light
> and roaring on the naked dark like seas
> wracked by a war of winds...
> (Canto V, 28–30)

These winds serve to illustrate the "law of retribution." Because these shades sacrificed their intellects to their carnal desires, they are themselves buffeted by the "winds of passion." Without having cultivated a will of their own, they have succumbed to the will of their instincts. Their thinking is fully overcome by the luciferic impulses working through them. Dante sees, among the sinful, two earthly lovers with whom he wishes to speak. They are Francesca and Paolo, whose story is among the most touching of those in the *Inferno*. Dante wants them to recount their tragic fate. As the winds die down momentarily, Francesca relates their misfortune, evoking the word *love* three times.

> "...*Love*, which in the gentlest hearts will soonest bloom,
> seized my lover with passion for that sweet body
> from which I was torn unshriven to my doom.
>
> *Love*, which permits no loved one not to love
> took me so strongly with delight in him,
> that we are as one in Hell, as we were above.
>
> *Love* led us to one death. In the depths of Hell
> Caina waits for him who took our lives."
> This was the piteous tale they stopped to tell.
> (Canto V, 97–105; italics mine)

This declaration, recalling the tradition of courtly love, reflects only its earthly aspect. For as Francesca, herself, tells Dante, it was while reading the story of Lancelot that she and Paolo were overcome by the rapture of love and immediately discovered by her husband, Giovanni, the brother of Paolo, who killed them before they could repent. What is of significance here is that they succumb to their instincts while engrossed in a story that relates the higher aspect of love. For like the *Divine Comedy*, the tales concerning the tradition of King Arthur, have both an inner and outer meaning. Dante seems to provide a clue to resolving the mystery behind his own work for those with a keen sense of what can lie hidden within such a work of art, and that is that the reader of his *Comedy* should not be led astray by the mere physicality of Beatrice's being. Those who use the *Divine Comedy* as a model for earthly love will potentially suffer the same delusion as Francesca and Paolo. Upon hearing Francesca's account, Dante is overcome with pity and faints, "as a corpse might fall."

Dante again awakens to find himself in another circle—that of the Gluttonous, who lie in the mud, which they are forced to eat in all its filth, as a hard rain falls upon them. All the while, they are watched over by Cerberus, the three-headed dog whose master was Pluto, king of the Underworld, known earlier as Hades. Cerberus denies Dante and Virgil passage. His voraciousness aptly depicts the gluttonous nature of those who comprise this circle. Again, Virgil resolves the problem, by throwing dirt in each of its mouths, thus allowing him time to usher Dante safely into the circle. Like the Lustful, the Gluttonous were unable to cultivate the will by which to empower the intellectual forces, so as to overcome the influences of their desire body. The Gluttonous, however, differ from the Lustful, in that their actions benefit only themselves, whereas the Lustful normally commit their transgressions mutually. Thus, gluttony is more self-centered, more egoistic, and so it reflects a greater hardening of egoic consciousness. As Dante looks about, he notices a soul sitting up. Looking closely, he recognizes him as Ciacco (Hog), of whom little is known. Ciacco relates to him the future state of Florence.

Having finished his declaration, with Dante about to descend into the next circle, Ciacco asks,

> ...But when you move again among the living,
> oh speak my name to the memory of men!
> Having answered all I say no more.
> (Canto VI, 85–87)

The Inferno: Confronting the Dragon

The need for the dead to be remembered by the living is something that the sinners of greater crimes in the lowest depths below manifest to an ever-lesser degree, for, again, only those sinners within the sphere of luciferic influences have a greater possibility of redemption.

The next canto opens with one of the most incomprehensible utterances in the *Divine Comedy*.

> Papa Satan , Papa Satan, aleppy
> (Canto VII, 1)

Nonetheless, upon closer inspection, the meaninglessness of these words by the wolf-like Plautus, the ancient god of riches, alludes to the incomprehensible nature of our relationship to materiality, for this is the circle of the Spendthrifts and the Prodigals. Like the Lustful and the Gluttonous, they, too, sacrificed their intellect by submitting it to the ravaging nature of desire. Unlike the Gluttonous, however, their desire centered not on objects created by God, rather, on those created by human beings. Material wealth—i.e., objects devoid of life, to which only humanity ascribes value—had become the focus of their aspirations. And so, the obsession with hoarding, namely, the insatiable desire to have materiality all for oneself, manifests tendencies that are tinged with ahrimanic influences. This relegates them to an even lower circle.

Plutus, like Charon and Minos, forbids Dante and Virgil passage. As before, Virgil declares that the continuance of Dante's journey *has been willed* from beyond. Suddenly, Plutus, the god of wealth, inflates himself and falls limply to the ground. The message here is clear. Material riches lend themselves to a false sense of power and self-aggrandizement. The powerlessness of Plutus in Dante's presence marks a subtle transformation in Dante. His will has been strengthened. He demonstrates greater fortitude. No longer is he *so* beset by fear. Thus, as Dante penetrates evermore into the darkness of Hell, so too does he gradually cultivate for *himself* the will that the divine forces transmit through Virgil (intellect), which, in turn, allows him to mitigate the effects of the shades before him.

The Avaricious and the Prodigal, depicted as heaving weights against each other while shouting "why do you hoard," "why do you waste," are largely comprised of the clergy—priest, cardinals, and popes. It is upon their souls that the blasphemous curses of Plutus fall, for they have abused the "office" of Christ by mistaking material goods for spiritual wealth. Says Virgil,

> ...Not all the gold that is or ever was
> under the sky could buy for one of these
> exhausted souls the fraction of a pause.
> (Canto VII, 64–66)

They failed to understand how the wheel of Divine Fortune (Providence) brings to light the words of Job: "The Lord gave, and the Lord hath taken away. May the name of the Lord be praised." Thus, it is God who has power over earthly things, not human beings:

> ...The king whose perfect wisdom transcends all,
> made the heavens and posted angels on them
> to guide the eternal light that it might fall
>
> from every sphere to every sphere the same.
> He made earth's splendors by a like decree
> and posted as a minister this high Dame,
>
> the Lady of Permutations. All earth's gear
> she changes from nation to nation, from house to house,
> in changeless change though every turning year.
>
> No mortal power may stay her spinning wheel.
> The nations rise and fall by her decree.
> None may foresee where she will set her heel...
> (Canto VII, 73–84)

Here, Dante speaks of an important figure in medieval mythology, namely, the Lady Fortune—a female figure that holds a wheel which is continually turning and which symbolizes "chance." Though Lady Fortune has been thought to be somehow connected to God's Will, by mentioning her here in Hell, Dante seems to intimate that "chance" *often* appears to fall outside the visibly conscious intent of Divine Will, pointing implicitly, instead, to the seemingly indiscriminate nature of the karma that often arises from our lack of personal will. Thus, Lady Fortune often administers nothing other than that which we have created for ourselves, without us knowing.

Soon after Virgil's explanation of Fortune, they come upon the Styx, known in classical mythology as the River of Hate. This river borders the City of Dis, which serves to separate the upper realms of Hell from the lower ones. Dis marks the spot where humanity's actions begin to reflect the *willful misuse of the intellect*—a misuse still grounded in the somewhat unconscious realm of feelings. The Wrathful lie in the River Styx. Lacking the will to assert their intellectual forces, they are manipulated by their feelings while they haphazardly strike each other. A second group, whose hate is more sullen, lies at the bottom of the murky river and is seen emitting bubbles to the surface.

The Wrathful are found in the lowest circle of incontinence, for their acts of transgression harbor *the capacity to harm others*. Thus, Dante arrives at the point of perceiving, more visibly, how one's self-centered fallen nature can inextricably have an effect on the destiny of others.

The waters of original sin (Acheron) have been tainted by the impurities of incontinence. Phlegyas now leads Dante and Virgil across these new waters of the river Styx. As they board the boat, Dante's weight causes it to sink more than normal, cutting into those souls who suffer below in the water. This prompts one of them, Filippo Argenti, to rise and shout out:

> Who are you that come here *before* your time?
> (Canto VIII, 33; italics mine)

This utterance provides another clue intimating the true nature of Dante's journey. For, usually, it is only the dead who venture into the "land of the dead." Though Argenti perceives Dante as being *alive*, Phlegyas erroneously thinks that he is among the departed shades, when he asks.

> So, do I have you at last, you whelp of Hell?
> (Canto VIII, 18)

Unlike Filippo Argenti who identifies Dante, Phlegyas does not know him. Upon recognizing Argenti, Dante curses him for his political undertakings. Argenti was part of the Adimari family, bitter enemies of Dante, who took possession of his belongings when he was exiled, and continually opposed the White Guelfs' return to Florence after they had been cast out. His outrage marks the first time during his journey that Dante firmly asserts himself. He has begun to develop a new attitude toward the damned. His indignation manifests in this Circle of Wrath, as he openly contests the adversarial forces confronting him. We must, therefore, not view his anger as an expression of evil, but one of courage and self-determination. This episode recalls the anger of Christ toward the moneylenders in the Temple, for just as Divine Justice plays a part in God's plan so, too, does Divine Punishment. Virgil voices his approval of Dante's actions,

> ...Then he embraced me saying:
> "Indignant spirit, I kiss you as you frown.
>
> Blessed be she who bore you..."
> (Canto VIII, 41–43)

According to Wallace Fowlie in his book, *A Reading of Dante's Inferno*, these last words bring to mind those "associated with the conception of Christ when Mary felt the stirring of the child within her."[6] They highlight the diminishing fear in Dante, which will eventually give rise to the initial stirring of the immanent *birth* of the force of Christ within him. And so, Virgil (Reason) catches sight of the burgeoning will in Dante, which shall eventually lead him to behold the cosmic creative activity of God.

Having crossed to the other shore, thousands of spirits bear witness to the fact that Dante is *alive* in the realm of the dead (materiality), thus indicating that he has embarked on *an initiatory experience*.

The Inferno: Confronting the Dragon

> ...Who is it that invades
> Death's Kingdom in his *life*?
> (Canto VIII, 81–82; italics mine)

Upon hearing the words of the fallen spirits, Virgil motions to them, indicating that he wishes to speak with them, to which they cry out:

> ...Come,
> but come alone. And tell that other one,
> who thought to walk so blithely through death's kingdom,
>
> he may go back along the same fool's way
> he came back by. Let him try his living luck.
> You who are dead can come only to stay.
> (Canto VIII, 85–90)

Here, the forces of reason, which have guided Dante until now, seem to be *abandoning* him, as Virgil attends to the unfettered adversarial impulses streaming in beyond Dante's control. This momentary abandonment of reason (Virgil) frightens Dante, as he feels the impact of these beings that seek to impede his passage:

> Reader, judge for yourself, how each black word
> fell on my ears to sink into my heart:
> I lost hope of returning to the world.
> (Canto VIII, 91–93)

Stranded between hope and fear, Dante begins to question whether or not he has the strength to carry on with his journey; whether or not he possesses the strength and the courage to will his thinking so as to penetrate evermore deeply into the realm of darkness.

> So the sweet Guide and Father leaves me here,
> and I stay on in doubt with yes and no
> dividing all my heart to hope and fear.
> (Canto VIII, 106–108)

This scene marks the first time since straying into the "Dark Wood" that Dante finds himself alone, left *momentarily* to his own devises. It is the first time in which he is able to reflect upon his own condition. Unwilling to succumb to fear, he holds firm and awaits the guidance of Virgil (reason) whose boldness versus the Wrathful reassures him. This scene calls to mind Christ overcoming temptation in the Garden of Gethsemane. Virgil comforts him,

> ... You need not be cast down
> by my vexation, for whatever plot
> these fiends may lay against us, we will go on.
>
> This insolence of theirs is nothing new:
> they showed it once at a less secret gate
> that still stands open for all that they could do...
> (Canto VIII, 118–123)

As they continue onward, Virgil foretells the coming of an angel who will open the Gates of Dis, where demons stand in wait.

The City of Dis, separated from The Circle of Wrath by the River Styx, is the metropolis of Satan (Ahriman) where fire torments the damned. The Wrathful serve as a prelude to the more heinous crimes beyond the city's gate. Whereas Filippo Argenti and others within his circle illustrate the incendiary, explosive nature of Wrath, theirs is a wrath that bursts uncontrollably from within. It is not premeditated. The intellect is not willfully misused to incite the feeling life for the attainment of wrongful ends. Up to the moment of their arrival at the Gate of Dis, each transgression or sin encountered by Dante and Virgil has fallen under the influence of the luciferic forces. From now on, the *willful* misuse of the intellect that they are soon to encounter will fall under the domain of Satan (Ahriman), for the misuse of that creative spark within their thinking, granted to them by God, *against* God, nature, and their fellow human being represents an inversion of Divine Will. *Thus, the City of Dis can be envisioned as the boundary between the influences of Ahriman and the more redeemable influences of Lucifer.* (Incidentally, this city [*bolgia*] of fire, demarcating the realm of Ahriman at the sixth circle, is in contradistinction to the

The Inferno: Confronting the Dragon

Empyrean (*Ring* of Fire) in Paradise, which will later signal Dante's entry into the "I" of God.)

Canto IX opens with Virgil a bit shaken from his encounter with the fallen spirits. However, he soon recovers and assures Dante that he is familiar with what lies within the depths of Hell, for he had once been sent down to its lowest circles to retrieve a spirit. If we consider the *Inferno* as the thinking sphere, then this account by Virgil attests to the degree of familiarity that the intellect (Virgil) can have with the boundaries of its dialectical limitations. This, in turn, would explain Virgil's incapacity to lead Dante far beyond the sphere of Satan (materiality) without the guidance of Divine Will.

Before long, three Furies—Alecto, Tisiphone, and Megaera—accost them. They threaten Dante with the head of Medusa. Virgil covers Dante's eyes so that he does not behold the frightful sight. At this point, Dante implores the reader to look beneath the surface of his words, so as to understand the *secret message* contained therein.

> *Men of sound intellect and probity,*
> *weigh with good understanding what lies hidden*
> *behind the veil of my strange allegory!*
> (Canto IX, 58–60; italics mine)

Here, we find the most *explicit* instance of how Dante's *Comedy* was, in fact, intended for those able to understand its secret meaning, and how he used subtle allusions to divert the attention of the *gente grossa*, while guiding those with "sound intellects"—namely, those privy to sacred knowledge—to the proper meaning intended. If we recall, Perseus cut off the head of Medusa, upon gazing at her *reflection* in his shield. The severed head of Medusa could be thought to symbolize the separation of thinking from the forces of the heart and the will. So it stands to reason that if Dante merely observes the reflective nature of his thinking symbolized by the head of Medusa, then his journey toward the living aspect of his thinking (*Divine Wisdom/Beatrice*) would be denied him.

> Turn your back and keep your eyes shut tight;
> for should the Gorgon come and you look at her,
> never again should you return to the *light*.
>   (Canto IX, 52–54; italics mine)

At this point there descends an indignant angel, who frightens away all the sinners, and with the touch of its wand, opens the gates of Dis, declaring,

> ...Why do you set yourselves against that Throne
> whose Will none can deny, and which, times past,
> has added to your pain for each rebellion?..."
>   (Canto IX, 91–93)

This angel symbolizes the grace of God that comes to aid human beings in times of difficulty. He opens the way for Dante to enter ever deeper into the realm of darkness so as to experience, to an ever-greater degree, the nature of sin and, therefore, his estrangement from the *light* of thinking.

As Dante and Virgil proceed, they come across tombs all ablaze. Within them lie heretics. Situated in the sixth circle between the incontinent and the violent, these tombs contain those who display the prideful (or arrogant) nature of the intellect—a state of being rather than a deliberate or non-deliberate act of transgression. These open fiery tombs, which are not to be closed again until the Last Judgment, are largely comprised of Epicureans, who made

> the soul share in the body's death.
>   (Canto X, 15)

Since these so-called heretics denied the immortality of the soul, their own bodies will be made to suffer in the sepulchers that they, themselves, have fashioned through their beliefs. These "followers of Epicurus" have, through their adherence to the laws of intellectuality, imprisoned themselves in the tomb of their own ideas. Suddenly, a spirit of immense stature rises up out of the fire and startles Dante. It is Farinata, who having died the year before Dante's birth was politically opposed to Dante's party (Guelfs) in Florence. Though his Ghibelline party defeated the Guelfs, Farinata saved Florence from total destruction, and is, thus, attributed a degree of distinction. Farinata and Dante converse on the political situation of Florence, when, out from Farinata's tomb, appears Cavalcante dei Cavalcanti, the father of Dante's dearest friend, Guido Cavalcanti. Cavalcante is desperate to know something about the fate of his son:

> And if... you travel through
> this dungeon of the blind by power of genius,
> where is my son? Is he not with you?
> (Canto X, 58–60)

Here lies yet another hidden reference for those who are *keen* to the aim of Dante's work, for as we said before, Guido Cavalcanti was, for a time, the leader of the *Fedeli d'amore*. Though he partook of the secret knowledge that they possessed, Guido, as the son of the Epicurean Calvalcante, often displayed skepticism, for which he was not, according to Valli, considered a *truly* committed believer in the "virtue of the Cross." Because of this, he is unable to "die into Christ" and thereby tread the path of the *living*. Since his father does not see him with Dante, he wonders whether his son is still living on Earth:

> Instantly he rose to his full height:
> "He *held*? What is it you say? Is he *dead*, then?
> Do *his eyes no longer fill with that sweet light*?"
> (Canto X, 67–69; italics mine)

These words uttered by Cavalcante can be seen harboring two meanings, one exoteric (alluding to the earthly condition of Cavalcante's son) and the other esoteric, in reference to the *light* of knowledge hidden in the *sweet* verses of the *Fedeli d'amore*. Again, only those possessing this knowledge and *convinced* of its transformative power through experience were regarded as *living*. Cavalvante seems unaware of this. Dante, considering Guido as not yet among the living (metaphysically), fails to understand what Cavalcante specifically desires to know and, as a result, gives him no indication that his son is alive, physically or spiritually. Without further ado, Cavalcante falls back into the tomb and the passage is quickly given over again to Farinata, who resumes his argument and predicts the Ghibellines' return to power.

Noticing that these souls have the power of looking into the past and future, Dante, in turn, asks him why they cannot perceive the events of the present. Farinata replies that God only grants them the light by which to see far-off events. They are blind to what is close at hand.

> "We see asquint, like those whose twisted sight
> can make out only the far-off, " he said,
> "for the King of All still grants us that much light.
>
> When things draw near, or happen, we perceive
> nothing of them. Except what others bring us
> we have no news of those who are *alive*..."
> (Canto X, 100–105; italics mine)

This circle is thus comprised of those whose thinking projects itself into the future. They fail to develop what is most immediate to them in their pursuit of knowledge, namely, thinking rooted in the present. They not only misuse the intellect, but cannot, in any way, recognize its intrinsic value as an instrument to help them realize their spiritual nature. They cannot progress into the future. Instead, they are eternally enclosed within their fiery *tombs*. Therefore, those who adhere only to a speculative intellect see things "imperfectly." This being the case, Farinata says,

> ...So that you may understand that all we know
> will be dead forever from that day and hour
> when the Portal of the Future is swung to.
> (Canto X, 106–108)

Having realized that he had misinterpreted Cavalcante's question, Dante bids Farinata to tell Cavalcante that his son, Guido, is amongst the "living" (in the physical sense, though he was to die soon after) and that before, he could not answer Cavalcante because his own thinking had failed him. It lacked the vision to which Farinata referred:

> Then, as if stricken by regret, I said:
> "Now, therefore, will you tell that fallen one
> who asked about his son, that he is not dead,
>
> and that, if I did not reply more quickly,
> it was because my mind was occupied
> with this confusion you have solved for me."
> (Canto X, 109-114)

Dante continues his journey with Virgil, bewildered at having discovered that Frederick II, initiator of "Il Dolce Stile Novo" was amongst the Epicureans, who indulged in sensual delights. Virgil reminds Dante that though he should "let thy memory retain" what he has undergone, not until he attains *Divine Wisdom* will he begin to fathom his experience. In other words, unlike Frederick II who delighted in the sensual nature of his intellect, Dante should push forward until he beholds the "sweet ray" of *light* (living thinking) radiating from the eyes of Beatrice.

> ...when finally you stand before the ray
> of that Sweet Lady whose bright eye sees all,
> from her you will learn the turnings of your way.
> (Canto X, 130-132)

From here, Dante and his faithful guide cross the sixth circle and come upon a rocky cliff that separates them from the circles below. Beset by a wretched stench that issues profusely from the tomb of Pope Anastasius, they rest there to accustom themselves to the foul odor. This, the eleventh canto, serves to expound upon the structure of Hell. Virgil explains, that within the walls of Dis, there exist three primary circles in which the "accurst" are placed, corresponding to the violent (lion), the fraudulent (leopard) and the traitor (she-wolf), respectively. However, the last two circles are more or less grouped together, insofar as they are both manifestations of a more consciously premeditated malice. *They comprise the lowest reaches of Hell, for they reflect the deliberate misuse of the intellect for reasons of personal gain.* The traitors that do harm to country, kindred, and God, lie in close proximity to Satan. The fraudulent are situated one circle above them. They exercised malice, individually, against their fellow human beings. Both of these forms of malice, employing intellectual forces as an instrument to harm others, are placed beneath the violent, whose misuse of the intellect arises spontaneously through ignorance. In other words, unpremeditated violence is reflective of bestiality and, thus, does not so clearly manifest the influences of the ahrimanic forces. Dante asks why the transgressors of incontinence above are not within the circle of Dis. Virgil promptly reminds him of what Aristotle had written in his *Ethics,* where it said that, of the three transgressions, incontinence "offends God less." It does so because it is neither premeditated nor fraught with beast-like violence, but merely reflects the lack of will within thinking. Thus, the *Inferno* (the thinking sphere) is divided into three main sections, each of which reflects a particular aspect of humanity's threefold activity. In essence, we have:

The *Inferno* (thinking sphere)	Incontinence (she-wolf): the impotence of the willing forces
	Violence (lion): lack of control of the emotional forces
	Fraud (leopard): malicious misuse of the intellect

We shall later see this "threefold" aspect repeated in reverse order in Purgatory.

Dante then questions Virgil on the nature of usury. His Master replies that just as nature proceeds from God so does art proceed from nature. Thus, art is referred to as the "grandchild" of God. We were meant to use both nature and art (labor) as means by which to sustain ourselves. Whoever fails to do so, disobeys the will of God.

The usurer, who profits from the interest that he demands in addition to the money owed him, disavows the saying in Genesis, "By the sweat of your brow you will eat your food."

Dante and Virgil descend the steep slopes leading into the seventh circle. There they meet the Minotaur who embodies half man and half bull. This beast symbolizes violence born of bestiality, in which the human being is ravaged by the raging nature of the astral body. The Minotaur's bloodthirsty disposition makes him the most fitting guardian over those who, during their earthly lives, committed acts of violence. Upon their arrival at the cleft in the rocks, Dante and Virgil appear threatened by this ominous figure looming before them. However, like before, Virgil proclaims that Dante's passage is directed from beyond the influence of the realm in which they find themselves and teases him with an allusion to Theseus, who killed him in the labyrinth where he lived on the island of Crete. Here, the labyrinth represents the intricacies of the human mind from which Theseus had to liberate himself, while pursued by the raging Minotaur. Virgil provokes the bull into an uncontrollable fit, thus enabling Dante and him to pass safely. With respect to Dante's journey, this symbolizes the control that Dante begins to exercise over his intellect, to temper the surges of emotionality that often manifest in acts of violence. In other words, he has *initiated* the process of transforming his emotions by way of willed thinking. The violence of this circle is differentiated from that of the Wrathful, in that, here, it results in well orchestrated acts of destruction.

Virgil now directs Dante's attention to the river of boiling blood (Phlegethon) that flows before them. There, sinners who were violent against their neighbors are immersed, as if in the very blood that boiled in their veins on Earth. Centaurs (half man/half horse), known for their violent eruptions, guard over them. Virgil wishes to speak with Chiron, who, being the most refined amongst them, once showed a predilection for such things as music and medicine. Chiron notices that Dante is *alive*. In confirming this, Virgil, again declares that Dante's journey has been willed from above.

> It is true he *lives*; in his necessity
> I alone must lead him through this valley.
> Fate brings him here, not curiosity...
> (Canto XII, 85–87; italics mine)

He then asks Chiron for the use of one of his Centaurs, so that they may easily find their way into the next circle. This is an interesting development, for it marks the first time Virgil, himself, asks to be guided. We are, thus, led to believe that Dante, by way of Virgil (intellect), is able to begin transforming the impulses of the emotional bestiality within him to fathom even greater atrocities that lie ahead. Dante describes his momentary guide, Nessus, himself a Centaur, as one with whom he can feel safe.

> ...So we moved beside our guide
> along the bank of the scalding purple river
> in which the shrieking wraiths were boiled and dyed.
> (Canto XII, 100–102)

Each of the sinners that they perceive is covered in blood. This blood reflects the degree in which they had once displayed their violent nature on Earth. Soon, Dante and Virgil are escorted to the opposite bank of the first round by Nessus who then turns back across the ford on his own. *Here,* Dante/Cross and Virgil/Eagle ride together on the back of a Centaur, which, interestingly, brings to mind *the Seal of the Knights Templar, in which two Templar knights are seen riding together on the back of a horse—a subtle allusion to Dante's affiliation with the Order.*

Canto XIII takes place in the second ring of the circle of violence. There, Dante and Virgil come upon a dismal wood made up of thorn trees in which the souls of those who had committed suicide during their previous life are confined. Since they denied the bodies given them by God, they are deprived of human form. Never again shall they wear their bodies like other souls after the "Last Judgment." Instead, they shall find them hanging upon the trees that envelop them. Of this wood, Dante says,

> Its foliage was not verdant, but nearly black.
> The unhealthy branches, gnarled and warped and tangled,
> bore poison thorns instead of fruit...
> (Canto XIII, 4–6)

And so, these knotted, contorted, lifeless trees yield no fruit for humanity, only pain. They effectively represent the *twisted* or convoluted thinking often conducive to suicide. Though suicide may have been considered a virtue among many pre-Christian societies, Christ taught that freedom is to be found within the human being. ("The Kingdom of Heaven is within.") Thus, the act of suicide not only violated human life (as in the previous circle), but also the *principle* of freedom *living* within human thinking, namely, *that* for which Christ descended to Earth and suffered death. It is a deeper crime than those committed out of a fit of rage against one's neighbors, for, typically, it is not as impulsive or reactionary. Whereas the murder of one's neighbor more often than not arises spontaneously from the untransformed emotional impulses (due to the absence of willed thinking), suicide is most often intentionally willed. One emotionally wills one's thinking against oneself. Thus, in the act of suicide, thinking is forced to work against itself. It is interesting that Dante should place this circle immediately after the one presided over by the Minotaur, for the latter, which recalls the myth of Theseus and the labyrinth (representing the complex nature of the mind), seems to presage those crimes that result from our inability to find our way out of the many folds that enclose us within our thinking. If the Minotaur is to represent violence born of emotionality, then the act of Theseus being chased by the bull is, in effect, a visual characterization of those whose thinking is driven to despair by unchecked emotional forces beyond their control. Dante seems to depict the complexity of this thinking when he says,

> I think perhaps he thought that I was thinking
> those cries rose from among the twisted roots
> through which the spirits of the damned were slinking
> (Canto XIII, 25–27)

This circle of the suicidal is guarded over by the Harpies—beings that are half man/half bird.

> Their wings are wide, their feet clawed, their huge bellies
> covered with feathers, their necks and faces human.
> They croak eternally in the unnatural trees.
> (Canto XIII, 13–15)

Unlike the Minotaur and the Centaurs, which represent the degradation of the lower self, the Harpies (whose animalistic aspect calls to mind the vulture, a perversion of the noble Eagle) reflect the perversion of the Higher Self.

Dante and Virgil hear voices rising out of the Wood, but see no one. Unable to spot anyone behind the trees, Virgil urges Dante to break off a leaf, which he does. Upon doing so, a voice cries out and frightens Dante. It is Pier della Vigna. During his life, he was the trusted minister of Frederick II, who held "both keys" to Frederick's heart, those of mercy and of punishment. It was Pier della Vigna, whom Frederick consulted regarding the laws of his kingdom. Pier della Vigna, however, suffered false accusations that resulted in his imprisonment. Beset by the misappropriated dishonor, he killed himself and upon doing so, was cast by Minos into the present circle, whereupon he sprouted "like a grain of spelt." Dante pities him, for, in effect, he was an honorable man who only victimized himself.

> ...inflamed all minds against me. These inflamed
> so inflamed him that all my happy honors
> were changed to mourning. Then, unjustly blamed,
>
> my soul, in scorn, and thinking to be free
> of scorn in death, made me at last, though just,
> unjust to myself...
> (Canto XIII, 67–72)

Dante, asked to reevoke the memory of Pier della Vigna upon his return to the world, listens to his tragic story. Suddenly, a trashing of leaves startles him and Virgil. They turn and perceive two spirits pursued by raging hounds. They are the Spendthrifts and Squanderers who destroyed themselves by abusing earthly goods. Having ripped the sinners to pieces, the hounds go off, leaving the bush, whose leaves had fallen, to cry out,

> ...what have you gained in making me your screen?
> What part had I in the foul life you led?
> (Canto XIII, 134–135)

This anonymous spirit, who resides in this tree, hanged himself in his very house and declares that the true symbol of Florence is not St. John the Baptist but, rather, the pagan god Mars, who previously served as its guardian. Upon hearing his words, Dante puts the fallen leaves of the sinner before him into a neat pile. This act of gathering, according to some, represents an *act of atonement* for having broken a twig from the tree housing Pier della Vigna, thus illustrating Dante's growing awareness of the inner workings of karma. Though the use of trees to house the bodies of the suicides may seem a bit unusual, it is not inconsistent with Dante's view of retribution, particularly with regard to the Last Judgment. Because they did away with their own bodies while on earth, thus denying their immortality bestowed to them by God, they are precluded from assuming such bodies for rest of eternity.

Having passed through the contorted wood, Dante and Virgil come across a great desert plain of burning sand. This desolate stretch of land is the setting for the next three cantos, where situated are those who have done violence to God, nature, and art. The burning sand prohibits the growth of anything living, and, thus, symbolizes sterility or, better yet, the absence of fertility. Instead of rain, gentle falling flakes of fire torment the shades.

Here, we find the Blasphemers of God lying supine and naked upon the sands. These are those shades that curse He who has given them life—He who is Life, the Christ. Whereas those who commit suicide transgress the principle of freedom that lives within them, these Blasphemers curse the very *source* from which that principle arises in all humanity. Lacking the ability to actualize *Divine Wisdom* (living thinking), they perceive only their materialized "conception" of God—a conception, which, divorced from the fount of its own becoming, is invariably devoid of life. Their nakedness reflects the barrenness of death, while the burning sands perpetuate this lifeless state. Hence, death begets death. Fire, symbolic of the creative principle of life, falls upon the shades, inflicting them with pain and destruction. It reflects the misdirected use of creative activity. The anger directed at God manifests as the anger against one's self. While those who tend to commit suicide are often subjected to emotional forces that rule over thinking, misguiding it, those blasphemous toward God, willfully direct their emotions at God. They hurl words of death at Life and, thus, victimize themselves by their arrogance and pride.

The first of the shades that Dante and Virgil encounter is Capaneus who was one of the Seven against Thebes. As he was before death, so is he now—defiant and still cursing God. Though killed by a thunderbolt hurled by Zeus, this shade declares that he has not been subdued, nor will he be by all the thunderbolts hurled at him. Virgil responds by pointing out to him that his rage—the fire that burns within his soul—is a more fitting torment than the flakes of fire that fall upon him.

> O Capaneus, by your insolence
>
> you are made to suffer as much fire inside
> as falls upon you. Only your own rage
> could be fit torment for your sullen pride.
> (Canto XIV, 60–63)

Dante and Virgil carry on their journey until reaching a small stream that is so red it frightens Dante. It is a tributary of the Phlegethon, the "boiling river of blood." This stream prompts Dante to ask Virgil about the origin of the rivers that he encounters in Hell. Virgil directs Dante's attention to the island of Crete, where, during the Golden Age, a chaste King (Saturn) had once lived. He was

The Inferno: Confronting the Dragon

told that he would be dethroned by one of his sons. Upon this island where the Orient meets the Occident, rises Mount Ida. Once green, it has become dry and lifeless. There the goddess Rhea, wife of the envious and jealous Saturn, hid her son from him so that his life could be saved. Meanwhile, she requested that noise be incited so as to distract the King from hearing the child's cries. And so, within the mountain there exists a magnificent being whose shoulders face Damietta (Egypt), while his face turns toward Rome. This statue, known as the Old Man of Crete, has a head made of gold, arms and breasts made of silver, an abdomen made of copper, legs made of iron, and the right foot made of clay. These five aspects are alluded to in the second book of Daniel. Except for the head of gold, the other four parts of the body represent periods of degeneration in the spiritual evolution of humanity.

From an anthroposophical point of view, the head of gold represents the first post-Atlantean epoch (Indian) when humanity still had a direct perception of the spiritual forces that lent themselves to the world's creation. The arms and breast, made of silver, point to the Persian epoch when thinking consciousness began to separate from these spiritual forces, thus giving birth to duality. The bronze torso corresponds to the Egyptian–Chaldean period in which the element of "necessity" began to enter human thinking. The iron legs represent the Greco–Roman period in which thinking was brought down into the earthly sphere, and one felt a more pronounced separation from nature. Finally, the right foot of clay represents our own tenuous epoch in which the spirit has completely withdrawn from our perception of reality. The cracks that begin to appear in the right foot of The Old Man indicate that the consciousness of present-day humanity is incapable of sustaining the weight of the ever-growing materialization of human thought. Thinking must, itself, be resurrected from the weight of earthly forces. Only in this way can humanity avoid a total collapse into materiality. Thus, Crete is significant in that it points to the Christ impulse issuing forth from Jerusalem, as it spreads its way toward Rome and the Western world, where the earthly nature of human thinking must, in turn, be enlivened so as to lead humanity back again to the New Jerusalem.

From the four degenerate stages of human evolution—symbolized by the elements of silver, copper, iron, and clay—spring the tears of humankind that collect to form the rivers of Hell (the Acheron, the Styx, the Phlegethon, and the Cocytus). No tears flow from the head made of gold.

Dante asks about the river Lethe and is told that it is not part of the infernal abyss. Instead it is the river of *forgetfulness*, whose waters trickle down from another realm (which he will eventually experience). Each of the rivers that he comes upon in Hell symbolizes the *remembrance* of sin. Satisfied with what he has heard, Dante is led by Virgil along the edge of the stream so to avoid the fiery sand of the desert.

Having walked to where they can no longer see the wood, they come upon a troop of shades forced to march upon the sand for "a hundred years." They are the Sodomites who having committed acts of sexual violence, are confined to a state of perpetual movement. As they could not control the passions burning within them and were, thereby, driven to act out of their lower natures, so are they thrust into motion by the scorching sands. These shades, however, made up largely of learned men, committed "unnatural" sexual acts, which were not *life engendering*. Thus, by moving incessantly upon the sterile sands, the Sodomites characterize those whose sexual acts, born of passion, bear no fruit. They are, in effect, seen as acts that violate the laws of nature, and, thereby, tend to undermine the *procreative* activity set into motion by God. Here, we see how human thinking fails to accord itself with the Will of God but, rather, begins to assert itself independently of God's procreative intentions and becomes, instead, an instrument that the unfettered emotional forces utilize for mere physical gratification. Sodomy thus represents the inability to cultivate the will by which thinking can transform the emotions and, thereby, lead to a natural reintegration of our androgynous nature. And so, such acts are seen as unnatural in the *Divine Comedy,* not merely because they fail to engender human life, but also because they lead us away from the living aspect of human consciousness embodied in the feminine principle, namely *Divine Wisdom*.

One of the spirits that approaches Dante grabs him "by the skirt" and exclaims "What a wonder!" It is Ser Brunetto Latini, teacher and friend of Dante, whose spiritual vision, according to Steiner, enabled Dante to compose his *Divine Comedy*. Dante's great respect for Brunetto is succinctly illustrated by the way in which he carries himself.

> I did not dare descend to his own level
> but kept my head inclined, as one who walks
> in reverence meditating good and evil.
> (Canto XV, 43–45)

In this episode, we witness one of the most touching and memorable scenes of the *Inferno*. Ser Brunetto, wanting to know how it is that Dante finds himself there, is told,

> Up there in the happy life I went astray
> in a valley... before I had reached
> the fullness of my years. Only yesterday
>
> at dawn I turned from it. This spirit showed
> himself to me as I was turning back,
> and guides me home again along this road.
> (Canto XV, 49–54)

Ser Brunetto assures Dante that had he lived, he would have encouraged Dante to continue on with his task. And so, Dante should follow the destiny that has been prepared for him.

> Follow your star, for if in all
> of the sweet life I saw one truth shine clearly,
> you cannot miss your glorious arrival.
>
> And had I lived to do what I was meant to do,
> I would have cheered and seconded your work,
> observing Heaven so well disposed toward you...
> (Canto XV 55–60)

Such words can be understood to have two separate and distinct meanings. Though it is true that a longer life may have enabled Brunetto to assist Dante in his work, the words, "had I lived to do what I was meant to do," could perhaps also refer to some unfinished work connected to the Goddess Natura (*Divine Wisdom*), or even his affiliation to the Knights Templar. Dante's allusion to *Il Tesoretto*, Brunetto's homage to the Mother Earth as a manifestation and procreator of the divine creative forces, is the key by which we are to understand the influence that Dante received from his master. Like Dante, Ser Brunetto was a Guelf. Exiled from Florence after the battle won by the Ghibellines in 1260, he sought refuge in Paris where he wrote, *Li Livres dou Tesor*, a longer more detailed version than that which he was to rewrite in Italy upon his return. Looking at his work, there arise, both in style and content, similarities to *The Plaint of Nature* by Alan de Lille, which supports the notion that he belonged to the Platonic stream at the school of Chartres. For, if anything, the literature of the Platonists had a more poetic (or pictorial) quality than that of the Aristotelians, who soon superseded them. As previously mentioned, this imaginative element was able to influence Dante in writing his *Divine Comedy*. Nonetheless, Ser Brunetto seemingly did not attain a *conscious* initiation leading to *morte mistica*. Rather, he experienced a spontaneous initiatory vision (partially induced by a sunstroke) that he later related to Dante. Though a great part of the exchange between Dante and Ser Brunetto centers on the political situation in Florence, what is most important is the relationship they established in their quest for spiritual understanding. Says Dante,

>...for that sweet image, gentle and paternal,
>you were to me in the world when hour by hour
>you taught me how man makes himself eternal,
>
>lives in my mind, and now strikes to my heart;
>and while I live, the gratitude I owe it
>will speak to men out of my life and art.

The Inferno: Confronting the Dragon

> What you have told me of my course, I write
> by another text I save to show another Lady
> who will judge these matters, if I reach her height…
> (Canto XV, 82–90)

Thus, we can see that Ser Brunetto was the one who instilled in Dante a spiritual vision of life, and it is while Dante "lives" that he feels the need to tell the world what Ser Brunetto has taught him of the path leading to the suprasensory. All of this will be verified if Dante attains to Beatrice—*Divine Wisdom*. Brunetto leaves Dante, mentioning his book, *Il Tesoretto*, so that he may be remembered on Earth. Only by living in the memory of those on Earth, do the shades of the *Inferno* find consolation and the hope of being redeemed by Christ when He reappears. The desire to be remembered will, again, diminish the further Dante ventures into the darkest regions of the abyss. There, the shades do not want to be remembered, which indicates the degree to which they have fallen from God's grace and into the clutches of Satan's influence. Though Ser Brunetto possessed much knowledge regarding the spiritual world, this was eclipsed by his inability to direct his thinking toward the transformation of his instinctive emotional nature. Dante, therefore, shows that the acquisition of knowledge is but a first step in realizing the being of Christ within us. Also needed is the cultivation of the will.

Meanwhile, Virgil has been silent this whole time. In a sense, Ser Brunetto has *momentarily* replaced him as teacher in this canto. Dante thus follows the path to "eternity" that leads from Brunetto to Beatrice, namely from earthly knowledge of the spiritual to Divine Knowledge itself. Virgil is the trusty guide who directs Dante from one to the other.

What follows in Canto XVI is a continuation of Dante's experience in the circle of those who are violent against Nature. There, he is accosted by three shades, each recognizing Dante as a fellow Florentine. Identifying themselves as members of Dante's own party, one of them utters,

> ...may our earthly fame move you to tell
> who and what you are, who so securely
> set your *live* feet to the dead dusts of Hell...
> (Canto XVI 31–33; italics mine)

Though Dante does not tell them his name, he gives them an idea of why he is there,

> ...Led by my Guide and his truth, I leave the gall,
> and go for the sweet apples of delight.
> But first I must descend to the center of all.
> (Canto XVI 61–63)

Here lies hidden yet another clue by which we can understand the *Divine Comedy* as a journey depicting our reentry into the suprasensory world. The sweet apples signify partaking of the Tree of Life, where human beings are immersed in the creative activity of God. Our participation in this creative activity was denied us when we partook of the Tree of Knowledge and, thus, descended into the realm of materiality.

Having commented on the corruption of Florence, Dante is again asked to help restore to memory the existence of these three shades upon his return to Earth. As Virgil leads him along the burning sand, they hear the sound of a waterfall, whose course connects all the manifestations of violence experienced by Dante. When they arrive at the precipice, Virgil asks Dante to untie the cord he has around his waist—the one by which Dante had hoped "to catch the leopard." This cord was Dante's defense against the sins of incontinence. Virgil, in taking it from him, hurls it over the edge of the cliff. This act summons what soon comes up to meet them from below. Meanwhile, Dante thinks to himself,

> ...how cautiously a man should breathe
> near those who see not only what we do,
> *but have the sense which reads the mind beneath!*
> (Canto XVI, 118–120: italics mine}

These words foretell the state of affairs that Dante will soon encounter, for the sins that occupy the region below them are those perpetrated through deliberate, ever-greater misappropriations of thinking. Human beings ought not merely rest their eyes on the deeds of others, but should look into the thoughts and *motivations* that manifest such deeds. Here, as we shall see, Dante alludes to those sinful acts that thinking *wills* into being. Virgil (reason) tells Dante that he will soon behold with wonder the manifestation of errant thinking—Geryon, the embodiment of fraud.

> You will soon see arise
> what I await, and what you wonder at;
> soon you will see the thing before your eyes.
> (Canto XVI, 121–123)

To describe fraud correctly, Dante makes us aware that words, themselves, often serve as a vehicle toward its manifestation.

> To the truth which will seem falsehood every man
> who would not be called a liar while speaking fact
> should learn to seal his lips as best he can.
> (Canto XVI, 124–126)

Dante feels he must relate his experience of the "picture of fraud" as it rises up (from within) to greet him. He shows how fraud—embodied by Geryon, the mythological figure with the head of a man, the hairy arms of a lion, and the body of a snake—results from the corruption of the human being's threefold nature. Its human head denotes the degradation of thinking; its lion-like arms reflect corruption of willing and its serpent tail points to the debasement of feeling. Geryon, thus, symbolizes those sins that result from our deliberate misuse of the intellect. Wallace Fowlie states that in medieval tradition, Geryon was thought to have attracted strangers into his power and then killed them. Here, thinking is set into motion not according to the dictates of its higher aspect but, rather, its lower reflected one. In other words, all the manifestations of fraud are a result of a mirrored thinking, whose instinctive self-perpetuating nature reflects the degree to which it is linked to the emotionally charged forces of willing.

As Dante and Virgil await Geryon's arrival, they perceive three souls sitting on the sand whose features are hardly distinguishable. Each of them has a crested pouch hanging from his neck. These are the Usurers, those who commit acts of violence against humanity's own creations. Virgil tells Dante to go and speak with them on his own. This scene is important insofar as it marks the first time in which Dante is urged to confront a terrifying aspect of sin by himself. The pouches the Usurers wear identify them. These shades cannot be recognized by way of their earthly deeds, namely, by what they, *themselves*, brought forth out of themselves. In usury, money generates money; it does not arise out of human activity (the will). Rather, it perpetuates itself as a lifeless manifestation. Death begets death. The dehumanizing nature of usury is portrayed in the lifelessness of the souls who lose their sense of self as their features fade into the desert sand. As a lifeless activity, usury reflects the self-perpetuating process of dialectical thinking. The fact that Dante confronts the three Florentine souls on his own denotes the continuing strength of will that he acquires in fathoming the very depths of thought (*Inferno*).

Dante, having listened to the souls, departs from them without saying a word. This act is itself important, in that it shows how Dante begins to recognize and distance himself from what is least fruitful in the sphere of human activity—empty words. He consequently begins to divorce himself from the emotional effects of his experience in Hell. Figuratively, he begins to perceive mirrored thinking in the act of self-proliferation. Upon returning to Virgil, he finds him already mounted on Geryon. Virgil encourages him to be bold and sit at the front of the monster, so that its tail will not hurt him.

> ...this beast must be our stairway to the pit:
> mount it in front, and I will ride between
> you and the tail, lest you be poisoned by it.
> (Canto XVII, 76–78)

The Inferno: Confronting the Dragon

Geryon conveying Dante and Virgil. *William Blake*

Thus, Dante seats himself on the part of Geryon that is in close proximity to its head—the thinking forces. Virgil (reason) in a *coup de grâce* separates Dante from its tail, "armed" as in scorpions, so that Dante will not have to suffer its sting. The rest of the Canto is dedicated to describing the long circular motions of Geryon as he descends, eel-like, far down into the circle of the Fraudulent, whose wailings can be heard in the impenetrable darkness.

As they descend, Dante describes the configuration of what lies below. Far beneath the circles of Violence, a circular wall of dark solid rock surrounds them. It forms the outer boundary of the Circle of Fraud. Up against the foot of this wall rise ten concentric rings, each containing a different class of sinner, each connected to the other by a bridge. These rings are more like chasms, leading down to the brim of what Dante calls a great "well" at the very center. Of this well, we shall speak later. It is important to bear in mind that the *solidity* of the great cliff encompassing them characterizes the ahrimanic realm, insofar as it resembles a skull harboring the crystallizing forces of thought. This dark foreboding abyss is where the will has been intentionally misguided by thought. It is also where Dante must counteract this misguided will by continually willing his thinking evermore decisively toward the manifestation of good, so that the process of reintegration can eventually take root in his feeling life (Purgatory). This reintegration of willing and thinking is later symbolized by his meeting with Beatrice who leads him through the "Garden of Earthly Paradise," where his ascent toward *revelation* begins—namely, his vision of God (the creative forces of life.)

Geryon leaves Dante and Virgil in the first ring of the Fraudulent, where the Panderers and Seducers are punished. These souls utilized their intellects to desecrate the human body. Unlike Francesca and Paolo, whose willing and thinking were overcome by the emotional forces, the Panderers and Seducers *prostitute* the intellectual forces to obtain earthly gratification. The Panderers do it for money, the Seducers for self-gratification. Both cases reflect a violation of the principle of reintegration, to the extent that the sanctity of the male/female dichotomy is corrupted. This dichotomy, as we have said, is reflected by the harmonious relationship that willing should have to thinking, which, in the case of these shades, has been disrupted in such a way that willing becomes the instrument of thinking.

Normally, our inner longings reflect the unconscious desire to reintegrate the two human spheres of activity. The inability to unite them results in the predomination of our instinctual nature, where, in the case of the Panderers and Seducers, thinking plays an active role. Here, then, lies the difference between the natural love of the Lustful in Canto V (or even its "perverted" aspect, as witnessed in the sodomites in Canto XV), on the one hand, where two human beings come together out of a *mutual* desire (or passion) that totally overwhelms the intellect devoid of will, and the Panderers and Seducers, on the other, who, for the purpose of self-gratification, *intentionally* utilize their thinking to lure other human beings *against their will*. The latter *deliberately* violates the reunification of the male/female principles (willing/thinking) severed by the Fall.

Just as the Panderers and Seducers violated the will of others so, too, is their will violated in Hell, as they are scourged into perpetual movement by the demons (or ahrimanic forces) that had prompted their action while on Earth. As was the case with the Avaricious and the Prodigals in the realm of incontinence, both the Panderers and Seducers are forced into opposite directions. Amongst the Panderers, Dante recognizes Venedico Caccianemico, who, as procurer for his sister, Ghisola, gave her to the Marquis Obbizo da Este, with whom his family was politically allied. Amongst the Seducers, Dante recognizes Jason, the leader of the Argonauts, who was known for having seduced the fierce women of Lesbos. Having sailed from Colchis, where he received the Golden Fleece, he later seduced Medea, whom he, in turn, abandoned for Creusa.

As Dante and Virgil move onward into the second ring, they notice the souls of Flatterers who are immersed in their own excrement. Of these, Dante notices Alessio de' Interminelli of Lucca, whom he recognizes, and the harlot Thais, seen scratching herself with her filthy nails. Like those in the preceding ring, Flatterers misuse the intellect to take advantage of others. However, they seduce the will of others by manipulating the feelings they have of themselves. He gives them a false impression of themselves and, thereby, subverts their "I" by diverting attention to its lower aspect. This permits Flatterers to penetrate more deeply into the emotional sphere, so that their manipulation is more firmly rooted there. For this reason, Flatterers find themselves farther down in regions of Hell than do the Panderers and Seducers. The excrement in which the Flatterers are immersed is lifeless. It is a visual representation of the *unfruitful effect* their words have on others. Just as excrement, devoid of nutritional value, is unable to sustain one's bodily forces, so, too, are the Flatterers words, whose dialectical nature lacks the transformative power conducive to realizing the living aspect of one's being.

In a previous chapter of this book, we alluded to the events that comprise much of Canto XIX, where, Dante and Virgil come upon the Simonists, who prostitute the "things of God" for money. From the very outset of the canto, Dante denounces them, by calling out the name of Simon Magus, from whom they derive their name:

> O Simon Magus! O you wretched crew
> who follow him, pandering for silver and gold
> the things of God which should be wedded to
>
> love and righteousness! O thieves for hire,
> now must the trump of judgment sound your doom
> here in the third fosse of the rim of fire!
> (Canto XIX, 1–6)

These shades, having followed the example of Simon of Samaria, who believed that God's sacredness could be bought with money, are put in close proximity to the Panderers and Seducers. In much the same way that the latter sold the honor of men and women for material gain, the popes and priests, whose understanding of God's divinity was largely materialistic in nature, prostituted the honor of the Church—the "Bride of Christ." Thus, the Simonists also embody the fundamental trait of fraudulence, that is, the misdirected use of intellectual forces. This misdirection is, as we have often alluded, a natural manifestation of a thinking that has succumbed to the influences of ahrimanic impulses. For this reason, we find the Simonists placed upside down in holes made of stone, with their feet protruding out and set on fire. This characterization represents an inversion of the role assigned to those of the Holy Office. Their head, thrust into the Earth in the direction of Satan (Ahriman), depicts the hardening power that Ahriman has over their thinking. Just as we associate fire with the creative activity manifested by the Holy Spirit, so, too, can we see how, by placing the soles of the sinner's feet on fire, Dante depicts how the tongues of fire that descended upon the heads of the Disciples have been perverted by the Simonists who claim to baptize by way of the Holy Spirit. This, thus, illustrates the degree to which the clergy *lacked* the knowledge that leads to the Christ by way of the Holy Spirit. Their transgression was rooted in their *ignorance* of the knowledge they believed to be true.

Virgil asks Dante if he wishes to speak to one particular sinner whom he sees writhing in pain, to which Dante answers,

The Inferno: Confronting the Dragon

The Simoniac Pope, *William Blake*

> *What you will, I will.* You are my lord
> and know I depart in nothing from your wish;
> and you know my mind beyond my spoken word.
>   (Canto XIX, 34–36; italics mine)

Though seemingly insignificant, these words by Dante reveal the healthy relationship that he maintains with Virgil (reason). Dante is "grateful" to follow the *will* that is inextricable to *conscious thinking.* Unlike the shades who surround him, Dante does not allow himself to be guided by undisciplined thoughts, divorced from a consciously directed will—namely, by thinking that adheres to the activity of bodily forces.

As Dante approaches the sinner, he stands over him "like a friar who gives the sacrament to a hired assassin," and discovers that it is Pope Nicholas III, who, in turn, mistakes Dante for Pope Boniface. Virgil urges Dante to tell Nicholas III that it is not Boniface who has arrived. Soon, Nicholas relates the nature of his own punishment, saying that Boniface VIII and Clement V will follow him. Clement V was responsible for the virtual extermination of the Knights Templar, while Boniface chose Charles of Valois, brother of Philip the Fair, to restore order between the Black Guelfs (aristocrats) and the White Guelfs, the popular party to which Dante belonged. Instead, Charles ruthlessly turned on the Whites, exiling and ruining many of them, including Dante. Having listened to Nicholas' account, Dante lashes out at him, stating:

> ...now tell me how much cash
>
> our Lord required of Peter in guarantee
> before he put the keys into his keeping?
> Surely he asked nothing but "Follow me!"
>
> ...Nor did Peter, nor the others, ask silver or gold
> of Matthew when they chose him for the place
> the despicable and damned apostle sold.
>
> Therefore stay as you are; this hole well fits you—
> and keep a good guard on the ill-won wealth
> that once made you so bold toward Charles of Anjou...
> (Canto XIX, 84–93)

Dante then refers to the Church as the great whore of Babylon, "who sits upon the Waters locked with the kings in fornication" and, then, denounces Constantine for having given the Church a dowry enabling it to exercise temporal power over Italy:

> ...Ah Constantine what evil marked the hour—
> not of your conversion, but of the fee
> the first rich Father took from you in dower!
> (Canto XIX, 109–111)

For the first time Dante indignantly reprimands a sinner after hearing his confession and is embraced by Virgil, thus symbolizing, to an ever-greater degree, the *merging* of intellect and will, so that not only will he later be able to ascend the slopes of Purgatory but, eventually, as Albert Steffen says, become the "judge in the sense of the Roman Church at her purest."[7]

Virgil carries Dante to the bridge of the next chasm, where below he perceives a people "silent and weeping," whose distorted bodies are such that they cannot see in the direction they walk. Their heads are turned backward, so that as they weep their tears fall upon their buttocks. This group of sinners comprises Magicians, Fortune tellers, and Soothsayers. The punishment allotted to them is graver than that of the Simonists. Whereas the latter subverted the Church for want of money, the soothsayer, by revealing the future for profit and tampering with the destinies of individuals, threatens to undermine the Will of God, thereby corrupting the laws by which we may realize our spiritual nature. The Will of God is the very force by which Dante is led through the three realms of being. By enabling us to know the future, the fortuneteller deprives us of the ability to *develop* Free Will. Depriving human beings of their Free Will, robs them of the thinking upon which Free Will depends. It deprives them of their allotted karma. So it is, that the fortunetellers, sorcerers, witches, etc. are forced to look backward in this chasm—backward because, there, one may understand what it is in one's past that holds the key to one's future. Since looking into the future is independent of a speculative dialectical mind, the sinners are portrayed as silent. Unlike others in Hell who can look into the past and future, these shades weep as they are denied the ability to look into the future, a gift that they had abused on Earth.

As Dante observes sorrowfully, Virgil scolds him for his pity, before identifying some of the shades before them. He names Amphiaraus, the prophet of Argos, Tiresias the Theban soothsayer and father of Manto, and Aruns, the Etruscan soothsayer. Then, Virgil points out Manto, the sorceress who allegedly settled in the region where Virgil was born (Mantua). By using her, Dante takes the opportunity to dispel the notion that Virgil practiced white magic. If, as many critics claim, this is so, then, it would seem to stand that Dante wishes to dispel any notion that reason, or the intellect (Virgil), has powers beyond its sense-based nature. In effect, the intellect should not be used for mastering the black arts that subjugate others and deprive them of the opportunity to exercise their will.

In Canto XXI, we find Dante and Virgil in the ring of the Grafters or Barrators, who used their intellects for personal, material gain in affairs of the State. Like the Simonists, these sinners abused their positions of influence. However, the negative effects of their actions weigh more than those of the Simonists, for their misdoings affect *society at large*, whereas simony affects mostly those members of the clergy and their congregation. To understand the gravity of the Barraters' transgressions, one must remember that Dante sees the affairs of both the Church and State as being *equally guided by the hand of God*. Thus, the intellect here is used—as in the case of the Simonists—as an instrument of deceit by which to overturn Divine Will. In addition to this, the Grafter, by depriving society of certain goods, restricts the Free Will of others by directing their thinking toward materiality and not spiritual development. The dichotomy between thinking and willing, in the development of *being,* is thus widened. Thinking is employed to manipulate the will of others. As with all the sins of the lower circles, such transgressions reflect the *effects* of the separation of these two poles of human activity. The shades' placement with respect to one another indicates the degree to which their actions counter the Will of God. One can only value what lies in the suprasensory realm if one has justly understood and revered the physical world *as a reflection* of the suprasensory world. In other words, reverence for God's worldly creations is intrinsic to the love for the creative forces that brought them into manifestation. As Christ says, "If man love not his brother whom he has seen, how shall he love God whom he has not seen?" Thus, unlike the Grafters, one must *respect* the intellect, for it contains the force by which one may ascend into the "heavenly heights."

As Dante looks into the fifth ring, he sees a black pitch that reminds him of the arsenals of Venice:

> As in the Venetian arsenal, the winter through
> there boils the sticky pitch to caulk the seams
> of the sea-battered bottoms when no crew
>
> can put to sea—instead of which, one starts
> to build its ship anew, one plugs the planks
> which have been sprung in many foreign parts;
>
> some hammer at a mast, some at a rib;
> some make new oars, some braid and coil new lines;
> one patches up the mainsail, one the jib—
>
> so, but by Art Divine and not by fire,
> a viscid pitch boiled in the fosse below
> and coated all the bank with gluey mire.
> (Canto XXI, 7–18)

The sticky, boiling pitch that Dante sees, reminiscent of the Phlegethon (where the Wrathful boil), is guarded by a troop of demons with hooks. In this pitch are the Grafters trying to find opportune moments by which to come up and gasp for air. The pitch, like glue, sticks to whatever makes contact with it, and thus, provides a vivid characterization of the effects of grafting and its far-reaching influence over society. Dante uses the word *invisciare* (here translated as "over-glue"), which conveys not only stickiness, but also baseness (in the sense of evil). As Dante continues to look, he perceives a huge black demon carrying a senator of Lucca—the rival city of Florence known for grafting—down into the pitch. To avoid detection, Virgil urges Dante to lower himself behind the ruins of a bridge, thus reassuring him that he is familiar with this path, having already traveled it before. Thus, we again see the will that is intrinsic to the intellect assert itself in times of difficulty. Virgil, then, exposes himself to the band of demons who come rushing at him like a pack of wild dogs. Upon reaching him, they stop in their tracks. This gives their leader, Malacoda (bad tail), a chance to speak with Virgil, who, in turn, warns him that this journey with Dante has been willed from above:

> "Do you think, Malacoda," my good Master said,
> "you would see me here, having arrived this far
> already, safe from you and every dread,
>
> without Divine Will and propitious Fate?
> Let me pass on, for it is willed in Heaven
> that I must show another this dread state."
> (Canto XXI, 82–87)

This again demonstrates how the will to press onward makes itself manifest through reason (Virgil), born of the intellect. Therefore, Virgil's confrontation with Malacoda reflects the ability of willed thinking to overcome those corruptive impulses arising from the depths of one's lower nature. Dante draws close to his Master, while looking at the demons that have gathered around him. This was "not good," says Dante, for

> They swung their forks saying to one another:
> "Shall I give him a touch in the rump?" and answering:
> "Sure; give him a taste to pay him for his bother."
> (Canto XXI, 103–105)

In other words, by diverting his eyes (attention) from Virgil, Dante is besieged by voices of temptation that wish to subvert his faith in his trusty guide (Reason). Malacoda quiets them, and then proceeds to tell them that the bridge leading to the sixth ring is broken, adding that not far ahead exists another bridge that they could use instead. Malacoda says that the bridge was broken as a result of Christ's descent into the depths of the Earth:

> ...In just five hours, it will be, since the bridge fell
> a thousand two hundred sixty-six years and a day;
> that was the time the big quake shook all Hell...
> (Canto XXI, 112–114)

Malacoda agrees to send ten escorts with Dante and Virgil so that they can find their way to the chasm below. This proposal terrifies Dante, for it represents abandoning the use of the good intellect (Virgil) by placing it into the hands of fraud. Virgil again reassures him that the demons are only concerned with the "boiled wretches."

As they continue their way along the pitch, Dante relates how the Grafters in it resemble dolphins in the high seas:

> As dolphins surface and begin to flip
> their arched backs from the sea, warning the sailors
> to fall-to and begin to secure ship—
> (Canto XXII, 19–21)

or frogs "at the edge of a ditch":

> ...the frogs squat about
> hiding their feet and bodies in the water,
> leaving only their muzzles sticking out—
> (Canto XXII, 25–27)

The comic nature of Dante's description is soon effaced when one of the demons, Graffiacane (scratch dog), hooks a sinner who failed to submerge himself into the pitch in time. This sinner is Ciampolo who, as a "domestic of King Thibault," committed acts of barratry. He is being flayed by the demon Rubicante (red nose), and ripped by the tusks of Ciriatto (boar tusk). Then, as he is held by Barbariccia (curly beard), he is made to answer the questions put to him by Virgil, who seeks to know which other souls are immersed in the pitch. Ciampolo mentions one from Sardinia who, at the service of Nino Visconti of

Pisa, favored the escape of various prisoners for which he was hanged. Upon hearing these words, Libicocco (libbicock) hooks his arm and makes off with a piece of it. Virgil then asks Ciampolo for the name of the sinner to whom he has referred and is told:

> It was the shade
>
> of Friar Gomita of Gallura, the crooked stem
> of every Fraud: when his master's enemies
> were in his hands, he won high praise from them.
>
> He took their money without case or docket,
> and let them go. He was in all his dealings
> no pretty bursar, but a kingly pocket...
> (Canto XXII, 81–87)

As Ciampolo tells of others down in the pitch, another demon, Farfarello (hell bat) threatens to strike. Ciampolo, to save himself, offers to reveal the names of spirits from Tuscany and Lombardy, if the demons keep their distance. Cagnazzo (harrow hound), upon hearing these words, suspiciously lifts his snout and utters:

> ...Listen to the grafter
> spinning his tricks so he can jump from the brim!
> (Canto XXII, 107–108)

As the demons, deciding what to do, quibble, Ciampolo dives safely into the water. Two go after him, but are too late. The guilt of having been deceived by Ciampolo causes them to fight one another. As a result, they fall into the pitch where they are rescued by their fellow demons. This affords Dante and Virgil the opportunity to escape.

Though this canto is a continuation of the last, it curiously depicts how thought is *conducive to the act of grafting*. The confusion that arises amongst the demons reflects disorderly thinking—a thinking that lacks discipline. Though it is the demons' responsibility to guard those skilled at the art of deception, they are, themselves, deceived. This illustrates how sensory thinking, by not taking hold the inner *dynamics* of its own nature, is often victimized by it. In Ciampolo, we witness the first time a sinner commits the very act for which he finds himself in Hell. Thus, the events and characterizations of this canto could serve as a picture to better fathom the process of thinking behind the transgressions that comprise the lower circles of fraud.

Dante and Virgil begin to make their way into the sixth chasm. They briefly contemplate what has gone on before them. Fearing the pursuit of the demons who wish to avenge their misfortune, Dante expresses his fear of Malebranche. Virgil quickly answers,

> Were I a pane of leaded glass. I could not
> summon your outward look more instantly
> into myself, than I do your inner thought.
> (Canto XXIII, 22–24)

That is to say, if Virgil were a mirror, he could not reflect the image of fear evident in Dante's face "more instantly" than the "inner thought" that arose in him. Here, the instantaneousness of thought—whose movement precedes its reflection—can be interpreted as the initial perception of the inner movement of thought awakening in Dante. Suddenly, Dante is swept into Virgil's arms while descending into the chasm below.

> Seizing me instantly in his arms, my Guide—
> like a mother wakened by a midnight noise
> to find a wall of flame at her bedside...
> (Canto XXIII, 34–36)

Though one may argue that Virgil's actions are more or less a reflex from encroaching danger, one must allow for the possibility that some degree of *foresight* is present in Virgil for which Dante is saved. For pure instinctive will is primarily conducive to *self*-preservation. The fact that Virgil takes Dante in his arms and leads him to safety reflects a degree of intuitive thinking, however slight, on his behalf, whereby Divine Will intercedes and directs the intellect (Virgil) to act on behalf of another human being.

As Dante and Virgil arrive into the sixth chasm, they perceive:

> ...a painted people, weary and defeated.
> Slowly, in pain, they paced it round and round
>
> All wore great cloaks cut to as ample a size
> as those worn by the Benedictines of Cluny.
> The enormous hoods were drawn over their eyes.
>
> The outside is all dazzle, golden and fair;
> the inside, lead, so heavy that Fredrick's capes,
> Compared to these, would seem as light as air.
> (Canto XXIII, 56–63)

These sinners, forced to walk slowly as if carrying a heavy burden, are the Hypocrites. They wear cloaks and hoods whose glitter dazzles the eyes. However, these robes, lined with lead, impel them to present a more subdued and proper attitude. This depicts their earthly habit of concealing vicious acts under the cloak of righteousness. Here, we find that thinking *contradicts* the will (action). One seeks to manipulate others not by merely undermining their will, but doing it in such a way that one's own will is compromised. The glittering intellect, used to manipulate others into a false belief, weighs down one's own freedom to *act*. Hence, its nuanced sophistication is more reproachable than the other forms of fraud that we have encountered until now.

Dante and Virgil are accosted by the voices of two sinners who, having recognized their Tuscan speech, wish to speak with them. These were jovial friars, named Catalano and Loderingo, a Guelf and a Ghibelline, who were to govern Florence together. As Dante begins to scold them for their evil deeds, he notices a figure lying staked to the ground. It is Caiaphas, who ordered the death of Christ. According to him, it was better for one man to die than to have a whole nation perish. Alongside him are his father-in-law, Annas, and other members of the Council who had condemned Jesus to death. Now, lying spiked to the ground (as Jesus was nailed to the Cross) they must support the weight of all the Hypocrites who walk over them. Having observed him for a long while, Virgil asks if there is a bridge leading out of the chasm mentioned by Malacoda. Friar Catalano answers that they had *all* been destroyed, but that Dante and Virgil could easily climb out amongst ruins nearby. Hearing this, Virgil realizes that Malacoda, whom Catalano called the "father of lies," had deceived him and is "darkened a bit with anger." And so, what at the beginning of Canto XXIII manifested as fear associated with the intellect (Virgil), has now been transformed to anger. Here, we see the initial signs of instability in Virgil, who has been outwitted. We can thus assume that the deeper Dante ventures into Hell (thinking sphere) the more his reason (Virgil) must continually tame his emotionality. Virgil's anger, or apparent lack of self-control, seems to indicate a slight loss of confidence regarding his ability to lead Dante onward, in spite of the fact that he and Dante are ultimately being guided by a will higher than his own.

Upon witnessing his Master's anger, Dante is reminded of a poor Italian peasant who thinks that he will lose his herd of sheep for lack of food in winter. Throughout the poem, Virgil has seemed mostly impervious to the various influences affecting Dante. He has demonstrated a steadfastness and tranquility reflected in his countenance. Here, however, we see Dante at a loss for knowing what to do as Virgil momentarily loses equanimity, which Dante needs to penetrate into the few remaining regions of the abyss. This concern of Dante's, however, is soon alleviated as he and Virgil reach the remains of the bridge. There, Virgil once again takes hold of Dante and directs him up over the scattered ruins. With great fatigue, Dante reaches the top of the pile of stones and stops to catch his breath. Virgil is quick to remind him that his journey is comprised of much greater ascents than what he has just experienced:

> "Up on your feet! This is no time to tire!"
> my Master cried. "The man who lies asleep
> will never waken fame, and his desire
>
> and all his life drift past him like a dream,
> and the traces of his memory fade from time
> like smoke in the air, or ripples on a stream.

> Now, therefore, rise. Control your breath, and call
> upon the strength of soul that wins all battles
> unless it sink in the gross body's fall.
>
> There is a longer ladder yet to climb:
> this much is not enough. If you understand me,
> show that you mean to profit from your time.
> (Canto XXIV, 46–57)

Again, we see Dante's intellect/reason (Virgil) calling on the will forces that have momentarily abandoned him. Each realm to which Dante is subjected leaves its mark on him. And so, here, immediately after having perceived the weight of suffering endured by the sinners of the sixth chasm, Dante is beset by the weightiness of his thoughts, further reflected by the ascent that he finds so difficult. Thus, his intellectual forces must be further strengthened by the will to carry on, which he does, once he is reminded of what lies in wait for him, namely, Beatrice. It is as though *Divine Wisdom* rays its light into the intellect, freeing it of earthly influence.

As they make their way up along the edge of the cliff, Dante hears a voice shout out in anger. Unable to make out the words, he and Virgil walk to the remains of the bridge, which lies between the seventh and eighth chasm. Gazing down below, Dante perceives a mass of serpents. Their cold-bloodedness makes his blood turn *cold*. Here, we should remember that the serpent represents human consciousness before the coming of the Christ—a consciousness that depended on the blood-ties and, therefore, lacked what could resurrect one's fallen nature, namely, independent thinking. As Massimo Scaligero states in *Il Graal: Saggio sul Mistero del Sacro Amore*, "the secret of the serpent is cold blood."[8] This serpent, having lured Adam and Eve into eating the "forbidden fruit" precipitated their loss of "the gift of immortality." He adds,

> By means of the neurocerebral system, that is, by means of the lifeless organ of reflective consciousness, from which we draw a sense of ourselves, our culture and the contents of our existence, we are

fettered to the Earth—not the living Earth that is invisible to us but, rather, the Earth as dead materiality. All forms of reflective thinking are devoid of life, for which we are confined to adhere without residuals to such earthliness, to identify with it, with its indeterminate surface, which we are confined to drag ourselves across like a serpent. To see the serpent gives us a sense of repugnance and shame because it arouses in us an inner, though even obtuse, perception of our real condition on the Earth, of our lowering of consciousness to the exclusive life of matter. This identity with matter, in its excluding of the "living," cannot but give rise to illness and death. After having eaten the fruit suggested by the Serpent, Adam and Eve lose the gift of immortality. If immortality had not been a gift, we would not have been able to lose it.

The nervous system, to have become an organ devoid of life, cold unto itself, receiving life from the warm blood of the blood–muscular organism is the condition of the Serpent. From the head to the dorsal spine, the nervous system assumes the form of the Dragon: the symbol of an inferior ghoulishness, of a savage egoism, of which we can become healed only by suffering, fear, and death. (tr. mine)[9]

Scaligero goes on to say that the redemption of Lucifer arises out of our ability to liberate ourselves (or, more precisely, our thinking) from the clutches of materiality. For this reason, the "Serpent symbolizes a degree of initiation."[10]

As Dante looks at the serpents, he notices human souls running naked among them without any means of escape:

> Their hands were bound behind by coils of serpents
> which thrust their heads and tails between the loins
> and bunched in front, a mass of knotted torments.
> (Canto XXIV, 94–96)

These are the thieves who misused their intellects to deny others the fruit of their labor. Serpents bind their hands. The nimbleness for these snakes arrests the nimbleness of their hands, which they so deftly used to deprive others of what was rightfully theirs. Such sinners are victims of their own subtle dexterity. As "nimble fingers make nimble minds," the snakes' deft movements around their hands also reflect the nimbleness of the thief's mind—a mind characterized by ever-recurring movements forever conditioned by the same patterns of behavior. It is a cycle that is self-perpetuating—one that conditions the development of their being. This is illustrated by one of the sinners who, bit by a serpent, falls to the ground in a blaze of fire and soon burns to ashes, before being resurrected ever again to suffer the same torment. Thievery is a recurring behavior that takes many forms. This metamorphic quality—reminiscent of Ovid's *Metamorphoses*—seeks to illustrate the unconscious associative pattern of dialectical thinking, where one thought connects with another only to be metamorphosed time and time again. However, this type of transformation should in no way be considered synonymous with the resurrection of thinking attributed to beholding the Christ. To attain Christ consciousness, dialectical thinking, itself, must be transformed so that an organ of perception develops by which one can behold the spiritual world. The serpent/sinner symbolizes the dialectical, sense-based thinking that merely manifests a multitude of patterns, or forms, without end.

Such was the shade that fell to the ground. Having gotten back on his feet, his rage and vengeance are directed at God with such force that not even Capaneus could duplicate it. This shade is Vanni Fucci, who finds himself here for having stolen the sacristy from a church in San Zeno. No sooner does he raise his hands in defiance of God, than a serpent coils itself around his neck, silencing him. Another wraps his wrists to his hips so that he is denied upper body movement. He flees and is pursued by a creature covered with snakes, bearing a fire-breathing dragon on his back. This is Cacus, the fire-breathing giant and son of Vulcan, who, having stolen some of Hercules' cattle, was clubbed to death. In this scene, he represents both sinner and punisher.

As Dante and Virgil watch the pursuit, three men arrive. Dante then delineates the two terrifying transformations that occur before him. A six-legged serpent seizes one of the shades before sinking his fangs into the sinner's face. This prompts the two bodily forms to become indistinguishable, so that eventually the shade becomes the serpent, and the serpent the shade. As this occurs, a tiny black evil-looking reptile bites the second shade. Smoke rises from the reptile's mouth and the sinner's wound. As the two trails of smoke meet, the legs of the shade unite in the form of a tail, while the tail of the reptile divides into two. The shade's skin becomes scaly, while the reptile's grows softer. The transformations persist until the shade goes away hissing like a serpent, while the serpent utters the sound of a human being. The third shade of the group remains unchanged.

Thus, Canto XXV describes the vivid transformations that occur between serpent and shade. We have previously witnessed how Dante utilizes beings, some half man half beast (Minotaur, centaurs, harpies), others monstrously configured (Cerberus), as guardians over the various circles in the upper regions of Hell. Here, however, the shades watch over each other. Since thieves commit transgressions that often elude the attention of others, Dante personifies the slithery nature of their thinking in the form of a serpent that acts as guardian over them. Thieves do not distinguish between what is theirs and what is someone else's. They lack the discernment that arises out of the rectitude of thinking. There is no sense of Self, in its higher sense. In the case of these sinners, their indiscriminate behavior reflects a thinking that is unable to consciously determine the degree to which they will their actions. Thus, the transformations of their physical nature mirror the unconscious mutability of their thinking. Just as sensory thinking is in constant flux, thereby revealing its instinctive nature, so, too, does Dante depict the transformations between the human being and the serpent as though they were guided by an unbridled will—a will acting indiscriminately on its own.

Dante begins Canto XXVI by crying out against the corruption of his native Florence, whose banners swell like the beating wings of a bird, and whose name "expands through all of Hell."

> Joy to you, Florence, that your banners swell,
> beating their proud wings over land and sea,
> and that your name expands through all of Hell!
> (Canto XXVI, 1–3)

This image serves as a precursor to the image of Satan further below, whose wings beat over the river Cocytus, transforming it into a frozen lake.

As they make their way up through the ruins of the bridge from which they descended, Dante and Virgil see what appear to be fireflies glowing in the dark, such as "the peasant sees when he rests on a hill and looks into the valley." These are the Evil Councilors who, enveloped in flames, comprise the eighth chasm. Amongst them is a double flame, which conceals the souls of Ulysses and Diomede. Together, they had stolen the Palladium, which guaranteed the safety of Troy, thus handing the Greeks a victory over the Trojans. Having described the fate of Ulysses in a previous chapter, we said that he had, according to the myth told by Dante, attempted to reach Purgatory by way of the sea, thus bypassing the depths of Hell. This represented humanity's attempt to ascend into the spiritual world so as to behold the creative principle of Life, without willfully penetrating the materiality of thought. Thus, Ulysses' actions reflected the influence of Lucifer, which tends to direct us away from the earthly realm, thereby, preempting us from attaining a true initiation into the suprasensory world. For only by following the example set forth by Christ, that is, by resurrecting the material nature of our thinking, can we realize a transformation of our earthly being. In this way, Dante's account of Ulysses symbolizes, in many respects, the ancient path of initiation, pre-dating the entry of Christ *into* the world. However, Ulysses is not punished in the circle of fraud for his seaborne flight toward Purgatory. As we have said, those who find themselves in this circle had committed sins of a more ahrimanic nature. Instead, he is being punished for having induced many men, including Achilles, to take flight with him upon the high seas. Deidamia, the wife of Achilles, was so overcome by the fate of her husband that she died of grief. Ulysses is presented as a man whose thirst for knowledge was so great that, not only did he neglect his family, but *manipulated* others into helping him try to achieve his aims.

> Shipmates," I said, "who through a hundred thousand
> perils have reached the West, do not deny
> to the brief remaining watch our senses stand
>
> experience of the world beyond the sun...
> (Canto XXVI, 106–109)

His deliberate misuse of the intellect (for luciferically inspired ends) can therefore also be seen to reflect the influences of ahrimanic thinking. In Ulysses' case, we witness neither the manipulation of another's intellect by appealing to one's lower nature (Panderers, Seducers, Flatterers, Sorcerers), nor the manipulation of human necessities (Simonists, Grafters, Hypocrites, Thieves). The Evil Councilor, by way of his intellect, *seeks to directly subvert the intellect of others*. Thus, he *misguides* others by dissuading them from applying their thinking in a manner suited to their stage of karmic development. Although Ulysses' aims may seem commendable, they were self-centered. By way of the intellect, Ulysses not only undermines the thinking of his fellow human beings, but also their will. Thus, he, too, severs thinking from the will. *He does so by intentionally affecting another's conviction in the "truth" of a given reality by way of his own*, unlike the hypocrites who *purposely* deceive others to simply justify their own behavior (to themselves) by an outright lie. Thus, the Evil Counselor's actions embed themselves more deeply into the fabric of consciousness and are, therefore, more difficult to overcome for they manipulate the *intent* of others by affecting the thinking by which one finds meaning in life.

We can see how the flames that engulf the Evil Councilors serve to isolate them from each other and, thus, bring to light the lack of intimacy in their interrelationships. In Ulysses' case, it was also the fire that burnt inside him (in his desire for knowledge), which is mirrored by the flames that engulf him:

> ...Aeneas came and gave the place that name,
> not fondness for my son, nor reverence
> for my aged father, nor Penelope's claim

> to the joys of love, could drive out of my mind
> the lust to experience the far-flung world
> and the failings and felicities of mankind...
> (Canto XXVI, 88–93)

Having described the details of his precarious journey, Ulysses departs with Virgil's permission and is soon followed by another flame, from whose top came a "confused sound," which Dante likens to that of the bellowing of a brass bull used to torture others. This shade asks whether there is peace or war in his native "Latian" land. Dante is quick to point out that, at present, there is no war, and briefly delineates the series of events that have taken place there. After which, he asks the shade to reveal himself and tell his story. The shade agrees and identifies himself as Guido di Montefeltro, who was once a soldier. Later, after repenting his sins he became a Franciscan monk. Though he had sinned, he was determined to mend his evil ways and seek Heaven. He would have succeeded had Pope Boniface VIII not convinced him (by absolving him of sin in advance) to devise a plan of deceit against his fellow Christians.

> ...the Great Priest—may he rot in Hell!—
> who brought me back to all my earlier sins;
> and how and why it happened I wish to tell
>
> in my own words: while I was still encased
> in the pulp and bone my mother bore, my deeds
> were not of the lion but of the fox...
> (Canto XXVII, 67–72)

In this case, however, we see that the fox was, himself, outfoxed. Boniface's plan was a success. Afterward, upon the death of Montefeltro, St. Francis descended from Heaven to take his soul, as was customary with all who were part of his order. As he did, a demon suddenly snatched him, laying claim to his soul, for Montefeltro had not repented before dying. Even the absolution of the pope could not erase his ill-fated destiny. This scene illustrates the doctrine of the Church, which says that the fate of a person's soul depends on its condition immediately preceding the moment of death. In other words, the act of penitence was thought to actualize the idea that, though one may have deviated from the spiritual path, one still possessed the moral qualities necessary to realize God's kingdom. These qualities, faint as they may be, were inextricably related to the understanding, cultivated through earthly life, of the relationship that we have with our Maker—an understanding born of dialectical thought. Thus, we witness God's mercy and love, insofar as we are given a chance (until the very end) to atone for our transgressions—an atonement that can result from the slightest acceptance of God's love. Those sinners, who, like Montefeltro, lack the inner resolve to acknowledge this love, are thought to have *completely* lost the "good of the intellect." Thus, we can see how the Church recognized that thought, even in its degenerate, dialectical form possesses the key by which we may be led to salvation.

In Canto XXVIII, Dante and Virgil come upon the Schismatics or "sowers of discord," responsible for having tried to divide, or split open, an institution during their earthly life. The four institutions affected by their actions are church, state, community, and family. As Dante nears them, their mutilated bodies discompose him. The nature of the punishment in this, the ninth chasm, is clear. To tear open an institution results in one's own body being torn asunder. This concept is derived from chapter 12 of the first letter to the Corinthians, in which Paul declares that the Church can only function well if each and every member works in harmony with the other, so that the unification of the body of Christ is maintained.

> The body is a unit, though it is made up of many parts; and though all its parts are many, they form one body. So it is with Christ....
> But God has combined the members of the body and has given greater honor to the parts that lacked it, so that there should be no division in the body, but that its parts should have equal concern for each other. If one part suffers, every part suffers with it; if one part is honored, every part rejoices with it.[11]

Thus, Christ manifests Himself to the extent that we are able to reflect His *Love* toward one another. This *Love* that forms the body of Christ is not derived by way of the senses, but by our ability to free ourselves from the influences of the bodily forces. The "love" we ordinarily experience is tainted by the impulses derived from our lower nature. Such impulses lack the fundamental qualities that reveal the nature of the Christ. In fact, they can be seen as impediments to the spiritual unification of humanity, in as much as they derive their source from the luciferic sphere of activity. Here, we are given a striking example of how the luciferic and ahrimanic influences—though each striving toward its own individual ends—work harmoniously in opposition to the Christ. For the "sowers of discord," while lured by the wiles of Lucifer, construe by way of willfully misdirected thinking (manifested by Ahriman), schemes by which to destroy the union between human beings. Such a union can only be brought about by the *Love* of Christ—a *Love* that can only arise from a thinking that is free of earthly influences. As our ordinary thinking is pulled from the left (Lucifer) and from the right (Ahriman), we are prevented from acknowledging the unifying force common to us—*living thinking*. Only by realizing what inherently lives within each of us can we, as human beings, find peace. The Schismatics represent those who, having been manipulated by the adversaries of Christ, construe philosophical or theological principles for all of humanity to follow. This represents a return to the tenets of the Old Testament in which humanity is united by common law (furthered by the Romans) and not by the principle of freedom intrinsic to thinking. This principle of freedom, in which we act out of the force of *Love* working within us, is what, in part, allows us to partake in the "body of Christ." It is this very principle that is violated by those punished in this chasm, for the Schismatics divide human beings by preying upon their thinking, so that such thinking becomes an instrument of division, further removed from the source of its own creation.

The first Schismatic that Dante sees is Muhammad, whose religious beliefs undermined the unity of the Church. Dante is horrified by his gruesome condition;

> A wine tun when a stave or cant-bar starts
> does not split open as wide as one I saw
> split from his chin to the mouth with which man farts.
>
> Between his legs all of his red guts hung
> with the heart, the lungs, the liver, the gall bladder
> and the shriveled sac that passes shit to the bung.
> (Canto XXVIII, 22–27)

Following Muhammad is his son-in-law, Ali, who succeeded him and now goes about with "his head cleft from the top-knot to the chin." As Dante listens to Muhammad, he learns that the sinners here, mutilated as they are, are forced to circle the chasm. In so doing, their wounds heal but are reopened by a devil with a sword. This essentially represents the inability of the body to properly heal itself of affliction (or division) because it lacks the curative or regenerative forces derived from the *light* of the Christ.

Having described the nature of his punishment, Muhammad asks Dante to identify himself, for he thinks that Dante is purposely trying to delay his punishment. Here lies another clue by which we can understand Dante's journey as one of *initiation*. Virgil relates that Dante, unlike the shades before them, is not *dead* (to the sacred knowledge) but *alive*. His journey into Hell symbolizes the death of his lower egoic nature that will eventually result in the attainment of *Divine Wisdom*. Such an experience is even a mystery to Virgil (reason), his guide, who declares himself to be *dead*. For, again, having preceded Christ's entry into the world, he died without the possibility of partaking in the substantiality of His being. In other words, his thinking *cannot become living*, and, therefore, conducive to the conscious perception of the *divine* spiritual world. Says Virgil,

> "Death has not come for him, guilt does not drive
> his soul to torment...
> *That he may experience all while yet alive*

> I, who am dead, must lead him through the drear
> and darkened walls of Hell, from round to round:
> and this is true as my own standing here."
> (Canto XXVIII, 46–51; italics mine)

Again, Virgil represents reason born of a dialectical thinking, which, in itself, cannot fathom *life*. This realization will eventually dawn on Dante the more he *wills his thinking* to actualize *Divine Wisdom*.

By this time, hundreds of shades come to witness the new spectacle. Suddenly, a sinner who recognizes Dante accosts him. It is Pier da Medicina who, having belonged to the Bianchini family was driven from Romagna in 1287. He later succeeded in pitting the rulers of Romagna against each other, which inevitably resulted in its division. Pier da Medicina is himself followed by another mutilated human form, Curio, who urged Caesar to cross the Rubicon that divided Gaul from the Roman Republic. This resulted in a declaration of war against the republic. For his advice, Curio must eternally suffer the harrowing pain of having a split tongue. He and Pier da Medicina both serve as examples to those who foster schisms within the State.

The next shade approaches Dante with his hands cut off. As he lifts his arms, blood drips from his stubs onto his face. He is Mosca dei Lamberti, whose decision to have Buondelmonte killed resulted in the war between the Guelfs and the Ghibellines. Buondelmonte rejected a girl born of the Amedei family, so as to marry another from the Donati family. Unsure of what to do, the Amedei family turned to Mosca dei Lamberti who advised them to have Boundelmonte killed, proclaiming, "a thing done has an end." This led to a bitter feud that effectively divided the city into two separate factions, which then became bitter enemies. Here, Mosca de' Lamberti is punished for having severed a community.

Dante now sees something that really startles him. It is a headless shade that carries his severed head in his hand. He approaches Dante. Swinging his head like a lantern, he lifts it up before Dante and speaks of his tragic fate. This shade is Bertrand de Born who, as the noble Lord of Hautefort, is being punished for having set Prince

Henry against his father. Having done so, he committed an act that is synonymous to severing one's head from their body. Thus, his punishment is retribution for having created division within the family structure.

Interestingly, the severing of Mosca's hands and that of Bertrand's head can serve as a picture by which to visualize the separation of willing and thinking forces. By placing these two scenes in succession, Dante inadvertently calls attention to the degree of separation between the two spheres of human activity that he sees in Hell.

Dante is so overcome by what he has just experienced that his eyes fill with tears. Virgil reminds him that they must continue, for it is getting late. As they begin to exit the chasm, Dante contemplates the fate of a family member, whom he suspects is somewhere amongst the Schismatics. It is Geri di Bello, his father's cousin. Virgil declares that he had seen this kinsman threateningly point his finger at Dante, while Dante was talking with the other spirit. Geri di Bello, having caused discord among the Sacchetti family, was killed, and Dante sorrowfully tells Virgil that Geri's anger probably stems from the fact that his death has yet to be avenged.

While conversing, Dante and Virgil come upon the tenth and final chasm of the eighth circle. Here, they are overcome by the wailings below, which are so strong that Dante is forced to put his hands over his ears to buffer the noise. This chasm contains the Falsifiers. Their overpowering stench arises from having to eternally withstand the degeneration of their disease-infested bodies. Making their way across the bridge to the lower edge of the chasm, they see these shades gathered in heaps, some crawling about the others. Four categories of Falsifiers are castigated here: those who pervert things, words, money and people. Unlike the Schismatics, whose bodies are mutilated from without, the Falsifiers, beset by disease, witness the degeneration of their human forms as it occurs from *within*. Thus, the disintegration of their physical bodies reflects their corruption of nature. This chasm brings to mind the last circles of violence where acts of abuse were rendered unto God, nature, and art. The difference is that, here, the

Falsifiers do not act by way of unbridled emotions—as do the Sodomites or Capaneus—but, rather, by way of their intellects. Theirs is a more conscious aberration that does not merely reflect the incapacity to control emotional impulses arising from within the depths of being but, rather, arises from *the voluntary manipulation of the physical world.* In other words, they seek power by manipulating outer nature, unaware of the strength that can be derived from the transformation of one's own thinking. Only in this way can the outer world be changed so as to benefit oneself, as well as the whole of humanity. To change oneself is to elicit a change in the world! The Falsifiers, on the other hand, manifest a behavior that arises from a lack of self-understanding. They, in essence, subvert that very thing from which the act of self-transformation can take root—thinking. This, in turn, leads to the disintegration of the physical realm so important as a basis for human development. And thus, their falsification of the physical world reflects the misuse (or distortion) of thinking, which, in its lifeless form, must be resurrected through willing.

Therefore, it is not surprising that the first sinners with whom Dante comes into contact are those who *falsely* (or materially) tried to create gold—the alchemists. Here, Dante alludes to those alchemists who misconstrued the aims of individuals such as Albertus Magnus, whose particular alchemy consisted in the transformation of the lunar forces (mirrored thinking = silver) into the solar forces (*living thinking* = gold) and who, non-coincidentally, is found in the *Sun* (*gold*) *sphere* of the *Paradiso* alongside Thomas Aquinas and other great lovers of wisdom. Massimo Scaligero in *Il Graal: Saggio sul Mistero del Sacro Amore,* describes this inner transformation of consciousness, *symbolized* by the attainment of gold (Christ consciousness)—or the actualization of the Sun forces—as Opertis Solare. Those, however, driven by the lunar aspect of dialectical thought and the thirst for materiality, were unable to recognize the esoteric significance of gold as an element corresponding to Christ. As a result, their behavior reflects the degree in which mirrored thinking is conducive to the degeneration of the physical world, *in as much as it, too, is a reflection of that degeneration.*

Dante sees two shades scratching each other and pulling off scabs "the way a knife scrapes bream." They are Griffolino di Arezzo and Capocchio di Siena who come from his native land. Griffolino, as the story has it, received an allotment of money from Alberto da Siena for promising to teach him how to fly. Upon realizing that he had been tricked, Alberto convinced his father, the Bishop of Siena, to have Griffolino burnt to death. Nonetheless, he was not condemned to the tenth chasm for his lie, but because he was an alchemist.

> ...But Minos, the infallible, had me hurled
> here to the final bolgia of the ten
> for the alchemy I practiced in the world.
> (Canto XXIX, 118–120)

After hearing the words of Griffolino, Dante asks Virgil if there were ever a people more vain than the Sienese. A shade, overhearing Dante's question, replies by giving the names of four men who squandered their money on extravagant living. The spirit who speaks is Capocchio, who was also burnt for having practiced alchemy. Believed to be a friend of Dante's, Capocchio ends Canto XXIX by declaring:

> ...So you will see I am the suffering shadow
> of Capocchio, who, by practicing alchemy,
> *falsified* the metals, and you must know,
>
> unless my mortal recollection strays
> how good an ape I was of Nature's ways.
> (Canto XXIX, 136–140; italics mine)

By concerning himself only with the metals of the physical world, Capocchio tried to mimic the processes of Nature. Unlike those in the School of Chartres who sought to uncover the creative forces behind Nature, Capocchio was interested *only* in the physical manifestation of those creative forces—forces that most likely he fails to even conceive. Again, he does not desire what gold *symbolizes*—namely, the transcendence of lunar consciousness (dialectical thinking) and the realization of Opertis Solare conducive to the perception of the Christ—but, rather, the physical element embedded within the Earth itself.

Canto XXX begins with two mythological examples depicting the nature of mental illness that characterizes the second type of falsification—the act of impersonation. First, he describes the madness that motivated the homicidal nature of Athamas, who was driven to insanity by the anger of his wife, Juno, for having had an affair with her sister, Ino. Then, Dante speaks of Hecuba, wife of Priam of Troy, who witnessed both the sacrifice of her daughter and the death of her son while being deported as a slave to Greece. The sight of such a tragedy induced her to madness, causing her to bark like a wild dog. While Dante conjures these mythological images in his mind, Capocchio is attacked by a ravaging spirit who

> ...sank his tusks so savagely
> into Capocchio's neck, that when he dragged him,
> the ditch's rocky bottom tore his belly.
> (Canto XXX, 28–30)

This rabid shade is Gianni Schicchi, who once impersonated a dead father to alter his will and receive a considerable fortune. As this happens, Dante asks Griffolino the identity of another spirit who has accompanied Schicchi. He is told that it is Myrrah, who once disguised herself to make love with her father, the King of Cyprus. These impersonators are punished for having *falsified their own being* for personal gain. They thus desecrate what differentiates them as human beings—their identity of Self. In as much as mental illness often reflects the degree of displacement of the "I" from the rest of one's spiritual constitution, these shades (impersonators) are represented as having completely lost that connection to their "I." Therefore, we see their instinctive, astral nature predominate. Whereas the falsifiers of metals reflect the perversion of knowledge conducive to the realization of their higher nature, the impersonators pervert both their bodies and their sense of Self, necessary to attain such knowledge.

After these shades have gone, Dante observes a sinner suffering from dropsy. His shape is so swollen that he looks like a lute. This is Master Adam of Brescia who craves "a drop of water," as he recalls

> ...The rivulets that run from the green flanks
> from Casentino to the Arno's flood,
> spreading their cool sweet moisture through their banks...
> (Canto XXX, 64–66)

Master Adam is punished for having counterfeited the florin, a Florentine coin, stamped with a picture of John the Baptist (the Water Bearer)—the patron saint of Florence. His insatiable thirst for money is now reflected by his thirst for water. Just as he perverted money, the means by which one barters for objects to sustain oneself, so, too, is his own body distorted to reflect the accumulation of vile fluid substances which, in their unadulterated form, once sustained human life. Thus, by forging money, one undermines that which was conceived for the maintenance of social interrelations and the continuance of physical life.

Upon hearing Master Adam's dilemma, Dante asks him the names of two shades lying nearby. They are Potiphar's wife, who accused Joseph of trying to seduce her, and Sinon, "the Greek from Troy" who tried to coax the Trojans into taking the wooden horse inside the walls of the city. Both shades suffer a burning fever. They are the falsifiers of words—the means by which human beings relate to one another. Esoterically, they represent those whose actions attempt to desecrate the archetype of all forms of speech—the *Word* itself. Since they sought to undermine the creative principle of life symbolized by fire, they are made to feel the burning of their own bodies—a manifestation of that creative activity.

Dante listens intently to the bickering that has developed between Master Adam and Sinon the Greek. As he does, Virgil reprimands him, saying

> Now keep on looking
> a little longer and I quarrel with you.
> (Canto XXX, 131–132)

Virgil notices that Dante is ashamed for having shown interest in the shades' argument, at which point, Virgil reassures him of his loyalty. Nevertheless, Dante must take care to never again be lured by the vulgarity of the sinners, for "the wish to hear such baseness is degrading." Once again, Virgil, representing reason, functions as an overseer, alerting Dante to the perils of giving way to impulses that seek to divert him from his true course. The Falsifiers represent the various forms of deceit that cunningly subvert our journey toward God. And so, we witness in Dante the slackening of will due to the hypnotic effect that the sinners' words have on him. Fortunately, however, Virgil (reason) quickly reasserts himself and willfully redirects Dante onto the straight path. Dante must avoid the lures of idle curiosity, which so often undermines intent. The forcefulness of Virgil's reproach reflects the further strengthening of will forces. This willfulness asserts itself the more deeply Dante advances into that realm of Hell, where the separation of will and thought is most manifest among the shades.

Dante and Virgil now venture into the ninth circle, an extension of the circle of fraud. It contains the Traitors—those whose acts are the most reprehensible. Here also lies the well that Dante and Virgil perceived as they looked down into the eighth circle, while sitting upon the back of Geryon. It is the river, Cocytus, known to the Greeks as the river of wailing. The beating of Satan's *machine-like* wings has caused it to become a frozen lake. The ice symbolizes the cold, fixed nature of the human intellect, totally divorced from the realm of feeling (Purgatory) and Divine Will (Paradise). Whereas Dante has, up to this point, been exposed to the *effects* of evil influences, now he comes upon their ultimate *cause*—Satan. This encounter is a necessary prerequisite of his journey. For by willfully penetrating the very core of Hell (dead intellectuality), Dante will slowly be able to detach himself from its influences. His thinking—transformed by the inner forces (will) guiding Dante's use of the intellect—will gradually bridge him to the heart forces, later symbolized by his encounter with Beatrice. In representing *Divine Wisdom*, the presence of Beatrice will mark the point in which Dante's thinking has primarily detached itself from the body's influence. This is represented later in the "Garden of Earthly Paradise" in the *Purgatorio*.

For now, Dante must continue to endure the terrifying scenes that await him below. As he and Virgil make their way up the banks of the chasm, they are enveloped by virtual darkness. Suddenly, they hear the thunderous sound of a horn that reminds Dante of the one Roland used to summon Charlemagne to his side in times of defeat. To understand what he has heard, Dante looks in the direction of the sound and perceives what he thinks are the towers of a city. Virgil tells him that he is mistaken. Here, no city can possibly exist, for a city implies community. Instead, what Dante sees are the giants of antiquity embedded from the navel downward in ice. These giants serve as a prelude to Dante's encounter with Satan. Just as Lucifer rebelled against God and was, thus, cast out of the Heavens, so, too, did these giants rebel against the gods who destroyed them. They, in fact, represent the elemental forces of the Earth that sought to subvert the spiritual beings of the hierarchies guiding all humanity. Presumably of lower rank than Lucifer or Ahriman, they have the similar aim of diverting humanity from the path leading to God. Here, they are "immobilized" by the same earthly forces that once epitomized their strength.

As the air clears, Dante makes out the first giant he encounters. It is Nimrod. Upon seeing him, Dante declares that the enormous beasts on Earth such as elephants and whales, are just and prudent manifestations of Nature. These giants, on the other hand, render humankind defenseless because

> ...the instrument of intelligence
> is added to brute power and evil will...
> (Canto XXXI, 55–56)

This allusion to the adverse effect of those beings upon humanity's spiritual development is reinforced by his description of Nimrod, who is most remembered for having used a tower in his attempt to reach Heaven. God, seeing that the people of the world who were busy creating this tower spoke one language, confused their tongues so that they could not understand one another, and then, scattered them throughout the Earth. This act represents the fall of atavistic consciousness and the instigation of the gradual emergence of individualized consciousness. Hence, Nimrod represents those forces that futilely try to reach the heavenly world by earthly means. He represents the attempt to circumvent individualization of consciousness by which a resurrection into the spiritual world can be attained. Thus, this individualization of consciousness, necessary to realize the Cosmic Word, is absent in Nimrod, who can only sputter the chaotic and incomprehensible words:

> Rafel mahee amek zabi almit...
> (Canto XXXI, 67)

To this, Virgil replies,

> ...he is Nimrod, through whose evil
> mankind no longer speaks a common tongue.
>
> Waste no words on him: it would be foolish.
> To him all speech is meaningless; as his own,
> which no one understands, is simply gibberish.
> (Canto XXXI, 77–81)

Nimrod's acts are seen as "evil," for they counter the Will of God by attempting to disrupt the divine evolutionary blueprint of our spiritual evolution.

As Dante and Virgil journey on, they meet a second giant, "far more fierce and large," who has his right arm pinned behind him and his left in front.

> "This piece of arrogance," said my Guide to me,
> "dared try his strength against the power of Jove;
> for which he is rewarded as you see.

The Inferno: Confronting the Dragon

Antaeus Setting down Dante and Virgil, *William Blake*

He is Ephialtes, who made the great endeavour
with the other giants who alarmed the Gods;
the arms he raised then, now are bound forever."
(Canto XXXI, 91–96)

Like Nimrod, Ephialtes tried reaching the gods by earthly means, namely, by piling the mountain Ossa on Mount Olympus, and Mount

Pelion on Mount Ossa. Again, we witness the fate of one who defies the spiritual world by attempting to overcome Zeus (Jove), a being of the angelic hierarchy. Therefore, Nimrod and Ephialtes tried to subvert the spiritual beings guiding humanity.

Dante wishes to see Briareus, but he is too far away. The only guest that he will be able to see is Antaeus. Frightened by the clamoring of Ephialtes, Dante and Virgil move on, when suddenly Antaeus emerges from a cavern. Virgil addresses him, recalling the time Antaeus killed a thousand lions. Virgil insists that had he joined his brothers (giants) in the fight against the gods, they might have won their battle. As a reprieve for having abstained from participating in the war against the gods, Antaeus is the only giant whose movements are *not* bound by the ice. In convincing Antaeus to set them down on the frozen river (Cocytus), Virgil tells him that Dante will help him achieve notoriety upon his return to Earth.

Hearing this, Antaeus lifts them up and gently sets them on the ice. He then raises himself "as in a ship the mast." At this point, Dante is reminded of Antaeus' wrestling match with Hercules who defeated him by lifting him from the ground. Antaeus was powerless once he lost contact with the Earth, thus reinforcing the relationship that these beings had to the terrestrial forces symbolized by Ahriman, who is placed here in close proximity to them.

As Dante looks about the icy pit, he cannot muster the words to describe what he perceives.

> ...it is no easy undertaking, I say,
> to describe the bottom of the Universe;
> nor is it tongues that only babble child's play.
> (Canto XXXII, 7–9)

To help him, he invokes the aid of the Muses who helped Amphion play the lyre while he drew stones from Mount Cithaeron—stones that formed the walls of Thebes. Dante angrily addresses the spirits imprisoned there, where neither light nor heat ever penetrates, by telling them:

> O most miscreant rabble, you who keep
> the stations of that place whose name is pain,
> better had you been born as goats or sheep!
> (Canto XXXII, 13–15)

This ninth circle is divided into four rounds or concentric rings, each of which houses a different kind of Traitor. The first round is Caina, named for Cain, who slew his brother Abel. This round is reserved for those treacherous to kin. Antenora contains traitors to their country; Ptolomea harbors those who betrayed guests; Judecca is reserved for those who conspired against their benefactors or masters. Each of these rounds extends ever closer to Satan, rooted at the very center of Hell. The principle factor that differentiates them is *how* the shades are placed into the ice. The traitors of this circle have committed graver sins than those of the previous circle, for here, acts of treachery were, in essence, perpetrated by outright cruelty. If one, again, looks at those of the eighth circle, such as the seducers, flatterers, grafters, evil counselors, etc., one perceives acts committed upon the misuse of the intellectual forces. However, the principle objective was merely one of personal gain. Ulysses, for example, convinced his crew to sail the seas, not because he wanted to do them harm, but because his obsessive quest for personal knowledge impeded him from being able to see beyond himself. Violence was not an intentional part of his scheme. In the ninth circle, however, the sinners' acts of deception either result in or have as their main objective violence. This is the realm in which thought has resulted in acts of *destruction*. In other words, unlike sense-free thinking that has liberated itself from degenerating bodily influences and is, thus, able to receive the creative impulses originating from the Godhead, the thinking in this lowest of earthly realms is one which, having been subjected to the degenerating influences of the sense-based reality, is reflected in forms of violence or destruction. As love is the fruit of creative living forces, hatred is what arises from an activity that finds its reflection in death.

Dante hears a voice from the first round, Caina, warning him not to step on the heads of the "forworn and miserable brethren."

As Dante looks upon the icy lake, "so frozen it seemed to be made of glass," he perceives the heads of "doleful shades" who "beat their teeth like storks." Looking around, Dante spots two shades so close to each other that "the hair of their heads had grown together." He asks them their names, but they do not answer. Instead, they weep, so that

> the cold froze them
> between the lids, sealing them shut again
>
> tighter than any clamp grips wood to wood
> and mad with pain, they fell to butting heads
> like billy goats in a sudden savage mood.
> (Canto XXXII, 47–51)

A third shade, whose ears have frozen off, tells Dante that the two shades are brothers, Alessandro and Napoleone, sons of Count Alberto degli Alberti. They killed each other while fighting over an inheritance. And so, they are condemned to an eternal punishment reflective of their violence on Earth.

As Dante makes his way to the center of the ice with Virgil, his foot strikes against the face of a sinner. He is not quite sure whether it was his "will, or chance, or fate" for which he committed such an offense. Nonetheless, we are led to believe that Dante's actions may have been intentional. Upon hearing the trampled sinner question Dante's motive for having stricken him, Dante reproaches the sinner with a forcefulness that underscores his ability to *act* on his own behalf. This marks the first time he does so since finding himself in the "Dark Wood."

> "Master," I said, "grant me a moment's pause
> to rid myself of a doubt concerning this one;
> then you may hurry me at your own pace."
>
> The Master stopped at once, and through the volley
> of foul abuse the wretch poured out, I said:
> "Who are you who curse others so?" And he:

> "And who are *you* who go through the dead larder
> of Antenora kicking the cheeks of others
> so hard, that were you alive, you could not kick harder?"
>
> "I *am* alive" I said...
> (Canto XXXII, 82–91)

> *I grabbed the hair of his dog's ruff* and I said:
> "Either you tell me truly who you are,
> or you won't have a hair left on your head."
> (Canto XXXII, 97–99; italics mine)

These lines are significant for they reveal a visible manifestation of Dante's transformation in the *Inferno*. Though some may argue that he simply reflects the emotional climate of the Antenora, Dante's behavior is deliberate. It marks the first time in which he *initiates* an action independently of Virgil. His actions thus reflect the degree to which his will has been strengthened, thereby allowing him to cast off the evil influences that threaten him ("...that I may rid me of a doubt respecting him"). This scene is also important, for it is here that Dante declares himself to be *alive*. No longer does Virgil define him. Instead, Dante defines himself by recognizing what *lives* within him. In other words, as Dante looks about the inner landscape of death, he, for the first time, perceives that which can draw him toward *Divine Wisdom* (Beatrice) and eventually toward the threefold aspect of God, namely, a thinking whose creative *activity* has until now been obscured by the forces of crystallization. Like a fountain in winter, whose water, gently pouring up from the ground, freezes into intricately shaped ice crystals along the periphery, leaving the tiny flowing stream unaffected at its center, so, too, does the living activity of thinking in Dante, begin to differentiate itself from its creation, symbolized by the sea of ice surrounding him.

The shade, afraid of exposing his identity, refuses to reveal his name. Dante, perturbed, grabs him by the hair and threatens to pull every lock from his head. In spite of the fact that Dante does indeed pull out a few tufts of hair, the shade still refuses to identity himself:

> Not though you snatch me bald, I swear
> I will not tell my name nor show my face.
> Not though you rip until my brain lies bare.
> (Canto XXXII, 100–102)

At this point, another shade shouts out the name Bocca, thereby identifying him as Bocca degli Abati, a Ghibelline turned Guelf. In fighting with the Guelfs at Montaperti, he cut off the hand of a Florentine soldier, thus causing panic among the troops. Bocca, realizing that Dante will relate his fate to the world, names others who find themselves there alongside him.

Dante and Virgil move on when, suddenly, Dante notices two shades, so close together in the ice that

> one head made a helmet for the other.
> (Canto XXXII, 126)

This scene is among the most gruesome in the *Inferno*, for Dante notices that

> As a famished man chews crusts—so the one sinner
> sank his teeth into the other's nape
> at the base of the skull, gnawing his loathsome dinner.
> (Canto XXXII, 127–129)

Taken aback by the horror that he witnesses, Dante asks the sinner whose teeth are entrenched deep into the head of the other, his name so that he can tell their stories. The shade answers that if his story succeeds in exposing the traitor who caused him so much grief, he will gladly do it. This is the tale of Ugolino, who in Canto XXXIII represents both the betrayer and the betrayed. Here, he is being punished for his acts of betrayal. In 1288, the Guelfs held power in his city of Pisa. Yet, the party had two factions, one headed by Count Ugolino of Gherardesca and the other by one of his grandsons, Nino de' Visconti. The Archbishop of Pisa, Ruggieri degli Ubaldini (whose head Ugolino presently has between his teeth) led the party of the Ghibellines. In trying to claim power for himself, Ugolino conspired with Ruggieri against Nino. This, however, caused the Guelfs to lose their political stronghold. The Archbishop, realizing this, double-crossed Ugolino and threw him and his four sons in prison, where after eight days, they died of starvation. And so, we see Ugolino here, satisfying the insatiable hunger that he had suffered, by chewing on the head of the one who betrayed him. This narration by Ugolino evokes one of the most powerful images in the *Divine Comedy*. It forms a counterimage to the plight of Francesca and Paolo. Whereas the latter were eternally united by love, Ugolino and Ruggieri are eternally united by hatred. Buffeted by the winds of passion, Francesca and Paolo were victims of their emotional nature—an emotionality that willed itself over thinking. Ugolino and Ruggieri, on the other hand, find themselves embedded in the ice, which reflects their malicious use of a cold, hardened intellect. Both Francesca and Ugolino weep as they tell their stories, while the silence of Paolo and Ruggieri seem to bear testimony to the truth of what is told.

Though Ugolino is a traitor, Dante portrays him more as a victim of despair. As we empathize with his terrifying fate of having to helplessly watch his sons die one by one, and the immense love which he felt upon losing them, we can not help wonder how he is equally capable of so much hatred. Yet, we realize that hate and love are equally present within all of us as expressions of unbridled emotionality, connected to our lower animal natures. This is consistent with where Ugolino finds himself, for there all sense of humanity is inexistent. The human being has become beast-like, having totally misused the intellect to commit acts of premeditated violence.

Upon hearing Ugolino's tale, Dante, moved by the compassion for the fate of his sons, utters a sharp cry against the evil of Pisa. Then, moving on into the round of Ptolomea, Dante encounters a shade lying in the ice, where

> Their very weeping closes up their eyes;
> and the grief that finds no outlet for its tears
> turns inward to increase their agonies:

> for the first tears that they shed knot instantly
> in their eyesockets, and as they freeze they form
> a crystal visor above the cavity.
> (Canto XXXIII, 94–99)

The shade asks Dante to remove the ice from his face. Dante, in turn, tells him that if he wants such a favor, he must reveal his identity, adding that if he is not given a reply, he will go to the bottom of the ice to get it. The shade declares that he is Friar Alberigo, a member of the Manfredi family of Faenza. After a bitter dispute with a younger brother, Manfred, Albergio acted as though he had forgiven him by inviting both him and his son to dinner. Having finished the main course, Alberigo, announcing dessert, called out, "bring out the fruit," a signal for the servants to kill Manfred and his son. Thus, Alberigo says to Dante:

> I am Friar Alberigo...
> the same who called for the fruits from the bad garden...
> (Canto XXXIII, 118–119)

Though Alberigo has *yet* to physically die, his soul has been cast down here in Ptolomea. According to Church doctrine, a person, physically alive, could lose their soul for committing an act of treachery.

> "What! Are you dead already?" I said to him.
> And he then: "How my body stands in the world
> I do not know. So privileged is this rim
>
> Of Ptolomea, that often souls fall to it
> before dark Atropos has cut their thread..."
> (Canto XXXIII, 121–125)

Here we see how a physical, living person can become dead to their spiritual Self. Instead of "dying in Christ," so as to be reborn spiritually, one does the opposite by unwittingly sacrificing their *spiritual nature* to physical desire. This is accomplished through one's adherence to the hardening forces of thought, which run counter to the influence of the Christ. Though physically alive, one is "dead" to the spiritual forces working within them.

Friar Alberigo, in trying to convince Dante to scrape the ice from his face, says,

> ...And that you may more willingly free my spirit
>
> of this glaze of frozen tears that shrouds my face,
> I will tell you this: when a soul betrays as I did,
> it falls from flesh, and a demon takes its place,
>
> ruling the body till its time is spent.
> The ruined soul rains down into this cistern...
> (Canto XXXIII, 126–131)

Here, we are explicitly told that an act of betrayal—born of a thinking divorced from its inner life forces—is directed by a demon "ruling the body" of those who have sacrificed their Self ("I"). This presages the fate of the ahrimanic forces, which, in their battle against the Christ, will one day inherent the dead corpse of the Earth, devoid of all life. This scene is a prelude to Dante's encounter with Satan in Judecca, the last round within the ninth circle.

Nonetheless, Alberigio mentions Ser Branca d'Oria, confined right behind him. Dante is convinced that Branca is still alive. However, Alberigio tells him that Branca's soul has been here for many years and that Michel Zanche (above in the boiling pitch), whom Branca treacherously killed, had yet to arrive when the soul of Branca was cast into Ptolomea. Though Branca d'Oria appears to be alive, a demon has taken the place of his soul. And so, we are given a picture of how the adversarial forces can possess the human soul and direct its actions. Though one may have the appearance of being alive, one is, in fact, *dead*. Those forces that seek to confine us to our physical nature do so by taking over our consciousness. In other words, as we act out of the impulses arising from our bodily nature, we are, in effect, possessed by beings whose mission it is to keep us from realizing our "I."

As Alberigio finishes his story, he cries out: "open my eyes!" But Dante does not open them for him, "for to be rude to him was a courtesy." Though one may interpret this as an example of coldheartedness on Dante's part, it would be missing the point. For one thing, the ice that seals shut one's eyes allegorically represents the hardened forces of the intellect that prevent one from *perceiving life*—that which streams from within thinking. Ice is the frozen aspect of water, which symbolizes life. Alberigio, wishes to see *without* the necessary understanding, namely without actualizing the force of the Christ within his thinking. As we are reminded in the Bible, only Christ can heal the blind! Even Dante, himself, has yet to resurrect his own thinking so as to perceive the spiritual world. Thus, how could he possibly help others to see, if they completely shut themselves off from the hope of ever doing so? Even if Dante could help Alberigio, he would be essentially working against Divine Justice, namely, against the very Will of God by which he is drawn in his journey. His actions would, thus, be in opposition to the Christ. Dante's realization of his own incapacities reflects his awareness of the limitations of dialectical thought, insofar as he has virtually penetrated to the core of evil—the very limits of sense-based thinking.

Dante's journey into the "underworld" has prepared him to behold the very force that manifests all malice. It is interesting to note that Virgil's presence is hardly felt in these lower realms, reinforcing the notion that Dante has almost mustered the strength of will to face the embodiment of all his karma, that is the repulsive, horrifying reflection of all his misdeeds—the Greater Guardian of the Threshold. Up to now, Dante has encountered all his misguided emotions, thoughts or actions in life, namely, the manifestations or effects of sense-based thinking. *Now, he is about to witness that from which they find their expression, that which is also their composite reflection.*

In traversing Caina and Antenora, Dante bore witness to those who betrayed family and country. These are considered lesser sins for the sinners' relationship to them results from emotional influences—tied to their self-identity—that are beyond their control. However, in Ptolomea and Judecca, where he presently finds himself, the shades are punished for having betrayed guests and Masters, respectively. Here, the nature of one's transgression is more severe, for the sinners—divorced from any attachment to their own sense of Self—intentionally and *detachedly* fabricate the circumstances leading to their acts of brutality.

As Dante ventures into the realm of Satan, he notices the shades totally submerged in the ice so that they "shone through like straw in glass." They are represented as having no contact with one another, and so, reflect the complete loss of that intellect which *connects* the various sensorial representations that one experiences in life. They are also, in a sense, immobilized by the complete abandonment of the will, for they are denied the slightest movement. As Fowlie makes note, "after watching the change from man to beast, we see the change from man to ice or stone"[12] Thus, one has become totally transformed by the crystallization of thought, so that the living aspect of speech is frozen in time as well. The only sound that Dante hears is the wind blowing over the cold ice as a result of the beating wings of Satan. Here lies the most extreme desolation.

As Dante proceeds, he hears Virgil uttering a hymn by Venantius Fortunatus of the sixth century, who said *"Vexilla regis prodeunt"* (On march the banners of the King). By adding the word *inferni*, Virgil draws attention to Ahriman. Upon seeing this monstrous form, Dante notices how its machine-like wings beat furiously, as it tries to lift itself from the ice in which it is embedded. Dante is horrified. Hiding behind Virgil, he musters the strength that allows him to behold the terrifying aspect of the three-headed beast chewing, in each of its mouths, a separate victim. This threefold aspect of Satan is the *negative* counterimage to what Dante will encounter in the *Paradiso*. The three heads that Dante perceives, each of a different color—red, yellow, and black, namely, hatred, impotence, and ignorance—reflect qualities *opposite* to the Holy Trinity (Love, Omnipotence, Omniscience).

At the sight of this hideous monster, Dante says,

> I did not die, and yet I lost life's breath:
> imagine for yourself what I became,
> deprived at once of both my life and death.
> Canto XXXIV, 25–27)

Lucifer–Satan, *William Blake*

This uncertainty on the part of Dante, as to whether he was dead or alive, describes the *experience of crossing the threshold from death to life*. The clue revealing the transcendent nature of Dante's experience is—as was before—concealed in his address to the Reader.

> Do not ask, Reader, how my blood ran cold
> and my voice chocked up with fear. I cannot write it:
> this is a terror that cannot be told.
> (Canto XXXIV, 22–24)

The Inferno: Confronting the Dragon

Dante sees the three mouths of the monster chewing up the bodies of Judas, Cassius, and Brutus. Judas (who betrayed Christ) and Cassius and Brutus (who betrayed Caesar) represent those forces that lead to the disintegration of human religious (Cross) and social (Eagle/Empire) life. These shades are the sustenance for that evil being who had once inspired their actions. In this way, evil feeds upon itself! Any show of compassion by Dante would be an evil act. Seen more esoterically, our proliferation of death is reflected by our unwillingness to bridge ourselves to the stream of life, as it arises from within the depths of thinking. Our incessant dependence on dead thinking perpetuates the death of humankind and the Earth itself. We can only help resurrect the Earth to the degree that we have resurrected thinking. Otherwise, we assist the adversarial forces that intentionally impede such a resurrection. In this way, humankind becomes a source of nourishment for such powers—as is depicted by the eating of Judas, Cassius, and Brutus. Therefore, Satan not only represents the mechanization of thinking but our estrangement from the only means by which humankind can ascend to the perception of the eternal Self—living thinking. After seeing Satan, Virgil tells Dante,

> There is no way
> but by such stairs to rise above such evil.
> (Canto XXXIV, 83–84)

As they descend upon the "shaggy" body of Satan, "between the tangled hair and frozen crusts"—as if descending a ladder—they suddenly find themselves turned upside-down so that their descent becomes an ascent. This point of transition, both physical and spiritual, is located at Satan's navel—the center of gravity (or materialization). From here, they begin their ascent toward Purgatory. Having been led through an opening in the rocks, Dante looks back and sees Lucifer's legs "turned upward." This greatly confuses him. He asks Virgil to explain this mystery to him. Virgil, then, tells him that they have crossed the center of the Earth and are now in the Southern

Hemisphere. This accounts for the transformation from evening to morning that they experience. He adds,

> ...You are under the other hemisphere where you stand;
> the sky above us is the half opposed
> to that which canopies the great dry land.
>
> Under the midpoint of that other sky
> the Man who was born sinless and who lived
> beyond all blemish, came to suffer and die.
>
> You have your feet upon a little sphere
> which forms the other face of the Judecca.
> There it is evening when it is morning here...
> (Canto XXXIV, 112–120)

As Dante and Virgil venture up toward the mount (Purgatory), whose meridian lies opposite to Jerusalem, Virgil explains Lucifer's fall from the Heavens. He says that Hell, located beneath Jerusalem, was created as a result of the impact of his fall onto Earth. Before his fall, "the southern hemisphere was covered with land, but after his plunge, the land sunk below the sea and shifted to the northern hemisphere."[13] As a result, what land that lay at the center of the Earth was thrust back upward thus forming the Mount of Purgatory. It sits alone, surrounded by water in the Southern Hemisphere. From it flows a tiny brook whose trickling waters flow back toward the center of Hell, carrying the impurities of those who have purged themselves of sin. It is the Lethe, the stream of *forgetfulness*, which, as a hidden path, guides human beings in their "return into the bright world." As Virgil leads Dante up along its waters, they reach a round "opening the beauteous things which Heaven bears." From there, they issue out "to see the Stars." These Stars conclude each of the three canticles in the *Divine Comedy* and, thus, delineate the course of Dante's journey toward God.

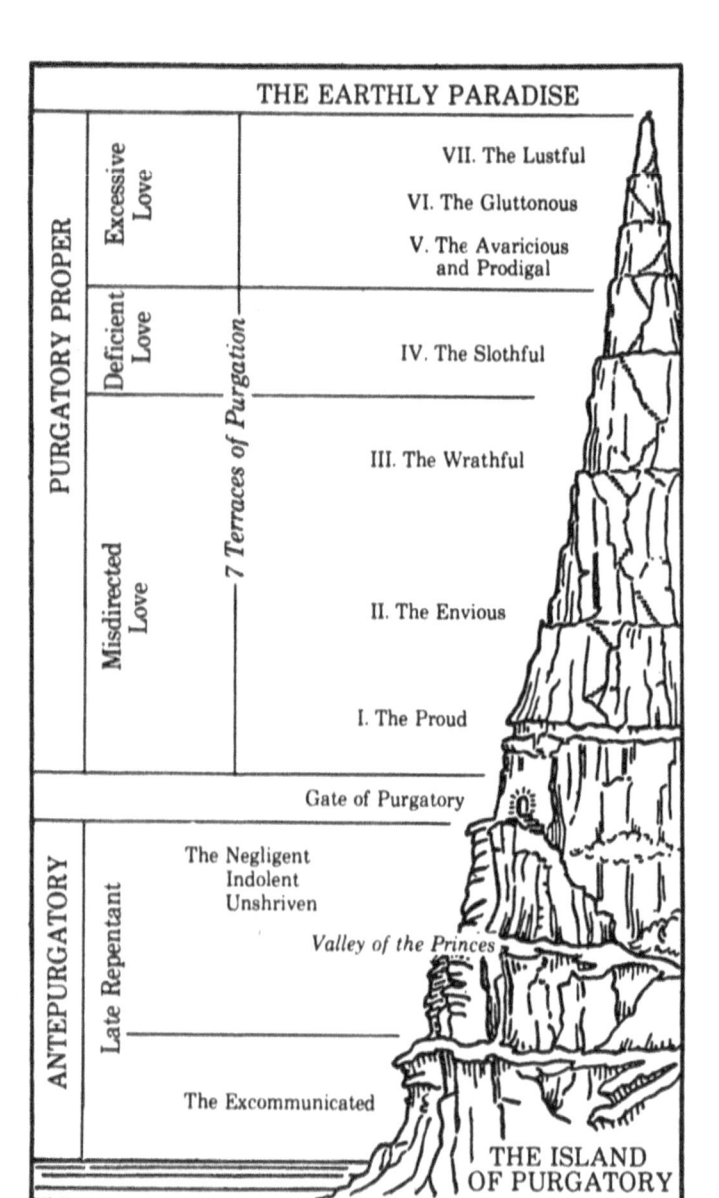

THE *PURGATORIO*
ASCENDING THE SLOPES OF REDEMPTION

At the end of the *Inferno*, Dante and Virgil make their way up toward the source of a rivulet that trickles down into the center of the cold, forsaken Earth. There, it merges with the Cocytus, containing the sins of humankind. Like the thread of Ariadne, which enabled Theseus to find his way out of the labyrinth and free himself of the Minotaur, this tiny stream, the Lethe, provides Dante with the means by which he, too, can liberate himself from the intricate configuration that has enveloped him. Just as both the circular labyrinth-like structure of Hell represents the complex nature of circuitous reflected thinking from which we must free ourselves, so, too, can the waters of the Lethe be likened to *thread* of Ariadne, for they symbolize the current of living thinking before it is seized by the bodily forces. As we stated in the previous chapter, the Lethe is the river of *forgetfulness*. Esoterically, it marks the point at which we pass from the Microcosm into the Macrocosm. With regard to sleep (but equally attributable to the state of death or initiation), Rudolf Steiner, in *Macrocosm and Microcosm*, states,

> The fact that in sleep he [the human being] is poured out, like a drop in a large vessel of water, into the Macrocosm, means that at the moment of passing out of the Microcosm into the Macrocosm, *he must pass through the stream of forgetfulness*. (italics mine)[14]

Thus, Dante's passage from the earthly depths of Hell to the Mount of Purgatory, by way of the Lethe, represents the moment his thinking begins to detach itself from the influences of the sense-based world. At the base of the Mount, which rises precipitously up from the sea, Dante initiates the process of purging himself of the *causes* of sin. Purgatory represents a period of atonement where souls perform acts of penitence to rise up toward the Heavens.

In his descriptions of the life between death and rebirth, Rudolf Steiner often mentions how, at the moment of death, we begin to relive our earthly lives in reverse order, from death all the way back to our birth. Though this series of events that we undergo immediately after death precedes our experience of Purgatory (or Kamaloca) as described by Steiner, Dante hints at this inverted process in his graphic illustration of the purging that he witnesses on the Mount of Purgatory. If we exclude, for the moment, the sins that resulted in the imprisonment of those suffering eternal damnation in the lower *ahrimanic* realm of the *Inferno*, and look at the less heinous (more redeemable) transgressions committed by those lying within its upper *luciferic* realm, we find the same transgressions that essentially constitute the upper part of Purgatory. In fact, by looking at the order in which Dante places the sins of Purgatory with respect to each other, we find that, for the most part, Purgatory is a mirror image of Hell.

Purgatory	Lustful
	Gluttonous
	Prodigal, Avaricious
	Slothful
	Wrathful
	Wrathful
	Prodigal, Avaricious
	Gluttonous
Hell	Lustful

What differentiates the sinners in Hell from the penitents on Purgatory is the degree of harm that their actions on Earth had upon the life of other human beings. Whereas the shades of the underworld committed acts that adversely affected the destiny or karma of others (as well as their own), the actions of the penitent on Purgatory did not. As a result, the penitents on Purgatory are seen purging themselves of *tendencies or predispositions* toward the various sins such as pride, envy, sloth, anger, lust, etc., In other words, their behavior on Earth reflected "states of being" (or consciousness) that harbored predispositions or tendencies toward sin, which ensue from the inability of the "I" to transform the astral body. Just as the shades in Hell manifest behaviors that arise from their inability to extricate thinking from its attachment to sense-based reality, the penitents on Purgatory have only the *tendency* to do so. Their souls have not been so corrupted that they cannot be redeemed.

Whereas the *Inferno* represents the *thinking* realm, the *Purgatorio* corresponds to our *feeling* life. We see this reflected, among other things, in Dante's encounter with Beatrice, in his explication of love and in the penitents' degree of joy and gratitude in spite of their suffering. Within this sphere of emotional activity, we also witness the influences that thinking, feeling, and willing have on one another. The baser transgressions (such as excommunication and negligence), located at the foot of the Mount—and, thereby, nearer to the center of the Earth—reflect the human will diverted by intellectual forces. Sins such as lust, pride, and envy show how thinking is misdirected by feeling. On the other hand, those aberrant tendencies such as wrath and gluttony demonstrate the degree to which the emotional forces are subject to willing. So that, again, we have what, in the *Purgatorio*, may be described as a sort of counterimage to the *Inferno*:

| Purgatory | feeling subject to willing |
| | thinking subject to feeling |
	willing subject to thinking
	thinking subject to willing
	feeling subject to thinking
Hell	willing subject to feeling

Another interesting relationship between the *Inferno* and the *Purgatorio* is reflected in the *direction* of Dante's path. The *Inferno* begins with Dante in the "Dark Wood." From there, he descends the circles of Hell by always moving to his left, which, in Italian, is translated by the word *sinistra* (sinister). On Purgatory, he climbs its slopes by always keeping to his right, until he comes upon a "Garden," illuminated by the rays of *divine light*. Though conceptually, Dante appears to go in opposite directions, he is, in effect, always going in the same direction. Upon traversing the center of the Earth (Satan's navel) where everything suddenly seemed to flip upside-down, he immediately finds himself in a part of the world diametrically opposed to that from which he had descended—a world reflected as its counterimage. Therefore, what seems to be a change in direction—namely, going from left to right and then from right to left—is really an illusion. This can be experimented in front of a mirror. By moving a pencil from our right to our left, we can see its reflection going from our left to our right.

Thus, Dante's graphic depiction of Purgatory illustrates the inversion of one's earthly experiences immediately after death as described by Rudolf Steiner, where one experiences the events from death to birth. Dante has further contrasted the *Purgatorio* with the *Inferno* by other descriptive means. For example, in the *Inferno*, only sighs and wailings are heard. Meanwhile, in the *Purgatorio*, Dante hears songs of praise, in spite of the pain that the penitents bear. In the *Inferno*, everything is shrouded in darkness, thus signifying the apparent absence of Christ's *light*—a *light* that, incidentally, comprises the whole of the *Paradiso*. In the *Purgatorio*, darkness and light alternate as night and day. Interestingly, only when the Sun shines, can the penitents progress up the slopes of the Mount toward the "Garden of Earthly Paradise," whose very name embodies the influences of earthly and spiritual forces. Thus, the penitents can resolve their karma only to the extent that the Christ force (represented by the Sun) is manifest. Lastly, *green* is the color that marks the boundaries of his journey up the precipitous slopes of Purgatory. Not only does green represent the *hope* that is absent in Hell, it also reflects the burgeoning life that is largely absent there, as well.

During the early hours of dawn, Dante and Virgil arrive at the foot of Purgatory, otherwise called anti-Purgatory. This realm precedes Purgatory proper. *It is the dawn of Easter Sunday, the day of Resurrection.* The year is AD 1300. Once again, Dante invokes the Muses—specifically Calliope, the Muse of Epic Poetry. He asks her to fill him with the music performed at the defeat of the Pierides, who challenged the Muses to a contest in song. This invocation marks the first of three references in this canto to the most important prerequisite for scaling the cliffs before them: *humility*. The Pierides exuded pride—i.e., the opposite of humility—in their desire to contest the song of the Muses. Pride is the gravest transgression on Purgatory proper, for it permeates the feeling life so as to preclude one from forgiving the transgressions of others and, thereby, bridging oneself to the Christ. Humility, on the other hand, allows for a greater receptivity to the Christ in our feeling life. As Steiner has often said, *wonder* should be transformed into devotion and reverence. This process requires humility. Only, then, can the heart's etheric forces be strengthened.

As Dante looks around, he is gladdened by the

> Sweet azure of the sapphire of the east
> ...gathering on the serene horizon
> its pure and perfect radiance—a feast...
> (Canto I, 13–15)

Unlike the *Inferno*, the atmosphere in the *Purgatorio* is peaceful and serene. The penitents are relatively undisturbed by outside influences. To arrive at self-purification, their work must arise from *within*, so that, there, they can eventually experience the birth of Christ through the contemplation of their earthly attitudes. Amid this tranquility, Dante directs his gaze to the planet of love—Venus—whose rays veil the constellation of the Fishes (Pisces). This symbolic representation is important, for the sign of the Fishes heralds the coming of *Christ, the Cosmic Power of Love*, which at this particular stage in

Dante's spiritual development, is concealed by the planetary influence of Venus. Says Rudolf Steiner in *Macrocosm and Microcosm*, "the influence which takes effect on waking (from sleep) is called the force of 'Venus.'" He adds, "The force that drives Venus around the Sun is similar to that which regulates the Sentient Soul by day."[15]

Thus, the force associated with the Sentient Soul is also associated with Venus. And so, the process of transforming our Sentient Soul, which thereby, initiates the total transformation of our astral nature leading to the development of the Spirit Self, is connected to that force which regulates the activities of Venus. Considering the fact that, in the *Paradiso*, Dante will traverse the zodiacal constellation to which he, here, makes reference, we can interpret Dante's characterization of Venus and the Fishes as a reference to his inability, at this point, to *directly* perceive the Christ. Nonetheless, having begun to free himself from the sensorial elements of his thinking, Dante begins the process of purification, which will eventually culminate in his ability to behold the Christ—the Prime Mover of his intellectual faculties.

As Dante turns to the right, he beholds four stars. They represent the four Cardinal Virtues—prudence, temperance, fortitude, and justice—largely seen and understood by the "first mankind." Looking down, he sees them reflected on the countenance of an old man in such a way that those "rays of holy light"

> ...made his face glow
> with such radiance that he looked to me
> as if he faced the sun...
> (Canto I, 37-39)

This man is Cato of Utica, who opposed the dictates of both Pompey and Caesar. To free himself of them, he committed suicide. Though he was a pagan, Dante places him here because he represents "the pursuit of liberty." He is not punished among the suicides in Hell, for, during Cato's time, suicide was not viewed as an act violating the Will of God. Cato asks how Virgil has come to the shores of Purgatory. Virgil tells him that he has not arrived there by his own powers.

The Purgatorio: Ascending the Slopes of Redemption

Rather, he has been chosen to help Dante find his way toward salvation. In other words, it is by way of the *light*, which ultimately proceeds from God, that Dante's path is illuminated. Virgil alludes to the journey that both he and Dante have thus far taken, adding that it is his task to show Dante "those whose suffering makes them clean."

Cato, guardian of anti-Purgatory, is remarkably different from those who preside over the various circles of Hell below. For one thing he demonstrates a deeply felt sense of compassion and forgiveness. This is most evident when Virgil reveals the plight of Cato's beloved Marcia, whose soul lingers in Limbo—the realm shared by Virgil himself down below. Cato's relationship with Marcia is a remarkable one. As the daughter of Philippus, she bore Cato three sons. Afterward, by way of a transaction approved by her father, she married Cato's friend Hortensius. After Hortensius' death, Cato remarried her. Because of the selfless nature of his actions, he is a most suitable exemplar to illustrate the disposition of soul necessary on Purgatory.

Realizing the nature of Dante's quest, Cato gives him the right of way. He urges Virgil to "bind a smooth *green* reed about his waist," wash the filth from his face in a nearby stream, and wipe the tears from his eyes. It would be inappropriate for Dante to appear before an angel of Heaven bearing the traces of the underworld. These acts set into motion a series of rituals outlining the stages of Dante's spiritual initiation on Purgatory. The reed that Dante must strap around his waist not only denotes *hope* (green), but just as important, *humility*. The reed brings to mind the cord that Dante wore in the *Inferno*, which was used to summon the monster Geryon up from the depths of Hell; its purpose then was to ensnare the leopard (incontinence). Now, the reed around Dante's waste represents the humility of submitting to God's Will, to consciously participate in God's divine plan. This humility is further symbolized by Dante's need to descend to the lowest regions of Purgatory to pluck the reed growing in the marshes. According to Ciardi, the reed around Dante's waist brings to mind Matthew 27:28–30, where the scourging and crowning of Christ is described.

They stripped him and put a scarlet cloak on him; and then twisted together a crown of thorns and set it on his head. They put a staff in his right hand. Then they knelt in front of him and mocked him... They spit on him, and took the staff and struck him on the head again and again.[16]

By *recalling the footsteps of the Christ, Dante's journey outwardly reevokes the path of Christian initiation.* Cato forbids them to go back the way they came. Instead, they are told to pursue the rising Sun, which, esoterically, is the *light* (of Christ) slowly about to break through the materiality of Dante's thinking. Virgil leads Dante to the low-lying marsh where he cleans his face of the "residues of Hell's black air." He, then, plucks a reed that is instantly replaced by another, sprouting from the same stalk. According John Ciardi, this symbolizes the eternal and nondiminishable nature of grace that is bestowed from God to humankind, by way of the passion of Christ.[17]

As Dante and Virgil stand by the shore pondering the journey they have before them, they notice a boat hurrying toward them with tremendous speed. Guided by an angel, it is brimming with the newly deceased. Virgil commands Dante to kneel before the "Angel of God." Needing neither oars nor sail, this angel covers great distances by way of "his eternal plumes" that do not "molt like feathers or human hair." The angel is so radiant that Dante must lower his head. Leading a great number of souls who sing, *"When Israel came out of Egypt"* (Humanity being led to the Promised Land), he represents the heavenly forces that guide our experience through the spiritual world. Dante is blinded at the sight of him. Esoterically, this may symbolize his initial glimpse of the etheric light within his thinking. However, it is just a flicker that bathes Dante's soul, for the angel vanishes immediately upon appearing.

The souls, whom the angel has guided, are unsure of where to ascend and, thus, ask Dante and Virgil for directions. Portrayed as children, they seem lost on the slopes of this solitary island. And so, in a sense, they represent those who cross the Guardian of the Threshold into the spiritual world unconsciously. Unlike Dante, they had not been visibly guided by a thinking (Virgil) *directed* from the Divine World. Suddenly the souls recognize, by Dante's breath, that he is *living*. Amazed, they draw near to him. One of them joyfully embraces him. It is his friend, the musician Casella. Upon Dante's request, Casella sings a song of Dante's that he had set to music, "*Amor che ne la mente mi ragiona*." This song introduces the third treatise of Dante's *Convivio*, in which is written:

> ...The Sun that circles all the world
> Sees nothing so gentle as at that time
> When it shines upon the place where dwells
> The lady of whom Love makes me speak.
> Every intelligence admires her from above,
> And those down here who are in love
> Still find her in their thoughts
> When Love makes felt the peace he brings...
> (*Convivio: Canzone* II, book 3; tr. by R. H. Lansing)[18]

In these verses, we can see that the beatification of woman as it relates to the principle of Love is that which characterizes "*Il Dolce Stil Novo.*" This Love (Christ)—the bearer of peace—is, as we have seen, intimately connected to the Eternal Feminine, or *Divine Wisdom*. In these verses, we discover that the *light* of Christ (Sun) is born of the feminine aspect of consciousness (thinking), which had been separated from its masculine counterpart (will) as a result of the Fall. This *Divine Wisdom* exists within the thinking of those who come to the *light* of the Christ. Thus, the word *Love* in the title of the poem, "*Amor che ne la mente mi ragiona*" (Love that reasons in my mind), is not a mere sentimental reference to love on the part of Dante, but an acknowledgement of the presence of Christ living within human thinking. In presenting Casella, Dante does not merely refer to the quality of music on Purgatory; rather, he addresses those who are keen to the true significance of his poem. *He intimates that it is the activity of Christ lost within thinking that is the object of his search*, and so, the song points to the ultimate aim of the *Fedeli d'amore*—i.e., the attainment of *Divine Wisdom*.

As the souls rejoice to the music of Casella, Cato descends upon Virgil and Dante, as well as the newly arrived, startling them and scattering them up the slopes. He cries out,

> ...Negligence! Loitering! O laggard crew
> run to the mountain and strip off the scurf
> that lets not God be manifest in you!
> (Canto II, 118–120)

Already, we see that they lack the *will* necessary to ascend the Mount rising up before them. This willing must be cultivated by all the souls on Purgatory. In fact, the various forms of atonement there reflect the degree to which the human will had been cultivated and rightly employed on Earth. Cato symbolizes *conscience*, which has within it the power to incite the will to action.

Dante and Virgil, having been chased off by Cato, find themselves at the base of Purgatory. As Dante looks at Virgil, he notices how remorseful he seems, for, like the other souls, he, too, felt the pangs of conscience (Cato). Having had to scamper hurriedly, Virgil has revealed himself to be less infallible than he was within the depths of the Earth. His haste reflects an act *not* born of the "I." Says Dante, "haste...urges men to mar the dignity of each act." Thus, each human act is dignified, insofar as it consciously bears responsibility in determining one's reality. Each act, if conscientiously carried out, is part of the conscious unfolding of God's creation. Actions that are done in haste do not *consciously* arise from the depths of the "I," namely, the "I" linked to the "I" of God. Therefore, they disrupt the continuity of one's will to that of God, since one invariably alters that which is willed from above—namely, Divine Willing itself.

As Dante and Virgil proceed with the Sun at their backs, Dante is startled to see only one shadow stretching before him—his own. He turns around thinking his guide has abandoned him, but finds him there as always. Says Virgil,

> Why are you still uncertain? Why do you doubt
> that I am here and guide you on your way?...
> (Canto III, 23–24)

Virgil (reason) reassures Dante that there is no need to panic, for, unlike Dante, Virgil is spirit and, therefore, cannot possibly cast a shadow. Seen esoterically, Dante's consciousness, still sense-based, is on the verge of a transformation that would allow him to behold thought's incorporeal aspect. The Sun now shining at his back hints at the emergence of Christ consciousness hidden from view. Thus, we see Dante awakening to the difference between the *light* of thinking and thought's dialectical form. What he perceives as his own shadow is figuratively a thought form born of his mediated perception of that light.

Seen from another point of view, Virgil, having symbolized reason (or intellect) tied to the sense world, can also be thought to *harbor an activity* separate from the form that manifests to Dante—an activity to which Dante is beginning to awaken. For this reason, Virgil states:

> "...If now I cast no shadow, should that fact
> amaze you more than the heavens which pass the light
> undimmed from one to another?..."
> (Canto III, 28–30)

Nonetheless, in his attempt to further explain the mystery of the spiritual world's relationship to the physical, Virgil begins to show, more than ever, how reason (or the intellect) is limited in penetrating certain mysteries. Says he,

> "...We react
> within these bodies to pain and heat and cold
> according to the workings of That Will
> which does not will that all Its ways be told.
>
> He is insane who dreams that he may learn
> by mortal reasoning the boundless orbit
> Three Persons in One Substance fill and turn.

> Be satisfied with the *quia* of cause unknown,
> O humankind! For could you have seen All,
> Mary need not have suffered to bear a son.
>
> You saw how some yearn endlessly in vain:
> such as would, else, have surely had their wish,
> but have, instead, its hunger as their pain.
>
> I speak of Aristotle and Plato...
> —Of them and many more." And here he paused,
> and sorrowing and silent, bowed his head.
> (Canto III, 30–45)

In Virgil's address, we can sense the futility encountered by reason, as Virgil ponders the reality that lies beyond the sensory world. He tells Dante to be content with the knowledge he has gained in life, since to expect more from dialectical thinking, often leads to desperation and sorrow—a sorrow of which he is reminded at the mention of those in Limbo. The mysteries of the world can only be revealed through the *light* of Christ; for this reason, Mary (the archetype of *Divine Wisdom*) conceived Jesus, so that we might one day realize, by means of the Christ, that *force* through which all things were created. Though Virgil is "aware" of the importance of the Christ, he is seen, here, having lacked the capacity to realize this spiritual force within him, since the *light* of Christ did not permeate the Earth until after Virgil's death in 19 BC. ACCORDING TO RUDOLF STEINER, CHRIST'S CRUCIFIXION TOOK PLACE ON AD APRIL 3, 33.

Dante and Virgil observe in dismay the sheer cliffs that rise above them. They seem unapproachable. As Virgil painstakingly ponders which direction up the slopes they should take, Dante notices a throng of penitents moving slowly toward them. They move as if motionless. These are the first of the Late Repentant who, before rising up to the next stage of purification, must wait thirty times longer to receive God's grace than their show of contumacy on Earth. These souls are not undergoing penitence for merely disobeying the Church, but for *sluggishly* turning their hearts toward God. Their laziness reflects a lack of will. Therefore, they must wait patiently to cultivate it. Though they feel no pain, they languish in the frustration of not actualizing their desire to be with God. By failing to recognize the sanctity of the Church, in spite of its corruption, they *precluded themselves of the will* necessary to penetrate its dogma and thereby uncover the mystery of the Christ buried within it. Thus, they were excommunicated for disobedience.

Among the souls that Dante encounters is Manfred, King of Sicily and the son of Frederick II. Though he had often opposed the Papal States, he was too powerful to be excommunicated while alive. Only after his death was he excommunicated, but this could not keep him from finding his way toward *Divine Love*. Though his sins were awful,

> ...infinite
> is the abiding Goodness which holds out
> its open arms to all who turn to It...
> (Canto III, 121–123)

Therefore, the slightest intimation of our acceptance of God's *Love* renders the heart forces predisposed to receive it—regardless of our many earthly transgressions. In revealing how his bones were scattered over unconsecrated grounds by the Archbishop of Cosenza, Manfred tells Dante:

> ...No man may be so cursed by priest or pope
> but what the Eternal Love may still return
> while any thread of green lives on in hope...
> (Canto III, 133–135)

As Dante and Manfred are about to leave each other, Manfred instructs him to inform his daughter Constance of his condition upon his return to the world, adding "for much is gained here through the help of you there." His request discloses an interesting fact regarding the interconnectedness between souls; the *living*, by seeking through prayer and meditation the divine forces of love working within them on Earth, are able to accelerate the process of purification that another undergoes in the spiritual world. In his lecture, *Links Between the Living and the Dead*, Rudolf Steiner says by directing the forces of *love* toward the dead, one "eases his path, removes hindrances from him." He adds,

> In order that this may be rightly understood, it must be stated that nourishment after death can be drawn only from the ideas and thoughts of those with whom there was some connection during life; nourishment cannot be drawn from those with whom there was no connection at all.[19]

Canto IV opens with Dante pondering Plato's concept of multiple souls, which postulates that a human being has three souls, each situated in a particular organ within the body. The Vegetative soul is seated in the liver, the Emotional soul in the heart, and the Intellectual soul in the brain. Aristotle and St. Aquinas, however, later contested this, as does Dante. Having embraced Plato in *La Vita Nuova*, Dante now seems to find it difficult to reconcile Platonism with Christianity. Thus, he asks how is it possible for one sensorial impression to draw our undivided attention, as it does, if we are made up of three spiritual bodies, each with a different function?

> When any sense of ours records intense
> pleasure or pain, then the whole soul is drawn
> by such impressions into that one sense,
>
> and seems to lose all other powers. And thus
> do I refute the error that asserts
> that one soul on another burns in us.
> (Canto IV, 1–6)

Here, Dante dismisses Plato's assertion regarding the inner workings of the human being's "threefold" spiritual nature, where, according to Plato, each "soul," within the human being, manifests a different cognitive capacity. Instead, Dante argues that since the *whole* human being experiences the feeling of pain or pleasure, there cannot be but one soul. When we are absorbed by a sensorial impression, we lose connection to the surrounding world, which, of course, implies that no other body (or soul) within us asserts itself to consciously discern the effect that other forces may have upon us. He thus attempts to correct the "error" of Plato and accept the idea put forth by Aristotle, Aquinas, and the Church—namely that the Vegetative, Emotional, and Intellectual souls manifest as one cognitive capacity. He attempts to prove this by showing how our sense of time is eclipsed by such an experience.

> And, for this reason, when we see or hear
> whatever seizes strongly on the soul,
> time passes, and we lose it unaware.
> (Canto IV, 7–9)

The excommunicated spirits soon interrupt Dante's thoughts and point out the path that he and Virgil are to take. While scaling the rocks leading up to the next ledge, Dante asks Virgil for directions. Again, Virgil is unable to indicate the way, for the intellect is unable to fathom the realm of feeling (Purgatory), a realm unfamiliar to it. Thought knows not the ways of the heart! Instead, they must once again ask the penitents for help. Meanwhile, Virgil (reason) spurs an exhausted Dante onward, encouraging him to exercise his will, which Dante must manifest to an ever-greater degree if he is to ascend higher. Though his intellect contains the light that can lead him to the higher realms of Purgatory, this light buried within the will can only break through the dialectical nature of Dante's consciousness if such a will is strengthened.

Having eventually arrived upon the slopes bearing the Indolent, Dante and Virgil face eastward toward the rising Sun and begin to contemplate its movement around the Earth. Dante, with Virgil's help, begins to visualize how Purgatory and Mt. Zion are antipodal. He sees that the equator is only as far to the north of one as it is to the south of the other. After their astronomical discussion, Dante asks Virgil to estimate how long their journey up the slopes of Purgatory will take. Virgil answers,

> Such is this Mount that when a soul
> begins the lower slopes it most must labor;
> then less and less the more it nears its goal.
>
> Thus when we reach the point when the slopes seem
> so smooth and gentle that the climb becomes
> as easy as to float a skiff downstream,
>
> then will this road be run, and not before
> that journey's end will your repose be found.
> I know this much for truth and say no more.
> (Canto IV, 88–96)

Thus, once again, Dante's ascent will be made easier the more he exerts his will to overcome the inertia of his thinking—an inertia that fetters souls to the lower slopes of the Mount. Seen esoterically, this can only become manifest to the degree in which he has purified his thinking of all earthly influences by way of the will, which has the strength to transform those karmic tendencies that inhibit the purification of his soul (Purgatory). Ultimately, the more he wills his thinking, the more the *light* intrinsic to it will begin to emerge ever more quickly—as evidenced by his ascent up the Mount—until he becomes fully immersed in this *light* (Paradise).

Having listened intently to Virgil, Dante hears a voice nearby utter, "Maybe by that time you'll find you need to sit before you fly!" They drag themselves to where the voice issues, and, there, lying on the ground is Belacqua. Because he was slow in seeking God, he finds himself amongst the Indolent and must repent on this ledge for the length of time he spent on Earth. Unlike the excommunicated, these souls do not suffer for having not accepted Church doctrine. Instead, their present predicament is *solely* a result of laziness—a lack of will. Belacqua seems so lazy that to even contemplate his ascent before its due time is not worth the effort. And so, thinking that is not led to conceive the importance of its own activity, also lacks the will to induce such action.

We see from this episode that he and Dante were good friends, for Dante says, "Belacqua, your fate need never again trouble my mind." Like Manfredi, Belacqua wishes for those on Earth to pray for him; again, only their prayers can aid his spiritual development. Having felt the joy of knowing that his friend, Belacqua, can one day find the *light* of salvation, Dante is urged to proceed.

Before long, Dante and Virgil find themselves walking among another group of penitents—those who died a violent death without the possibility of repentance. Though they, too, failed to cultivate the will that leads to God, outer circumstances robbed them of the opportunity to do so late in life. Because they were often the victims of karmic necessity, they are placed just a little higher up the Mount than the Indolent. Of course, one can argue that they, themselves, are responsible for the karma that befalls them. However, since not everything can so easily be traceable to the workings of karma, they are given the benefit of the doubt and by "God's grace" have a slightly more favorable predicament than those below them.

The souls on this slope notice that Dante is *alive*, for, again, they can see his shadow—yet another clue to the initiatory nature of Dante's journey! This light and dark contrast can be envisioned as an allegorical device used to denote the fragmented nature of Dante's dialectical thinking, despite the emergence of Christ's *light* slowly about to emerge within his consciousness. This is particularly evident as Dante pays too much attention to the voices of the penitent, who, still manifesting the effects of their transgressions, represent those forces of dialecticism that inadvertently suppress the human will—thus diverting Dante from his true course. Virgil, in fact, commands him to abstain from such idle curiosity,

> ...toward every wisp, he loses true direction
> sapping his mind's force with continual change.
> (Canto V, 17–18)

These souls, noticing that Dante is *alive*, quickly surround him—each hoping to receive a favor from him upon his earthly return. They ask him if he recognizes any of them. Dante does not, but he asks them to relate their wishes, so that he can try to oblige them by "that peace" he seeks "in following the footsteps" of his Guide, namely, "that peace which draws me on from world to world to my own good." To this, one replies:

> No soul among us doubts you will fulfill
> all you declare, without your need to swear it,
> if lack of power does not defeat your will...
> (Canto V, 70–72)

Here, Dante promises that he will do whatever he can for them by that force of *Love* (peace) to which his intellect (Virgil) leads him, for only then can his actions really accord themselves with the Will of God. The souls do not doubt Dante's sincerity. They realize that Dante can only help them to the degree that his will becomes one with that of God. As long as God's Will manifests in his thinking, Dante will be granted the opportunity to consciously incite a change in the conditions of many in the afterworld.

The first of three spirits comes up to greet Dante. It is Jacopo del Cassero da Fano, a Guelf captain who was hunted down by the hirelings of Azzo VIII of Este. During his escape, he fell into a morass and met his doom. He asks that those still living on Earth direct their thoughts to Heaven and pray for his forgiveness. The second penitent is Count Bonconte of Montefeltro whose father, Guido, was among the Evil Councilors in Hell. Bonconte's story forms the counterpoint to that of his father. As a Ghibelline leader, Bonconte fought the Guelfs at the battle of Campaldino—where even Dante had taken part. There, he was killed. But unlike his father who died without the absolution of sin, Bonconte crossed his arms upon his breast, and with a tear in his eye, pronounced the name of the Virgin Mary at the moment of his death. Suddenly, an angel swooped down from Heaven and saved him, just as a black demon was about to snatch his soul. The demon furiously retaliated by raging havoc on his body. This picture presented by Dante illustrates how even the slightest display of openness to the creative force of life leads to the path of salvation. In the black demon, we witness the ahrimanic forces' future relationship to humanity, where they inherit only what is *dead*. What comes into contact with such forces inevitably undergoes a process of disintegration.

The third spirit who approaches Dante is Pia, a quiet and courteous lady who was killed by her husband, Count Nello Pannocchieschi for no apparent reason. She, like the others, asks to be remembered on Earth,

> ...oh speak my name again with living breath
> to living memory. Pia am I...
> (Canto V, 139–140)

Therefore, the spirits whom Dante encounters on Purgatory disclose the presence of an insoluble connection between the living and the dead. Within *living memory* there exists the *force* by which one is linked to another human being. Our salvation is, thus, intrinsically related to that of others. Christ enkindles the memory inherent within our etheric bodies. He is the ubiquitous link between all human beings. Dante is soon swarmed by a host of spirits all wishing that their names be remembered on Earth.

After they leave the group, Dante asks Virgil if he did not, in fact, say that earthly prayer for the departed could not sway what was decreed for them in Heaven.

> ...Can all their hope be in vain? Or have I missed
> your true intent and read some other there?
> (Canto VI, 32–33)

Virgil answers that the intensity of *Love* revealed to the soul can transform unfulfilled karma in an instant. The prayer that he referred to in the *Aeneid VI*, in which Palinurus implores The Sybil to carry his message across the Styx, had no direct access to God, for, as a pagan, Palinurus had no comprehension of—nor openness toward—the *light* of the Christ at work within consciousness. Thus, the grace of God could not manifest itself to him. Virgil adds that one person does not diminish Divine Justice by taking on the karmic debts of another. However, the deeper Virgil ventures into the question posed by Dante, the more difficulty he encounters. So, once again, we witness the fading of intellectual forces, which in our attempt to fathom the nature of spiritual reality, futilely rely on a system of logic formulated upon earthly principles. With each ascent, Virgil's (intellectual) powers diminish, until they inevitably succumb to "faith"—the heartfelt conviction in the existence of higher powers of spiritual reality (and of cognition).

Having attempted somewhat unsuccessfully to answer Dante's question, Virgil tells him that Beatrice will decipher such perplexing mysteries for him high above the slopes of Purgatory. There, she will essentially be his "lamp between the truth and intelligence." Upon hearing her name, Dante desires to speed ahead. But Virgil insists that the road ahead of them is arduous and that, regardless of his haste, Dante will not reach the mountaintop before the appointed time. Again, each step Dante takes must be deliberate and consciously undertaken.

After a while, Virgil notices a lone spirit observing them. He asks him for directions. But the spirit refuses to answer until Virgil identifies the place of his birth. As soon as Virgil tells him, the spirit leaps to his feet and cries,

> O Mantuan, I am Sordello
> of your own country!
> (Canto VI, 77–78)

They embrace. At this point, Dante launches into a prolonged diatribe against Italy, which he continues until the end of the canto.

Sordello, born around 1200, was a Troubadour who wandered through the countries bordering the Mediterranean. Though only forty or so of his poems still exist, he was also known to have penned highly charged political works. Dante places him here as a political dissident who abandoned Italy on principle. His unanticipated reunion with Virgil, a fellow Mantuan, illustrates the importance of *brotherly love* as a guiding force necessary for the world's spiritual evolution. Says Dante,

> That noble spirit leaped up with a start
> at the mere sound of his own city's name,
> and took his fellow citizen to his heart...
> (Canto VI, 82–84)

Against this image of brotherhood, Dante cries out:

> Ah servile Italy, grief's hostelry,
> ah ship unpiloted in the storm's rage,
> no mother of provinces but of harlotry!
> (Canto VI, 79–81)

> ...while still, within you, brother wars on brother,
> and though one wall and moat surrounds them all,
> your living sons gnaw at one another!
> (Canto VI, 85–87)

Dante's passionate reproach of Italy resonates because of the silence between Virgil and Sordello—a silence that shelters the "kindling" of heart forces that not even the impassioned rage of Dante's invective can extinguish. Within their silence exists the presence of Christ's all pervading Love. Dante seems to be crying out that nothing should be so fundamental as the love for one's fellow human being. Yet, his tirade against his homeland reveals the many levels of love that have been corrupted there. A mere intellectual understanding of love cannot suffice. Instead, a process of reintegration resulting in the harmonious unification of thinking and feeling must be incited by the will to action. Only then, can the *light* of the Christ streaming through human hearts be actualized. The two poets who stand united before Dante exemplify the harmonization of thinking and feeling. Virgil, of course, is representative of reason/intellect and Sordello, who sang courtly rhymes of love, symbolizes feeling.

Canto VII opens with Virgil and Sordello embracing. In fact, they embrace three or four times before Sordello asks, "Who are you?" Virgil tells him. Sordello, taken by surprise, embraces him again, this time with great reverence and asks how is it that he finds himself there. Virgil tells him

> Through every valley of the painful kingdom
> I passed... A power from Heaven
> marked me this road, and in that power I came.
>
> Not what I did but what I had left undone,
> who learned too late, denies my right to share
> your hope of seeing the Eternal Sun.
>
> There is a place below where sorrow lies
> in untormented gloom...
> (Canto VII, 22–29)

Here, Dante lays the groundwork for what lies ahead, for they are about to enter a lush *green* valley that is the antithesis of Limbo. For now, Virgil asks Sordello to lead them to the Gate of Purgatory. Sordello agrees, but tells him that it will be impossible for them to make much progress in the face of the impending darkness. Once the shadows fall, the penitents cannot make any progress toward God. Virgil, confused as to the meaning of Sordello's words, asks for clarification for, again, having lived before the Mystery of Golgotha, he lacks the *light* of the Christ.

> "Once the sun sets," that noble soul replied,
> "you would not cross this line"—and ran his finger
> across the ground between him and my Guide.
>
> "Nor is there anything to block the ascent
> except the shades of night: they of themselves
> suffice to sap the will of the most fervent..."
> (Canto VII, 52–57)

Without the *light* of Christ, humankind cannot find its way to God. Only this *light*, hidden within thinking, harbors those forces

The Purgatorio: Ascending the Slopes of Redemption

that can guide human beings toward higher realms of experience. Therefore, Sordello suggests that any progress in ascending toward the higher spheres of consciousness necessitates the cultivation of will. Otherwise, one merely wanders about the darkened regions of dialecticism, where energy is exhausted and progress never realized.

Sordello leads them into the valley that he has described. It is an enchanting glade where flowers scent the air and sparkle in the lush *green* grass like gems. There, they hear the hymn *Salve Regina* rising toward Heaven, sung by a choir of souls hidden from view. This place is reserved for the rulers of humanity who were negligent toward God. So preoccupied were they with the good of others, that they had little time to devote themselves to their Creator. As we have seen until now, the souls in Anti-Purgatory are those who failed to cultivate the will, for their thinking had often been focused elsewhere, or misdirected as in the case with the Excommunicated, though not maliciously. Here, the luminosity of the valley in which the rulers are placed reflects the brilliance of their worldly fame. Since they sacrificed themselves for others, they inhabit the most beautiful place in the lower reaches of Purgatory. Thus, they are being recognized for the good that they were able to manifest—a good that reflects, even to the most infinitesimal degree, the activity of the higher forces working within humanity. Among the souls to which Dante gives heed are the Emperor Rudolph, Ottocar II, Wenceslaus IV, Henry III, Phillip III, Henry the Fat of Navarre, Peter III of Aragon, Charles I of Anjou, and William, Marquis of Monteferrato and Canavese. Dante and Virgil will spend the night among such nobility. There is, as we have noted, a parallel between this valley and Limbo, in that both contain figures of nobility but with radically different destinies. Here, the *greenness* of the valley signals the *hope* of Eternal life, which is reflected by the flowers glistening in the Sun's rays. Limbo, on the other hand, sighs with the knowledge that glows dimly in the darkness of despair, for without the *light* of the Christ, there is no hope, nor shall there be.

As night falls, Dante gazes down into the *flowering valley* and sees a spirit signal for attention, with palms joined in prayer, he faces the East and says,

> I have no thought except that Thou art there.
> (Canto VIII, 12)

East is the direction of the rising Sun. Therefore, we can assume that he directs the spirits in the valley to await the dawn, when the Sun's rays slowly begin to reveal what was veiled by the darkness. Allegorically, the East, of course, signifies the dawning of Christ's *light* within the human being. In Dante's case, this moment represents his attentiveness to the first sign of *life* arising from within his thinking—namely, the dawning of the *light*. In witnessing the birth of *light* within thinking, one can perceive how this *light* (life) precedes the emergence of materialized thought (form). And so, the spirit, whom Dante watches, sings the evening hymn *Te Lucis Ante* (To Thee before the light is done). It is a hymn intended to protect the penitents from the imminent darkness about to envelop them.

As the spirits in the valley finish their song, Dante again posits yet another clue for deciphering the mysterious message concealed within his *Comedy*. Says he,

> Reader, if you seek truth, sharpen your eyes,
> for here the veil of allegory thins
> and may be pierced by any man who tries.
> (Canto VIII, 19–21)

This scene recalls Dante at the gates of Dis, when the arrival of heavenly aid rescued him from the terrifying face of the Medusa. There, he beckoned the reader to take similar note: "Men of sound intellect and probity, weigh with good understanding what lies hidden behind the veil of my strange allegory" (Canto IX, *Inferno*, 58–60).

Here, two angels, dressed in *green*, each with a fiery blunted sword in hand, swoop down from the Heavens. They take their positions on opposite sides of the valley sheltering the group of repentant souls.

> "They are from Mary's bosom," Sordello said,
> "and come to guard the valley from the Serpent
> that in a moment now will show his head."
> (Canto VIII, 37–39)

Dante breaks into a cold sweat at the mention of the Serpent. Sordello, relatively unconcerned, suggests that they go and visit some of the souls below. As they begin to make their way toward them, Dante notices, in the darkened air, the figure of Nino Visconti of Pisa. As Judge of Gallura, he sentenced Friar Gomita to his death. Dante, however, portrays him as a worldly man who had neglected his own spiritual development, having instead devoted himself to his duties. Nino asks Dante to explain how he finds himself there. Dante answers:

> ...I came by the pits of woe—
> this morning, *I am still in my first life,*
> *though I gain the other on the road I go.*
> (Canto VIII, 58–60; italics mine)

Again, Dante describes the nature of the journey—one that permits him, *while still alive* ("I am still in my first life"), to gain life in the spiritual world. Dante's ability to fathom the nature of his journey is more and more reflected in the slow, but gradual, fading of Virgil. As we have already intimated, this is possible because Dante has begun to assert his will to an ever-greater degree to go beyond dialectical understanding and arrive at the *light* of thinking, or *Active Intelligence*— symbolized by Beatrice (*Sophia*)—which eventually enables him to behold the celestial hierarchies.

Taken aback that Dante—though *alive*—finds himself among the dead, Nino asks him to implore Giovanna for her prayers. As soon as Nino finishes speaking, Dante gazes up at the Heavens and beholds three stars that he had never seen before. They represent the three theological virtues—Faith, Hope, and Charity. They have replaced the four Cardinal virtues representing the *active life*, which have disappeared from view and now shine on the other side of the Earth. These three Christian virtues, on the other hand, appearing immediately before Dante's entrance into Purgatory proper, symbolize the *contemplative life*. Here, an interesting dichotomy arises between the two groups of stars. The four Cardinal virtues manifest as the Sun begins to rise in the early dawn, whereas the three Christian virtues reveal themselves as the Sun's light disappears. In this interplay, we can see humanity's spiritual evolution being represented. Under the guidance of the four stars—long before Christ's entry into the world—we human beings beheld the process of creation, but only as mere spectators of this creative process. We were unable to participate in it, for our consciousness had yet to be individualized. The three Christian virtues, on the other hand, point to those soul qualities necessary for the transformation of being *by way of the Christ,* which in turn enables humankind to consciously participate in God's creation. Viewed from a more individualized perspective, we can see how these two groups of stars characterize the relationship between willing and thinking. The Cardinal virtues incite the human will in the act of doing. They herald the work that is to be done as the Sun rises. On the other hand, the Christian virtues direct human beings *inward* (as night approaches) so as to behold the unseen forces within thinking. *Thus, these two constellations, alternating over Purgatory, visually symbolize the interplay between willing and thinking within the realm of feeling (Purgatory).*

All of a sudden, Sordello points to a place in the grass and shouts,

> Our Adversary! There he is!
> (Canto VIII, 96)

As Dante looks, he sees that

> Straight through the valley's unprotected side
> a serpent came, perhaps the very one
> that gave bitter food for which Eve cried.
> (Canto VIII, 97–99)

Important to note here is *how* the serpent approaches. The manner of its approach illustrates the guile possessed by the luciferic forces in deviating humanity from its true course. The serpent makes its way toward Dante and the penitent through the *unprotected* side. If the valley symbolizes the precondition necessary for the soul's purification, conducive to humanity's spiritual reascension, then the serpent, as Massimo Scaligero points out in *Il Graal: Saggio sul Mistero del Sacro Amore* symbolizes "the degeneration of the originating force and the point from which this force must rise again."[20] The serpent must thus be understood as the being initially responsible for the separation of thinking and willing, that hastens Dante's climb up the slopes of redemption (Purgatory), so that Dante can reintegrate these two aspects of consciousness—a process to be consummated once he encounters Beatrice. The angels that come to Dante's aid reflect the "Grace of God," for, with their blunted fiery swords, they bestow upon him the *temperance*, by which Dante can fend off the influences that seek to *divert* him from achieving his aim. We see another reference to the flaming swords of the Cherubim at the Garden of Eden in Genesis 3:24:

> The Lord God made garments of skin for Adam and his wife and clothed them. And the Lord God said, "The man has become like one of us, knowing good and evil! He must not be allowed to reach out his hand and take also from the tree of life and eat, and live forever!" So the Lord God banished him from the Garden of Eden to work the ground from which he was taken. After he drove the man out, he placed on the east of the Garden of Eden cherubim and a flaming sword flashing back and forth to guard the way to the tree of life.[21]

The Tree of Life, as we have mentioned, is symbolic of the creative forces intrinsic to our thinking, unhindered by materiality. Having been corrupted by the luciferic impulses, we human beings (represented by Adam and Eve) had to be cast from the "Garden of Eden," so that we could one day free ourselves of their influence and, thereby, restore the sanctity of the Tree of Life.

Just as the Cherubim, in the "Garden of Eden," "turned every way to guard the way" to this sacred tree, so, too, do we see them, here, in the valley, descend upon the snake and frighten it away. Humanity is thus protected from the forces that seek to disrupt the reintegration of thinking and willing. Having witnessed, with Dante, the angel's power over the serpent, Nino Visconti turns to him and says,

> So may *the lamp* that leads to what you seek
> find oil enough...in your own will
> *to light your way* to the enameled peak...
> (Canto VIII, 112–114; italics mine)

This metaphor reinforces the notion that human thought (lamp: Virgil) must be rekindled by the will (oil), so that Dante may find the *light* of Christ that can guide him into the suprasensory world.

At this point, Dante is sitting among a group of spirits, longingly awaiting the return of the Sun.

> Now pale upon the balcony of the East
> ancient Tithonus' concubine appeared,
> but lately from her lover's arms released
>
> Across her brow, their radiance like a veil,
> a scroll of gems was set, working in the shape
> of the cold beast whose sting is in his tail
>
> And now already, where we were, the night
> had taken two steps upward, while the third
> thrust down its wings in the first stoke of flight;
>
> when I, by Adam's weight of flesh defeated,
> was overcome by sleep, and sank to rest
> across the grass on which we five were seated.
> (Canto IX, 1–12)

Here, Dante describes the Moon as the concubine of Tithonus. However, according to classical mythology, when Tithonus married the daughter of the Sun (Dawn), he implored Jove to grant him immortality. In so doing, Tithonus forgot to ask for eternal youth. Thus, Tithonus grew ever so old next to his young bride, who was ageless. By depicting Tithonus flirting with the Moon, Dante creates

The Purgatorio: Ascending the Slopes of Redemption

Lucia Carrying Dante in His Sleep, *William Blake*

an interesting prelude to the series of events that are about to ensue. Here, the Moon is seen standing out on the balcony of the East (i.e., the eastern horizon before the coming of the Sun) with the constellation of Scorpio imprinted, like a gem, upon her forehead. Night, having taken two steps, that is, having lasted two-thirds its normal length of time, initiates the last third of its duration. Says Dante, "the third thrust down its wings in the first stroke of flight." At his point, he begins falling into a dream:

> and when the mind, escaped from its submission
> to flesh and to the chains of waking thought,
> becomes almost prophetic in its vision…
> (Canto IX, 16–18)

Dante dreams that, like Ganymede, an Eagle has taken him to Heaven. Ganymede, the most beautiful of mortals, was taken at the request of Jove into Heaven where he was made cupbearer to the gods. This Eagle that descends from God has wings of gold (sense-free thinking) spread outward (embrace of Divine Love) as it approaches. It snatches Dante and takes him up into the *sphere* of Fire. *This marks a pivotal point in the spiritual transformation of Dante.*

The intensity of the *light* was so powerful that it shocked Dante back into the sense world.

> It seemed that we were swept in a great blaze,
> and the imaginary fire so scorched me
> my sleep broke and I wakened in a daze.
> (Canto IX, 31–33)

Having awakened, Dante finds himself on the Mount of Purgatory, unaware of his whereabouts, or how he has arrived there. His situation recalls that of Achilles who, while sleeping, was stolen from Chiron by his mother, Thetis, and taken to Scyros. Disguised as a girl, he was coaxed by Ulysses and Diomede to follow their dream upon the high seas. Virgil tells Dante that while he was asleep a lady, calling herself Lucia, had come. Lucia represents *divine light*. Having taken the form of an eagle (also a symbol of divine light or spiritual vision), she had carried Dante from the beautiful valley up to the Gate of Purgatory. Dante has ingeniously represented the transformation from the lower self to the higher self by the juxtaposition of the scorpion and the eagle—both representative of the Constellation of Scorpio. The fact that Dante is taken hold of by the Eagle under the influence of Scorpio symbolizes the *birth* of his higher self, through the transformation of his lower self. (Incidentally, the Eagle may also be thought to represent *Divine Justice* as it relates to the Roman Empire.)

As he and Virgil begin to ascend the steep slope before them, Dante says,

> Reader, you know to what exalted height
> I raised my theme. Small wonder if I now
> summon still greater art to what I write.
> (Canto IX, 70–72)

The Purgatorio: Ascending the Slopes of Redemption

Dante and Virgil Approaching the Angel
Who Guards the Entrance of Purgatory, *William Blake*

These verses bear witness to the fact that the powers of thought are too feeble to describe the *initiatory experience* about to unfold, and that only by means of a *pictorial representation* can such an experience be more accurately conveyed.

As Dante and Virgil arrive at the gate, they notice an Angel dressed in the color of ashes. In its one hand, it bears two keys (one silver and one gold); in its other hand, it holds a sword. He stands upon the last of three steps, each of a different color. The first step is white and luminous: the second is dark and burnt with vertical and horizontal lines running across its surface; the third is porphyry, a color deeper than red.

This scene calls to mind the act of confession in the Roman Catholic Church. The Angel, speechless and motionless, serves as the confessor. Dressed in the color of ashes, he displays humility, for the priest is himself also a penitent. The sword that he bears in one hand represents Divine Justice, as it reflects the Sun's rays—a *light* so bright that Dante is forced to look away, for it is difficult to behold the reflected splendor of God's *light* without *the necessary preparation*. The two keys that the Angel holds in his other hand have been attributed various meanings, the most common of which says that gold represents the divine authority to pardon, while the silver symbolizes the understanding necessary for directing the penitent and "loosening...the knot" (the entanglement of sin). The three steps before Dante have also been interpreted in a variety of ways. As Ciardi states, the step made of white marble is said to mirror the soul of the penitent as "he truly is and not in its outward seeming."[22] It symbolizes Contrition of the Heart. The step that is burnt containing the lines running across its surface reflects the shame that envelops the penitent while confessing. The cracks that develop are said to reflect the imperfect nature of the sins confessed. This step represents Contrition of the Mouth. The third step is dark red—as "flaming as blood." It is emblematic of humanity's flaming desire to atone for its sins through deed.

These symbolic interpretations are not the only ones that can be used to depict the inner nature of the human being about to undergo a purgatorial experience. The three steps, for example may also represent the field of activity upon which the process of purification takes place. The white shiny marble acts as a mirror and can be thought of as the etheric body, which uses the brain to reflect cosmic activity in the form of thoughts. The dark and burnt step, containing cracks, can represent the astral body, the human being's most imperfect of the three bodies not visible to him. Its rough surface reflects the degree to which the untransformed astral forces have contributed to the manifestation of sin. Dante likens the step that looks like porphyry to the blood running through the arteries, which can be considered the vehicle of the human "I." The silver and gold keys that the Angel carries may relate to the forces of dialectical thought (Moon/silver) and the *light* of thinking (Sun/gold), respectively. And so, just as the Moon reflects the light of the Sun, so, too, does dialectical thought reflect cosmic thinking. In other words, the brain (Moon) *reflects* the *light of thinking* (Sun/Christ), which alone can enable humankind to reascend the heights from which it descended.

As Dante approaches the Angel, he begins the second ritualistic act of initiation, that of Communion. Here, he actively *begins* the first initiatory steps toward the eventual realization of the Christ being. Upon reaching the steps, he is asked,

> What is your business here?
> Answer from where you stand. Where is your Guide?
> Take care you do not find your coming dear.
> (Canto IX, 85–87)

Virgil tells the Angel that a "Lady well-versed in these matters" has sent them. The Angel replies,

> And may she still assist you, once inside,
> to your soul's good! Come forward to our three steps.
> (Canto IX, 91–92)

This Angel stands on the third and highest step, thus, symbolizing the point of connection between the forces descending from God—via the Angel—and the Higher Self, or "I" of the human being. Dante climbs carefully onto each step as if in contemplation. At this point, Virgil (intellect/reason) whispers into Dante's ear, instructing him to ask the Angel for admittance. Dante quickly obeys with the utmost devotion. He beats upon his breast three times, thus conforming to the classical tradition for penitence in which the sinner asks to be forgiven in thought, word, and deed. Dante has revealed his soul to his Guardian Angel, who, standing on the step of porphyry, is portrayed as anchored in the "I" of Dante. Having revealed both his etheric and astral nature to the higher forces, Dante thus greets the Angel from his own "I."

The Angel, as a witness to Dante's contrition, carves seven Ps on Dante's forehead, each signifying a vice purged on the ledges above—pride, envy, wrath, sloth, avarice, gluttony, and lust. Each vice of which Dante is able to purge himself results in the elimination of a P. The Angel then takes the two keys, silver and gold, and places the first (silver) one into the keyhole. Says he,

> Whenever either of these keys is put
> improperly into the lock and fails to turn it,
> ...the door stays shut.
> (Canto IX, 121–123)

Having turned both keys, the Angel warns Dante not to look behind him for, if he does, he will find himself *outside* the Gate once again. As the enormous portals swing open, Dante hears a thunderous roar of voices singing *"Te Deum Laudamus"* (*We Praise Thee O God*). This marks his entrance into Purgatory proper where his penitence begins.

The scenes that ensue on the slopes of Purgatory depict the elimination of the *causes* of sin. The eventual elimination of these *causes* will enable Dante to become so pure as to be a "mirror of God." This purification will consequently lead to Dante's perception of the cosmic forces (God) that weave the world into being.

Until now, we have seen penitents confined to a state of *waiting* before being allowed entry into Purgatory, for such spirits lacked the will in earthly life to consciously direct their thinking toward God. In fact, it was undisciplined thinking that determined the penitent's predicament. In the case of the Excommunicated and the Negligent Rulers, we found that thinking was willfully employed but not directed toward the spiritual world. On the other hand, the Indolent were victims of a thinking that lacked will. Now, just as the will misdirected thinking in the lowest circles of Hell, here, in the lowest regions of Purgatory, thinking misguides the will. Therefore, the transition from an earthly state of being to a more spiritual one, presents itself (as we have previously alluded) in the form of a mirrored image.

The Purgatorio: Ascending the Slopes of Redemption

As Dante and Virgil enter Purgatory proper, they also make their way ever more deeply into the *feeling* realm, where we find thinking subjected to feeling. All of our transgressions—such as pride, envy, avarice, etc.—reflect the degree to which our emotions keep the force of thinking from adhering to a path that leads to the realization of our own divine nature. The "Seven Deadly" sins that must be purged on the cornices further up the Mount can be understood as the *causes* of the aberrant forms of behavior that we find manifested as *effects* in the various regions of Hell. At the entrance to each cornice, Dante finds examples of virtues opposite the sin punished there. There are always three examples, the first of which is taken from the life of the Virgin Mary. Such examples comprise what Dante calls the Whip of a particular sin, for they are to "spur" the sinners "on to emulation." Following the Whip is a scene in which the penitents purge themselves. This is finally succeeded by the Rein, which depicts the result or consequence of a particular sin such as pride, to remind the penitents of the ramifications of their actions. Here, Dante also chooses exemplary, historical examples to illustrate his point. Therefore, each human vice comprises three individual cantos.

Having entered the Gate of Purgatory, Dante and Virgil cross

> ...the threshold of that gate
> so seldom used because man's perverse love
> so often makes the crooked path seem straight.
> (Canto X, 1–3)

Here, once again, Dante drops yet another subtle clue in reference to his *initiatory* experience. For the *"seldom"*-used gate into the spiritual world can only be entered by those *few* who are conscious of what lies *inside* the Gate of the path they trod. Furthermore, had Dante been merely describing an after-death experience, there would have been no need to point out the fact that one enters the Gate by being *conscious* of the right path, for he adds,

> I knew by the sound that it had closed again;
> and had I looked back, to what water ever
> could I have gone to wash away that stain?
> (Canto X, 4–6)

The road leading up to the First Cornice is arduous. Virgil implores Dante to hug the walls of the cliff. Dante likens their experience of this treacherous tract to that of passing through "the eye of the needle." The difficulty described by Dante recalls Matthew 19:24, where it is said, "it is easier for camel to go through the eye of a needle than for a rich man to enter the kingdom of God."[23] This reference is connected with the seldom-used gate mentioned above. This continuum of events, of course, requires that we continually envision aspects of Dante's journey not only graphically (as he visually presents them), but also as the flow of consciousness in continual transformation. In this particular case, the courage to confront one's mortality is paramount to one's ability to reach the heights of the spiritual world. This courage necessitates that thinking be rightly balanced with feeling. One must have equanimity of mind to enter the spiritual world. Dante, in following the footsteps of the Christ, adheres to the model by which these two spheres of activity, working within us, are brought into delicate balance.

Eventually Dante ends his climb to the next terrace. There, he comes upon a flat plain where he sees white marble lining the sheer bank that forms the wall of the Cornice of Pride. Curved into this marble are examples of humility. The first example shows the Annunciation. The Virgin Mary who, upon hearing from Gabriel that she had been chosen to give birth to Jesus, humbly responds, *"Ecce ancilla Dei"* (Behold the handmaiden of God). Next to the panel depicting the Virgin Mary, is a depiction of David dancing before God in humility after bringing the Ark to Jerusalem from the house of the Gittite. The third panel portrays the Emperor Trajan dismounting from his horse on the way to battle so as to comfort a widow who sheds tears for her slain son.

As Dante and Virgil observe the bas-relief of the Virgin Mary, Virgil tells Dante, "Do not give all your thought to this one part." In other words, Dante is *to shun the static nature of sense-based thinking*, even if it regards the archetype of *Divine Wisdom*. He is thus essentially told to avoid forming a "graven image." Dante stands on the side of Virgil "where one has one's heart." This juxtaposition symbolizes the fact that Dante's heart forces are permeating his thinking. Only then can he be so transformed as to overcome the influences of pride that have stained his soul.

Nonetheless, Dante presents these artistic representations as *living imaginations*. Upon seeing them, he says,

> The Maker who can never see or know
> anything new, *produced that "visible speaking"
> new to us, because not found below.*
> (Canto X, 91–93: italics mine)

Thus, the reproductions on the cornices of Purgatory attempt to depict the moral impulses working in the spiritual world—impulses that cannot be experienced, unless we attain a consciousness that allows them to be perceived. This stage corresponds to what is known as **Imagination** in Anthroposophy. It represents the point where our etheric body gradually lifts itself from the physical, thereby enabling us to begin perceiving the cosmic flow of ether forces through which the Christ is made manifest. Says Steiner,

> If we ascend to Imaginative consciousness in a healthy way, we first become free of our bodily nature. We weave in the ether life. Our mental images will thereby cease to have sharp contours; they will be Imaginations flowing into one another.[24]

As Dante "relishes the art and thought of those high images ("dear in themselves, and dearer yet as works His hand had wrought"), Virgil notices a group of penitents crawling toward them. They are the Proud. They each have an enormous stone placed on their backs—a stone so heavy that it "doubles them to the very earth." Dante rebukes the human aspect of pride:

> O you proud Christians, wretched souls and small,
> who by the dim lights of your twisted minds
> believe you prosper even as you fall—
>
> can you not see that we are worms, each one
> born to become the Angelic butterfly
> that flies defenseless to the Judgment Throne?
> (Canto X, 118–123)

The nature of pride does not allow us to see how we, as earthbound creatures, can transform ourselves into angelic beings. Dante seems to be implying that this process of metamorphosis cannot be grasped by "the dim light" of mere logic whose fixed forms adhere to the contours of the physical world. Pride is the greatest of all sins punished on Purgatory, for it underlies all others. It is intrinsic to our intellectual nature, which forms the basis of our understanding of the world. The intellect, by nature, dismisses those earthly events or manifestations that defy or transcend logic. It does so, however, with an unfounded certainty, which in itself reflects the inner workings of pride. The Fall of Humanity arose out of pride—our very first sin. By disobeying God's Will, Adam and Eve succumbed to the influences of Lucifer, who, himself, was cast from Heaven because of pride. Since it is the Primal transgression of humankind, it lies at the base of Purgatory proper. Those penitents, bearing slabs of rock on their backs, must endure the weight of worldliness that thrusts them ever closer to the Earth. Pride, in fact, may be viewed as our most immediate and greatest impediment, for its essential role in the Fall was, again, to sever thinking from willing—both of which are to be reintegrated in the form of Divine Will.

Canto XI begins with the penitent singing *The Lord's Prayer*. Since it is usually the first prayer a child learns, Dante (according to Ciardi) seems to be implying that humanity must revert to the most fundamental creed in the Christian faith. Contained in *The Lord's Prayer* is the verse, "lead us not into temptation." This clearly refers to the Fall, in which temptation was responsible for having taken away our "daily bread," namely, our connection to spiritual life. Thus, this prayer is, in a sense, an imagination, sung incessantly by the penitents, to reinforce the *memory* of what led them to their present state. By reevoking the childhood state in which pride had yet to *fully* establish itself in them, the penitents can gradually lessen their burden, namely, the *earthly* influence of the intellect. These spirits pray for those individuals still alive on Earth who are vulnerable to the clutches of temptation.

As Virgil approaches the penitent, he wishes them a speedy ascent and asks them for direction. We see, again, that Dante is less dependent on Virgil and more on himself. These souls, burdened by the weight on their backs, think nothing of the fact that Dante is *alive*, bearing the flesh of Adam, as told to them by Virgil. Here, we have yet another instance in which the influences of the earthly realm are not so manifest in Dante. For, unlike in Anti-Purgatory, Dante has begun to actualize evermore the living aspect of his thinking, which perfectly accords itself with the spiritual path of these souls. Virgil and Dante, having heard a sound issuing from underneath a rock, hear a soul tell them:

> Your way is to the *right*, along with ours.
> If you will come with us, you will discover
> *a pass within a living person's powers...*
> (Canto XI, 49–51; italics mine)

Note, again, yet another clue for those "with eyes to see"! The word *pass* refers to a point of transformation where the human being ascends to a higher level of spiritual perception, lying within the powers of thinking and willing.

Virgil asks a heavily burdened soul—Omberto Aldobrandesco, son of Guillim Aldobrandesco—about the path leading to the ascent. Omberto represents those who show pride for their lineage of birth. As Dante bends down to see him (sign of humility), he notices another soul following Omberto. It is Oderisi da Gubbio, a reknown illuminator of manuscripts. In order to see him, Dante must bend down even further. Oderisi confesses to have done his utmost to diminish the fame of another artist, Franco Bolognese, now celebrated in the world. He, thus, represents the pride of talent. Oderisi tells Dante that fame is like the wind blowing "this way and that," of which nothing will remain. He also refers to Guido Cavalcanti and Guido Gunizelli, adding that someone already born may surpass them. Here, Dante seems to hint at his superiority over Guido Cavalcanti who, by disdaining Virgil, is thought to have shown no appreciation for higher models of poetic inspiration. Nonetheless, Dante is purposely ambiguous here, for it is not at all clear that he is specifically referring to himself and, thus, exhibiting the pride to which he admitted in Hell. The last of the sinners whom Dante meets is Salvani, who represents pride of temporal power. Previously, all of Tuscany "sounded" with his fame. Now, no mention is made of him. Like the unrepentant, Salvani took no time for repentance. What saved him from Anti-Purgatory was a great act of humility. In his attempt to save a friend captured by Charles of Anjou, Salvani begged in the streets for his ransom, thereby debasing himself in the interest of his fellow man; he did what was unthinkable for a proud Ghibelline leader.

Virgil (reason) cuts Dante's discourse with the penitent short, and by doing so, reveals how Dante's thinking has become more discerning and restrained. It exhibits greater self-awareness born of the will. As they make their way from the cornice, Virgil bids Dante to look down at the sculpted forms on the floor beneath them. They are there for the dead to see how they "looked while yet alive," for

> ... often at the sight a thought will stir
> the passer-by to weep for what has been—
> though only the compassionate feel that spur.
>
> (Canto XII, 19–21)

These stone engravings form the Rein of Pride. Among the figures, Dante sees Thymbraeus, Mars, Pallus, Nimrod, Niobe, Saul, Troy,

The Purgatorio: Ascending the Slopes of Redemption

and others. They represent the downfall of those who succumb to pride, and serve as a reminder to those who have become humble.

As other commentators have shown, Dante displays, here, an ingenious poetic device in his attempt to illustrate how pride is inherent in "MAN"—V (U)OM=UOMO. In describing the thirteen figures that he sees before him, Dante begins each of the first four tercets (depicting each of the first four panels) with the word *Vedea,* the second four panels with the word *O,* and the last four with the word "*Mostrava.*" If we consider that V is the same as *U* in Latin, by taking the first letter of each word (*Vedea O Mostrava*), we have a combination that reads *UOM* or "MAN." Thus, pride is depicted as being *synonymous* with humankind. Moreover, the first word of each of the next three tercets (depicting the thirteenth panel) form the words *Vedea Qual Morti (UOM),* "I saw such dead," thus essentially emphasizing the idea that a proud person is a dead person—that is, dead to one's Higher Self. He adds:

> The *dead seemed dead,* and the *living alive.* A witness
> to the event itself saw it no better
> than I did, looking down here at its likeness.
> (Canto XII, 67–69; italics mine)

So well depicted were these engravings (imaginations in the esoteric sense), that those who were dead actually looked it, and those who were alive seemed to be living. Here, Dante insinuates that the aspect of death was reflected in those who, because of their prideful nature, were precluded from partaking in the knowledge leading to the realization of the *light* within them. Likewise, whoever cultivates knowledge of their divine nature, based on this living principle, manifests this life outwardly. *This marks the spot where Dante differentiates life from death.*

As they continue onward, the "ever watchful" Virgil (intellect) commands Dante to look up. There, an Angel is seen descending to greet them and show them the way up to the next cornice. The Angel calls out:

> Come... the stars are near, and now
> the way is easy up the mountainside.
>
> Few, all too few, come answering to this call.
> O sons of man, born to ascend on high,
> how can so slight a wind-puff make you fall?
> (Canto XII, 92–96; italics mine)

Here, again, we find yet another allusion to the esoteric nature of Dante's journey, for few are those who actually arrive at the point where they can behold the *light* of thinking manifest before them. Having overcome the influences of pride, Dante feels the Angel of Humility brush a P from his forehead, thus, making it easier to ascend to the next slope. With the purging of each sin, Dante's ascent becomes easier.

Dante and Virgil, having made their way up to the next cornice, hear the chant, *Beati pauperes spiritu* ("*Blessed are the poor in spirit, for theirs is the kingdom of heaven*" [Matt. 5:3]). Feeling lightness in his steps, Dante asks Virgil to explain. Virgil answers:

> When the P's that still remain,
> though fading, on your brow, are wiped away
> as the first was, without a trace of stain—
>
> then will your feet be filled with good desire:
> not only will they feel no more fatigue
> but all their joy will be in mounting higher.
> (Canto XII, 121–126)

In childlike disbelief, Dante touches his forehead and finds only six P's remaining. In this series of events, we see how Virgil (reason) continues to interpret the nature of Dante's experience for him. Once Dante has purged himself of all earthly "stains" (effects of earthly thinking), then Virgil will no longer be needed.

Having arrived at the next cornice occupied by the Envious, Dante finds no sculptures or engravings. Instead, the terrace rock is dark and seemingly deserted. There are no signposts to help him on his way. Looking around, Virgil addresses the Sun, imploring it to guide them,

> O Blessed Lamp, we face the road ahead
> placing our faith in you: lead us the way
> that we should go in this new place...
>
> You are the warmth of the world, you are its light;
> if other cause do not urge otherwise,
> your rays alone should serve to lead us right.
> (Canto XIII, 16–21)

Virgil (intellect) recognizes the Sun as the *Light of the World*, for it was from there that the Christ descended, so as to enlighten our thinking and kindle our feeling life. That is to say, this "visible" Sun once harbored the being of Christ, whose *light* the intellect (Virgil) needs in order for Dante to find his way toward the *sphere of the Sun*—far beyond the slopes of redemption upon which they now find themselves.

On this cornice, Dante acknowledges the Whip of Envy in the form of song, for the air is permeated by musical hymns of love and generosity. The first voice that Dante hears sings out *"Vinum non habent,"* (*"They have no wine"*). This refers to the Wedding Feast at Cana in Galilee, in which Mary, noting that there was not enough wine for everyone, did not envy those who had some, but spoke to Jesus of her sadness for those who had none. Whereupon, Jesus changed water into wine, thus performing his first miracle. Before this voice finishes singing, another interrupts saying "I am Orestes" and speeds quickly by. Orestes was known for his deep friendship with Pylades, who upon hearing that Orestes was condemned to death, declared himself to be Orestes. This, in turn, prompted Orestes to claim his own identity so that he might save Pylades. Each of them insisted on being Orestes to save the other. As soon as Dante hears Orestes' voice, another penitent yells out the indelible words spoken by Christ in his Sermon on the Mount, "Love your enemies." For only *love* purges envy.

As Dante and Virgil look up ahead, they catch sight of a group of souls dressed in course cloth. They are huddled together against the inner cliff, their eyes sewn together by fine wire. These are the Envious, who are forced to depend upon one another for love and support. They are dressed in the livid color of the rocks upon which they sit, which makes it impossible for them to stand out and differentiate themselves. The significance of this is clear. Because of their selfish desire to be superior to others on Earth, they are forced to be indistinguishable from one another. Their inability to humbly acknowledge that *Love* (Christ) connects all human beings has resulted in their present state of temporary blindness. Leaning on each other, they slowly purge themselves of envy by recognizing how they are but a reflection of one another. In this way, the element of fear, which differentiates envy from pride, can be transcended. Whereas before, they feared the good fortune and joy of others, now they are represented as beggars waiting to receive the grace of God. Thus, their blindness is only overcome through the development of conscience. This is represented by the voices fleeting around them, continually reminding them of the need to manifest acts of *love*.

Dante, seeking Virgil's permission to question the penitent, asks whether any of them are from his native land, when a voice cries out:

> We are all citizens of one sublime
> and final city, brother; you mean to ask
> who lived in Italy in his pilgrim time.
> (Canto XIII, 94–96)

Already we witness the effects of their purging, for not even country divides them here. Instead, they are portrayed as brothers and sisters, connected by the love they cultivate for each other. The spirit who utters these words, describes having been Sienese. She is Sapia of Siena, who was so filled with envy over her nephew, Provenzano Salvani, and his rise to power, that upon his defeat and beheading, she thanked God, asking Him to do with her whatever He wanted. After Dante recounts the journey he has undertaken, she asks Dante to help restore her memory to humanity, so that her spiritual development can be accelerated.

The Purgatorio: Ascending the Slopes of Redemption

Two other penitents, Guido del Duca and Rinieri da Calboli, overhear Dante's conversation. Wanting to know Dante's identity, they ask that he reveal his name and native city. Dante tells them that he is from the region of the Arno. But he refuses to disclose his identity, for he is still unknown. This is a most appropriate response, for, by not revealing his identity, Dante eliminates the *cause* of envy and helps to facilitate the soul's purification. In other words, he chooses to portray himself as one of them: one who cannot be differentiated and, thereby, become the object of the very envy from which they strive to rid themselves. Upon hearing that Dante is from the region of the Arno, Guido del Duca delivers an invective against those living along this river. For he perceives them as ruthless—ever more so, the more one approaches Florence and Pisa. In describing the malice found along the river, he says that dogs grow fewer and wolves (Florentines) grow thicker until they give way to foxes (Pisans). The Pisans are so fraudulent that "they fear no trap set by a mortal mind." Guido, in speaking to Rinieri, delivers a prophecy concerning the cruelty committed by Rinieri's grandson, Fulcieri da Calboli in Florence. Dante, at this point wishes to know the names of these two penitents before him. Guido identifies himself and acknowledges the seed of envy that he planted while on Earth. Upon revealing the identity of Rinieri, Guido lashes out against the corruption of his native Romagna.

As Dante and Virgil leave these souls, they hear voices resounding in the air. These voices recount examples of envy and, thus, form the Rein of Envy. First there is the voice of Cain, who was the first man to be punished for envy. He utters, *"Anciderammi qualunque m'apprende,"* (Everyone that findeth me shall slay me). The second voice that Dante hears is that of Aglauros, daughter of Cecrops (King of Athens). Mercury turned Aglauros into stone after she arranged a meeting between him and her sister Herse. Envious that Herse would sleep with a god, she turned Mercury away when he arrived for his appointment. She sings, *Io sono Aglauro che divenni sasso* (I am Aglauros who was turned into stone). Shocked by the thunderous roar, Dante steps to the right toward Virgil instead of proceeding onward.

This illustrates his lingering reliance on the diminishing power of the intellect to confront his experience.

Canto XV begins with a reference to the Sun whose late rays strike them "full in the face." This is symbolic of the Christ impulse piercing the veil of his earthly slumber, at which point, Dante feels the burden of sin lessen as an Angel removes another P from his forehead. It is the Angel of Charity. The *light* cast onto Dante's eyes temporary blinds him. "Enter to a path less steep than before," shouts the splendorous figure, whereupon, Dante and Virgil hear the hymn, "*Blessed are the Merciful.*"

As they proceed, Dante asks Virgil to explain Guido del Duca's comment that the human heart is often set on those things where sharing is forbidden. This question serves as a prelude to Virgil's discourse on *Love*, in which he explains how the limited nature of material goods often precludes the possibility of sharing. The more earthly goods one possesses, the less others are able to possess. It is the opposite with regard to spiritual (or immaterial) reality, such as human love or knowledge. The more these are shared the more there is to share. Such sharing is founded on *Love* (the Christ), which brings human beings closer to one another and to God. The living Christ that permeates our being is what every individual has in common. Envy, on the other hand, seeks to undermine the essence (Love) of our connection to one another and, ultimately, to God. Our adherence to the world's materiality obfuscates our perception of the interconnecting principle of *Love*. And so, envy obscures the *light* of reason that would otherwise allow us to acknowledge the truth of our oneness with one another. It is, in many ways, a less insidious sin than pride, for its negative effects are more recognizable and, thus, subject to the human will. For this reason, it is more easily redeemed.

Another aspect in Virgil's response to Dante is revealed when he says,

> Because within the habit of mankind
> you set your whole intent on earthly things,
> *the true light falls as darkness on your mind…*
> (Canto XV, 64–66; italics mine)

Here, Virgil implies that our adherence to the materiality (of thought) inhibits the *light* of the Christ from entering into our field of consciousness. Massimo Scaligero, in *Trattato del Pensiero Vivente,* refers to the light of thinking that falls into materiality as *"il pensiero pensante."* It is "thinking in the act of reflecting itself"[25]—namely, thinking whose light falls into the darkness of dialecticism. Consequently, we are denied the *light* that can help us overcome the negative influences (such as fear) arising from thought's adherence to our physical being.

Upon hearing Virgil's explanation, Dante, on the next cornice, is absorbed by a series of visions, each of which are examples of meekness. The first vision is that of the Blessed Mary gently admonishing the Child Jesus for having strayed away into the Temple without her knowing. Despite feeling great anxiety over his whereabouts, Mary is able to contain her anger, stating, "My son my son, why do you treat us so? Your father and I were seeking you in tears." The second vision consists of Pisistratus, ruler of Athens, refusing to grant his wife's wish to have her daughter's lover be put to death. Says he, "What shall we do to those that wish us harm if we take vengeance upon those that love us?" The third vision recalls St. Stephen praying to God to forgive those who are stoning him to death.

Virgil awakens Dante, who is still in a trance, and tells him that the purpose of the visions is to keep him focused on the *peace* that flows into humanity from the Eternal Fount—the Christ. Thus, they represent the force of imagination connected to the moral impulses arising from the heart of creative activity. We can assume that Dante himself displayed the anger to which these visions correspond. The brilliance of their illumination is in stark contrast to the blindness experienced by the penitent on the preceding cornice.

As Dante and Virgil travel onward, they perceive a dark cloud of smoke approaching them. This cloud seems to envelop the Sun, so that there is no "refuge from it anywhere." Dante says, "It took our sight from us, and the pure air." As Dante feels the sting of dark smoke in his eyes, he grasps the shoulder of Virgil like a blind man.

Virgil encourages him to hold fast. "Take care. Do not let go of me. Take care," he says. Once again, in the face of the blind emotionality, Dante adheres to reason.

Dante and Virgil have arrived at the Cornice of the Wrathful. The smoke that engulfs the penitents illustrates the nature of anger. It clouds our vision of the world. As with envy, thinking becomes captive to anger (the feeling realm).

From within the approaching cloud of smoke, Dante hears *Agnus Dei*, the Litany of the Mass, being sung by the penitents who are praying for *peace*. In so doing, they seek to purge themselves of the incendiary forces within them. One of the spirits, Marco Lombardo, overhears Dante speaking with Virgil and assures them that they are on the right path. As they carry on, Dante is burning to ask Marco a question that has been gnawing at him so much that he will explode if not provided an answer. Here, we see that this new environment conditions Dante to act like those who surround him once did, when they were on Earth. On the other hand, it might be assumed that Dante is outwardly *experiencing the influence that he once had on others as he relives (and purges himself of) the effects that his actions had upon them*. In fact, Rudolf Steiner, in many of his lectures regarding life after death, describes how in Purgatory (Kamaloca), we experience the emotions that we had inflicted on others, as they themselves experienced it on Earth. Regarding the nature of our relationship with others, Steiner in *Life Between Death and Rebirth* says,

> We know, for instance, that a dead friend is there outside us in the spiritual world. We perceive him through our visions. We feel *entirely at one* with him. We know *exactly* how we are related to him. What we chiefly perceive, however, is what happened between us on earth. (italics mine)[26]

Dante wishes to know the reason for which there is so much evil in the world. Is it due to planetary forces or is it because of something inherent within the Earth itself? Says Marco in response,

> Ah!...Brother,
> the world is blind and you are its true son.
> (Canto XVI, 65–66)

Marco's response seems to acknowledge Dante as one who, living in a world without light, *seeks to find the source of illumination* to share it with others on Earth. His answer leads directly to the question of *Free Will*. Marco Lombardo says that if the Heavens alone were responsible for evil in the world, that would essentially mean that we are precluded the freedom to act out of our own will. What justice would there then be in rewarding bliss for virtuousness, or administering pain for evil? He adds,

> ...The spheres *do* start your impulses along.
> I do not say *all*, but suppose I did—
> the light of reason still tells right from wrong:
>
> and Free Will also, which, though it be strained
> in the first battles with the heavens, still
> can conquer all if it is well sustained.
>
> You are free subjects of a more immense
> nature and power which grants you intellect
> to free you from the heaven's influence...
> (Canto XVI, 73–81)

Though the suprasensory world is responsible for many human "impulses," we still have the *light* of reason (force of Christ) by which we are able to guide our actions. This force, as we have repeatedly stated, can only be incited if we strengthen the will that had initially become separated from thought. Moral impulses, arising from the spiritual activity of the will, have *the potential* to transform our thinking so as to free us from "unfortunate" influences of the Heavens (stars).

Marco attributes the bad state of the world to "bad leadership." He blames the Church for assuming temporal power:

> ...Rome used to shine in two suns when her rod
> made the world good, and each showed her its way:
> one to the ordered world, and one to God...
> (Canto XVI, 106–108)

No longer does there exist a system of checks and balances. When the crock and sword become one, evil follows.

In the *Inferno*, we witnessed the condemnation of those members of the clergy who misused their authority for reasons of profit. Here, Dante criticizes the Church for impeding the secular freedom of its people. Interestingly, this is connected to the issue of Free Will, for, by preventing one from governing one's own earthly affairs, the Church not only misrepresents the teaching of Christ by politicizing them, but it also (as we have said earlier) undermines the thinking by which one can eventually arrive at the Christ through self-determination. In other words, Dante considers the Church (as constituted during his time) to be humanity's greatest *opponent* of Free Will.

As Marco reaches the end of his time allotted to Dante, he perceives, shining through the smoke, a light that issues from the Angel of Meekness. It is the signal for him to depart. Here, as the poets emerge from the smoke, the *light* of the Sun gradually makes itself present to them, thus symbolizing Dante overcoming the remnants of spontaneous emotionality within him.

Dante's attention is immediately focused on visions that comprise the Rein of Wrath—visions which, again, must be understood as *imaginations*. There, Dante says, "a light forms in Heaven of itself, or of His will who sends its rays to men." The first vision is the destruction caused by the wrath of Procne, who is portrayed as a nightingale for having killed her son. Then, Dante sees the wrath by which Haman tried to persuade Ahasuerus to declare the death of all the Jews in Persia. Instead, he was himself crucified. The last vision that Dante experiences is that of Amata killing herself in a fit of rage upon hearing the false rumor that Turnus, whom she had hoped would marry her daughter Lavinia, was killed in battle. As soon as this last vision vanishes, a shining light blinds Dante once again. It is the Angel of

Meekness who removes yet another P from his forehead. His voice whispers *Beati Pacifici* (Blessed are the Peacemakers).

It is almost nightfall, and already Dante feels his legs weaken. The poets have ascended to the top step of the next cornice—the Cornice of the Slothful.

Here, we have arrived at the **halfway point** of the *Divine Comedy*— the very *heart* of the poem. And so, it is most appropriate that Virgil gives a discourse on the nature of *Love*. He explains that *Love*, be it natural (as in the action of animal) or rational (mind-directed), moves God and every one of his creatures. Natural love can never be led into err, for it arises instinctively from the inner forces of the human being. Rational love, instead, is prone to err in that "it can strive to bad ends, or by too little, or too much fervor." When love is directed toward Eternal Good, which is God, or a secondary good, that which God has provided us for our pleasure, it cannot lead to sin. However, if love is overzealously directed toward God's gifts, or even if it lacks zeal, it can lead to sin. Thus, "Love," says Virgil, is the "true seed of every merit in you and of all acts for which you must atone." Nor can we truly hate our Creator, for no effect can hate its primal cause. Just as thought cannot direct its aversion toward the unperceived, suprasensory aspect that brought it into manifestation, so, too, are human beings unable to feel aversion toward their Maker. If anything, the aversion one might feel would be directed against the *concept* one has of the Creator, in which case, hate directs its destructive tendencies toward itself, inasmuch as it is generated by our dialectical nature. The perverted love that Virgil has been discussing refers to the three forms that are purged below—pride, envy and wrath. One who manifests pride seeks to rise above others at their expense; the envious, on the other hand, fear that the rise of others may result in a diminution of their own power; and the wrathful manifest uncontrolled acts of vengeance. Love, pursued with too little zeal, is purged on the terrace upon which they presently find themselves. There are yet other types of love that are excessive in their "devotion" to good. Such forms of "love" are purged on the three terraces above them.

They are avarice, gluttony, and lust, though Virgil does not disclose their nature to Dante.

It is interesting to note that Virgil does not explain the nature of *Divine Love*, for we must again remember that he appeared before the dawning of the Christ on Earth. He therefore symbolizes the intellect, which, in and of itself, rarely reveals the capacity to actualize the *light* of Christ. Virgil is able only to expound on the nature of that love which does not stream as a moral impulse from the thinking that is freed of bodily influences and flows from the etheric forces of the heart. In effect, the love of which Virgil speaks is that love which is prone to err, a love understood dialectically, namely, by way of thinking connected to our physical nature.

In Canto XVIII, Virgil continues his discourse on *Love*, for he has seen, by Dante's inquisitive expression, that his explanation, until now, has merely increased Dante's desire for knowledge. Virgil tells Dante that the soul, "being created prone to love" is drawn to whatever pleases it. Love, itself, "passes to action in three stages." First, the intellect observes, "that which really is," and then extracts from it a form, which it then imprints upon the soul. Secondly, the *force of love* draws the mind, which expresses a natural propensity for form, toward it. Thirdly, just as fire rises naturally upward toward the sphere of Fire, so, too, is the soul drawn toward what it yearns. Thus, love is "spiritual motion" that never finds rest until it unites with the object it desires. This object does not always, of necessity, exemplify good. Virgil tells Dante that often love is attracted to that which is not worthy of it.

Having listened with great intent, Dante asks:

> ...if love springs from outside the soul's own will
> it being made to love, what merit is there
> in loving good, or blame in loving ill?
> (Canto XVIII, 43–45)

In other words, if the soul is obliged to love but has no say in what it loves, what value is there in loving what is good? Or, how can one even be blamed for loving what is bad? Here, we arrive at the question of Free Will. Virgil tells Dante that he can *only* relate what reason "sees." If he wishes for more, he must wait for Beatrice, since the answer to his question lies within the "Mystery of Faith." Nonetheless, he continues his discourse by saying that substantial form (soul) is united with matter, and possesses an invisible force that can be ascertained only by way of its effects. No one knows "whence springs the light of his first cognizance." Here, the light to which he unknowingly refers is the Christ force within us, for all knowledge, in dialectical form, manifests as a product of thinking cut off from the creative force (*light*) of life. Nonetheless, Virgil argues that reason has the power to *enable us with the choice* of Free Will. What we choose, as a result of our Free Will, is, in effect, something for which we inevitably are held accountable. Individuals like Aristotle and Plato, who were able to perceive this "innate liberty" within humanity, were responsible for providing human beings with a "moral science." Virgil concludes by reminding Dante that he has the power by which to control errant love.

The close historical proximity of Virgil's life to that of the Christ can be gleaned from his discourse, for we see that Virgil actually touches upon *that* aspect of human thinking which reveals itself as the *living* force of Christ. But because he himself could not *experience* it, he is unable to identify it within himself. He merely observes that the *powers* of reason are associated to Free Will, but seems to lack the capacity to identify the force of Christ as necessary to the *actualization* of Free Will.

It is almost midnight and, once again, the penitents cannot ascend without the *light* of the Sun. As Dante begins to fall asleep, he is awakened by the noise of souls who, once slothful on Earth, now race around the cornice. As they pass, they shout out examples of Zeal, which, themselves, constitute the Whip of Sloth. The first example is of the Virgin Mary hurrying to visit Elizabeth after the Annunciation. The second example recalls Caesar's fervor in conquering the town of Lerida. The souls are in such haste that they have little time to point the way for Dante and Virgil to get up to the next cornice. Fortunately, one soul, San Zeno, tells the poets to follow them, for he will indicate the way.

San Zeno and the Slothful must be distinguished from the Indolent in Anti-Purgatory. For one thing, the Slothful are actually in the process of purging themselves from their earthly transgressions, whereas the Indolent are merely awaiting the opportunity to do so. Unlike the Indolent, who were *late in turning toward God*, the Slothful recognized God but were slow in pursuing the good of the world that would hasten their journey toward God. In other worlds, the Indolent were primarily slow in thought, while the Slothful were slow in deed. The purging, which the Slothful undergo, is meant to quicken them into accepting the good, which on Earth they were slow to accept. As an interesting poetic illustration of this quickening, Dante incorporates the Whip of Sloth, the sinner's actual purging, and the Rein of Sloth, all into one canto.

After San Zeno passes them, Dante hears the Rein of Sloth from two souls who hurry past. The first refers to those who refused to follow Moses and were, thus, doomed to die in the wilderness. The second recalls those followers of Aeneas who, choosing to live a life of comfort in Sicily, did not partake in the glorious founding of Rome. Taken by the thoughts that these visions and experiences provoke, Dante once again falls into a dream.

In this second dream, Dante sees the Siren of classical antiquity who was known to have lured seagoing sailors, including Ulysses, to their deaths. Ciardi states that she is symbolic of the three remaining sins found above—Greed, Gluttony, and Lust—which reflect one's "abandonment to physical appetites." Here, the Siren is depicted as a "stuttering crone, squint-eyed, clubfooted, with both her hands deformed, and her complexion like a whitewashed stone." However, Dante's gaze soon transforms her into a beautiful woman whose voice rings with such sweetness that "only with great pain" could Dante pull away from "her soliciting." At this point, a "Heavenly Voice" (an unidentified Saintly Lady) arrives and cries, "O Virgil, who is this?" with such indignation that Virgil "seized the witch, and with one rip laid bare all her front, her loins and her foul belly." Dante awakens from the stench that issues forth. The intent of this dream is to call attention to the transgressions of incontinence purged on the next three cornices. As a sort of prelude to this dream, Dante alludes to the effects of Saturn, known as the cold planet or the crystalizing planet of death. It is the planet of restriction or contraction and points to the need to curb our proclivity toward such incontinence. It was under such an influence that Dante succumbed to the dream. The Siren embodies, of course, the sins "of the flesh"—sins where we overindulge in our love for earthly pleasure. Though one may consider these sins to be "perverted," they are here deceptively transformed into enchanting beauty. Only with the aid of higher reason (Virgil) can they be exposed for what they are.

There is yet another interpretation to this dream. It has to do with how our perception of reality is inextricably linked to thinking rooted in our lower nature. Though the Siren is most repulsive to the eyes, Dante is able to envision her as ravishing, for the luciferic influences of sensuality obscure his ability to perceive reality in its true form. Since this episode occurs shortly before Dante's meeting with Beatrice, we must understand it as an admonishment to those who seek *Divine Wisdom* purely through their attraction to the physical aspect of women. One must be free of the influences of the emotional or astral body, to behold the *light* of Christ. Thus, one's attraction to the *bodily* nature of a woman reflects the subjugation of the "I" to the astral forces associated with sense-based thinking and perception. The impermanence of our union with the physical (deadened or Saturnian) nature of love is represented by the stench that issues forth from the navel of the Siren.

Virgil calls Dante three times. This number *three* pervades the whole of the *Divine Comedy*. Given the ritualistic nature of these events, we can easily envision this dream as a part of an *initiatory* experience in which Virgil plays the part of a hierophant.

It is now day. As Virgil and Dante continue on their path, they come upon the next cornice where the Angel of Zeal removes another P from Dante's forehead, thereby announcing that he has been purged of sloth. Seeing Dante unable to shed the effects of his dream, Virgil says:

> Did you see the ageless witch...for whom
> —and for no other—those above us weep?
> And did you see how men escape her doom?
>
> Let it teach your heels to scorn the earth, your eyes
> to turn to the high lure the Eternal King
> spins with his mighty spheres across the skies.
> (Canto XIX, 58–63)

Upon hearing these words, Dante hurries to the ledge of the next cornice where he perceives souls lying face downward, crying, "My soul cleaves to the dust." Virgil asks them for direction. These are the Avaricious. One of them, Pope Adrian V, answers and immediately prompts Dante's curiosity to speak with him. Adrian tells him that he was pope for little over a month. Always motivated by avarice, it was not until he put on the pope's mantle that he realized the perversion and emptiness of worldly ambition. Having always loved earthly things, he quickly became a man who sought and loved the spiritual. Since the Avaricious focus their sole attention on earthly things, they must do penitence by turning their eyes away from the *light* of God. For this reason, they are held fast to the Earth. Only by being forced to look and meditate on the *source* of their materialistic desires can the Avaricious truly understand their emptiness. Only, then, will they be able to understand why such desires are so difficult to control. Since these souls were overzealous in their desire for earthly goods or pleasure, they can begin to see how feeling, propelled by the will, was unable to find a rightful balance with thinking. In fact, the Avaricious, the Gluttonous, and the Lustful all manifest, to some degree, the absence of conscious reflection, which keeps the feeling life (or emotional impulses) in check. Again, on Purgatory, the penitents are dealing with the *source (or cause)* of their sins. Unlike the Avaricious in Hell, whose aims were willfully directed against one another causing harm, the penitent here did not *consciously* seek to injure others on Earth. The uncontrolled feelings manifested by those souls in Hell drove them toward unredeemable acts of lust and greed. Meanwhile, on Purgatory we see its inverted reflection. Restrained feeling eventually reigns the more one is *consciously* able to guide the will.

As Dante finishes listening to Adrian, he is seen kneeling beside him, reverently. Adrian admonishes him, by saying,

> Straighten your legs, my brother! Rise from error!
> ...I am, like you and all the others,
> a fellow servant of one Emperor...
> (Canto XIX, 136–138)

Adrian asks that Dante remind his niece Alagia of him, since she is the only one left on Earth to pray for him.

The poets leave along a narrow passage amid the Slothful, when Dante curses the She-Wolf, which in this case, is the symbol of avarice—but, more specifically, the Papacy.

> Hell take you, She-Wolf, who in the sick feast
> of your ungluttable appetite have taken
> more prey on earth than any other beast!
> (Canto XX, 10–12)

This unfulfilled desire for earthly goods outwardly reflects the insatiable appetite of materialistic thinking (She-Wolf), which constantly needs an object to appease it. And so, the insatiable desire for earthly goods is rooted in sense-based thinking whose fervent adherence to matter does not allow it to be free. Only the *light* of thinking would lead to freedom by banishing the sense-based desire symbolized by the she-wolf. Dante immediately alludes to this in the following verses:

> You Heavens, in whose turnings, as some say,
> things here below are changed—when will he come
> whose power shall drive her from the light of day?
> (Canto XX, 13–15)

As Dante's attention centers on those suffering souls, he hears a voice that cries out the Whip of Avarice. It is Hugh Capet. First, he makes reference to the poverty of the Blessed Mary, when she gave birth to the child Jesus in a stable. He then speaks of Fabricius Caius Luscinus, the Roman Consul in the second century AD who refused to take the bribes customarily offered to those in high office. As a result, he died of poverty and had to be buried by the State. The third example is that of St. Nicholas, Bishop of Myra in Lycia, who gave all his wealth away to the needy and became so poor that he couldn't even afford dowries for his daughters.

Hugh Capet speaks of himself and declares that he had much to do with the root of that "malignant tree which casts its shadow on all Christendom so that the soil bares good fruit only rarely"—an allusion to the French Dynasty, which culminated with the rein of Philip the Fair who attacked Pope Boniface VIII, Dante's archenemy. Boniface, having been declared a heretic by Philip, sought to excommunicate him, at which point, Philip sent an army to Alagna, where they took hold of Boniface and threatened him with execution. They threw him into prison and, after a few days, he was released. However, at eighty-six, the shock of this experience seemed to have had a devastating effect on him, for, soon after, he died of "hysterical seizures." Here is an explicit example of how Dante, though he detested Boniface and the corruption of the Church, honors the "Office of the Pope"—the "Vicar of Christ" on Earth. Thus, Dante differentiates between the *representative figure of Christ* (Pope) on Earth and the particular individual responsible for upholding that office. The Pope for Dante should manifest those qualities that are reflective of the Christ. He must be Christlike. By offending the "papacy," Philip offends the Christ and, once again, reenacts the Crucifixion:

> ...But dwarfing all crimes, past or yet to be,
> I see Alagna entered, and, in His Vicar,
> Christ Himself dragged in captivity.

> I see Him mocked again and crucified,
> the gall and vinegar once more sent up.
> He dies again—with *live* thieves at His side...
> (Canto XX, 85–90)

Many have suggested that Dante saw, in France's growing power, the seeds to the destruction of the temporal and spiritual law, embodied by Empire and the Church. Though Boniface, himself, corrupted these two institutions by having the Church assume the responsibilities of the State—thereby, misrepresenting the teachings of Christ—Dante's sympathy for the papacy reflects the degree of faith that he has in its redemption. The events of France, which Capet delineates, pose a greater threat to Dante's dream of the twofold system of government, for they gave rise to a sort of nationalism that Dante believed would oppose the international power of the "Empire."

Capet then tells Dante how, during the day, the penitents relive examples of poverty and generosity, and how at night they meditate on examples of avarice. These latter examples comprise the Rein of Avarice. Among them, Dante includes Pygmalion, Midas, Achan, Sapphira, Polymnestor, and Crassus.

From here, the poets move onward, when, suddenly, they feel the whole mountain shake and hear the chant *Gloria in excelsis Deo* (Glory to God in the Highest). They stand motionless until the tremor subsides, and soon continue on their way, puzzled by what has just happened.

Dante is burning with the desire to understand what made the Mount tremble, when, suddenly, a spirit overtakes them and greets them with the words, "Brothers, God give you peace." Virgil is quick to return the greeting and tells him that Dante has the mission of experiencing the spiritual worlds while still *alive*, but not without the help of Divine Will:

> ...Therefore, his soul, sister to yours and mine,
> since it cannot see as we do, could not
> climb by itself. And, therefore, Will Divine

> has drawn me out of the great Throat of Woe
> to guide him on his way, and I shall lead him
> far as my knowledge gives me power to go...
> (Canto XXI, 28–33)

Virgil then asks the spirit what caused the tremor. The spirit replies:

> ...Only what Heaven draws
> out of itself into itself again—
> that and nothing else—can be a cause...
> (Canto XXI, 43–45)

In other words, Purgatory belongs to the heavenly realms and is not tainted by the influences of the physical world. Therefore, what occurs there is not the result of external influences but, rather, of the transformation of the penitents' inner nature. That is to say, the penitents rise up to Heaven not by external means, but by acts of purgation that connect them to God. "Heaven draws out of itself into itself once again." *When the Mount shakes, it is because a soul has purified itself by means of its own will.* Though the penitents wish to climb the mountain, "High Justice" induces each of them to "will pain as he willed crime," so that they may each become purified of their transgressions. The tremor resulted from the ascent of penitents up the mount after having purged themselves of sin. Meanwhile, the voices of other penitents rejoice in their liberation. The soul who explains this is Statius, who lived from AD 45 to 96. There seems to be no specific reason for which he was chosen at this stage to serve as an intermediary between Virgil and Beatrice, apart from the fact that Virgil's intellectual powers seem greatly diminished with respect to his ability to explain the mysteries that Dante is about to encounter. Virgil (Reason) is unable to fathom the question of "faith," which presupposes the presence of an inner *light* conducive to higher, unseen worlds. The choice of Statius, instead, would be consistent with regard to this "inner light," for having been born *after* Golgotha, he would have been able to receive the Christ impulse (sustenance) that had already entered the Earth. Thus, he could ideally serve as the link between Virgil and Beatrice, who is soon to appear—namely, between reason and *Divine Wisdom.*

Statius, without knowing that Virgil is beside him, speaks of his admiration for the *Aeneid.* He adds that had he been able to live during Virgil's time he would gladly endure another year purging himself on the slopes of Purgatory. Virgil motions to Dante to be quiet. However, Dante cannot help but smile at the peculiarity of the situation. The silence of Virgil and the gesture of Dante bewilder Statius. Dante, with Virgil's permission, reveals the identity of his guide, whereupon Statius falls to his knees and embraces Virgil's feet. Virgil reprimands him by reminding him that they are both spirits.

The Angel who guards the sixth cornice has already removed another P from Dante's forehead. This enables him to ascend the slope behind them without having to labor. Virgil, showing respect for Statius, wants to know what had brought him to the fifth cornice. Statius, noting that Virgil seems to assume that he is being punished for avarice, tells him:

> ...Often, indeed, appearances give rise
> to groundless doubts in us, and false conclusions,
> the true cause being hidden from our eyes...
> (Canto XXII, 28–30)

Here, in a most subtle way, Dante uses Statius to illustrate how reason (Virgil) often deduces wrongly concerning questions pertaining to the suprasensory realm. In other words, since the causes of sin originate in the spiritual world, they cannot *always* be discerned by a sense-bound intellect. One cannot easily fathom the nature of one's transgressions unless thinking has been transformed into an *organ of perception* that allows for the perception of their hidden *causes.* In this case, Statius, himself, represents that point of transition whereby reason (Virgil) gives way to *Divine Wisdom* (Beatrice), thereby enabling Dante to fathom the nature of sin.

Statius explains that he is doing penitence not because of avarice, but because of his prodigality. "How many," says Statius, "shall rise bald to Judgment Day because they did not know this sin to grieve it in life?" Though wastefulness is not normally recognized as a sin, it denies everyone the opportunity to equally partake in the abundance of God's goodness. Therefore, it trivializes our relationship to the things around us, for each good possessed is not fully valued. Thinking spent on trivialities is not conducive to transforming one's consciousness and, thus, is, in a sense, a wasting away of life. Statius goes on to thank Virgil for having been spared the fate of the Prodigious in Hell, for it was Virgil who set him on the path to faith so that he could be baptized.

> You were the lamp that led me from that night.
> You led me forth to drink Parnassian waters;
> then on the road to God you shed your light...
> (Canto XXII, 64–66)

Statius refers to the lines in Virgil's *Fourth Prologue*, which during the Middle Ages was considered to be an "unconscious prophecy" of Christ's birth.

> ...When you declared, "A new birth has been given.
> Justice returns, and the first age of man,
> And a new progeny descends from Heaven"—
>
> you were as one who leads through a dark track
> holding the light behind—useless to you,
> precious to those who followed at your back...
> (Canto XXII, 67–72)

Here, we witness Virgil (reason) on the verge of an intuition that transcends the material influences of the world.

After Virgil appeases Statius' desire to know of those who suffer with him in Limbo, the poets come upon an enormous tree "laden with fruits." Though the nature of this tree has been a source of great debate among scholars, many believe that it alludes to the tree from which Adam and Eve ate the forbidden fruit, for the voice that issues from within it, strongly admonishes the Gluttonous from eating from

The Purgatorio: Ascending the Slopes of Redemption

it. In fact, this voice, in citing examples of abstinence and moderation, constitutes the Whip of Gluttony. The first example is the Virgin Mary who abstained from eating at the Marriage of Cana so that others could partake in the feast. The second example cites the custom of the noble matrons of Rome to not drink wine. They were thus said to have found "joy in water." The next example points to Daniel's decision to avoid corrupting himself with the king's wine and meat. Also admired here are those who lived during humanity's Golden Age, in which human beings were one with nature and had yet to develop cooking instruments such as forks and spoons that inevitably led to gluttony. Finally, an example from the *Gospels* is included as well, namely, John the Baptist who found his way to God by eating only honey and locusts in the desert.

Dante looks back up into the tree to see whose voice he heard, but Virgil urges him to carry on with his journey. Suddenly, they hear the words *Labia mea, Domine* (O Lord, open Thou my lips). Dante turns around and sees a group of souls, "silent and devout," pass them. They are comprised of the Gluttonous; their emaciated features startle him:

> The sockets of their eyes were caves agape;
> their faces death-pale, and their skin so wasted
> that nothing but the gnarled bones gave it shape.
> (Canto XXIII, 22–24)

Next to a tree laden with the fruit that entices the penitents to satisfy their hunger, there passes a crystal brook tempting them to quench their thirst. However, these souls must endure such temptations, since they were unable to control their appetite during their earthly lives. In other words, they must cultivate the *will* that they lacked on Earth to overcome the instinctual demands of the body. The fruit and drink before them outwardly stimulate the mental images that provoked their gluttony. Since they were unable to sufficiently muster the will to subdue the cravings of the physical body, they must now painfully endure them. By so doing, they purge themselves of influences that weaken the will. In *Founding a Science of the Spirit*, Rudolf Steiner speaks of how in Purgatory (Kamaloca) we purge ourselves of desires that we developed on Earth. There, he states,

> To take a simple example, suppose a someone eats avidly and enjoys the food. The clairvoyant will see the satisfaction of that desire as a brownish-red form in the upper part of the person's astral body. Now suppose that one dies: what is left is the person's desire and capacity for enjoyment. Only the means of enjoyment belongs to the physical part of a human being: thus we need gums and so on to eat. Pleasure and desire belong to the soul, and they survive after death. But one no longer has any means of satisfying those desires because the appropriate organs are absent, and this applies to all kinds of wishes and desires. We may want to look at some beautiful arrangements of colors—but we lack eyes; or to listen to some harmonious music, but we lack ears.
>
> How does the soul experience all this after death? The soul is like a wanderer in the desert, suffering from a burning thirst and looking for some spring at which to quench it; and the soul has to suffer this burning thirst, because there is no organ or instrument for satisfying it. It must feel deprived of everything, so to call this condition one of burning thirst is very fitting. This is the essence of Kamaloka. The soul is not tortured from outside, but has to suffer the torment of the desires it still has but cannot satisfy.
>
> Why does the soul have to endure this torment? *The reason is that human beings have to wean themselves gradually from the physical wishes and desires, so that the soul may free itself from the Earth to purify and cleanse itself. Once that is achieved, the Kamaloka period ends and one ascends to Devachan.* (rev. translation; italics mine)[27]

The voice that Dante hears within the tree is the voice of conscience, continually reminding the penitents of the task before them. One can thus understand the motivations of the Gluttonous by realizing that the Fall, prompted by Adam and Eve's eating of the "forbidden fruit," symbolizes humanity's separation from the divine forces that had once given birth to (and nourished) human existence. Unable to partake any longer in God's infinite blessing, humanity was compelled to depend on earthly creations for sustenance. No longer was humanity guided by the spiritual impulses that it had once beheld. As a result, the human being was forced to respond evermore to the urgings of the physical body. Only by purging themselves of their desires can they eventually reconnect with the divine world.

As Dante looks at the emaciated bodies before him, he can hardly recognize any of their faces. Suddenly he is, himself, recognized by Forese—a poet and close friend of Dante who died five years earlier. After Forese describes the pain suffered by the Gluttonous, Dante is perplexed. He cannot understand why his friend is not with the Late Repentant but, rather, so high up on the Mount. Forese tells him he has risen up the slopes due to the prayers of Nella, his beloved, whose virtue can be best understood when compared to the immodesty of the women of Florence—at which point, he shouts out an invective against them. He wonders how Dante has arrived at this cornice. Dante, reminding Forese of the quality of their time on Earth, tells him that Virgil rescued him from that life and has led him through Hell and Purgatory so that he can encounter Beatrice.

As the poets move on, Statius slows his pace in order to stay a bit longer with Virgil. In so doing, he also slows Dante's ascent toward God—thus, making God wait for his arrival. Statius inadvertently opposes the law of Divine Will. Nonetheless, the presence of Statius is central to the topic of discussion at this point of the *Divine Comedy*—namely, poetry and its relation to *love*. Here, a congregation of poets has assembled. Dante alludes to *"Il Dolce Stil Novo"* (The Sweet New Style), practiced by the *Fedeli d'amore*. Among these poets are Virgil, Statius, Forese, Dante, and the soon-to-be Bonagiunta di Lucca—all of whom partake in a short discussion concerning the nature of this new poetry that has arisen in Italy. This discussion, appearing shortly after the discussion of *Love* at the heart of the *Divine Comedy*, hints at the importance of such poetry with respect to *Divine Wisdom* (Beatrice), soon to appear.

Having been introduced to a good number of the Gluttonous, Dante is accosted by Bonagiunta who mutters the name "Gentucca." Dante asks the penitent to speak. Says Bonagiunta:

> Though men may mock my city...
> she who will teach you how to treasure it
> is born there, though she is not yet a bride.
>
> This presage you shall take with you from here,
> and if you misconstrue what I first muttered
> the facts themselves, in time, will make it clear...
> (Canto XXIV, 43–48)

Bonagiunta alludes to a pleasant reception awaiting Dante in the city of Lucca, by a lady known as Gentucca. As we remember, the *Fedeli d'amore*, who wrote their verses (in *"Il Dolce Stil Novo"*), used the names of women when referring to *Divine Wisdom*. In fact, we notice, here, how this Gentucca is "not yet a bride." These verses by Bonagiunta are somewhat enigmatic. But upon closer inspection, they seem to reveal that in the city of Lucca there exists a group or sect (*Fedeli d'amore*) that holds the keys to *Divine Wisdom*. Having alluded to this esoteric reference, Bonagiunta continues by asking Dante:

> ...But is this really the creator of
> those new *canzoni*, one of which begins
> "Ladies who have *the intellect of Love*"?
> (Canto XXIV, 49–51; latter italics mine)

Of all Dante's sonnets, this particular sonnet beginning with "Ladies who have the intellect of Love," more than any other (even by its very title), points to *Love* as the force that reintegrates the masculine (willing) and feminine (thinking) polarities of our consciousness. The fact that she is "not yet a bride" refers to the separation of these two polarities, namely to the fact that *Divine Wisdom* has yet to be realized in Lucca. The "ladies" referred to in this poem are, again, either members of the *Fedeli d'amore*, or the individualized feminine representations of *Divine Wisdom*, which, realized by way of sense-free thinking, harbor the impulse of *Love* (the Christ). Dante seems to confirm that he is cognizant of this *Love*, which, in turn, has inspired his writing:

> And I: "When Love inspires me with delight,
> or pain, or longing, I take careful note,
> and as he dictates in my soul, I write."
> (Canto XXIV, 52–54)

These words conceal what distinguished Dante and his school of poets from others, such as Guittone d'Arezzo and Jacopo da Lentino, who did not take part in *"Il Dolce Stil Novo"* and its connection to *Divine Wisdom*.

> And he, "Ah, brother, now I see the thong
> that held Guittone, and the Judge, and me
> short of that sweet new style of purest song.
>
> I see well how your pens attained such powers
> by following exactly Love's dictation,
> which certainly could not be said of ours.
>
> And if one scan the two styles side by side,
> that is the only difference he will find."
> With that he fell still, as if satisfied.
> (Canto XXIV, 55–63)

Since Bonagiunta, still purging himself, is now within the vicinity of the blessed, he can comprehend the significance of Dante's words. No longer is he completely bound to the earthly thinking that had obscured his vision. He is now able to conceive how *Love* directed the pen of Dante, and not the influences arising from his lower nature that he is attempting to purge.

At this point, the rest of the penitents race ahead. Only Forese remains with the Poets. He asks Dante when they will see each other again. Dante does not give a clear answer. Instead, he alludes to the corruption of Florence, adding that, once back on Earth, he will, *after earthly death,* eagerly return to the shores of Purgatory to begin his final ascent toward God.

With Forese out of sight, the poets round a curve and behold yet another tree, the Tree of Knowledge. Under its branches, souls strive to reach the fruit like

> ...greedy children beg and screech
> or what they may not have, the one they cry to
> holds it in plain sight but beyond their reach
>
> to whet their appetites...
> (Canto XXIV, 106–109)

The poets near the tree, when they hear a voice inside it say:

> Pass on. Do not draw near. The tree whose fruit
> Eve took and ate grows further up the slope,
> and this plant sprouted from that evil root.
> (Canto XXIV, 115–117)

This voice constitutes the Rein of Gluttony. The first example is that of Eve, who, in her desire for the forbidden fruit, rejects the wishes of God. She symbolizes the supreme form of gluttony since her actions resulted in the Fall, from which humanity must now resurrect itself so as to, once again, enter God's heavenly realm. The second example depicts the Centaurs who became so drunk at the feast of the Lapithae that they attempted to steal away the bride. Pursued by Theseus and the Lapithae, they were seized and killed in great numbers. The third example is based on the Book of Judges, when Gideon—in choosing his army against Midian—was told (by the Lord) to take men down by the river and observe how they drink. Those who drank by plunging themselves into the water were to be avoided, while those who drank cautiously in wait of the enemy were to be chosen. By so doing, Gideon was able to march to victory.

Having heard the voice shout out these admonishments, the three poets behold the Angel of Temperance. This angel appears to Dante as a softly glowing red light. The color red symbolizes, of course, the passions of a raging appetite and foretells the lust purged on the cornice above. The softness of its glow, on the other hand, denotes the tempering of such passion. Having brushed another P from Dante's forehead, the Angel paraphrases the words "Blessed are those who hunger (and thirst) after righteousness."

The poets ascend to the seventh and final cornice, that of the Lustful. As they make their way up the narrow slope, Dante is puzzled by a perplexing problem: how can the Gluttonous seem to suffer from hunger and thirst when they lack the substantial bodies of living human beings but, rather, have "airy" bodies which do not need food nor drink? Statius answers him in three parts. First, he discusses the generative principle in the human being; then he explains the birth of the human soul; and finally he touches upon the formation of aerial bodies. His explanation, medieval in character, reflects the limitations of humanity's general understanding at the time.

Statius begins his discussion of the generative principle of human beings by drawing Dante's attention to the blood—more particularly, to what is not absorbed into the bloodstream:

> ...Perfect blood—that pure blood that remains
> as one might say, like food upon the table,
> and never goes to slake the thirsty veins...
> (Canto XXV, 37–39)

Here, what Statius calls the "perfect blood" is the generative principle that precedes the formation of the blood commonly known to us—the blood that the "I" utilizes as a vehicle of expression. John Ciardi says that generative principle was referred to as the *formative* power by the Scholastics of the Middle Ages.[28] This "perfect blood," according to Statius, "acquires, within the heart, the formative power over all human organs." In other words, the blood in its "pre-manifested" form flows through our veins to give our organs form. The actual development of these organs falls into three stages. First, the "perfect blood" once again flows into the father's heart where it is transformed into sperm. From there, it flows down to "that place better left unmentioned" (genitals), where, in the act of conception it "drips over another blood" in the female's womb ("its natural vase"). Man's blood was considered active, woman's blood passive. Man's blood is active because it flows from "that perfect place" (the heart). A woman's blood is passive because it is not inclined to take form.

As these two bloods "commingle," the active blood causes the passive blood to clot. Matter is thus formed and quickly takes life. The act of conception is complete.[29]

Ciardi goes on to explain the process by saying that upon conception, the soul is born as a result of the active force within the father's blood that issues from the heart. The passive blood of the woman merely provides the matter through which the active principle can begin to mold the developing being. At this point, the newly developed "soul" is comparable to that of a plant; the only difference is that the plant's "soul" has reached the end of its development, whereas the human being's has merely begun.[30] (Seen from an Anthroposophical point of view, the formation of this plant-like "soul" seems to refer to the development of the human etheric body.) From this "vegetative body," the human soul acquires the "faculties of sensation and motion."

> ...It then begins to form
> those powers of sense of which it is the seed.
>
> Now, my son, the formative power expands
> and elongates within, till every member
> takes form and place as nature's plan commands...
> (Canto XXV, 56–60)

In other words, the undifferentiated organism begins to take on an animal form. More important, however, the faculties of "sensation" and "motion" that ensue would point to the development of humankind's astral nature. Here, Statius tells Dante that many have been led astray, including "a wiser head" than his (Dante's). Reference is being made to Averroes who believed that

> ...the *possible intellect* was thought
> (since it occupied no organ) to be disjoined
> from the *vegetative soul*—and so he taught...
> (Canto XXV, 64–66)

The Purgatorio: Ascending the Slopes of Redemption

The human being, according to the thinking of Scholasticism, possessed three bodies other than the physical—the vegetative soul that might be compared to the etheric body; the sensitive (or animal) soul that might be likened to the astral body; and finally the rational soul or "possible intellect" that enables us to reason. We may associate this with the "I." Since the vegetative and sensitive faculties, which were thought to be the only ones capable of receiving external impressions, and were assumed to have the brain as the common organ between them, the question arose as to which organ corresponded to the "possible intellect." It is obvious from such a description that the emphasis put on the organ is itself what is in error, for humanity at that time failed to see that the mere presence of an organ such as the brain, does not necessitate the presence of a faculty such as reason. As Ciardi elucidates, Averroes, unable to attribute the faculty of reason to an organ (since the brain was thought to be shared by both man and beast, thereby precluding its relationship to the rational self), believed that we, human beings, acquired the faculty of rationality from a Universal Mind, to which it was relinquished upon death. And so, by not possessing our own individual rational soul, we could not be subjected to Eternal Judgment.[31] Instead, our condition would be like that of the animal to a certain extent, in that we would lack the *individual* Free Will by which the motivations of our actions could be judged. This, of course, was totally discredited by the Church and St. Thomas Aquinas, himself.

Statius tells Dante that the human brain is completely formed within the human fetus. Once formed, God "breathes" an all-powerful spirit into it, thus differentiating us from the animal. At this point, this newly formulated soul draws into itself the vegetative and animal souls, thereby forming one single soul that is alive, sensitive to its environment and conscious of itself. This human soul is, thus, the immortal part of the human being.

From here, Statius goes on to describe the development of the aerial body that Dante has encountered. He says that after death, one's lower powers are "passive and mute," but "memory, intelligence, and will" are "more active than they were, and more acute." In other words, we preserve those characteristics that comprise our (human) individuality after death. They are eternally part of us. Once across the threshold of death, the soul (formative power), enclosed in the new atmosphere, "sends out rays," like it did in giving shape to the sense organs. These rays recall those of the Sun that work upon the air. It is given the name "shade" because it creates these organs of sense from the air, of which it, too, is made.

> ...From air it draws its visibility. Hence,
> it is called a *shade*. And out of air it forms
> the organs of sight, speech, and every sense...
> (Canto XXV, 100–102)

The appearance of the shade is subject to the changes it experiences in the ebb and flow of desires and feelings. Unlike earthly human beings who are able to hide their thoughts and feelings, the shade can do nothing but reveal them, for they are what, in essence, comprise it.

As we briefly ponder the assertion made by Statius regarding the development of humankind, both spiritually and physically, we see that such a description contains elements also found in Anthroposophy, though in rudimentary form. Much of this, of course, is due to the fact that human beings had yet to attain a consciousness that would enable them to perceive all of the implications of such a development. In fact, since the notion of reincarnation had not entered the thinking of the general population at that time, it was quite acceptable to envision the soul's development as proceeding from the heart or any physical origin, at the moment of conception. Nonetheless, we can see how the description given of the rational soul in its relation to the vegetative and animal souls does resemble, to some degree, Rudolf Steiner's perception of life between death and new birth. In Anthroposophy, the "I," having shed the etheric and astral bodies (though retaining an extract of each), ventures off into the cosmic expanse only to return to Earth. As it nears the physical Earth, it reacquires an astral body from the "astral world" and an etheric body from the "etheric world" before penetrating into the womb of the mother. In light of the fact that the question of "unbornness" eluded the thinking of most scholars during the Middle Ages, one can regard the conception of life reached by such people as Aquinas as a precursor to the germinating impulse that was to flower centuries later in Steiner.

The poets have arrived at the last Cornice, which is filled with flames, save a narrow passage along the edge. The poets can go ahead only one at a time. From within the flames, Dante hears the hymn *Summae Deus clementiae* (God of Supreme Clemency), after which a voice from within the fire calls out examples that form the Whip of Lust. First, reference is made to the Virgin Mary, who, upon being told by the Archangel Gabriel that she was to conceive a son, declares, "I know not a man." These words pointed to the Immaculate Conception. The second example regards Diana, the huntress, who expelled the nymph Helice for having exposed herself to Jove and conceived a son. Finally, praise is given to those "husbands and wives who were chaste as virtue and marriage vows require."

The poets arrive at the Cornice of the Lustful where the penitents, in the act of being purified by the flames of the passion that led to their lustful transgressions on Earth, move from east to west (symbolizing the natural order). These penitents perceive that Dante's shadow causes the red flames to grow redder, prompting one of them to declare, "*He seems to be no shade, but a living man!*" Some of the penitents draw near to him, careful to remain within the purging fire. The penitent continues:

> ...how is it that you cast a shadow yet,
> making yourself a barrier to the Sun,
> as if death had not caught you in its net?
> (Canto XXVI, 22–24)

Dante hardly has time to begin his explanation when, from the opposite direction, west to east (symbolic of an unnatural order) a new group of penitents arrives. Moving in the direction opposite to Dante, they exchange kisses with this first group that Dante has met. The second group of souls is comprised of sodomites. In their encounter with the first group, who once exhibited excessive lust, they exchange a brief greeting, each group then continuing on its way. Together, these two groups cry out the Rein of Lust. The first example is of Sodom and Gomorrah, whose homosexual practices resulted in the destruction of ancient cities. The second example is of Pasiphae, daughter of Apollo, who was made to fall in love with the bull that Minos refused to sacrifice. Having had Daedalus construct an effigy of a cow with wooden ribs, she spread cowhide over them and hid inside so that the bull could possess her. From the union was born the Minotaur. The souls, having completed the exchange, continue on their separate ways.

The first group, once again, accosts Dante in order to hear his story. He obliges them by saying:

> ...I did not leave my limbs beyond the flood,
> not green nor ripe, but bear them with me here
> in their own jointure and in their own blood.
>
> I go to be no longer blind. Above
> there is a lady wins us grace, and I,
> still mortal, cross your world led by her love...
> (Canto XXVI, 55–60)

Thus, Dante "crosses" into the world of the afterlife while still bearing his limbs "in their own jointure and in their own blood." We, again, witness how Dante's journey into the world beyond the threshold of the physical realm, is one that he undertakes while still *alive*. No longer is he blind to the light within him. By the *love* reflected in "the lady above" (Beatrice), he is being led to the light's source—the Christ.

Having finished his talk, Dante asks the spirits to explain the spectacle he has just witnessed. A spirit tells Dante that the departed group committed acts of "unnatural" lust—i.e., homosexuality. Their shame feeds the fire that purifies them and helps them rise up to the next cornice. This illustrates how one's behavior is not alone in determining the fate of those who cross the threshold of death, but equally important is their *attitude* after having committed such an act. These penitents, though they committed acts against the will of God, demonstrated contrition—namely, the acknowledgement of their wrongdoings and the desire to be forgiven. The group that remains before him, on the other hand, committed natural acts of lust, but they did so excessively. They recall Pasiphae, who by following her instinctive desires to their extreme, gave birth to the beast of violence. They also exercise contrition. The soul who relates all this to Dante is his old friend, and founder of *"Il Dolce Stil Novo,"* Guido Guinizelli.

Staring in amazement, Dante cannot find the words to address Guinizelli. Unlike Brunetto Latini, Guido Guinizelli fully repented before he died, and thus is spared the abominable damnation below. Dante feels a deep love for this penitent, since

> ...he had fathered me
> and all the rest, my betters, who have sung
> sweet lilting rhymes of love and courtesy.
> (Canto XXVI, 97–99)

Guinizelli, is referred to by Dante as "he who had fathered me," for he was Dante's teacher in the art of *"Il Dolce Stil Novo."* Though Guido, himself, was keen to the esoteric wisdom inherent within he poetry of his time, he was still *unable* to shed the effects of his lustful nature. As he stands before Dante, he, like many before him, is amazed that Dante has been able to enter into the spiritual world while *alive*. Dante offers to serve him in any way he can, to which Guido responds:

> What you say has made
> such a profound impression on my mind
> as Lethe cannot wash away, nor fade.
>
> But if the words you swore just now are true
> let me know why you show by word and look
> such love as I believe I see in you?
> (Canto XXVI, 106–111)

Guido asks Dante to explain how he is able to manifest the love that he sees shining from his eyes. Dante praises Guido by telling him:

> Your songs so sweet and clear
> which, for as long as modern usage lives,
> shall make the very ink that writes them dear.
> (Canto XXVI, 112–114)

Therefore, Dante's success in actualizing *Divine Wisdom* is largely attributable to the "sweet" poetry penned by Guido. Dante claims that Guido's poetry is so precious that the "ink," with which it is written, is "dear." His praise of Guido's writings is not merely to extol the beauty of his lyrics, but their significance in *guiding* others to *the source of knowledge* conducive to God. In other words, Guido's poetry contains the key to uncovering the path of salvation. For this reason, even the ink is "dear." Guido gracefully accepts Dante's praise, but tells him that there is another nearby who "was in life a greater craftsman of the mother tongue," who "in his love songs and his tales in prose, was without peer." Guido asks Dante to pray for him and disappears into the fire, like "a fish does to the dark depths of the sea." Looking toward the spot indicated by Guinizelli, Dante sees yet another penitent (also a poet), who briefly explains in the *langue d'oc*—his provincial tongue—that he, too, is undergoing purification. It is Daniel Arnaut. He asks Dante to be "mindful of his pain," while ascending the slope. Then, quickly, he vanishes into the fire.

There is a line of succession between the three poets. Arnaut brought forth the rudimentary elements of Provencal poetry that led to the formation of *"Il Dolce Stil Novo"* by Guinizelli, which, in turn, prompted Dante to use his mother tongue to bring this poetic tradition into even greater fruition in the form of his *Divine Comedy*. Thus, Dante effectively traces the development of love poetry by having Guinizelli direct our attention to Arnaut, who used common language (the vernacular) as a means to forge a new style. Immediately preceding Dante's entrance into the "Garden of Earthly Paradise,"

The Purgatorio: Ascending the Slopes of Redemption

these poets form a prelude to Dante's encounter with Beatrice, for they, having sung these mysterious love songs, are the very ones to have attained the highest possible *earthly* human connection to the spiritual world.

The symbolism of fire surrounding the Lustful is quite clear. Just as they burned with passion while on Earth, now they are seen burning away such desires by way of fire. Fire can also be associated with the Holy Spirit, through which humanity is led to the Christ. In Genesis 3:24, we encounter the flaming sword of the Cherubim whose mission it was to guard the entrance to Eden after humanity's expulsion. This sword, which according to Church tradition turned every which way to protect the "Tree of Life," formed a complete wall around Eden, so that, not only does the fire symbolize the element of purgation, but it also represents a "final barrier to the place of innocence." Only those who have completely removed every stain of sin are able to enter the realm in which humanity had once belonged.

The poets come upon the Angel of Chastity, who stands beyond the reach of the fire and sings *Beati mundo corde* (Blessed are the pure in heart). He tells them that they must pass through the Wall of Fire. Upon hearing his words, Dante stands motionlessly "as one laid in his tomb." This Wall of Fire, meant to purify the imperfect love within one's heart, reminds Dante of the human bodies he "once saw burned" (a possible reference to the burnings of the Inquisition). But Virgil quickly comforts him by saying that, though he may feel torment, his passage there will not result in death. Unable to persuade Dante of his safety, Virgil evokes the thought of Beatrice. Upon hearing her name, Dante recovers from his shock and expresses his desire to proceed with "the trial by fire," in spite of the scorching flames. Virgil instructs Statius, who until now has stood between them, to walk behind Dante while he leads him into the fire. In helping Dante overcome his anxiety, Virgil continues to speak of Beatrice, saying, "I seem already to see her eyes." Here, Virgil is instrumental in his delicate hierophant-like role. Suddenly, from the other side of the fire, "rose a paean" that guided them through the flames to where the final

The Angels Inviting Dante to Enter the Fire, *William Blake*

ascent began. There, a light shone *so brightly* into Dante's face that he had to turn away. From that light came the words *Venite benedicti patris* (Come all the blessed of my Father). Thus spoke the Guardian Angel of Earthly Paradise, urging the poets to hurry to the top of the slope "while the last brightness lingers in the west." As they heed the Angel's advice, the Sun sets in the West and prevents the poet's ascent up the remaining slope.

Forced to await the rising Sun, Dante looks beyond the rocks and sees the stars growing in the sky to a size normally unseen. Lost in thought, he is soon overcome by a sleep that "oftentimes presents the fact before the event." He dreams of an "innocent and beautiful" maiden, gathering flowers while singing. It is Leah who finds joy in work. Says she:

> Say I am Leah if any ask my name,
> and my white hands weave garlands wreath on wreath
> to please me when I stand before the frame
>
> of my bright glass. For this my fingers play
> among these blooms. But my sweet sister Rachel
> sits at her mirror motionless all day.
>
> To stare into her own eyes endlessly
> is all her joy, as mine is in my weaving.
> She looks, I do. Thus live we joyously."
> (Canto XXVII, 100–108)

Leah and her sister Rachel symbolize the *active life* and the *contemplative life*, respectively. The *active life* symbolized by Leah is cherished in Christianity for it signifies the "doing of good works" upon the Earth. It represents the continuity of God's creative activity. Though humanity is presently subjected to fashioning the material world, it will one day create "out of the spirit." Thus, it prefigures a future age in which we—by actualizing the *light*, or the creative principle, within us—will eventually become co-creators of the cosmos. Yet, this *active life* must be accompanied by a *life of contemplation*, otherwise it will not be able to penetrate the spiritual world, for it will be distracted by its own activity. The *contemplative life*, represented by Rachel, permits humanity to devote its attention solely to the Presence of God, so that one creates in conformity to the creative impulses streaming in through the spiritual world. In Dante's dream, Leah foretells of his encounter with Matilda, while Rachel presages the arrival of Beatrice.

When Dante awakens, Virgil tells him that the day for which his soul has yearned has finally arrived. Having climbed the final stairs to the top of the Mount, Virgil turns, fixes Dante with his eyes, and says:

> My son... you now have seen the torment
> of the temporal and the eternal fires;
> here, now, is the limit of my discernment.
>
> I have led you here by the grace of mind and art;
> now let your own good pleasure be your guide;
> you are past the steep ways, past the narrow part...
> (Canto XXVII, 127–132).

This, in effect, is where Virgil (reason) has reached the limit of his ability to lead Dante in his journey toward the threefold aspect of God. Reason can no longer penetrate into the realm of the spiritual. This is illustrated by Virgil's inability to *fully* enter the "Garden of Earthly Paradise." Having finally arrived at the Garden's gate from which humankind was expelled, Dante is told by Virgil:

> ...Expect no more of me in word or deed:
> here your will is upright, free, and whole,
> and you would be in error not to heed
>
> whatever your own impulse prompts you to:
> lord of yourself I crown and mitre you.
> (Canto XXVII, 139–143)

At this point, Dante has become lord of his physical self (crown) and lord of his soul (miter: bishop). He has prepared himself for the arrival of Beatrice and the attainment of *Divine Wisdom*. That is to say, Dante has, for the most part, overcome the influences of earthbound consciousness, which subjected him to the transgressions represented in the various realms below. For this, he is crowned. He has taken the first major step in fully beholding the *light* conducive to the realization of the Christ.

The Enchanted Garden of the Soul

At the beginning of this chapter, we showed how the *Inferno* and the *Purgatorio* mirror each other in many respects. We have seen the effects of "unrepented" sin, as portrayed in the *Inferno*, purged of their causes in the *Purgatorio*; how suffering and pain are transformed into music and joy; how the separation of thinking from willing resulted in the Fall. We have also witnessed how the heart forces, descending from Beatrice, have, in turn, tempered this thinking, so that it can receive the impulses that stream in from the spiritual world. In effect, what we have really been observing is the metamorphoses of the human soul in its struggle to reclaim the vision of God that had been denied it by the luciferic and ahrimanic impulses. The "Dark Wood," in which Dante had found himself in the *Inferno*, was, in essence, the condition of his soul impregnated by such impulses. Now, he finds himself in the "Garden of Earthly Paradise." In order to arrive there, he has had to purge himself of influences that had obscured his vision of the heavenly spheres. He has arrived at a point in which his soul is no longer totally subjected to the influences of the physical body. The crowning and mitering of Dante symbolizes the degree to which he has become the master of himself, He has transformed his thinking by way of willing. His thinking and willing have become one. From now on, Dante shall be drawn toward the heavenly spheres by the force of Divine Will, with Beatrice (*Divine Wisdom*) as his guide. Thus, the "Garden of Earthly Paradise" represents the point in which materialized thinking loses its connection to the physical body, so that the *light* of thinking becomes the vehicle that allows Dante to perceive the spiritual worlds. *Divine Wisdom (Active Intelligence) is not merely a doctrine but, rather, a state of consciousness attained by freeing thought from earthly influences, so as to behold the being of Christ within our hearts.*

Having said this, we find Dante hastening to enter the "Garden of Earthly Paradise," a place of dazzling virgin beauty, graced by the early morning rays of the Sun. This description is significant in depicting the state of consciousness at which Dante has arrived. The *green* forest, of course, recalls our primordial condition when we were one with the divine forces. However, it is a virgin forest, differentiated by the fact that Dante has become *conscious of himself* in his relation to the new world. This new and purified region of his soul is *fully* graced by the first rays of Christ's *light* as manifested by the Sun.

Dante has ventured so far into the "Garden" that he cannot see the place he entered. Soon, he comes upon a stream that blocks his path. It is the Lethe, which, as we have said, cleanses the memory of sin, carrying it down the slopes all the way to the bottom where it trickles into the pit of Hell. There, it deposits all the traces of sin responsible for humanity's separation from God. Thus,

> The purest waters known to man would seem
> to have some taint of sediment within them
> compared to those, for though that holy stream
>
> flows darkly there, its surface never lit
> in its perpetual shade by any shaft
> of sun or moon, nothing could hide in it.
> (Canto XXVIII, 28–33)

Unable to carry on, Dante glances around him, when, suddenly, he sees a lady singing and picking flowers, her path perfumed by their scents. She is Matilda who was foreshadowed in his dream of Leah. Dante asks her to draw closer to him, so that he can understand her song. Says he:

> ...You make me see in my imagining
> Persephone as she appeared that day
> her mother lost a daughter; she, the Spring.
> (Canto XXVIII, 49–51)

By envisioning Matilda as Persephone, Dante recalls yet another account of the Fall, in which Persephone, while picking flowers in springtime, was captured by Hades and sent into the underworld. There, Hermes rescued her. Yet, having eaten a quarter of the fateful pomegranate, she could spend only three-quarters of the year on Earth; the other quarter would have to be spent in the netherworld with Hades.

Matilda grants Dante his wish and appears before him. Not only can he hear the music that she sings, but he can also make out the words. Looking into her eyes, he is struck by their radiance. They remind him of Venus. There, on the opposite bank, she picks flowers that "sprang up without seeds." This description recalls Genesis, where it is said that the forces of creation brought forth the Earth in all its manifestations. In other words, suprasensory forces gave birth to the physical world, symbolized by the "seed," which represents regeneration through death. The "seedless flowers" that Matilda picks, however, are symbolic of the *spiritual forces* continually at work in the act of creation.

The stream, three paces wide, recalls the three steps at the Gate of Purgatory, where Dante underwent contrition. To help the poets better understand her joy, Matilda mentions the psalm, *Delectasti me,* taken from the verse ("For Thou, Lord, hast made me glad through Thy work"). She, like Leah, represents the *active life*. She is now there to answer all of Dante's questions. Having been told by Statius that neither rain nor wind exists above the entrance to Purgatory proper, Dante desires to know how it is that the trees sway gently in the breeze and a stream flows. Matilda explains that Dante presently finds himself in the "Garden," where God originally placed all humanity. However, because human beings wished to replace "innocent laughter and sweet play" for "tears and toil," their stay there was brief. She informs Dante that the Mount of Purgatory suffers no earthly disturbance. Instead, the atmosphere moves from the East to the West around the Earth by way of the movement transmitted to it by the Primum Mobile. The air also moves in that direction, thereby giving birth to the breeze that he feels. The Earth, fixed in relation to the heavens, "intercepts" the motion, which causes leaves to rustle. By way of this wind, there arise the formation of new species.

> ...Know, too, the sacred soil on which you stand
> is bursting-full of species of all sorts,
> and bears fruit never picked by human hand...
> (Canto XXVIII, 118–120)

From this, Ciardi states that earthly plants seem to have:

> their origins in "virtues" or powers" (somehow distinct from seeds). They impart these virtues to the wind that bears them around the world as wind-borne gifts of heaven. On earth, if soil and climate favor, these "virtues" cause new species to spring up (which then reproduce themselves from their own seed). But since no earthly soil or climate is perfect (unchanging), no zone on earth can raise all plants, whereas in the Earthly Paradise *all* created plants may be found, including species unknown to man since the Fall. [32]

Thus, the "Garden of Earthly Paradise" allows for the generation of an infinite number of species, born of the "virtues" or "powers." And so, differentiated within this "Garden" is the *archetype* of all plant life, recalling Goethe's theory on the metamorphoses of plants. According to Goethe all the plants on Earth have their archetype in the spiritual world. Dante has thus ventured into a realm (state of being) in which his consciousness enables him to perceive the forces that result in the proliferation of the plant world. It is the point where the creative forces, originating from beyond the planetary spheres, are transformed into earthly effects.

Matilda continues her explanation by telling Dante that the Lethe has its source in the "Will of God." In fact, this Divine Will is responsible for the creation of two streams: the Lethe, which removes the memory of sin, and the Eunoe that "strengthens the memory of every good deed done." She informs Dante that the Golden Age recalled by the ancient poets in song seems to allude to this "Garden," with its limitless fruit and sacred waters. Upon hearing these words, Dante turns to see Virgil and Statius "with smiles that lingered on their faces"—smiles of recognition.

Matilda continues to sing, *"Beati quorum tecta sunt peccata"* (Blessed are those whose sins are hidden). She walks along the stream and is followed by Dante on the other side, until both face eastward, in the direction of the rising Sun (symbolizing the dawning rays of Christ.) All of a sudden, Dante witnesses a "flood of radiance" and hears "a sweet melody fill the bright air," inducing him to question the ill-fated decision of Eve, which denied humanity, including himself, the opportunity of tasting the "delights sooner," and enjoying them longer. As Dante partakes of the joy around him, he summons the Muses of Helicon and soon hears the melody strengthen until it is transformed into a chanting choir by The Nine Muses. Here begins a most complex series of representations that ushers in the presence of Beatrice (*Divine Wisdom*). These symbolic images—used by Dante—form a pageant or procession (divided into two sections), which traces the spiritual evolution of humanity.

At first, Dante sees what he believes are seven golden trees approaching from a distance. As they near, Dante instead notices a candelabrum, whereupon he hears the chant of *Hosanna*.

> Above the gold array flamed seven times seven
> candles more lucent than the mid-month moon
> at midnight in the calm of clearest heaven.
> (Canto XXIX, 52–54)

Dante, amazed by what he sees, turns to Virgil (reason) who remains silent. Unable to fathom the mystery before him, Virgil is in awe. Matilda quickly admonishes Dante for his fixation on the bright lights and, instead, directs his attention to what follows. There, he sees "people walking like attendants behind their lords...clothed in robes so white earth has no snow of such resplendence." Dante notices a river that "shone bright as a mirror." Gazing at it, he sees that it reflects his left side. He positions himself better to watch the spectacle that is gradually drawing near. The glowing candles leave rainbow-colored streams of light in the air. Following these streams are twenty-four elders dressed in white and crowned with lilies, who sing "Blessed art thou among the daughters of Adam! Blessed thy beauty to eternity!" Once they pass, these elders are followed by four beasts, wearing wreathes of "living *green*." Each of them has three pairs of wings, full of eyes. These beasts surround a two-wheeled triumphal cart "harnessed to the neck of a great Griffon," whose wings, stretching in between the colored streams of light, are lost to human sight.

The Griffon is part bird, part beast; its bird-like parts are gold, the rest white dappled with red. By the right wheel of the cart, three ladies are dancing. One is red, one green and another white. Four nymphs in purple are dancing by the left wheel. Behind the cart are two elders. One seems to be a physician; the other has a sharp and shiny sword in his hand. Four men, walking humbly, follow these two. Finally, there is a lone man who seems to be walking in a trance, his face "firm but keen." These last seven—like the preceding twenty-four—are dressed in white, only they are crowned in roses, and not lilies. A loud thunderclap is heard as the cart reaches the stream opposite Dante. There it comes to a halt.

The candelabra with the seven softly glowing flames have been thought to represent the seven gifts of the Holy Spirit: wisdom, understanding, council, might, knowledge, piety, and fear of God. However, they may also be seen to represent the seven spiritual bodies that humankind shall acquire during the seven evolutionary stages of the Earth. These seven bodies—physical, etheric, astral, "I," Spirit-Self, Life-Spirit, Spirit-Man—reflect the evolution of human consciousness through time. Furthermore, they correspond to the seven planetary spheres through which Dante will venture while guided by *Divine Wisdom*. The twenty-four elders represent the books of the Old Testament. For this reason, they come before the cart, which represents the Church. The white robes and crown of lilies that they wear denote purity. Dante, upon seeing them, notices that the Lethe reflects his *left* side, or his sinister side, which recalls the memory of shame before the eyes of God. These elders in white represent all forms of revelation preceding the birth of Christ for they have "three sets of wings full of eyes"; a revelation that was based not upon the *living principle* (light) within thinking, but upon the unconscious (atavistic) connection that humanity had to the spiritual world before Christ's entry into the world. The purity of their faith in the coming of a new age—the Age of Christ—is, of course, reflected by the whiteness of their dress. However, these twenty-four elders can also represent those whom we meet in the Apocalypse. They are the twenty-four elders who look down upon present-day humanity. Seven of them are from the Saturn phase of the Earth's development, Seven from the Sun, Seven from the Moon, and three from the present phase of earthly evolution. According to Steiner, in his *Apocalypse of St. John,* they are the "guides of evolution, the directors of time."[33] The four beasts around the cart take the forms of man, lion, ox, and eagle, each of which represent the four Gospels that follow the Old Testament. They are crowned in *green,* symbolizing the hope that these Gospels hold for humanity's spiritual development. The triumphal cart is, of course, the Church, but not that which has been perverted by the sins of humanity—namely, the Church of Rome, but, rather, *the community of individuals who unite by way of the principle of Christ* (Love) *operating within them*. This cart, therefore, represents the triumph of the human spirit. A Griffon, half-bird (eagle) half-beast (lion) draws it. It speaks of the dual nature of consciousness conducive to the Christ—divine (eagle) and human (lion). That is to say, the Griffon symbolizes the unification of willing (lion) and thinking (eagle) that engender spiritual perception. They have merged within Dante and must merge within all of humanity, if the "Church of Christ" is to truly become a reality on Earth. The eagle is gold in color, which, of course, represents our connection to the solar forces. The red and white are indicative of the Sacrament, more precisely of flesh and blood (bread and wine). The idea of a gold head and white and red body may also have been taken from the *Song of Solomon,* where it is said with regard to those enamored of Love, "My lover is radiant and ruddy.... His head is pure gold."

The wings of the Griffon, extending into the heavenly heights, represent the power of human perception spiritualized by the *light* of thinking (Christ). Around the right wheel of the cart are three ladies (red, white, and green) representing the three Christian virtues: Charity, Faith, and Hope. Charity, otherwise known as Christian love, alternates with Faith in leading the dance, while Hope can only submit herself to their lead. In other words, our Hope of salvation, which involves beholding the divine forces of creation, is dependent upon our very Faith in their existence, as well as the Love that we are able to cultivate by actualizing the Christ within us. The four women in purple represent the four Cardinal Virtues: Prudence, Justice, Fortitude, and Temperance. The color purple denotes the Empire, whose temporal guidance of humanity comes under the jurisdiction of God. These four virtues also represent the attitude of soul necessary for the reception of the three Christian virtues; all of which are important to the human being's spiritual development. The seven elders who follow represent the seven books of The New Testament, aside from the four gospels. They are Luke, Paul, James, Jude, John and Peter, followed again by John of the Book of Revelation. Luke and Paul symbolize the Acts; Paul, James, John and Peter represent the Epistles. These men, crowned in red roses, denote the new form of initiation achievable through the Holy Spirit. Thus, the white lilies and red roses represent two forms of baptism. The white lilies represent baptism by water (Old Testament) and the red roses represent baptism by fire, or the Holy Spirit (New Testament). Finally, the theological virtues are not only represented by the red, white, and green ladies, but also by the three groups of figures connected to the cart—the preceding twenty-four elders crowned in *white*, the four winged creatures crowned in *green*, and the seven elderly men crowned in *red*.

The elder prophets face the cart that has stopped, when one of them begins to sing *Veni, sposa de Libano* (Come, O bride of Lebanon), from the Song of Solomon. This song is followed by another: *"Benedictus qui venis, Manibus o date lilia plenis"* (Blessed is he who cometh: O, with full hands give lilies). These songs usher the arrival of Beatrice, whose initial presence Dante likens to the Sun:

> Time and again at daybreak I have seen
> the eastern sky glow with a wash of rose
> while all the rest hung limp and serene,
>
> and the Sun's face rise tempered from its rest
> so veiled by vapors that the naked eye
> could look at it for minutes undistressed.

> Exactly so, within a cloud of flowers
> that rose like fountains from the angels' hands
> and fell about the chariot in showers,
>
> a lady came in view: an olive crown
> wreathed her immaculate veil, her cloak was green,
> and the colors of live flame played on her gown.
> (Canto XXX, 22–33)

Once again, the colors of the three theological virtues are represented in Beatrice, whose presence overwhelms Dante. His soul now feels "the mastery of enduring love" by some power which shines from her "above the reach and witness" of his "mortal eyes." In other words, Dante feels the presence of the irradiating *Love* of the Christ streaming into his consciousness; yet, the source of that *Love* transcends his ability to behold it. Then, Dante makes a slight autobiographical reference, whose significance might easily be passed over. Says he:

> The instant I was smitten by the force,
> which had already once transfixed my soul
> before my boyhood years had run their course...
> (Canto XXX, 40–42)

Many critics have exclusively considered these lines to refer to a *physical* encounter that Dante may have had with Beatrice Portinari at the age of nine. They fail to acknowledge that Dante's experience of Beatrice was not based solely on her physical aspect, but primarily on the spiritual aspect of her being. As a consequence, they have mistaken Dante's *initiatory* experience of *Divine Wisdom* for his childhood infatuation of the physical Beatrice.

Nonetheless, having had a glimpse of *Divine Wisdom*, Dante turns to Virgil, as would a child who seeks the embrace of his mother, and says,

> ...I recognize
> the tokens of the ancient flame.
> (Canto XXX, 47–48)

But *Virgil is not there*; he has disappeared. No longer can Dante depend upon Virgil (reason) to help him discern the enigmas of the afterworld. Instead, he has arrived at a new level of consciousness, symbolized by his encounter with Beatrice, which allows him to decipher the spiritual realities that are about to unfold before him.

In spite of his newfound joy of finding himself in the "Garden of Earthly Paradise," Dante cannot suppress the tears that race down his cheeks. Suddenly, he hears his name being called by Beatrice.

> Dante, do not weep yet, though Virgil goes.
> Do not weep yet, for soon another wound
> shall make you weep far hotter tears than those!
> (Canto XXX, 55–57)

Upon hearing his name, Dante directs his attention to himself; he awakens to his "I."

As Beatrice addresses the Spirit of Dante, he looks to the side of the cart and sees her eyes piercing him. She says,

> Look at me well. I am she. I am Beatrice.
> How dared you make your way to this high mountain?
> Did you not know that here man lives in bliss?
> (Canto XXX, 73–75)

Dante looks into the stream and beholds his shame. In that reflection, he bears witness to the very shame that resulted from the Fall. Quickly, he looks at the grass to avoid his reflection. Beatrice reminds Dante that, in a sense, his tenacious adherence to the intellect represents a denial of the Absolute Truth to which *Divine Wisdom* is the vehicle.

As the words of Beatrice come to an end, Dante hears an angelic chorus sing, *"In te, Domine, speravi"* (In Thee, O Lord, have I put my trust). Hearing the Angels' compassion for him, he again bursts into tears. These tears dissolve the ice—born of anguish—that had crystallized around his soul. Beatrice, however, is unyielding as she addresses the angelic host who sought her compassion. She says that

Dante must grieve for his guilt. Though he had been born with rare genius (a gift from Heaven), such good may be easily transformed into evil if not properly cultivated. She reveals how she had kept him on the right path until her death, after which he strayed by "letting others shape his will." We should remember that Beatrice's death—as well as that of other women connected to the *Fedeli d'amore*—represented the attainment of "mystical intuition," or *excessus mentis*. So, as long as Dante stayed on track by cultivating the knowledge leading to *Divine Wisdom*, she was *alive*. But he had to go further; he had to strive toward attaining spiritual vision, which was possible through the *death* of Beatrice. Such a vision evidently lay beyond his apparent desire. Instead, he pursued "false images of good"—namely, good as it presents itself to human thinking, stripped of its connection to Christ by the adversarial forces. Dante had drifted so far from the vision of God that only by entering Hell—the region of the dead—could he find "salvation." For this, Beatrice implored Virgil (reason) to help him. Now, she speaks firmly to Dante so that he can shed "tears of penitence," which would, in turn, enable him to avoid offending the Will and Law of God.

Beatrice continues her stern accusations. "Is not what I have said true?" she asks. Dante is numb and unable to answer; his voice dies in his throat. Beatrice persists, "What are you thinking? Speak up, for the waters have yet to purge sin from your memory." Then, with a voice so faint that only by reading his lips could one make out his words, Dante answers, "yes." He then succumbs to a flood of tears. Beatrice, however, is not finished. She wants to know what had caused him to forsake her. Dante, virtually unable to resuscitate the dying voice in his throat, answers, "The things of the world's day, false pleasures and enticements, turned my steps as soon as you had ceased to light my way." Hearing this, Beatrice is unmoved by Dante's response and tells him that her death should have spurred him toward a higher goal (spiritual perception). Her death should have at least made him realize the transitory nature of the physical world and all its pleasures:

> ...And if my dying turned that highest pleasure
> to very dust, what joy could still remain
> in mortal things for you to seek and treasure?...
> (Canto XXXI, 52–54)

Dante watches Beatrice as she turns toward the Griffin. He now sees her face more clearly than ever. He is so overwhelmed by grief that he falls into a swoon. Only Beatrice, he says, can remember what happened to him thereafter.

Regaining consciousness, Dante finds himself being transported across the river Lethe by Matilda. This scene, incidentally, brings to mind the first time that Dante fainted, namely, when Virgil had taken him across the Acheron. It thus forms a polarity with that in the *Inferno*. As Matilda nears the bank, he hears her singing, *"Asperges me"* (Thou shall purge me), at which point she takes his head between her arms and dips him into the waters "that make clean." These waters that remove the memory of sin recall the Baptism at the river Jordan, in which the indwelling "I" in the body of Jesus, relinquished its place to the Christ.

Once Matilda lifts Dante's head up from the water, he is led to the circle of the four nymphs dressed in purple. They represent the Cardinal virtues that had *prepared the way for the coming of the Christ* and the founding of his Church. They are the handmaidens of Beatrice, whose function now is to lead Dante to the Griffon where he can look into the eyes of Beatrice. There, Dante gazes into the *light* capable of revealing the twofold nature of Christ symbolized by the Griffon: His human aspect and His godlike aspect. The Griffon is comprised of the eagle and the lion. The eagle represents spiritual perception and the lion is symbolic of the human will and heart forces. At this point, Dante does not perceive this twofold aspect simultaneously; only later in the *Paradiso* does he succeed in doing so. Instead,

> ...the twofold creature
> shone from the deep reflection of her eyes,
> now in the one, now in the other nature.
> (Canto XXXI, 121–123)

The Purgatorio: Ascending the Slopes of Redemption

It is important to note that Dante does not experience this vision by looking directly at the Griffon but, rather, *by looking directly into the eyes of Beatrice*. Still, even this first beatific vision is not enough. Dante needs the help of three other maidens, those representing Hope, Faith, and Charity, who now come forth and suggest to Beatrice that she turn her eyes upon her lover who has ventured far to see her. They implore Beatrice to remove her veil so that Dante may bear witness to the second vision, namely, *the Divine Love reflected by her smile*. No attempt by Dante to describe the beauty before him would ever do it justice. And so, Dante is content to merely behold the heavenly sight that is revealed to him.

In trying to understand the spectacle that Dante has perceived until now, we can assume that his vision of the Griffin, as reflected in the eyes of Beatrice, represents the first time in which the transformation of his consciousness permits him to perceive, more deeply, the spiritual nature of his thinking and its dialectical reflection. Up to now, he has been unable to witness them simultaneously and also understand the interrelationship between them—namely, how one arises from the other. The dual aspect of Jesus Christ (human and divine) is, in essence, a reflection of this twofold aspect in human consciousness. Nonetheless, Dante has come to behold the creative force within his own thinking—the principle of Divine Love reflected in the smile of Beatrice.

Dante stares so intensely into the smiling face of Beatrice that he "forgets everything else." His attention is then disrupted by the Three Virtuous Ladies who tell him that he stares "too fixedly." Heeding their advice, Dante looks away and realizes that he is momentarily blinded, as if, for just an instant, he has looked into the Sun. When Dante again regains his sight, he notices that the procession has veered toward the East. The vanguard, having passed the cart, now also has its place in the march. As the Griffon pulls the sacred cart into the forest, Dante and Statius take their place at the right wheel of the cart. The entire group marches into the forest, which has been deserted since the time of Adam.

Beatrice Addressing Dante from the Cart, *William Blake*

The procession stops before a barren tree—the Tree of Good and Evil—that rises to enormous heights. As Beatrice descends from the cart, Dante hears everyone murmur "Adam"; then, circling around the tree, all sing a song of praise:

> Blessed art thou, Griffon, whose beak has rent
> no morsel of the sweet wood of this tree,
> for it grips the belly with a raging torment!"
> (Canto XXXII, 43–45)

The Griffon responds, "Thus is preserved the seed of every good." It then pulls the cart to the tree and ties its mast or pole to the tree's trunk. The pole of the cart (or Chariot) is said by some to represent the True Cross. Instantly, the tree bursts into bloom. The souls then begin singing a hymn unfamiliar to Dante. Unable to understand it, he falls asleep. Dante foregoes the description of his drowsiness, and, instead, recounts his awakening. Says he,

> ...a radiance tore the veil of sleep; a voice
> cried out: "Arise! What are you doing there?"
> (Canto XXXII, 71–72)

As Dante awakens, he finds Matilda bent over him. "Where is Beatrice?" he cries out. Matilda directs his attention to the tree, where Beatrice sits alone, surrounded by the Seven Graces. As Dante again fixes his gaze upon her, she tells him:

> Here briefly in this forest shall you dwell;
> and evermore, with me, be of that Rome
> in which Christ is a Roman. Hence, look well
>
> there at the great car, and that you may be
> a light to the dark world, when you return
> set down exactly all that you shall see."
> (Canto XXXII, 100–105)

Dante gives himself to her command by directing all his attention to the scene before him. Suddenly, an eagle swoops down upon the tree, "ripping the flowers, the leaves, even the bark, with its fierce claws and beak." It attacks the Chariot with such a "tremendous blow" that the cart staggers like a "storm-battered ship." A fox, "so gaunt and angular it seemed to know no fit food," then pounces on the triumphant cart. Beatrice intercedes by sending it "reeling back from there as fast as such a bag of bones could go." Again, the eagle descends into the cart, filling it full of golden feathers from end to end. A voice then cries down from the sky, "Oh what a load you bear, my little ship!" Soon a crack opens in the Earth between the two wheels of the cart. Out from it comes a dragon, which sinks its tail into the cart. As it draws its tail (stinger) out, the bottom of the cart is ripped open; its remains are immediately covered with feathers:

> So changed, the holy ark began to sprout
> heads from its various parts: three from the pole,
> one from each corner. Seven in all grew out.
> (Canto XXXII, 142–144)

At this point, a harlot, virtually undressed, rides upon the back of the beast, "her eyes darting with avarice." Next to her, a giant provides protection, "ready to risk all to keep her for himself." They kiss from time to time. Suddenly, the haggish woman looks at Dante with lustful, hungry eyes, whereupon her "savage lover in a bestial rage" whips her "from head to foot unmercifully." He then unties the monster from the tree and drags it into the wood where it is out of sight.

This complex vision depicts the corruption of Catholic Church. As we have said, the "Church" that Christ entrusted to Peter was to be founded on the *living principle* within human consciousness, namely, the *force of the Christ Himself.* By beholding this stream of living thinking, we arrive at a morality based not upon dogmatic principles but, rather, upon the life-giving qualities of the Christ. Moreover, by realizing the *light* of the Christ within us, we can also behold our oneness with other human beings. Only, then, can a true community arise amongst us.

Quite a different impulse arose from the Church of Rome, which has primarily based its understanding of Christ's teachings on a consciousness rooted in dialectical thinking. Dante allegorically depicts the perversion of morality that ensues from the Church in this the penultimate canto of the *Purgatorio*. Unable to behold the *living* Christ, it resorted to "faith" when confronted with the mysteries that it found inexplicable—a faith that, in effect, required blind submission, by its adherents, to the Church's *interpretation* of the Christ Mystery. However, this "faith" in the Church's dogmatic teachings became the instrument by which the Church would maliciously impose its will upon the faithful, often persecuting—by way of the Inquisition—anyone who would even question its authority. It is, in effect, the eradication of the freedom of thought that largely accounts for Church's portrayal by Dante as the seven-headed beast we see in *Revelations.*

In interpreting the symbolism of the procession described by Dante, we shall begin with the Tree of Knowledge to which the Griffon ties the cart (or Chariot). This tree, otherwise known as the Tree of Good and Evil and whose offshoot was seen sprouting from one

The Purgatorio: Ascending the Slopes of Redemption

of the ledges below, is the one associated with Adam. For this reason, the souls murmur his name upon seeing it. It symbolizes the point in which humanity begins to lose sight of the spiritual forces at work behind the physical world. Thus, it also marks the initial development of thinking, and the gradual loss of our perception of cosmic activity. This tree is barren, for it lacks the capacity to engender life. In other words, the dead thinking that arises from the Tree of Knowledge during the course of human evolution is sterile.

And so, as the Griffon approaches the tree, all give him praise for not eating of the tree, that is, for not partaking in the proliferation of the dying process to which humanity has succumbed. Also, by not eating of the tree, the Griffon does not partake of the materialization that manifests from this dying process. This materialization is symbolized by the material wealth that the Church has acquired. Thus, only by abstaining from such corruption, by rendering "unto Caesar the things which are Caesar's," can the seed of every good "be preserved." Now, we must understand that the True Cross, according to medieval thought, is cut from the Tree of Good and Evil. The pole of the cart that the Griffon has been dragging represents the True Cross, namely, *the living impulse of the Christ*. By tying it to the Tree of Knowledge, which has been barren from the time of Adam, the Griffon causes it to bloom—that is, he imbues it with *life*, thereby resurrecting it. Thus, what we have depicted here is the resurrection of human thought by way of the Christ.

Because the righteousness first bestowed upon Adam was, to some degree, thought to be manifest in the laws of the Roman Empire, many have alleged this tree to also symbolize the Holy Roman Empire. In this way, the tree can represent both divine law and temporal law. For them, the cart, representative of the Church in its *true* form, is tied to the tree (the Roman Empire) and permeates it with life, thus causing something "less than rose" to turn more than violet (Imperial purple). That is to say, the Church, by truly representing the impulse of Christ, would enable the Empire to assert its rightful power in guiding humanity according to the Will of God.

Up to now, the series of events that has unfolded before Dante induces him into slumber. Suddenly, a radiant light penetrates his veil of sleep. He awakens to hear a voice cry, *"Arise!"* This is the word used by Christ to raise Lazarus from the dead. Thus, we can interpret all of this as Dante's awakening to "Eternal Life," for the radiance which tears open the veil of sleep, is, in essence, the *light* of the Christ that has broken through the luciferic and ahrimanic influences of his earthly consciousness—which is *itself* a form of sleep. When Dante opens his eyes, he sees only Matilda, who is bending over him. Dante proceeds to compare this experience to that of Peter, John, and James at the Transfiguration:

> After six days Jesus took with him Peter, James, and John the brother of James, and led them up a high mountain by themselves. There he was transfigured before them. His face shone like the sun, and his clothes became as white as the light...they fell facedown on the ground, terrified. But Jesus came and touched them. "Get up," he said. "Don't be afraid." When they looked up, they saw no one except Jesus [34.]

To this image, Dante adds another—namely, the "flowering of that Tree which makes the angels hurry for its fruit and sets a feast in Heaven eternally." The flowering, here, represents the *promise* of the Christ impulse, blossoming in human souls. This, in turn, "will follow the fruit of eternal rejoicing."[35]

While Dante slept, the Griffin and the Heavenly Pageant ascended back into the spiritual world, leaving Beatrice (*Divine Wisdom*), of course, to keep watch over the cart (Church). She sits on the ground by the Tree that has been resurrected. Therefore, she is the guardian of this newly found Church—a community of souls connected by their direct *realization of Christ's light*. We may, again, *also* interpret the Tree as the Holy Roman Empire and its roots, Rome. The cart (the Church) rests on the very roots (Rome) of this Tree (Empire). Says Beatrice to Dante:

> Here briefly in this forest shall you dwell;
> and evermore, with me, be of that Rome
> in which Christ is a Roman...
> (Canto XXXII, 100–102)

What follows vividly represents Dante's perception of the Church's downward evolution. From the sky, the bird of Jove shoots down into the tree, ripping the flowers, leaves, and even the bark with its sharp claws and beak. This bird is taken from Ezekiel 17, the "Parable of the Eagle and the Cedar." Whereas, there, the eagle represents the persecution of the Jews in Babylonia, here, it represents the Romans' persecution of Christians. In effect, the Romans inflicted damage on the newly found Christ impulse by cutting off many believers who sought a living connection to it. Though the Romans were unable to keep Christianity from taking root, they succeeded, to a large extent, in disrupting it at a most critical phase, namely, when knowledge of the Christ was fresh in the hearts of human beings. Even before humanity had mostly lost sight of the spiritual worlds (c. AD 400), many of the possible connections that could have led to a more living understanding of the Christ had been severed.

After the eagle swoops down, a fox pounces upon the cart and is frightened off by Beatrice. This fox is commonly thought to represent the many "heresies" that posed a threat to the *early* Church. Such heresies were tolerated by the early Church Fathers. Though some of these "heretical" movements, such as Gnosticism, still harbored, as Rudolf Steiner indicates, a vestige of spiritual perception, they later became feared by the Church, which claimed that they misrepresented the "true" teachings of the Christ. Therefore, in the *eyes of the Church*, the fox represented the falsification of Christ's teachings. Nonetheless, as history has shown, the Church *itself* propagated, evermore, the idolized worship of the Christ as the spiritual world receded from view during the early years of Christianity. This idolization of the Christ reflected an ever-emerging consciousness born of luciferic impulses. The corruption exhibited by the popes was often instigated by a cunningness that could be likened to that of the fox. More than not, Dante could also have implied that the fox symbolizes the false teachings of the popes he despised.

Once again, the eagle descends from above. This time, it showers the cart with a heap of golden feathers. Here, the eagle is thought to represent the generosity of Constantine—first Christian Emperor—who corrupted the Church by bestowing material riches upon it. Thus, the foxes (the luciferic element) are complimented by the eagle, which, by endowing the Church with material wealth, ushers in an ahrimanic impulse. Moreover, we also see how the gift of Constantine results in the passing of temporal power from the Empire to the Church, to which we hear Peter's voice cry out, "Oh what a load you bear, my little ship."

The Dragon that rises up from the crack in the Earth is, of course, representative of those adversarial impulses that corrupted the very foundation of the Church founded by Peter. In other words, the true Church of Christ, founded on humanity's direct connection to the being of Christ, himself, is destroyed by the materialistic impulses that begin to impregnate human consciousness. For this reason, we see the bottom of the cart destroyed by the deadly "sting" of the dragon's tail. Though the cart is badly damaged, the golden feathers (material riches) completely covering the cart, keep it fast to the Earth (Satan's domain). They act as fertile soil for the seven heads that sprout from the "holy ark"—three from the pole and one from each corner. The three "were horned like oxen" (having two horns each), while the other four each had one evil horn. This, of course, brings to mind the passage in the Book of Revelation: "There I saw a women sitting upon a scarlet beast that was covered with blasphemous names and had seven heads and ten horns." Thus, we can see how the corruption of the Church, spurred by the acquisition of material wealth, manifests as the seven-headed beast that rises from the waters in the Book of Revelation. We are speaking of Lucifer, who is portrayed by Dante as having "ahrimanic traits." In other words, the Church, having once been founded purely upon impulse of the Christ, has slowly succumbed to the influences of humanity's great Adversaries. Many, including Ciardi, have pointed out that the three heads, which bear two horns each, represent the worst of the Seven Deadly Sins—Pride, Avarice, and Wrath. They are the sins that most offend God and one's neighbor. The other four heads offend God but not necessarily one's neighbors. For this reason, they are thought to have a single horn.

In light of the fact that the Church has been besieged by the incarnation of demonic forces, Dante presents a final, yet lasting, image in the canto. Atop the seven-headed monster, there appears a harlot, immodestly dressed, whose eyes were "darting with avarice." This harlot replaces Beatrice (*Divine Wisdom*). As previously stated, the Church, incapable of realizing the spiritual impulses by which Christ and his disciples sought to found a sacred community, declared itself to be the bride of Solomon's verses, that is, *Divine Wisdom*. In other words, the Church, under the spell of adversarial forces, perverted the understanding of *Divine Wisdom* by equating this suprasensory state of consciousness with its own dogmatic teachings. The Giant with whom she finds herself represents France under the rule of King Philip the Fair who made the Church his marionette by transferring the seat of the Papacy from Rome to Avignon. The Giant dragging the monstrous cart deep into the woods thus symbolizes King Philip the Fair's control over the Church; the woods represent the world of darkness—bereft of Christ's light and reminiscent of the "Dark Wood" of the *Inferno*. Therefore, the Church is seen as being evermore further removed from the *light* of Christ. The harlot can also represent the Papacy under the guidance of the two popes that Dante considered most corrupt, Boniface VIII and Clement V. Clement V was complicit in the demise of the Knights Templar. The Giant, of course, represents Philip the Fair, the king of France who subjugated the Church to have the Knights Templar excommunicated and eventually destroyed. Rudolf Steiner speaks of how Philip the Fair was possessed by ahrimanic forces in his desire to rob them of their wealth, especially gold. In a lecture given by Steiner on September 25, 1916 (*Inner Impulses of Evolution: The Mexican Mysteries and the Knights Templar*), he says,

Pope Clement V, former Bishop of Bordeaux, resided in Avignon and was a tool completely in the hands of Philip. Gradually, under the working of Philip's powerful will, he had reached the point of no longer having a will of his own, but used his ecclesiastical power only to serve Philip, carrying out all he desired. Philip was filled with a passionate desire to make himself master of all the then available wealth. After he had seen what a different significance gold could have in other hands, it was no wonder that he wished above all things to exterminate those other hands, the Knights Templar, so that he might confiscate their gold and possess their treasure himself.[36]

At the sight of what has just transpired, the Seven Saintly Ladies sing *Deus venerunt gentes* (O God, the heathen are come into thine inheritance). This sorrowful hymn is sung for the grief they feel for the Church. Beatrice is so transformed by the compassion she feels in her heart, that she now resembles Mary at the Cross (at Golgotha); she has been witness to the crucifixion of the Church. Upon finishing their song, the Seven Virtuous ladies look to Beatrice. She answers, "*Modicum et non videbitis me; et iterum...modicum, et vos videbitis me*" (A little while and ye shall not see me; and again, a little while, and ye shall see me). These are the words spoken by Christ announcing his Resurrection. Here, they refer to the resurrection of the Church that can only manifest when human beings actualize the *light* of the Christ as a living, creative force. In other words, only through the resurrection of our thinking that allows for the perception of the Christ in one another, will a community arise that can be called the "New Jerusalem."

Beatrice bids Dante, Statius, and the Seven Nymphs to follow her. As they proceed into the woods, she draws Dante near to her and invites him to question her. Dante, too shy to speak with her, remains silent, whereupon she asks him, "Dear brother, why are you not moved to question me as we move on?" Overcome by the sight of her, Dante barely answers, "My Lady, all my need and all that is my good is known to you." These words spoken between Dante and

Beatrice represent the first bridge of communication between the two, thus reflecting yet another step in Dante's realization of *Divine Wisdom*. As Steiner has repeatedly stated, nothing frightens one so much as actually coming into contact with the spiritual within oneself. Here, we see this fear manifested. Once again, Beatrice must reproach him, this time more gently than before:

> ...My wish is that you break
> the grip of fear and shame, and from now on
> no longer speak like one but half awake ...
> (Canto XXXIII, 31–33)

Having said this, she delivers a prophecy, though obscure, regarding the spectacle Dante has just witnessed. She begins by saying, "The cart the dragon broke was, and is not." These words are also taken from *Revelations,* in which it is said, "The beast which you saw, once was, now is not." Soon, she makes it clear that nothing will diminish the wrath of God who will take vengeance against those responsible for the corruption that he saw symbolically represented in the procession. She goes on to say that the true heirs to the Roman Empire—represented here by the Eagle—will regain what is rightfully theirs:

> ...The eagle you saw shed its plumes back there
> to make the cart a monster and a prey,
> will not remain forever without her heir...
> (Canto XXXIII, 37–39)

Though Beatrice admits that her prophecy is clothed in enigmatic references, she attests to the fact that, in little time, all will be made clear. She then asks Dante to take careful note of her words so that he may relay them to the living on Earth, "whose life is no more than a race toward death." Here, Beatrice directs Dante's attention to the process of death normally occurring within human consciousness, for it is *that* death which is responsible for the unfortunate turn of events described. This fallen state of consciousness has twice resulted from the desecration of the Tree. The first refers to Adam and Eve eating of the Tree of Knowledge, and the second to the recklessness of the eagle, which, in the vision, signified the persecution of early Christians that eventually resulted in humanity's loss of the true meaning of *Divine Wisdom*. Beatrice goes on to say that anyone who "breaks the boughs" of the Tree offends God who created it. In other words, those who partake of His creation resulting in its gradual destruction, perform the work of the adversarial forces whose intent is to "deaden the spiritual." Beatrice, then, seems to refer to the five-thousand-year period of Kali Yuga (the Dark Age), often mentioned by Steiner, which eventually resulted from Adam's eating of the forbidden fruit:

> "...For just one bite, the First Soul's tears were spilt
> five thousand years and more, yearning for Him
> who suffered His own flesh for that guilt..."
> (Canto XXXIII, 61–63)

Beatrice tells Dante that, had he not been asleep, he would have been able to understand the implicit meaning of the vision presented to him. Beatrice again tells Dante that her wish is for him to tell others on Earth what has transpired, for his mind is like a "stone"—that is, it cannot allow Dante to behold the *light* shining from higher worlds. Even if his mind could allow the beholding of this *light*—as it eventually will—he will not be capable of expressing the cosmic happenings in their fullness. Dante replies,

> As pressed wax will retain
> a faithful imprint of a signet ring,
> so is your seal imprinted on my brain...
> (Canto XXXIII, 79–81)

Dante then asks, why is it that each time she speaks, he is unable to grasp the meaning of her words, and the more he tries to grasp the meaning, the less he is able. Beatrice responds by telling him that the phenomenon of which he speaks bears testimony to the fact that his philosophical studies have not been an adequate preparation for him to understand the deeper mysteries of life. Dante then tells her that he has no recollection of having estranged himself from her. At this point, Beatrice smiles and tells him that he has drunk from the Lethe, whose waters *remove* the memory of all sinful acts. It also marks the beginning stage of **Inspiration**, in which the formative forces that he experienced with respect to his encounter with Beatrice (Divine Wisdom) are erased, thus giving way to a deeper initiation into the spiritual world. From now on, she says, all will become clear to him.

At this point, the Seven Nymphs have stopped before the waters of the Eunoe—the stream that *restores* the memory of the spiritual world from which humanity came into being. This enkindles his memory of a world free of error and marks the gradual awakening of **Intuition**, in which the spiritual world reveals itself to him. Dante, overcome by the sight of the waters, asks, "What is this flood that pours forth from one source and then parts from itself to either side?" Beatrice has Matilda answer him, though Matilda tells of already having done so. Beatrice asks her to take Dante to the water. This she does, bidding Statius to follow. Dante drinks from the stream and says:

> I came back from those holiest waters new,
> remade, reborn, like a sun-wakened tree
> that spreads new foliage to the Spring dew
>
> in sweetest freshness, healed of Winter's scars;
> perfect, pure, and ready for the Stars.
> (Canto XXXIII, 142–146)

The key to understanding the significance of these final words in the *Purgatorio* rests with the word *Stars,* which foretells of Dante's journey into the heavenly spheres of God's creation. The waters of the Eunoe, having restored Dante's memory of the spiritual world, can be seen as marking the beginning stage of **Intuition**, in which the faculty of spiritual perception has been formed in order for Dante to experience the *realities* of the spiritual world that exist within the planetary spheres and beyond, through which he is now about to enter. In other words, by bringing forth imaginations and then erasing them, Dante has developed his consciousness to the point of beholding in all their glory, the spiritual beings/forces that arise during the initiatory stage of *Intuition*.

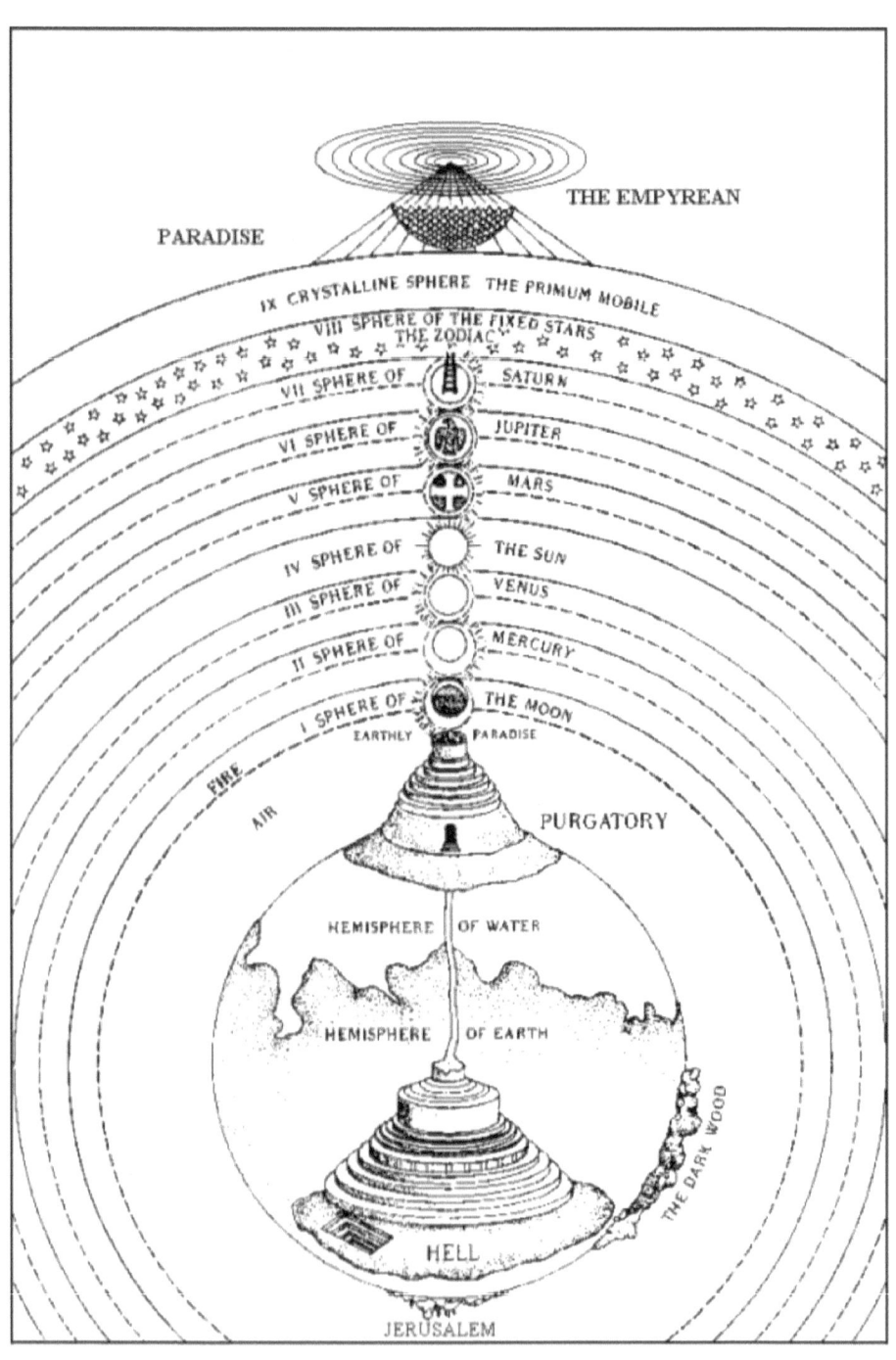

Dante's Scheme of the Universe

The *Paradiso*: Into the "I" of God

At the end of the last canto of the *Purgatorio*, Dante says, "I came back from those holiest waters new...healed of Winter's scars; perfect, pure, and ready for the Stars." Unlike the conclusion of the *Inferno* in which Dante perceives the distant stars shining into the earthly sphere, here we find Dante about to enter into the *activity* of the Macrocosm, after having purified his lower (astral) nature. In fact, we can interpret Dante's journey through the various planetary spheres and the fixed stars in the *Paradiso* as a journey through the spiritual realms of creative activity where the human "I" unites with the "I" of God. Having united thinking and willing—the feminine and masculine polarities of consciousness—Dante has laid the groundwork for his reintegration into the spiritual world. He has, in a sense, resurrected his thinking from the forces of death that had bound him to the material world.

The world into which Dante now enters is a world of *music* and *light*. These are perceptible manifestations that bear witness to the Will of God, guiding him up through the suprasensory world. Though Dante's journey is allegorically depicted as one bounded by space and time, we must continually envision both light and sound as metaphors for the suprasensory activity that suddenly discloses itself to the initiate. It is the activity to which John refers with regard to the Logos, namely, *the light and the life through which all things are made.* This cosmic experience that Dante shares with us is depicted as a journey beginning with the planetary spheres and continuing on into the zodiacal constellation of the fixed stars, the Primum Mobile (where Dante perceives the angelic hierarchies existing within the Empyrean), the Empyrean (*Ring* of Fire), the Mystic Rose, angelic hierarchies and, finally, therein, the three concentric circles representing the Trinity. Thus, the structure of the *Paradiso* is based on Ptolemy's geocentric conception of the universe, in which the human being on Earth was thought to be at the center of the cosmos. Immediately surrounding the Earth was the *Sphere* of Fire (musical sphere) followed by that of the Moon, Mercury, Venus, Sun, Mars, Jupiter, and Saturn, respectively. This, of course, largely coincides with the description given by Rudolf Steiner of the spiritual world through which we journey after death. In other words, the Ptolemaic conception of the universe was one based on the interrelationship of the planetary spheres on the *spiritual* plane. Robert Powell in his book, *The Sophia Teachings,* writes

> In the Christian esoteric tradition, the millions upon millions of stars shining in the heavens can be understood as an outer manifestation of the realm of the Father. As Jesus said: *In my Father's house are many mansions*. The fixed stars of the zodiac are considered the central belt of this whole world of stars, and after death the soul ascends through the succeeding planetary realms of the Moon, Mercury, Venus, the Sun, Mars, Jupiter, Saturn, to enter this world of the fixed stars. The journey of the soul after death is described in Dante's great work the *Divine Comedy*. Rudolf Steiner also chronicled this journey of the soul after death[37.]

As humanity's perception of the suprasensory world diminished more and more at the dawn of the fifteenth century (the beginning of the Consciousness Soul Age), so, too, did Ptolemy's conception of the universe, which was supplanted by a cosmological model that postulated physical bodies in space orbiting the Sun. The perception of these planetary bodies was, therefore, commensurate with the emergence of dialectical thinking, which had, by then, largely asserted itself in human consciousness. This heliocentric conception of the universe is, of course, attributed to Copernicus who first laid the foundation for his claims in a treatise called *Concerning the Revolutions of Celestial Spheres* (1543).

In analyzing the *Paradiso* from an esoteric perspective, it will be necessary to remember that just as the *Inferno* represents the thinking realm and the *Purgatorio* the realm of feeling, the *Paradiso* is symbolic of willing. However, there exists a slight modification in the way it is structured in relation to the other two canticles. Whereas the *Inferno* and the *Purgatorio* (as we have seen) largely reflect one another, both structurally and constitutionally, the *Paradiso* is the realm in which thinking, feeling, and willing are merged into harmonious unity. In other words, no longer do we find each of these individual human activities acting upon one another; instead they lose their distinctiveness and flow as unified stream of consciousness. Thinking is willed and permeated by the heart forces. The integration of this threefold activity becomes the very force that connects us to God, namely *Divine Willing*, which is depicted by the light and sound that enable Dante to venture into the furthest reaches of the cosmos.

Another important element to consider is the function of Beatrice (*Divine Wisdom*). Unlike in the *Inferno* and the better part of the *Purgatorio* (in which the cause of sin had yet to be purged), Virgil is not needed in the *Paradiso*, for, here, there is nothing of the sensory world to which the intellectual forces can adhere. Instead, Beatrice, representing the point in which intellectuality is transformed into an instrument of perception, becomes Dante's vehicle through the spiritual worlds. For this reason, he often makes reference to her eyes. By gazing into them, Dante finds the *light* he needs to enter into the realm of cosmic activity—namely, the *light* of the Christ that leads toward the realization of the human "I."

At the beginning of Canto I, Dante implores Apollo to help him describe, as well as can be done, his experience of the brightest regions of the spiritual world. It is a state of being that transcends both dialectical knowledge and the powers of description. Yet, Dante states, "I was there" ("*fu 'io*"), attesting to the fact that what he describes is, in fact, *an objective experience*. In so doing, he quickly makes us aware that just as the intellect cannot fathom the depths of the suprasensory world, memory cannot "plumb" the depths of the soul.

> For as our intellect draws near its goal
> it opens to such depths of understanding
> as memory cannot plumb within the soul.
> (Canto I, 7–9)

And so, he summons Apollo, the God of poetry, to help him. It is interesting that of the Greek gods associated with a planetary sphere, Apollo is the one connected to the Sun—the abode of the Christ. Not only that, but by having killed the Python (dragon) which guarded the oracle of Delphi, Apollo prefigures the Archangel Michael, who, of all the archangels, heralds the dawning of the Christ in human consciousness. In fact, Rudolf Steiner often referred to him as the "countenance of the Christ (Sun)." Dante acknowledges the difficulty of his undertaking and admits that he needs the support of both peaks of Parnassus, if he is to succeed. However, he pledges to strive for the crown made of laurel, bestowed upon those few poets who achieve victory in translating spiritual imaginations into pictorial representations—the art of poetry in its very essence. It is such a difficult task that Dante declares:

> O power divine, but lend to my high strain
> so much as will make clear even the shadow
> of that High Kingdom stamped upon my brain,
>
> and you shall see me come to your dear grove
> to crown myself with those green leaves which you
> and my high theme shall make me worthy of.
> (Canto I, 22–27)

At this point, Dante proclaims that, because of our adherence to mortal desires, only few are able to "increase the joy" of the Delphic god. Struck by the arrow of Cupid, Apollo is inflamed by the passions of the heart. He pursues Daphne, who upon being touched by him, is instantly transformed into a laurel, the symbol of poetic representation. And so, Dante's invocation of Apollo can be viewed as an appeal to *Imaginative consciousness*. His own pursuit of the laurel is one to gladden Apollo, for "in his mind" Dante seeks to experience his own Daphne—namely, Beatrice. His description of higher worlds is, in fact, only possible by way of a more sublime consciousness.

Having finished his invocation of Apollo, Dante looks up to see the Sun illuminating all of Purgatory. It is the vernal equinox when God was said to have created the world. Dante comments on the various stations or points in which the Sun rises on the celestial horizon during the year. In doing so, he makes light of the fact that four circles join with three crosses. These four circles are comprised of 1) the "equinoctial colure" running through both poles of the Earth, 2) the celestial equator that is the extension of a plane of the Earth's equator stretching into the celestial sphere, 3) the ecliptic—i.e., the path the Sun travels in a year, and 4) the celestial horizon. These four circles meet to form three crosses, suggestive of the four cardinal virtues and the three theological virtues that Dante had witnessed during his climb of Purgatory.

Here, however, they depict Dante's initial experience of the cosmic interplay between the Earth and the Sun, namely, matter and spirit. Whereas the virtues were previously perceived as distant stars, now, they gradually enter into his field of experience. For his journey takes him through the spiritual world, to the Christ. Therefore, it is easy to understand how the vernal equinox ushers a happier course (longer and brighter days), symbolizing an ever-greater presence of the Sun (Christ). Those who consciously approach the Christ, experience the spiritualization of their earthly nature,

> ...it [the Sun] warms and seals the wax of the world
> closer to its own nature and high function.
> (Canto I, 41–42)

This symbolic aspect of the vernal equinox explains the apparent contradiction in the following lines:

> That glad conjunction had made it evening here
> and morning there; the south was all alight,
> while darkness rode the northern hemisphere;
> (Canto I, 43–45)

These two statements represent separate and distinct characterizations that Dante ingeniously juxtaposes so as to provoke the reader to search for inner meaning. Whereas the darkness in the Northern Hemisphere and the light in the South seem to contradict the depiction of evening in Southern Hemisphere and the morning in the North, this may essentially be a pictorial reference to the presence of Christ consciousness. This characterization can specifically relate to the fact that the *light* of thinking hidden within the darkness (evening) of the will must emerge from the *reflected* light (darkness) of day consciousness.

The Eighth Sphere (*the fixed stars*), Botticelli

Dante turns to notice Beatrice staring at the Sun, her gaze more fixed at "its shining" than that of an eagle. Just as the eagle represents spiritual vision, Beatrice has the power to sustain that vision so as to behold the essence of the Sun, namely, the spiritual being of the Christ. Dante follows Beatrice and stares into the *light* so intensely that he says had it happened on Earth it would have "blinded him." *This, again, is an allusion to the esoteric nature of his journey,* for Dante is not looking at the physical Sun but, rather, at its imperceptible, suprasensory *light*.

Soon, he notices the Sun appearing to grow in size, as he lifts his consciousness from the terrestrial realm up toward the Ring of Fire. He then looks away from the light and gazes into the eyes of Beatrice whose attention is now fixed on the "eternal spheres." Thus, she directs his inner vision from the Sun sphere toward the Primum Mobile, from which one can view the Empyrean—the center of creative activity out of which arose the cosmos. In other words, his gaze is guided from the *abode* of Christ (Son) to that of Godhead (Father). At this point, Dante imagines what Glaucus must have felt when transformed into a sea-god. Dante does not yet fully realize that he has risen to a higher level of perception. He is unsure as to whether the transformation that he experiences is one that takes place within him physically or spiritually ("that part of me created first"). He is only aware that he has been *"transhumanized,"* suggesting an alchemical transformation of being, whereby the eyes of Beatrice become his own. They represent a heightened level of perception, which transforms his very being. Just as Goethe stressed that our eyes were born of the light, which in turn allowed us to behold the light, so, too, does Dante's perception of the spiritual world allow him to be transformed by the Sun's irradiating spiritual *light*. Through the harmony (Music of the Spheres) and light that fill his being, Dante feels himself drawn to the Cause of that which enables the Great Wheel (Primum Mobile) to turn—the *Love* of God. The Music of the Spheres, as Massimo Scaligero states, recalls a "remote vision of an invisible construct of the Universe, whose 'dynamis' is the creative sound."[38] He adds that, "the forces of the original sonority operate in us at a given moment, dominating the lower lunar aspect within us" (tr. mine).

Suddenly, Beatrice explains to Dante that, though he thinks he is still on Earth, he has risen into the *sphere* of Fire faster than a lightning bolt descends to the Earth. What makes it difficult for him to comprehend his ascension into the heavenly worlds are his "preconceptions"—namely, the lingering residuals of dialectical memory. Dante asks Beatrice how he can possibly ascend through "such airy substance" in a gross body. Says she,

> The elements
>
> of all things,...whatever their mode,
> observe an inner order. It is this form
> that makes the universe resemble God...
> (Canto I, 102–105)

In other words, within all living things, forces ("elements") exist that weave the universe into being. These forces originate in the spiritual world and "observe an inner order" that enables them to configure the universe so as to "resemble God." This "inner order" that *"draws the Earth together and makes it one"* is the *light* of God that draws us toward Him—namely, the *light* of thinking. The fact that Dante's "gross body" is not of consequence, once again, implicitly refers to the initiatory nature of Dante's experience. Beatrice tells Dante that his ascent is as natural as water falling from a mountaintop to the valley floor and that had he not ascended—having purified his inner being of the weight of sin—that, *itself*, would have been as astonishing as a "still flame in the mortal plain."

As Dante and Beatrice soar up toward the sphere of the Moon, Dante warns the unprepared reader not to follow his "great ship" into the deep "unchartered" waters, for one runs the risk of "losing" him. By losing him, all becomes lost.

> O you who in your wish to hear these things
> have followed thus far in your little skiffs
> the wake of my great ship that sails and sings,
>
> turn back and make your way to your own coast.
> Do not commit yourself to the main deep,
> For, losing me, all may perhaps be lost.
> (Canto II; 1–6)

Here, the "little skiffs" refer to the dialectical thoughts by which we seek to follow his journey into the spiritual world. His "great ship," on the other hand, refers to the *light* of thinking—the only vehicle that ultimately leads to the infinite depths of God.

This allusion to the ship recalls the beginning of the *Purgatorio*, in which the Angel boatman brings the newly deceased across the waters to the base of Purgatory. It suggests that Dante is about to become the master of *his own destiny*, thus fulfilling the role provided by the Angel. Whereas in the *Inferno* and in the *Purgatorio*, Dante called upon the Muses, in the *Paradiso*—where a heightened eloquence is needed to describe the subtle complexity of what lies before him—he invokes Apollo (Christ), Minerva (Goddess of Wisdom), and nine new Muses. The inspiration that they provide enables Dante to make his way to where no one before him had ever sailed. Only those who have partaken in the "bread of angels"— "comic thought"—are able to

> follow in the furrow of my wake
> ahead of the parted waters that close back.
> (Canto II, 14–15)

That is to say, only by paying strict attention to Dante's message can one grasp its *hidden meaning* before the opportunity to do so is lost.

Soon, Dante and Beatrice are enveloped by the Moon sphere that

> ...seemed to me a cloud as luminous
> and dense and smoothly polished as a diamond
> struck by a ray of sun...
> (Canto II, 31–33)

This is the comic boundary of the angelic world that Rudolf Steiner has often described, especially in *Spiritual Hierarchies and their Reflection in the Physical World,* as we will see.

Having penetrated into this smooth pearl-like realm, Dante wonders how it is that two apparent solid bodies can occupy the same space, for he still imagines himself to be of physical form when beholding this world into which he has entered.

> We were received into the elements
> of the eternal pearl as water takes
> light into itself, with no change in its substance.

> If I was a body (nor need we in this case
> conceive how one dimension can bear another,
> which must be if two bodies fill one space)
>
> the more should my desire burn like the sun
> to see that Essence in which one may see
> how human nature and God blend into one.
> (Canto II, 34–42)

In these lines, we see how Dante and Beatrice were received by the "elements" just as water receives light into itself so that its substance does not become altered. The "elements" are the creative forces or hierarchical beings of the Moon sphere ("eternal pearl"). Just as water is unaltered by the rays of light that penetrate it, so, too, is he with respect to the sphere of the Moon. Esoterically, Dante is referring to how his burgeoning suprasensory consciousness is able to interpenetrate the beings that occupy the Moon sphere. Dante invariably misdirects the *gente grossa* from realizing that it is not literally a physical body, *per se*, that has ventured into a nonmaterialized reality. Instead, by way of suprasensory consciousness, he beholds the imperceptible activity of the suprasensory world, while remaining firmly fixed to the Earth in his bodily form. This distinction is significant if one is to understand the *Divine Comedy* as an esoteric work, or as an outline of initiation. What would seem to be a cloud-like region to an ordinary, earthly observer becomes one of cosmic activity when viewed with spiritual eyes. It is only by way of such interpenetrating consciousness that he will be able to *perceive* how "Essence" (being of Christ) can be connected to both human nature and God. Thus, the "I"'s interpenetration of the spiritual world has become an objective reality. He says,

> There we shall witness what we hold in faith
> not told by reason but self-evident;
> as men perceive an axiom here on earth.
> (Canto II, 43–45)

Dante then asks Beatrice to explain the dark spots on the Moon. She answers him by asking for *his* opinion. Dante posits the notion that the variations on the Moon's surface are caused by bodies of differing densities. Here, again, we find that even with regard to suprasensory *light*, Dante still retains a residual of sensory logic. Beatrice quickly alerts him to the inaccuracy of his reasoning by telling him

> ... The eighth sphere shines with many lamps, and these
> may be observed to shine with various aspects,
> both in their qualities and quantities...
> (Canto II, 64–66)

In other words, each of the fixed stars in the eighth sphere, or sphere of the fixed stars, possesses a different virtue or moral quality that results in varying intensities of color and brightness. Her allusion to the *moral* aspect of the stars brings to mind Rudolf Steiner's assertion of a star being comprised of spiritual beings. It is not hard to imagine, therefore, that the moral qualities corresponding to our suprasensory nature are reflected in the moral impulses that constitute the spiritual world. In other words, the virtues inherent within a star are reflected within the human "I." She goes on to say that if rarefied matter did extend to the Moon sphere then, during an eclipse, the Sun's light should fall onto the Earth through those points where the Moon's surface is more rarefied.

Beatrice refutes another hypothesis, which claims that rarefied regions of varying depths on the Moon's surface reflect the degree of the Sun's light relative to their distance from it. Beatrice answers this claim by means of an experiment. She proposes that an observer stand equidistant from two mirrors and that there be added a third further away. In addition, a light should be placed behind the observer so that he or she can see its reflection in the mirror. It will thus be shown that the light reflected furthest away in the mirror, shines just as brightly as the two situated closer to the observer. By this, Dante seeks to illustrate that the interrelationship between the furthest reaches of the cosmos and the human "I" cannot be determined purely by spatial means, thus leading us to realization that the macrocosmic world that extends beyond the earthly realm is mirrored within our microcosmic being.

At this point, Beatrice explains to Dante how the spiritual energy of the cosmos is transmitted through the entire universe from the Godhead (Empyrean)—where all being has its source. From the Empyrean, it is passed onto the Primum Mobile, which contains "the being of all things." Then, he sees the next sphere all lit up—namely, the realm of fixed stars, which

> ...distributes this power to many essences
> distinct from itself, yet all contained within it...
> (Canto II, 116–117)

In referring to the Empyrean (*Ring* of Fire) from which the universe derives its creative impulse, Rudolf Steiner states,

> All that came to us during the earliest phase of earthly development before Saturn was thus transferred outside, beyond the zodiac. In primeval wisdom this is called "the Crystal Heaven." It is where the deeds of beings belonging to a previous evolution were deposited. They formed the basis on which new beings could become creative.[39]

Thus, we can see here the hint of a deeper elaboration by Steiner applicable to Dante's description of the transference of power from the highest spiritual regions to the lowest. For, as Dante himself states, "the motion and power of the sacred gyres...must flow from the Blessed Movers." Therefore, we see that according to Dante

> ...The other spheres, in various degrees,
> dispose the special powers they have within
> to their own causes and effects, All these
>
> great universal organs, as you now know,
> proceed from grade to grade. Each in its order
> takes power from above and does its work below...
> (Canto II, 118–123)

This handing down of power from the Father (Godhead) to the lowest regions of the cosmos is the task of the Intelligences.

> ...And as the soul within your mortal clay
> is spread through different organs, each of which
> is shaped to its own end; in the same way
>
> the high angelic Intelligence spreads its goodness
> diversified through all the many stars
> while yet revolving ever in its Oneness...
> (Canto II, 133–138)

As Rudolf Steiner states in *The Spiritual Hierarchies and their Reflection in the Spiritual World*,

> ...What the Godhead has given to the Seraphim, Cherubim, and Thrones must be so arranged that the commands and impulses received are translated into reality. The Kyriotetes (or Dominions) receive from the periphery of Saturn, through the intermediary of the highest hierarchy, what has to be transformed and made to harmonize with the interior of Saturn.
>
> A further transformation comes about through the Mights (Spirits of Motion, Dynameis). Whereas the Dominions are concerned with the highest arrangements within Saturn, the Mights carry out, as it were, their directives. The Powers, on the other hand, insure that what has been constructed according to the intentions of the universe should endure as long as is necessary without disappearing immediately.... The Spirits of Form (Powers) are the maintainers. So, within Saturn the Dominions are the organizers, the Mights carry out directives, and the Powers preserve what has been formed by the Mights.[40]

Each of the Intelligences, in relation to humanity, has its particular task and finds its outer boundary in the various planetary spheres surrounding the Earth. The sphere of Saturn, for example, represents the "outer workings" of the Thrones; the sphere of Jupiter constitutes the outer boundary (or the organizing principle) of the Kyriotetes (Dominions); Mars demarcates the region of the Dynamesis (Mights); the Sun sphere delineates that of the Exusiai (Powers); the sphere of

Venus marks the outer boundary of the Archai, while that of Mercury makes up the outer region of the Archangels. The Moon sphere, as we have said, is the region where the activity of the Angels manifests. According to Steiner, only the Seraphim, Cherubim, and Thrones enjoy "the immediate sight of the Godhead."

To illustrate how Dante's cosmological characterization coincides with the schematic delineation of the activity of the Spiritual beings above, we need only to quote a passage from the aforementioned book by Steiner regarding the Seraphim, Cherubim, and Thrones. Says he,

> It is of extreme importance to know that these beings beheld God from the time of their origin, and that they continue to do so. They accomplish everything out of their gazing upon God, and God works through them. They could not do otherwise but act as they do for the sight of God is such a powerful force, has such an influence on them, that with unerring certainty and immediate impulse they accomplish what the Godhead ordains. Anything resembling deliberation or judgment does not exist in the sphere of these beings; here there is only a beholding of the commands of the Godhead, which provides the immediate impulse to accomplish what must be done. They behold the Godhead in its true original form, as it really is. They consider themselves only as those who fulfill the will and wisdom of the divine. Thus it is for the highest hierarchy.
>
> In descending to the next hierarchy, to the beings called Dominions, Mights, and Powers, or Spirits of Wisdom, Movement and Form, we find they do not have such an immediate view of the Godhead. They no longer behold God in his immediate form; they behold his manifestation, as he reveals himself, if I might put it so, through his countenance. For them it is unmistakably the Godhead, and they too have the immediate impulse to carry out the manifestations of the Godhead as was the case for the Seraphim, Cherubim and Thrones. The impulse is not quite so powerful but it is, nevertheless, still an immediate one. It would be impossible for the Seraphim, Cherubim and Thrones not to accomplish what they behold as ordained by the Godhead; that would be unthinkable because of their proximity to the Godhead. But it would be equally out of the question for the Dominions, Mights and Powers to undertake something that was not willed by the Godhead himself.[41]

Thus, Rudolf Steiner vividly depicts, with great consistency, the transference of God's Will as intimated by Beatrice to Dante.

With regard to Beatrice's explanation of the light and dark areas on the Moon, it is not a matter of quantitative differences that account for their presence—for we are not effectively concerned here with natural law—but, rather, *qualitative* differences that reflect the moral law of the spiritual world. Thus, just as the capacity to perceive the Godhead diminishes with respect to the diminution of moral impulses, so, too, are the Moon's darkened areas—as inferred by Beatrice—a manifestation of the lower spiritual forces permeating the Moon's surface.

Having understood Beatrice's explanation of the Moon and the spiritual hierarchies, Dante begins to acknowledge his error, when a vision suddenly seizes him. Looking intently about him, he compares his surroundings to a "still and limpid pool whose waters are not so deep that the bottom is lost from sight." Here, Dante fittingly represents the lower degree of radiance reflected by this sphere—a radiance that corresponds precisely to the *clarity* of his suprasensory consciousness at this point of his journey. Though water absorbs light without any change to its substantial nature, it does modify (or distort) what is *seen* by way of the light. Such is how Dante seeks to depict the state of consciousness attained in this sphere as opposed to what he will later encounter in his journey toward the Godhead. Furthermore, the Moon sphere is associated with the theological virtue of Faith, whose incomprehensible nature is, in fact, depicted by the translucent atmosphere surrounding him—an atmosphere that lacks the clarity capable of revealing the reality of what lies therein.

What is also significant is how the "Garden of Earthly Paradise," the sphere of the Moon, the sphere of Mercury, and the spheres of Venus and of the Sun, each symbolize "initiation" into a sphere represented by one of the four alchemical elements of creation. The "Garden of Earthy Paradise," of course, is reflective of the Earth; the Moon sphere, as we have seen, corresponds to water; the sphere of Mercury is connected to the element of air; and the Sun sphere (as well as that of Venus) is the creative realm of fire, connected to the Christ.

Beyond the Sun sphere, Lucifer is benevolent toward humanity. Previous to the Sun sphere, he is adversarial. Dante seems to demonstrate this by pointing out that the Moon, Mercury, and Venus (the lower aspect of cosmic fire—love) manifest some taint of earthliness as each of these planets fall within the Earth's shadow during an eclipse. Beyond the Sun sphere exists the element of ether—which is the living force connecting all four elements in their interrelated aspects and which extends on through the spheres of Mars, Jupiter, and Saturn. The presentation of earth, water, air, and fire, here, in the *Paradiso* is, unlike in the *Inferno*, reflective of humanity's immersion into the creative forces that have begun to take on a more prominent role in his consciousness. If we remember correctly, in the *Inferno*, these four elements were represented by Dante in caricature to denote our subjugation to the earthly realm. We experienced them as the buffeting winds of lust (which sweep Francesca and Paolo) in the second circle; the rains beating incessantly upon the glutton, Ciacco, in the third circle; the earth as mud in which the wrathful live in the fifth circle; and finally, the fire from which Farinata emerges in the tomb in the sixth circle.

Thus, Dante arrives at the Moon sphere where he notices "many faces" eager to speak with him. At first, Dante considers these beings to be reflections and, thus, alludes to Narcissus who fell into the opposite error—namely, of mistaking his reflection for his real face. Turning away to perceive the source of what he thinks are reflections, he finds empty space. Beatrice, with sweet reproach, asks, "Are you surprised that I smile at this childish act of reasoning, since even now you dare not trust your sense of the true fact, but turn, as usual, back to vacancy?" Once again, Dante has reverted to sense-based logic, by thinking that these figures can only be a reflection of a more substantial reality. Beatrice urges Dante to speak with the spirits who approach him, explaining that they are the Inconstant, who, for some reason or other, were unable to maintain the vows that they had made on Earth. Says Beatrice, "the True *Light* that fills them permits no soul to wander from its ray" (italics mine). They are filled with the blessedness that irradiates from the Godhead and, thus, what they say is true.

Dante turns to the spirit that seems most eager to speak with him. It is Piccarda, who in this spiritual realm appears more beautiful than when she was on Earth. Therefore, Dante does not easily recognize her. Like others in this sphere who were unable to keep their vow, Piccarda rejoices in the eternal life that extends to all the regions of Heaven. As the daughter of Simone Donati and the sister of both Forese and Corso Donati, Piccarda was a nun at the convent of St. Clare until her brother Corso took her away from there. He then forced her to marry Rossellino della Tossa of Florence to form a political alliance. Having been forced to marry against her will, she died of grief. Dante asks Piccarda if she wishes to ascend to a higher spiritual realm. She responds by saying, "What we desire, we have. There is in us no other thirst than this." The desire for more would counter the Will of God. Their happiness is complete for *Divine Love* has determined their place in the cosmological scheme. Says she, "In His will is our peace." This, she says, requires that the will of human beings be in line with the Will of God, so that "our wills are one and all agreeing." Dante realizes that all the souls in Heaven—though allotted varying degrees of blessedness—are equally content to be in God's *light.*

Piccarda, having spoken about herself, directs Dante's attention to a spirit next to her, whom she calls "the great Constance." Like Piccarda, the Empress of the Two Sicilies (Sicily and Naples) was forced to leave the convent to marry Henry VI and, though the "shadow of the veil was ripped away" from her, Constance succeeded in veiling the sanctity of her heart to the very end. It is interesting how, at the very outset of the *Paradiso*, Dante presents these two women as having equal rank to demonstrate that social rank on Earth is of no consequence in the spiritual world. All are equal in the eyes of God. Having concluded her speech, Piccarda sings *Ave Maria* as her image disappears into the watery atmosphere.

(Incidentally, as a testament to Dante's meticulous attention to symmetry, these two women—Piccarda and Constance—are chosen to represent the Moon sphere, the feminine polarity of human consciousness, while, as we will later see, two men—St. Aquinas and St. Bonaventure—are chosen to represent the Sun sphere, the masculine polarity.)

At the beginning of Canto IV, we find Dante perplexed by two questions, each of which is of great importance to him. He is unable to decide which question to ask first, thus proving Aquinas' assertion that human beings, when presented with equal choice, find themselves unable to act. Beatrice resolves his dilemma, for she is able to read the thoughts written on his face.

Beatrice begins with the question concerning the soul's immortality as described in Plato's *Timeaus*. Do all spirits, as Plato asserted, inhabit a particular sphere in Heaven from which they descend, whereby they each embody a characteristic of that sphere—or, do they all reside in the Empyrean? In helping Dante come to a greater understanding of the spirit's journey through the spiritual world, Beatrice tells him that all the spiritual beings that he has already come into contact with, as well as all the others that he will encounter, dwell in the Empyrean. They only *appear* to reside exclusively in the various planetary spheres because of the limited nature of his powers of discernment. In the Empyrean, the spirits of Moses, John, and Samuel, for example—reflective of a specific level of spiritual consciousness—are equally a part of God, as are the highest beings of the spiritual hierarchy, such as the Seraphim and Cherubim. They differ only in terms of "how much of the Eternal Breath they feel." In other words, the sphere seemingly occupied by the heavenly spirits reflects the degree of beatitude that they possess. It is our dialectical nature that makes it seem that they are allotted different *spatial* relationships with respect to the Godhead.

> ...So one must speak to mortal imperfection,
> which only from the *sensible* apprehends
> whatever it then makes fit for intellection...
> (Canto IV, 40–42)

In clarifying her point, Beatrice alludes to Scripture, which describes God as possessing human-like attributes, or to the Holy Church, which portrays Gabriel, Raphael, and Michael in "mortal guise," so that the human intellect can more readily grasp the spiritual world. With respect to Plato's *Timaeus*, Beatrice seems to disagree with the notion (if taken literally) that the soul returns to the star from which it was separated before earthly existence. She suggests that Plato could have intended a "second meaning," a metaphorical meaning, which would allow for a certain level of truth in Plato's assertion that the stars have an influence on earthly beings, for, of course implicit to such an assertion, is the issue of Free Will. Can human beings have Free Will, if the stars govern their behavior? Also inescapably connected to Plato's idea is the question of reincarnation, for if a soul returns to the star from which it was separated before entering the Earth, one must then ask how did the soul originally arise in its relation to the star? Nonetheless, Beatrice explains that because Plato's words were largely misunderstood, characteristics were assigned to the planets based on Mythology, which drove "almost the whole world to attach to planets such names as Mars and Mercury and Jove"—names that may have intimated a given influence on the behavior of various individuals.

The second problem that Beatrice resolves for Dante is the question of whether or not one can be blamed for an action that is forced upon them against their will. Beatrice explains that one is not to be blamed for having been forced to do something. Rather, fault lies in one's acceptance of such condition. In other words, when there arises the possibility to return to the previous state to which one had made a vow and one does not do so, then that implies that the will from which one had been torn, was not rooted in the Will of God. For, had it been, it would have returned to its original state. Those, like Piccarda and Constance, should have— when faced with the opportunity—returned to the life they had once led in the convent, before being forced against their will. Beatrice says that one person who exemplified this steadfastness, or "perfect will," was St. Lawrence.

When asked by the Roman Perfect, Valerius, to hand over the treasure belonging to the Church, he brought forth the poor, declaring that *they* were the treasure. For this, he was burnt on a grill.

Beatrice concludes the canto by explicating the difference between Absolute Will and Conditioned Will. Says she,

> ...Absolute will does not will its own harm,
> but fearing worse may come if it resists,
> consents the more, the greater its alarm.
>
> Thus when Piccarda spoke as she did to you,
> she meant the absolute will; and I, the other.
> So both of us spoke what is true.
> (Canto IV, 109–114)

In other words, Absolute Will is precluded by its own nature from willing harm against itself. It cannot will evil, especially against its own creation. Conditioned will, however, when confronted with violence accepts a small proportion of harm so as to avoid that which is more menacing. Having understood these words, Dante exclaims,

> Beloved of the First Love! O holy soul!
> ...You whose words flow over me,
> and with their warmth quicken and make me whole,
>
> ...There is not depth enough within my love
> to offer you due thanks, but may the One
> who sees and can, answer for me above...
> (Canto IV, 118–123)

Dante asks if it is possible to atone for one's past action by way of virtuous deed. Beatrice, in response, looks at him, "her glad eyes...afire with their divinity, shot forth such sparks of love" that Dante is entranced by their splendor. Again, we see how the light in Beatrice's eyes is the pathway to the "eyes of God." The radiance in Beatrice's eyes reflect *the degree in which Dante's own perception of the spiritual world is illuminated*—an illumination that allows him to bear witness to the inner workings of that world as a living reality.

In fact, each time that Beatrice glows with greater radiance, Dante enters a higher sphere. His consciousness is taken to new heights. Says Beatrice at the beginning of Canto V,

> If, in the warmth of love, I manifest
> more of my radiance than the world can see,
> rendering your eyes unequal to the test,
>
> do not be amazed. These are the radiancies
> of the perfected vision that sees the good
> and step by step moves nearer what it sees...
> (Canto V, 1–6)

Thus, the questions that came to Dante's mind are explained by way of such illumination. Beatrice attests to the fact that the higher self in Dante has begun to awaken:

> ...Well do I see how the *Eternal Ray*,
> which, once seen, kindles love forevermore,
> *already shines on you*. If on your way
>
> some other thing seduce your love, my brother,
> it can only be a trace, misunderstood,
> of this, which you see shining through the other...
> (Canto V, 7–12; italics mine)

From here, Beatrice addresses the question that Dante harbors in his soul, that is, can one compensate for a broken vow through good deeds? She begins her explanation by saying that the most precious gift that God bestowed upon humanity is Free Will, for it is the gift "which is most like Him." In other words, the freedom to *consciously* act out of our inner impulses is the one quality that we possess that differentiates us from the lower realms of creation. *It is the basis for all creative activity.* To sacrifice this most valuable gift, namely, to surrender one's will to the Will of God is the highest deed of which we are capable. It is, in effect, this sacrifice that constitutes a vow. Here, however, it is most important to note that the merging of our will with that of God is a metaphysical act that enables us to act within the consciousness of God. Thus, we have, in a sense, attained the highest possible good by doing so, for not only do we manifest our inner creative forces, we work according to the "design" provided by higher beings. To compensate for having broken a vow by doing a good deed is a worthy act, but it is one that can be executed without necessarily having to sacrifice the whole of our being, for we can do a good deed and still not relinquish our Free Will.

In elucidating her point, Beatrice explains that each vow is really made up of two parts:

> ...The essence of this sacrificial act
> lies, first, in *what* one does, and second, in *how*—
> the *matter* and *manner* of the pact...
> (Canto V, 43–45)

The *manner* in which the "pact" with God is executed—namely, the disposition of the "I" in its relationship with God—cannot be compensated, because it reflects the degree to which we connect with the Godhead and the higher beings of the spiritual world. The *matter* of the pact can be replaced by other deeds provided that:

> ...no man by his own judgment or whim
> take on himself that burden unless the keys
> of gold or silver have been turned for him...
> (Canto V, 55–57)

In other words, only by attaining to a consciousness (through grace) that enables us to see the *effects* of our actions (on our karma), can our compensation not be arbitrary or mechanical, but fully in accordance with the dictates of Divine Will. In addition, the compensation should be one that reflects an increase in the substance of our vow.

Beatrice then explains that a distinction should also be made between a vow that is acceptable to God and one that is not, for not all vows are acceptable in His eyes. She cites two examples from antiquity to illustrate her point. First, she recalls the story of Jephthah, King of

Israel, who in his fight with the Ammonites vowed to sacrifice the first thing he perceived exiting his house. The first person he saw was his daughter and, so, as it is said in Judges 11, he sacrificed her. Beatrice also cites the myth of Agamemnon, who vowed to sacrifice the most beautiful child born during that year to Artemis, not knowing that it, too, would be his yet-to-be-born daughter, Iphigenia. Years later, when the Greek ships were kept motionless at Aulis, Agamemnon was blamed for not having kept his vow. As a result, Iphigenia was sent away and sacrificed. Thus, Beatrice warns Christians to move slowly when making a vow and not "like a feather in the wind." One must have the "shepherd of the church" (Christ) as a guide to be rooted in the consciousness of the "I" before making a vow. Says She,

> ...You have the Testaments, both old and new,
> and the shepherd of the church to be your guide;
> and this is all you need to lead you true...
> (Canto V, 76–78)

Suddenly, Beatrice turns to "that part where the world is quickened most by the True Light." As Dante gazes at her, he notices that she increases in brilliance, a sign that he has risen into a higher planetary sphere (of consciousness). In effect, he has perceived (on the Moon sphere) the inner workings of our connection to the Godhead and how our actions on Earth must be in consonance with what we have directed toward our Maker.

Now, he has arrived in the sphere of Mercury where the radiance of Beatrice illuminates the planetary sphere:

> My lady glowed with such a joyous essence
> giving herself to the light of that new sky
> that the planet shone more brightly with her presence.
> (Canto V, 94–96)

Her radiance is born of joy—a joy that increases the more she rises up through the planetary spheres. Her joy is commensurate with her radiance.

Dante, too, is transformed by what he sees:

> And if the star changed then and laughed with bliss
> what did I do, who in my very nature
> was made to be transformed through all that is?
> (Canto V, 97–99)

Thus, Dante alerts those "with eyes to see" that his transformation resulted from the joy of heightened consciousness. By entering the planetary spheres via the *radiance* of Beatrice, he begins to notice that he, himself, becomes his experience, that his will is made divine. As soon as Dante realizes this change of being, he is surrounded by "a thousand splendors," each crying out, "Here is what will give increase to our love!" These souls are the Seekers of Honor: those who sought good, but for the least good of all imaginable reasons. As Ciardi states, these souls are "lost to Dante's sight in their own radiance,"[42] for just as the planet Mercury often disappears within the glow of the Sun, so, too, are these souls obscured by the brilliance of their joy within the sphere of Mercury. Because they are not easily revealed to Dante, he must ascend to perceive them.

One of the leading spirits who approaches Dante acknowledges the unique grace bestowed upon him—a grace that permits him to visit the heavenly realms while still *alive*. He states,

> O well-born soul, permitted by God's grace
> to see the thrones of the Eternal Triumph
> while still embattled in the mortal trace,
>
> the lamp that shines through all the vaults in Heaven
> is lit in us; if, therefore, you seek the light
> on any point, ask and it shall be given.
> (Canto V, 115–120)

Here, we see that these spirits within the sphere of Mercury are endowed with godlike qualities, as they transmit the *light* of God to Dante. In fact, Beatrice says

> ...Speak. Speak with full assurance.
> And credit them as you would deities!
> (Canto V, 122–123)

As previously mentioned, the sphere of Mercury represents the outer boundary of activity of the Archangels. Unlike the Angels who are the guardians of individual human beings, the Archangels guide the activities of folk souls or nations. It is, therefore, interesting to note that the spirit approaching Dante at the end of the fifth canto is Justinian, Emperor of the Roman Empire. For Dante, he reflects the wisdom and light that manifests in that realm, namely, that of guiding a nation or people. Thus, as Justinian begins speaking, he glows in brilliance, indicating that there exists within him the *light* that rays down from the higher regions of the Empyrean.

In identifying himself, Justinian begins by describing how Constantine "turned the eagle's wing against the course of Heaven," so that the center of the Empire in Rome was transferred to Byzantium around AD 330. Since Dante believed that the Church of God and the Roman Empire were—by heavenly decree—to be situated in Rome, the transference of the imperial seat from Rome to Byzantium was an act against Divine Will. Justinian depicts this graphically when he says that the eagle's wing turned "against the course of Heaven"— namely, from West to East, the direction *opposite* to that in which the Heavens are revealed to us. After two hundred years of corruption, Justinian restored the Empire to its "rightful" place. Also, by God's Will, he "pruned the law of waste, excess and sham." Justinian confesses to Dante that, at one time, he did not believe in the dual nature of Christ. It was Agapetus who was able to show him the "true way." Says he,

> ...I see the truth as clearly as you see
> how a contradiction is both false and true...
> (Canto VI, 20–21)

Justinian explains that upon comprehending the mystery of Christ, he was moved to codify the Roman law. Yet, Dante's adoration of the Roman Empire as the seat of spiritual and temporal power overlooks the unfortunate consequences that Justinian's prohibition of the Greek schools had on the evolution of human consciousness. In *Three Streams in the Evolution of Mankind*, Rudolf Steiner states,

> Just take the event, of very little interest to ordinary people, but all the same an extraordinarily significant event—take the event of the year 529, when the Emperor Justinian prohibited the further functioning of the Greek schools of philosophy—those schools which were the shining light of antiquity. So all the scholarship of olden times which had been drawn into the Greek schools of philosophy, and had produced an Anaxagoras, a Heraclitus, and later a Socrates, a Plato, an Aristotle—all this was swept away in 529 by a decree of the Emperor Justinian. True, it is possible to gain from history some idea of why Justinian swept away the old knowledge in Europe; but if we reflect honestly upon these matters, we shall remain dissatisfied with any of the explanations given. We feel the working of unknown forces. And it is strange that this event coincides—not exactly, but historical facts often appear to belong together when they are looked at from a later time—this event ties up with the expulsion of the philosophers from Edessa in the year 489 by the Isaurian, Zeno Isauricus. So from the most important places of that world the most learned men were driven out. And these men, who had preserved the ancient wisdom that had not yet been influenced by Christianity, were obliged to wander forth. They fled to Nisibis, journeyed then to Persia and founded the Academy of Jundí Sábúr.[43]

Sergei O. Prokofieff, in his book, *The Case of Valentin Tomberg: Anthroposophy or Jesuitism*, states,

> After he had driven out the still living Greek wisdom, the same emperor then decided to codify the old Roman law in order to consolidate his absolute imperial power. Rudolf Steiner put it thus: The "Roman state idea, taken up into pure jurisprudence and jurisdiction" was thus victorious in Constantinople. This was the final victory of the "state imperialism of Romanism." So in reality Justinian's codification meant the death of that law which had in the preceding centuries still contained vestiges of an inner

aliveness and thus its original connection with the spiritual world (revelation).[44]

By adhering to the notion that an idealized Catholicism, untainted by the corruption of its organizational structure, held the promise of humanity's spiritual evolution and salvation, Dante did not seem to acknowledge the *consequences* of Justinian's actions with regard to the ancient Greek schools. Thus, Dante was still, in some respects a product of his time. His understanding was, to a degree, influenced by the religious and philosophical structures reflective of the Middle Ages.

Justinian, from here, delineates for Dante the history of the Roman Empire and alludes to how certain factions, specifically the Guelfs and the Ghibellines, each undermine the true aims of the Empire—the Ghibellines by bribing imperial rule to accomplish their own goals, and the Guelfs by replacing its rule with that from local quarters. Justinian then speaks of the founding of Rome by Aeneas, the defeat of Hannibal, the defeat of Pompey by Caesar, the peaceful reign of Augustus, and Tiberius, during whose rule Christ was crucified. He also speaks of Titus, whose vengeance against the Jews was meant to atone for their offense against God, and the heroics of Charlemagne who defended Rome against the Lombards. In conclusion, Justinian issues a warning to the Guelfs and the Ghibellines against usurping the influence of the Empire.

Justinian explains that within the sphere of Mercury is the light of those who sought fame and honor. In fact, they sought such reward so fervently that they overlooked the true motive for serving as leaders of human beings—their devotion to God. As with the spirits in the Moon sphere, the spirits in this sphere also fall within the Earth's eclipse and, thus, they content themselves with the degree of beatitude allotted them by God. Justinian identifies another spirit amongst them (Romeo) who on Earth rose to the high position of minister within the court of Raymond Berengar. Defamed by envious members of the court, he was driven into exile.

An interesting correlation arises here in Canto VI of *Paradiso* with respect to Cantos VI of the *Inferno* the *Purgatorio*—namely, that all three cantos reference the political corruption in society during Dante's time. Florentine politics forms the basis in Canto VI of the *Inferno*, regional politics in Canto VI of the *Purgatorio*, and the politics of the Roman Empire in Canto VI of the *Paradiso*. Taken all together these three political cantos form the "number of the beast" (6 + 6 + 6 = 666) in the Apocalypse of John 13:18. Nevertheless, there is an implicit evolution toward the realization of good, even within the realm of politics and earthly affairs. This evolution proceeds from the center outward, not only in geographical terms as it pertains to Italy, but also from the center of one's being as one ventures from the darkness of dialecticism out toward the *light* radiating from the Empyrean. This symmetrical pattern is consistent with the whole of the *Divine Comedy*. What is noteworthy is how in each canticle—even in the depths of Hell—an example of justice is praised. In the *Inferno VI: 70*, Ciacco praises two identified individuals in Florence as "just" (*giusti*). In the *Purgatorio VI: 133*, Dante points to examples of "others" outside Florence who "have Justice at heart" (*giustizia in cuore*). Finally, in the *Paradiso,* Justinian—whose very name denotes Justice—leads the just to realize their heavenly reward.

Canto VII opens with a song sung by Justinian, who is joined by other spirits in dance. Afterward, they disappear into the distance like shooting sparks. Dante stands silently perplexed by a question that he is afraid to ask Beatrice. Knowing that he lacks the strength to ask her, she proceeds to answer the question on her own. Beatrice, able to perceive the thoughts of Dante, explains to him how a "just vengeance can be justly avenged." She says that Adam, having fallen from his divine state, induced the Fall, which resulted in human suffering. The punishment suffered by Jesus Christ was to counteract this event. In other words, Christ took upon himself the karma of all humanity. For this reason, Beatrice states that His suffering was "justified" in atoning for Adam's sin. On the other hand, *injustice* was perpetrated against the *divinity* of Christ. Therefore, the vengeance brought by

Titus against the Jews in destroying Jerusalem was due punishment for having committed such an act of sacrilege. Dante's logic here is rooted in Scholasticism and, again, reflects the degree in which the materialistic conception of Christ's divine nature was reflected in the thinking of that time. Because the idea of vengeance is un-Christlike, it follows the precepts of the Old Testament, which Christ had come to supplant. Thus, Dante, in this particular instance, reverts to the logic of the Middle Ages and not to the esoteric principles born of suprasensory perception.

The second question puzzling Dante is why God chose such a form of redemption for humanity. Beatrice, again anticipating Dante's bewilderment, answers by saying that in the beginning God made human beings pure and free of sin. However, this soon changed with the transgression of Adam and Eve in the "Garden of Eden." With regard to humanity, she says,

> ...Sin is the one power that can take away
> its freedom and its likeness to True Good,
> whereby it shines less brightly in Its ray...
> (Canto VII, 79–81)

Therefore, sin impedes us from shining more radiantly in God's light, which is to say, the brightness of His light shines most in those beings that resemble Him most. The word *sin* is not confined to an act of transgression but extends to the consciousness that induces it, which is shared by all humanity bereft of Christ's *light*. This sense-based consciousness (loss of Paradise) arose from Adam, whose actions represent the "seed" of all sins:

> ...Your nature, when it took sin to its seed,
> sinned totally. It lost this innate worth,
> and it lost Paradise by the same deed...
> (Canto VII, 85–87)

Paradise, thus, refers to the state in which *the human being is one with God*. The redemption of our spiritual nature could only come about in one of two ways—either by atoning for our transgressions, or through the mercy of God's intervention, which alludes to Christ's deed at Golgotha. According to Beatrice, human beings often lack the "humility" by which they could ascend toward God. Instead, their pervasive pride is commensurate with the increased materiality of human consciousness after the Fall. Though the seed of all sin—intellectuality—had already implanted itself firmly into human consciousness at that time, this burgeoning intellectuality could not, in and of itself, lead humanity to a perception of the spiritual world. Having descended from the spiritual heights, Christ penetrated the Earth with His *substantiality* at Golgotha. In this way, His regenerative force could enter human consciousness and resurrect it, thereby, providing humanity with the means by which it could atone for its fall from grace. Herein lies the great significance of Christ's sacrifice.

> ...There was not, nor will be, from the first day
> to the last night, an act so glorious
> and so magnificent, on either way.
>
> For God, in giving Himself that man might be
> able to raise himself, gave even more
> than if he had forgiven him in mercy.
>
> All other means would have been short, I say,
> of perfect justice, but that God's own Son
> humbled Himself to take on mortal clay.
> (Canto VII, 112–120)

Beatrice concludes by answering the last question troubling Dante, namely, how can all the earthly things that are corruptible or temporal be reconciled with the fact that God's creations have the mark of perfection? She explains that spiritual beings such as the Angels are incorruptible and suffer no diminution of God's splendor. However, earthly elements are created by "powers that had themselves to be created."

> ...Created was the matter they contain.
> Created, too, was the informing power
> of the stars that circle them in Heaven's main...
> (Canto VII, 136–138)

What is corruptible, according to Beatrice, are the four principle elements—earth, water, air, and fire—out of which all *material* things were made. These elements are themselves manifestations of "certain directly created powers in nature."[45] They are not the "direct effects of God." The human spirit, on the other hand, is a creation of God's own likeness. Beatrice states that God's breath of life (Spirit) into humanity is evidence of our link to the divine world:

> ...And from this you may
> infer the sure proof of your resurrection,
> if you once more consider in what way
>
> man's flesh was given being like no other
> when He made our first father and first mother.
> (Canto VII, 145–149)

It is interesting to note here how the word *your* insinuates that Dante himself, by following the path of Christ, will be resurrected, for "man's flesh was given being like no other." Here "being" refers to the "I," the incorruptible principle that distinguishes the human being from all other earthly creations, a principle that connects to the power of Christ through *living* thinking. Again, Dante drops yet another clue for "those with the eyes to see," which points to the presence of an esoteric reality at the heart of his cosmological creation.

Canto VIII opens with Dante alluding to the misunderstanding that the ancients had of Venus. It was believed that this planet within the third heavenly sphere "rayed down love-madness"—i.e., it's rays drove men and women to madness. Venus's position along the epicycle, the center line of the Third Sphere, gave humanity the impression that it "wooed" the Sun, "now shining at its nape, now at it brow"—namely, as an evening star and as a morning star. Therefore, Venus represents the *lower* aspect of Love and like the Sun, it is symbolized by the element of fire. It is the sphere in which the Archai exert their activity. Like the Moon sphere and the Mercury sphere, Venus also falls within the Earth's shadow during an eclipse. Thus, it is among the lowest in rank with respect to the heavenly spheres. Here, the sphere of Venus is represented by the Amorous, who were so influenced by the rays of Venus that they nearly succumbed to earthly passion. However, through God's *Love* they were able to transform physical passion into "true caritas." The spirits in this sphere are the last that Dante encounters who bear some resemblance to human form.

Dante immediately realizes that he has risen into this spiritual realm by way of an increase in Beatrice's radiance. Again, her increased radiance denotes a heightening in the degree of consciousness. Dante perceives "lights" circling at various speeds within the bright light of that heavenly sphere, each "proportioned to its eternal vision of delight." (It is interesting to note that Dante, by so describing the spirits, preserves the notion of one's individual "I" as being distinct from that of others, thus discrediting Averroes, who believed that upon earthly death, the soul loses its individual corporeal component while its eternal aspect returns to the "cosmic pool" of creation as an indistinct merging essence.)

These spiritual beings—who rejoice while singing *"Hosanna"* among the Seraphim (within the Empyrean)—have descended with lightning speed so as to appear before Dante. Then, a spirit approaches him, declaring that all the beings present in this sphere are disposed to increase his pleasure. He also states that these spirits move with the High Principalities (Archai) to whom Dante in his *Convivio* (while on Earth) cried *"Voi ch' ntendendo il terzo ciel movete"* (O you whose intellects turn the third great wheel). Having listened to the intention of these beings, Dante turns to Beatrice:

> I raised my eyes to the holy radiance
> that was my lady, and only after she
> had given them her comfort and assurance,

> did I turn to the radiance that had made
> such promises. "Who are you?" were my words,
> my voice filled with the love it left unsaid.
> (Canto VIII, 40–45)

Here, again, Dante probes the depths of *Divine Wisdom* for the strength to confront the new realities before him. Questioning this spirit, Dante notices its glow increase with *joy* upon knowing that Dante has urged himself on high into loftier realms. Dante thus characterizes how these higher beings, having sacrificed themselves for humanity, experience human striving toward the spiritual world with great anticipation and joy.

The spirit who has spoken to Dante identifies himself as the one who ruled the Danube region below the German borders and who should have ruled the left bank of the Rhone, as well as Southern Italy. He claims that had he done so, much evil could have been avoided. As a result, Dante and others would have witnessed more than the mere potential of his aims but, rather, the flowering fruit of his deeds. In short, he would have attempted to harmonize opposing forces backed by the Vatican. This soul—though he does not name himself—is Charles Martel, the son of Charles II and grandson of Charles of Anjou. He was married to the daughter of Emperor Rudolph I. His brother Robert was King of Naples who wrought much havoc against the poor of his region. This Charles Martel is not to be confused with the more famous Charles Martel, grandfather of Charlemagne. Martel delineates, by way of references, the various connections that Charles had to family members and concludes the historical description of his family tree by stating that he would still govern Sicily had members of the Anjou dynasty not misruled. Instead, the House of Anjou was overthrown in what became known as the "Sicilian Vespers," as the people "cried out through all Palermo's streets 'Death! Death' [to the French]."

The description that Charles outlines prompts Dante's curiosity, for he cannot understand how family members often manifest a variety of temperaments so radically different from one another. Says Dante,

> Sire, I hold dearer this felicity
> that fills me when you speak, believing it
> *as visible to you as it is to me,*
>
> *there where every good begins and ends.*
> *And this, too, I hold dear—that you discern it*
> *in looking on Him from whom all love descends.*
>
> You have given me joy. Now it is in your power
> to give me light. For your words leave me in doubt:
> how, if the seed is sweet, may the fruit be sour?"
> (Canto VIII, 85–93; italics mine)

Though we are within the planetary sphere of Venus, the spirits who appear to Dante reside "where every good begins and ends"—the Empyrean. There, these spirits discern what is being spoken by looking in the direction of Him "from whom all love descends." And so, we witness the actual transference of *light* (truth) as it proceeds from the Godhead, by way of the Christ, down through the levels of consciousness, represented by the beings occupying the planetary spheres of spiritual activity.

So, how can the fruit that issues from a sweet seed be sour? In response to his question, Charles directs Dante's attention to the stars, for they harbor the powers (or qualities) that affect human characteristics on Earth. According to Charles, if not for the stars, one would be left to think that the characteristics of a given individual are readily transmitted to his or her offspring. Interestingly, the idea that our ancestors do not transmit to us certain characteristics seems to accord itself with something that Rudolf Steiner stated in *Life Between Death and Rebirth*. There, however, he did not attribute it to the stars but, rather, to ourselves:

> Science believes that a person takes on the characteristics of his ancestors. Actually he influences the characteristics of his ancestors from the spiritual world. In a certain sense we ourselves are responsible for the way our great-great-great-grandparents were. Obviously, we cannot influence all their characteristics and

yet, among others, those must be present that we ourselves later require. What one inherits from one's ancestors one first has oneself instilled in them.[46]

Nonetheless, Charles implies that the influence the stars have on one's destiny serves God's purpose by providing society with individuals gifted in various capacities of social life. Thus, individual talent is largely determined by means of what one gathers from the planetary spheres and the fixed stars. This seems to be in accordance with what was said by Rudolf Steiner when he describes how the spirit of a human being, between death and rebirth, often sojourns in one planetary sphere longer than in another so as to receive from it the influences necessary to fulfill its karma on Earth.

The lack of consideration given to reincarnation by Dante prevents him from approaching the question of talent from the perspective of karmic development, thus forgoing how individuals confront the question of necessity and freedom. Instead, by relegating all the responsibility to the Divine World, Dante *seems* to be pointing to the idea of predestination, thereby diminishing the role of Free Will. Yet, if we pay close attention to the verses, it becomes clear that we are always free to do as we please. However, it is only when we strictly observe the nature of our own development that we can consciously perceive how our particular gift or talent conforms to our destiny and that of the world. Only then can we understand how we have chosen this destiny that invariably is in consonance with God's Will. Those who seek to live harmoniously within the scheme of God's plan accept the gift allotted to them by Providence, knowing that they have chosen to work constructively toward the realization of His purpose. Says Charles to Dante:

> ...If the world below would learn to heed the plan
> of nature's firm foundation, and build on that,
> it then would have the best from every man...
> (Canto VIII, 142–144)

Thus, danger arises when a person whose intellect is made for writing sermons becomes king and another who is "born to strap on a sword and shield" takes the cloth.

Dante addresses Clemence, most likely the wife of Charles, and reveals Charles' prophesy, which alludes to the many attacks upon their house: attacks which shall be chastised. Shortly after Charles turns his attention to the Sun "to be renewed," Dante is approached by another spirit. With Beatrice's consent, Dante addresses the spirit by saying:

> O blessed spirit, be pleased to let me find
> my joy at once,...Make clear to me
> that you are a true mirror of my mind!
> (Canto IX, 19–21)

Here, we are made aware that the spirits living in the afterworld are able to perceive the thoughts of others. Rudolph Steiner has said that in the spiritual world lies *cannot* exist. For, there, the human "I" perceives what on Earth can be hidden. What those living in the spiritual world are able to behold is the *light* (or will) intrinsic to dialectical thinking. Dialectical thought, whose inner *light* is normally imperceptible on Earth, is what makes it difficult for humanity to see truth. It is that which Dante's journey has led him to transcend.

The spirit responds to Dante's request by identifying herself as Cunizza da Romano who lived in that "sinful land," which "lies between Rialto and the springs from which Brenta and Piave flow." Daughter of Ezzolino II, Cunizza admits to having succumbed to the influence of that "burning star" (Venus) during her youth. Now, however, she gladly embraces her fate and rejoices there—"although it may seem hard to the crowd below" to understand. Though many have wondered why she is allotted a place in Paradise, the most convincing explanation is that she underwent a "true contrition" before her death. She therefore exemplifies the level of atonement achievable on Earth.

Cunizza points to the "star" beside her and declares that he will have fame for five hundred years. She continues foretelling the fate of others by denouncing the wickedness of those living near her native Treviso. Among other things, she predicts that the "Paduan blood" (of soldiers) will soon "stain the water that bathes Vicenza," for the Paduans refused to ally themselves with the empire under the reign of Can Grande della Scala. As a result, Rizzardo da Cammino (Lord of Treviso) will be murdered. In addition, the Bishop of Feltro will betray a group of Ghibelline refugees from Ferrara, whom he accepted as guests before having them beheaded. As a consequence, the Bishop will immediately be cast into the Ptolomea, where others who once betrayed their guests lie. Cunizza reveals that the Thrones reflect God's judgment to them. This enables her to foretell the fate of individuals who commit treacherous acts. Here we are led to believe that spirits are able to perceive the inner workings of karma, for such perception is aligned with that of God. At this point, Cunizza falls silent and joins her fellow spirits.

Soon, the other spirit of whom she spoke reveals itself "like a fine ruby struck by the sun's ray." In addressing this being, Dante reiterates what has just been said regarding the capacity of spiritual beings to perceive the thoughts of others.

> God sees all, and your insight, blessed being,
> makes itself one with His...and thus,
> *no thought or wish may hide beyond your seeing...*
> (Canto IX, 73–75; italics mine)

We notice that these beings have the potential to perceive the thinking and feeling of others. Knowing this, Dante cannot help but wonder why the spirit before him does not satisfy his curiosity by revealing his identity. He says,

> ...Had I the intuition
> with which to read your wish as you read mine,
> *I* should not be still waiting for *your* question!
> (Canto IX, 79–81)

Though Dante has risen to a state of consciousness that allows him to perceive beings of the suprasensory world, he still has not yet completed the process by which to perceive ever-higher states of being.

In response to Dante's plea, the spirit identifies himself as having come from a land situated between Spain and Italy, precisely opposite to the city of Bougiah in North Africa. This would indicate that he was from Marseilles, where Caesar had stationed Brutus to defeat the troops of Pompey, while he descended on Spain. The spirit reveals himself as Folquet, whose ray here "marks all this sphere, as its [the sphere's] ray marked [his] birth." However, like Cunizza, there is no remorse here for the past, only joy:

> ...But none repents here; joy is all our being:
> not at the sin—that never comes to mind—
> but in the All-Ordering and All-Foreseeing...
> (Canto IX, 103–105)

To repent or to feel remorse would not be in keeping with the nature of this celestial sphere, for sin—as an aberration of divine perception—cannot manifest itself within the Mind of God, which is the source of all Truth. Thus, the force that drove them toward "amorous ends" on Earth is the inversion of the same force that led them to the Christ.

What is interesting is the manner in which Folquet describes his birthplace. The reader gets the impression that they are truly looking down upon the Earth from the heavenly heights. Yet, the very fact that those regions on the Earth are describabable is yet another clue that Dante still has not completely freed himself from the Earth's influences (for Venus, again, falls under the Earth's influence when the Suns' light is eclipsed). Nonetheless, we get the sense that he is about to do just that very thing.

Folquet states that in the sphere of Venus,

> ...all our thoughts are fixed upon the Love
> that beautifies creation, and here we learn
> how the world below is moved by the world above...
> (Canto IX, 106–108)

At this point, the reader is able to acknowledge that Dante, having arrived at his present state where he witnesses the activity of the creative forces ("Love that beautifies creation"), *begins to perceive the process by which cosmic activity actually affects (or even manifests) the physical world.*

Folquet reveals the identity of the spirit beside him by reading Dante's mind:

> ...You wish to know who is within this blaze
> you see in all its splendor here beside me,
> like purest water lit by the sun's rays.
>
> Know, then, that in it Rahab finds her good;
> and that, one with our choir, she seals upon it
> the highest order of beatitude...
> (Canto IX, 112–117)

Rahab, a harlot of Jericho, earned salvation, in spite of her sinful life, as she aided Joshua in capturing Jericho, thus, helping the "people of Israel regain the promised land." At this point, Folquet speaks of how unfortunate it is that Popes place so little importance on the Holy Land.

Folquet, then, denounces Florence, "founded" by Mars, the god of war. Under the guidance of the "One who first turned on his Maker" (Lucifer), there arose the "cursed flower of gold" (florin) that corrupted the Church, which, as "the shepherd," changed "into a ravenous wolf by whom the sheep are scattered from the fold." As a consequence, the Gospels and the Church Doctors became neglected. Only *the Decretals* (Canon Law) are given serious thought. These volumes of canon law, which "covered the temporal rights and privileges of the Church's vast power and wealth," became the primary focus of study within the Catholic Church. And so, the true meaning of Christianity found within the *Gospels* and the teachings of the Church Doctors became lost. Folquet, however, predicts that the Vatican and other parts of Holy Rome, which have been a "cemetery of those faithful hearts that followed Peter," will soon be free of such "adultery."

Dante begins Canto X with a reference to the Holy Trinity. The "First Presence," namely the Creator, in "Contemplating His Son," breathed forth together with Him the "Third Essence" (Holy Spirit). Dante says the Father created everything in the universe with such perfection "that to look upon it is to be seized by the love of the Maker's grace." He, therefore directs the reader, to turn his gaze toward the starry sphere, but more specifically, to where the "sun's ecliptic crosses the celestial equator." As Ciardi states,

> These two circles are the "one motion and another." (The Sun is now at the vernal equinox.) The apparent equatorial (or diurnal) motion is from east to west. The apparent order in which the signs of the Zodiac appear along the ecliptic is from west to east. It follows, therefore, that the influences of the planets, following the zodiacal path, vary from north to south of the equator striking the earth variously but in a fixed progression that is part of God's inscrutable plan. Were the courses of the equator and the elliptic to run parallel, or were the angles between them to change, the influences of the spheres would be weakened, and earth that stands ever in need of those influences ("earth that calls on them") would lose the full good of their powers.[47]

Thus, the motions of the "two circles" reflect how the influences of the planetary spheres upon the Earth are at their highest point of perfection, and that a slight change in their relative positions would be devastating to the physical and spiritual development of humanity. In short, this astronomical observation points to the delicate balance of God's cosmological design and its importance with regard to all earthly and human activity.

And so, we are given an illustration of humanity's dependence on the cosmos and how the course of human evolution is orchestrated by the activities of those forces lying beyond the earthly realm. Dante invites the reader to seriously consider the scope and implications of his observations:

> Stay on at the table, reader, and meditate
> upon this foretaste if you wish to dine
> on joy itself before it is too late.

> I set out food, but you yourself must feed!
> For the great matters I record demand
> all my attention and I must proceed.
> (Canto X, 22-27)

The food that Dante sets out, of course, is the spiritual knowledge by which we, through contemplation, can find our way to God. We, however, play our part by *activating the will* so as to unite it with that of God.

Dante suddenly realizes that he has entered into the sphere of the Sun.

> And I was with the Sun; but no more aware
> of my ascent than a man is of a thought
> that comes to mind, until he finds it there.
> (Canto X, 34-36)

There are two things to consider here. First of all, Dante shows that with our sense-based consciousness, we are unable to perceive the process by which a thought makes itself visible to us. As repeatedly stated, this is the basis for understanding how we can transcend the dialectical mind. Secondly, this is a metaphorical illustration of Dante's ascension into the Sun sphere, where he has yet to perceive the coming into being of the cosmic influences that he gradually beholds. Just as a physical thought manifests by way of unseen creative forces (*its inner light*), so, too, are the forces that have drawn him upward into the Solar realm (*Light of the Christ*) still eclipsed from view by a consciousness which, to some degree, is still permeated by a remnant of lunar influences. Only through Beatrice can this incapacity be transcended. Says Dante:

> It is Beatrice, she it is who leads our climb
> from good to better, so instantaneously
> that her action does not spread itself through time.
> (Canto X, 37-39)

Dante has arrived at the sphere that marks the outer boundary of the Exusiai's activity. It is also the sphere beyond which, according to

Steiner, Lucifer begins to have a benevolent effect upon humanity, and no longer presents an obstacle in our journey through the spiritual world. From the Sun sphere outward, Lucifer helps to guide humanity into the furthest reaches of the cosmos. In *Esoteric Christianity and the Mission of Christian Rosenkreutz*, Rudolf Steiner says,

> Up to the period of Sun existence, we stand under the leadership of Christ. From the Sun existence onward we need a Leader whose task it is to guide us to the further realms of cosmic space. Lucifer now comes to our side. If we have fallen prey to him on the physical plane, it is bad for us; but if on the Earth we have lightly understood the Christ Impulse, then we are strong enough on the Sun to follow even Lucifer without danger. From then onward he has charge of the inner progress of the soul, just as on this side of the Sun, Christ has had charge of our ascent. If on the Earth we have received the Christ Impulse, Christ is the Keeper of the soul on the path to the Sun. Beyond the periphery of the Sun sphere, Lucifer leads us out into the Cosmos *within* the periphery of the Sun, he is the Tempter.[48]

This differentiation with regard to the role of Lucifer was, of course, most likely unknown to Dante.

Individual lights whose brightness is inconceivable to humankind on Earth, surround Dante. He is witness to the fact that they manifest the creative activity of the Godhead. The radiance that Dante beholds is far greater than that of our ordinary Sun.

> Such, there, was the fourth family of splendors
> of the High Father who fills their souls with bliss,
> *showing them how He breathes forth and engenders.*
> (Canto X, 49–51; italics mine)

Beatrice instructs Dante to give thanks to the "Sun of Angels," "by whose grace he has been lifted to this physical one!" Thus, it was by the grace of the Christ, working through the hierarchy of beings connected to the Sun sphere, that Dante has been able to ascend into the sphere of His manifested activity. Having listened to Beatrice's words, Dante is so moved by his love for God that

> The heart of mortal never could so move
> to its devotion, nor so willingly
> offer itself to God in thankful love,
> as mine did...
> (Canto X, 55–58)

The key, here, are the words *"the heart of mortal,"* for Dante seems to imply that there has occurred a transformation by which he begins to feel the burgeoning of the forces that lend themselves to the development of the etheric heart—the organ that corresponds to the solar forces. The feeling that has taken hold of him is so strong that it momentarily eclipses his perception of Beatrice. He thus feels the presence of the Christ so strongly that it momentarily restricts him from acknowledging the consciousness by which he has ascended into the present realm. It is not incidental that Dante, within this sphere of the *Sun*, draws attention to the heart, for it is, as we have previously stated, the solar region within the human being most associated with the activity of the Christ.

Dante becomes aware of those beings surrounding him by looking into Beatrice's eyes—namely, into light of suprasensory activity.

> Nothing displeased, she laughed so that the blaze
> of her glad eyes pierced my mind's singleness
> and once again divided it several ways.
> (Canto X, 61–63)

What Dante sees here is a circle of individual lights similar to the corona of the Moon. These are the Doctors of the Church. Dante insists that what he perceives are gems "so precious and so lovely that they cannot be taken from the kingdom." Humanity's everyday consciousness is unworthy of their splendor. Only by lifting his level of perception can he actively partake in their beauty. ("Who does not grow wings that will fly him there, must learn these things from the tidings of the tongueless here below.") Singing a celestial melody, the circle of lights dance around Dante and Beatrice *three* times. Three obviously symbolizes the Trinity, which is, here, prefigured by the concentric rings of *light*—namely, the threefold aspect of God's being—which Dante will eventually perceive.

From the garland of flowers circling luminously about Dante, a spirit comes forth and tells Dante that because a "ray of grace from which true love is kindled" shines within him virtually nothing can prevent his ascent. Realizing that Dante wishes to know the identity of the spirits surrounding him, this soul identifies the spirit to his right as his teacher, Albert of Cologne (Magnus), before identifying himself as Thomas of Aquinas. Like Aquinas, Albert Magnus was a Dominican who sought enlightenment through study and contemplation. Aquinas then introduces Dante to the other spirits surrounding him. First, there is the twelfth-century scholar, Gratian who brought into balance ecclesiastical law with civil law. Next to him is Peter Lombardus "who gave all he had" to the Holy Church, namely a compilation of scriptures. Next, Aquinas refers to the other spirits by way of their deeds. There is Solomon, who "shines forth from so magnificent a love," human beings on Earth thirst for knowledge of him, for within him shone the depths of wisdom. Next to him is Dionysius of Areopagite, who perceived the order of the spiritual hierarchy. The "lesser lamp" to Aquinas' right is Paulus Orosius whose treatise *Historiarum Adversus Paganos*, "led Augustine toward the light," so that the Roman Empire could be permeated by Christianity. The eighth spirit whom Aquinas identifies is Boethius, known most notably for his *Consolation of Philosophy*. Aquinas, then, identifies the spirits of Isidore who wrote *"Etymologiae"* and was canonized St. Isidore, the biblical scholar Venerable Bede who wrote the *Ecclesiastical History of the English Nation*, and Richard of St. Victor known as the Great Contemplator for his work *"Contemplations."* The last spirit that Dante beholds is Siger of Brabant, an Averroist philosopher, who was declared heretical by the Church. Aquinas' complimentary description of Siger as one who "syllogized *truths* for which he would be hated" seems a bit paradoxical here, for their views were antagonistic to one another at the University of Paris. In Paris, Siger was known to have espoused truths by way of logic, whereas Aquinas did so according to Church Doctrine. Nonetheless, there is perfect harmony among the souls in this sphere. For, here, they find themselves before a Higher Truth than that of the intellect. Dante perceives the circle of lights, which he has come to know, begin to wheel around him—each light (spirit) singing in perfect harmony.

Dante begins Canto XI by denouncing the pursuit of earthly vanities:

> O senseless strivings of the mortal round!
> How worthless is that exercise of reason
> that makes you beat your wings into the ground!
> (Canto XI, 1–3)

How trivial are the indulgences of one who strives for physical comfort and pleasure through the senses-based reason, when compared to the spiritual realities revealed to Dante by way of Beatrice! The luminous spirits stop circling around Dante, when Aquinas steps forth and addresses him. He states that Providence governs humanity with wisdom too deep for mortal humans to comprehend. To insure that there be a perfect marriage between the Church (Bride) and Christ (Groom), Providence chose two men (Princes).

> ...One, in his love, shone like the seraphim.
> The other, in his wisdom, walked the earth
> bathed in the splendor of the cherubim...
> (Canto XI, 37–39)

The man of the heart was St. Francis of Assisi; the man of keen mind was St. Dominic. Most interesting here is the fact that St. Francis is compared to the Seraphim, the highest hierarchy of spiritual beings, while St. Dominic is associated with the next highest rank, the Cherubim. By this, Dante seems to infer that the heart forces are closer and more intimately connected to the essential nature of the Christ than are the thinking forces. Though most of this canto is devoted to St. Francis, we find that it is a Dominican (Aquinas) who lauds him. A similar scene occurs in the next canto in which the Franciscan, St.

Bonaventure, praises St. Dominic—an example of symmetry as an illustration of *Divine Justice*.

Aquinas begins to describe the life of St. Francis by referring to the region from which he came.

> ...Between the Tupino and the little race
> sprung from the hill blessed Ubaldo chose,
> a fertile slope spreads up the mountain's face.
>
> Perugia breathes its heat and cold from there
> through Porta Sole, and Nocera and Gualdo
> behind it mourn the heavy yoke they bear.
>
> From it, at that point where the mountainside
> grows least abrupt, a sun rose to the world
> as this one does at times from the Ganges' tide...
> (Canto XI, 43–51)

Thus, situated between Tupino and Gubbio ("the hill the blessed Ubaldo chose"), which run north, Perugia to the west, and Nocera and Gualdo to the east is Assisi where a "sun rose to the world" (birth of St. Francis). It rose from there, says Aquinas, just as the Sun itself rises from the Ganges, which, located along the Tropic of Cancer, marks the point where the Sun "is at its brightest."[49] Aquinas then alludes to the sacredness of Assisi by saying that no one should refer to it as was then common, *Ascesi* (I have risen) but, rather, as *Oriente* (a sun/son has risen), for the latter refers not only to the East where the Sun rises—thereby evoking the image of the Risen Christ—but also to the principle bearer of the Christ impulse during his time, St. Francis of Assisi.

Having described the birthplace of St. Francis, Aquinas tells how this humble saint was born into a wealthy family, whose inheritance he renounced by devoting himself to "that lady," poverty. In so doing, he followed in the footsteps of the Christ. For this reason, Aquinas states that not long after birth, the "first comfort of his glorious powers began to make its warmth felt on earth." The "warmth," of course, alludes to the presence of the Christ force working through him. In a lecture given by Rudolf Steiner on May 29, 1912 regarding the life of St. Francis, he states:

> ...He was born in the year 1182. We know that the first years of the life of a human being are devoted principally to the development of the physical body. In the physical body is developed chiefly that which comes to light through external heredity. Hence, there appeared in him first of all that which originated through external heredity from the European population. These qualities gradually came out, as his etheric body developed from the seventh to the fourteenth year, like any other human being. In this etheric body appeared primarily that quality which as the Christ-impulse had worked directly in him in the mysteries on the Black Sea. From his fourteenth year, at the dawn of his astral life the Christ power became particularly active within him, in such a way that there entered into his astral body that which had been in connection with the atmosphere of the earth since the Mystery of Golgotha. *For St. Francis of Assisi was a personality who was permeated by the external power of Christ, owing to his having sought for the Christ power, in his previous incarnation, in that particular place of initiation where it was to be found.* (italics mine)[50]

Steiner also says that the mysteries on the Black Sea cultivated, as their highest ideal, the teachings of Buddha, particularly those concerned with one's transformation from a Bodhisattva to a Buddha. These mystery teachings permeated by the Christ impulse, enabled humanity to understand Buddha's contribution to humanity. St. Francis was, himself, a member of that school in his previous incarnation. For this reason Steiner says:

> ...No wonder, then, that in him there was the wisdom that he had received, knowledge of the brotherhood of humankind, the equality of all human beings, and the necessity to love everyone equally; no wonder that this teaching pulsed through human souls and that those souls were permeated and strengthened by the Christ impulse.[51]

Again, we find the presence of the Christ-impulse working in St. Francis when Aquinas says, "The first comfort of his glorious powers began to make its warmth felt on the earth." The "warmth" is not only in reference to the physical Sun but also the "son" that arose in Assisi—St. Francis—who was *permeated by the Christ impulse*. Aquinas speaks of various incidences in the life of this great saint beginning with his refusal to partake in the earthly riches that were to be his inheritance. Not only did he refuse to lay claim to what one day would be his, but he took off his very clothes and gave them to his father saying, "Until this hour I called you my father on earth; from this hour I can say in full truth 'our Father which art in Heaven.'" And so, in renouncing his material inheritance by giving back to "Caesar what belongs to Caesar," St. Francis follows the path of Christ. Here, Aquinas tells Dante that St. Francis was the Lady of Poverty's "First Groom" since Christ Himself. Of this lady (Poverty), Aquinas says:

> ...Bereft of her First Groom, she had had to stand
> more than eleven centuries, scorned, obscure;
> and, till he came, no man had asked her hand...
> (Canto XI, 64–66)

In describing the relationship between Christ and Lady Poverty, Aquinas says that at the time of the crucifixion, "She climbed the Cross to share Christ's agony." Acknowledging the marriage of St. Francis to "Lady Poverty," others such as Bernard, Egidius, and Sylvester joined him by going barefoot, dressing in course cloth, and girding themselves with a cord, all of which denoted humility. Pope Innocent III sanctioned the order of St. Francis, though only provisionally. Then, as more people joined his cause, Pope Honorius III approved the order of the Franciscans, having been "moved by the Eternal Breath." Aquinas then describes St. Francis' crusade to Egypt, where he unsuccessfully took the message of Christ to the "haughty Sultan." Finally, he speaks of the stigmata that St. Francis received on the crag of Mt. Alvernia upon experiencing the vision of Christ. Once

St. Francis completed his mission, he returned to the "bosom" of Lady Poverty, namely, the bare ground to which he urged his followers to dedicate their lives.

Aquinas concludes the canto by alluding to the unheeded commands of another important saint—St. Dominic. He is described as St. Francis' "fellow helmsman, holding Peter's ship straight to its course across the dangerous sea." Aquinas, himself a Dominican, takes a moment to denounce many of the members of St. Dominic's order who obsessively lust after material goods. Says Aquinas,

> ...The more his vagabond and distant sheep
> wander from him, the less milk they bring back
> when they return to the fold. A few do keep
>
> close to the shepherd, knowing that the wolf howls
> in the dark around them, but they are so few
> it would take little cloth to make their cowls...
> (Canto XI, 127–132)

As soon as Aquinas finishes speaking, the wheel of lights, comprised of twelve souls, begins to circle once again. Before concluding its first revolution, a second wheel, also made up of twelve souls and "matching it tone for tone, motion for motion" surrounds it. This second wheel, issuing from the first, is made up of Franciscans. Its spokesperson is St. Bonaventure. As the Dominicans represent wisdom, the Franciscans are emblematic of love:

> ...those sempiternal roses wove
> their turning garland round us, and the outer
> *answered the inner with the voice of love.*
> (Canto XII, 19–21; italics mine)

Through the interweaving of love and wisdom, humanity is led to the Christ. Just as the second radiant wheel seems to be born from the bosom of the first, so, too, is love born of wisdom. As Dante watches the festivity before him, he notices how it harmonizes into oneness ("as does the eyes of man when he sees"). A voice issues forth from one of the splendors and addresses Dante, whose soul is "drawn to that glorious flame." It is St. Bonaventure who seeks to relate the life of St. Dominic. He begins by saying how St. Francis and St. Dominic must both be mentioned in the same breath, for, though their means were different, both were chosen by Christ to reunite the Christians scattered over the world:

> ...The troops of Christ, rearmed at such great cost,
> were struggling on behind the Holy Standard,
> fearful, and few, and laggard, and half lost,
>
> when the Emperor who reigns eternally—
> of His own grace and not for their own merit—
> took thought of his imperiled soldiery;
>
> and, as you have heard say, He sent His bride
> two champions by whose teachings and example
> the scattered companies were reunified...
> (Canto XII, 37–45)

St. Bonaventure alludes to the struggles that the two eulogized saints waged in their efforts to restore the sanctity of the Church, which had become lost over time. Dante seems to be inferring that those struggles must be construed as being directed against the adversarial *forces* of the Church. Thus, St. Dominic, who sought a "scholarly" way to bridge humanity to Christ, represents the struggle to lead human beings to a conscious understanding of the Christ impulse by way of thinking. St. Francis, on the other hand, being a man of the heart, counteracted the adversarial forces through the feeling life.

Unfortunately, one of the great inconsistencies of Dante—which reveals his lingering attachment to the impulse of Augustine—regards his perception of St. Dominic, whose role as the founder of the Inquisition, belies the Christlike nature that Dante believes St. Dominic emulated. As history has shown, St. Dominic's initial attempts to convert many of the heretics through reason and discourse, harbored a militaristic (ahrimanic) impulse (Inquisition), by means of which the Catholic Church was able to decimate scores of people, who were seeking, in their own way, the sacred knowledge (or *light*) that lies at the heart of Dante's quest.

As was the case in Aquinas' account of the life of St. Francis, Bonaventure begins with a geographical description of St. Dominic's birthplace. In a land to the West (Spain) from where the warm winds of Spring blow, not far from the sea that hides the Sun from "all mortal sight," there exists a "fortunate village" (Calahorra), guarded by a "great shield," "on which two lions are seen, one subjugating and one in subjection." Here reference is made to the region in which St. Dominic was born, namely, Castile (castle) and Leon (lion). One of the emblems portrays the castle subjected to the lion, and the other, the lion subjected to the castle. Seen esoterically the castle is representative of the Higher Self, whereas the Lion (Leo) can be seen as connected to the sphere of the Sun (or Christ)—namely, the heart–will forces. Their alternation seems to point to the inextricable interrelationship that exists between the two.

Bonaventure then goes on to portray St. Dominic as a "true knight of the Christian faith," giving "bread to his followers, to his foes a stone." St. Dominic was gifted with a mind of such spiritual powers that, even before his birth, while still in the womb, he was able to endow his mother with a prophetic vision. Legend has it that she dreamed that she was to give birth to a black and white dog, whose colors symbolized the Dominican order. Just as St. Francis was to marry Lady Poverty, St. Dominic is said to have had Lady Faith as his bride. Once married, his godmother dreamed that he had a star on his forehead, in recognition of the fact "that he would bring God's light to men." Since St. Dominic was to bear the Word of Christ, he was given the name Dominic, meaning "of the Lord." When his nurse once asked him why he was meditating on the floor, he replied, "for this end I have come." According to Bonaventure, it is little wonder why his father was named Felix (Felicity) and his mother Giovanna (God's Grace). Unlike many who sought fame and fortune, St. Dominic strove for the spiritual knowledge by which he could tend to God's Church—a Church that withers without the *light* of knowledge leading to the Christ. He was

> ...a mighty doctor, and began to go
> his rounds of that great vineyard where the vine,
> if left untended, pales and cannot grow...
>   Canto XII, 85–87)

St. Dominic pleaded for the right to establish his order before the Papacy, which had once tended to the poor. He wanted neither wealth nor personal recognition, but merely the opportunity to combat heresy ("license in the sick world there below to battle for that seed from which are sprung the four and twenty plants that ring you now"). That seed is, of course, the germinating force of the Christ, from which spring the plants (the teaching of Church Doctors) now surrounding Dante. Once granted permission, he sought to tame and reform heresy—amongst which was Catharism—through preaching and dialogue. Unfortunately, however, under Innocent III a movement was initiated to undo Catharism, and it wasn't long before the Cathars were massacred and nearly eradicated, thus undercutting the initial efforts of St. Dominic.

Just as Aquinas spoke of the degeneracy of his own order, Bonaventure declares that he, too, will speak against the order of the Franciscans to which he belongs. He begins by stating that the two wheels Dante beholds—represented by Franciscans and Dominicans—move the cart upon which the Church of Christ rests. However, the track of the wheel's great circumference (Franciscan Order) has been "abandoned." The casks of wine—the results of humanity's spiritual harvest—are empty; they no longer contain the residue of wine but, rather, its mold. The followers of St. Francis no longer trace his footsteps, but walk backward on them so that what is printed is " toe on heel, and heel on toe." Therefore, humanity is confused regarding which direction to take. It is without guidance. Bonaventure then points out the two men responsible for the schism within the order—Ubertino of Casale who tightened the rules of the order and Matteo of Acquasparta who relaxed them.

Having revealed his identity to Dante, Bonaventure begins identifying the other members of the circle. He mentions two of St. Francis' earliest followers, Illuminato and Augustino, as well as Hugo of St. Victor, philosopher and theologian. Next, he names Peter Mangiadore, Dean of the Cathedral of Troyes, who wrote *Historia Scholastica* on biblical history and, Peter of Spain who was known to have penned, *Summulae logicales,* twelve small books on the principle of logic. Then comes the prophet Nathan, followed by St. John Chrysostom, who like Nathan, denounced the transgressions or sins of rulers. Next, we find St. Anselm who strove to have the king recognize and accept the Pope, as well as Donatus, who had written an influential book on grammar during Dante's time. The last two spirits mentioned by Bonaventure are Rabanus, who wrote a manual for clerics called *De clericorum institutione,* and Joachim of Fiore, a Cisterian mystic.

It was the figure of Joachim of Fiore, however, whose teachings revealed the tenuous alliances amongst the monastic orders of the Middle Ages. This was most evident in the Franciscan Order where its two factions—the Spirituals and the Convectuals—were at odds over his teachings. The Convectuals opposed the movement of Joachim of Fiore—to which Dante was thought to have associated. While, on the other hand, the Spirituals—who were much stricter and opposed to St. Bonaventure—had a Joachite group form within its ranks. Joachim spoke of three ages. The first age was that of the Father, namely of the Old Covenant. This was followed by the Age of the Son, which referred to the Christian world. Finally, the third age was that of the Holy Spirit, within which there was to be revealed an "Eternal Gospel" that would essentially fulfill and replace the Church. Joachim of Fiore prophesized that the second age would end in 1260, after which the Antichrist would become manifest. His prophecy was based on his interpretation of the *Book of Revelation.* Because he predicted that the Church would *no longer be necessary*—an idea, incidentally, that was in accordance with Steiner's assertion that the Church had already primarily outlived its role by the twelfth to thirteenth centuries—his teachings were viewed as a threat. The Fourth Council of the Lateran denounced a number of his ideas.

Having presented all the members of the circle to Dante, Bonaventure asserts that Aquinas' eulogy for St. Francis inspired his own for St. Dominic.

At the beginning of Canto XIII, we find the two wheels of light merged together in the form of a double crown, wheeling in opposite directions. This image exemplifies the nature of their interrelationship. Though the Dominican and Franciscan orders functioned in directions opposite one another, each in its own way is considered here a bridge to the mystery of Christ.

In *Karmic Relationships* vol. 4, Rudolf Steiner speaks of the relationship between Platonism and Aristotelianism in the Middle Ages. These two streams, represented by individuals of different intellectual dispositions, worked together to prepare the way for St. Michael's impulse to enter humanity near the end of the nineteenth century. The Platonists, represented by the likes of Bernardus Sylvestris and Alanus ab Insulis, sought to find the Goddess Natura within the activity of nature. Steiner says that their teachings were often believed to be heretical by official Christianity. Many of the individualities of the School of Chartres, he adds, were members of the Cistercian order, which to some degree resembled the Franciscans. In fact, if we remember correctly from the previous canto, Joachim di Fiore was, himself, a Cistercian, placed amongst the Franciscans in the circle headed by Bonaventure. If one studies the literature of those such as Alan of Insulis, one will notice there a highly polished poetic imagination that recalls the pictorial nature of Platonic consciousness—a consciousness that retained elements of atavistic clairvoyance.

While the Platonic stream at the School of Chartres was busy working on the Earth, the Aristotelian stream prepared for its descent from the heavenly realms. As many of those in the Platonic stream died, there was in the spiritual world "a suprasensory exchange of ideas" between them and the Aristotelians about to descend. The Aristotelians differed significantly from the Platonists for they were representative of a thinking that had begun to take on a more abstract nature. One need only observe the writings of St. Aquinas to notice that the poetic quality of the Platonists had already given way to a more shadow-like form of thinking. In essence, the Aristotelian stream derived its fundamental character through the impulse of Aristotle, who, more than Plato, had lost the "pictorial" quality of thought conducive to perceiving the spiritual activity of the gods within nature. Rudolf Steiner explains that many Aristotelian souls operated within the Dominican order. Furthermore, given the fact that Dante's teacher, Brunetto Latini, wrote *Li livres dou* Tresor—a poetic inspiration—while at the School of Chartres, it is easy to imagine Dante implicitly associating members of the Aristotelian and Platonic streams with the two rings of light, encircling each other within the Sun sphere.

Finally, one could say that the Franciscans and the Dominicans each seemed to embody the inextricable relationship between *contemplative life* and *active life*, symbolized by Rachel and Leah. As Dante suggests, only through their interconnected roles can humankind come to know the dual nature attributed to Christ—human and divine.

To understand the brilliance of the twenty-four stars wheeling around him, Dante asks the reader to imagine seeing the fifteen brightest stars in the heavens and adding to them the seven stars of the Big Dipper and the two most luminous stars of the Little Dipper, so that they form two circles, each like the Corona Borealis, which was made of the bridle wreath of Ariadne after she has been taken to Heaven by Dionysius. Only, then, can the reader have a *dim* understanding of the radiance that Dante beholds. Again, the *image* of light that we normally conceive is derived from the sense-bound world and can, thus, in no way accurately reflect our actual perception of the *inner light* within the creative activity of the cosmos.

The two wheels of light "sang of Three Persons in One Divine Nature / and It and human nature in One Person," so that:

> The song and circling dance ran through their measure,
> and now those holy lights waited on us,
> turning rejoiced from pleasure to new pleasure.
> (Canto XIII, 28–30)

Ciardi says, "from pleasure to new pleasure" refers to the transition from the pleasure of praising God to that of serving Him.[52] To serve God is to *prepare* for the coming of Christ in the etheric realm, and one can only prepare for the *light* of Christ by wrestling oneself free of dialecticism. Only in this way can Dante behold the *light* of the resurrection born of the Mystery of Golgotha. This is what forms the basis of Dante's relationship to the circling *lights*. They prepare him to venture beyond the sphere of the Sun so that he can directly *perceive the Christ*.

Once again, St. Aquinas speaks to Dante to resolve the mystery of Solomon's superior wisdom. Aquinas explains that one must differentiate what was directly created by God from that which was brought forth through His "nine ministers":

> ...All things that die and all that cannot die
> are the reflected splendor of the Form
> our Father's love brings forth beyond the sky.
>
> For the *Living Light* that streams forth from the Source
> in such a way that it is never parted
> from Him, nor from the Love whose mystic force
>
> joins them in Trinity, lets its grace ray down,
> as if reflected, through nine subsistent natures
> that sempiternally remain as one...
>   (Canto XIII, 52–60; italics mine)

Here, we find that all things—mortal and immortal—are reflections of God's creative impulse (Platonic Idea), for the Christ ("Living Light") streams forth from God to reconnect human beings to their Creator. God remains "one" with this creative principle—the Christ. The "*Love*" originating from the Father is the very force that transforms human consciousness so as to be receptive of the Christ. This *Love* reaches down into humanity through the Spiritual Hierarchies, "from thing to thing" to the last the "potencies" (matter). It thus brings forth "brief contingencies," which are "the *generated things* the moving heavens bring forth from seeds or not, as the case may be." These higher beings "press" the "wax" (matter) so as to give the "contingencies" ("generated things") form. Hence, physical life manifests in such a way that each form reflects God's *light* in varying degrees. Aquinas explains that this is what makes people of different talents or plants of varying levels of beneficence. He then goes on to say that things made *directly* by God are *perfect*:

> ...But if the Fervent Love move the Pure Ray
> of the First Power to wield the seal directly,
> the thing so stamped is perfect in every way...
> (Canto XIII, 79–81)

Therefore, Aquinas agrees with Dante that no one possessed more wisdom than Adam or Christ, for they were direct creations of the Father. The Wisdom of Solomon, though not perfect, was supreme because it was born of his desire to *guide* his people. Such wisdom was unlike the knowledge typically sought during the Middle Ages, where human beings grappled with such things as the number and degree of angels, or the principles of logic, which lead human beings to the realm of dialecticism, or abstract speculation, and thus away from the Will of God in their quest for understanding. *The Wisdom of Solomon was, instead, wisdom that attuned itself to the aims of the Godhead for which* "No mortal ever rose to equal this one" (Solomon).

Aquinas then urges Dante to avoid prejudgment. Says he,

> ...And lead weights to your feet may my words be,
> that you move slowly, like a weary man,
> to the "yes" and "no" of what you do not see.
>
> For he is a fool, and low among his kind,
> who answers yea or nay without reflection,
> nor does it matter on which road he runs blind.
>
> Opinions, too, soon formed often deflect
> man's thinking from the truth into gross error,
> in which his pride then binds his intellect...
> (Canto XIII, 112–120)

Aquinas concludes that we should judge neither a pickpocket nor a person of charity as if we possessed the eyes of God, for the first may rise while the latter may fall. Steiner has spoken about this idea of prejudgment in various books and lectures, including *How to Know Higher Worlds*, where he says:

> This is sometimes called faith or trust. We must learn to approach every person, every being, with trust. Such trust or confidence must inspire all our actions. We should never say, in reply to something said to us, "I don't believe that because it contradicts the opinion I have already formed." Rather, when faced with something new, we must always be willing to test our opinions and views and revise them if necessary. We must always remain receptive to whatever approaches us. We should trust in the effectiveness of whatever we undertake. All doubt and timidity should be banished from our being. If we have a goal, we must have faith in the power of our goal. Even a hundred failures should not be able to take this faith from us. This is the *"faith that can move mountains."*[53]

Thus, Dante provides a fundamental guideline to the esoteric tradition. By exercising our opinions, we prevent ourselves from fathoming the deeper impulses at work behind the object of our criticisms. As a result, we merely strengthen the pretention of a thinking, which, by adhering to only the sense-based world, must be transcended. Instead, the element of faith could be reinforced in us if we forego opinion and, thereby, muster the *courage* to enter the spiritual worlds.

Dante begins Canto XIV by illustrating the interesting relationship that the rings of light and Beatrice have to each other. In the opening stanzas, just as Aquinas finishes uttering his last word, it occurs to Dante that

> The water in a round vessel moves about
> from center to rim if it is struck from within,
> from rim to center if it is struck from without.
> (Canto XIV, 1–3)

Thus, as Aquinas speaks on behalf of the circles of light surrounding him, Dante notices that his words are filled with the wisdom raying down from the Empyrean, down through the celestial spheres and into humanity—namely, "from the rim to the center if it is struck from without." Whereas that which goes "from the center to the rim" is symbolized by Beatrice, for she is, as we have said again and again, the *Divine Wisdom* that reaches from the depths of human consciousness out into the heavenly spheres all the way to the Godhead. Therefore, Dante immediately presents us with a picture depicting how the Microcosm is a reflection of the Macrocosm. Just as God's *light* is able to reach humanity from the Empyrean down through the Spiritual Hierarchies, so, too, does humanity reach "up" to God through the *light* of thinking reflected in the eyes of Beatrice (*Divine Wisdom*).

Speaking to twenty-four new souls, comprising two rings—one of philosophers and another of theologians—Beatrice asks them to explain to Dante one more problem that is unclear to him. (Here, we must remember that Beatrice *symbolizes* the consciousness by which Dante is able to penetrate the higher suprasensory realms, where he can discover the answer to his questions. He is becoming more and more capable of *intuiting* spiritual realities. Which is to say, that he is gradually able to read by way of Beatrice that which is written in spiritual world.) Nevertheless, Beatrice addresses the spirits regarding the need Dante has of understanding a question that relates to the origin of his physical being ("holy root"). Says she,

> There is another need this man must find
> the holy root of, though he does not speak it,
> nor know, as yet, he has the thought in mind.
>
> Explain to him if the radiance he sees flower
> about your beings will remain forever
> exactly as it shines forth in this hour;
>
> and if it will remain so, then explain
> how your restored eyes can endure such brilliance
> when your beings have grown visible again.
> (Canto XIV, 13–18)

In essence, what Beatrice asks them to answer for Dante is how after Judgment Day, having again taken on their flesh, can human souls possibly endure, with physical eyes, the ever-increasing luminosity irradiated within them and without? In response to Beatrice's question, the wheels of light spin ever faster. Moved by *joy,* they begin to sing in harmony. Dante has reached ever deeper into inner regions of the cosmic activity where he comes to *know* one of the most enigmatic mysteries regarding the evolution of his being.

Before he is given an answer, Dante clues the reader once again as to the *initiatory* aspect of his journey:

> Those who mourn, here, that we must die to gain
> the life up there, have never visualized
> that soul-refreshing and eternal rain.
> (Canto XIV, 25–27)

In other words, those who believe that it is possible to see God only upon death, do so because they fail to perceive or even conceive the rays of His eternal *light.* Such rays represent the current of life (living thinking) that streams like rain within consciousness, renewing the soul.

A voice from within the inner circle gently informs Dante that the souls' degree of radiance (God's *light*) indicates the degree of ardor that burns within them with respect to their dedication to *"caritas"* (love/charity). Furthermore, their individual radiances indicate the level of divine vision they have each attained, a vision granted by the grace of God in relation to an individual soul's worthiness. As a gift from God, this grace can even extend beyond the merit of each soul. Consequently, the human body, once resurrected, will have undergone a transformation that enables it to endure the increased intensity, just as a coal, in giving off a flame, shines through it and maintains its integrity:

> ...Thereby shall we have increase of the light
> Supreme Love grants, unearned, to make us fit
> to hold his glory ever in our sight.

> Thereby, it follows, the vision shall increase;
> increase the ardor that the vision kindles;
> increase the ray its inner fires release."
>
> But as a coal, in giving off its fire,
> outshines it by its living incandescence,
> its form remaining visible and entire;
>
> so shall this radiance that wraps us round
> be outshone in appearance by the flesh
> that lies this long day through beneath the ground;
>
> nor will it be overborne by so much light;
> for the organs of the body shall be strengthened
> in all that shall give increase of delight.
> (Canto XIV, 46–60)

Having concluded his explanation, the souls cry out, "Amen," revealing their desire to wear their flesh again.

With regard to the "resurrection body" it is said in Catholicism that upon Jesus' return to Earth, he will physically raise all those who have died, giving them back the *bodies* they lost at death. These resurrection bodies, the same ones people had in earthly life, will not die but will be transformed into a "glorified" state, freed from suffering and pain. The arising of Christ is, according to Catholic doctrine inextricably linked to the resurrecting of these dead bodies. Said Paul, "if the dead are not raised, then Christ has not been raised..."

Here, we may be reminded of Steiner's mention of the Phantom Body which is much more difficult and subtle to understand, and which must not be confused with the concept of resurrected bodies spoken of in Catholicism. The Phantom body is the "reconditioned spiritual essence of the physical body" of *all* humanity, namely, the resurrected *body* of Adam lost during the Fall, which is to be restored at the end of Earth's evolution, immediately preceding that known as Jupiter. Thus the restoration of the Phantom Body precedes the transformation of the human being's lower sheathes during the succeeding evolutionary stages of the Earth's development, where, from the spiritualization of the astral body (during the Jupiter stage of the earth's evolution) there will arise Spirit-Self; through the metamorphoses of the etheric or life body (during the Venus stage), the Life-Spirit will be born; and finally the transformation of the *physical body* (during Vulcan stage), will give rise to Spirit-Man. Steiner speaks of this phantom body in his book *From Jesus to Christ*. There, he states,

> This phantom is the shape form that, as a spiritual texture, works up the physical substances and forces, so that they fill out the form, which we encounter as the human being on the physical plane. The sculptor can bring no statue into existence by merely taking marble or something else and striking away wildly so that single pieces spring off only as the substance permits. Just as sculptors must have a "thought" that they impress on the substance, likewise a "thought" is related to the human body.... The phantom belongs to the physical body as an enduring part—a more important part than the external substances. The external substances are merely loaded into the network of the human form, as one might load apples into a cart.... The substances that fall apart after death are essentially those we meet externally in nature. They are merely caught up by the human form.[54]

He continues,

> [The phantom body] is a transparent body of force. What the physical eye sees are the physical substances that a person eats and takes in, and they fill out the invisible phantom. When the physical eye looks at a physical body, it sees the mineral part that fills the physical body, but not the physical body itself.[55]

Suddenly, another circle slowly appears to Dante before bursting into splendor. It encircles the other two wheels of light with such brilliance that he is forced to look away. Dante identifies it as the "essence of the Holy Ghost," which, together with the other two rings of light (in which one ring issues from the first, just as Christ from the Father), *symbolize* the Trinity. Having been temporarily blinded, Dante sees before him the gradual return of Beatrice, thus restoring his perception of the spiritual worlds:

> But Beatrice let herself appear to me
> So glad in beauty, that the vision must lie
> With those whose glory outdoes memory.
>
> From her I drew again the power of sight
> and looked up, and I saw myself translated,
> with her alone, to the next estate of light.
> (Canto XIV, 79–84)

And so, *within the Sun sphere, Dante has his first true glimpse of the threefold nature of God.* This allows him to perceive more deeply into the eyes of Beatrice. Dante realizes that he has risen into this next sphere "by the enkindled ardor of the red star." Dante offers himself to God in prayer, when two rays of light appear, intersecting to form the *Cross*. Within the red glow of light, Dante has a vision of Christ:

> As, pole to pole, the arch of the Milky Way
> so glows, pricked out by greater and lesser stars,
> the sages stare, not knowing what to say—
>
> so constellated, deep within that sphere,
> the two rays formed into a holy sign
> a circle's quadrant lines describe. And here
>
> memory outruns my powers. How shall I write
> that from that cross there glowed a vision of Christ?
> What metaphor is worthy of that sight?
> (Canto XIV, 97–105)

The color red (of the star) signifies the "blood of Christ," which bears the cosmic "I" that enables the "I" (of Dante), born by human blood, to behold Him. Thus, the *light* of Christ (the suprasensory creative force of life) fashions the spiritual eyes by which it can become visible, just as the physical light shapes our mortal eyes so that it, too, can be seen. This momentary vision of Christ, which Dante fails to accurately describe in words, will become manifest to *those* who bear their own cross in life and follow the Christ—namely, *those* who, by accepting their *suffering*, use it to transform themselves. "Suffering," as Steiner often said, is "crystallized wisdom"—a wisdom that is conducive to the perception of the spiritual world:

> But whoso takes his cross and follows Christ
> will pardon me what I leave here unsaid
> when *he* sees that great dawn that rays forth Christ.
> (Canto XIV; 106–108)

Within the Cross itself, Dante sees "bright lights moving, crossing and rejoining." Upon meeting one another, these lights glow even more brightly. He compares his perception of the spirits glinting within this *light* (of Christ) to the particles floating in a beam of light within a dimly lit room. These spirits proceed to sing a hymn that enraptures Dante, though he does not understand its meaning. Nothing that he has ever experienced compares to the sight and sound of what lies before him. Up to this moment, Dante has, with each new experience, gazed into the eyes of Beatrice. Now, however, it is the beauty of what he beholds that absorbs him. We notice the further strengthening of his "I," which allows for an even higher level of consciousness to guide him. The *joy* that he experiences through Beatrice seems to lift him into the spiritual worlds. Says he, "my sacred pleasure in those eyes can only become purer as we rise."

Having arrived at the sphere of Mars, the planet of war, Dante finds himself at the outer boundary where the Dynameis have their activity. Within this realm of the *Paradiso* are the "soldiers of faith" who represent the virtue of *fortitude*. As instruments of God's Will, these spirits sing Him praise. Upon setting their sights on Dante, they abruptly stop their singing, thus giving the impression that God wishes to hear from him. In one of his few references to the damned suffering below in Hell, Dante says that their relentless concern with the temporal world *justifies* their exclusion from the heavenly spheres.

Suddenly, from the right arm of the *Cross*, a light streaks down to its foot. It reminds Dante of a shooting star, for it does not abandon the other lights within the *Cross*, but moves through them to reach the point nearest to Dante. Dante recalls Anchises who goes forth to meet Aeneas in

Elysium. The spirit who rushes to address Dante is Cacciaguida, his great-great-grandfather. Says Cacciaguida, "O blood of mine! O ever-abundant grace of God poured over you! To whom was the gate of Heaven ever thrown open twice, as it is to you." (The fact that the gate of Heaven is "thrown open" twice hints at the initiatory nature of Dante's journey, for this present journey will later be followed by that which comes after death.) Upon hearing these words, Dante looks at Beatrice and is astounded by the fire of love in her eyes. Not only does Dante consciously reestablish his connection to Beatrice—from whose eyes he had looked away to witness the *Cross*—he reaffirms the importance of Beatrice's role in his beholding of the Christ. At first, Cacciaguida's words reach far beyond Dante's level of experience, for they have their source in God.

> Nor did the spirit's words elude my mind
> by his own choice. Rather, his thoughts took place
> above the highest target of mankind.
> (Canto XV, 40–42)

However, Cacciaguida gradually finds his target as his lofty words descend to Dante's level of understanding. Says Cacciaguida,

> Praised by Thou, O Triune Unity
> which showeth me such favor in my seed!
> (Canto XV, 47–48)

The very sight of Dante satisfies the hunger that Cacciaguida felt burning within him. Cacciaguida bestows praise upon Beatrice, whose *Love*, he says, has made it possible for Dante to ascend into the heavenly realm. Just as all numbers have their source in the number one (symbol of unity), so, too, does Dante's thought exist within the Mind of God. For this reason, Cacciaguida understands Dante's initial hesitation to question his ancestor regarding his identity, for

> ...here in Paradise
> greatest and least alike gaze in that Mirror
> where thoughts outsoar themselves before they rise...
> (Canto XV, 61–63)

Here, Dante seems to imply that the thoughts of all those ("greatest and least alike") who gaze into the Mirror (Mind of God) transcend dialectical form, and thus extend far into the suprasensory realm where wordless communication is possible. Beings that mirror the higher aspects of God's thinking are already aware of what is on Dante's mind. Although Cacciaguida presages Dante's response, he nevertheless wishes to hear, for himself, the *sound* of Dante's voice. Note, here, that the voice (or words) of Dante is important insofar as it echoes the cosmic principle of creation—the Word, which manifests in Dante the closer he nears God. In response, Dante humbly expresses the wish to know the name of the spirit that has presented itself to him, asking to be excused for not adequately clothing his thoughts in words. Without hesitation, Cacciaguida metaphorically depicts his genealogical relation to Dante by declaring himself to be the "root" of their family tree and Dante, "the leaf":

> O leaf of mine, which even to foresee
> has filled me with delight, I was your root.
> (Canto XV, 88–89)

The word *leaf* seems to herald the flowering of Dante's Eternal Self, which Cacciaguida foresees happening before the Mystic Rose. The word *root*, on the other hand, points to the solid foundation on Earth that has inevitably contributed to Dante's rise into the cosmic heights—namely, to the realization of his "I." Cacciaguida tells Dante that he who took on the name Alighiero ("your present surname") was the father of Dante's grandfather, namely the son of Cacciaguida, himself. Dante is told that he should pray for his spirit, presently on the first round of Purgatory.

Cacciaguida then proceeds to give a brief account of ancient Florence. He says that, once, within her "ancient walls" the church rang with peace and purity, for, unlike in Dante's time, the vanity of self-indulgence was inexistent. Newborn daughters were not thought of as an impoverishment to their fathers. "No mansions were left uninhabited," says Cacciaguida, a reference to the frivolous use made of them by the aristocracy during Dante's time. Cacciaguida refers to Bellincion Berti, a nobleman, who was not decorated with expensive ornaments but was "belted in leather and bone." He also spoke of his wife whom, unlike the women of Dante's day, did not return from the mirror with a painted face. The same goes for the lords of Vecchio and Nerli who wore "plain leather" and whose wives tended to their household tasks. These souls, as Cacciaguida says, could be sure of their own "burial place"—a reference to Dante's forced exile at the hands of ignorant Florentine leaders.

Cacciaguida then mentions Mary, to whom his mother prayed to lessen the pain of his birth. As a result, he received the blessing of a "sweet birth" in Florence. In the Baptistery of San Giovanni, he was Christianized. Cacciaguida declares Moronto and Eliseo to be his brothers. His wife, from whom Dante received his surname, came from the region of the Po. Cacciaguida mentions his crusade to the Holy Land, for which he received knighthood under "the Emperor Conrad." There, he was killed while trying to wrestle the Holy Land from the followers of Islam, who were able to lay claim to it because of the Popes' inability to assert their will ("shepherds sin") so that it might remain in Christian hands:

> ...With him I raised my sword against the might
> of the evil creed whose followers take from you—
> because your shepherds sin—what is yours by right.
>
> There, by that shameless and iniquitous horde,
> I was divested of the flesh and weight
> of the deceitful world, too much adorned
>
> by many souls whose best hope it destroys;
> and came from martyrdom to my present joys...
> (Canto XV, 142–149)

Thus, for Dante, Cacciaguida exemplifies the true "soldier of Faith" represented within the sphere of *Mars*.

Canto XVI opens with Dante contemplating the strong relationship between earthly pride and noble birth, for even here in Heaven he can't help but feel a sense of pride as he stands before Cacciaguida. Dante recognizes that the pride of noble birth felt on Earth quickly diminishes, unless it is constantly renewed. In other words, because "kings" once represented humanity's connection to the spiritual world, each of their descendants must *sustain* those qualities that made their ancestor a spiritual leader among human beings. Otherwise, family pride is of little significance. If, on the other hand, one does attempt to attain to those higher spiritual aspects of a noble ancestry—as is the case with Dante in regard to Cacciaguida—then pride is a valid inner experience. We witness such "spiritual" pride in Dante, a pride that does not arise out of selfishness or elitism. Instead, it reflects the goodness one feels in having attained a spiritual state conducive to administering God's love.

Dante speaks again, addressing Cacciaguida with the formal *voi*, thereby revealing his respect and affection for him. Says Dante:

> You are my father...
> You give me confidence to speak out boldly.
> So uplift me. I am more than I...
> (Canto XVI, 16–18)

At this point, Dante asks Cacciaguida to help him understand who his ancestors were, and what prominent families lived in Florence during that time on Earth. By uttering, "I am more than I," Dante pays respect to those responsible for helping bring about his incarnation on Earth. Such knowledge is what only Cacciaguida can provide him.

> ...Tell me, then, dear source of my own blood,
> who were your own forefathers? when were you born?
> and what transpired in Florence in your boyhood?"
>
> Tell me of St. John's sheepfold in those days.
> How many souls were then within the flock,
> and which of them was worthy of high place?
> (Canto XVI, 22–27)

Here, the allusion to St. John the Baptist is in reference to Florence, for he is its patron saint having replaced Mars. There are two important aspects to consider here. First, St. John is seen as a shepherd watching over his flock, until, of course, the arrival of the Christ who was to "increase" while John "decreased." In a similar way, Dante is to increase in stature, thereby eclipsing Cacciaguida who (like John the Baptist) baptizes him. Secondly, we must take note of the fact that Dante, within the sphere of Mars, asserts that it is John the Baptist who represents Florence, and not the god Mars, himself. He thus alludes to the city's need to be Christianized—something that Dante hopes to help bring about as a man "baptized" by God in the spiritual world. Thus, the question of nobility, addressed earlier, is not one of pride but of the "glory of God."

Having heard Dante's request, Cacciaguida intensifies in radiance. He indicates the year of his birth by telling Dante that the planet Mars had made about 580 revolutions since the time of the Annunciation of Christ's birth. This would indicate the time of Cacciaguida's birth to be about AD 1150.

> ...From the day when *Ave* sounded forth
> to that in which my mother, now a saint,
> being heavy laden with me, gave me birth,
>
> this flame had come back to its Leo again
> to kindle itself anew beneath his paws
> five hundred times plus fifty plus twenty plus ten...
> (Canto XVI, 34–39)

Known for its courage and fearlessness, Leo (the Lion), had kindled the flame of Mars as it circled the Sun about 580 times. Cacciaguida tells Dante that he and his ancestors were from the quarter in Florence where the "Feast of St. John" is celebrated, adding that silence is most appropriate when alluding to his forefathers, for only it can do them honor. Furthermore, it curbs the excesses of pride to which Dante has always been prone. Cacciaguida says that, during his time, Florence stretched "between Mars and the Baptist"—namely, from Ponte Vecchio to the Baptistery of St. John—and had one-fifth the population than that of Dante's time. It was a population that was not yet "mongrelized by the blood of Campi, Certaldo and Figghine." Florence, he argues, would have fared better had it not extended its boundaries to incorporate neighboring villages. Moreover, had the Church not shown a "hard stepmother's face and greed to Caesar" but been more like a "loving mother" in its relation to the Empire, Florence would not have been involved in the capture of towns throughout all of Tuscany, which, in turn, resulted in the increase of refugees within her boundaries. Cacciaguida, then, lists many prominent Florentines, some of whom had a marked influence on the historical development of Florence during Dante's time. Says Cacciaguida:

> ...It has always been a fact that the confusion of blood
> has been a source of evil to city-states,
> just as our bodies are harmed by too much food...
> (Canto XVI, 67–69)

In a series of Lectures given by Rudolf Steiner, *The Gospel of John in Relation to the Other Gospels*, he makes light of the fact that one of the most important contributions of the Roman Empire to the spiritual evolution of humanity (though unintended) was that it accelerated the mixing of the blood between peoples, thereby strengthening it in such a way that it could be a more suitable vehicle for the human "I." Up to that time, it was taboo for people to marry outside their tribe (or group) and thereby create new blood ties. Therefore, their blood had become weakened. The strengthening of the blood provided humankind with a more suitable vehicle by which to receive the Christ that was to flow into all of humanity. In light of this, Cacciaguida's declarations seem to reflect a kind of "localized folk-soul consciousness" and would, at first, seem to contradict the Christian ideal that all human beings are "equal in the eyes of God" and must strive to live in harmony.

Nonetheless, Cacciaguida's concern with the so-called mixing of the blood that arises out of greed and corruption seems to regard the *unseen* social consequences that ensue. Not only do families dwindle, claims Cacciaguida, but cities do, too. In fact, he says:

> ...All mankind's institutions, of every sort,
> have their own death, though in what long endures
> it is hidden from you, your own lives being short.
>
> And as the circling of the lunar sphere
> covers and bares the shore with never a pause,
> so Fortune alters Florence year by year...
> (Canto XVI, 79–84)

Thus, just as it is hard to perceive the eternal forces of destiny at work in life due to its brevity, so, too, does Fortune (Wheel of Fate) escape human awareness as it unpredictably alters Florence year by year. Given this, Cacciaguida tells Dante that it should not seem "wondrous" that behind the veil of corruption incessantly changing the face of Florence, the positive influences of many good people have gone unnoticed. He mentions a few—Ughi, Catellini, the Alberichi, the Ravignani, etc. — whose names, once noble, have virtually fallen into obscurity. Finally, Cacciaguida alludes to the strife caused by two families in Florence (as we have discussed in the *Inferno*), the Boundelmonti and the Amidei. Their conflict resulted in the separation of the Guelfs and Ghibellines, thereby dividing the city in two warring factions.

At the beginning of Canto XVII, Dante describes how he felt when questioning Cacciaguida about certain prophesies that haunted him. He refers to Phaeton, son of Clymene and Apollo who, having been told by Epaphus that Apollo was not his father, ran to his mother to be reassured. By persuading Apollo to let him prematurely ride the chariot toward the Sun, Phaeton epitomizes those children who make their fathers wary of being easily obliged to give their consent. Beatrice already reading Dante's mind convinces him to ask the question. By conversing with spirits of the heavenly world, he will be better prepared to convey the knowledge of his experiences there, once he has returned to Earth. With great reverence, Dante addresses Cacciaguida, whose consciousness is aligned with God:

> Dear root of my existence, you who soar
> so high that, as men grasp how a triangle
> may contain one obtuse angle and no more,
>
> you grasp contingent things before they find
> essential being, for you can see that focus
> where all time is time-present in God's mind...
> (Canto XVII, 13–18)

Here, Dante seems to allude to the Archetypal World of Ideas. Just as ordinary human beings grapple with the spatial configuration of a triangle, Cacciaguida is able to grasp "contingent things"—namely, things that may or may not exist. The existence of such things depends on necessity. In other words, he is able to see into the "primary" realm where all things originate. By being able to grasp "contingent things before they find essential being," Cacciaguida is immersed within the "Eternal Mind," that is, the cosmic activity that results in the manifestation of being. Dante asks him to explain the misfortunes that await him on Earth, as foretold him by some of the spirits in the lower world.

Cacciaguida responds in clear, well-ordered thinking that reflects the implicit order of perfection of the higher worlds. Says he:

> *Contingency*, whose action is confined
> to the few pages of the world of matter,
> is fully drawn in the Eternal Mind;
>
> but it no more derives *necessity*
> from being so drawn, than a ship dropping down river
> derives its motion from a watcher's eye...
> (Canto XVII, 37–42)

In other words, "contingency"—what can or cannot exist within the world of matter—does not owe its existence to the exclusion of Free Will, anymore than a ship going down a river is guided by an onlooker's eyes. Likewise, Cacciaguida's foreknowledge, or spiritual perception of future events, cannot bestow necessity so as to affect the manifestation of being. In describing the future events in Dante's life, Cacciaguida declares that his eyes receive such a vision by looking into the Primal Mind, which, again, is responsible for manifesting the physical world.

Dante is then told that he will be forced to leave Florence:

> ...So is it willed, so does it already unfold,
> so will it soon be done by him who plots it
> there where Christ is daily bought and sold...
> (Canto XVII, 49–51)

This stanza refers to Pope Boniface VIII, who used the Church as a seat of economic and political power. Because Dante opposed the politics of the Pope, he was essentially condemned for his opposition to the Church. Though Cacciaguida's prophecy was declared twelve to fifteen years after the beginning of Dante's exile—during which time he wrote the *Divine Comedy*—Dante relates that this journey into the spiritual world occurred in the year 1300, just shortly before he was banished from Florence in 1301. Thus, the reader must realize that his *Divine Comedy* retells the events that had allegedly *already* happened to him and, of course, not a moment-by-moment account of his experiences as they occurred.

Cacciaguida continues by saying that the outcry against Dante will be immediate, but the truth regarding his situation will not be revealed until later. First, he prophesizes that Dante will have abandoned what is most dear to him—namely, Florence and his involvement with the White Guelfs. He will thereby understand the bitterness of the "bread of others," which he compares to "salt and stone." However, the pain that he will have to most bitterly endure is the "foul and foolish company" that he "will fall into on that barren coast"—namely, the *betrayal* as leader of the White Guelfs by the members of his own party.

> ...Ingrate and godless, mad in heart and head
> will they become against you, but soon thereafter
> it will be they, not you, whose cheeks turn red.

> Their bestiality will be made known
> by what they do; while your fame shines the brighter
> for having become a party of your own...
> (Canto XVII, 64–69)

Regardless of their attack on Dante, Cacciaguida says it will be his followers who will feel the shame of their thoughtless actions, which resulted in the internal strife felt by Florence. Having been betrayed by both the White and Black factions of the Guelfs, Dante was forced to form a party of his own which was comprised only of himself, for he became aware that the existing political parties offered little hope in resolving the social problems of the time. He, thus, was to become the spokesperson for those higher Ideals which lend themselves to the realization of a unified society, whereby the Church and Empire, in their own allotted ways, could manifest the expression of God's Will on Earth.

Cacciaguida then tells Dante that his first place of refuge will be provided by the Great Lombard—Bartolomeo della Scala, Lord of Verona. Of interest here is the symbol of della Scala's family crest, which depicts an Eagle sitting up above a ladder. For the Eagle, as mentioned, represents spiritual vision, while the ladder—as will be evident in the sphere of Saturn—represents the means of ascension into the Higher Worlds. Though the Eagle can also be thought to signify the Roman Empire (as well as the family, della Scala, which can bring the Empire to realization), only a vision that beholds the cosmic principle at work in the world can unify such an Empire. Cacciaguida goes on to say that Dante and Bartolomeo will forge a relationship that transcends the normal course of giving and receiving. There shall also come into Dante's life another person who is part of the family crest—Francesco (Bartolomeo's brother). A renowned "warrior," Francesco—also known as Can Grande—will destroy and abolish the evil forces besetting Italy. Thus the "greyhound," of which Dante has already spoken in the *Inferno*, is reintroduced here within the sphere of Mars. Again, this sphere is comprised of the "soldiers of faith" whose actions serve a higher purpose designated by God. *Mars, the warring planet, is thus the realm from which the impulse to transform the configuration of earthly power toward the attainment of freedom takes place.* Seen anthroposophically, this striving toward freedom and independence can be associated with the transformative impulse that is presently occurring in the Mars sphere itself. In a lecture by Rudolf Steiner on January 14, 1913 Steiner says,

> Thus, in the Mars sphere people can be emancipated from the tendency to uniformity caused by the effects of public opinion that are detrimental for their progress on Earth. Whereas in earlier times Mars was said to be the planet of warlike traits, it is now the Buddha's task to transform these warlike traits gradually so that they become the foundation of the sense for freedom and independence needed in the present age. Whereas nowadays people have a tendency to surrender their sense of freedom and succumb to the fetters of public opinion, on Mars, between death and rebirth, they will strive to throw off those fetters and not bring them into life on Earth when they return again to new incarnations.[56]

In *Karmic Relationships* (vol. 5), Steiner says,

> Those whose main karmic impulses take shape in the Mars existence become as Voltaire. All their thoughts are concerned with life on Earth—criticizing it, fighting it, sometimes (in Voltaire's case with genius) epitomizing it in caustic, aphoristic sayings.[57]

Cacciaguida tells Dante that the world has yet to take notice of Can Grande, for he is only nine years of age. But people will gradually begin to see how he will transform the plight of the poor so that they can partake in the wealth of the nation. Cacciaguida then secretly reveals the various events that will take place by whispering them in Dante's ear, "and he said things about him (Can Grande) to astonish even those who shall be present." Though Dante's dream of a unified Italy, born of the moral impulses arising from a Church and State *restored* as agents of God, would never be realized as he had hoped, it is interesting to see how he lures his readers—by way of his silent discourse with Cacciaguida—to reflect more seriously about Can Grande and his eventual role in their lives.

(Incidentally, this prophecy that Cacciaguida unveils must not be confused with the kind of fortune-telling mentioned in Hell. We must remember that what reveals itself to Dante here is the result of his ability to decipher the mysteries of the suprasensory world and is thus the fruit of his spiritual development commensurate with the perfection of his being.)

Cacciaguida concludes his prophecy, assuring Dante that he will live to see the time when the injustices that he has had to suffer are avenged. He tells Dante not to hate his neighbors, for his "future stretches far beyond the reach of what they do."

Dante then asks if he should reveal to people on Earth what he has learned in the spiritual world:

> ... Yet if, half friend to truth, I mute my rhymes,
> I am afraid I shall not live for those
> who will think of these days as "the ancient times."
> (Canto XVII, 118–120)

Dante's concern, here, is whether his actions affect the balance of karma in such a way as to harm his people, since there are those who, not understanding the implications of what has been revealed to him, may react unwisely. Cacciaguida responds that Dante must reveal his entire vision regardless of who is prepared or unprepared to understand it ("let them scratch where it itches"), for it will nourish those who accept the truth of his experience, no matter how bitter it is to swallow.

> ... For if your voice is bitter when first tested
> upon the palate, it shall yet become
> a living nutriment when it is digested...
> (Canto XVII, 130–132)

In fact, Cacciaguida tells Dante that the *purpose* of his entire journey is to make the *Will of God* (as told by those who inhabit the higher regions of His Creation) known to all humanity. If Dante does not impart the knowledge of his experience to all humanity, he runs the risk of benefiting only himself and not others. However, by making all that is hidden from humanity manifest, Dante will help lead the *crusade* against those powers adversarial to the Christ. He will, in essence, be a true "soldier of faith."

> ...Therefore you have been shown—here in these spheres,
> there on the mount, and in the valley of woe—
> those souls whose names most ring in mortal ears;
>
> for the feelings of a listener do not mark
> examples of things unknown, nor place their trust
> in instances whose roots hide in the dark;
>
> nor will men be persuaded to give ear
> to arguments whose force is not made clear.
> (Canto XVII, 136–143)

Having uttered these last words, Cacciaguida is now absorbed in his thoughts. Meanwhile, Dante can taste the bitter sweetness of the prophecy he has just heard. Having perceived this, Beatrice encourages Dante to turn his attention "along a happier course," reminding him that She dwells with the "One" where *Justice* is manifest. Again, Beatrice lifts Dante up from the heaviness of earthly concerns. She bears the *light* of the Holy Spirit that is to manifest in Dante. Having heard her spoken words, Dante turns and perceives the *Love* streaming from her eyes. It transcends the power of his words,

> my powers of speech fail, but my memory
> cannot return so far above itself
> unless Another's grace be moved to guide me.
> (Canto XVIII, 10–12)

Dante reveals that his will became free of all earthly desire while looking at Beatrice. For her face shone with the ray of Eternal Bliss, which "gladdened his soul." The heaviness of Dante's thoughts here marks one of the few times in all the *Paradiso* where any inclination toward earthliness arises in Dante. However, Beatrice succeeds in directing his attention to the cosmic forces all around him when she says, "Turn and listen: not in my eyes alone is Paradise." Dante again directs his attention to Cacciaguida ("the holy ray"). As Rudolf Steiner has often said, the inner nature of the human being, which can easily be hidden from others here on Earth, is instantly revealed in the spiritual world. This fact is intimated by Dante:

> ...so, in the flaming of the holy ray
> to which I turned, I read the inner wall,
> and knew that it had something more to say.
> (Canto XVIII, 25–27)

Here, Cacciaguida feels that he must reveal the identity of those spirits near Dante who, as great "soldiers of faith" sparkle within the Cross. He refers to the sphere of Mars as the "fifth limb of the tree whose life is from its crown, and bears forever, and never sheds a leaf"—namely, the Tree of Life (life's cosmic force) rooted in God. Thus, Dante pictorially associates Paradise to the Tree of Life, from where burgeon eternal life forces that give birth to all earthly matter, as well as thought, itself. Among the spirits mentioned by Cacciaguida are Joshua who succeeded Moses in leading the chosen people into Israel, Judas Maccabaeus who freed Israel from Syria, Charlemange who cast the Moors out of Europe and Roland his mightiest knight, William of Orange who as a most faithful Christian knight died a monk, Rinoardo Rainouart who was William's chief lieutenant, Godfrey of Bouillon, the Knight Templar, who led "the first crusade and became the first Christian king of Jerusalem" and, finally, Robert Guiscard who fought in the war against the Saracens in the South of Italy, where he became the duke of Puglia and Calabria. We see that many of the spirits whom Cacciaguida presents are, in fact, those who led or participated in the crusades, those who tried to preserve the living flame of knowledge regarding the Christ.

Once again, Dante turns to gaze at the *light* in Beatrice's eyes. As he beholds the increase in radiance, he has the impression of turning with the Heavens—"through a greater arc."

Dante has now entered into the sphere of Jupiter—the "temperate star"—where he notices that the red light of Mars has become white. This, he masterfully describes as if he were witnessing the transformation in the face of a lady, who, touched by shame, was restored to her former self;

> And such a change as fair-skinned ladies show
> in a short space of time, when from their faces
> they lift the weight of shame that made them glow—
>
> such change grew on my eyes when I perceived
> the pure white radiance of the temperate star—
> the sixth sphere—into which I was received.
> (Canto XVIII, 64–69)

Within the "jovial face of Paradise" (the word *jovial*, of course, derived from Jove = Jupiter), Dante perceives the force of Love which provides humanity with the "means of speech." In other words, he penetrates even further into the cosmic Word where he is able to literally *read* the forces themselves and thereby witness the qualities inherent within the sphere. Dante beholds this as a visually imaginative experience. At first, he watches spirits rise up like birds and begin to form letters—first *D*, then *I*, then *L*, and so on—until formed are the words *Diligite Iustitiam qui Iudicatis Terram* (love justice, you who judge the earth). Dante immediately invokes the Pegasean Muses to assist him in describing what has unfolded before him. Says he:

> ...so fill me with your light, that as it shines
> I may show forth their image as I conceive it:
> let your own power appear in these few lines!
> (Canto XVIII, 85–87)

Thus, in this sphere, whose outer boundary is marked by the activity of the Kyriotetes, the central message is *temperance*. Whoever seeks to represent the Christ on Earth must arrive at a consciousness devoid of the earthly passion or desire that would impede them from beholding the forces that manifest a given reality.

As Dante gazes at the final M—where the spirits "stayed aligned, and silvery Jupiter seemed washed in a gold glow around them"—more beings descend atop the M, singing "a hymn to the Good that draws them to Its grace." Then, over a thousand spirits arise like sparks, each to a different height, according to the degree of grace bestowed upon them. Dante now gradually perceives the outline of an *Eagle*. Thus, as each light follows the Will of God to its rightful place, Dante is able to *intuit* how God Himself is the artist behind the form, through which the imagination before him takes place:

> The One who paints there needs no guide's behest.
> He is Himself the guide. From Him derives
> the skill and essential form that builds the nest.
> (Canto XVIII, 109–111)

Just as birds obey the imperceptible forces that guide them in building their nests, so, too, have the spirits followed such forces in forming the *Eagle* that appears before Dante. Other spirits form lilies around the M before it is completely transformed into the shape of an *Eagle*. Many have interpreted the lilies to be symbolic of the French Monarchy that was thought to have played an instrumental role in uniting and helping to preserve the Empire symbolized here by the *Eagle*. Furthermore, just as the *Eagle* represents spiritual vision, the lily symbolizes the purity required for such a vision. Therefore, *the formation of the Eagle illustrates Dante's ability to see form* (M) *manifesting from light*, the creative force within thought. It graphically illustrates his attainment of spiritual perception.

Dante addresses Jupiter by saying that earthly justice is an effect of its moral impulses at work in the heavenly world. It is the *ideal* of earthly justice that has been depicted for Dante.

> O lovely star, how rich a diadem
> shown forth to let me understand our justice
> flows to us from the heaven you bejewel.
> (Canto XVIII, 115–117)

Dante then lashes out against the Papacy, which, instead of representing Heavenly Justice on Earth, has perverted it by abusing its power to excommunicate. Such actions have thereby impeded human beings from searching the Grace of God by way of the sacraments. Says he:

> In earlier eras wars were carried on
> by swords; now, by denying this man or that
> the bread the Heavenly Father denies to none.
> (Canto XVIII, 127–129)

At the end of Canto XVIII, Dante relates how the Papacy abandoned the living ideals of Peter and Paul by coveting the Florin (Florentine money), which bore the *image* of John the Baptist's head—an image that recalls the gruesome compensation made to the daughter of Herodias for having entertained Herod, who upon witnessing her dance offered her "whatsoever she would ask." She asked for the Baptist's head. For Dante, the Papacy's insatiable desire for a coin ("the root of evil") that bore the image of such a revered figure proved the extent to which materialistic impulses had taken possession of the Church.

As Dante gazes at the *Eagle*, each spirit within it appears as a ruby penetrated by the Sun's rays. Never, says he, has a similar experience presented itself to humanity, for all of the spirits comprising the *Eagle* address Dante in unison. With a single voice, they use the pronouns *I* or *mine* when referring to themselves. This uniformity reflects, above all, how each spirit, drawn together by the Will of God, partakes in the formation of a true spiritual community. Instead of manifesting individual will, their will is united in that of God. The unity exemplified by these spirits seems to result from the interpenetration of being, which, according to Steiner, is common among spirits in the heavenly world whose interest and intent on Earth were the same. Steiner says, "The fundamental principle of knowledge in the suprasensory world is that of *interpenetration*. The knower enters into the being of that which he knows and, as it were, shares its very being and its knowledge of itself."[58] This participation is predicated on the fact that the personal element is no longer an obstacle in forming intimate connections between human beings. In other words, each spirit equally partakes in a community united within the "I" of the Father.

And so it is on Earth. Only when human beings overcome the dialecticism that divides them and partake in living thinking can a community centered on Christ consciousness arise. The *Eagle* declares that a *"memory"* of justice and piety had been left behind on Earth, though many "evildoers" avoid its good examples. This memory, of course, regards the Christ who descended onto the Earth to lead humanity into the spiritual world. No longer is there a person on Earth who exemplifies the teaching of the Christ in all its perfection. Only The Bible and the various accounts of Christ's deed can lead humanity to where Universal Justice has its source. The spirits that speak must not be regarded as individual beings that once acted out of their earthly understanding of justice. Rather, they represent the *force of Justice* that had once made its way to the Earth and survives only as a memory. Says the *Eagle*:

> For being just and pious in my time
> …I am exalted here in glory
> to which, by wish alone, no one may climb;
>
> and leave behind me, there upon the earth,
> a memory honored even by evildoers,
> though they shun the good example it sets forth.
> (Canto XIX, 13–18)

Dante asks the *Eagle* to explain the mysteries of Divine Justice, for on Earth his soul could find "no other food with which to break its fast." He adds that even if Divine Justice created its "holy mirror" in some other realm, the *Eagle* has a clear view of it. This "holy mirror" refers to the kingdom of the Thrones, which as Ciardi points out, Dante describes as "mirrors" reflecting "God's judgment to us" (Par. IX, 61–63).

In its response, the *Eagle* preens itself to "show its readiness," and then sings as a hymn,

> ...The One who wheeled
> the compass round the limits of the world,
> and spread there what is hidden and what revealed,
>
> could not so stamp his power and quality
> into his work but what the creating Word
> would still exceed creation infinitely...
> (Canto XIX, 40–45)

In other words, nothing created by God is greater than He, Himself. The *Eagle* then reveals this as the reason for which Lucifer, who prided himself as God's equal, fell from the heights of cosmic activity. No creature of God can "contain the Good which has no end." Our attempt to comprehend God's creation is like trying to perceive the ocean depths with our naked eyes. Only the *light* of God can lead to clarity, whereas the reflected light of the human intellect is but darkness leading to the sins (poison) of the flesh. The *Eagle* tells Dante that much has already been revealed to him. However, detecting a question burning inside Dante, it seeks to provide the answer.

> ...For you used to say, "A man is born in sight
> of Indus' water, and there is none there
> to speak of Christ, and none to read or write.
>
> And all he wills and does, we must concede,
> as far as human reason sees, is good;
> and he does not sin either in word or deed.
>
> He dies unbaptized and cannot receive
> the saving faith. What justice is it damns him?
> Is it his fault that he does not believe?"...
> (Canto XIX, 70–78)

The *Eagle* asks how can human beings judge something a thousand miles away when they cannot perceive the ground upon which they walk. Such is the nature of human logic, for it fails to understand its own *foundation*—namely, its own inner *light*—by which it can perceive what lies beyond it. The *Eagle* then points to *The Bible*, and says that the Primal Will of God does not move toward the good "created" by humanity, but is *Itself* the fount from which good is made manifest in the hearts of human beings. He adds that no spirit who was not a believer in Christ has ever risen to such heights as Dante. Yet, there are many people with the word *Christ* always at the tip of their tongues who, in essence, shall be further away from Him on Judgment Day than those who, "without sin in word or deed," are oblivious to Him.

The *Eagle* implies that it is inconceivable for us to truly realize our divine nature unless we find our way to the Christ—namely, to the Word through which the world was made manifest. *This, of course, becomes a reality the more we behold the light born by Divine Wisdom and perceive its significance in the course of human development.* Many are those who speak of Christ and, yet, are unaware of this *light*. Fewer still are those who actualize it. Those individuals who concern themselves only with a "conception" of the Christ, who linger within the sphere of earthly consciousness wherein they are prone to "sin," are no closer to Christ than someone who has never even heard of Him but acts out of the impulse of Good born of Him. In other words, one who speaks of Christ but does not act in accordance with His teachings reflects a greater separation from Him than one who never utters His Name yet acts out of the Good that He manifests.

The *Eagle* goes on to name individuals who abused their noble positions on Earth. Among them are the Emperor Albert of Austria who invaded Bohemia; Philip "the Fair" who, having debased the French currency and destroyed the Knights Templar, will face the tusks of a boar; Edward I of England and the Scottish Wallace, whose greed will manifest as they incessantly fight over their borders; Ferdinand IV and Wenceslas IV who "knew nothing of valor, and chose not to know"; Charles II of Anjou ("Cripple of Jerusalem") who bestowed the title of "King of Jerusalem" upon himself, yet failed to restore the Holy Land to Christian rule (his good deeds are marked with the number 1 and his misdeeds with the letter M, as in one thousand). He also names Frederick II of Sicily, King James of Majorca, James I of Aragon, Dionysius of Portugal, Haakon of Norway, Stephen of Rascis who was known for having counterfeited Venetian coins and Henry II of Lusignan who maintained French rule over Cyprus.

Canto XX begins with a hymn, in which the spirits each sing with their own voice. Dante compares the alternation between the *Eagle*'s speech (comprised of unified voices) and the hymn of many voices that participate individually in transforming day into night, to the Sun being replaced by countless stars in the Heavens:

> When the sun, from which the whole world takes its light,
> sinks from our hemisphere and the day fades
> from every reach of land, and it is night;
>
> the sky, which earlier it alone had lit,
> suddenly changes mode and reappears
> in many lights that take their light from it.
>
> I thought of just that change across night's sill
> when that emblem of the world and of its leaders
> had finished speaking through its sacred bill;
>
> for all those living lights now shone on me
> more brightly than before, and began singing
> a praise too sweet to hold in memory.
> (Canto XX, 1–12)

This image, which Dante evokes to illustrate the dual nature of our relationship to the spiritual world, is indeed all-encompassing. On the one hand, all human beings are united in the Christ (Sun), and speak in unison of *Divine Justice* as it is reflected to them by the higher beings within the celestial hierarchy; on the other hand, each spirit *individually* reflects the Will of God by manifesting the *light* of Christ within itself.

The *Eagle* once again speaks to Dante. This time it asks him to focus his attention on its eye: "Look closely now into that part of me that in earth's eagles can endure the Sun." The *Eagle*, which ancient humanity once believed could look directly into the Sun, symbolizes the potential to perceive the Higher Self through the *light* of thinking—namely, the *light* of the Christ who had once descended directly from the Sun. Making up the *Eagle's* eye are its noblest members. Therefore, the spirits nearest to God constitute the eye of *Divine Justice*—those most able to accurately *perceive* "with the eyes of God."

At the very center of the *Eagle's* pupil, within which *light* (Christ) enters humanity, is David who brought the "Ark of the Covenant" back to the Holy Land. Forming the eyebrow of the *Eagle's* eye are five spirits. Closest to the beak is the Emperor Trajan who, in an act of great humility, consoled a poor widow for her dead son. This act, as previously mentioned, was depicted on the bas-reliefs on the terrace of Pride on Purgatory. The *Eagle* informs Dante that though Trajan now partakes of the "sweet life," he has "known the bitter way," for he had spent much time in Limbo. Due to the prayers of St. Gregory, he was converted and, thus, died a true Christian. The next spirit in line is Hezekiah, a former King of the Jews, who interceded with his own prayers, thereby delaying his death so that he could redeem himself and his way of life. He, says the *Eagle*, knows how a prayer can change the plan of God without altering it. The next spirit is the Emperor Constantine who moved the Empire to Greece, which resulted in great harm to humanity at that time. Thus, we have a spirit here whose intentions were good, even though the consequences of which bore "bad fruit." Because his heart was directed toward good, he cannot be punished for the bad effects that result from it. Dante seems to imply that one's karma is related to the *inner disposition* of one's soul. This would be in compliance with Aquinas who utters the same thought in his *Summa*. One need only remember how the disposition of the soul resulted in completely different fates for Guido da Montefeltro and his son Bounconte. Thus, not everything that results from an action can be linked directly to it, for many things have their source in other deeds that seem unrelated. Next to the Emperor is William II of Sicily, who has been replaced by two tyrants, Charles and Frederick II. The *Eagle* then asks Dante who, in the erring world below, would ever believe that Ripheus the Trojan would be the sixth soul among the sacred in this sphere? Other than a passing mention by Virgil in the *Aeneid*, nothing more is known of him, other than his justness. Dante freely depicts him as one of the converted and, thus, resolves, by way of example, the question of the preceding canto as to whether or not one who is not born a Christian can eventually enter the realm of Heaven.

Having heard the declarations of the *Eagle*, Dante is amazed at how such spirits hold a position of blessedness before the Eye of God. "How can this be?" he cries out. The *Eagle* says in response:

> I see that you believe these things are true
> because I say them. Yet, you do not see how.
> Thus, though believed, their truth is hidden from you...
> (Canto XX, 88–90)

In other words, Dante believes the *Eagle* on faith alone and *not* the capacity to penetrate the inner causes of things. In fact, the Bird of Justice says to him,

> ...You are like one who knows the name of a thing
> whose quiddity, until it is explained
> by someone else, defies his understanding...
> (Canto XX, 91–93)

The term *quiddity* in Scholasticism refers to "the essence of a thing"—that is, the suprasensory force from which arises the form of a given thing or event. This being the case, the *Eagle* sets out to clarify one of the most difficult theological questions for Dante, namely, how can two pagans (such as Trajan and Ripheus) find their way into the "Kingdom of God."

The *Eagle* states that the God is immoveable, yet, as the fount of *Love*, He is responsible for moving the entire cosmos while allowing Himself to be moved by acts of love. Thus, by being moved (conquered), He, Himself, conquers:

> ...By every living hope and ardent love
> that bends the Eternal Will—by these alone
> the Kingdom of Heaven suffers itself to move.
>
> Not as men bend beneath a conqueror's will.
> It bends because it wishes to be bent.
> Conquered, its own beneficence conquers still...
> (Canto XX, 94–99)

The *Eagle* informs Dante that both Trajan and Ripheus "did not leave their bodies...as pagans, but as Christians." Moreover, one grieved "in firm faith in the pierced feet" (of Christ) while the other was still to grieve (for the Crucifixion was yet to come). The *Eagle* says that Trajan rose from Hell "into the flesh." In other words, Trajan's life was restored to him as a result of "living hope," which had the "power of love" to make good the prayers by St. Gregory, who had come to help him renew his will. As a result, Trajan came to believe in God.

> ...One rose again from Hell—from whose dead slope
> none may return to Love—into the flesh;
> and that was the reward of living hope;
>
> of living hope, whose power of love made good
> the prayers he raised to God to bring him back
> to life again, that his will might be renewed.
>
> And so the glorious soul for whom he prayed,
> back in the flesh from which it soon departed,
> believed in Him who has the power to aid...
> (Canto XX, 106–114)

In this picture, we see how Trajan is permeated by the Holy Trinity, in that the "living hope" (Holy Ghost), which is our connection to the suprasensory aspect of our own thinking, contains the "power of love"—namely, the presence of the Christ force that descends from the Father to enkindle the human will necessary for humanity to consciously experience God. Thus, his first death, which follows his experience of Hell, must be understood in the light of the Christian initiation practiced in the early centuries after Golgotha. For it was effectively similar to the death that was so much a part of Rosicrucian initiation. The "second death" to which the *Eagle* refers is, of course, Trajan's actual physical death.

> ...Believing, he burst forth with such a fire
> of the true love, that at his second death
> he was worthy of a seat in this glad choir...
> (Canto XX, 115-117)

The issue of Ripheus' place in Paradise hinges on a somewhat legendary account created by Dante, for, again, very little is known about him. Dante declares that because Ripheus was granted a vision of the Coming Christ—a vision that he *believed*—he was a Christian before Christ had even descended to the Earth. As a result, he was baptized by the three Christian virtues, faith, hope, and charity. This is essentially what differentiates Ripheus from Virgil. Thus, Dante hints in *veiled* language the reason for which many spirits before the time of Christ are unable to partake of Paradise; they lacked the *substantiality* of Christ's being in the world, of which Ripheus was able to partake in his vision.

The canto concludes with a reference to the question of predestination. Says the *Eagle*:

> ...Mortals, be slow to judge! Not even we
> who look on God in Heaven know, as yet,
> how many He will choose for ecstasy...
> (Canto XX, 133-135)

Thus, the Will of God is not known to anyone but God Himself. What exists within the field of His creative activity proceeds from an Intelligence that transcends the capacities of even those who are able to behold it. To perceive future events does not imply actively partaking in their manifestation. Regardless if one eventually creates out of oneself (as a higher spiritual being), one still creates within the Will of

God, therefore, in accordance with His design. One's creative activity is thus aligned to that of higher beings, which, in turn, is aligned to the source of all creative forces, namely, God Himself. Thus, our ability to create lifeless form, as well as our ability to create life itself one day—exists in accordance to what is willed from above, namely *Divine Will*.

It is important to note here that the events from Canto XIV to Canto XX are overseen by the Cross and the Eagle, respectively. Just as the question of *Love* lies at the *heart* of the *Purgatorio*, here in the *Paradiso*, the *Cross (Church) and the Eagle (Roman Empire)* take center stage. They constitute the core of Dante's conception of Justice in its purest form and are central to his perception of a society's wellbeing—a wellbeing founded on the separation of Church and State. For him, both the Cross and the Eagle were of equal importance in resurrecting our spiritual and temporal lives, since they were representative of the *contemplative* and *active* life respectively. Moreover, their juxtaposition at the heart of the *Paradiso* subtly alludes to the Knights Templar, for, as we have previously mentioned, together they formed the insignia of the Templars.

Canto XXI opens with Dante beholding the face of Beatrice. With his eyes fixed on her, Dante's thoughts flee into oblivion, except those he has of Her. Once more, he is seen penetrating the depths of *Divine Wisdom* (Beatrice). Beatrice does not smile, otherwise Dante would be burnt to ashes, as was Semele, who, having been tricked by Juno into asking Jupiter to reveal himself as the gods perceived him, was burnt to death. So overpowering is Beatrice's radiance now, as they ascend into the sphere of Saturn! Note how, in the Saturn sphere, Beatrice exercises temperance in revealing herself to Dante. In other words, the deepening of one's consciousness must occur gradually, if one is to avoid danger of being "shattered." Says she,

> ...because my beauty, which, as it goes higher
> from step to step of the eternal palace,
> burns, as you know, with ever brighter fire;

> and if it is not tempered in its brightening,
> its radiance would consume your mortal powers
> as a bough is shattered by a bolt of lightning...
> (Canto XXI, 7–12)

Having arrived at the seventh sphere, that of Saturn, Dante finds himself where the Thrones manifest their activity. Beyond Saturn, as Rudolf Steiner has said, the Cherubim, but more so, the Seraphim stand in direct sight of the Godhead. As stated in Cantos IX (61–63) and XIX (28–33), the Thrones were thought to reflect the activity of the Godhead onto the Earth. In fact, in *The Spiritual Hierarchies and the Physical World,* Steiner describes how they "are the first to exert their activity on the fiery form that we call ancient Saturn. They have reached a stage of development that enables them to pour forth their own substance."[59] In other words, from within their beings they "poured forth their own substance," thus initiating the first stage of the Earth's creation. This first stage was comprised of warmth, which much later, after long stretches of time, eventually materialized in what we know as the Earth today. In this way, the Thrones reflected the activity of the Godhead on Earth. In a similar vein, Steiner says:

> The Thrones, the third rank of the hierarchies, counting from above, have the task—figuratively speaking, of course—of putting into practice the lofty cosmic thoughts that have been conceived in wisdom, thoughts received by the Seraphim from the Gods and pondered over by the Cherubim.[60]

Beatrice explains to Dante that they have arrived at the Saturn sphere, which at this moment is in conjunction with Leo (the Lion).

> ...We have soared to the Seventh Splendor, which is now
> beneath the Lion's blazing breast, and rays
> its influence, joined with his, to the world below...
> (Canto, XXI, 13–15)

Beatrice bids Dante to make his eyes "the mirror of the vision this mirror (Saturn) will reveal to you." In other words, Dante is to let the *light* reflected by Saturn (Thrones) from the Godhead be reflected in his eyes. As he looks around, Dante is enraptured by what he sees, for within that "crystal" sphere, there rose a golden ladder so high that it transcended the depths of Dante's perception:

> Within the crystal that bears round the world
> the name of its great king in that golden age
> when evil's flag had not yet been unfurled,
>
> like polished gold ablaze in full sunlight,
> I saw a ladder rise so far above me
> it soared beyond the reaches of my sight.
> (Canto XXI, 25–30)

The golden ladder recalls the ladder of Jacob in Genesis 28, where it is said, "...He had a dream in which he saw a stairway resting on the Earth and its top reaching to heaven and the angels of God were ascending and descending on it."[61] In fact, Dante himself describes it is such:

> And I saw so many splendors make their way
> down its bright rungs, I thought that every lamp
> in all of heaven was pouring forth its ray.
> (Canto XXI, 31–33)

The symbolism of the ladder is clear. It represents the pathway leading from the planetary spheres, within which the spiritual hierarchies exercise their dominion, to the Empyrean. In other words, it is the path toward an even higher state of consciousness that allows for the Father to be seen, so that no longer does one remain within the sphere of reflected cosmic activity but, instead, becomes part of the creative process manifested in the various realms below. The *Zohar*, the fundamental book of the Kabbalah, remarks that Jacob's ladder had seventy-two rungs, thus denoting the line of descent from the Nathan Jesus all the way back to Adam—namely, from the body wherein dwelt the Christ to that formed directly by the Father. The ladder's *golden* aspect refers to the Solar Logos, the Christ, which rays down from the Father so that human beings can find their way back up to Him.

The spirits who occupy the sphere of Saturn are monks, for this realm contains those who dedicate themselves to what, in the Middle Ages, was considered the highest of Christian virtues—*contemplation*. In a sense, the aspect of Rachel and Leah are both represented here, for though this sphere is devoted to contemplation, it is filled with the activity of those who *joyously* ascend and descend the spiritual heights, each carrying out God's Will.

One of the spirits descends the stairs to where Dante and Beatrice are situated and increases in brightness. Dante is sure he knows "with what love" the spirit glows. He looks at Beatrice but realizes, by her silence, that it is not yet time to ask questions. As Beatrice sees "in the vision of He who sees all things," she perceives the yearning within Dante's soul and thus gives him permission to speak. This illustrates how *Divine Wisdom* is a source of revelation for Dante's entry into the spiritual world. Dante reverently asks the spirit why he has come down the ladder and why he hears no music, unlike in the sphere below. The spirit answers the second question first by saying that the song resounding in the Saturn sphere is too strong for mortal ears, just as the smile of Beatrice is too radiant for mortal eyes. The reason for which he has come to greet Dante is to make his spirit "gladder." He adds, "The high love that makes us prompt to serve the Judge who rules the world, decrees the fate of every soul among us." Dante, realizing that each spirit drawn to the Eternal Will needs no command, is still a bit puzzled and asks why, among all the spirits before him, has this particular one come to speak with him. (This affords Dante the opportunity to later address the mystery of predestination.) The spirit, having heard Dante's question, spins in ecstasy, and

> ...then the Love within the lamp replied:
> "I feel the ray of God's light focused on me.
> It strikes down through the ray in which I hide.
>
> Its power, joined to my own, so elevates

> my soul above itself, that I behold
> the Primal Source from which its emanates...
> (Canto XXI, 82–87)

Here, the Will of God predestines the fate of all spirits—that is, Divine Will naturally draws each spirit here toward *Love,* to serve Him. Though this may seems paradoxical, in effect, it is not, for the spirits *wish* to be permeated by God's *Love* by serving Him. Out of their own volition, they act in accordance with Divine Will in order to enter a state of Eternal Joy. Thus, God assigns the fate of each spirit in relation to that spirit's particular qualities, so that the inner disposition of each individual spirit enables it to fulfill a particular task. A ray of God's *Light* had focused on this spirit to help Dante perceive the "Primal Source" from which the power of God emanates. The spinning motion, as Ciardi points out, can be understood as a "contemplative soul revolving around its own center (*love*)."[62] Though the spirit is able to contemplate or perceive the Godhead by way of His Eternal Ray of Love, it cannot fathom the reason for which it has been chosen to speak with Dante, for not even the highest beings closest to God (Seraphim) can comprehend the nature of His actions:

> ...But in all Heaven, the soul granted most light,
> the Seraph that has God in closest view,
> could not explain what you have asked me to know...
> (Canto XXI, 91–93)

In fact, so far hidden in Eternal Law is the truth of this assertion that all those beings with "created vision" are cut off from seeing it. The spirit encourages Dante to make this known to mortal ears upon his return to the earthly world. He adds;

> ...On earth the mind is smoke; here, it is fire.
> How can it do there what it cannot do
> even when taken into heaven's choir?
> (Canto XXI, 100–102)

Dante, having listened to the spirit's response, asks him his identity. The spirit begins by describing a series of mountains, amongst which exists a hermitage on Mt. Catria, "once given entirely to meditation and prayer." The spirit adds that he had once been rooted there, subsisting only on "lenten olive food." That monastery, says the spirit, once sent many contemplative souls to the regions of the Higher World, but now, "all its works are in vain." The spirit identifies himself as Peter Damiano, who in Ravenna, "by the Adriatic," was known as Peter the Sinner. He was an emissary there, having resided at the Monastery of Santa Maria Pomposa. He later became a cardinal, wearing a hat passed *down* to him from cardinal to cardinal—thus, intimating the gradual degeneration of that position. Peter Damiano denounces the present clergy, who have failed to uphold the offices of Peter and Paul. Instead, the clergy have grown so fat and rich that each must be propped up by a man on all four sides of him. The other spirits, moved by the justice of Damiano's words, rejoice as they descend the ladder. Their song is so loud that Dante's senses reel from the thunderous sound. He cannot even make out the words that he hears.

Shaken, Dante turns toward Beatrice, who tells him,

> Do you not know that you are in the skies
> of Heaven itself? That all is holy here?
> That all things spring from love in Paradise?...
> (Canto XXII, 7–9)

She makes Dante aware that he is not quite ready to witness the manifestation of God's presence embodied in their song. Beatrice tells him that the roar that reeled his senses was a cry against the clergy—a cry that hid from Dante a vengeful prayer calling on God to show His Wrath toward those responsible for the clergy's corruption.

Dante directs his gaze at the great souls around him and sees that "a hundred shining globes entwined their beams, soul adding grace to soul in Paradise." Dante remains silent, fearing that his questions would offend them. At this point, the largest glowing light among them approaches him and declares that these spirits have the desire of bestowing *joy* upon him. This glowing light then begins to address Dante's question. He identifies himself as St. Benedict, the one who first brought "the holy name of Him who came on earth" to the region of Montecassino, where paganism flourished. He tells Dante that, while spreading knowledge of the Christ, human beings were saved "from the seductions of the impious creed" (cult of Apollo) by the grace that had shone upon him. He then points out two contemplative spirits who devoted themselves totally to the cloister, St. Maccarius, and St. Romualdas, founder of the Camaldolese Order.

Dante tells the spirit, St. Benedict, that the *Love* he feels in this sphere has opened his confidence, just as the petals of a rose open to the warmth of the Sun. He then asks St. Benedict to unveil himself before Dante's mortal eyes. The spirit answers that this can only occur when Dante reaches the highest heavenly sphere, for only, *there*, is all desire for higher knowledge answered. At this point of Dante's journey, St. Benedict cannot unveil himself, for Dante would be blinded by his radiance. Only when Dante has risen into the higher spheres of divine activity—that is, only when he has *fully* developed the faculty of spiritual perception—will he be able to endure the spiritual essence of the spirit before him. For, just as the physical Sun that blinds, conceals the Spiritual Sun within it, so, too, does the *light* of this glowing spirit conceal this being's suprasensory nature from eyes not trained to perceive it. Says he,

> ...There, every wish is perfect, ripe, and whole.
> For there, and there alone, is every part
> where it has always been; for it has no pole,
>
> not being in space. It is to that very height
> the golden ladder mounts; and thus you see
> why it outsoars the last reach of your sight...
> (Canto XXII, 64–69)

Thus, the golden ladder rises up to where "there is no pole," to where there is no space, so that the levels of consciousness (rungs of the golden ladder) by which one rises into the highest reaches of the Macrocosm, extend to where mortal eyes cannot reach, namely, to the source of God's *Love*, where it is, in turn, renewed by human deeds. What is, therefore, represented in spatial terms by Dante (ladder, spheres, etc.) is meant to enable the intellect to grasp the inner reality that transcends it.

St. Benedict says that ever since Jacob dreamed of the ladder covered by angels, few men have striven to climb it. Therefore, the book of rules that he, St. Benedict, wrote to help the contemplative soul rise toward the spiritual world lies in waste on the very parchment upon which it was written. He adds that religious buildings have become a "den for beasts" and that even usury offends God less than the avarice committed by the Church members, who confiscate material goods from the poor to enrich their own families. Just as on Earth a seedling well planted does not always bear fruit, so, too, is a "good beginning" often insufficient to ensure a fruit of goodness. As examples of good beginnings gone astray, he cites the folds of Peter, who desired neither gold nor silver; St. Francis, who, through poverty, drew men to his fold; and even himself, who continually fasted and prayed.

> ...And if you look at the origins of each one,
> then look again at what it has become,
> you will see that what was white has changed to dun...
> (Canto XXII, 91–93)

Peter's attempt to illustrate the corruption of the Church has largely been interpreted in primarily one of two ways—one that is hopeful, one that is not. Says he,

> ...Yet Jordan flowing backward, and the sea
> parting as God willed, were more wondrous sights,
> than God's help to His stricken church would be.
> (Canto XXII, 94–96)

As Ciardi points out, the hopeful scenario is that if God can part the Red Sea and make the Jordan River flow backward, certainly he can reverse the tide of the Church's corruption. The second interpretation reflects the futility of converting the Church to its original state of goodness, for that would be more extraordinary than the "parting of the sea" or the "Jordan flowing backward." This ambivalence is interesting for Dante maintains the idea of God's omnipotence while conveying the magnitude of the work yet to be done regarding the Church.

Having uttered these words, St. Benedict disappears into the group of souls around him and whirls away into the higher regions, far from Dante's sight. At that point, Beatrice lifts Dante up the ladder, "conquering my nature with her power divine." This marks yet another point of transformation with regard to Dante's consciousness. *Divine Wisdom* (Beatrice) elevates him so high that what remained of his lower vision is overcome by the *intuitions* of even higher realms in the Divine World. Dante rises so quickly into those exulted regions that there is no suitable means of comparison on Earth. Given that the light that we commonly recognize is but a *reflection* of the living force from which it arises, so, too, can its motion through physical space be seen as an aftereffect of the *Love* that drives it—a *Love* that is God.

Quickly, Dante finds himself in the House of Gemini, the sign of the zodiac under which he was born and to which he expresses gratitude for his poetic genius.

> O glorious constellation! O lamp imbued
> with great powers, to whose influence I ascribe
> all my genius, however it may be viewed.
>
> When I drew my first breath of Tuscan air
> the Sun, the father of all mortal life,
> was rising in your rays and setting there.
> (Canto XXII, 112–117)

Gemini is also the sign through which he ventures into the realm of the Fixed Stars. Dante directs his prayers to this constellation in recognition of the great passage that still lies before him. It is interesting that just as he is born on Earth under the sign of Gemini, so, too, is he "born" into the higher regions of the spiritual world under the same sign. This is yet another example of the symmetry underlying Dante's poem.

Beatrice alerts Dante to God's close proximity before directing his attention to the spheres of the universe through which he has journeyed. Looking down through those spheres, Dante perceives a globe so small that he has to "smile at such a sorry show." Upon witnessing what appears to be "a pebble in the skies," he declares that the truly wise do not direct all their attention only toward the earthly realm.

Dante then beholds Latona's daughter, the Moon, "glowing there without that shadow that had once misled me to think her matter was part dense, part rare." Thus, Dante is looking at the "dark side of the Moon"—namely, that which is never visible on Earth. It is now illuminated by the Sun, situated between him and the Moon. It is important to note that we must not envision the planets that Dante sees as mere physical bodies in space at this point of his journey. For by attributing mythological characteristics to the planets, Dante is alluding to the *living planetary influence* of the spheres that he beholds. The *light* of the Sun illuminates the "dark side of the Moon." Thus, by making it completely visible, he dispels his mistaken notion that the Moon's matter is "part dense, part rare." This realization illustrates how Dante has reached the point in which he can see all sides of a given reality simultaneously. The planetary spheres that Dante perceives are in perpetual motion, for upon seeing the Sun sphere, Dante beholds that of Mercury (*Maia*) and Venus (*Dione*). Looking up from those, he then perceives the Jupiter sphere mediate between "his father and son"—namely, Saturn, an extremely cold planet and Mars, an extremely hot one. For this reason, Jupiter has been called the "temperate planet." All seven planetary spheres reveal themselves to Dante so that he perceives the simultaneous workings of the Hierarchies manifesting God's Will in their motion about the Sun.

> And all the seven, in a single view,
> showed me their masses, their velocities,
> and the distances between each in its purlieu.
> (Canto XXII, 148–150)

As Dante turns "with the Eternal Twins," he once again takes note of the Earth, "the dusty little threshing ground that makes us ravenous for our mad sins." "Threshing ground," here, denotes a violent separation of seed from shaft, namely of the life force and its offspring, that which is in marked contrast to the peaceful harmony of the heavenly spheres. In this way, it can be viewed as the center of karmic activity, where the lower forces (threshing ground) lead us to hunger (ravenous for our mad sins) after that which separates us from God. Having taken note of this, Dante turns his eyes again toward Beatrice.

Amid the fixed stars, where the Seraphim and Cherubim have a direct view of the Godhead, Dante follows Beatrice's gaze upward into the higher regions. Just "as a bird in its sweet canopy of green covers the nest of its beloved young through all the night when nothing can be seen," Beatrice stands looking expectantly on "the predawn glow" of the Sun. All the while, Dante, while observing her "blissful expectation," yearns "with sweet anticipation" for what is to come. But their wait is not long, for

> ...the interval between *when* and *when* was slight—
> the *when* of my *waiting*, I say, and the *when* of seeing
> the sky begin to swell with a new light.
> (Canto XXIII, 16–18; italics mine)

Beatrice tells Dante that the light he sees descending from the Empyrean and extending across the sky is "the militia of Christ's triumph, and all the fruit harvested from the turning of the spheres." This "militia" contains the souls of individuals who had, with all their concentrated energy, worked to participate in the activity of the Resurrected Christ. They were affected by the influences of the spheres, so that "good" could manifest. Note Dante's reference to the word *waiting*, which in meditative practice is of the utmost significance. Says Massimo Scaligero in *The Secrets of Space and Time*,

> Those of us who are schooled to perceive the thinking used to think about space and time, are aware of the attitude that begins introducing us to the secret of space and time—waiting.

Waiting is the inner exercise that draws from the living current of time.

Waiting is the calm within agitation; it is the patience that disenchants the imprint of exterior space–time within the soul.

The art of waiting calmly enables us to enter the mystery of ever-existing time; it allows us to enter a space that feels like the vestment of what we call eternity.[63]

At this point, Beatrice tells Dante,

> ...Before you now appears
> the militia of Christ's triumph, and all the fruit
> harvested from the turning of the spheres.
> (Canto XXIII, 19–21)

Of all the beings in Heaven ("the militia") that share in God's triumph, only the souls of those who are redeemed comprise the "harvest." This would exclude the hierarchical beings above humankind, whose existence was not subjected to *time,* as the word *harvested* implies.

Thus, what Dante sees descending from the luminous heights is *the light of the Christ Himself, manifested among those souls populating the heavenly spheres.* Up to now, the Christ has primarily revealed Himself indirectly, through his reflected aspect, that is, by way of pictorial representations, such as the Cross glowing within the Mars sphere. All the while, however, Dante has felt, streaming into him more and more, the irradiations of His Essence. Now, for the first time, he has briefly seen the *Light* itself, surrounded by a host of others much smaller in size.

> As Trivia in the full moon's sweet serene
> smiles on high among the eternal nymphs
> whose light paints every part of Heaven's scene;
>
> I saw, above a thousand thousand lights,
> One Sun that lit them all, as our own Sun
> lights all the bodies we see in Heaven's heights;

> and through that *living* light I saw revealed
> the Radiant Substance, blazing forth so bright
> my vision dazzled and my senses reeled.
> (Canto XXIII, 25–33; italics mine)

Previously, Dante was able to look more easily at the Sun, insofar as it was the aspect of the Christ's being that was *reflected* down through the spiritual hierarchies. Now, however, he has briefly sustained a direct glimpse at the *living* light of the Christ Himself, which "reels" his senses. Says Beatrice to him, "What blinds you is the very power nothing withstands, and from which none may hide." It is this *Light*, glimpsed only momentarily, that strengthens his capacity for perceiving the increased radiance in Beatrice:

> Open your eyes and turn them full on me!
> You have seen things whose power has made you able
> to bear the bright smile of my ecstasy!
> (Cato XXIII, 46–48)

Whereas before, Dante lacked the strength to perceive the "smile of ecstasy," now, having only briefly glimpsed the *Light* of the Christ, he has cultivated the inner fortitude to withstand the radiance of Beatrice at its highest point; that is to say, he is able to more fully partake of *Divine Wisdom* (Beatrice). Having slowly come to his senses, Dante says that he is filled with a thankfulness which "shall live on forever within the *book* where what is past is proved" (italics mine). In once, Dante makes it known that his experience can be verified by those who attain the consciousness that allows them to read from the "book" (Akashic records), where all that has transpired on the face of the Earth is inscribed.

Dante says that "if there should sound now all the tongues of Polyhymnia with her eight sisters nourished" they could not help to reveal the "glory" which made the features of Beatrice glow. Dante's allusion to Polyhymnia and her sisters herald the Virgin Mary who is soon to appear before Dante. As the Muse of sacred songs, Polyhymnia and her sisters gave nourishment (sweetest milk) to poets, that is, the "power of song" by which they could describe through words the imagination of the spiritual worlds that were revealed to them. A correlation exists between Polyhymnia and her sisters, on the one hand, and the Virgin Mary on the other. Just as Polyhymnia and her sisters, as virgins, were able to maintain a supply of milk (inspiration) to nourish poets and their imaginations, so, too, was the *Virgin* Mary able to nourish the development of Jesus. In other words, the "milk" of the Muses represented the power to help the poets incarnate—through words—the imaginative forces that they perceived. Likewise, the Virgin Mary was the earthly manifestation of the Sophia—the Holy Spirit—through which the Christ was able to manifest Himself to all humanity. For it is through the Holy Spirit (Divine Wisdom/Sophia) that the Christ is able to stream into the consciousness of human beings. Emil Bock alludes to the significance of the Virgin Mary in his book *The Childhood and Youth of Jesus*, when he says;

> In completely pristine purity and perfection, a divine archetype that surrounds humanity in the spiritual world was mirrored in her being and countenance. Even as the archetype of the child and childlikeness—a focal point on earth of all childlike qualities— was reflected and embodied in the child that she was to bear, so too the Mary of Luke seemed like the archetype of all virginal womanhood come down to earth, the incarnation of eternal femininity, the woman of women.... Here in all outward unpretentiousness, a human soul was through and through surrounded and imbued by the world soul and, through it, by the pure light being of the cosmos, the same which in the ancient world was called Isis–Sophia and, in Christianity, the "Holy Spirit."[64]

Beatrice's radiant presence will reveal itself evermore to Dante. For now, however, he finds it impossible to describe the eternal aspect of Beatrice's smile that he perceives in all its glorious light. He alludes to the enormous burden of describing what lies in Heaven and asks "what thoughtful man will blame me for trembling under it for fear I fail?" Yet, once again, he makes mention of the fact that upon the "seas" of such an experience there is little room for small ships or helmsmen who "cringe in fear."

As Dante continues to gaze at the countenance of Beatrice, she urges him to cast his eyes onto the "garden that flowers there in the radiance of Christ's grace." And so he does, shifting his gaze from Beatrice to the Rose (Virgin Mary) surrounded by lilies (the Apostles and all those who have exemplified purity). It is the point in which Dante' is guided toward the perception of the Holy Spirit, that through which the Christ being was incarnated. This perception of the Holy Spirit is made possible, in part, by the work of the Apostles and those who (by their written works) have created the *pictures* by which humankind could gradually be led to the spiritual worlds:

> ...The Rose in which the Word became incarnate
> is there. There are the lilies by whose odor
> men found the road that evermore runs straight.
> (Canto XXIII, 73–75)

As Dante raises his eyelids to "do battle with that radiance" that had caused him to swoon, he perceives, as if shielded by clouds, the "field of flowers blazing in glory." It is as if a beam of sunlight raying down from above touched them. However, he does not dare, at this point, to fix his gaze on the Christ—*the source of that light in all its purity*. For if he did, he would be unable to withstand its brilliance. Instead, he sees all that which His *light* illuminates.

Beatrice tells Dante to look upon the brightest ray (Virgin Mary) that has descended upon the garden. As he does, he watches a crown of light come down out of the Heavens and surround her:

> from Heaven's height a torch of glory came,
> shaped like a ring or wreath, and spinning round her,
> it wound and crowned her in its living flame.
> (Canto XXIII, 94–96)

This light is the Archangel Gabriel, the Angel of the Annuncia- *Thus, just as Gabriel announced the birth of Christ Jesus to*

Mary, here he heralds the birth of Christ within the being of Dante. The Rose is surrounded by a melody so sweet that it would make the most beautiful earthly harmony sound like "thunder from a shattered cloud." Gabriel identifies himself:

> I am the Angelic Love that wheels around
> the lofty ecstasy breathed from the womb
> in which the hostel of Our Wish was found;
>
> so shall I wheel, Lady of Heaven, till
> you follow your great Son to the highest sphere
> and, by your presence, make it holier still.
> (Canto XXIII, 103–108)

The circling diadem of light sings a hymn in honor of the Virgin Mary, while the other lights call out her name. Above Dante, the "royal mantle" (Primum Mobile), which encircles the Empyrean, turns "its inner shore" so that Dante can no longer perceive it. He cannot follow the flight of the "crowned flame" that soared even higher into the Heavens so as to be united with her Son (Christ). Each of the lights, which were as flowers in the garden, express their love for the Virgin Mary as she ascended. They then sing *Regina Coeli* (*Queen of Heaven*). "What treasure lies in wait for those who reap the seed of good on Earth!" This is what runs through Dante's mind as he ponders those who gave up all on the Earth—often suffering in exile—in preparation for "the treasure they now enjoy." This series of events serves as an introduction for St. Peter who

> ...sits in triumph under the lofty Son
> of God and the Virgin Mary in His triumph
> and in the company of everyone
>
> crowned from the New or the Old Consistory,
> (Canto XXIII, 136–139)

Peter is the "soul who holds the keys to such glory." Beatrice, addressing the spirits gathered around St. Peter, asks that they give their consent to grant Dante a foretaste of the crumbs that fall from their table as they partake in the supper of the Lamb of God. As a re-creation of the Last Supper, Peter, surrounded by other spirits, is represented here as Christ's vicar after the Resurrection. For, as we have just seen, the ascension of Christ's *light* into the Empyrean is a reenactment of His resurgence following the Mystery of Golgotha.

In light of this, Peter is left to carry on the mission of Christ by gathering round him a community of individuals. By feeding on the grace of God's revelation (Lamb) to humankind, they lay down the first stone in building the Eternal Church of Christ on Earth. Thus, Beatrice asks the company of souls to help satiate Dante's thirst for the "waters of that spring for which he yearns."

Heeding the words of Beatrice, the spirits form a circle or "sphere revolving on fixed poles," so that its interior seemed stationary, while its outer edge turned with great velocity. Appearing as lighted wheels, they express their joy to varying degrees, which, in turn reflect the gradations in the souls' evolution of consciousness. Nonetheless, their individual actions synchronize as one. As they turn, one particular light grows so radiant that it outshines the rest. Three times it encircles Beatrice while singing with such sublime harmony that Dante is unable to re-imagine it. It is St. Peter. Dante says that it is impossible to recapture the truth of a spiritual event by way of memory:

> Therefore my pen leaps and I do not write;
> not words nor fantasy can paint the truth:
> the folds of heaven's draperies are too bright.
> (Canto XXIV, 25–27)

Here, we must imagine that Dante—through Beatrice (*Divine Wisdom*)—reaches deep into the mysteries that led St. Peter to found the Church.

St. Peter, declaring that the "ardor" of Beatrice's love entered his "state of bliss" within that sphere, seeks to satisfy her request. Beatrice then asks him to test Dante on the nature of *faith*, which is among the most fundamental elements of the Church's teachings. Says she:

The Paradiso: Into the "I" of God

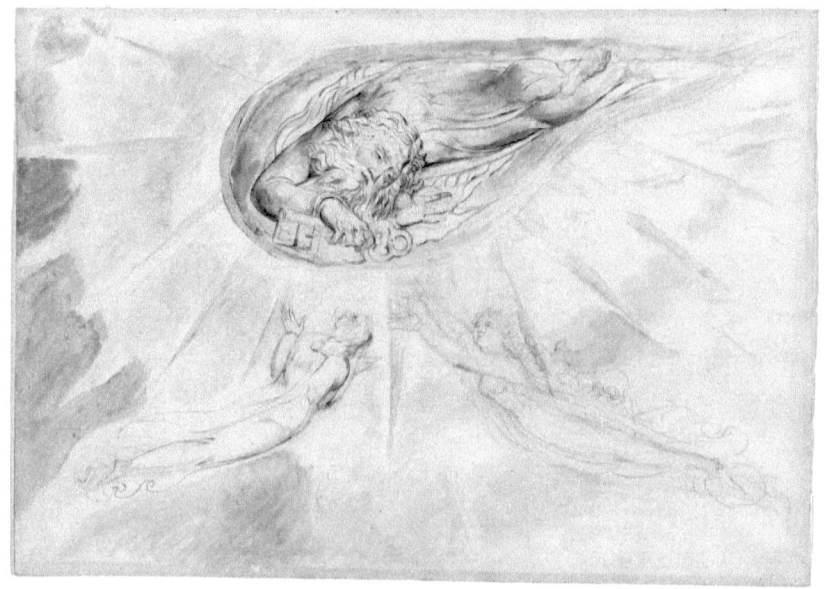

St. Peter, Beatrice, and Dante, *William Blake*

> ...Eternal Light of the great priest
> to whom Our Lord brought down and gave the keys
> to the sublimities of this joyous feast;
>
> at your own pleasure, whatever it may be,
> test this man on the greater and lesser points
> of the faith in which you once walked on the sea...
> (Canto XXIV, 34–39)

Here, Beatrice refers to Matthew 14:28:

> "Lord if it is you," Peter replied, "tell me to come to you on the water." "Come," he said. Then Peter got down out of the boat, walked on the water and came toward Jesus. But when he saw the wind, he was afraid and, beginning to sink, cried out, "Lord, save me!" Immediately Jesus reached out his hand and caught him. "You of little faith," he said, "why do you doubt?" And when they climbed into the boat, the wind died down. Then those who were in the boat worshipped him, saying, "Truly you are the Son of God."[65]

While Beatrice speaks to St. Peter, Dante braces himself as if he were a doctorial candidate about to be questioned by his examiner. The first question posed to Dante is, essentially, "What is faith?" Dante raises "his eyes to the light from which these words had been breathed forth," then, looks back at Beatrice who urges him on. He answers St. Peter by referring to the words of St. Paul:

> ...faith is the *substance* of what we hope to see
> and the *argument* for what we have not seen.
> This is its *quiddity*, as it seems to me.
> (Canto XXIV, 64–66)

Thus, for Dante, faith is the "substance" (*sub + stare*), namely, what gives support by "standing under." It is what supports us in our search for that which we one day "hope to see," namely, the source of activity that enables the world to become manifest. As the "argument" of things unseen, it also gives human beings on Earth the means by which to fathom the truth of such an activity—though in a limited way—so that one may not lose the hope to one day actualize it through the light of consciousness.

St. Peter, acknowledging that Dante has touched upon the essence of faith, asks him why St. Paul classifies it first with "substance" and then with "argument." Dante answers that the mysteries in Heaven, revealed in all clarity, are hidden from humanity on Earth. Their existence in the heavenly world provides the "substance" of one's belief on Earth.

> ...On belief the structure
> of high hope rises. It is *substant*, therefore,
> or "standing under" by its very nature...
> (Canto XXIV, 73–75)

Since we are forced on Earth to reason from mere beliefs, we must utilize those as evidence for what does not further reveal itself to us. Thus, belief "partakes, by nature, of *argument*." In other words, as dialectical thinking can only give rise to belief, we have only such belief as evidence of some underlying principle actively at work in creation. It is our search for truth by way of "belief" that gives birth to argument.

St. Peter declares that if everyone could understand the workings of moral impulses as Dante has done, then the Sophists, who were skeptical about absolute knowledge, would find little audience for their arguments. Instead, by gearing their philosophy toward the practical aspects of life, they directed human thinking toward the material aspect of reality. As a result, their teachings were more conducive to practical politics and the like, thereby ignoring the unseen forces capable of establishing a social order based on the emancipation of the human "I."

St. Peter asks Dante whether or not he possesses the *faith* that he has described. Dante asserts that he does, so much so, that it is like a coin that has not been worn nor consumed. St. Peter, then, asks him how he came upon his understanding of faith, to which Dante answers:

> ...The shower of gold
> of the Holy Ghost, which pours down endlessly
> over the sacred Scrolls, both New and Old,
>
> reasons it to such logical certainty
> that, by comparison, all other reasoning
> can only seem confused and dull to me.
> (Canto XXIV, 91–96)

Note, here, that Dante does not say his understanding is derived from his mere reading of the scriptures but, rather, from the Holy Ghost (Sophia), which "showers gold over them." Because Dante is rooted firmly in this direct spiritual experience of the force that inspired the scriptures, no logic born of sense-bound thinking can sway him from the certainty of his belief.

In response to Dante's statement, St. Peter asks Dante why he accepts both the Old and New Testaments as being "divinely true." Dante answers that evidence regarding the truth within Scripture lies in the "works" performed—namely, the "miracles" that have been described. This is especially true of Christ, Who performed miracles that reflected the power of the Father working through Him and all humankind. For nothing within the laws of nature could bring about the deeds by which Christ revealed the activity of the spiritual world. That is to say, nothing with regard to dialectical thinking, from which the spiritual world often seems excluded, could bring about proof of a suprasensory realm of existence. If miracles did not attest to the truth of the spiritual world, how could the spread of Christianity throughout much of the world occur without the intervention of divine forces—an intervention often witnessed in the form of miracles?

St. Peter, then, asks Dante how he can be sure that the miracles of which he speaks really occurred? Dante answers by saying that had they not occurred, the spread of Christianity throughout the world would be a miracle a "hundred times greater than the rest." In other words, Christianity could never have survived as a mere philosophical or theological postulation. Instead, it is a *living impulse*, which having streamed into the souls of humankind, could only be sustained, throughout the centuries, by proof of the suprasensory world's existence. This proof, of course, came in the form of "miracles." Had they not occurred, argues Dante, human beings would have long ago abandoned their faith in the existence of such a suprasensory world. This, in turn, would have resulted in the gradual disappearance of Christianity. Thus, what is intimated by the word *miracle* is nothing other than the existence of the "unexplainable"—that which transcends the boundaries of reason. Moreover, the ever-changing meaning of the word *miracle* reflects the deterioration that has taken place with the loss of our connection to the spiritual world—a connection that could have explained the existence of the unfathomable. Only within small esoteric circles did few individuals, who still maintained such a connection, preserve the sacred wisdom so that a phenomenon in the physical world could be understood by way of those forces responsible for its manifestation.

Having heard Dante's response, the spirits gathered around St. Peter sing out the words *"Te Deum Laudamus!"* (Thee, O God, We Praise). St. Peter shows his approval for what Dante has explained through the "grace whose loving good had pledged itself" to Dante's mind. In other words, Dante is able to respond with a knowledge derived from grace, which allowed for his perception of the spiritual world by way of the Holy Spirit, whose *light* he had just witnessed.

Next, Dante is asked *what he believes* and what is the *source* of his belief. Dante quickly responds by pointing out that St. Peter wishes to know the form of his belief, namely the "idea or eternal aspect" which constitutes the very foundation for what he believes. Dante begins his answer by saying that he believes in one God, whose *Love* moves the Heavens. The mention of "one God," of course, begins the Apostolic Creed and is used by Dante to dispel any notion of polytheism that had been prevalent among the pagans as a direct result of the influences that had primarily stemmed from the Greeks. The Greeks deemed the hierarchy of angels immediately above humanity to be gods. In fact, such paganism extend into the Middle Ages, particularly near Montecassino, where pagans revered the god Apollo, before St. Benedict indoctrinated them into the mystery of Christ.

Dante says that his faith in God lies in both "physical and metaphysical evidences," namely, in his perception of what has manifested and their creative forces. In addition, he also finds cause for belief in the writings of the Old Testament, as well as the New Testament—which, of course, includes the works of St. Peter himself. Dante then affirms his belief in the Trinity, stating that the "teachings of the Evangels" have stamped their truth "on the wax of his mind" like a "living seal." Here, Dante again deftly circumvents the *gente grossa* by stating that it was the "teachings" (or examples) in the Evangels that enabled him to ascertain the truth of his experience. Not only do they enable us to verify the validity of our spiritual experiences but they give us the courage to further our understanding and one day hopefully impress upon our consciousness (on the "wax of the mind") the living imaginations that are the creative forces of life (living seal)—imaginations that reveal the spiritual world. In this way, a "spark" of realization can "widen" into a "living flame" that shines "like a star in Heaven" within the depths of our beings.

> ...This is the beginning, the spark shot free
> that gnaws and widens into living flame,
> and, like a star in Heaven, shines in me.
> (Canto XXIV, 145–147)

Pleased by what Dante tells him, St. Peter blesses him "in a glad chant of praise" and circles him three times as he did upon meeting him, which symbolizes being protected by the Holy Trinity.

Dante begins Canto XXV with a declaration. He states that if ever the merits of his poem allow the cruel gates of Florence to open up to him, he will go the Baptistery of St. John to receive the poet's laurel crown. For it was there that he was baptized into the Christian faith—the *faith* for which he has just been blessed.

> If ever it comes to pass that the sacred song,
> to which both heaven and earth so set their hand
> that I grew lean with laboring years long,
>
> wins over the cruelty that exiles me
> from the sweet sheepfold where I slept, a lamb,
> and to the raiding wolves an enemy;
>
> with a changed voice and with my fleece full grown
> I shall return to my baptismal font,
> a poet, and there assume the laurel crown;
>
> for there I entered the faith that lets us grow
> into God's recognition; and for that faith
> Peter, as I have said circled my brow.
> (Canto XXV, 1–12)

Notice that Dante refers to himself as a "lamb," thus alluding to the Christ's presence within him—a lamb that the "wolves" regarded as an enemy. The wolf symbolized the Church whose avarice and greed led it to consume those blessings intended for the poor. With his "fleece full grown," Dante has strengthened himself against the storms raging around him, so as to return one day to where he was baptized into the "faith" that has led to his "recognition of God." By referring to the laurel, Dante prefigures the second theological virtue to be addressed by him, namely, *hope*, for green—the color of the laurel—is its symbol.

Soon, from the "same sphere," descends another light. Beatrice cries out "Look! Look there! It is the baron for whom men throng to Galacia there below," namely, St. James, the Apostle of Hope, whose tomb in Galacia has been the object of many pilgrimages.

As Dante observes his arrival, he notices St. Peter and St. James each circling about one another like doves, "praising the diet (love) that regales them there." Here, the dove is not only used to denote the aspect of *caritas*, the third theological virtue, which will result from the interaction between the first two (*faith and hope*), but it also symbolizes the presence of the Holy Spirit which descends into humankind (Dante) as a result of the interaction between the three virtues. Having greeted one another, they turn to Dante who is overcome by their brilliance. Beatrice asks St. James to speak about *hope*, since he not only personified it in his life on Earth but he wrote of it in his *Epistles*. Here, as many have noted, Dante seems to be combining the two St. James into one, for the James of the *Epistles* should not be confused with the Apostle from Santiago de Compostela in Spain.

St. James encourages Dante to look up at him, for the *light* that shines will not blind him but strengthen him, so that he can prepare himself for his encounter with God. Then, he tells Dante that since *he has been chosen while still a mortal man to behold God in all His glory*, he should make known the power that has helped him attain such heights:

> Since of His grace Our Lord and Emperor calls
> and bids you come while still in mortal flesh
> among His counts in His most secret halls;
>
> that you, the truth of this great court made clear,
> may make the stronger, in yourself and others,
> the hope that makes the men love the good down there,

> say what it is, what power helped you climb,
> and how you bear its flowering in your mind.
> (Canto XXV, 40–47)

Dante is thus invited to be among the "counts" of God, that is, among those who have, while on Earth, been able to attain the consciousness enabling them to ascend into the highest spheres of spiritual activity ("secret halls").

Before Dante answers the question of hope, Beatrice interjects, declaring that no "child" is more grounded in hope than Dante. Evidence of this lies in the fact that he is able to venture into the realms of Paradise while he is still *alive* on Earth. In other words, Dante not only harbors hope, but he has used it as a vehicle for his *initiation* into the spiritual world. Dante's presence among the Fixed Stars could not have been possible had Dante not been rooted in hope.

> Church Militant, as is written in the Sun
> whose ray lights all our hosts, does not possess
> a single child richer in hope—not one.
>
> It was for that he was allowed to come
> from Egypt to behold Jerusalem
> before his warring years had reached their sum...
> (Canto XXV, 52–57)

Here, "Egypt" signifies bondage to the Earth, while "Jerusalem" denotes ascension into the heavenly realms. Beatrice allows Dante to answer two other points raised by St. James, namely, "What is *hope*?" and "What are its sources?" Dante answers that hope:

> ...is the certain expectation
> of future glory. It is the blessed fruit
> of grace divine and the good a man has done...
> (Canto XXV, 67–69)

The source of his knowledge is derived from the *light* of many stars (the fixed stars) connected to the activity of the spiritual beings surrounding him. The *light* (or cosmic activity) of the spiritual beings (stars) appears to humankind as a direct revelation. This *light*, he says, was "distilled" into his heart by David, the "ultimate singer of the Ultimate Majesty," who, in the *Psalms* sang, "Let them hope in Thee, whoso doth know Thy name." Dante also alludes to the *Epistle* of St. James where it is said, "Blessed is the man who preservers under trial, because when he has stood the test, he will receive the crown of life that God has promised to those who love him."[66] In other words, *hope* is the "fruit of grace divine and the good a man has done."

As Dante speaks, the *light* of St. James "trembles" with elation, as "love burns within him." He asks Dante what *hope* holds for him. Dante responds that from the Old and New Testaments comes a symbol that points to the blessings resulting from hope: Heaven. This good is, in turn, what directs Dante toward hope. Dante draws reference to Isaiah who says that those called to be with God "shall be dressed in double raiment in their native land." This "double raiment" refers to the human spirit joined to the resurrected flesh. And so, we are born into the "I" of God by resurrecting our fallen nature—the fallen light within thinking. Dante, then, alludes to St. James' brother, John, to whom he gives credit for the Book of Revelation. Says he:

> ...And your brother, where he writes so ardently
> of the white robes, sets forth this revelation
> in great detail for all of us to see.
> (Canto XXV, 94–96)

Having answered the question of *hope* to the satisfaction of those within the sphere of the Fixed Stars, Dante hears the sound of *"Sperent in te"* (They hope in Thee) ringing from above. Then, from within the choir, streams forth a star, which, together with the other two (St. Peter and St. James), joyfully dance around Dante. As they dance, Beatrice keeps "her eyes fixed on their glory," which reflects the fact that Dante is able to sustain the brilliance of the spiritual light that reflects the *joy* of their union with God. These three represent the theological virtues that prefigure the Trinity.

In introducing the third light that has joined St. Peter and St. James, Beatrice says,

> This is he who lies upon the breast
> of Our Pelican; and this is He elected
> from off the cross to make the great behest.
> (Canto XXV, 112–114)

The "Pelican," here, refers to the Christ. It recalls the sacrifice made by Christ on the Cross on behalf of all humanity (his children). The pelican often nourished its young by striking its own breast with its beak; it thereby sacrificed its own blood so that they could live. This recalls the sacrifice made at Golgotha, when the blood of Christ had fallen onto the Earth—blood that contained the cosmic etheric forces necessary for the resurrection of humankind, as well as the Earth itself, thereby gradually transforming it into a "sun." Steiner says that blood is the *vehicle of the "I."* The *resurrection* of sense-based thinking into *living thinking*, thus enabling the human being to behold the spiritual world, occurs through the purification of the blood.

This purification of the blood, incidentally, can account for Dante's vision of the Mystic Rose. As Steiner has shown, the Rose was particularly used by the Rosicrucians to symbolize the purification of the astral forces within the human being, so that one could ascend into the heavenly world by the *light* of the Holy Spirit.

Having developed this capacity to perceive into the spiritual world, St. John was able to speak of the future of humanity. He has now descended from the "breast" of Christ to question Dante on the third theological virtue, *caritas* (Love). It was St. John who was chosen to be a son for Mary after the Crucifixion of Christ. By way of the Holy Ghost that had shone in Mary, St. John could perceive into the etheric and become a witness to the future "glory" of Christ.

At this point, the spirit-light leaves the group of spirits and presents himself before Dante. Beatrice, having identified him as St. John, keeps her gaze fixed on his *light*, so that, as Dante beholds her gaze,

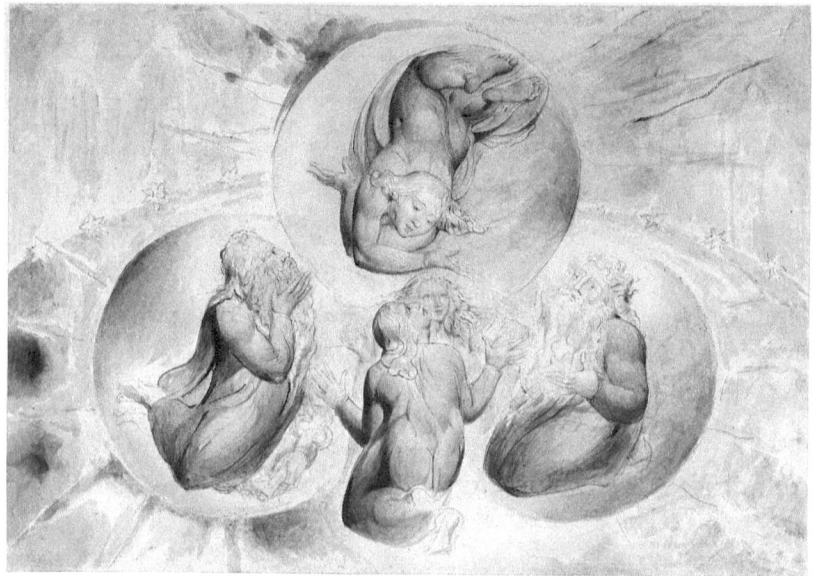

*St. Peter, St. James, Dante, Beatrice with St. John the Evangelist,
William Blake*

he is blinded. In other words, the light of St. John's revelation was so bright that Dante cannot see him.

> As one who stares, squinting against the light,
> to see the Sun enter a partial eclipse,
> and in the act of looking loses his sight...
> (Canto, XXV, 118–120)

Instead, Dante looks for some semblance of him, at which point, St. John reprimands him for seeking out a form where it has no true place. He adds that only "Two Lamps" (Jesus and Mary) rose into Heaven in their physical bodies. Dante only knows that he is in close proximity to Beatrice there in Paradise. He is only aware of the state of consciousness that has enabled him to ascend to this point. The fact that this blinding light or revelation occurs when it does is not coincidental, for it takes place before St. John, whose writings reflect the presence of the *light* by which he, himself, was able to perceive into the future of the world's evolution.

As Dante stands bewildered, "a breath" (St. John) calls out, assuring him that his sight will be restored by Beatrice, who has "in a single turning of her eyes, the power that lay in Ananias' hand." Ananias was asked by God to cure the blindness of Saul who, having persecuted many disciples of God, was to become His chosen vessel. This act by Ananias constituted the baptism of Saul, whereby he could recover his sight "and be filled with the Holy Spirit." By referring to Ananias, we are given a prelude to Dante's own baptism by the power of the Holy Spirit as administered through Beatrice. Nonetheless, St. John informs Dante that, while blinded, he has an opportunity to address the question of *Love*, the third theological virtue. Though temporarily blinded, Dante is content to be cured by Beatrice, for she brings the fire (namely, the love irradiating from Holy Spirit) that enkindles him. The heart of *Love*, he adds, resides in the Will of God.

St. John again addresses Dante. He asks "what made you draw your bow at this exalted target—what and who?" Here, the exulted target is none other than *Love*, itself. Dante responds that by philosophical arguments and the authority that rays down from the Godhead, *Love* has "stamped its seal" on him. The degree to which one's imperfect nature can grasp the goodness inherent within the Good (God) enkindles the *Love* therein. Therefore, the radiance of this *Love* is determined by our capacity to "understand its excellence," namely, the *perfection of goodness*. Each and every good that is not immediate or *directly* connected to the Christ who manifests such perfection, is to be considered nothing more than a reflection of His ray. Yet, it is *toward the Christ, Himself, that the human mind must move*, once it has perceived the *truth* that "compels" human love.

> ...To the Essence then in which lies such perfection
> that every good thing not immediate to It
> is nothing more than Its own ray's reflection—
>
> to It, above all else, the mind must move
> once it has seen the truth that is the proof
> and argument that so compels man's love...
> (Canto XXVI, 31–36)

In other words, we must direct our minds to the solar aspect of *Love* and not its lunar aspect, or the reflected light, experienced as dialectical thought. The truth of which Dante speaks reveals itself through the inspired works of those who have witnessed the manifestations of "Good." Plato, in his *Symposium,* first unveiled this truth of Absolute Good or Absolute Love, where *Love* was thought to be the primal essence of the cosmos. However, this idea was further expanded by Aristotle who believed that the initiatory principle of creation is the "unmoved mover," which becomes the object of human striving, for this "unmoved mover" is but the Creator of *Love,* who sets the universe in motion (*Metaphysics XI*), namely, the *Love* descending from Holy Spirit. It is, thus, Aristotle to whom Dante refers when he says:

> ...That truth he made evident to me
> whose proofs set forth the First Cause and First Love
> of every sempiternal entity...
> (Canto XXVI, 37–39)

Next, Dante alludes to two Biblical passages—one from the Old Testament and one from the New. First, he refers to Moses' vision of the Burning Bush that announced the descent of the Christ onto the Earth from the Sun:

> Then Moses said, "Now show me your glory." And the LORD said, "I will cause all my goodness to pass in front of you, and I will proclaim my name, the LORD, in your presence. I will have mercy on whom I will have mercy, and I will have compassion on whom I will have compassion. But," he said, "you cannot see my face, for no one may see me and live." Then the LORD said, "There is a place near me where you may stand on the rock. When my glory passes by, I will put you in a cleft in the rock and cover you with my hand until I have passed by. Then I will remove my hand and you shall see my back, but my face must not be seen."[67]

This passage, as we have said, points to the moment in time when the Christ, in descending from the Sun, made His *Light* and the warmth of His *Love* known to humankind through Moses. Yet, such love was, in a sense, a reflection of the *Love* that was later to permeate humankind, for, as the Lord said, "man could not see him and live." In other words, humanity had yet to attain the spiritual constitution apt for beholding the "face" of Christ—his solar aspect. Instead, it could only behold His "back," which we designate with the term *Jehovah*. This is, in effect, the lunar aspect of his being, that which *reflects* the light of the Sun.

As this example predates Golgotha, Dante posits yet another example, one that reveals the vision of God after the descent of Christ into humankind. He says,

> ...And proved by you in the high proclamation
> that cries to earth the secrets of this heaven
> more clearly than any other revelation.
> (Canto XXVI, 43–45)

Here, Dante refers to Revelations 1:8, where it is written,

> "I am the Alpha and the Omega," says the Lord God, "who is, and who was, and who is coming, the Almighty."

Whereas Moses perceived the *light* of the Christ as it descended into the etheric body of the Earth, St. John speaks of that same *light*, which after Christ's resurrection embraces the whole of time. It is that aspect of *Love,* having entered and transformed the Earth, which reaches far into future worlds as a manifestation of the creative forces of life. These *living* forces intrinsic to the being of Christ are those to which he refers when he said, "I am with you all days, even unto the consummation of the world."

Having given these two Biblical references as proof of the presence of God's *Love* for humankind, Dante is asked if there exist other ties which bind him to such *Love*. Asks St. John, "With what teeth does this love consume you?" Here, St. John, who was commonly referred to as the Eagle of Christ (an allusion to his suprasensory perception), uses the word *teeth* to denote the degree to which we *adhere*

The Paradiso: Into the "I" of God

to our love for God. In response to St. John's question, Dante points to Christ's sacrifice of taking on death so that we could find the *life* that leads to our future salvation. What moves Dante's soul is the fact that Christ, as the greatest of all avatars, having descended from the Sun, would, at Golgotha, permeate the world with the living force of His *Being*, thus providing us with the possibility to reascend into the spiritual world by resurrecting our thinking. In this way, we can, once again, perceive the suprasensory world:

> ...The existence of the world, and my own, too;
> the death He took on Himself that I might live;
> and what all believers hope for as I do—
>
> these and the *living* knowledge mentioned before
> have saved me from the ocean of false love
> and placed me by the true, safe on the shore...
> (Canto XXVI, 58–63; italics mine)

Thus, Dante is saved from the "ocean of false love," that is, those luciferic impulses that arise from the lunar element of consciousness. For, as the rhythms of the ocean conform to the movement of the Moon, so, too, does lunar consciousness (dialectical thinking) arise out of a separation from its solar aspect (*living thinking*), thereby manifesting as the reflected light of mirrored thinking. This mirrored thinking, lacking the light (will) by which we can extricate ourselves from our lower nature, is, thus, a vehicle by which these lower forces can find expression within us.

Dante concludes his argument by insinuating that human love is determined by God's love for us. God, the Eternal Gardener (Cultivator of Life) administers his *Love* (creative forces) to His grove (world) so that the leaves (humankind) can green (be imbued with life). Says Dante, "I love to the degree that each receives the dew and ray of His all flowering love."

Dante falls silent. Suddenly, all of Heaven rejoices by singing, "*Holy, holy, holy!*" Slowly, just as the rays of the early morning light awaken a sleeping man, "piercing lid by lid," so too, is Dante awakened. This "early morning light" represents the dawning *light* of Christ by way of the Holy Spirit. It is the actual *force of light* that he has begun to see more consciously. Just as we are not sure of what we see until we totally regain our faculties, Dante feels the light of Beatrice's eyes penetrating his own, driving away "every last impediment," thereby restoring his sight more clearly than before.

> and the man so roused does not know what he sees,
> his wits confounded by the sudden waking,
> till he once more regains his faculties;
>
> so from my eyes, my lady's eyes, whose ray
> was visible from a thousand miles and more,
> drove every last impediment away;
>
> in consequence of which I found my sight
> was clearer than before...
> (Canto XXVI, 73–80)

In *Esoteric Christianity and the Mission of Christian Rosenkreutz*, Rudolf Steiner has this to say in regard to Faith, Love, and Hope,

> Faith, love, hope constitute three stages in the essential human being; they are necessary for health and for life as a whole; we cannot exist without them. Just as work cannot be done in a dark room until light is found, it is equally impossible for human beings to carry on in their fourfold nature if their three sheaths are not permeated, warmed through, and strengthened by faith, love, and hope. Faith, love, hope are the basic forces in our astral body, our etheric body, and our physical body, and from this one instance you can judge how the new revelation makes its entry into the world and permeates the old language with thought content. Are these three wonderful words not urged upon us in the Gospel revelation—these words of wisdom, *faith, love, hope*, that ring through the ages?[68]

Having been blinded by the *light* of revelation (St. John), Dante's sight is transformed so that he can penetrate deeper into the cosmic forces of creation. Understood as such, the *light* of St. John deepens

Dante's spiritual perception. Thus, what issues from Beatrice can manifest itself to an even greater extent. This light enables Dante to ascend into the World of the Archetypes. Says Beatrice:

> In that ray's Paradise
> the first soul from the hand of the First Power
> turns ever to its maker its glad eyes.
> (Canto XXVI, 82–84)

Here, Dante confronts "the first man" created by God—Adam. Though the tendency is often to visualize Adam as an individual human being, it might be helpful to consider Adam as the Archetypal being associated with all humanity, which existed as androgynous during the period of Lemuria. Adam, in effect, represents the archetypal form that humanity possessed, as it became visible on a physical plane. For this reason, Dante refers to him as "the first and only fruit Earth ever saw spring forth full ripe," since he represented the first manifestation of God's love. Says Steiner:

> This cosmic being from whom the man of today and all the kingdoms of nature have issued, is referred to in the Cabala as Adam–Cadmon. Adam–Cadmon embraced all the manifold aspects of man as we know him today in the various races and peoples.[69]

Wishing to hear from Adam, Dante waits for him to speak, for he realizes that Adam is aware of what Dante desires to know. In fact, as Adam says,

> Without any need to hear
> what you would say, I know your wish more surely
> than you know what you take to be most clear.
>
> I see it in the True Mirror, itself the perfect
> reflector of all things in Its creation,
> which nothing in creation can reflect...
> (Canto XXVI, 103–108)

Here, the "True Mirror" is the Mind of God that can reflect "all things in its creation"—including all human thoughts. The word *reflected*, in this case, means to be seen within the Mind of God, which itself, however, cannot be reflected, for it is the source of all *living thinking*. Adam proceeds to address the questions that linger in Dante. Says he,

> ...You wish to know how many years it is
> since God created me in the high garden
> where she prepared you for these stairs to bliss;
>
> and how long my eyes enjoyed the good they prized;
> and the true reason for the great rejection;
> and the tongue I spoke, which I myself devised...
> (Canto XXVI, 109–114)

Adam begins by stating that his "exile" did not result from partaking of the Tree of Knowledge but, rather, from "violating" God's decree. Adam begins to answer the questions not in the order in which Dante presents them, but by order of importance, for the Fall of Humanity is central to our re-ascension into the spiritual world. Adam explains that it was not the act of plucking an apple from the tree that caused the Fall but, rather, the materialistic *impulse* that arose within human consciousness, which ultimately led to humanity's separation from God. This impulse, again, was the emergence of sense-based thinking, which provided humanity with the possibility of *choice*. The act of taking the apple was the *manifestation* of this new impulse.

The second question that Adam answers is the date of his appearance on Earth and the length of his stay there. He states that, having lived to see the Sun circle the signs of Heaven (the Zodiac) 930 times, he then spent 4,302 years in Limbo before being able to ascend into Heaven. The 4,302 years in Limbo ("where your lady summoned you") represent the length of time in which he could not enter into the spiritual world—"supposedly" the number of years before the resurrection of Christ that made it possible. Add to this the 930 years of his life and we can, according to such calculation, estimate his birth to have been roughly 5200 BC.

In regard to the language Adam spoke, he says:

> ...The tongue I spoke had vanished utterly
> long before Nimrod's people turned their hands
> to the work beyond their capability,
>
> for nothing of the mind is beyond change:
> man's inclination answers to the stars
> and ranges as the starry courses range.
>
> That man should speak is nature's own behest;
> but that you speak in this way or in that
> nature lets you decide as you think best...
> (Canto XXVI, 124–132)

In examining these initial verses by Adam, we see that the language that he spoke was, in fact, one that had radically "vanished" by the time of Babel. The Tower of Babel represented humanity's failed attempt to connect itself to Heaven. From the Cosmic Word out of which Adam was created and through which he communicated, Babel marks the time in which the formation of many languages came into being as this cosmic creative sound impressed itself into the material world. These languages attest to the fact that the greater part of humanity could not readily reascend into the cosmic heights, for the primordial connection amongst human beings had been lost. These languages were inextricably linked to the continuing emergence of sense-based thinking. As the multiplicity of languages arose more and more from such thinking, they complicated the development of interrelationships between human beings, and made virtually impossible their reconnection with God. It is the arbitrariness associated with such thinking connected to our bodily nature that leads Adam to say, "that you speak in this way or in that nature lets you decide as you think best."

Adam declares that until the time in which Christ penetrated the depths of the Earth, God sent down his ray known on Earth as EL, and then, later, as JAH. Since humanity could only perceive the reflection of the Christ (Jehovah) at one time, it is interesting to note here, *how* the sounds that Adam articulates illustrate the descent of the Cosmic Word onto the Earth in Its reflected (and thereby, inverted) aspect. In other words, just as Jehovah is a *reflection* of the Christ being as He descended onto the Earth, so, too, does the combination of EL (god) and JAH denote an inverted *reflection* of the word *Jehovah*—namely a reflection of the Word (Christ) Itself.

After Adam ends his discourse, Dante hears the heavenly host sing *"Glory to the Father, Son and Holy Ghost!"* It appears to him that the universe is "alight with a single smile," as his senses become inebriated.

> O joy! O blessedness no tongue can speak!
> O life conjoint of perfect love and peace!
> O sure wealth that has nothing more to seek!
> (Canto XXVII, 7–9)

The four brightest lights (Peter, James, John, and Adam) stand radiating before Dante, when, all of a sudden, St. Peter, in taking on the color red, begins to glow more intensely than the rest. This transition from a state of temperance to passionate indignation is depicted thus,

> As Jupiter might appear if it and Mars
> were birds and could exchange their glowing plumes—
> such it became among the other stars.
> (Canto XXVII, 13–15)

Silence forms around him as he begins to denounce the Papacy for its corruption and degeneracy. Says he:

> …You need not wonder that I change hue,
> for as I utter what I have to say
> you shall see all these beings change theirs, too.
>
> The usurper of the throne given to me,
> to me, to me, there on the earth that now
> before the Son of God stands vacant, he
>
> has made a sewer of my sepulcher, a flow
> of blood and stink at which the treacherous one
> who fell from here may chuckle there below.
> (Canto XXVII, 19–27)

Peter primarily addresses the deeds of Boniface VIII, who has made his tomb a "sewer." Dante, then, compares the transformation of Peter's face to clouds opposite a sunrise or sunset and says, "I saw the sweet face of all heaven burn." Beatrice, too, changes complexion, so that "such eclipse came over heaven then as when Supreme Might suffered humankind's death." Here, we see that the *light* by which Dante has been guided into the spiritual world—that very light streaming through the Heavens—was so changed by the wrath raining down from the stars, that it prevented Dante from seeing any further. Dante compares this darkening to that immediately following Golgotha where in Matthew 27:45 it is said, "From the sixth hour until the ninth hour darkness came over all the land." Thus, just as Christ's *light*, having descended into the center of the Earth before being resurrected within the Earth's etheric body, was overshadowed by a darkening of the Earth's atmosphere immediately upon the death of Jesus, so, too, has the light of Peter—which he carried from the Christ into the world—been eclipsed. Now, Dante is momentarily without the *light* of Beatrice to guide him through Heaven. The denunciation of the Papacy seems to point to a second crucifixion, one in which humankind is robbed of the *light* born by the Virgin Sophia (Holy Ghost)—the very light that leads us into the spiritual worlds. We must, in fact, remember that the Church, by declaring itself the "Bride of Christ" induced humanity to seek out the Holy Spirit through her institutionalized form.

As St. Peter continues to speak, his voice is still full of indignation. He refers to the early popes of the Church, who through sacrifice and the loss of their own blood, sought to maintain its sanctity. He adds that the Church was not founded in order to attain gold. Never did the Church founders intend for individuals to oppose each other by sitting on the left and right of the popes. Here, Peter most likely refers to the warring factions of the Guelfs and Ghibellines. However, we can just as easily infer that the two wings of the Papacy—namely, the luciferic (left) and ahrimanic (right) forces—deceived human beings who strove to live a devout Christian life. Furthermore, Peter declares that the "keys" given to him were not meant to "fly as emblems from a flag unfurled against the baptized in a Christian land." However, what seems to make Peter's bitterness insurmountable is the fact that the Papacy unscrupulously used a seal bearing the image of his head on many corrupt documents.

Peter says that we see "wolves dressed as shepherds" everywhere. He then alludes to the Cahorsines and Gascons who influenced the Papacy with members from their regions. Pope Clement V, a Gascon, was responsible for the transference of the papal seat from Rome to Avignon. Meanwhile, John XXII lined his pockets with money by excommunicating noblemen who could afford to be reinstated. Peter declares that "high Providence" will return to the Earth to avenge the wrongs of his Church. Before leaving Dante, Peter bids him to tell the world about what he has just revealed.

Dante watches all those souls who remained behind when Mary ascended into the Empyrean now ascend like a snowfall in reverse. Beatrice asks him to look down upon the Earth to see "how far the heavens have revolved." Casting his gaze downward, Dante notices that he lies somewhere between Spain and Jerusalem. His gaze spans from the western shore of Spain—where Ulysses braved the waters in his mad journey to Purgatory, to Phoenicia, namely, the eastern shore of the Mediterranean, where Zeus, transformed into a bull, took Europa on his back to the island of Crete. Given this perimeter, we could, therefore, imagine Dante to be directly over Rome, as he ascends into the Primum Mobile—the Rome whose corrupted church Peter has just denounced.

Dante's ascension over Rome recalls the *Ascension of Christ*. Here, while being resurrected above the Church that has fallen into a state of decay and death, Dante serves as an earthly representative of the Christ. He is thus seen as *heralding the light of Christ as he ascends into the higher regions of the spiritual world.*

What lies outside the *light* of the Christ, is subject to the influence of the earthly forces. Dante claims that *that* part of the Earth is not clearly visible to him. He is in the constellation of Gemini, while the

Sun is rising ahead of him by "a sign and more." Given that roughly every two hours of the day the Sun rises in a different astrological sign, we can estimate that, presently, it is rising a couple hours or so away to the East of Rome, where it is predawn—which is to say that it is approaching Jerusalem.

The mind of Dante, which, as he says, "ever found its Paradise in thinking of my lady," now "burns with desire" to look into the eyes of Beatrice. Again, by looking into Her eyes, Dante receives the inspiration that deepens his contemplation of the spiritual world that he has entered. In fact, we find that each time Dante reaches the boundary of a particular celestial realm, he, again and again, gazes into the eyes of "his lady" in order to find the *light* by which he can ascend even higher. Having, thus, been enlightened by her smiling face, Dante says:

> In one look I then felt my spirit given
> a power that plucked it out of Leda's nest
> and sent it soaring to the swiftest heaven.
> (Canto XXVII, 97–99)

Leda's nest refers to the constellation of Gemini, the sign of the Twins—Castor and Pollux—who were conceived when Zeus appeared to Leda as a swan. Dante's resurrection coincides with the dawning *light* of the Sun (Christ) in the sign of Gemini (The Mind). Thus, Dante, having been born into the earthly world while the Sun shone in the constellation of Gemini, *enters the Primum Mobile under the same sign.*

As Dante enters into the ninth sphere, he notices that he is without a point of reference. Beatrice immediately explains to him that this is where the lower spheres in the universe find the impetus for their motion. This motion receives its power from the Mind of God. It is, in essence, the force of his *Love* that causes the sphere—and, consequently, the whole universe—to turn.

> The order of the universe, whose nature
> holds firm the center and spins all else around it,
> takes from this heaven its first point of departure.

> This heaven does not exist in any place
> but in God's mind, where burns the love that turns it
> and the power that rains to it from all of space...
> (Canto XXVII, 106–111)

The center, here, is the Earth, around which, the planetary spheres revolve. Therefore, one can envision, in this Ptolemaic conception of the universe, the realms in which higher hierarchical beings interact to aid humankind in its spiritual development. These planetary realms move in accordance with the *power* raying down from God's *Love*. The Primum Mobile, its own motion "unfactored," determines the motion of the lower spheres.

> ...Its own motion unfactored, all things derive
> their motions from this heaven as precisely
> as ten is factored into two and five...
> (Canto XXVII, 115–117)

Beatrice compares the Primum Mobile to the root of a tree, for just as the *source of time* (by which the motion of the heavenly spheres are measured) is unseen, so, too, are the roots of a tree that allow for springing forth of leaves and fruit.

> ...So may you understand how time's taproot
> is hidden in this sphere's urn, while in the others
> we see its spreading foliage and its fruit...
> (Canto XXVII, 118–120)

Having explained the nature of the Primum Mobile, Beatrice issues an invective against the covetousness that has polluted the world. Only in childhood, she says, do "faith and innocence" exist. However, they fade from view before children are old enough to have the first hair "sprout from their cheeks." She, then, denounces the Church for its corruption, adding that evil in the world exists because no one is there to keep it in check; no one is there to govern. She predicts, however, that a *light* from Heaven will come to guide humanity back to its proper course.

The Paradiso: Into the "I" of God

At the beginning of Canto XXVIII, Dante looks into the eyes of Beatrice and presages the presence of God gradually dawning upon his consciousness:

> just as a man before a glass can see
> a torch that burns behind him, and know it is there
> before he has seen or thought of it directly;
>
> and turns to see if what the glass has shown
> is really there; and finds, as closely matched
> as words to music, the fact to is reflection;
>
> just so, as I recall, did I first stare
> into the heaven of those precious eyes
> in which, to trap me, Love had set its snare.
> (Canto XXVIII, 4–12)

The eyes of Beatrice, here, reflect the *light* of the spiritual hierarchies within the planetary spheres, thus anticipating Dante's actual perception of them as creative forces or beings:

> just so, as I recall, did I first stare
> into the heaven of those precious eyes
> in which, to trap me, Love had set his snare;
>
> then turned, and turning felt my sense reel
> as my own were struck by what shines in that heaven
> when we look closely at its turning wheel.
> (Canto XXVIII, 10–15)

What Dante perceives, is a "Point" so luminous that he must turn away, or else lose his sight. Just as looking into the physical Sun can affect our vision, so, too, does Dante risk losing his bearings in the suprasensory world as he attempts to directly behold the Godhead. The "Point" denotes God's infinite nature, void of spatial properties. Surrounding this point (or center) are nine concentric circles that house the spiritual hierarchies; the highest of them (Seraphim) immediately surrounds the Godhead (point), while the lowest (Angels) is furthest away. This inversion reflects our experience in the afterworld as conveyed by Steiner in a lecture on October 21, 1921, when he said, "When we are on earth and look out into cosmic space we have one particular view; it is the view we have between birth and death. Between death and rebirth we have a different view, for we are inside the sphere and look back to the central core. We have, in a sense, a world that is the opposite of our present world."[70] George Adams in his book, *Physical and Ethereal Spaces*, also quotes from this lecture, when he writes, "the cosmic world that was formerly at the periphery surrounding us—therein we feel ourselves to be *within*; while on the other hand, what was formerly the earthly world on which we stood—we feel it henceforth as our *concentric outer world.*"[71] He adds,

> "We shall come nearer to the idea of a "peripheral space" or counterspace which has here been suggested, if we call to mind how we ourselves in certain stages of our life before birth or after death live in another kind of space than on Earth. For we go out into the cosmic ether and into the realms of the Sun and Stars. As we live here in a point-center—in a space which takes its start, for our experience, from the given center where our earthly body is—so we there live in the circumference, in the periphery.... If this be so, there is indeed, even in real experience, such a thing as a "centric outer world"—an outer world, not spread around us as a circumference, but such that we ourselves indwell the whole circumference and look toward a center as our outer world. *We look into the infinite, not as into the wide expanse of a circumference, but rather inward as into a cosmic center.*" (italics mine)

Thus, we can see that by having the ninth hierarchy (Angels), as seen from the Empyrean, comprise the furthest circle from the center, Dante adheres to this principle.

Therefore, infinity (God) is represented as a "point" on the physical plane. This principle of inversion, however, is further alluded to as Dante describes how the circles such as Primum Mobile (realm of the Seraphim), Fixed Stars (realm of the Cherubim), and so on, immediately surrounding the "point," revolve more swiftly than do those that lie at the periphery. In other words, the closer an angelic hierarchy is to the point of light, the quicker the circle moves and the more luminous it is, because it is inflamed with God's *Love*. Says Dante,

> so close around the Point, a ring of fire
> spun faster than the fastest of the spheres
> circles creation in its endless gyre...
> (Canto XXVIII, 25–27)
>
> and so the eighth and ninth, and each ring spun
> with an ever slower motion as its number
> placed it the further out from the first one,
>
> which gave forth the most brilliant incandescence
> because, I think, being nearest the Scintilla,
> it drew its fullest share of the true essence.
> (Canto XXVIII, 34–39)

This description of the planetary spheres and the spiritual hierarchies that comprise them seems to present a sort of counterimage to our solar system as we experience it here on Earth. Our sense-based perception of the solar system is commensurate with a dialectical consciousness responsible for its spatial–temporal dimensions. Dante seems to infer that the counterimage of the spiritual hierarchy is possible only to a consciousness not bound by space and time, namely a consciousness that transcends reflective thinking.

Again, Beatrice explains to Dante that it is by virtue of God's *Love* that the innermost circle moves most swiftly. John Ciardi explains, in his notations to his translation of the *Paradiso*, that, the "hierarchy of angels"

> ...surround God as the heavenly spheres surround the Earth, but their motions, contrary to those of the heavenly spheres, are greater as they lie closer to the center. Opposition (paradox) is a natural part of the language of mysticism. These spheres seem at first to be a sort of counter-universe. But note that the principle of both "universes" remains the same, *for in either system, the spheres have greater motion and greater "virtue" as their placement draws nearer to God.* (italics mine)[72]

The cosmology that Dante postulates appears to strike a balance between the planetary spheres and their relation to both the earthy realm and the Empyrean. Since the Copernican view did not appear until the early sixteenth century, Dante seems to combine two different vantage points by which to view our relationship to the universe. Seen in this way, it is possible to imagine how the luminosity and velocity of the planets encircling the Earth (considered the center of the universe by Ptolemy) increase the closer they are to the Earth—the Moon being the fastest, then Mercury, Venus, the Sun, Mars, Jupiter, and Saturn. At the same time, this cosmological design was itself part of an even larger construct, whereby Saturn, the farthest removed—though seemingly the slowest when viewed from the physical Earth—is from the Empyrean the quickest and brightest. And so, seen from the Empyrean, the Moon, comprised of angels, is seen as slower, further removed and less "godlike" with respect to Saturn, comprised of the Thrones.

This inversion that occurs can be liked to the inversion of our bodily organs after death. Steiner often intimated that, after death, our organs are "turned inside out" so that they become part of the macrocosmic universe. Says he.

> Here on the Earth, we are situated at a point on the Earth's surface. Our organs are within us, while the starry heavens are outside. The opposite is true after death. Then we grow to a cosmic dimension. Once we have expanded up to the Moon sphere, the spiritual that belongs to the Moon becomes an organ within us. After death, it becomes what the brain is for us as physical human beings on Earth. Each planetary body becomes an organ for us after death, inasmuch as we have expanded to its orbit. The Sun becomes a heart for us. Just as we bear the physical heart within our body here, there we carry the spiritual part of the Sun within us.[73]

Thus, it would not be difficult to imagine this inversion with respect to the "I"'s journey after death. Seen from the Earth, the Moon sphere is the smallest and quickest sphere while Saturn is the largest and slowest. This is reversed with regard to the Empyrean, in which case

Saturn is the smallest and quickest sphere (as it encircles the Fixed Stars, the Primum Mobile and the Empyrean) while the Moon is the slowest and most removed. The "I," in the process of excarnating and incarnating, experiences the inversion of these spheres in the form of a lemniscate, namely, a "figure eight." And so, Dante is able to point at the planetary sphere of Saturn as more "godlike" when seen both from an earthly point of view as well as from the vantage point of the Empyrean, where the sphere of Saturn is closer to the "point" of all creation, namely, the "I" of God.

At this point, Dante asks Beatrice to explain for him the apparent contradiction. She begins by stating that the planetary spheres are "graduated in size according to the power that infuses each," so that, what in the spiritual world lies closer to God is also what has the capacity ("greater grace") to "contain" "greater good." In other words, while each sphere is permeated equally by God's power, it is the nature of such power (virtue) that differs in each circle. The greater the capacity of beings to contain power as it rays from God, the smaller is the circle needed to contain it. Likewise, the lesser the capacity of beings to contain the power of God's ray, the greater the circle.

We can understand from this that the most powerful *planetary* sphere is that which is closest in proximity to God, namely, the sphere of Saturn—governed by the Thrones. Aside from the Seraphim and the Cherubim who reside in the *Primum Mobile* and the fixed stars, respectively, the Thrones are the most powerful of the hierarchical spiritual beings.

This, however, is not the case as seen from the physical realm where the sphere of Saturn is both outermost and the largest of all the planetary spheres. Similarly, the Moon sphere—the sphere closest to the Earth with the smallest orbit—in the spiritual realm is seen as being the furthest circle from God. Consequently, the Angels that comprise it are the least powerful of hierarchical beings. *Strangely*, however, Beatrice seems to assert the opposite, namely, that the Moon or angelic sphere is that which "most loves and most knows." Herein lies an inconsistency—one of a very few—in which she seems to overlook the sphere's proximity to God as the determining factor in its spiritual rank.

> ...This sphere, then, that spins with it as it goes
> all of the universe, must correspond
> to the angel sphere that most loves and most knows.
>
> ...If you will measure not by what appears
> but by the power inherent in these beings
> that manifest themselves to you as spheres,
>
> you will observe a marvelous correspondence
> of greater power to larger, and lesser to smaller,
> between each Heaven and its Intelligence.
> (Canto XXVIII, 70–78)

Dante compares Beatrice's reply to the Boreas, that is, the wind that blows over Italy from the northwest and disperses cloudy activity that may exist, for which he now sees the truth shining before him "like a star." In his sight are the angelic spheres in all their transparency as they sparkle before him. The "sparks" that Dante perceives in each sphere, of course, allude to the beings that maintain their individuality while joyously illuminating the sphere as a whole. Each sphere is comprised of hierarchical angelic beings and earthly human spirits. However, the once-earthly spirits with whom he comes into contact should be considered differently—namely, in relation to their degree of earthly *spiritual development*. Their position in the various hierarchal spheres (Moon, Mercury, etc.) reflects their level of karmic development. Only in this way can we begin to reconcile the question of reincarnation with what may seem to be a stagnant representation of humanity's after-life by Dante.

(Unlike Steiner's description of the various angelic beings residing *within* the planetary spheres themselves, Dante places each of the angelic hierarchies within the Empyrean in nine concentric rings, while intimating that their influence [and presence] simultaneously extends respectively down through all the planetary spheres.)

As Dante observes the hierarchies, he hears voices sing a hymn of praise to God. This singing is a manifestation of their love—*a love that moves the universe.* Dante chooses to characterize this love in the form of song, which is but a manifestation of the creative principle, the Word.

Beatrice proceeds to name the beings of the hierarchy, beginning with the first triad or trinity comprised of the Seraphim, Cherubim, and Thrones. Of the first two, she states, "they chase the reins in their eagerness / to resemble the Point the more, and they can the more, / the more they look upon its blessedness." As Steiner says in *The Spiritual Hierarchies and the Physical World,* the Seraphim receive the ideas of the Trinity while the Cherubim ponder over them.[74] The Thrones, as we have already seen, put these ideas into action. Beatrice tells Dante that the degree of blessedness possessed by each member of the hierarchy depends on the *act* of perceiving, that is to say, on their ability to "penetrate the Truth":

> ...Hence one may see that the most blest condition
> is based on the act of seeing, not of love,
> love being the act that follows recognition...
> (Canto XXVIII, 109–111)

Thus, the human soul also moves closer toward God the more it can "look upon Its blessedness." Love is born of recognition, that is, one's ability to perceive the divine within oneself as a reflection of God. Says Steiner in *The Spiritual Hierarchies and the Physical World,*

> The Seraphim, Cherubim, and Thrones represent for us the highest hierarchy among divine beings because they have already accomplished their development as a solar system and have risen to an exalted rank of cosmic sacrificial service.
>
> As a result, these beings have come into the closest vicinity of the most exalted divinity of which we can speak, the threefold divine power, or the Trinity. We must, therefore, picture the Godhead as beyond the Seraphim. We find this threefold divinity among almost all peoples as Brahma, Shiva, and Vishnu, and as

the Father, the Word, and the Holy Spirit. The creative source of every new cosmic system also arises within this exalted Trinity.[75]

Beatrice, then, directs Dante's attention to the next triad, comprised of Dominations (Kryiotetes), Virtues (Dynamsies), and Powers (Exusiai), each of which sing *"Hosannah"*—their melodies reflecting the differing degrees of blessedness. Finally, she names the last triad, composed of Principalities (Archai), Archangels, and Angels, adding that, though their gaze is directed upward (toward God), their power descends into the physical world. Thus, their activity is also centered in the Will of God, as they manifest their "eagerness to resemble the Point more."

Beatrice concludes the canto by recognizing Dionysius the Areopagite, who identified and named the spiritual hierarchies. Dionysius, says Beatrice, was told of the hierarchies by "one still in the weight of mortal dust" (St. Paul), who was thought to have ascended into "the third heaven" (II Cor. 12:2). Here, Dante seemingly mistakes Psuedo-Dionysius of the late fifth to early sixth century, indeed the writer of *The Celestial Hierarchies* for St. Dionysius of Areopagite, an Athenian member of the judicial council, the Areopagus, the one converted to Christianity by Paul.

The "children of Latona" (Sun and Moon) are suspended equidistant, yet opposite of each other, one rising and the other setting. The Sun, in Aries, and the moon, in Libra, visible for a fleeting instant, reflect the delicate *balance* of creation as Beatrice silently fixes her eyes on the Fixed Point. Then she addresses one of the questions that Dante has on his mind—namely, the purpose of God's creations. Says she:

> ...Not to increase Its good—no mil nor dram
> can add to true perfection, but that reflections
> of his reflection might declare "I am"—
>
> in His eternity, beyond time, above
> all other comprehension, as it pleased Him,
> new loves were born of the Eternal Love...
>   (Canto XXIX, 13–18)

Therefore, God created other beings so that they could partake in his *Love* by having the possibility to reflect His being and declare the words *I AM,* which, as Rudolf Steiner has so often pointed out, cannot refer to anyone but the individual who utters them. It is a faint but tangible echo of the "eternal" aspect of one's being, namely, the "I." The beings that share in God's Eternal nature are beyond the realm of time and space, as is our "I," where the creative activity of God—that preexisted the Word's descent from the Sun—resides ("Nor did He lie asleep before the Word sounded above these waters").

Beatrice, then, tells Dante that "pure essence" (angelic beings), pure matter (physical substance of the Earth), and their synthesis (humankind) arose simultaneously. At first sight, we can perceive an inconsistency with regard to Steiner's description of the relationship that matter has to essence, if by "essence" one refers to the life force out of which matter arose. However, if we consider the process of Earth's evolution with respect to the sacrifice made by the spiritual hierarchies and the emergence of the constitutional elements comprising the Earth's formation, then some degree of truth can be gleaned from what Beatrice says. However, we must envision this process to encompass long stretches of time. They do not appear instantaneously as Beatrice's claim seems to infer. The formation of our Earth (pure matter) that initially arose as warmth during the planetary stage of Saturn giving birth to the incipient form of the physical body, later underwent a process of densification as other elemental forms arose such as light/gas, water, and then solid matter. These were commensurate with the successive planetary stages of the Earth's evolution—namely, Sun, Moon, and Earth itself—in which there arose three further constitutive *components* of our being (etheric, astral, and pure spirit "I"), each respectively comprising the lowest bodies of the three angelic hierarchies immediately above the human being. Creation, itself, reflects order imposed upon chaos, so that those beings that are able to create from their inner living impulse, were, themselves, a direct manifestation of the "pure act." Humankind, the recipient of those creative impulses, lives instead as "pure potential." For we have still to *develop* the capacity to individually create *life* from within ourselves. In other words, we are, at present, unlike those hierarchical beings above us that are both creators and receivers of *life* streaming down from the above.

> ...Order was the co-created fact
> of every essence; and at the peak of all,
> these angel loves created as pure act.
>
> Pure potential held the lowest ground;
> between, potential and act were tied together
> so tight they nevermore shall be unbound...
> (Canto XXIX, 31–36)

Beatrice informs Dante that Hieronymus was wrong to speak of the "procreation of the angels" in one of his epistles. His declarations were overturned by the "Scribes of the Holy Ghost," those who wrote the Scriptures. Beatrice asserts that the perfection of Angels is to be found within the level of their own creative activity. And so, the function of the angelic beings reflects the nature of their perfection. The higher the rank, the higher their perfection, and the more they have influence over those below them. They have resulted from a pure act, while humankind has been endowed with pure potential. Between "potential" and "act" were created the Heavens. These Heavens are subject to the influences of what lies above (God), while they influence what lies below (humanity).

Having touched upon the particulars regarding the creation of the hierarchies, Beatrice then alludes to a band of angels who were cast from the spiritual worlds for their rebelliousness so as "to roil the bedrock of the elemental core." She says that they fell because of their pride, which opposed the Will of God. This band of Angels, as we know from Anthroposophy, could be thought to consist of the hosts of luciferic (lagging Angels) and ahrimanic (lagging Archangels) beings. Having forgone their evolutionary development, they did not progress to the next highest hierarchical stages (Archangel and Archai, respectively). Therefore, they did not progress toward God, but sought to exercise their influence upon the Earth. Though it is common to think of the Devil and Satan as evil forces, they can also be thought of as beings that sacrificed their own development so as to prepare us to receive the Christ impulse through the development of our will. Nonetheless, Dante does not perceive the work of the rebel spirits as sacrificial but, rather, as one that is self-centered.

Again, Beatrice makes reference to those beings who were "changeless in their will," namely, those who were not affected by pride. They did not seek to will against God but, rather, to focus "their will" in that of God. "The good of grace," she says, "is in exact proportion to the ardor of love that opens to receive it." This, of course, refers to the grace of higher vision, for only by being receptive to the *love* or *light* of the Christ, can one gradually open one's eyes to perceive Him.

At this point, Beatrice alerts Dante to the human misconceptions regarding the faculties ascribed to the hierarchical beings. Unlike what is commonly believed, she says, angels have no need of memory, for

> ...these beings, since their first bliss in the sight
> of God's face, in which all things are revealed,
> have never turned their eyes from their delight.
>
> No angel's eye, it follows, can be caught
> by a new object; hence, they have no need
> of memory, as does divided thought...
> (Canto XXIX, 76–81)

Memory only pertains to us as human beings, since we have the physical bodies upon which the etheric body can impress an image of the sensory world. Angelic beings, however, unbounded by spatial or temporal relationships, lack the physical component that can register an imprint of memory, for the angel's experience of the Earth consists only in *perceiving the forces that materialize form*. Therefore, memory is something that lies outside their field of experience.

Nearing the end of her speech, Beatrice tells Dante of the damage done by preachers when they promote their speculations on truth at the expense of the *Gospels*. Instead, she says:

> ...the ignorant sheep turn home at night
> from having fed on wind. Nor does the fact
> that the pastor sees no harm done set things right.
>
> Christ did not say to His first congregation:
> "Go and preach twaddle to the waiting world."
> He gave them, rather, holy truth's foundation...
> (Canto XXIX, 106–111)

Beatrice associates these negligent preachers with pigs. She mentions Anthony's pig, "rooting" at his feet. Beatrice tells Dante that while human beings feed on the empty promises, swinish monks (pigs) feed on the ignorance of such human beings until they have their fill. Such a feast is paid for by empty promises ("money never minted").

> ...On such St. Anthony's pig feeds on, unstinted,
> and others yet more swinish feast and guzzle
> and pay their way with money never minted...
> (Canto XXIX, 124–126)

Beatrice, once again, directs Dante's attention toward higher beings, to whom the "Primal Light sends down Its ray."

Just as the stars begin to fade, one by one, into the light of dawn, so do the concentric rings of light spinning around the Fixed Point, fade from Dante's sight as he ascends into the Empyrean. There, he turns his gaze to Beatrice as love "commanded" him and declares that if all the descriptions of her coalesced as one, they would scantly approach the beauty that he now beholds. Dante adds that only our Maker can comprehend her beauty. And so, Dante concedes defeat, for her degree of beauty depends on the level of his ability to behold her. In other words, the higher the level of consciousness Dante attains, the more beautiful Beatrice appears. The more beauty Dante is able to behold, the more deeply he is able to enter into God's realm. (This brings to mind his discourse on *Love* on the Mount of Purgatory where we discover that the more we share love the more love there is to share.)

The Paradiso: Into the "I" of God

Beatrice announces that Dante has ascended into the realm of "pure light," which she declares to be the "*light* of the intellect," namely, the Christ Himself— "love unending." Says she:

> ...here you shall see both hosts of Paradise,
> one of them in the aspect you shall see
> when you return the day all bodies rise.
> (Canto XXX, 43–45)

Among the Blessed are great human spirits occupying a place in the Mystic Rose. The beings there are considered to have reached the highest point of spiritual development possible to humanity at the time of Dante. This Mystic Rose, as Dante seems to present it, has no specific correspondence to the picture of human evolution as presented by Steiner. To do so, would bind us to the realm of pure abstract speculation and, therefore, commit us to error.

Having listened to the words of Beatrice, Dante is immediately engulfed by a flood of light that prevents him from seeing. Beatrice says that God prepares whoever enters into this Kingdom by extinguishing the "candle" of his soul so that he might behold God's splendor. Again, such incidents of momentary blindness prepare Dante to gaze into the higher realms.

> The Love that keeps this Heaven ever the same
> greets all those who enter with such salutation,
> and thus prepares the candle for His flame.
> (Canto XXX, 52–54)

Upon hearing these words, Dante's powers of perception are heightened "beyond themselves" so that, "transcendent and elated," his eyes

> ...were lit with such new-given light
> that they were fit to look without distress
> on any radiance, however bright.
> (Canto XXX, 58–60)

Here, we can assume that Dante has arrived at the final stages of *excess mentis*, where he attains "direct intuition of divine truth." This ability to see the *light* of the God's Essence marks the point in which Dante no longer perceives by way of Beatrice. For, as we shall see, she, too, will shortly be replaced as Dante's guide. At this point, Dante is able, more and more, to directly perceive the *light* within the Empyrean. However, this *light* will soon give way to the Archetypes that comprise this realm.

Dante sees a river of light flowing between two flowery banks. From the river, sparks shoot up and fly to the flowers, and then return to the river as though they were inebriated. All the while, other sparks repeat the process. Dante says that the sparks that settle on the flowers seem like rubies set in gold. In this vision, Dante makes it clear that the river symbolizes divine grace; the sparks are the Angelic beings; and the flowers are the Blessed. So, in effect, we see the Angelic beings administering divine grace to the Blessed.

Dante in the Empyrean, Drinking from the River of Light,
William Blake

Beatrice bids Dante to drink from the *river of light by touching it with his eyes*. Says she:

> ...The river and jewels (topaz) you see
> dart in and out of it, and the smiling flowers
> are dim foretastes of their reality.
>
> Not that these fruits are in their natures tart
> and unformed, but that you still lack the vision
> of such high things. The defect is on your part.
> (Canto XXX, 76–81)

Here, Dante specifically refers to the gem "topaz" for, as Ciardi says, it was used to reflect things without distorting them.[76] Again, Dante finds himself at the threshold of this vision most high. He drinks eagerly from the River of *Light,* from which flows the grace that makes "better mirrors of our eyes." Quickly, the river widens into a sea, while the sparks and flowers transform into "a greater festival." At this point, Dante uses the words *"I saw" three times* to emphasize the active partaking of God's *light.* Unlike before, where things reveal themselves to him, here, he *actively partakes of them.* As always, however, this active participation on his part is possible through the grace of God, which, in turn, depends on the degree to which he submits to Divine Will:

> ...and I saw
> the vision of both courts of Paradise.
>
> O splendor of God eternal through which I saw
> the supreme triumph of the one true kingdom,
> grant me the power to speak forth what I saw!
> (Canto XXX, 95–99)

This emphatic affirmation of his newborn sight bears witness to the fact that, for the first time, Dante has reached the highest stages of **Intuition,** thereby partaking directly of the "I" of God. He has, thus, arrived at the threshold of that experience which was the ultimate aim of his journey.

Dante describes what he sees as a bright light that forms a circle whose circumference is greater than that of the Sun. "It," says Dante, "is made up of the reflection of rays that strike the top of the first-moved sphere." It is what gives that sphere its "power and motion." *This circle of light takes the form of a rose,* within which:

> ...tier on tier, mounting within that light,
> there glowed, reflected in more than a thousand circles,
> all those who had won return to heaven's height.
> (Canto XXX, 112–114)

Dante's vision is reflected in the sea of light that has been transformed from the flowing river. He thus does not apprehend the rose directly. The flowing light can be thought of as the stream of Christ-consciousness within the etheric realm. This etheric stream of thinking leads Dante into the etheric realm (sea) wherein dwells the Christ. The Mystic Rose appears to Dante as a stadium whose tiers (made up of petals) mount ever higher until they disappear from Dante's sight. This indicates that he is at the bottom of the Rose. As J. E. Cirlot says in *The Dictionary of Symbols,* the rose is the "symbol of completion, of consummate achievement and perfection."[77] Its white color denotes purity. At its very center is the ever-present *light* of God, surrounded by rows upon rows of angelic beings and saints. Thus, what Dante had perceived as a classification of hierarchies (and blessed souls) within the planetary circles or spheres, was but a projection of what exists *here* within the "I" of God. For, as we have said, all spiritual beings represented in those spheres dwell *simultaneously* in the Empyrean. Dante, possessing a vision unfettered to earthly forces, has the capacity to accurately gaze far into the distant regions of the Rose.

> Nor were my eyes confounded by that sea
> and altitude of space, but took in all,
> both number and quality, of that ecstasy.
> (Canto XXX, 118–120)

Dante is drawn "into the gold of the rose that blooms eternal"—namely, its corona, where the *essence* of God reveals itself. There, Beatrice directs his attention to the petals, each of which is given to

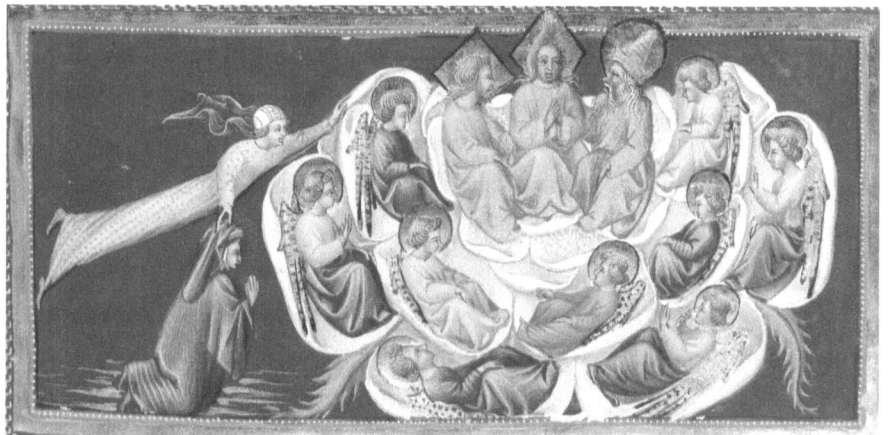

Paradiso 57, Celestial Rose, *Giovanni di Paolo*

an Angel or Blessed Soul. Only few places remain for those who are still left on Earth.

Beatrice points out an empty seat marked with a crown and tells Dante that it is reserved for Emperor Henry VII, whose destiny is to try and free Italy (though his attempt will be unsuccessful). She then directs her invective against the Italians who like hungry, screaming children push away their nurse. A pope who professes his cause in public while privately working to defeat it will oppose the Emperor. This pope is none other than Boniface VIII who, upon his death, will find himself within the Third Bolgia of the Eighth Circle of Hell, stuffed into a pit headfirst because of his corruption, especially that regarding his role in the downfall of the Knights Templar.

At the beginning of Canto XXXI, Dante sees the "first host of the sacred soldiery," made up of all the Blessed, but mortal beings that comprised the spheres below. They are those whom "Christ in his own blood espoused"—namely, those who by their deeds on Earth heeded the Will of God. The blood of the Christ denotes the "I," whose *light* has entered their consciousness. The second host is comprised of the angelic hierarchy, singing and rejoicing in God's glory. Dante compares them to a "swarm of bees who in one motion dive into the flowers and in the next return the sweetness of their labors to the hive." These beings fly incessantly from the *light* of God to the petals of the Rose, bringing with them the sweetness of God's *Love*. From the petals they, in turn, bring the "bliss" of the souls to God. On the one hand, these bees that transport the sweetness of God's *Love* can represent the activity of the Christ Himself, who having descended from the Father brought to all humankind the essence of God's *Love*. What the bees take back to the heart of the Rose is the *human will*, which, by conforming to that of God, furthers His creation. In other words, the *Love* (Christ) that God brought forth into the world, out of Himself, is what, in turn, enables humanity to lift itself from the material realm to redeem itself.

The angelic beings, by spreading "the ardor and the peace they had acquired in flying close to Him (God)" from tier to tier, do not block the rays of God's *light* upon the souls who receive it according to merit. Thus, no soul among the blessed can receive less of God's radiance than what is appropriate at its level of spiritual development. In turn, all the souls direct their eyes and love toward a star that shines with a triple light. Dante utters:

> O Threefold Light which, blazoned in one star,
> can so content their vision with your shining,
> look down upon us in the storm we are!
> (Canto XXXI, 28–30)

As Dante looks upon this vision of the Trinity, he compares his astonishment to what the Goths ("barbarians") must have felt upon entering Rome and perceiving the works that exceeded those of all humanity. Stupefied, Dante says nothing. Instead, he lets his eyes wander out to the tiers from rank to rank, up and down and around. Here, Dante partakes in the vision of God's glory, that is, "the form and general plan of Paradise," which was revealed to him by Beatrice.

With his desire rekindled, Dante wheels about to see his "sweet lady," *but she is not there*. In her place stands "an elder in the robes of glory." Says Dante,

> His eyes and cheeks were bathed in the holy glow
> of loving bliss; his gestures, pious grace.
> He seemed a tender father standing so.
> (Canto XXXI, 61–63)

As was the case before with Virgil, Dante is distraught at having lost Beatrice. "Where is she?" he cries. A voice then answers, "To lead you to the goal of all your wish Beatrice called me from my place." It is St. Bernard—the final guide to lead Dante into the "I" of God. St. Bernard directs Dante's gaze toward the "third circle down from the highest rank upon the throne her merit has assigned her." Dante, looking up to that height, sees Beatrice wrapped in an aureole that reflects the "Eternal Light" (of God).

This transference from Beatrice to St. Bernard can best be understood when we consider the fact that St. Bernard was a twelfth-century French monk who worked perseveringly to deepen humanity's veneration of the Virgin Mary during the Middle Ages. He was deeply devoted to her. It was under his guidance that the Cistercian order gained strength—an order whose monasteries were dedicated to the *contemplation* of the Virgin Mary (*Sophia/Divine Wisdom*). It was also he who had given impetus to the founding of the Knights Templar. Here, he represents the arrival of Virgin Sophia, which, as Emil Bock has suggested, is the archetype of the human soul. Thus, Beatrice, who represents *Divine Wisdom*, must be understood as the sense-free consciousness that permits us to behold the living imaginations constituting the foundation of our world. The attainment of this consciousness allows the Holy Spirit to enter Dante's soul. And so, Dante, having been guided by reason (Virgil) and *Divine Wisdom* (Beatrice), is now set to partake in the Oneness of all creation, wherein exist the archetypal beings that can only be seen by the power of the Holy Spirit.

Though Dante finds himself far removed from where she sits on her throne, he is able to perceive the image of Beatrice "unblurred by the atmosphere." St. Bernard here represents **Revelation**. The beings or forces in the spiritual world, imagined by us spatially, must be seen as interpenetrating. Therefore, distance, or what seems "further away," merely reflects different levels of spiritual development. With his *Intuitive* powers, Dante is able to behold the activity of all beings, in spite of their hierarchical differences.

Dante, at this point, expresses his gratitude to Beatrice for all the help she has given him. Says he:

> O lady in whom my hope shall ever soar
> and who for my salvation suffered even
> to set your feet upon Hell's broken floor;
>
> through your power and your excellence alone
> have I recognized the goodness and the grace
> inherent in the things I have been shown.
>
> You have led me from my bondage and set me free
> by all those roads, by all those loving means
> that lay within your power and charity.
>
> Grant me your magnificence that my soul,
> which you have healed, may please you when it slips
> the bonds of flesh and rises to its goal.
> (Canto XXXI, 79–90)

Upon finishing his address, Dante notices that Beatrice smiles at him and then turns back to behold the "Eternal Fountain," namely, the ever-flowing source of *Light*—God.

St. Bernard, having waited for Dante to recognize the vehicle of *Love* that has guided him to the Empyrean, now declares himself to be the one to help him reach the "perfect consummation" of his ascent. He bids Dante to look around the "garden" whose radiance will prepare him to *directly* behold the "Trinal Ray." Just as Beatrice had summoned Virgil to help Dante, the Virgin Mary (Sophia) now summons St. Bernard. Having declared that "prayer and sacred love" sent for him, Bernard says,

> ...The Queen of Heaven, for whom in whole devotion
> I burn with love, will grant us every grace
> because I am Bernard, her faithful one.
> (Canto XXXI, 100–102)

As we have seen, the point of transference from Beatrice to St. Bernard enables Dante to ascend higher into the heavenly regions; *Divine Wisdom* leads to *Revelation*.

At this point, Dante is reminded of a Croatian (Croat) who embarked on a distant pilgrimage to see Veronica, a devout follower of Christ and, thereby, likens the effect of the Croatian's perception of Veronica (*vera*-icon, or true image)—who had used her handkerchief to wipe the blood from the face of Jesus—to his experience of having come before St. Bernard, "the living love of him who in this world, through contemplation, tasted the peace which ever dwells above." We can thus assume that this father-like figure (St. Bernard) was initiated into the spiritual world by way of the Virgin Sophia, whom he now wishes to present to Dante. He then tells Dante to let his eyes

> ...mount to the last round
> where you shall see the Queen to whom this realm
> is subject and devoted, throned and crowned.
> (Canto XXXI, 115–117)

Dante looks up at the highest tier where the brightest point seems to shine. There, surrounded by a thousand singing angels, distinct and radiant, is the Virgin Mary (Sophia), who Dante sees smiling at the holy festivity around her. Once again, Dante does not even attempt to describe what he sees; it simply lies beyond his descriptive abilities. This has increasingly been the case the higher he has ventured into the spiritual world. For words lack the capacity to clothe the infinite beauty of the spiritual world. If anything, Dante's inability to describe the overwhelming beauty of what he sees is meant to incite us to cultivate our own powers of spiritual imagination (or perception). Finally, the moment arrives in which Dante is led to perceive the Virgin Sophia. Says Dante:

> Bernard, seeing my eyes so fixed and burning
> with passion on his passion, turned his own
> up to that height with so much love and yearning

> that the example of his ardor sent
> new fire through me, making my gaze more ardent.
> (Canto XXXI, 139–143)

This new fire, of course, indicates the presence of the Holy Spirit. Thus, he has completely resurrected his faculty of vision so that, with spiritual eyes, he can witness the Holy Trinity.

As Bernard gazes at the Mystic Rose, he begins identifying the Blessed that hold positions of honor. He points to the lady who dealt the first wound to humankind, Eve, sitting at the feet of the Virgin Mary. Below Eve sits Rachel and next to Rachel is Beatrice. On the subsequent tiers below Rachel are Sarah, Rebecca, Judith and Ruth respectively, followed by a line of Hebrew Women, forming "a part in the tresses of the rose." Hence, the Virgin Mary (Mother of God) sitting *above* Eve (mother of humankind) symbolizes the resurrection of the spiritual faculties dormant within human beings. She transmits her blessedness to Eve by way of Contemplation—namely, Rachel (representative of the *Contemplative Life*). Beatrice, who sits to the side of Rachel, represents *Divine Wisdom* living within individual human beings (Dante). Below Rachel extends the line of Hebrew women, who, because of their physical spiritual constitution, enabled the development of a suitable physical body for the indwelling Christ.

The row of feminine figures creates a wall that divides two classes of Christians. On the one side, there are those "whose faith was founded upon Christ to Come." St. Bernard says of them, "the flower is in full bloom," meaning that all the spaces in the Mystic Rose are completely occupied. The other side, made up of those "whose living faith was fixed on Christ Descended," contains places not yet occupied.

Now, opposite the Virgin Mary on the highest tier of the Mystic Rose sits John the Baptist, who "bore the desert, martyrdom, and Hell's distress," for he had to wait a period of two years (in Limbo) before being saved by the *light* of the Resurrected Christ. It is interesting that John, symbolizing ancient initiation by water and not fire (Holy Spirit), should be placed opposite the Virgin Mary.

The Queen of Heaven in Glory, William Blake

Next to Mary's right sits Peter, who founded the Church in Rome. Next to him is John the Evangelist. It is interesting that John and Mary flank Peter, the representative of the true Church of Christ. At the Crucifixion, these two beings were seen kneeling at the foot of the Cross. Thus, we have Mary, mother of the Nathan Jesus—who, according to Rudolf Steiner had assumed the "I" of the mother of the Jesus of Solomon—to the one side of Peter, and John (the resurrected Lazarus) to the other.

These two individualities, Mary and John, therefore, represent the highest manifestations of human nature at the time of Golgotha. Thus, what is revealed on a physical plane is a picture of the unification of the male–female polarity (willing/thinking) of human consciousness, linked by the *light* of the Christ. That is to say, it is a cosmic picture of the future unification of human consciousness made possible by Christ's entrance into the Earth.

Seated below John the Baptist are St. Francis, St. Benedict, St. Augustine followed by other Christian saints, tier after tier, all the way to the center of the Rose. They, too, form a wall, that essentially continues the one formed by the Hebrew women. With regard to John the Baptist, Georg Kühlewind in *Becoming Aware of the Logos* says,

> The grouping of the blessed in Dante's *Paradiso*, in the white rose, gives the Baptist what he could not attain, his connection with the mother of Jesus. The Mother of God takes her seat in the highest rank in the rose, but the Baptist has his seat opposite to her in the circle, equally in the highest rank, the furthest away from her, but facing her in eternal contemplation. In the same way St. John's Tide and Christmas, the festival of the birth-giving human soul, stand opposite each other in the cycle of the year.[78]

Bernard, then, explains that the upper section of the Rose is made up of those adults who consciously devoted themselves to the Christ. The lower section is, instead, made up of children who were too young to consciously direct their love toward God before their premature death. These children were awarded a place in the Rose because of the prayers of others who had a profound faith in Christ.

Bernard, then, intuits the question Dante has on his mind, namely how are these children, who could not take moral responsibility for themselves, classified? St. Bernard answers by telling him that there exists an "infinite order" that precludes mere "accidence." In other words, everything is "fixed by decree of the Eternal Law." He insists that we should "let the effect suffice," since the cause exists deep within the unseen recesses of God's Infinite Mind. He points to Jacob and Esau, the twins who were always at odds, even while they were within the womb of their mother. Like many other children, they are not allotted a place according to their deeds on Earth, but "by variance only in original grace." Says St. Bernard,

> ...In the first centuries of man's creation
> their innocence and the true faith of their parents
> was all they needed to achieve salvation...
> (Canto XXXII, 76–78)

"But," says St. Bernard "when the age of grace came to mankind, unless perfectly baptized in Christ, such innocents went down among the blind."

St. Bernard bids Dante to look at the Virgin Mary (the visible manifestation of the Sophia), for "only the great glory of her shining can purify your eyes to look on Christ." As Dante looks, he witnesses the Intelligences (angelic beings) imbuing the Virgin Mary (Sophia) with *light* from God.

Just as the Archangel Gabriel had descended before the Blessed Virgin proclaiming the Annunciation with the hymn, *"Ave Maria gratia plena,"* he now appears, once again, with his wings extended. In response to this hymn, the "blessed court joined in song." Dante asks Bernard the identity of this angel. Bernard explains that:

> ...it was he who brought the victory
> to Mary when the Son of God had willed
> to bear the weight of human misery...
> (Canto XXXII, 112–114)

Just as Gabriel's proclamation of "victory" prefigured the Annunciation, here, it heralds the birth of Christ's *light* in Dante.

At this point, St. Bernard directs Dante's gaze to many of the other Blessed Ones who comprise the Mystic Rose. Sitting at each side of the Virgin Mary (Sophia) are the Rose's "eternal roots," St. Peter (Father of the Church) on the right and Adam (Father of Humankind) on the left. Again, to the right of St. Peter is John the Evangelist, whose Book of Revelation delineates the future evolution of humanity. Moses "to whom manna fell to feed the ingrate and rebellious clan" sits to the left of Adam. He is recognized, above all, for helping humanity transition from the old mysteries to the new by establishing a homeland for the "chosen people" in their exodus from Egypt. Across from Peter is Anna, the mother of the Virgin Mary. So filled with bliss is she for her daughter that she does not remove her eyes from her. Opposite Adam is Lucy, who sent Beatrice to summon Virgil, after having been asked by the Virgin Mary (Sophia). Again, the word *Lucy* (*Lucia*) is significant for it means *light*. She, thus, symbolizes the *light* of the Christ that enables Dante (humanity) to find its way to the Father by going from Virgil (reflected thinking) to Beatrice (imaginative consciousness) to Bernard (revelation).

St. Bernard now prompts Dante to turn his eyes to the "Primal Love." As his "powers advance with looking toward him," he may "penetrate as deep as may be through His radiance." Thus, Dante is able to venture toward the very essence of God depending on the grace bestowed upon him. Such grace, says St. Bernard, is contingent on prayer. At this point, he begins to pray to the Virgin Mary and bids Dante to follow his example. Dante is thus urged by St. Bernard to invite the Virgin Sophia to imbue him with the *light* by which he can experience the threefold nature of God. For prayer is the act of asking the grace of God to enter into the human heart.

The final canto of the *Divine Comedy* opens with St. Bernard praying to the Virgin Mary on Dante's behalf. He begins by saying,

> Virgin Mary, daughter of thy son;
> humble beyond all creatures and more exulted;
> predestined turning point of God's intention...
> (Canto XXXIII, 1–3)

Here, Mary is seen as the figure, within whom, God can again make Himself manifest to all humankind. She is the "turning point of God's intention," for she bore the man who bore the Christ—the being that permeated the Earth with new life forces. Just as Jesus of Nazareth provided the physical vehicle for the Christ, Mary can be understood as the physical manifestation of the Virgin Sophia. In as much as Mary enabled Jesus of Nazareth to enter the world, so, too, did the Virgin Sophia enable Christ to enter human consciousness. Thus, as St. Bernard says "the Creator did not scorn to make Himself the creature of His creature." And so, God, in the aspect of Christ Jesus, was willing to be born on Earth through the human being so that the human being, in turn, could be reborn through Christ. Thus, we see:

> ...The Love that was rekindled in Thy womb
> sends forth the warmth of the eternal peace
> within whose ray this flower has come to bloom...
> (Canto XXXIII, 7–9)

"Love," here, refers to the Christ. The "flower" represents Dante who seeks to awaken to the Christ within him. However, St. Bernard implies that this "flower" cannot bloom without the "living fountain of eternal hope," namely, the stream of Christ-consciousness as it flows (from the Holy Spirit) into the human soul.

St. Bernard prays (to the Virgin Mary) that Dante be granted the vision of God, for he says:

> ...Now comes this man who from the final pit
> of the universe up to this height has seen,
> one by one, the three lives of the spirit...
> (Canto XXXIII, 22–24)

These "three lives" can, of course, refer to the threefold aspect of the human being—thinking, feeling, and willing, reflective of the realms through which Dante has traversed. Having totally aligned his will to that of God, Dante wishes to partake in "the all-healing final revelation." St. Bernard, in complete selflessness, declares, "And I, who never more desired to see the vision myself than I do that he may see It." He concludes by praying for Dante's protection once Dante returns to the world below (earthly consciousness). In particular, he prays for protection against "man's clay," that is, the forces that drag human consciousness down. He says:

> ...I pray thee further, all-persuading Queen,
> keep whole the natural bent of his affections
> and of his powers after his eyes have seen...
> (Canto XXXIII, 34–36)

Having felt gratified by the prayer of St. Bernard, the Virgin's eyes turn toward God (the "Eternal Ray"), whereupon Dante feels his soul "grow calm with rapture." Though St. Bernard incites him to look up, Dante has already fixed his sight on God, so that

> Little by little as my vision grew
> it penetrated further through the aura
> of the high lamp which in Itself is true.
> (Canto XXXIII, 52–54)

This "lamp" is the *source* of the *light*. Here, Dante penetrates the glow of *light* until he perceives its Essence. This Essence is "true" to the degree that every other light is but a reflection.

What Dante, then, perceives transcends the limits of human speech. Memory, itself, "swoons and falls away." Says he:

> As one who sees in dreams and wakes to find
> the emotional impression of his vision
> still powerful while its parts fade from his mind—
>
> just such am I, having lost nearly all
> the vision itself, while in my heart I feel
> the sweetness of it yet distill and fall.
> (Canto XXXIII, 58–63)

Here, Dante still preserves the memory of his experience in his *feeling life* for it is there that his experience can be best contained. Surely, the suprasensory imaginations that he has beheld cannot be contained in earthly pictures or thoughts, for they are themselves, symbols of the spiritual impressions gathered directly by way of a higher consciousness. Only through *feeling* is the immediate impact of the experience preserved so that one can, though often unconsciously, attempt to reconnect oneself with it. Instead, in the Sun (of the intellect) "the footprints fade from the snow." Dante implies that it is up to his readers to reconstruct his journey based on the indications that he has given them—indications that he compares to the leaves upon which Sybil had written her oracles before casting them into the wind, thereby scattering them about the land. One could only understand these oracles by gathering them and placing them in the correct order.

Dante supplicates God to give him a "glimpse" of what he had seen and to make his tongue eloquent so that he can "speak a single clue" to all humankind of "the glory of Heaven."

So "dazzling" is Dante's vision that had he looked away he would have lost his senses. By turning away, he would have lost the *Love* and Goodness that results from looking at God. Had he done so, then, the redeeming factor that flows into humanity—the Christ—would have been forsaken. While gazing at the physical Sun can damage our senses, gazing at God (its spiritual aspect) heals them. One is healed from the effects of death. Dante's power of perception is again increased, not decreased, in directly beholding the *Light* of God.

> And so it was, as I recall, I could
> the better bear to look, until at last
> my vision made one with the Eternal Good.
> (Canto XXXIII, 79–81)

By beholding the Eternal Light, Dante perceives how within that *light,* the creative forces of the universe manifest all things as interrelated reflections of His Love. These things are like leaves scattered in the universe. That is to say, they are the symbolic representations of the very forces that create them, so that humanity can only find its way to God by reading into the universe (gathering and ordering of the leaves). This indicates the importance of "order" in the Middle Ages. Order, as exemplified in the artistic expressions of that time, was a means by which to understand the delicate interrelationships woven by thought as it reflects the activity of the cosmos—expressions that reflect the creative forces at work within the universal order. Says he:

> I saw within Its depths how It conceives
> all things in a single volume bound by Love,
> of which the universe is the scattered leaves;
>
> substance, accident, and their relation
> so fused that all I say could do no more
> than yield a glimpse of that bright revelation.
> (Canto XXXIII, 85–90)

We see Dante, the writer, trying to recall his experiences with the utmost clarity when he says:

> I think I saw the universal form
> that binds these things, for as I speak these words
> I feel my joy swell and my spirits warm.
> (Canto XXXIII, 91–93)

Dante has, indeed, beheld the World of the Archetypes revealed to him as the "universal form" connecting all the strewn images of the world surrounding us. He declares that not since Neptune had seen the Argo's keel has humankind experienced the awe that he now feels. So entranced is he, as he stares "fixed and motionless upon that vision," that he could never think of "turning from It." Dante is "ever fervent to see in the act of seeing." He has arrived at the state of Pure Perception, where thinking has been completely transformed into its higher aspect. "Good," says Dante, "the will's ultimate object," is "subsumed in God."

Dante hardly has the power to describe the rest of his experience. The power he has to speak is less than that of "any infant wetting its tongue...at its mother's breasts." This, he says, is not due to the changing aspect of the Living Radiance that he beholds, for it is "unchanging." Instead, he says:

> ...as I grew worthier to see,
> the more I looked, the more unchanging semblance
> appeared to change with every change in me.
> (Canto XXXIII, 112–114)

The change that Dante thinks he perceives in God reflects the transformation unfolding within *him*. For, to behold the essence of God ever more clearly, his own powers of perception must be heightened evermore. In this way, he is able to experience God to an ever-greater degree in such a way that his Maker seems to change before him.

Dante says that three circles shown in that "abyss of light," each equally reflecting the other. Thus,

> Within the depthless deep and clear existence
> of that abyss of light three circles shown—
> three in color, one in circumference:
>
> the second from the first, rainbow from rainbow;
> the third, an exhalation of pure fire
> equally breathed forth by the other two.
> (Canto XXXIII, 115–120)

We see here how the Father and the Son are like a self-generating rainbow. From the breath (creative impulse) of the first two principles of God, rises the pure fire of the Holy Spirit—the creative force of humankind bridged to the Father by way of the Christ.

Dante once again remarks on the inadequacy of human speech to grasp the essence of his experience. Finally, within the second circle, he sees what seems to be the human image:

> that second aureole which shone forth in Thee,
> conceived as a reflection of the first—
> or which appeared so to my scrutiny—
>
> seemed in Itself of Its own coloration
> to be painted with man's image. I fixed my eyes
> on that alone in rapturous contemplation.
> (Canto XXXIII, 127–132)

This "human image" refers, of course, to the human aspect that Christ took upon himself so that He could fully experience mortality and, thus, lead humanity to the realization of its divine nature. Dante fixes his undivided attention on that image. The "coloration" of which Dante speaks is what can be connected to the following verse, so that, just as the whole of the *Divine Comedy*, in its intricate, meticulous, and symmetrical order brings to mind the great Gothic cathedrals of his day, so, too, does the coloration of this human image—in all its mystery—relate to their rose windows, for

> Like a geometer wholly dedicated
> to squaring the circle, but who cannot find,
> think as he may, the principle indicated—
>
> so did I study the supernal face.
> I yearned to know just how our image merges
> into that circle, and how it there finds place...
> (Canto XXXIII, 133–138)

We see that Dante, in his attempt to fix his attention wholly on the mystery before him, is like a geometrician who seeks to find the principle of a circle as derived from a square. Though this principle was intensely sought during Dante's time, it was never found. The idea of a square transformed into a circle can itself be a metaphor for the process of transforming rigidly contoured thinking into its fluid, malleable and universal living aspect. Although Dante finds it difficult to fathom the mystery before him, "the truth" he had hoped for appears to him "in a flash of light"—as an act of grace. This *light* represents the highest level of spiritualization that one could attain at that time, so that Dante's "I" is permeated by the purest aspect of God's being.

Dante cannot recall by way of memory the totality of his experience that lives within his feeling life. Nevertheless, he feels himself balanced like a wheel set into motion by the *Love* of God "that moves the sun and the stars." It is most interesting that Dante perceives his consciousness as moving in conformity to the Heavens through which he has ventured, for this circular motion is precisely that which has been pervasive throughout the whole poem, from the depths of Hell to the rounds of Purgatory to the circling planetary spheres and beyond in Paradise. Whereas each canticle forms a mandala, the configuration of *Paradiso* can also be likened to a *rose window*. Such a geometrical pattern enables Dante to focus on the center point—the Christ (or the *light* of thinking).

Finally, if we bear in mind that Dante, from the base of Purgatory, ascends vertically and that the planetary spheres through which he travels extend horizontally, we can behold—as Éliphas Lévi suggests in *The History of Magic*—*a cross, upon whose intersecting point is placed the Mystic Rose.* He says that Dante's Heaven "is composed of a series of Kabalistic circles divided by a cross, like the pantacle of Ezekiel; in the center of this cross a rose blossoms, thus for the first time manifesting publically and almost explaining categorically the symbol of the Rosicrucians."[79]

Notes to Part One

Preface

1. Morris Berman, *The Twilight of American Culture*, p. 50.
2. Owen Barfield, *Saving the Appearances: A Study in Idolatry*, p. 11.

The Tower of Babel and the Problem of Dialecticism

3. Terry Eagleton, *Literary Theory: An Introduction*, p. 104.
4. Ibid., p. 12.
5. Ibid., p. 4.
6. Ibid., p. 100.
7. Ibid., p. 132.
8. Ibid., pp. 100–101.
9. Rudolf Steiner, *The Karma of Untruthfulness*, vol. 1, pp. 210–211.
10. Rudolf Steiner, *The Arts and their Mission*, p. 85.
11. Rudolf Steiner, "La concezione religiosa medievale nel Poema dantesco" (Lecture on February 11, 1904, from O. 97), p. 30–31.
12. Georg Lukacs, *Studies in European Realism*, p. 1.
13. Massimo Scaligero, *Il Pensiero come Anti-Materia*, p. 40.

Metamorphoses of the Soul

14. Rudolf Steiner, "Lost Unison between Speaking and Thinking," pp. 23–45.
15. Rudolf Steiner, *The Search for the New Isis, Divine Sophia*, p. 22.
16. René Querido, *The Golden Age of Chartres*, p. 25.
17. Rudolf Steiner, "La concezione religiosa medievale nel Poema dantesco" (Lecture on February 11, 1904, from O. 97), p. 32.
18. Rudolf Steiner, *True and False Paths of Spiritual Investigation*, pp. 86–87.

Behind the Scenes

19. Rudolf Steiner, *From Symptom to Reality in Modern History*, p. 35.
20. Rudolf Steiner, *Gospel of St. John in Relation to the Other Gospels*, p. 206.
21. Rudolf Steiner, *From Symptom to Reality in Modern History*, pp. 33–34.
22. Rudolf Steiner, *Transforming the Soul*, vol. 2, p. 124.
23. Rudolf Steiner, *Learning to See into the Spiritual World*, p. 7.
24. Rudolf Steiner, *Three Streams in Human Evolution*, p. 113.
25. Rudolf Steiner, *From Symptom to Reality in Modern History*, p. 22.
26. Ibid., p. 26.
27. William C. Heckethorn, *The Secret Societies of All Ages and Countries*, vol. 1, pp. 175–176.
28. Ibid., p. 172.
29. Ibid., p. 174.

The Secret Message

30. Mircea Eliade, *Rites and Symbols of Initiation: The Mysteries of Birth and Rebirth*, p. 127.
31. Henri Corbin, *Avicenna and the Visionary Recital*, pp. 269–70.
32. Ibid., p. 268.
33. Rudolf Steiner, *Karmic Relationships: Esoteric Studies*, vol. 6, p. 176.
34. Ibid., p. 177.
35. Benedetto Croce, *Giornale Critico della filosofia italiana*, vol. 1 ("La metodologia della Critica Letteraria e La "Divina Comedia"), pp. 254–55.
36. Rudolf Steiner, *Art as Spiritual Activity: Rudolf Steiner's Contribution to the Visual Arts*, pp. 275–278.
37. William Anderson, *Dante the Maker*, p. 191.
38. Henri Corbin, *Avicenna and the Visionary Recital*, pp. 268–269.
39. Gabriele Rossetti, *Disquisitions on the Antipapal Spirit which Produced the Reformation*, vol. 1, p. 201.
40. Valli, Luigi, *Il Linguaggio Secgreto di Dante e dei Fedeli d'Amore*, p. 153.
41. Ibid., p. 154.

Deciphering the Meaning of Love

42. Joseph Tusiani, *The Age of Dante*, p. 101–102.
43. Rudolf Steiner, *Love and Its Meaning in the World*, p. 16.
44. Rudolf Steiner, *Redemption of Thinking*, p. 32.
45. Ibid., p. 32.
46. Ibid., p. 41.
47. Massimo Scaligero, *Graal: Saggio sul Mistero del Sacro Amore*, p. 129.
48. Rudolf Steiner, *True and False Paths of Spiritual Investigation*, pp. 86–87.
49. Rudolf Steiner, *Love and Its Meaning in the World*, p. 11.
50. Dante Gabriel Rossetti, *Dante and his Circle*, p. 197.
51. Luigi Valli, *Il Linguaggio Segreto di Dante e dei Fedeli d'amore*, p. 396.
52. Ibid., p. 60.
53. Ibid., pp. 60–61.
54. Dante Alighieri, *Dante's Vita Nuova*, p. 39.
55. Luigi Valli, *Il Linguaggio Segreto di Dante e dei Fedeli d'amore*, p. 61.
56. Guido Cavalcanti, *Poetry of Guido Cavalcanti*, p. 43.
57. Ibid., p. 45–47.
58. Dante Gabriel Rossetti, *Dante and his Circle*, p. 187.
59. Ibid., p. 190.

Goddess of the Sun

60. Dante Alighieri, *Dante's Vita Nuova*, p. 4.
61. Rudolf Steiner, *True and False Paths of Spiritual Investigation*, p. 139.
62. Rudolf Steiner, "La concezione religiosa medievale nel Poema dantesco" (Lecture on February 11, 1904, from O. 97), pp. 30–31.
63. Rudolf Steiner, *Isis Mary Sophia: Her Mission and Ours*, pp. 119–120.
64. Henri Corbin, *Avicenna and the Visionary Recital*, p. 267.
65. Dante Alighieri, *Dante's Vita Nuova*, pp. 7–8.
66. Ibid., p. 9.
67. Luigi Valli, *Il Linguaggio Segreto di Dante e dei Fedeli d'amore*, p. 279.

68. Ibid., p. 279.
69. Dante Alighieri, *Dante's Vita Nuova*, pp. 7–8.
70. Ibid., p. 9.
71. Ibid., p. 11–12.
72. Ibid., p 14.
73. Charles G. Osgood (Ed.), *Boccaccio on Poetry*, p. 53.
74. Luigi Valli, *Il Linguaggio Segreto di Dante e dei Fedeli d'amore*, p. 265.
75. Corinne Heline, *The Sacred Science of Numbers*, p. 75.
76. Ibid., p. 79.
77. Dante Alighieri, *Dante's Vita Nuova*, p. 62.
78. Luigi Valli, *Il Linguaggio Segreto di Dante e dei Fedeli d'amore*, p. 313.
79. Dante Alighieri, *Dante's Vita Nuova*, p. 62.
80. Ibid., p. 23.
81. Dante, *Convivio* (tr. By Richard H. Lansing), p. 219.
82. Adam Maclean, *The Triple Goddess*, p. 10.
83. Ibid., p. 14.
84. Robert Powell, *The Sign of the Son of Man in the Heavens*, p. 5.
85. Ibid., pp. 6.
86. Rudolf Steiner, *Isis Mary Sophia: Her Mission and Ours*, p. 121.
87. Ibid., p. 118.
88. Ibid., p. 119.
89. Ibid., p. 125.

Excessus Mentis/ Morte Mistica

90. *The Bible, Song of Solomon*, NIV Study Bible, p. 999.
91. Luigi Valli, *Il Linguaggio Segreto di Dante e dei Fedeli d'amore*, p. 91.
92. Ibid., p. 91.
93. Ibid., p. 92.
94. Ibid., p. 92
95. Ibid., p. 99.
96. Ibid., p. 98.
97. Dante Alighieri, *Dante's Vita Nuova*, p. 59.
98. Ray C. Petry, *Late Medieval Mysticism*, pp. 84–85.
99. Luigi Valli, *Il Linguaggio Segreto di Dante e dei Fedeli d'amore*, p. 95.
100. Ibid.
101. Giovanni Pascoli, *Tutte le operere di Giovanni Pascoli*, vol. 2 (*La Mirabile Visione: abbozzo d'una storia della Divina Commedia*), p. 815.
102. William Anderson, *Dante the Maker*, p. 337.
103. Dante Alighieri, *Dante's Vita Nuova*, p. 60.
104. Luigi Valli, *Il Linguaggio Segretto di Dante e dei Fedeli d'amore*, pp. 308–309.
105. Dante Alighieri, *Dante's La Vita Nuova*, p. 61.
106. Ibid., p. 61.
107. Luigi Valli, *Il Linguaggio Segreto di Dante e dei Fedeli d'amore*, p. 310.
108. Rudolf Steiner, "La concezione religiosa medievale nel Poema dantesco" (Lecture on February 11, 1904, from O. 97), pp. 33–34.
109. Rudolf Steiner, *The Redemption of Thinking*, p. 67.
110. Luigi Valli, *Il Linguaggio Segreto di Dante e dei Fedeli d'amore*, p. 98.
111. Luigi Valli, *La Struttura Morale dell'Universo Dantesco*, p. 179.

112. Rudolf Steiner, "The Need for Understanding the Christ," O. 224, pp. 14–15.
113. Rudolf Steiner, *How Can Mankind find the Christ Again?*, pp. 48–50.
114. Ibid., p. 52–53.
115. Kühlewind, Georg, *Stages of Consciousness*, pp. 27–28.

Resurrecting the Temple

116. Rudolf Steiner, *The Temple Legend*, p. 158.
117. Virginia Sease and Manfred Schmidt-Brabant, *Thinkers, Saints, Heretics: Spiritual Paths of the Middle Ages*, p. 153.
118. Ibid., pp. 154–155.
119. Ibid., pp. 156–157.
120. Ibid., p. 157.
121. Thomas Merton, *The Last of the Fathers: Saint Bernard of Clairvaux and the Encyclical Letter Doctor Mellifluus*, p. 56.
122. Rudolf Steiner, *The Temple Legend*, p. 21.
123. Ibid., p. 160.
124. Ibid., pp. 56–59.
125. Ibid., p. 66.
126. Dante, *De Monarchia*, p. 92.
127. Rudolf Steiner, *Inner Impulses of Evolution*, p. 113.
128. Sylvia Francke, *The Tree of Life and the Holy Grail*, p. 67.

The Heresy of Romantic Love

129. Denis de Rougemont, *Love in the Western World*, p. 75.
130. Morris Berman, *Coming to Our Senses*, p. 206.
131. Walter Nigg, *The Heretics: Heresy Through the Ages*, p. 179.
132. William C. Heckethorn, *The Secret Societies of All Ages and Countries*, vol. 1, p. 90.
133. Franz Cumont, *The Mysteries of Mithra*, p. 207.
134. Rudolf Steiner, *How Can Mankind Find the Christ Again?*, p. 44.
135. Ibid.
136. Rudolf Steiner, *Driving Force of Spiritual Powers in World History*, p. 30.
137. Ibid., p. 31.
138. Ibid., pp. 43–44.
139. Morris Bergman, *Coming to Our Senses*, p. 199.
140. Jeffrey B. Russell (ed.), *Dissent and Reform in the Early Middle Ages*, p. 58.
141. Morris Bergman, *Coming to Our Senses*, p. 189.
142. Denis de Rougemont, *Love in the Western World*, p. 79.
143. Ibid., pp. 79–80.
144. Ibid., p. 66.
145. Ibid.
146. Ibid.
147. Ibid.
148. Sergei O. Prokofieff, *The Occult Significance of Forgiveness*, pp. 59–60.
149. Ibid., p. 108.
150. Ibid.
151. Isabel, Cooper-Oakley, *Masonry and Medieval Mysticism*, p. 103.

152. Manly P. Hall, *Orders of the Quest: The Holy Grail*, pp. 46–47.
153. Isabel Cooper-Oakley, *Masonry and Medieval Mysticism*, p. 125.
154. Gabriele Rossetti, *Disquisitions on the Antipapal Spirit which Produced the Reformation*, vol. 2, pp. 113–114.
155. Ibid., p. 114.
156. Denis de Rougemont, *Love in the Western World*, pp. 83–84.
157. Veronic M. Fraser, *The Songs of Peire Vidal*, p. 77.
158. Zoe Oldenbourg, *Massacre at Montsegur*, p. 26.
159. Ibid., p. 27.
160. Isabel, Cooper-Oakley, *Masonry and Medieval Mysticism*, pp. 113–114. (Here she quotes from Eugene Aroux's *Le mysteres de la chevalerie et de l'amour platonique au moyen age*, pp. 161–169.)
161. Ibid., p. 114.
162. Ibid., p. 117.
163. Rudolf Steiner, *The Temple Legend*, p. 65.
164. William C. Heckethorn, *The Secret Societies of All Ages and Countries*, vol. 1, p. 144.
165. Ibid., p. 144.
166. Frederick Goldin, ed., *Lyrics of the Troubadours and Trouvères*, p. 291.
167. Alexander J. Denomy, *The Heresy of Courtly Love*, pp. 21–22.
168. Ibid., pp. 29–30.
169. Ibid., pp. 30–31.
170. Ibid., p. 26.
171. Isabel Cooper-Oakley, *Masonry and Medieval Mysticism*, p. 114. (Here she quotes from Eugene Aroux's *Le mysteres de la chevalerie et de l'amour platonique au moyen age*, pp. 161–169.)
172. Denis de Rougemont, *Love in the Western World*, p. 86.
173. Ibid., p. 86.
174. Frederick Goldin, ed., *Lyrics of the Troubadours and Trouvères*, p. 219.
175. Robert John, *Dante Templare*, p. 318.

The Sufis and their Influence

176. Denis de Rougemont, *Love in the Western World*, p. 102.
177. Ibid., p. 102.
178. Ibid., pp. 102–103.
179. George Santayana, *Interpretation of Poetry and Religion*, pp. 121–122.
180. Theodore Richards, *Cosmosophia: Cosmology, Mysticism and the Birth of a New Myth*, p. 81.
181. Ibid., p. 82.
182. Luigi Valli, *Il Linguaggio Segreto di Dante e dei Fedeli d'amore*, pp. 102–103.
183. Denis de Rougemont, *Love in the Western World*, p. 105.
184. Dante Alighieri, *Dante's Vita Nuova*, p. 39.
185. Frederick Goldin, ed., *Lyrics of the Troubadours and Trouvères*, p. 99.
186. Ibid., p. 71.
187. Ibid., p. 71.
188. P. L. Wilson and N. Pourjavady, eds., *The Drunken Universe*, p. 63.
189. Denis de Rougemont, *Love in the Western World*, p. 107.
190. Ibid., pp. 103–104.
191. Morton M. Hunt, *The Natural History of Love*, p. 130.

192. Ibid., p. 129.
193. Eithne Wilkins, *The Rose-Garden Game*, p. 141.

Unearthing the Forces of Darkness

194. Theodore Richards, *Cosmosophia: Cosmology, Mysticism and the Birth of a New Myth*, p. 82.

Notes to Part Two

Tripartition of the *Divine Comedy*

1. Rudolf Steiner, *The Bridge between Universal Spirituality and the Physical Constitution of Man*, p. 57.
2. Rudolf Steiner, *Macrocosm and Microcosm*, p. 23.
3. Rudolf Steiner, *The Search for the New Isis*, p. 23.
4. Rudolf Steiner, *Transforming the Soul*, vol. 2, p. 124.

The *Inferno*: Confronting the Dragon

5. Massimo Scaligero, *Graal: Saggio sul Mistero del Sacro Amore*, p. 42.
6. Wallace Fowlie, *A Reading of Dante's Inferno*, p. 65.
7. Albert Steffen, *Mystery Drama: From Ancient to Modern Times*, p. 26.
8. Massimo Scaligero, *Graal: Saggio sul Mistero del Sacro Amore*, p. 79.
9. Ibid., pp. 139–140.
10. Ibid., p. 140.
11. *The Bible (NIV Study Bible)*, 1 Corinthians 12, pp. 1752–1753.
12. Wallace Fowlie, *A Reading of Dante's Inferno*, p. 210.
13. Ibid., pp. 212–213.

The *Purgatorio*: Ascending the Slopes of Redemption

14. Rudolf Steiner, *Macrocosm and Microcosm*, p. 25.
15. Ibid., p. 44.
16. *The Bible (NIV Study Bible)*, Matthew 27:28-30, p. 1485.
17. John Ciardi, *The Purgatorio*, p. 190.
18. Dante, *Il Convivio* (tr. by Richard H. Lansing), p. 83.
19. Rudolf Steiner, *Links Between the Living and the Dead*, p. 16.
20. Massimo Scaligero, *Graal: Saggio sul Mistero del Sacro Amore*, p. 64.
21. *The Bible (NIV Study Bible)*, Genesis 3:21-24, p. 11.
22. John Ciardi, *The Purgatorio*, p. 237.
23. *The Bible (NIV Study Bible)*, Matthew 19:24, p. 1467.
24. Rudolf Steiner, *Cosmosophy*, vol. I, p. 58.
25. Massimo Scaligero, *Trattato del Pensiero Vivente*, p. 11.
26. Rudolf Steiner, *Between Death and Rebirth*, p. 85.
27. Rudolf Steiner, *Founding a Science of the Spirit*, pp. 22-23.
28. John Ciardi, *The Purgatorio*, p. 338.
29. Ibid., p. 338-339.
30. Ibid., p. 339.
31. Ibid., p. 339.
32. Ibid., p. 359.
33. Rudolf Steiner, *The Apocalypse of St. John*, p. 101.
34. The Bible (*NIV Study Bible*), Matt. 17:1-8, pp. 1463-1464.
35. John Ciardi, *The Purgatorio*, p. 383.
36. Rudolf Steiner, *Inner Impulses of Evolution*, p. 115.

The *Paradiso*: Into the "I" of God

37. Robert Powell, *The Sophia Teachings*, p. 121.
38. Massimo Scaligero, *Graal: Saggio sul Mistero del Sacro Amore*, p. 132.
39. Rudolf Steiner, *The Spiritual Hierarchies and the Physical World*, p. 124.
40. Ibid., p. 62.
41. Ibid., p. 127.
42. John Ciardi, *The Paradiso*, p. 423.
43. Rudolf Steiner, *Three Streams of Human Evolution*, pp. 86-87.
44. Sergei O. Prokofieff, *The Case of Valentin Tomberg*, p. 30.
45. John Ciardi, *The Paradiso*, p. 435.
46. Rudolf Steiner, *Life between Death and Rebirth*, p. 294.
47. John Ciardi, *The Paradiso*, p. 455.
48. Rudolf Steiner, *Esoteric Christianity and the Mission of Christian Rosenkreutz*, p. 312.
49. John Ciardi, *The Paradiso*, p. 461.
50. Rudolf Steiner, *The Spiritual Foundation of Morality*, pp. 46-47.
51. Ibid., p. 45.
52. John Ciardi, *The Paradiso*, p. 474.
53. Rudolf Steiner, *How to Know Higher Worlds*, pp. 121-122.
54. Rudolf Steiner, *From Jesus to Christ*, p. 113.
55. Ibid., p. 114.
56. Rudolf Steiner, *Between Death and Rebirth*, p. 130.
57. Rudolf Steiner, *Karmic Relationships*, vol. 5, p. 101.
58. Rudolf Steiner, *The Redemption of Thinking*, pp. 175-176.

59. Rudolf Steiner, *The Spiritual Hierarchies and the Physical World*, p. 98.
60. Ibid., p. 58.
61. The Bible (*NIV Study Bible*), Gen. 28, p. 48.
62. John Ciardi, *The Paradiso*, p. 526.
63. Massimo Scaligero, *The Secrets of Space and Time*, p. 94.
64. Emil Bock, *The Childhood and Youth of Jesus*, pp. 158–159.
65. The Bible (*NIV Study Bible*), Matt. 14:28–33. p. 1460.
66. The Bible (*NIV Study Bible*), Epistles of St. John, p. 1880.
67. The Bible (*NIV Study Bible*) Ex. 33:19–23, p. 135.
68. Rudolf Steiner, *Esoteric Christianity and the Mission of Christian Rosenkreutz*, pp. 166–167.
69. Rudolf Steiner, *An Esoteric Cosmology*, p. 131.
70. Rudolf Steiner, *Cosmosophy*, vol. 2, p. 28.
71. George Adams, *Physical and Ethereal Spaces*, p. 36.
72. John Ciardi, *The Paradiso*, p. 570.
73. Rudolf Steiner, *Life between Death and Rebirth*, p. 304.
74. Rudolf Steiner, *The Spiritual Hierarchies and the Physical World*, p. 58.
75. Ibid., p. 58.
76. John Ciardi, *The Paradiso*, p. 582.
77. J. E. Cirlot, *The Dictionary of Symbols*, p. 263.
78. Georg Kühlewind, *Becoming Aware of the Logos*, p. 164.
79. Éliphas Lévi, *The History of Magic*, pp. 260–261.

Bibliography

Adams, George. *Physical and Ethereal Spaces*. London: Rudolf Steiner Press, 1965.

Alan of Lille. *The Plaint of Nature*. Toronto: Pontifical Institute of Mediaeval Studies, 1980.

Alessandrini, Mario. *Cecco d'Ascoli*. Roma: G. Casini, 1955.

———. *Dante Fedele d'Amore*. Roma: Atanor, 1960.

Aligheri, Dante. *Il Convivio* (tr. R. H. Lansing). New York: Garland, 1990.

———. *Il Convivio* (tr. E. Pryce Sayer). London: George Routledge, 1887.

———. *Dante's* Vita Nuova: *A Translation and Essay by Mark Musa*, Bloomington, IN: Indiana University, 1973.

———. *La Divina Commedia*. Milano: Editore Ulrico Hoepli, 1974.

———. *The Divine Comedy* (tr. J. Ciardi). New York: Norton, 1977.

———. *The Inferno*. London: J. M. Dent and Sons, 1930.

———. *De Monarchia* (tr. D. Nicholl). Westport, CT: Hyperion, 1979.

Anderson, William. *Dante the Maker*. New York: Crossroad, 1980.

Aristotle. *Metaphysics XI* (tr. H. Lawson-Tancred). London: Penguin, 1998.

Aroux, Eugene. *Dante hérétique, révolutionnaire et socialiste, revelations d'un catholique sur le moyen age*. Paris: V. J. Renouard, 1854.

———. *Le mysteres de la chevalerie et de l'amour platonique au moyen age*. Paris: V. J. Renouard, 1858.

Asin, Miguel. *Islam and The Divine Comedy* (tr. H. Sutherland). London: John Murray, 1926.

Bamford, Christopher. *An Endless Trace: The Passionate Pursuit of Wisdom in the West*. New Platz, NY: Codhill, 2003.

Barfield, Owen. *Saving the Appearances: A Study in Idolatry*. New York: Harcourt Brace Jovanovich, 1965.

———. *Worlds Apart: A Dialogue of the 60's*. Middletown, CT: Wesleyan, 1963.

Benini, Rodolfo. *Dante tra gli splendori de'suoi enigmi risolti: con disegni vari e tavola cromolitograficha dell'itenerario di Dante per I cieli*. Rome: A. Sampaolesi, 1919.

Berman, Morris. *Coming to Our Senses: Body and Spirit in the Hidden History of the West*. New York: Simon and Schuster, 1989.

———. *The Twilight of American Culture*. New York: Norton, 2006.

Bernard of Clairvaux. *Bernard of Clairvaux: Treatises III, In Praise of New Knighthood.* Kalamazoo, MI: Cistercian Publications, 1977.

Bock, Emil. *The Childhood and Youth of Jesus.* Edinburgh: Floris, 1980.

Cerchio, Bruno. *L'ermetismo di Dante.* Roma: Edizione Mediterranee, 1988.

Cirlot, J. E. *A Dictionary of Symbols.* New York: Philosophical Library, 1962.

Cooper-Oakley, Isabel. *Masonry and Medieval Mysticism.* London: Theosophical Publishing House, 1977.

Corbin, Henri. *Avicenna and the Visionary Recital.* Princeton, NJ: Princeton University, 1988.

———. "Pour l'hymnologie manicheenne" (1937).

Croce, Benedetto. "La Metodologia della Critica Letteraria e La 'Divina Comedia'" from *Giornale Critico della filosofia italiana*, vol. 1. Messina: Casa Editrice Giuseppe Principato, 1920.

Cumont, Franz. *Mysteries of Mithra.* New York: Dover, 1956.

de Lorris, Guillaume, and Jean de Muen. *The Romance of the Rose* (tr. H. W. Robbins). New York: Dutton, 1962.

de Rougemont, Denis. *Love in the Western World.* New York: Pantheon, 1956.

de Saint-Victor, Richard. *On the Four Grades of Violent Love* (tr. A. B. Kraebel). Turnhout: Brepols, 2011.

———. *Richard of St. Victor: The Book of the Patriarchs, The Mystical Ark, Book Three of the Trinity* (Classics of Spirituality). New York: Paulist Press, 1979.

de Salvio, Alphonso. *Dante and Heresy.* Boston: Dumas, 1936.

Delaforge, Gaetan. *The Templar Tradition in the Age of Aquarius.* Putney, VT: Threshold, 1987.

Denomy, Alexander J. *The Heresy of Courtly Love.* Gloucester, MA: Peter Smith, 1965.

Durante, Ser (Dante). *The Fiore, and the Detto D'Amore: A Late 13th-Century Translation of the Roman de la Rose* (tr. D. Casciani and C. Kleinenz). Notre Dame, IN: Notre Dame University, 2000.

Eagleton, Terry. *Literary Theory: An Introduction.* Minneapolis: University of Minnesota, 1983.

Eliade, Mircea. *Rites and Symbols of Initiation: The Mysteries of Birth and Rebirth.* Dallas: Spring, 1994.

Evola, Julius. *The Hermetic Tradition: Symbols and Teachings of the Royal Art.* Rochester, VT: Inner Traditions, 1995.

———. *The Metaphysics of Sex.* Rochester, VT: Inner Traditions, 1983.

Faivre, Antoine. *The Eternal Hermes From Greek God to Alchemical Magus.* Grand Rapids MI: Phanes, 1995.

Foscolo, Ugo. *Studi su Dante* (Edizione nazionale delle opere di Ugo Foscolo, vol. 1). Firenze: F. Le Monnier, 1978–81.

———. *Ultime lettere di Jacopo Ortis. Discorso sul testo della Commedia.* Milano: Casa Editrice Sonzogno, 1925.

Fowlie, Wallace. *A Reading of Dante's Inferno.* Chicago: University of Chicago, 1981.

Francke, Sylvia. *The Tree of Life and the Holy Grail: Ancient and Modern Spiritual Paths and the Mystery of Rennes-le Chateau.* London: Temple Lodge, 2007.

Fraser, Veronica M. *The Songs of Peire Vidal: Translation and Commentary.* New York: Peter Lang, 2006.

Gardner, Edmund E. *Dante and the Mystics.* New York: Octagon, 1968.

———. *Dante's Ten Heavens.* New York: Books for Libraries, 1972.

Gettings, Fred. *The Secret Zodiac: The Hidden Art of Medieval Astrology.* London: Arcana, 1989.

Goldin, Frederick, ed. *Lyrics of the Troubadours and Trouvères.* New York: Anchor/Doubleday, 1973.

Guénon, René. *L'esoterismo di Dante.* Rome: Editrice Atanor, 1978.

Guzzardo, John J. *Dante: Numerological Studies.* New York: Peter Lang, 1987.

Hall, Manly P. *Orders of the Quest: The Holy Grail.* Los Angeles: The Philosophical Research Society, 1949.

Heckethorn, Charles William. *Secret Societies of All Ages and Countries* (2 vols.). New York: University, 1965.

Heer, Friedrich. *The Medieval World: Europe 1100–1350.* Cleveland, OH: The World Publishing, 1962.

Heline, Corinne. *Sacred Science of Numbers: A Series of Lectures Dealing with the Sacred Science of Numbers.* La Canada, CA: New Age Press, 1971.

Homer. *The Odyssey,* New York: Mentor 1937.

Hunt, Morton M. *The Natural History of Love.* London: Hutchinson, 1960.

John, Robert L. *Dante Templare: Una nuova interpretazione della Commedia.* Milano: Hoepli, 1987.

Johnson, Robert A. *We: Understanding the Psychology of Romantic Love.* San Francisco: HarperOne, 2009.

Klonsky, Milton. *Blake's Dante: The Complete Illustrations to the Divine Comedy.* New York: Harmony, 1980.

Kühlewind, Georg. *Becoming Aware of the Logos: The Way of St. John the Evangelist.* West Stockbridge, MA: Lindisfarne Press, 1985.

———. *Stages of Consciousness: Meditations on the Boundaries of the Soul.* West Stockbridge, MA: Lindisfarne Press, 1984.

———. *Thinking of the Heart and Other Essays.* Fair Oaks, CA: Rudolf Steiner College, 1987.

Lanza, Adriano. *Dante all'Inferno: I Misteri Eretici della Commedia.* Roma: Tre Editori, 1999.

———. *Dante e la Gnosi: L'Eesoterismo del Convivio*. Roma: Edizioni Mediterranee, 1990.

———. *Dante Eterodosso: Una lettura diversa della Commedia*. Bergamo: Moretti & Vitali Editori, 2004.

Latini, Brunetto. *Il Tesoretto* (The Little Treasure). New York: Garland, 1981.

Lea, Henry Charles. *A History of the Inquisition of the Middle Ages* (3 vols.). New York: Russell & Russell, 1955.

Lévi, Éliphas. *The History of Magic: Including a Clear and Precise Exposition of Its Procedure, Its Rites, and Its Mysteries* (tr. A. E. Waite). New York: Weiser, 1971.

Lukács, Georg. *Studies in European Realism*. London: Merlin, 1970.

Luke, Helen M. *Dark Wood to White Rose: Journey and Transformation in Dante's Divine Comedy*. New York: Parabola, 1989.

MacLennan, Bruce. "Dante and the Fedeli d'Amore" (http://web.eecs.utk.edu/~mclennan/Classes/US310/Dante-Fedeli-d-Amore.html).

Makin, Peter. *Provence and Pound*. Berkeley: University of California, 1978.

Mandonnet, Pierre. *Dante le théologien: Introduction à l'intelligence de la vie, des oeuvres et de l'art de Dante Alighieri*. Paris: Desclée de Brouwer, 1935.

McCaffrey, Ellen. *Astrology and Its Influence on the Western World*. New York: Weiser, 1970.

McLean, Adam. *The Triple Goddess: An Exploration Archetypal Feminine*. Grand Rapids, MI: Phanes, 1989.

Merton, Thomas. *The Last of the Fathers: Saint Bernard of Clairvaux and the Encyclical Letter "Doctor Mellifluus."* New York: Harcourt Brace Jovanovich, 1954.

Morizot, Pierre. *The School of Chartres*. Spring Valley, NY: St. George, 1987.

Nelson, Lowry, Jr. (ed. and tr.). *The Poetry of Guido Cavalcanti*. New York and London: Garland, 1986.

Nigg, Walter. *The Heretics: Heresy Through the Ages*. New York: Knopf, 1962.

Oldenbourg, Zoé. *Massacre at Montsegur: A History of the Albigensian Crusade*. New York: Pantheon, 1961.

O'Neil, George, and Gisela O'Neil. *The Human Life*. Spring Valley. NY: Mercury, 1990.

Osgood, Charles G. (ed.). *Boccaccio on Poetry*. Princeton, NJ: Princeton University, 1930.

Pagels, Elaine. *The Gnostic Gospels*. New York: Vintage, 1979.

Pascoli, Giovanni. "Tutte le Opere di Giovanni Pascoli," vol. 1 (*Sotto il Velame: Saggio d'un'Interpretazione Generale del Poema Sacro*). Milano: Arnoldo Mondadori, 1952.

———. "Tutte le Opere di Giovanni Pascoli," vol. 2 (*La Mirabile Visione: abbozzo d'una storia della Divina Commedia*, Livorno) Milano: Arnoldo Mondadori, 1952.

Perez, Francesco Paolo. *La Beatrice svelata: Preparazione all'intelligenza di tutte le opere di Dante Alighieri.* Palermo: Flaccovio Editore, 2001.

Petry, Ray C., and John Baillie. *Late Medieval Mysticism.* Philadelphia: Westminster, 1957.

Pizzi, Italo. *Storia della Poesia Persiana.* Torino: Unione tipografico-editrice, 1894.

Pound, Ezra. *The Spirit of Romance.* New York: New Directions, 1952.

Powell, Robert. *The Sign of the Son of Man in the Heavens: Sophia and the New Star Wisdom.* San Rafael, CA: Sophia Foundation, 2007.

———. *The Sophia Teachings: The Emergence of the Divine Sophia in our Time.* New York: Lantern, 2001.

Powell, Robert, and Kevin Dann. *Christ and the Maya Calendar: 2012 and The Coming of the Anti-Christ.* Great Barrington, MA: Lindisfarne, 2009.

Pozzato, Maria Pia (ed.). *L'Idea deforme: Interpretaztioni esoteriche di Dante.* Milano: Bompiani, 1989.

Prokofieff, Sergei O. *The Case of Valentin Tomberg: Anthroposophy or Jesuitism.* London: Temple Lodge, 1997.

———. *The Occult Significance of Forgiveness.* London: Temple Lodge, 1991.

———. *Rudolf Steiner and the Founding of the New Mysteries.* London: Temple Lodge, 1994.

———. *The Spiritual Origins of Eastern Europe and the Future Mysteries of the Holy Grail.* London: Temple Lodge, 1993.

———. *The Twelve Holy Nights and the Spiritual Hierarchies.* London: Temple Lodge, 1993.

Querido, René. *The Golden Age of Chartres: The Teachings of a Mystery School and the Eternal Feminine.* Edinburgh: Floris, 1987.

Ralphs, Sheila. *Dante's Journey to the Centre: Some Patterns in his Allegory.* Manchester, UK: University of Manchester, 1972.

Reeves, Marjorie. *Joachim of Fiore and the Prophetic Future.* New York: Harper Torch, 1976.

Richards, Theodore. *Cosmosophia: Cosmology, Mysticism, and the Birth of a New Myth.* Danvers, MA: Hiraeth, 2011.

Rincolfi, Alfonso. *Studi sui "Fedeli D'Amore."* Foggia: Edizioni Bastogi, 1983.

Rossetti, Dante Gabriel. *Dante and His Circle.* Boston: Roberts Brothers, 1887.

Rossetti, Gabriele. *Disquisitions on the Antipapal Spirit which Produced the Reformation.* London: Smith, Elder, Cornhill, 1934.

———. *La Beatrice di Dante.* Imola, Italy: Cooperative, 1935.

———. *Il Mistero dell"amore Platonico del Medioevo derivato da misteri antichi* (5 vols.). London: R. and G. Taylor, 1840.

Runciman, Steven. *The Medieval Manichee: A Study of Christian Dualist Heresy*. Cambridge, NJ: Cambridge University, 1947.

Russell, Jeffery Burton (ed.). *Dissent and Reform in the Early Middle Ages*. New York: Wiley, 1971.

Saly, John. *Dante's Paradiso: The Flowering of the Self*. New York: Pace University, 1989.

Santayana, George. *Interpretations of Poetry and Religion*. Cambridge. MA: MIT, 1989.

Scaligero, Massimo. *Dell'Amore immortale*. Roma: Tilopa, 1963.

———. *Graal: Saggio sul mistero del sacro amore*. Roma: Perseo, 1968.

———. *Iside–Sofia. La dea ignota*. Roma: Edizione Mediterranee, 1980.

———. *La Logica Contro L'uomo. Il mito della scienza e la via del pensioero*. Roma: Tilopa, 1967.

———. *Il Logos e i nuovi misteri*. Roma: Teseo, 1973.

———. *La Luce. Introduzione all'imaginazione creatrice*. Roma: Tilopa, 1964; *The Light (la Luce): An Introduction to Creative Imagination* (tr. E. L. Bisbocci). Great Barrington, MA: Lindisfarne Books, 2001.

———. *Il pensiero come anti-materia*. Roma: Perseo, 1978.

———. *Segreti dello spazio e del tempo*. Roma: Tilopa, 1963; *The Secrets of Space and Time* (tr. E. L. Bisbocci). Great Barrington, MA: Lindisfarne, 2013.

———. *Trattato del pensiero vivente*. Roma: Tilopa, 1960; *A Treatise on Living Thinking* (tr. E. L. Bisbocci). Great Barrington, MA: Lindisfarne Books, 2014.

———. *La via della volonta solare. Fenomenologia del"uomo interiore*. Roma: Tilopa, 1962.

Schwartz, Willi. *Studi su Dante e spunti di storia del cristianesimo*. Milano: Editrice Antroposofica, 1982.

Sease, Virginia, and Manfred Schmidt-Brabant. *Thinkers, Saints, Heretics: Spiritual Paths of the Middle Ages*. London: Temple Lodge, 2007.

Seward, Barbara. *The Symbolic Rose*. Dallas: Spring, 1989.

Shah, Idries. *The Sufis*. New York: Anchor, 1971.

Smoley, Richard. *Inner Christianity: A Guide to the Esoteric Tradition*. Boston: Shambhala, 2002.

Soresina, Maria. *Liberta' va cercando: Il catarismo nella Commedia di Dante*. Bergamo, Italy: Moretti e Vitali, 2009.

Steffen, Albert. *Mystery-Drama from Ancient to Modern Times*. Hillsdale, NY: Adonis, 1977.

Stein, Walter Johnannes. *The Death of Merlin: Arthurian Myth and Alchemy.* Edinburgh: Floris, 1984.

Steiner, Rudolf. *Anthroposophy and the Inner Life: An Esoteric Introduction.* London: Rudolf Steiner Press, 2015.

———. *The Apocalypse of St. John.* Hudson, NY: Anthroposophic Press, 1993.

———. *The Arts and their Mission.* New York: Anthroposophic Press, 1964.

———. *Art as Spiritual Activity: Rudolf Steiner's Contribution to the Visual Arts* (ed. M. Howard). Hudson, NY: Anthroposophic Press, 1998.

———. *Background to the Gospel of St. Mark.* New York: Anthroposophic Press, 1985.

———. *Between Death and Rebirth.* London: Rudolf Steiner Press, 1975.

———. *The Bridge between Universal Spirituality and the Physical Constitution of Man.* Spring Valley: NY: Anthroposophic Press, 1979.

———. *The Child's Changing Consciousness.* Hudson, NY: Anthroposophic Press, 1988.

———. *Cosmosophy*, vol. 1. Spring Valley, NY: Anthroposophic Press, 1985.

———. *Cosmosophy*, vol. 2. Gympie, Australia: Completion, 1997.

———. *Death as Metamorphosis of Life: Including "What Does the Angel Do in Our Astral Body?" and "How Do I Find Christ?"* Great Barrington, MA: SteinerBooks, 2008.

———. *The Deed of Christ.* N. Vancouver, BC: Steiner Book Centre, 1976.

———. *The Driving Force of Spiritual Powers in World History.* N. Vancouver, BC: Steiner Book Centre, 1983.

———. *The Effects of Esoteric Development.* Hudson, NY: Anthroposophic Press, 1997.

———. *Esoteric Christianity and the Mission of Christian Rosenkreutz.* London: Rudolf Steiner Press, 2013.

———. *An Esoteric Cosmology: Evolution, Christ, and Modern Spirituality.* Great Barrington, MA: SteinerBooks, 2008.

———. *The Evolution of Consciousness.* London: Pharos (Rudolf Steiner Press), 1979.

———. *The Fall of the Spirits of Darkness.* Bristol: Rudolf Steiner Press, 1993.

———. *The Foundation Stone / The Life, Nature, and Cultivation of Anthroposophy.* London: Rudolf Steiner Press, 1997.

———. *Founding a Science of the Spirit.* London: Rudolf Steiner Press, 2007.

———. *From Jesus to Christ.* London: Rudolf Steiner Press, 1991.

———. *From Symptom to Reality in Modern History.* London: Rudolf Steiner Press, 1976.

———. *Good and Evil Spirits: And their Influence on Humanity.* London: Rudolf Steiner Press, 2014.

———. *Gospel of St. John in Relation to the Other Gospels.* New York: Anthroposophic Press, 1982.

———. *How Can Mankind Find the Christ Again? The Threefold Shadow-Existence of Our Time and the New Light of Christ.* Hudson, NY: Anthroposophic Press, 1984. (See also: Steiner, *Death as Metamorphosis of Life: Including "What Does the Angel Do in our Astral Body?" & "How Do I Find Christ?"*)

———. *How to Know Higher Worlds: A Modern Path of Initiation.* Hudson, NY: Anthroposophic Press, 1994.

———. *Il Ponte fra La Spiritualita' Cosmica e l'Elemento Fisico Umano.* Milano: Editrice Antroposofica, 1979.

———. *Il Vangelo di Giovanni in Relazione con gli altri tre e specialmente col Vangelo di Luca.* Milano: Editrice Antroposofica, 1981.

———. *The Influence of Spiritual Beings upon Man.* Spring Valley, NY: Anthroposophic Press, 1982. (See also: Steiner, Good and Evil Spirits: And their Influence on Humanity.)

———. *The Influences of Lucifer and Ahriman: Human Responsibility for the Earth.* Hudson, NY: Anthroposophic Press, 1993.

———. *Inner Impulses of Evolution: The Mexican Mysteries and the Knights Templar.* Spring Valley, NY: Anthroposophic Press, 1984.

———. *Intuitive Thinking as a Spiritual Path: A Philosophy of Freedom.* Hudson, NY: Anthroposophic Press, 1995.

———. *Isis Mary Sophia: Her Mission and Ours.* Great Barrington, MA: SteinerBooks, 2003.

———. *Karma of Untruthfulness: Secret Societies, the Media, and Preparations for the Great War,* 2 vols. London: Rudolf Steiner Press, 2005.

———. *Karmic Relationships: Esoteric Studies,* 8 vols. London: Rudolf Steiner Press, 1977–2015.

———. *Knowledge of the Higher Worlds and Its Attainment,* New York: Anthroposophic Press, 1961.

———. "La concezione religiosa medievale nel Poema dantesco" (lect. Feb. 11, 1904), in *Graal: Rivista di scienza dello Spirito.* Roma: Tilopa, N. 29–30, 1990.

———. *Learning to See into the Spiritual World.* Hudson, NY: Anthroposophic Press, 1990.

———. *Life between Death and New Birth.* London: Rudolf Steiner Press, 1975.

———. *Life between Death and Rebirth.* Spring Valley, NY: Anthroposophic Press, 1968.

———. *Links between the Living and the Dead.* London: Rudolf Steiner Press, 1973.

———. "Lost Unison between Speaking and Thinking" (lect., July 18, 1915). Spring Valley, NY: Mercury Press, 1984.

———. *Love and its Meaning in the World*. Hudson, NY: Anthroposophic Press, 1998.

———. *Microcosm and Macrocosm*. London: Rudolf Steiner Press, 1985.

———. *Mission of the Folk-Souls*. London: Anthroposophical Publishing Co., 1929.

———. *The Mysteries of the East and of Christianity*. London: Rudolf Steiner Press, 1972.

———. *The Mystery of the Trinity: Mission of the Spirit* (rev. ed.). Great Barrington, MA: SteinerBooks, 2016.

———. *Mystery of the Universe: The Human Being, Model of Creation*. London: Rudolf Steiner Press, 2001 (previously *Man: Hieroglyph of the Universe*).

———. *Natura Interiore dell'Uomo e La Vita Fra Morte e Nuova Nascita*. Milano: Editrice Antroposofica, 1975.

———. "The Need for Understanding the Christ" (O. 224). Steiner Book Centre: N. Vancouver, BC, 1983.

———. *The Occult Movement in the Nineteenth Century and Its Relation to Modern Culture*. London: Rudolf Steiner Press, 1973.

———. *The Origins of Natural Science*. Spring Valley, NY: Anthroposophic Press, 1985.

———. *An Outline of Esoteric Science*. Hudson, NY: Anthroposophic Press, 1997.

———. *Philosophy, Cosmology, and Religion*. Spring Valley, NY: Anthroposophic Press, 1984.

———. *The Philosophy of Freedom*. London: Pharos Books, 1979. (See also: Steiner, *Intuitive Thinking as a Spiritual Path*.)

———. *Planetary Spheres and their Influence on Man's Life on Earth and in Spiritual Worlds*. London: Rudolf Steiner Press, 1982.

———. *The Redemption of Thinking*. Spring Valley, NY: Anthroposophic Press, 1983.

———. *Ritmi nel Cosmo e Nell'Essere Umano: L'Azione dell'eterico e dell'astrale sull'Uomo e Sulla Terra* (lect. June 28, 1923). Milano: Editrice Antroposofica, 1993.

———. *Rosicruianism and Modern Initiation*. London: Rudolf Steiner Press, 1982.

———. *La Saggezza dei Rosacroce*. Milano: Editrice Antroposofica, 1978.

———. *The Search for the New Isis, Divine Sophia*. Spring Valley, NY: Mercury, 1983.

———. *The Spiritual Hierarchies and the Physical World: Zodiac, Planets and Cosmos*. Great Barrington, MA: SteinerBooks, 2008.

———. *The Spiritual Hierarchies and their Reflection in the Physical World*. Spring Valley, NY: Anthroposophic Press, 1983.

———. *The Temple Legend: Freemasonry and Related Occult Movements: From the Contents of the Esoteric School*. London: Rudolf Steiner Press, 1985.

———. *Theosophy*. Hudson, NY: Anthroposophic Press, 1994.

———. *The Three Streams of Evolution of Mankind*. London: Rudolf Steiner Press, 1985.

———. *Transforming the Soul*, vol. 2. London: Rudolf Steiner Press, 2006.

———. *True and False Paths of Spiritual Investigation*. London: Rudolf Steiner Press, 1985.

———. *Universal Spirituality and Human Physicality: Bridging the Divide: The Search for the New Isis and the Divine Sophia*. London: Rudolf Steiner Press, 2014.

———. *A Western Approach to Reincarnation and Karma* (ed. R. Querido). Hudson, NY: Anthroposophic Press, 1997.

———. *Wonders of the World, Ordeals of the Soul, Revelations of the Spirit*. London: Rudolf Steiner Press, 1963.

Suhrawardi, Shihabaddin. *Opera metaphysica et mystica*, I (ed. H. Corbin). Bibliotheca Islamica 16. Istanbul, 1945.

Tusiani, Joseph. *The Age of Dante: An Anthology of Early Italian Poetry*. New York: Baroque Press, Inc., 1974.

Valli, Luigi. *Il Linguaggio Secgreto di Dante e dei Fedeli d'Amore*, 2 vols. Roma: Optima, 1928–1929.

———. *Il Segreto della Croce e dell'Aquila nella Divina Commedia*. Bologna: N. Zanichelli, 1922.

———. *La Chiave della Divina Commedia: Sintesi del Simbolismo della Croce e dell'Aquila*. Bologna: N. Zanichelli, 1925.

———. *La Struttura Morale dell'Universo Dantesco*. Roma: Ausonia, 1935.

———. *Lo Scema segreto del Poema Sacro*. Foggia: Bastogi,.1983.

Versluis, Arthur. *The Philosophy of Magic*. Boston: Arcana, 1986.

Vinassa de Regny, Paolo. *Dante e Pitagora*. Genova: I Dioscuri, 1988.

Wicksteed, Philip H. *Aquinas and Dante*. New York: Dutton, 1913.

Wilkins, Eithne. *The Rose Garden Game*. New York: Herder and Herder, 1969.

Wilson, Peter Lamborn, and Nasrollah Pourjavady, eds. *The Drunken Universe: An Anthology of Persian Sufi Poetry*. Grand Rapids, MI: Phanes, 1987.

Zohar. *The History of the Zodiac*. New York: Arco, 1972.

≈

The Bible, NIV Study Bible, Grand Rapids, MI: Zondervan Publishing House, 1995.

Index of Illustrations

Angels Inviting Dante to Enter the Fire, William Blake	378
Antaeus Setting down Dante and Virgil, William Blake	285
Beatrice Addressing Dante from the Cart, William Blake	394
Dante and Virgil Approaching the Angel Who Guards the Entrance of Purggatory, William Blake	331
Dante in the Empyrean, Drinking from the River of Light, William Blake	552
Dante Running from the Three Beasts, William Blake	212
Dante's Scheme of the Universe	408
Dantis Amor, Dante Gabriele Rossetti	58
Diagram of the Earth at the Center of the Universe	192
Eighth Sphere (the fixed stars), Botticelli	414
Empyrean, engraving by Gustave Doré to illustrate Dante's Divine Comedy	ii
Encounter of Dante and Beatrice, 14th-century miniature painting	82
Franciscan Friars witness a Cathar Consolamentum	144
Geryon conveying Dante and Virgil, William Blake	251
Inscription over Hell-Gate, William Blake	217
Lucia Carrying Dante in His Sleep, William Blake	329
Lucifer–Satan, William Blake	296
Map of Hell: Figurazione Generale dell'Inferno	208
Muhammad-Sharif Musawwir's miniature	174
Paradiso 57, Celestial Rose, Giovanni di Paolo	555
Portrait of Dante (c. 1495), by Sandro Botticelli	xiii
Queen of Heaven in Glory, William Blake	561
St. Peter, Beatrice, and Dante, William Blake	515
St. Peter, St. James, Dante, Beatrice with St. John the Evangelist, William Blake	525
The Simoniac Pope, William Blake	255
Troubadours, 14th century	144
Two Knights on Horseback; A Seal of the Knights Templar	126

www.ingramcontent.com/pod-product-compliance
Lightning Source LLC
Chambersburg PA
CBHW020259010526
44108CB00037B/158